PHILIP'S

ILLUSTRATED WORLD ATLAS

PHILIP'S

ILLUSTRATED WORLD ATLAS

Contents

Compiled by:
RICHARD WIDDOWS

Executive Editor
Caroline Rayner

Editor
Martha Swift

Executive Art Editor
Vivienne Brar

Design
Rubik Graphic Communications
Peter Burt
Alison Myer

Jacket Design
Stewart Cocking

Art Director
Andrew Sutterby

Maps
B.M. Willett
David Gaylard
Ray Smith
Jenny Allen
Craig Asquith

Picture Research
Caroline Hensman

Production
Chris Latcham

Index
Byte and Type Limited,
Birmingham, UK

Flags
Bosse Norrgård

Information on recent
changes to flags provided and
authenticated by the Flag
Institute, Chester, UK

First published in Great Britain in
1994 by George Philip Limited,
an imprint of Reed Consumer
Books Limited, Michelin House,
81 Fulham Road, London SW3
6RB, and Auckland, Melbourne,
Singapore and Toronto

Cartography by Philip's

Copyright © 1994 Reed
International Books Limited

A CIP catalogue record for this
book is available from the British
Library

ISBN 0-540-05861-0

Printed and bound in China

Picture Credits

BRUCE COLEMAN LTD: Brian J. Coates 98; Jeremy Grayson
13; Charles Henneghain 48 top; Kaufman Photography
54 bottom; Oliver Langrand 133; Frans Lanting 177 bottom;
George McCarthy 7 bottom left; Hans-Peter Merten 9 bottom;
Dieter and Mary Plage 189; Dr Eckart Pott 11 bottom;
Peter Terry 3; Rod Williams 25 top;

HUTCHISON LIBRARY: 121;

IMPACT PHOTOS: Wendy Aldiss 38 bottom; Carolyn Bates
108; Steve Benbow 177 top; Christophe Bluntzer 15 bottom;
Martin Black 37, 82 bottom; Gerald Buthaud/Cosmos 117; Piers
Cavendish 6, 66, 79, 180; Rupert Conant 45 top; Christopher
Cormack 126; Michael Dent 17; Ben Edwards 74; Alain Evrard 95
bottom; Paul Freestone front cover top left; Simon Grosset 143;
Mark Henley 90; Colin Jones 93, 100, 111, 122, 166, 186 bottom;
Alan Keohane 64 top, 65, 68, 104, 105; Alain Le Garsmeur 80,
72–73; Mike McQueen 57 top; Peter Menzel 10; Guy Moberly 8
top; Giles Moberly 119; Neil Morrison 181 bottom; Jeremy
Nicholl 120; David Palmer 97 top, 110, 118; Tony Page 134, 191;
Caroline Penn 73 top right, 106, 107; Vigen Rao/Vika 61; David
Reed 16 top; Panayiotis Sofroniou 63; Jorn Stjerneklar 127;
Wendy Levine 53;

JAMES DAVIS TRAVEL PHOTOGRAPHY: 21 bottom, 26, 57
bottom, 131;

PANOS PICTURES: Neil Cooper 112; Ron Giling 116; Jeremy
Hartley 60, 114; Rhodri Jones 49 centre, 50; Matthew Kneale 43
top; Alain Le Garsmeur 69 top; M.Kneale 175; Sean Sprague 56,
124, 164; Chris Stowers 46 centre; Hamish Wilson 113;

SOUTH AMERICAN PICTURES: 178; Tony Morrison 179,
186–187 top; Peter Williams 182;

TONY STONE IMAGES: 20, 24 bottom, 28 bottom, 52, 62, 78
top, 83 top, 88 bottom, 149, 153, 160 top, 163 bottom; Jerry
Alexander 181 top; Doug Armand 29; David Austen 137 left;
David Baird 168; Oliver Benn 4 top, 151 top, 172; Jon Bradley 32
top; Michael Braid 75; Marcus Brooke 85 top; Michael Busselle 5,
21 top, 22; Anthony Cassidy 76; Paul Chesley 87 top, 140 top,
142; Joe Cornish 36 top, 44; Cosmo Condina 163 top; Tony
Craddock 151 bottom; Sue Cunningham 183; Ron Dahlquist 146;
David Hanson 156; Nicholas DeVore 87 bottom; Gerard Del
Vecchio 103 top; Fred M. Dole 157; John Edwards 192; Johan
Elzenga 103 bottom; Richard Elliott 115; John Garrett 140
bottom; Sylvain Grandadam 39; David Hanson 18; Chris Harvey
130; Simeone Huber 36 bottom; Geoff Johnson 27 top; Stephen
Johnson 152; Zigy Kaluzny 138 bottom; Hilarie Kavanagh back
cover left; Rhonda Klevansky 188; Bob Krist 171; Hideo Kurihara
33; Ian Murphy 69 bottom, 129; David E. Myers 161; Donald
Nausbaum 184; John Noble front cover top centre; Dennis Oda
160 bottom; Richard Passmore 34; Nicholas Parfitt 101; Ed
Pritchard 85 bottom; Fritz Prenzel 137 right; Colin Prior 54–55
top; Mitch Reardon 125; Rohan 64 bottom; Dave Saunders 95
top; Ulli Seer 30 centre; Pete Seaward 78 bottom; Robin Smith
136, front cover top right; David Sutherland 77; Darryl Torckler
141 top; Jean-Marc Truchet 91; Henry Tse 82 top; Nabeel
Turner 67; Ken Walsh 141 bottom; Peter Wilkie 92;

JUDY TODD: 41 bottom, 42 bottom, 83 bottom, 174;

TRIP: 70, 71.

World Statistics

World Map Symbols viii

Europe 2

World Statistics: Countries

This alphabetical list includes all the countries and territories of the world. If a territory is not completely independent, then the country it is associated with is named. The area figures give the total area of land, inland water and ice.

Units for areas and populations are thousands. The annual income is the Gross National Product per capita in US dollars. The figures are the latest available, usually 1991.

Country/Territory	Area km² Thousands	Area miles² Thousands	Population Thousands	Capital	Annual Income US $
Adélie Land (Fr.)	432	167	0.03	-	-
Afghanistan	652	252	16,433	Kabul	450
Albania	28.8	11.1	3,250	Tirana	1,000
Algeria	2,382	920	24,960	Algiers	2,020
American Samoa (US)	0.20	0.08	39	Pago Pago	6,000
Amsterdam Is. (Fr.)	0.05	0.02	0.03	-	-
Andorra	0.45	0.17	52	Andorre-la-Vella	-
Angola	1,247	481	10,020	Luanda	620
Anguilla (UK)	0.09	0.04	8	The Valley	-
Antigua & Barbuda	0.44	0.17	77	St John's	4,770
Argentina	2,767	1,068	32,322	Buenos Aires	2,780
Armenia	29.8	11.5	3,416	Yerevan	2,150
Aruba (Neths.)	0.19	0.07	60	Oranjestad	6,000
Ascension Is. (UK)	0.09	0.03	1.5	Georgetown	-
Australia	7,687	2,968	17,086	Canberra	16,590
Australian Antarctic Territory	6,120	2,363	0	-	-
Austria	83.9	32.4	7,712	Vienna	20,380
Azerbaijan	86.6	33.4	7,451	Baku	1,670
Azores (Port.)	2.2	0.87	260	Ponta Delgada	-
Bahamas	13.9	5.4	253	Nassau	11,720
Bahrain	0.68	0.26	503	Manama	6,910
Bangladesh	144	56	115,594	Dacca	220
Barbados	0.43	0.17	255	Bridgetown	6,630
Belau (US)	0.46	0.18	15	Koror	-
Belgium	30.5	11.8	9,845	Brussels	19,300
Belize	23	8.9	188	Belmopan	2,050
Belorussia	207.6	80.1	10,374	Minsk	3,110
Benin	113	43	4,736	Porto-Novo	380
Bermuda (UK)	0.05	0.02	61	Hamilton	25,000
Bhutan	47	18.1	1,517	Thimphu	180
Bolivia	1,099	424	7,400	La Paz/Sucre	650
Bosnia-Herzegovina	51.2	19.8	4,364	Sarajevo	-
Botswana	582	225	1,291	Gaborone	2,590
Bouvet Is. (Nor.)	0.05	0.02	0.02	-	-
Brazil	8,512	3,286	153,322	Brasilia	2,920
British Antarctic Terr. (UK)	1,709	660	0.3	Stanley	-
British Indian Ocean Terr. (UK)	0.08	0.03	3	-	-
Brunei	5.8	2.2	266	Bandar Seri Begawan	6,000
Bulgaria	111	43	9,011	Sofia	1,840
Burkina Faso	274	106	9,001	Ouagadougou	350
Burma (Myanmar)	677	261	41,675	Rangoon	500
Burundi	27.8	10.7	5,438	Bujumbura	210
Cambodia	181	70	8,246	Phnom Penh	200
Cameroon	475	184	11,834	Yaoundé	940
Canada	9,976	3,852	26,522	Ottawa	21,260
Canary Is. (Spain)	7.3	2.8	1,700	Las Palmas/Santa Cruz	-
Cape Verde Is.	4	1.6	370	Praia	750
Cayman Is. (UK)	0.26	0.10	27	Georgetown	-
Central African Republic	623	241	3,039	Bangui	390
Chad	1,284	496	5,679	Ndjamena	220
Chatham Is. (NZ)	0.96	0.37	0.05	Waitangi	-
Chile	757	292	13,386	Santiago	2,160
China	9,597	3,705	1,139,060	Beijing (Peking)	370
Christmas Is. (Aus.)	0.14	0.05	2.3	The Settlement	-
Cocos (Keeling) Is. (Aus.)	0.01	0.005	0.70	-	-
Colombia	1,139	440	32,987	Bogotá	1,280
Comoros	2.2	0.86	551	Moroni	500
Congo	342	132	2,271	Brazzaville	1,120
Cook Is. (NZ)	0.24	0.09	18	Avarua	900
Costa Rica	51.1	19.7	2,994	San José	1,930
Croatia	56.5	21.8	4,784	Zagreb	-
Crozet Is. (Fr.)	0.51	0.19	35	-	-
Cuba	111	43	10,609	Havana	3,000
Cyprus	9.3	3.6	702	Nicosia	8,640
Czech Republic	78.9	30.4	10,299	Prague	2,370
Denmark	43.1	16.6	5,140	Copenhagen	23,660
Djibouti	23.2	9	409	Djibouti	1,000
Dominica	0.75	0.29	83	Roseau	2,440
Dominican Republic	48.7	18.8	7,170	Santo Domingo	950
Ecuador	284	109	10,782	Quito	1,020
Egypt	1,001	387	53,153	Cairo	620
El Salvador	21	8.1	5,252	San Salvador	1,070
Equatorial Guinea	28.1	10.8	348	Malabo	330
Estonia	44.7	17.3	1,600	Tallinn	3,830
Ethiopia	1,222	472	50,974	Addis Ababa	120
Falkland Is. (UK)	12.2	4.7	2	Stanley	-
Faroe Is. (Den.)	1.4	0.54	47	Tórshavn	23,660
Fiji	18.3	7.1	765	Suva	1,830
Finland	338	131	4,986	Helsinki	24,400
France	552	213	56,440	Paris	20,600
French Guiana (Fr.)	90	34.7	99	Cayenne	2,500
French Polynesia (Fr.)	4	1.5	206	Papeete	6,000
Gabon	268	103	1,172	Libreville	3,780
Gambia, The	11.3	4.4	861	Banjul	360
Georgia	69.7	26.9	5,571	Tbilisi	1,640
Germany	357	138	79,479	Berlin	17,000
Ghana	239	92	15,028	Accra	400
Gibraltar (UK)	0.007	0.003	31	-	4,000
Greece	132	51	10,269	Athens	6,230
Greenland (Den.)	2,176	840	57	Godthåb	6,000
Grenada	0.34	0.13	85	St George's	2,180
Guadeloupe (Fr.)	1.7	0.66	344	Basse-Terre	7,000
Guam (US)	0.55	0.21	119	Agana	6,000
Guatemala	109	42	9,197	Guatemala City	930
Guinea	246	95	5,756	Conakry	450
Guinea-Bissau	36.1	13.9	965	Bissau	190
Guyana	215	83	796	Georgetown	290
Haiti	27.8	10.7	6,486	Port-au-Prince	370
Honduras	112	43	5,105	Tegucigalpa	570
Hong Kong (UK)	1.1	0.40	5,801	-	13,200
Hungary	93	35.9	10,344	Budapest	2,690
Iceland	103	40	255	Reykjavik	22,580
India	3,288	1,269	843,931	Delhi	330
Indonesia	1,905	735	179,300	Jakarta	610
Iran	1,648	636	58,031	Tehran	2,320
Iraq	438	169	18,920	Baghdad	2,000
Ireland	70.3	27.1	3,523	Dublin	10,780
Israel	27	10.3	4,659	Jerusalem	11,330
Italy	301	116	57,663	Rome	18,580
Ivory Coast	322	125	11,998	Abidjan	690
Jamaica	11	4.2	2,420	Kingston	1,380
Jan Mayen Is. (Nor.)	0.38	0.15	0.06	-	-
Japan	378	146	123,537	Tokyo	26,920
Johnston Is. (US)	0.002	0.0009	0.30	-	-
Jordan	89.2	34.4	4,009	Amman	1,120
Kazakhstan	2,717	1,049	17,104	Alma Ata	2,470
Kenya	580	224	24,032	Nairobi	340
Kerguelen Is. (Fr.)	7.2	2.8	0	-	-
Kermadec Is. (NZ)	0.03	0.01	0	-	-
Kirghizia	198.5	76.6	4,568	Bishkek	1,550
Kiribati	0.72	0.28	66	Tarawa	750
Korea, North	121	47	21,773	Pyongyang	900
Korea, South	99	38.2	43,302	Seoul	6,340
Kuwait	17.8	6.9	2,143	Kuwait City	16,380
Laos	237	91	4,139	Vientiane	230
Latvia	63.1	24.4	2,700	Riga	3,410
Lebanon	10.4	4	2,701	Beirut	2,000

Country/Territory	Area km² Thousands	Area miles² Thousands	Population Thousands	Capital	Annual Income US $
Lesotho	30.4	11.7	1,774	Maseru	580
Liberia	111	43	2,607	Monrovia	500
Libya	1,760	679	4,545	Tripoli	5,800
Liechtenstein	0.16	0.06	29	Vaduz	33,000
Lithuania	65.2	25.2	3,751	Vilnius	2,710
Luxembourg	2.6	1	384	Luxembourg	31,080
Macau (Port.)	0.02	0.006	479	-	2,000
Macedonia	25.3	9.8	2,174	Skopje	-
Madagascar	587	227	11,197	Antananarivo	210
Madeira (Port.)	0.81	0.31	280	Funchal	-
Malawi	118	46	8,556	Lilongwe	230
Malaysia	330	127	17,861	Kuala Lumpur	2,490
Maldives	0.30	0.12	215	Malé	460
Mali	1,240	479	8,156	Bamako	280
Malta	0.32	0.12	354	Valletta	6,850
Mariana Is. (US)	0.48	0.18	22	Saipan	-
Marshall Is.	0.18	0.07	42	Dalap-Uliga-Darrit	-
Martinique (Fr.)	1.1	0.42	341	Fort-de-France	4,000
Mauritania	1,025	396	2,050	Nouakchott	510
Mauritius	1.9	0.72	1,075	Port Louis	2,420
Mayotte (Fr.)	0.37	0.14	84	Mamoundzou	-
Mexico	1,958	756	86,154	Mexico City	2,870
Micronesia, Fed. States	0.70	0.27	103	Palikir	-
Midway Is. (US)	0.005	0.002	0.45	-	-
Moldavia	33.7	13	4,458	Kishinev	2,170
Monaco	0.002	0.0001	29	-	20,000
Mongolia	1,567	605	2,190	Ulan Bator	400
Montserrat (UK)	0.10	0.04	13	Plymouth	-
Morocco	447	172	25,061	Rabat	1,030
Mozambique	802	309	15,656	Maputo	70
Namibia	824	318	1,781	Windhoek	1,120
Nauru	0.02	0.008	10	Domaneab	-
Nepal	141	54	18,916	Katmandu	180
Netherlands	41.9	16.2	15,019	Amsterdam	18,560
Neths. Antilles (Neths.)	0.99	0.38	189	Willemstad	6,000
New Caledonia (Fr.)	19	7.3	168	Nouméa	4,000
New Zealand	269	104	3,429	Wellington	12,140
Nicaragua	130	50	3,871	Managua	340
Niger	1,267	489	7,732	Niamey	300
Nigeria	924	357	108,542	Lagos/Abuja	290
Niue (NZ)	0.26	0.10	3	Alofi	-
Norfolk Is. (Aus.)	0.03	0.01	2	Kingston	-
Norway	324	125	4,242	Oslo	24,160
Oman	212	82	1,502	Muscat	5,220
Pakistan	796	307	112,050	Islamabad	400
Panama	77.1	29.8	2,418	Panama City	2,180
Papua New Guinea	463	179	3,699	Port Moresby	820
Paraguay	407	157	4,277	Asunción	1,210
Peru	1,285	496	22,332	Lima	1,020
Peter 1st Is. (Nor.)	0.18	0.07	0	-	-
Philippines	300	116	61,480	Manila	740
Pitcairn Is. (UK)	0.03	0.01	0.06	Adamstown	-
Poland	313	121	38,180	Warsaw	1,830
Portugal	92.4	35.7	10,525	Lisbon	5,620
Puerto Rico (US)	8.9	3.4	3,599	San Juan	6,330
Qatar	11	4.2	368	Doha	15,860
Queen Maud Land (Nor.)	2,800	1,081	0	-	-
Réunion (Fr.)	2.5	0.97	599	St-Denis	4,000
Romania	238	92	23,200	Bucharest	1,340
Ross Dependency (NZ)	435	168	0	-	-
Russia	17,075	6,592	149,527	Moscow	3,220
Rwanda	26.3	10.2	7,181	Kigali	260
St Christopher/Nevis	0.36	0.14	44	Basseterre	3,960
St Helena (UK)	0.12	0.05	7	Jamestown	-
St Lucia	0.62	0.24	151	Castries	2,500
St Paul Is. (Fr.)	0.007	0.003	0	-	-
St Pierre & Miquelon (Fr.)	0.24	0.09	7	St-Pierre	-
St Vincent/Grenadines	0.39	0.15	116	Kingstown	1,730
San Marino	0.06	0.02	24	San Marino	-
São Tomé & Príncipe	0.96	0.37	121	São Tomé	350
Saudi Arabia	2,150	830	14,870	Riyadh	7,070
Senegal	197	76	7,327	Dakar	720
Seychelles	0.46	0.18	67	Victoria	5,110
Sierra Leone	71.7	27.7	4,151	Freetown	210
Singapore	0.62	0.24	3,003	Singapore	12,890
Slovak Republic	49	18.9	5,269	Bratislava	1,650
Slovenia	20.3	7.8	1,963	Ljubljana	-
Solomon Is.	28.9	11.2	321	Honiara	560
Somalia	638	246	7,497	Mogadishu	150
South Africa	1,221	471	35,282	Pretoria	2,530
South Georgia (UK)	3.8	1.4	0.05	-	-
South Sandwich Is. (UK)	0.38	0.15	0	-	-
Spain	505	195	38,959	Madrid	12,460
Sri Lanka	65.6	25.3	16,993	Colombo	500
Sudan	2,506	967	25,204	Khartoum	400
Surinam	163	63	422	Paramaribo	3,610
Svalbard (Nor.)	62.9	24.3	4	Longyearbyen	-
Swaziland	17.4	6.7	768	Mbabane	1,060
Sweden	450	174	8,618	Stockholm	25,490
Switzerland	41.3	15.9	6,712	Bern	33,510
Syria	185	71	12,116	Damascus	1,110
Taiwan	36	13.9	20,300	Taipei	6,600
Tajikistan	143.1	55.2	5,680	Dushanbe	1,050
Tanzania	945	365	25,635	Dar es Salaam	100
Thailand	513	198	57,196	Bangkok	1,580
Togo	56.8	21.9	3,531	Lomé	410
Tokelau (NZ)	0.01	0.005	2	Nukunonu	-
Tonga	0.75	0.29	95	Nuku'alofa	1,100
Trinidad & Tobago	5.1	2	1,227	Port of Spain	3,620
Tristan da Cunha (UK)	0.11	0.04	0.33	Edinburgh	-
Tunisia	164	63	8,180	Tunis	1,510
Turkey	779	301	57,326	Ankara	1,820
Turkmenistan	488.1	188.5	3,838	Ashkhabad	1,700
Turks & Caicos Is. (UK)	0.43	0.17	10	Grand Turk	-
Tuvalu	0.03	0.01	10	Funafuti	600
Uganda	236	91	18,795	Kampala	160
Ukraine	603.7	233.1	51,940	Kiev	2,340
United Arab Emirates	83.6	32.3	1,589	Abu Dhabi	19,860
United Kingdom	243.3	94	54,889	London	16,750
United States	9,373	3,619	249,975	Washington	22,560
Uruguay	177	68	3,094	Montevideo	2,860
Uzbekistan	447.4	172.7	21,627	Tashkent	1,350
Vanuatu	12.2	4.7	147	Port Vila	1,120
Vatican City	0.0004	0.0002	1	-	-
Venezuela	912	352	19,735	Caracas	2,610
Vietnam	332	127	66,200	Hanoi	300
Virgin Is. (UK)	0.15	0.06	13	Road Town	-
Virgin Is. (US)	0.34	0.13	117	Charlotte Amalie	12,000
Wake Is.	0.008	0.003	0.30	-	-
Wallis & Futuna Is. (Fr.)	0.20	0.08	18	Mata-Utu	-
Western Sahara	266	103	179	El Aaiún	-
Western Samoa	2.8	1.1	164	Apia	930
Yemen	528	204	11,282	Sana	540
Yugoslavia	102.3	39.5	10,642	Belgrade	2,940
Zaïre	2,345	906	35,562	Kinshasa	230
Zambia	753	291	8,073	Lusaka	420
Zimbabwe	391	151	9,369	Harare	620

World Statistics: Physical Dimensions

Each topic list is divided into continents and within a continent the items are listed in size order. The order of the continents is as in the atlas, Europe through to South America. The bottom part of many of the lists are selective. The world top ten are shown in square brackets; in the case of mountains this has not been done because the world top 30 are all in Asia. The figures are rounded as appropriate.

World, Continents, Oceans

	km^2	$miles^2$	%
The World	509,450,000	196,672,000	–
Land	149,450,000	57,688,000	29.3
Water	360,000,000	138,984,000	70.7
Asia	44,500,000	17,177,000	29.8
Africa	30,302,000	11,697,000	20.3
North America	24,241,000	9,357,000	16.2
South America	17,793,000	6,868,000	11.9
Antarctica	14,100,000	5,443,000	9.4
Europe	9,957,000	3,843,000	6.7
Australia & Oceania	8,557,000	3,303,000	5.7
Pacific Ocean	179,679,000	69,356,000	49.9
Atlantic Ocean	92,373,000	35,657,000	25.7
Indian Ocean	73,917,000	28,532,000	20.5
Arctic Ocean	14,090,000	5,439,000	3.9

Mountains

Europe		m	ft
Mont Blanc	*France/ Italy*	4,807	15,771
Monte Rosa	*Italy/ Switz.*	4,634	15,203
Dom	*Switzerland*	4,545	14,911
Weisshorn	*Switzerland*	4,505	14,780
Matterhorn/Cervino	*Italy/ Switz.*	4,478	14,691
Mt Maudit	*France/ Italy*	4,465	14,649
Finsteraarhorn	*Switzerland*	4,274	14,022
Aletschhorn	*Switzerland*	4,182	13,720
Jungfrau	*Switzerland*	4,158	13,642
Barre des Ecrins	*France*	4,103	13,461
Schreckhorn	*Switzerland*	4,078	13,380
Gran Paradiso	*Italy*	4,061	13,323
Piz Bernina	*Italy/ Switz.*	4,049	13,284
Ortles	*Italy*	3,899	12,792
Monte Viso	*Italy*	3,841	12,602
Grossglockner	*Austria*	3,797	12,457
Wildspitze	*Austria*	3,774	12,382
Weisskügel	*Austria/ Italy*	3,736	12,257
Balmhorn	*Switzerland*	3,709	12,169
Dammastock	*Switzerland*	3,630	11,909
Tödi	*Switzerland*	3,620	11,877
Presanella	*Italy*	3,556	11,667
Monte Adamello	*Italy*	3,554	11,660
Mulhacén	*Spain*	3,478	11,411
Pico de Aneto	*Spain*	3,404	11,168
Posets	*Spain*	3,375	11,073
Marmolada	*Italy*	3,342	10,964
Etna	*Italy*	3,340	10,958
Olympus	*Greece*	2,917	9,570
Galdhöpiggen	*Norway*	2,469	8,100
Pietrosul	*Romania*	2,305	7,562
Hvannadalshnúkur	*Iceland*	2,119	6,952
Narodnaya	*Russia*	1,894	6,214
Ben Nevis	*UK*	1,343	4,406

Asia		m	ft
Everest	*China/ Nepal*	8,848	29,029
Godwin Austen (K2)	*China/ Kashmir*	8,611	28,251
Kanchenjunga	*India/ Nepal*	8,598	28,208
Lhotse	*China/ Nepal*	8,516	27,939
Makalu	*China/ Nepal*	8,481	27,824
Cho Oyu	*China/ Nepal*	8,201	26,906
Dhaulagiri	*Nepal*	8,172	26,811
Manaslu	*Nepal*	8,156	26,758
Nanga Parbat	*Kashmir*	8,126	26,660
Annapurna	*Nepal*	8,078	26,502
Gasherbrum	*China/ Kashmir*	8,068	26,469
Broad Peak	*India*	8,051	26,414
Gosainthan	*China*	8,012	26,286
Disteghil Sar	*Kashmir*	7,885	25,869
Nuptse	*Nepal*	7,879	25,849
Masherbrum	*Kashmir*	7,821	25,659
Nanda Devi	*India*	7,817	25,646
Rakaposhi	*Kashmir*	7,788	25,551
Kanjut Sar	*India*	7,760	25,459
Kamet	*India*	7,756	25,446
Namcha Barwa	*China*	7,756	25,446
Gurla Mandhata	*China*	7,728	25,354
Muztag	*China*	7,723	25,338
Kongur Shan	*China*	7,719	25,324
Tirich Mir	*Pakistan*	7,690	25,229
Saser	*Kashmir*	7,672	25,170
K'ula Shan	*Bhutan/ China*	7,543	24,747
Pik Kommunizma	*Tajikistan*	7,495	24,590
Aling Gangri	*China*	7,314	23,996
Elbrus	*Russia*	5,633	18,481
Demavend	*Iran*	5,604	18,386
Ararat	*Turkey*	5,165	16,945
Gunong Kinabalu	*Borneo*	4,101	13,455
Yu Shan	*Taiwan*	3,997	13,113
Fuji-san	*Japan*	3,776	12,388
Rinjani	*Indonesia*	3,726	12,224
Mt Rajang	*Philippines*	3,364	11,037
Pidurutalagala	*Sri Lanka*	2,524	8,281

Africa		m	ft
Kilimanjaro	*Tanzania*	5,895	19,340
Mt Kenya	*Kenya*	5,199	17,057
Ruwenzori	*Uganda/ Zaïre*	5,109	16,762
Ras Dashan	*Ethiopia*	4,620	15,157
Meru	*Tanzania*	4,565	14,977
Karisimbi	*Rwanda/ Zaïre*	4,507	14,787
Mt Elgon	*Kenya/ Uganda*	4,321	14,176
Batu	*Ethiopia*	4,307	14,130
Guna	*Ethiopia*	4,231	13,882
Toubkal	*Morocco*	4,165	13,665
Irhil Mgoun	*Morocco*	4,071	13,356
Mt Cameroon	*Cameroon*	4,070	13,353
Amba Ferit	*Ethiopia*	3,875	13,042
Teide	*Spain (Tenerife)*	3,718	12,198
Thabana Ntlenyana	*Lesotho*	3,482	11,424
Emi Kussi	*Chad*	3,415	11,204

Oceania		m	ft
Puncak Jaya	*Indonesia*	5,029	16,499
Puncak Trikora	*Indonesia*	4,750	15,584
Puncak Mandala	*Indonesia*	4,702	15,427
Mt Wilhelm	*Papua N. Guinea*	4,508	14,790
Mauna Kea	*USA (Hawaii)*	4,205	13,796
Mauna Loa	*USA (Hawaii)*	4,170	13,681
Mt Cook	*New Zealand*	3,753	12,313
Mt Balbi	*Solomon Is.*	2,439	8,002
Mt Kosciusko	*Australia*	2,237	7,339

North America		m	ft
Mt McKinley	*USA (Alaska)*	6,194	20,321
Mt Logan	*Canada*	6,050	19,849
Citlaltepetl	*Mexico*	5,959	19,551
Mt St Elias	*USA/ Canada*	5,489	18,008
Popocatepetl	*Mexico*	5,452	17,887
Mt Foraker	*USA (Alaska)*	5,304	17,401
Ixtaccihuatl	*Mexico*	5,286	17,342
Lucania	*Canada*	5,227	17,149
Mt Steele	*Canada*	5,073	16,644
Mt Bona	*USA (Alaska)*	5,005	16,420
Mt Blackburn	*USA (Alaska)*	4,996	16,391
Mt Sanford	*USA (Alaska)*	4,940	16,207
Mt Wood	*Canada*	4,848	15,905
Nevado de Toluca	*Mexico*	4,670	15,321
Mt Fairweather	*USA (Alaska)*	4,663	15,298
Mt Whitney	*USA*	4,418	14,495
Mt Elbert	*USA*	4,399	14,432
Mt Harvard	*USA*	4,395	14,419
Mt Rainier	*USA*	4,392	14,409
Blanca Peak	*USA*	4,372	14,344
Long's Peak	*USA*	4,345	14,255
Nevado de Colima	*Mexico*	4,339	14,235
Mt Shasta	*USA*	4,317	14,163
Tajumulco	*Guatemala*	4,220	13,845
Gannett Peak	*USA*	4,202	13,786
Mt Waddington	*Canada*	3,994	13,104
Mt Robson	*Canada*	3,954	12,972
Chirripó Grande	*Costa Rica*	3,837	12,589
Pico Duarte	*Dominican Rep.*	3,175	10,417

South America		m	ft
Aconcagua	*Argentina*	6,960	22,834
Illimani	*Bolivia*	6,882	22,578
Bonete	*Argentina*	6,872	22,546
Ojos del Salado	*Argentina/ Chile*	6,863	22,516
Tupungato	*Argentina/ Chile*	6,800	22,309
Pissis	*Argentina*	6,779	22,241
Mercedario	*Argentina/ Chile*	6,770	22,211
Huascaran	*Peru*	6,768	22,204
Llullaillaco	*Argentina/ Chile*	6,723	22,057
Nudo de Cachi	*Argentina*	6,720	22,047
Yerupaja	*Peru*	6,632	21,758
N. de Tres Cruces	*Argentina/ Chile*	6,620	21,719
Incahuasi	*Argentina/ Chile*	6,600	21,654
Ancohuma	*Bolivia*	6,550	21,489
Sajama	*Bolivia*	6,520	21,391
Coropuna	*Peru*	6,425	21,079
Ausangate	*Peru*	6,384	20,945
Cerro del Toro	*Argentina*	6,380	20,932
Ampato	*Peru*	6,310	20,702
Chimborasso	*Ecuador*	6,267	20,561
Cotopaxi	*Ecuador*	5,896	19,344
S. Nev. de S. Marta	*Colombia*	5,800	19,029
Cayambe	*Ecuador*	5,796	19,016
Pico Bolivar	*Venezuela*	5,007	16,427

Antarctica		m	ft
Vinson Massif		4,897	16,066
Mt Kirkpatrick		4,528	14,855

Ocean Depths

Atlantic Ocean	m	ft
Puerto Rico (Milwaukee) Deep [7]	9,220	30,249
Cayman Trench [10]	7,680	25,197
Gulf of Mexico	5,203	17,070
Mediterranean Sea	5,121	16,801
Black Sea	2,211	7,254
North Sea	660	2,165
Baltic Sea	463	1,519
Hudson Bay	258	846

Indian Ocean	m	ft
Java Trench	7,450	24,442
Red Sea	2,635	8,454
Persian Gulf	73	239

Pacific Ocean	m	ft
Mariana Trench [1]	11,022	36,161
Tonga Trench [2]	10,882	35,702
Japan Trench [3]	10,554	34,626
Kuril Trench [4]	10,542	34,587
Mindanao Trench [5]	10,497	34,439
Kermadec Trench [6]	10,047	32,962
Peru-Chile Trench [8]	8,050	26,410
Aleutian Trench [9]	7,822	25,662
Middle American Trench	6,662	21,857

Arctic Ocean	m	ft
Molloy Deep	5,608	18,399

Land Lows

		m	ft
Caspian Sea	*Europe*	–28	–92
Dead Sea	*Asia*	–400	–1,312
Lake Assal	*Africa*	–156	–512
Lake Eyre North	*Oceania*	–16	–52
Death Valley	*N. America*	–86	–282
Valdês Peninsula	*S. America*	–40	–131

Rivers

Europe		km	miles
Volga	*Caspian Sea*	3,700	2,300
Danube	*Black Sea*	2,850	1,770
Ural	*Caspian Sea*	2,535	1,574
Dnepr	*Volga*	2,285	1,420
Kama	*Volga*	2,030	1,260
Don	*Volga*	1,990	1,240
Petchora	*Arctic Ocean*	1,790	1,110
Oka	*Volga*	1,480	920
Belaya	*Kama*	1,420	880
Dnestr	*Black Sea*	1,400	870
Vyatka	*Kama*	1,370	850
Rhine	*North Sea*	1,320	820
N. Dvina	*Arctic Ocean*	1,290	800
Desna	*Dnieper*	1,190	740
Elbe	*North Sea*	1,145	710
Vistula	*Baltic Sea*	1,090	675
Loire	*Atlantic Ocean*	1,020	635
W. Dvina	*Baltic Sea*	1,019	633

Asia		km	miles
Yangtze [3]	*Pacific Ocean*	6,380	3,960
Yenisey-Angara [5]	*Arctic Ocean*	5,550	3,445
Huang He [6]	*Pacific Ocean*	5,464	3,395
Ob-Irtysh [7]	*Arctic Ocean*	5,410	3,360
Mekong [9]	*Pacific Ocean*	4,500	2,795
Amur [10]	*Pacific Ocean*	4,400	2,730
Lena	*Arctic Ocean*	4,400	2,730
Irtysh	*Ob*	4,250	2,640
Yenisey	*Arctic Ocean*	4,090	2,540
Ob	*Arctic Ocean*	3,680	2,285
Indus	*Indian Ocean*	3,100	1,925
Brahmaputra	*Indian Ocean*	2,900	1,800
Syr Darya	*Aral Sea*	2,860	1,775
Salween	*Indian Ocean*	2,800	1,740
Euphrates	*Indian Ocean*	2,700	1,675
Vilyuy	*Lena*	2,650	1,645
Kolyma	*Arctic Ocean*	2,600	1,615
Amu Darya	*Aral Sea*	2,540	1,575
Ural	*Caspian Sea*	2,535	1,575
Ganges	*Indian Ocean*	2,510	1,560
Si Kiang	*Pacific Ocean*	2,100	1,305
Irrawaddy	*Indian Ocean*	2,010	1,250
Tigris	*Indian Ocean*	1,900	1,180
Angara	*Yenisey*	1,830	1,135
Yamuna	*Indian Ocean*	1,400	870

Africa		km	miles
Nile [1]	*Mediterranean*	6,670	4,140
Zaïre/Congo [8]	*Atlantic Ocean*	4,670	2,900
Niger	*Atlantic Ocean*	4,180	2,595
Zambezi	*Indian Ocean*	3,540	2,200
Oubangi/Uele	*Zaïre*	2,250	1,400
Kasai	*Zaïre*	1,950	1,210
Shaballe	*Indian Ocean*	1,930	1,200
Orange	*Atlantic Ocean*	1,860	1,155
Cubango	*Okavango*	1,800	1,120
Limpopo	*Indian Ocean*	1,600	995
Senegal	*Atlantic Ocean*	1,600	995
Volta	*Atlantic Ocean*	1,500	930
Benue	*Niger*	1,350	840

Australia		km	miles
Murray-Darling	*Indian Ocean*	3,750	2,330
Darling	*Murray*	3,070	1,905
Murray	*Indian Ocean*	2,575	1,600
Murrumbidgee	*Murray*	1,690	1,050

North America		km	miles
Mississ.-Missouri [4]	*Gulf of Mexico*	6,020	3,740
Mackenzie	*Arctic Ocean*	4,240	2,630
Mississippi	*Gulf of Mexico*	3,780	2,350
Missouri	*Mississippi*	3,780	2,350
Yukon	*Pacific Ocean*	3,185	1,980
Rio Grande	*Gulf of Mexico*	3,030	1,880
Arkansas	*Mississippi*	2,340	1,450
Colorado	*Pacific Ocean*	2,330	1,445
Red	*Mississippi*	2,040	1,270
Columbia	*Pacific Ocean*	1,950	1,210
Saskatchewan	*Lake Winnipeg*	1,940	1,205
Snake	*Columbia*	1,670	1,040
Churchill	*Hudson Bay*	1,600	990
Ohio	*Mississippi*	1,580	980
Brazos	*Gulf of Mexico*	1,400	870
St Lawrence	*Atlantic Ocean*	1,170	730

South America		km	miles
Amazon [2]	*Atlantic Ocean*	6,450	4,010
Paraná-Plate	*Atlantic Ocean*	4,500	2,800
Purus	*Amazon*	3,350	2,080
Madeira	*Amazon*	3,200	1,990
São Francisco	*Atlantic Ocean*	2,900	1,800
Paraná	*Plate*	2,800	1,740
Tocantins	*Atlantic Ocean*	2,750	1,710
Paraguay	*Paraná*	2,550	1,580
Orinoco	*Atlantic Ocean*	2,500	1,550
Pilcomayo	*Paraná*	2,500	1,550
Araguaia	*Tocantins*	2,250	1,400
Juruá	*Amazon*	2,000	1,240
Xingu	*Amazon*	1,980	1,230
Ucayali	*Amazon*	1,900	1,180
Maranón	*Amazon*	1,600	990
Uruguay	*Plate*	1,600	990
Magdalena	*Caribbean Sea*	1,540	960

Lakes

Europe		km^2	$miles^2$
Lake Ladoga	*Russia*	17,700	6,800
Lake Onega	*Russia*	9,700	3,700
Saimaa system	*Finland*	8,000	3,100
Vänern	*Sweden*	5,500	2,100
Rybinsk Res.	*Russia*	4,700	1,800

Asia		km^2	$miles^2$
Caspian Sea [1]	*Asia*	371,800	143,550
Aral Sea [6]	*Kazakh./ Uzbek.*	36,000	13,900
Lake Baykal [9]	*Russia*	30,500	11,780
Tonlé Sap	*Cambodia*	20,000	7,700
Lake Balkhash	*Kazakhstan*	18,500	7,100
Dongting Hu	*China*	12,000	4,600
Issyk Kul	*Kirghizia*	6,200	2,400
Lake Urmia	*Iran*	5,900	2,300
Koko Nur	*China*	5,700	2,200
Poyang Hu	*China*	5,000	1,900
Lake Khanka	*China/ Russia*	4,400	1,700
Lake Van	*Turkey*	3,500	1,400
Ubsa Nur	*China*	3,400	1,300

Africa		km^2	$miles^2$
Lake Victoria [3]	*E. Africa*	68,000	26,000
Lake Tanganyika [7]	*C. Africa*	33,000	13,000
Lake Malawi [10]	*E. Africa*	29,600	11,430
Lake Chad	*C. Africa*	25,000	9,700
Lake Turkana	*Ethiop./ Kenya*	8,500	3,300
Lake Volta	*Ghana*	8,500	3,300
Lake Bangweulu	*Zambia*	8,000	3,100
Lake Rukwa	*Tanzania*	7,000	2,700
Lake Mai-Ndombe	*Zaïre*	6,500	2,500
Lake Kariba	*Zamb./ Zimbab.*	5,300	2,000
Lake Mobutu	*Uganda/ Zaïre*	5,300	2,000
Lake Nasser	*Egypt/ Sudan*	5,200	2,000
Lake Mweru	*Zambia/ Zaïre*	4,900	1,900
Lake Kyoga	*Uganda*	4,400	1,700
Lake Tana	*Ethiopia*	3,630	1,400

Australia		km^2	$miles^2$
Lake Eyre	*Australia*	8,900	3,400
Lake Torrens	*Australia*	5,800	2,200

North America		km^2	$miles^2$
Lake Superior [2]	*Canada/ USA*	82,350	31,800
Lake Huron [4]	*Canada/ USA*	59,600	23,010
Lake Michigan [5]	*USA*	58,000	22,400
Great Bear Lake [8]	*Canada*	31,800	12,280
Great Slave Lake	*Canada*	28,500	11,000
Lake Erie	*Canada/ USA*	25,700	9,900
Lake Winnipeg	*Canada*	24,400	9,400
Lake Ontario	*Canada/ USA*	19,500	7,500
Lake Nicaragua	*Nicaragua*	8,200	3,200
Lake Athabasca	*Canada*	8,100	3,100
Smallwood Res.	*Canada*	6,530	2,520
Reindeer Lake	*Canada*	6,400	2,500
Lake Winnipegosis	*Canada*	5,400	2,100
Nettilling Lake	*Canada*	5,500	2,100

South America		km^2	$miles^2$
Lake Titicaca	*Bolivia/ Peru*	8,300	3,200
Lake Poopo	*Peru*	2,800	1,100

Islands

Europe		km^2	$miles^2$
Great Britain [8]	*UK*	229,880	88,700
Iceland	*Atlantic*	103,000	39,800
Ireland	*Ireland/ UK*	84,400	32,600
Novaya Zemlya (N.)	*Russia*	48,200	18,600
W. Spitzbergen	*Norway*	39,000	15,100
Novaya Zemlya (S.)	*Russia*	33,200	12,800
Sicily	*Italy*	25,500	9,800
Sardinia	*Italy*	24,000	9,300
N. E. Spitzbergen	*Norway*	15,000	5,600
Corsica	*France*	8,700	3,400
Crete	*Greece*	8,350	3,200
Zealand	*Denmark*	6,850	2,600

Asia		km^2	$miles^2$
Borneo [3]	*S. E. Asia*	744,360	287,400
Sumatra [6]	*Indonesia*	473,600	182,860
Honshu [7]	*Japan*	230,500	88,980
Celebes	*Indonesia*	189,000	73,000
Java	*Indonesia*	126,700	48,900
Luzon	*Philippines*	104,700	40,400
Mindanao	*Philippines*	101,500	39,200
Hokkaido	*Japan*	78,400	30,300
Sakhalin	*Russia*	74,060	28,600
Sri Lanka	*Indian Ocean*	65,600	25,300
Taiwan	*Pacific Ocean*	36,000	13,900
Kyushu	*Japan*	35,700	13,800
Hainan	*China*	34,000	13,100
Timor	*Indonesia*	33,600	13,000
Shikoku	*Japan*	18,800	7,300
Halmahera	*Indonesia*	18,000	6,900
Ceram	*Indonesia*	17,150	6,600
Sumbawa	*Indonesia*	15,450	6,000
Flores	*Indonesia*	15,200	5,900
Samar	*Philippines*	13,100	5,100
Negros	*Philippines*	12,700	4,900
Bangka	*Indonesia*	12,000	4,600
Panay	*Philippines*	11,500	4,400
Sumba	*Indonesia*	11,100	4,300
Mindoro	*Philippines*	9,750	3,800
Bali	*Indonesia*	5,600	2,200
Cyprus	*Mediterranean*	3,570	1,400
Wrangel Is.	*Russia*	2,800	1,000

Africa		km^2	$miles^2$
Madagascar [4]	*Indian Ocean*	587,040	226,660
Socotra	*Indian Ocean*	3,600	1,400
Réunion	*Indian Ocean*	2,500	965
Tenerife	*Atlantic Ocean*	2,350	900
Mauritius	*Indian Ocean*	1,865	720

Oceania		km^2	$miles^2$
New Guinea [2]	*Ind./ Pap. NG*	821,030	317,000
New Zealand (S.)	*New Zealand*	150,500	58,100
New Zealand (N.)	*New Zealand*	114,700	44,300
Tasmania	*Australia*	67,800	26,200
New Britain	*Papua NG*	37,800	14,600
New Caledonia	*Pacific Ocean*	19,100	7,400
Viti Levu	*Fiji*	10,500	4,100
Hawaii	*Pacific Ocean*	10,450	4,000
Bougainville	*Papua NG*	9,600	3,700
Guadalcanal	*Solomon Is.*	6,500	2,500
Vanua Levu	*Fiji*	5,550	2,100
New Ireland	*Papua NG*	3,200	1,200

North America		km^2	$miles^2$
Greenland [1]	*Greenland*	2,175,600	839,800
Baffin Is. [5]	*Canada*	508,000	196,100
Victoria Is. [9]	*Canada*	212,200	81,900
Ellesmere Is. [10]	*Canada*	212,000	81,800
Cuba	*Cuba*	110,860	42,800
Newfoundland	*Canada*	110,680	42,700
Hispaniola	*Atlantic Ocean*	76,200	29,400
Banks Is.	*Canada*	67,000	25,900
Devon Is.	*Canada*	54,500	21,000
Melville Is.	*Canada*	42,400	16,400
Vancouver Is.	*Canada*	32,150	12,400
Somerset Is.	*Canada*	24,300	9,400
Jamaica	*Caribbean Sea*	11,400	4,400
Puerto Rico	*Atlantic Ocean*	8,900	3,400
Cape Breton Is.	*Canada*	4,000	1,500

South America		km^2	$miles^2$
Tierra del Fuego	*Argent./ Chile*	47,000	18,100
Falkland Is. (E.)	*Atlantic Ocean*	6,800	2,600
South Georgia	*Atlantic Ocean*	4,200	1,600
Galapagos (Isabela)	*Pacific Ocean*	2,250	870

General Notes

Philip's *Illustrated World Atlas* follows a geographical, rather than an alphabetical sequence, starting with Europe and proceeding through Asia, Africa, Australasia and the Pacific islands, to North and South America and ending with the islands of the Atlantic Ocean. Within each continent the progression is generally west to east and north to south.

The size of a country's article and the size of its map tend to reflect the importance and status of the country on a world scale. This is not fixed, however, and a few small countries appear at a map scale which is larger than they would normally merit. Large countries such as the USA, Canada and Russia have maps covering a double page, while for a few densely populated areas – such as south-east England or northern India – supplementary maps have been added at a scale larger than the main country map.

The maps are all positioned with north at the top, with the lines of latitude and longitude shown and labelled. Around the edges of the maps are a series of letters and figures, used for locating places from the index.

Place names are spelled in their local forms on the maps, but in the tables and text conventional spellings are generally used. For example, Roma (Rome) will appear with the Italian spelling on the map but in the text it will be referred to as Rome. The maps were corrected up to April 1994 and any changes to place names and boundaries were incorporated up to that time.

For ease of reference, an alphabetical list of the countries described in the main text is given below. Some islands, areas or territories that are a part of a country, but separated from it, have been omitted from this list (please refer to the Index on pages 193–200 for the full listing).

MAP SYMBOLS

SETTLEMENTS

| PARIS | Berne | Livorno | Brugge | Algeciras | Fréjus | Oberammergau | Thira |

Settlement symbols and type styles vary according to the scale of each map and indicate the importance of towns on the map rather than specific population figures

∴ Ruins or Archæological Sites   ˇ Wells in Desert

ADMINISTRATION

Boundaries

——— International

— — — International (Undefined or Disputed)

············ Internal

National Parks

International boundaries show the *de facto* situation where there are rival claims to territory.

Country Names
NICARAGUA

Administrative Areas
KENT
CALABRIA

COMMUNICATIONS

Roads

——— Primary

——— Secondary

‿‿‿ Trails and Seasonal

Railways

——— Primary

——— Secondary

········ Under Construction

✧ Airfields

⤬ Passes

╪---╪ Railway Tunnels

▭▭▭ Principal Canals

PHYSICAL FEATURES

⁓ Perennial Streams

····· Intermittent Streams

⬭ Perennial Lakes

Intermittent Lakes

Swamps and Marshes

Permanent Ice and Glaciers

▲ 2259 Elevations (m)

▾ 2604 Sea Depths (m)

408 Elevation of Lake Surface Above Sea Level (m)

Europe

EUROPE

Second smallest of the continents, Europe is topographically subdivided by shallow shelf seas into a mainland block with a sprawl of surrounding peninsulas and off-lying islands. Its western, northern and southern limits are defined by coastlines and conventions. Of the off-lying islands, Iceland, Svalbard, the Faroes, Britain and Ireland are included. So are all the other larger islands of the Mediterranean Sea, though more on the grounds of their conquest and habitation by Europeans than by their geographic proximity.

The eastern boundary, between Europe and Asia, is hard to define, and conventions differ. Geographers usually set it along the eastern flank of the Ural Mountains, the Emba River, the northern shore of the Caspian Sea, the Kuma and Marich Rivers (north of the Caucasus), and the eastern shores of the Azov and Black Seas, and include the small piece of Turkey west of the Bosphorous. Europe extends from well north of the Arctic Circle almost to the latitude 34°N, and includes a wide range of topographies and climates – from polders below sea level to high alpine peaks, from semi-deserts to polar ice-caps.

Its geological structure, and some of the forces that have shaped it, show up clearly on a physical map. In the far north lies a shield of ancient granites and gneisses occupying northern Scandinavia, Finland and Karelia. This underlies and gives shape to the rugged lowlands of this area. The highland formed later: north and east of the platform lay a marine trough, which was raised, compressed and folded by a lateral pressure about 400 million years ago to form the highlands – now eroded but still impressive – of Norway and north-west Britain.

To the south lay another deep-sea trough, from which a vast accumulation of sediments was raised about 300 million years ago, producing the belt of highlands and well-worn uplands that stretches across Europe from Spain to southern Poland. They include the Cantabrian and central mountains of Iberia, the French Massif Central and uplands of Brittany, the Vosges, Ardennes and Westerwald, the Black Forest, the hills of Cornwall, South Wales and south-west Ireland. A third trough, the Tethys Sea, formed still further south and extended in a wide swathe across Europe and Asia. Strong pressure from a northwards-drifting Africa slowly closed the sea to form the Mediterranean, and raised the 'alpine' mountains that fringe it – the Atlas of North Africa, the Sierra Nevada of Spain, the Pyrenees, the Alps themselves, the Apennines, the Carpathians, the Dinaric Alps and the various ranges of the Balkan Peninsula.

More recently still came the Ice Age. The first ice-sheets formed across Eurasia and North America from 2 to 3 million years ago; during the last million

years there have been four major glacial periods in the Alps and three, maybe more, in Scandinavia. The lowland ice melted 8–10,000 years ago, and the Scandinavian and Alpine glaciers retreated, only Iceland and Svalbard keeping ice-caps. The accompanying rise in sea level finally isolated Britain.

Physically, Central Europe is divided into three clear structural belts. In the south, the Alpine fold mountains are at their highest and most complex in Switzerland and Austria, but divide eastwards into the Carpathians and the Dinaric mountains of Yugoslavia, enclosing the basin in which Hungary lies. A second belt, the central uplands, consisting of block mountains, intervening lowlands and some of Europe's greatest coalfields, stretches from the Ardennes across Germany and the Czech and Slovak Republics to thin out and disappear in Poland. The third belt, the northern lowland, broadens eastwards, and owes its relief largely to glacial deposits.

Two great rivers dominate the drainage pattern: the 1,320 km [820 ml] Rhine rises in the Alps and crosses the central uplands and northern lowland to reach the North Sea. The east-flowing 2,850 km [1,770 ml] Danube cuts right across the fold mountains of Bratislava and again at the Iron Gates (Portile de Fier) on its way to the Black Sea. The Iberian Peninsula (586,000 sq km [226,000 sq mls]) is the largest of the three peninsula jutting southwards from

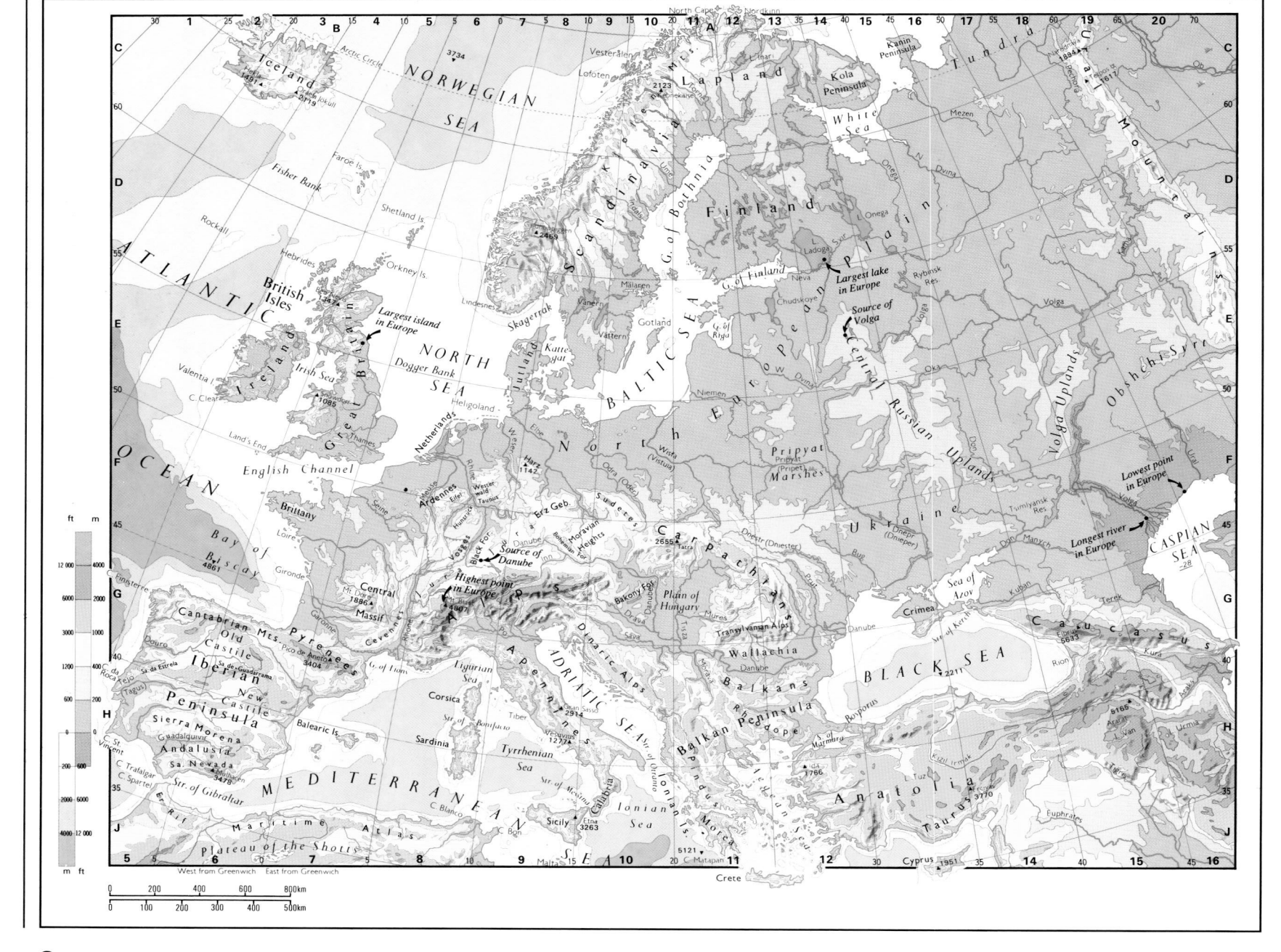

Europe into the Mediterranean Sea. Stretching through 10°, of latitude it reaches to within 15 km [9.5 mls] of the African coast and extends far enough westwards to merit the title of 'the outpost of Europe'. This position is reflected in the fact that the voyages of Columbus to the New World were launched from Iberian shores.

The core of the peninsula is the Meseta plateau, a remnant of an ancient mountain chain with an average height of 600–1,000 m [1,900–3,280 ft]. Huge faulted mountain ranges, such as the Sierras de Gata, de Gredos and de Guadarrama, traverse the plateau obliquely and terminate westwards in Portugal as rocky headlands jutting into the Atlantic. Between these upthrust ranges are the wide down-warped basins of Old and New Castile. The plateau is tilted

Well-watered cultivation brings life to the sparse natural environment of Greece – home of the first great modern European civilization.

towards the west and its high eastern edge forms a major watershed that overlooks narrow, discontinuous coastal lowlands on the Mediterranean side. The main drainage is through Portugal towards the

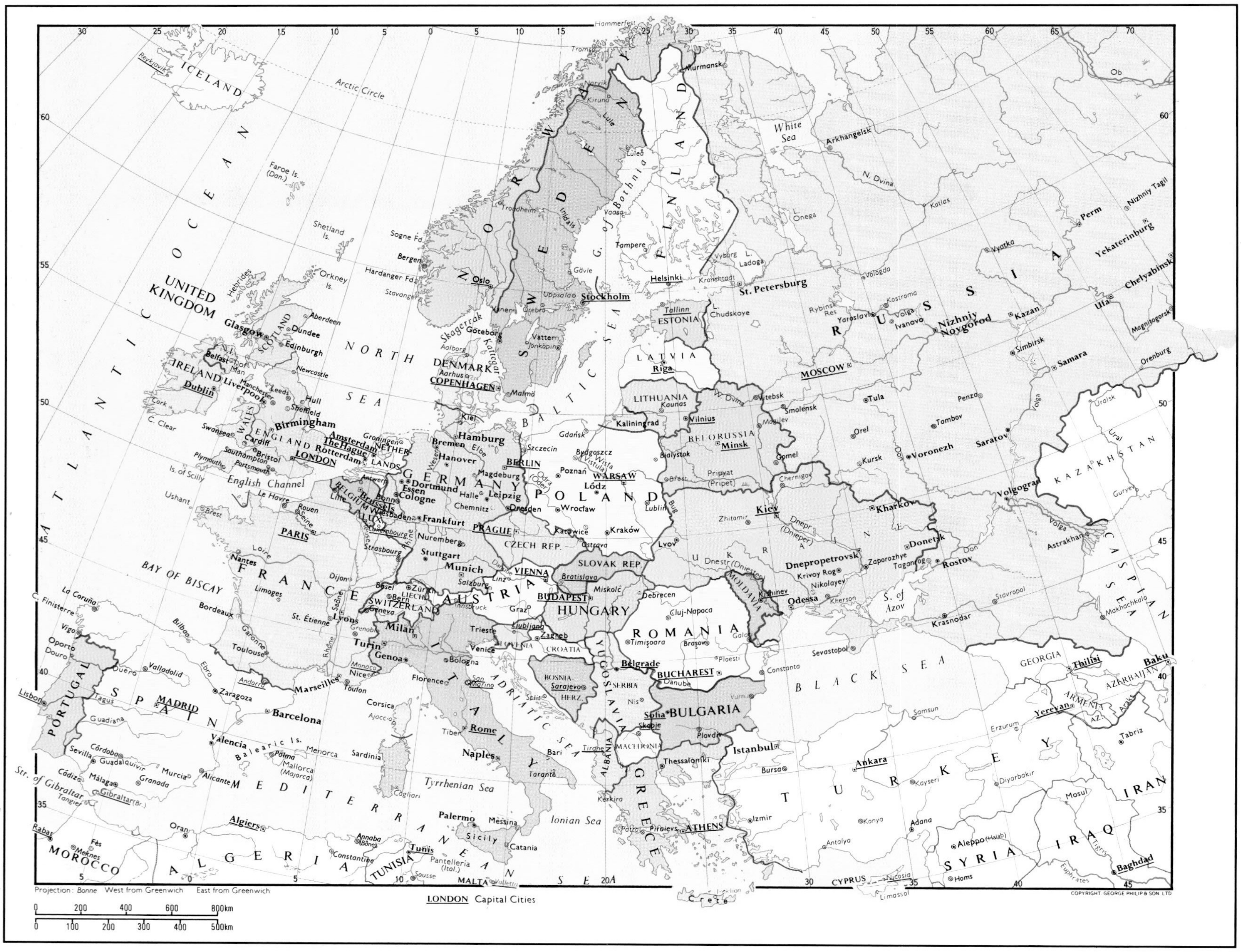

The clean chalk faces of the 'Seven Sisters' gaze out from Sussex across the English Channel towards France. Britain was separated from continental Europe at the end of the last Ice Age, some 8–10,000 years ago.

Atlantic. On its north-eastern and southern flanks the Meseta plateau drops abruptly to the Ebro and Guadalquivir (Andalusian) fault troughs; these rise on their outer sides to the lofty mountains of the Pyrenees and the Sierra Nevada respectively.

The Italian and Balkan peninsulas extend southwards into the Mediterranean Sea. In the north of Italy lies the Plain of Lombardy, drained by the River Po and its tributaries; towering above are the ranges of alpine fold mountains – southern outliers of the European Alps – that mark the boundary between Italy and neighbouring France, Switzerland and Austria. A further range of alpine mountains – the Apennines – runs through peninsular Italy and continues into Sicily.

The western Balkans are made up of alpine fold mountains, running north-west to south-east behind the western coasts – the Dinaric Alps of the former Yugoslavia and the Pindos Mountains (Pindos Oros) of Greece. The Balkan Mountains of Bulgaria represent the southern extension of the great arc of alpine mountains which loop round the lower basin of the Danube. Between them and the Dinaric Alps is a

stable, crystalline block, the Rhodopi Massif.

Eastern Europe is a relatively huge area, stretching from the Arctic Ocean to the Caspian Sea and the Adriatic to the Urals and including the continent's two largest 'nations' – (European) Russia and the Ukraine. The most common landscape here is undulating plain, comprising coniferous forest as well as massive expanses of arable farmland, but there are impressive mountains too, notably the Carpathians, the Transylvanian Alps and, in the east, the Caucasus and the Urals.

The tree line in Europe – the boundary marking the northern limit of tree growth – runs north of the Arctic Circle. Only the tundra-covered northern area of Lapland and the Kola Peninsula lie beyond it. Practically all of Europe that lay south of the tree line was originally forested. North of the 60th parallel lay dark, sombre evergreen forests, dominated by spruce and pine. Since the last glacial period the evergreen forests have occupied a swathe 1,200 km [750 mls] wide across central Scandinavia and Finland, broken by marshes, moorlands and lakes, and interspersed with stands of willow and birch. Much of this forest remains today, and is still the haunt of elk, red deer and small numbers of wolves, brown bears and lynx. To the south of the coniferous forest, Europe was covered with broad-leaved deciduous woodland – an ancient forest of mature oak, ash, birch, beech,

sycamore, and many other familiar species. Favoured by the mild damp climate, this rich forest grew in abundance over the lowlands, foothills and warmer uplands of Europe, but was limited in the south by dry Mediterranean summers, and in Hungary and the south-west by the aridity of the plains. Virtually the first industrial resource of European man, the forest suffered a thousand years of exploitation and only remnants survive today.

The large number of Europe's nationalities all speak Indo-European languages and can be grouped into racial types (Nordic, Germanic, Mediterranean and so on), but centuries of extensive intermixing and more recent immigration have blurred the distinctions. Christianity has exerted a profound influence on the continent's culture and remains the dominant religion, though its forms are many and varied.

Europe's modern history is one of conflict between nations, culminating in the 20th century with two world wars. While the period after 1945 saw unprecedented peace, the collapse of Communism after 1945 suggested a different political pattern for the new millennium ■

Created by the northward movement of the African plate, the Alps form a backdrop to the wooded slopes of Savoie in south-east France. Almost all of Europe below the tree line was originally forested.

ICELAND

Situated far out in the North Atlantic Ocean, Iceland is not only the smallest but also the most isolated of the independent Scandinavian countries. Though politically part of Europe, the island (nearer to Greenland than to Scotland) arises geologically from the boundary between Europe and America – the Mid-Atlantic Ridge. It is indeed a product of the ridge, formed almost entirely by volcanic outpourings at a point where the Earth's crust is opening at a rate measurable in centimetres per year.

A central zone of recently active volcanoes and fissures crosses Iceland from Axarfjördur in the north to Vestmannaeyjar in the south, with a side-branch to Reykjanes and an outlying zone of activity around the Snaefellsnes peninsula in the west. During the thousand years that Iceland has been settled, between 150 and 200 eruptions have occurred in the active zones, some building up substantial volcanic cones. Between 1104 and 1970 Mount Hekla, in the south-west, erupted at least 15 times. Its earliest outpourings of ash devastated local farms, some of which have recently been excavated.

A huge eruption in 1783 destroyed pasture and livestock on a grand scale, causing a famine that reduced the Icelandic population by a quarter. More recent eruptions include the formation of a new island – Surtsey – off the south-west coast in 1963, and the partial devastation of the town of Vestmannaeyjar-Karpstadur, on neighbouring Heimaey, ten years later. Paradoxically, Iceland is also an island of glaciers and ice-sheets, with four large ice-caps occupying 11% of the surface, and several smaller glaciers.

A deep-sea trawler pulls out of Akureyri, at the head of Eyjafjördur in northern Iceland. The economy's dependence on fishing has led Iceland into periodic 'Cod Wars', notably with Britain.

Colonized by Viking and British farmers in the 9th century, Iceland became a dependency first of Norway, then of Denmark, though mainly self-governing with a parliament (Althing) dating from AD 930. This is thought to be the world's first parliament in the modern sense, and is certainly the oldest. Recognized as a sovereign state from 1918, Iceland was united with Denmark through a common sovereign until 1944, when it became a republic.

Since the country was formerly pastoral, with most of the population scattered in farms and small hamlets, the standard of living depended on the vicissitudes of farming close to the Arctic Circle. Now the economy is based on deep-sea fishing; fish and fish products make up 70% of exports. About a fifth of the land is used for agriculture, but only 1% is actually cultivated for root crops and fodder. The rest is used for grazing cattle and sheep. Self-sufficient in

meat and dairy products, Iceland augments its main exports with clothing such as sheepskin coats and woollen products.

Geothermal and hydroelectric power provide cheap energy for developing industries, including aluminium smelting and hot-house cultivation; and most houses and offices in Reykjavík, the capital, are heated geothermally. About a quarter of the work-force is engaged in the production of energy and manufacturing – processing food and fish, making cement and refining aluminium from imported baux-ite. The population is concentrated mainly in settle-ments close to the coast, over half of them in or near Reykjavík. Living standards currently compare with those of other Scandinavian countries. In some respects they are better: Iceland boasts the lowest infant mortality rate in the world and the highest life expectancy outside Japan ■

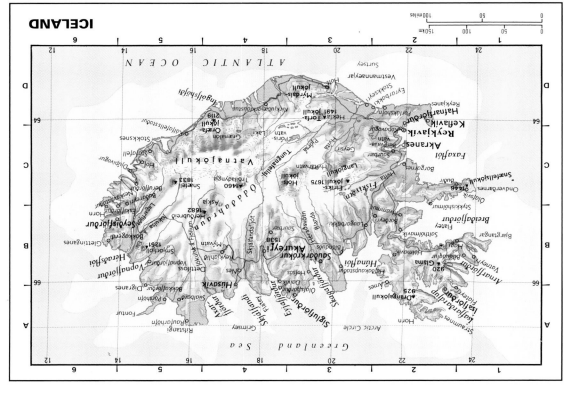

ICELAND

ATLANTIC OCEAN

Greenland Sea

FAROE ISLANDS

The Faroes are a group of rocky islands situated in the North Atlantic Ocean about 450 km [280 mls] from Iceland, 675 km [420 mls] from Norway and 300 km [185 mls] from the Shetlands. Like Iceland, they are composed mainly of volcanic material. They were dramatically moulded by glacial action and the landscape forms a forbidding setting for the Faroese farming and fishing settlements. Away from the villages and scattered hamlets, high cliffs are home to millions of seabirds.

Winters are mild for the latitude but the summers are cool. It is usually windy and overcast or foggy. Sheep farming on the poor soils is the main occupation but salted, dried, processed and frozen fish, fishmeal and oil – from cod, whiting, mackerel and herring – comprise the chief exports. Faroese motorvessels are found in all the deep-sea fishing grounds of the North Atlantic and the capital, Tórshavn, has ship-repairing yards. Denmark, Norway and Britain are the country's main trading partners.

The Faroes have been part of the Danish kingdom since 1386 and from 1851 they sent two representatives to the Danish parliament. Their own elected assembly, dating from 1852, secured a large degree of self-government as a region within the Danish realm in 1948.

The islands left the European Free Trade Association (EFTA) when Denmark switched membership to the European Economic Community (EEC) on 1 January 1973, but did not join the community – though they do have a special associate status allowing for free industrial trade. Since 1940 the currency has been the Faroese krøna, which is freely interchangeable with the Danish krone. The people speak Faroese, a Scandinavian language official (alongside Danish) since 1948. Of the 22 islands, 17 are permanently inhabited ■

A trio of puffins take a break from fishing on the Faroes. While the islands prove a tough environment for their human inhabitants, they are a magnet for a wide variety of seabirds.

NORWAY

One of the world's most distinctly shaped countries, the kingdom of Norway occupies the western part of the Scandinavian peninsula, from the North Cape at latitude 71°N to Lindesnes at 58°N, a north-south distance of over 1,600 km [1,000 mls]. It covers an area far larger than Poland, yet has a population of less than 4.3 million, most of whom live in the southern part of the country, where the capital, Oslo, is situated.

Nowhere in Norway is far from the sea. At the widest point it is only 430 km [270 mls] from west to east, and near the Arctic port of Narvik the Swedish border comes to within 6.5 km [4 mls] of the Norwegian coast. A third of Norway lies within the Arctic Circle, but the climate is not as severe as might be expected because the Norwegian coast benefits from the moderating effects of the warm waters of the North Atlantic Drift. Even on the Arctic coast, the ports of Hammerfest and Kirkenes remain unfrozen in most winters.

The sea has always been a major influence in Norwegian life. A thousand years ago Viking sailors from Norway roamed the northern seas, founding colonies around the coasts of Britain, Iceland and even North America. Today fishing, shipbuilding and the management of merchant shipping lines are of vital importance to the Norwegian economy, and its merchant ships, most of which seldom visit the home ports, earn profits which pay for a third of the country's imports.

Landscape

Norway is a rugged, mountainous country in which communication is difficult. The Norwegian landscape is dominated by rolling plateaus, the *vidda*, generally 300 to 900 m [1,000 to 3,000 ft] high, above which some peaks rise to as much as 1,500 to 2,500 m [5,000 to 8,000 ft] in the area between Oslo, Bergen and Trondheim. In the far north the summits are around 1,000 m [3,000 ft] lower.

The highest areas retain permanent ice fields, as in the Jotunheim Mountains above Sognefjord. The Norwegian mountains have been uplifted during three mountain-building episodes during the last 400 million years, and they contain rocks of the earliest geological periods. Intrusions of volcanic material accompanied the uplifting and folding, and there are great masses of granites and gneisses - the source of Norway's mineral wealth.

There are few large areas of flat land in the country, but in the east the *vidda* are broken by deep valleys of rivers flowing to the lowlands of south-east Norway, focused on Oslo. In glacial times the whole country was covered by the great northern ice-cap. When it melted about 10,000 years ago it left behind large deposits of glacial moraine, well represented around Oslo in the Raa moraines. Soils of better quality are used for crops and meadows, while the less productive sands and gravels remain forested.

The configuration of the coast – the longest in Europe – helps to explain the ease with which the Norwegians took to the sea in their early history and why they have remained a seafaring nation since. The *vidda* are cut by long, narrow, steep-sided fjords on the west coast, shaped by the great northern ice-cap.

The largest of these, Sognefjord – 203 km [127 mls] long and less than 5 km [3 mls] wide – is the longest inlet in Europe and the best known fjord, though not the most spectacular.

Along the coast there are hundreds of islands, the largest group of which, the Lofoten Islands, lie north of the Arctic Circle. These islands, known as the *skerryguard*, protect the inner coast from the battering of the Atlantic breakers, and provide sheltered leads of water which the coastal ferries and fishing boats can navigate in safety.

Until recently communications along the coast were easier by boat than by land. Oslo is linked by rail to the main towns of the south, and a line reaches north to Bodö at latitude 67½°N. Roads are difficult to build and costly to maintain, and are often blocked by snow in winter and spring (snow accumulates to March).

There are still several hundred ferries which carry cars across the fjords, but much money has been invested in the building of a north-south trunk road, with bridges across the fjords, to avoid the constant use of ferries. Air transport is of increasing importance and many small airstrips are in use, bringing remote communities into contact with the more populated south.

Resources

With two-thirds of the country comprising barren mountains, snowfields or unproductive wastes, and one-fifth forested, less than 3% of the land can be cultivated. The barrenness of the soil, the heavy rainfall, winter snows and the short growing season restrict agriculture, especially in the north, though in the long days of summer good crops of hay, potatoes, quick-growing vegetables and even rye and barley are grown. Near the coast, farming is confined to the limited areas of level or gently sloping ground beside these sheltered fjords. Cattle and sheep use the slopes above them in the summer but are fed in stalls during the winter. Everywhere fish is caught in the local waters.

Iron and lead ores are found in the north, copper in central Norway and titanium in the south. The

---

SCANDINAVIA

There are several possible definitions of the term Scandinavia. In the narrow geographical sense it refers to the peninsula shared by Norway and Sweden; in a broader cultural and political sense it includes the five countries of the Nordic Council – Norway, Sweden, Denmark, Finland and Iceland. All except Finland have related languages, and all have a tradition of parliamentary democracy: Finland and Iceland are republics, while the others are constitutional monarchies.

There are also strong historical links between them, beginning in the 8th century when their ancestors, the Norsemen, colonized large parts of northern Europe. All have at different times been governed together, Sweden and Finland separating in 1809, Norway and Sweden in 1905, and Denmark and Iceland as recently as 1944. Until 1995, only Denmark had joined the EU.

Because of their northerly position, and their exposure to Atlantic weather systems, the Scandinavian states have a cool, moist climate not favourable to crops. However, because of the long hours of daylight in the northern summer, some surprisingly good crops are grown north of the Arctic Circle.

Deep fjords accommodate an increasing number of cruise ships – part of a boom that now sees Norway welcome more than twice as many tourists as Sweden.

people own their houses, and many families have second homes on the shores of fjords and lakes. Today's Norwegians are also more generous than their Viking ancestors: the nation is by far Europe's biggest donor of foreign aid per capita, with a figure of 1.1% of GNP – well above the OECD (Organization for Economic Co-operation and Development) target of 0.7%. Norway rejected the EEC when Denmark, the UK and Ireland joined in 1973, but now aims for membership of the EU in 1995.

The pre-war economy, dependent on forestry, farming, fishing and seafaring, is still important, but the numbers employed in these industries are dwindling as more and more people move into the new industries and services in the growing towns. There are still few large towns, and all six of those with more than 50,000 population are on the coast. The largest are Oslo, Bergen and Trondheim ∎

extent of Norway's mineral resources is not fully known, and prospecting is still revealing new deposits. Oil and natural gas from the seabed of the North Sea have made a great contribution to the Norwegian economy in recent years, and comprise more than half of the country's export earnings; Statfjord B (816,000 tonnes) is the world's biggest oil platform. Exploitation of all these reserves provides more than enough for the country's needs.

There is no coal in mainland Norway, although some is found in the islands on the Svalbard archipelago in the Arctic Ocean. The lack of coal has been partly compensated for by the development of hydro-electricity, begun in the early 20th century, when the waterfalls of rivers flowing down the steep slopes above the fjords were first harnessed. Later, inland sites were developed, and the greatest concentration is in the Rjukan Valley, 160 km [100 mls] west of Oslo. Today Norway (which owns five of the world's highest waterfalls) derives more than 99% of its electricity from water power.

The availability of cheap power made possible the rapid growth of the wood-pulp, paper and chemical industries, and later stimulated the metal-working industries. Many of the industrial sites are on the shores of remote fjords, where cheap electricity and deep-water access for the import of raw materials and for the export of finished products are the determining factors in choosing the location. The aluminium and chemical industries of the south-west coast are typical.

Metal-working has developed in the far north since World War II. After primary treatment iron is exported from Kirkenes to a smelter at Mo-i-Rana, on the coast just south of the Arctic Circle, which uses coal imported from Svalbard. The port of Narvik was connected by rail to the Swedish system in 1903, so that Swedish iron ore could be sent from an ice-free port to supply the iron smelters of Germany and other continental markets.

Rapid industrial development since World War II has transformed the Norwegian economy, and has ensured that the Norwegians are among the most prosperous people in Europe. Few people are very wealthy – taxation rates are high – but few are very poor, and an advanced welfare state (common to all the Scandinavian countries) provides good services even to isolated communities. The great majority of

NORWAY, SWEDEN

SWEDEN

The kingdom of Sweden is the largest of the Scandinavian countries in both population and area. It occupies the eastern half of the Scandinavian peninsula, extending southwards to latitude 55°N and having a much smaller Arctic area than either Norway or Finland.

The 1,600 km [1,000 ml] eastern coast, along the shores of the Baltic Sea and the Gulf of Bothnia, extends from the mouth of the Torne River, which forms the border with Finland to Ystad in the south, opposite the Danish island of Bornholm and the German coast. Sweden also has a coastline facing west along the shores of the Kattegat – the strait that separates Sweden and the Jutland peninsula, which is part of Denmark.

Landscape

Sweden's share of the Scandinavian peninsula is less mountainous than that of Norway. The northern half of the country forms part of the Baltic or Fenno-Scandian Shield, a stable block of ancient granites and gneisses which extends round the head of the Gulf of Bothnia into Finland. This part of Sweden contains most of the country's rich mineral wealth. The shield land is an area of low plateaus rising westwards.

South of the plateaus area there is a belt of lowlands between the capital city, Stockholm, and the second city, Göteborg (Gothenburg). These lowlands contain several large lakes, the chief of which are Mälaren, near Stockholm, and the larger Vänern and Vättern, which are situated in the middle of the lowland belt.

These are all that remains of a strait which, in glacial times, connected the Baltic with the Kattegat. Changes in land and water level during the later stages of the Ice Age led to the breaking of this connection. Now linked by canals, these lakes form an important water route across the country. South of the lakes is a low plateau, rising to 380 m [1,250 ft] above Lake Vättern and sloping gently down to the small lowland area of Skåne (Scania).

Sweden's topography was greatly affected by the Ice Age: the long, narrow lakes which fill the upper valleys of many of the rivers of northern Sweden have been shaped by the action of ice. They are the relics of a much larger lake system which was fed by water from the melting ice-sheet and provide excellent natural reservoirs for hydroelectric stations. Some of the most fertile soils in Sweden were formed from material deposited in the beds of such glacial lakes. Elsewhere, glacial moraines and deposits of boulder clay are other reminders of the impact of the Ice Age.

Climate and agriculture

The high mountains which form the spine of the Scandinavian peninsula shut off the modifying influence of the Atlantic weather systems from northern Sweden. This area thus has colder, drier winters than places on the seaward side, but also enjoys warmer and less rainy summers. On the Norrland plateau annual rainfall is less than 508 mm [20 in], July temperatures average 15°C [59°F] and the long summer days of the high northern latitudes make summertime pleasant – although the long winters are dark and cold.

The southern part of Sweden, between the Kattegat and the Baltic, is open to Atlantic influences and has milder winters than the northern areas, but summers are cooler and wetter. Göteborg has average winter temperatures of 0°C [32°F], compared with Stockholm's –3°C [27°F], whilst at Haparanda, at the head of the Gulf of Bothnia, the coldest month of February has an average temperature of –12°C [10°F]. In summer, however, there is little difference between north and south, most areas having between 15° and 20°C [59° to 68°F].

There are extensive coniferous forests throughout northern Sweden; indeed, half the country's land area is covered with trees. In the south the original cover of mixed deciduous woodland has been cleared for agriculture from the areas of better soil, the typical landscape now being farmland interspersed with forest. This is usually spruce, often with birch.

There are better opportunities for agriculture in Sweden than elsewhere in Scandinavia. Cereal crops, potatoes, sugar beet and vegetables are grown for human consumption in Skåne and in central Sweden, but by far the greatest area of cultivated land is given over to the production of fodder crops for cattle and sheep. Dairy farming is highly developed, and Sweden is self-sufficient in milk, cheese and butter production.

Industry and population

Many farmers have left the land since World War II, attracted by the higher wages and more modern lifestyle of the towns. Sweden has been able to create a high standard of living based on industry – despite the fact that, apart from the large iron-ore deposits, many of the essential fuels and raw materials have to be imported. Most of the iron ore obtained from the mines at Kiruna and Gällivare in Arctic Sweden is exported via Narvik and Lulea to Germany.

The development of hydroelectricity has made up for the lack of oil and coal. Sweden is famous for high-quality engineering products such as ball bearings, matchmaking machinery, agricultural machines, motor vehicles (Saab and Volvo), ships, aircraft and armaments (Bofors). In addition to these relatively new industries, the traditional forest-based industries have been modernized. Sweden is the world's largest exporter of wood pulp and third largest exporter of paper and board – as well as Europe's biggest producer of softwood.

The bulk of the population lives in the lakeland corridor between Stockholm and Göteborg, and around the southern city of Malmö. These citizens, by their forebears working hard, exploiting their resources and avoiding war or occupation for nearly two centuries, now enjoy a standard of living that is in many ways the envy of most other Western countries. Sweden has by far the highest percentage figure for public spending in the OECD, with over 70% of the national budget going on one of the widest-ranging welfare programmes in the world.

In turn, the tax burden is the world's highest (some 57% of national income) and some Swedes are beginning to feel that the 'soft' yet paternalistic approach has led to overgovernment, depersonalization and uniformity. The elections of September 1991 saw the end of the Social Democrat government – in power for all but six years since 1932 – with voters swinging towards parties of lower taxation.

Other changes were in the wind, too. A founder member of EFTA – Stockholm played host to the inaugural meetings in 1960 – Sweden nevertheless applied for entry to the EEC in 1991, with hopes of EU membership pinned on 1995.

While some say that Sweden's biggest problems could be of its own making (though contrary to belief it is Denmark that has the world's highest known suicide rate), it is possible that it will be vulnerable to forces largely beyond its control. Like its neighbours, Sweden suffers from forest-killing acid rain generated mostly by the UK and Germany ∎

Mariefred sits quietly on the edge of Lake Mälaren, west of Stockholm. Within easy commuting distance of the capital, it typifies the towns of Sweden's neat and prosperous central lowland belt.

DENMARK

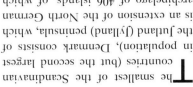

T he smallest of the Scandinavian countries (but the second largest in population), Denmark consists of the Jutland (Jylland) peninsula, which is an extension of the North German Plain, and an archipelago of 406 islands, of which 89 are inhabited. The coastline – about 7,300 km [4,500 mls] – is extremely long for the size of the country. The largest and most densely populated of the islands is Zealand (Sjaelland), which lies close to the coast of southern Sweden. This has recently been connected to the most important island – Funen (Fyn) – by the Storebaeltstunnel. Copenhagen (København), the capital city, lies on the narrow strait, The Sound, which leads from the Kattegat to the Baltic Sea.

Control of the entrances to the Baltic – the Great and Little Belts and The Sound – contributed to the power of Denmark in the Middle Ages, when the kingdom dominated its neighbours and expanded its territories to include Norway, Iceland, Greenland and the Faroe Islands. The link with Norway was broken in 1814, and with Iceland in 1944, but Greenland and the Faroes retain connections with Denmark. The granite island of Bornholm, off the southern tip of Sweden, also remains a Danish possession.

Structurally, Denmark is part of a low-lying belt of sedimentary rocks extending from north Germany to southern Sweden, which are geologically much younger than the rest of Scandinavia. The surface is almost entirely covered by glacial deposits, but the underlying strata are exposed as the 122 m [400 ft] chalk cliffs on the island of Møn. Nowhere in Denmark, however, is higher than 171 m [561 ft] and the country averages just 98 m [30 ft]. Along the west coast of Jutland, facing the North Sea, are lines of sand dunes with shallow lagoons behind them.

Agriculture and industry

Denmark has few mineral resources and no coal, though there is now some oil and natural gas from the North Sea. A century ago this was a poor farming and fishing country, but Denmark has now been transformed into one of Europe's wealthiest industrial nations. The first steps in the process were taken in the late 19th century, with the introduction of co-operative methods of processing and distributing farm produce, and the development of modern methods of dairying and pig- and poultry-breeding. Denmark became the main supplier of bacon, eggs and butter to the growing industrial nations of Western Europe. Most of the natural fodder for the animals is still grown in Denmark – three-quarters of the land is cultivated and more than 60% is arable – with barley as the principal crop.

Although less than 5% of the working population is actively engaged in farming, the scientific methods used and the efficient co-operative marketing system ensure that output remains high. Over a third of Denmark's exports are of food products, with Britain and Germany the chief customers.

From a firm agricultural base Denmark has developed a whole range of industries. Some – brewing, meat canning, fish processing, pottery, textiles and furniture-making – use Danish products, while others – shipbuilding, oil refining, engineering and metal-working – depend on imported raw materials. The port of Copenhagen is also the chief industrial centre and draw for more than a million tourists each year.

At the other end of the scale there is Legoland, the famous miniature town of plastic bricks, built at Billund, north-west of Vejle in eastern Jutland. Lego was first created here and went on to become the world's best-selling construction toy. The country is also the world's biggest exporter of insulin.

The number of storks that migrate north to Denmark are now down to a few pairs, the drainage of bogs having much reduced their feeding grounds.

Copenhagen's rich architectural heritage runs from the Dutch Renaissance of Rosenborg Castle to the imaginative modernity of the Carlsberg brewery.

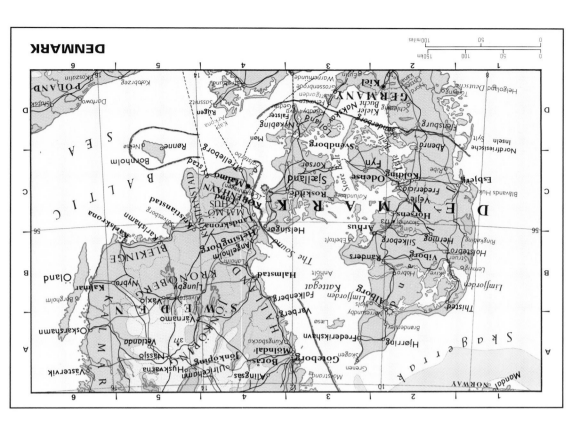

DENMARK

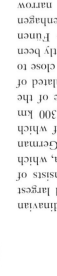

People and culture

Denmark is a generally comfortable mixture of striking social opposites. The Lutheran tradition and the cradle of Hans Christian Andersen's fairy tales co-exist with open attitudes to pornography and one of the highest illegitimacy rates in the West (44%). A reputation for caring and thorough welfare services – necessitating high taxation – is dented somewhat by the world's highest recorded suicide rate.

It is, too, one of the 'greenest' of the advanced nations, with a pioneering Ministry of Pollution that has real power to act: in 1991 it became the first government anywhere to fine industries for emissions of carbon dioxide, the primary 'greenhouse' gas. At the same time, Danes register Europe's highest rate of deaths from lung cancer.

Denmark gets on well with its neighbours and partners. On 1 January 1973, along with Britain and Ireland, it joined the EEC – the first Scandinavian country to make the break from EFTA – but it still co-operates closely on social, cultural and economic matters with its five Scandinavian partners in the Nordic Council. In a referendum in May 1992, Denmark voted to reject the treaty of Maastricht. Although this was reversed in 1993, the Danes remain inhibited Europeans.

Bornholm is a Danish island well away from the rest of the country and far nearer to the southern tip of Sweden (40 km [25 mls]) than to Copenhagen (168 km [104 mls]). A separate administrative region, it was occupied by Germany in World War II but liberated by the Russians, who returned it to Denmark in 1946.

Measuring 558 sq km [227 sq mls], Bornholm is composed mainly of granite and has poor soils, but deposits of kaolin (china clay) spawned a pottery industry. The principal town and ferry port is Rønne, the fishing port Nekso. Fishing and fish processing, agriculture (mainly cattle rearing) and tourism are the main sources of income – the last-named reliant partly on the island's fine examples of fortified churches ■

FINLAND

Located almost entirely between latitudes 60°N and 70°N, Finland is the most northerly state on the mainland of Europe, though Norway's county of Finnmark actually cuts it off from the Arctic Ocean. A third of its total area lies within the Arctic Circle, a far higher proportion than for its two large Scandinavian partners.

The climate of the northern province of Lappi (Lapland) is not as severe as in places which lie in similar latitudes, such as Canada and Siberia, because of the North Atlantic Drift. This influence keeps the Arctic coasts of Europe free from ice all year round.

Finland enjoys a short but warm summer, with average July temperatures at Helsinki of 17°C [63°F] and 13°C [55°F] in Lapland. Because of the high latitudes, summer days are extremely long; in the Arctic region there is virtually no night throughout June.

Winters are long and cold (Helsinki's January average is −6°C [21°F]) and the days are short. In severe winters the sea freezes for several miles offshore and ice-breakers have to be used to keep the ports open. Snowfall is not heavy, however, and rail and road transport is seldom badly disrupted, even in Lapland.

Landscape

Geologically Finland is made up of a central plateau of ancient crystalline rocks, mainly granites, schists and gneisses, surrounded by lowlands composed of recent glacial deposits. In the 600 million years between the formation of these ancient rocks and the last Ice Age, the surface of the land was worn down to a peneplain, and most of central and southern Finland is below 200 m [650 ft]. However, the roots of an old mountain system running north-west to south-east can still be traced across Lapland and

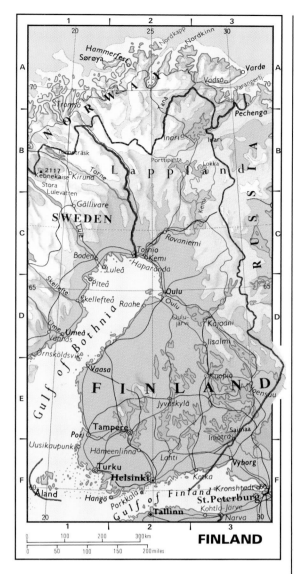

FINLAND

along the country's eastern border with Russia.

A tenth of the land surface is covered by lakes. Concentrated in the central plateau, they are in most cases long, narrow and shallow, and aligned in a north-west to south-east direction, indicating the line of movement of the ice-sheet which scoured out their basins. The number of lakes varies from 60,000 to 185,000, depending on the source of the information and the definition used; but whatever the exact figure may be, they dominate the landscape of the southern half of Finland and contribute to its austere beauty. The Saimaa area in the south-east, near the Russian frontier, is Europe's largest inland water system.

Although under increasing threat from pollution caused by wood processing and fertilizers as well as acid rain, the lakes are still rich in fish – mainly trout, salmon, pike and perch – and provide a prime source of recreation for huge numbers of Finnish people.

More than two-thirds of Finland is covered by lakes and forest – a fact that accounts for almost everything from the composition of its exports to the brilliance of its rally drivers.

Economy

Forests occupy almost 60% of the land surface, the main trees being pine, spruce and birch. Forest-based products – wood pulp, sawn timber, paper and board – still constitute 40% of Finland's exports, but since World War II engineering, shipbuilding and metallurgical industries have greatly expanded. A member of EFTA, Finland saw its economy grow at a faster rate than that of Japan during the 1980s. In 1992 Finland applied to become a member of the EU, with entry scheduled for 1995 ■

THE LAPPS

Hunters, fishermen and herdsmen living in Arctic Europe, some 35,000 Lapps are scattered between Norway (with 20,000), Sweden and Finland, with a small group in Russia. Physically, the short, dark Lapps – or Samer, as they call themselves – are different from other Scandinavians, though their language, Saarme, is related to Finnish.

Until the 17th century, when they first domesticated reindeer (*above*), they lived entirely by hunting and fishing; thereafter, many followed a semi-nomadic life, driving their herds each summer from their winter settlements at the edge of the forest to the high pastureland.

Mining and hydroelectric development has badly affected nomadic herding, and it now occupies only about 10% of Lapps. Most live in fixed settlements in coastal areas, and a steady trickle migrate south.

UNITED KINGDOM

The British Isles stand on the westernmost edge of the continental shelf – two large and several hundred small islands for the most part cool, rainy and windswept. Despite physical closeness to the rest of Europe (32 km [20 mls] at the nearest point – little more than the distance across London), Britain is curiously isolated, with a long history of political independence and social separation from its neighbours. In the past the narrow seas served the islanders well, protecting them against casual invasion, while Britons in turn sailed to explore and exploit the rest of the world. Now insularity is rapidly breaking down, and Britain is closer to federation with Europe than ever before.

The islands are confusingly named. 'Great Britain', the largest in Europe and eighth largest in the world – so named to distinguish it from 'Little Britain' (Brittany, in France) – includes the kingdoms of England and Scotland and the principality of Wales; Ireland was once a kingdom, but is currently divided into the Province of Northern Ireland, under the British Crown, and the politically separate Republic of Ireland. Great Britain, Northern Ireland, and many off-lying island groups from the Scillies to the Shetlands, together make up the United Kingdom of Great Britain and Northern Ireland, commonly known as the UK. Even isolated Rockall, far out in the Atlantic Ocean, is part of the UK, but the Isle of Man and the Channel Islands are separate if direct dependencies of the Crown, with a degree of political autonomy and their own taxation systems.

Climate

Despite a subarctic position Britain is favoured climatically. Most other maritime lands between 50°N and 60°N – eastern Siberia, Kamchatka, the Aleutian Islands, southern Alaska, Hudson Bay and Labrador – are colder throughout the year, with longer winters, ice-bound coasts and a shorter growing season. Britain's salvation is the North Atlantic Drift or Gulf Stream, a current of surface water that brings subtropical warmth from the southern Atlantic Ocean, spreading it across the continental shelf of Western Europe and warming the prevailing westerly winds.

The growing season, indicated roughly by the number of months in which mean air temperature exceeds 6°C [42°F], ranges from less than four months in the Scottish Highlands to nine months or more on the south-west coast. Most of lowland Britain has a growing season of seven to eight months, enough to ensure the prosperity of arable farmers in most years.

Britain's reputation for cloudiness is well merited. Mean duration of sunshine throughout the year is about 5 hours daily in the south, and only 3.5 hours daily in Scotland. At the height of summer only the south-west receives more than 7.5 hours of sunshine per day – less than half the hours available. In winter only the south coast, the Severn Estuary, Oxfordshire and a sliver of south-eastern Essex receive more than 1.5 hours per day, while many northern areas receive less than half an hour daily.

Despite a reputation for rain Britain is fairly dry. More than half of the country receives less than 750 mm [30 in] annually, and parts of Essex have less than 500 mm [20 in] per year. The wettest areas are Snowdonia with about 5,000 mm [200 in], Ben Nevis and the north-western highlands with 4,300 mm [172 in], and the Lake District with 3,300 mm [132 in].

The British climate is far from static. It was warmer at the time of the Domesday Survey (1086) when vineyards flourished as far north as York, and it cooled throughout the Middle Ages, when Arctic pack-ice was reported off Shetland and Eskimos are said to have visited northern Scotland in their kayaks. Cooling continued into the mid-19th century, followed by a long period of warming up to World War II and a succession of warm summers in the 1970s and 1980s.

Population and immigration

Despite insularity the British people are of mixed stock. The earliest immigrants – land-hungry farmers from the Continent – were often refugees from tribal warfare and unrest. The Belgic tribesmen escaping from Imperial Rome, the Romans themselves (whose troops included Spanish, Macedonian and probably North African mercenaries); the Angles, Saxons, Jutes, Danes and Normans, all in turn brought genetic variety; so too did the Huguenots, Sephardic and Ashkenazim Jews, and Dutch, French and German businessmen who followed them. Latterly the waves of immigrants have included Czechs – most, like their predecessors, fugitives from European wars, overcrowding, intolerance and unrest.

During the 19th century Britain often took in skilled European immigrants through the front door while steadily losing her own sons and daughters – Scots and Irish peasants in particular – through the back. Most recent arrivals in Britain are immigrants from crowded and impoverished corners of lands once part of the British Empire, notably the West Indies, West Africa, India and Pakistan. These and their descendants now make up about 4% of the population of Britain.

Under Roman rule the population of the British island numbered half to three-quarters of a million. By the time of the Domesday Survey it had doubled, and it doubled again by the end of the 14th century. The Black Death of the late 15th century swept away one in every three or four, but numbers climbed slowly; at the Union of 1707 some 6 million English and Welsh joined about 1 million Scots under a single parliament. By 1801 the first national census revealed 8.9 million in England and Wales, 1.6 million in Scotland; Ireland missed the first two ten-year counts, but probably numbered about 5 million. In 1821 the total British population was 21 million, and in 1851 31 million, and in 1921 47 million. Fortunately for all, the rate of increase has now declined, but some parts of Britain, notably the south-east and the conurbations, are among the most heavily populated areas of the world, with higher densities only in the Netherlands and Taiwan.

ENGLAND

Landscape: Visitors to England are often amazed at the variety of the landscape. Complex folding, lava outpourings, volcanic upheavals and eruptions, glacial planing, and changes of sea level have all left their marks on the present landscape.

From Northumberland to the River Trent, the Pennines extend southwards as an upland with rolling hills, plateaus and fine valleys, many known as 'dales'. The range includes two western outliers – the Forest of Rossendale north of Manchester, and the Forest of Bowland in north Lancashire. To either side lie lowlands – those of Lancashire to the west and of Yorkshire and Nottingham to the east.

The Eden Valley separates the northern Pennines from Cumbria, which includes the Lake District. This is England's most striking mountain mass, a circular area of peaks, deep valleys, splendid lakes and crags. The loftiest peak is Scafell, 978 m [3,210 ft]. In the south-west Exmoor is a fine sandstone upland, and Dartmoor a predominantly granite area with many prominent tors. Elsewhere are isolated hills, small by world standards but dramatic against the small-scale background of Britain, as shown by the Malvern Hills.

THE CHANNEL ISLANDS

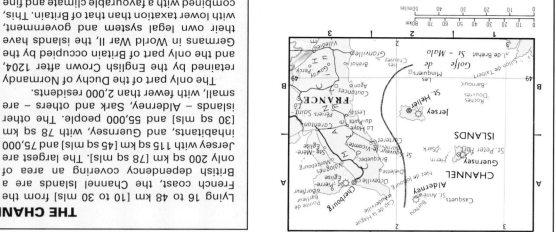

Lying 16 to 48 km [10 to 30 mls] from the French coast, the Channel Islands are a British dependency covering an area of only 200 sq km [78 sq mls]. The largest are Jersey with 115 sq km [45 sq mls] and 75,000 inhabitants, and Guernsey, with 78 sq km [30 sq mls] and 55,000 people. The other islands – Alderney, Sark and others – are small, with fewer than 2,000 residents.

The only part of the Duchy of Normandy retained by the English Crown after 1204, and the only part of Britain occupied by the Germans in World War II, the islands have their own legal system and government. This, with lower taxation than that of Britain, combined with a favourable climate and fine coastal scenery, has attracted a considerable number of wealthy residents.

The main produce is agricultural, especially early potatoes, tomatoes and flowers for Britain, and the countryside has a vast number of glasshouses. The soil is now fertile, having been made so by the farmers' skilful use of seaweed and other fertilizers. Jersey and Guernsey cattle are famous breeds, introduced to many countries. Holidaymakers visit the islands in large numbers during the summer months, travelling by air or by the various passenger boats, especially from Weymouth. English is the official language but French is widely spoken.

ISLE OF MAN

Covering 590 sq km [227 sq mls], the Isle of Man sits in the Irish Sea almost equidistant from County Down and Cumbria, but actually nearer Galloway in Scotland. The uplands, pierced by the corridor valley from Douglas to Peel, extend from Ramsey to Port Erin. Mainly agricultural, with some fishing and a few light industries, the island is now largely dependent on tourism, with the annual Tourist Trophy (motorcycle) races attracting many visitors. Douglas, the capital, has over a third of the island's population. Like the Channel Islands, the Isle of Man is a dependency of the British Crown with its own legislative assembly, legal system and tax controls – leading to a position as a financial centre and tax shelter.

of Worcester and the Wrekin near Shrewsbury.

Much of the English lowland consists of chalk downlands, familiar to continental visitors who enter England through Folkestone or Dover as the famous chalk cliffs. These are the exposed coastal edge of the North Downs, whose scarped northern slope forms a striking feature in the Croydon area of Greater London. The North Downs continue westwards through Surrey to the Hampshire Downs, then south and east as the South Downs, emerging at another coastal landmark – Beachy Head.

There is a northwards extension of downland through the Berkshire and Marlborough Downs to the Chilterns then north again into East Anglia to disappear under the edge of the fens near Cambridge.

Distinctive double-decker buses and black 'cabs' ply their trade along London's Oxford Street, the best-known thoroughfare of Europe's largest city.

Formerly forested, the downlands were cleared early for pasture and agriculture, and now provide a rich and varied mixture of woodlands, parklands, fields and mostly small settlements. Chalk appears again in the wolds of Lincolnshire and Yorkshire, emerging at Flamborough Head.

Older rocks, predominantly limestones, form the ridge of the Cotswold Hills, and the rolling, hilly farmlands of Leicestershire, the Lincoln Edge (cut by the River Witham at Lincoln), and finally the North York Moors. In these older rocks are rich iron deposits, mined by Cleveland to supply ores for the steel towns of the Tees Estuary until 1964, and still mined in the Midlands.

England is drained by many fine rivers, of which the greatest are the Thames, the Severn, the fenland Ouse, the Trent, and the great Yorkshire Ouse that receives its tributaries from the many picturesque valleys – the Dales – of the Pennine flank. There are many smaller rivers, and a large number of the old towns that dot England at intervals of 20 km [12 mls] or so were built at their crossing points – generally where dry ground existed above marshes and gave firm sites for building. Chester, for example, was founded on a patch of sandstone beside the Dee; one of the four gates of the Roman town is still called the Watergate. York, too, was built on firm ground by a river crossing, and so was Manchester. London arose on the site chosen by the Romans for the first convenient crossing place of the Thames, formerly a much broader and shallower river.

Agriculture: England has a rich variety of soils, derived both locally from parent rocks and also from glacial debris or 'drift'. During the 12,000 and more years since the ice retreated, soils have been enriched, firstly by such natural processes as flooding and the growth of forests, latterly by the good husbandry of

many generations of farmers. Husbandry improved particularly from the 18th century onwards; the Industrial Revolution was accompanied by an agricultural revolution that resulted in massive increases in crop yields and in the quality of livestock.

Through the 18th and 19th centuries farming became more scientific and more specialized; as the demands from the towns grew, so did the ability of English farmers to meet increasing markets for food. The eastern counties, particularly East Anglia and Holderness (now part of Humberside), became the granaries of England, while the rich, wet grasslands of the west and the Midlands turned pastoral – Cheshire cheese is a famous product of this specialization. There were other local products – the hops of Kent and Hereford, the apples of Worcester, and the fine wools that continued to be the main product of the chalk downlands. In south Lancashire potatoes and vegetables became major crops for sale in the markets of the growing northern industrial towns; market gardening and dairying on a small scale developed near every major settlement, taking advantage of the ready market close at hand.

Scenically England still gives the impression of being an agricultural country. Less than 10% of the area is rough moorland, about 5% is forest, and about another 10% is urban or suburban, leaving roughly three-quarters under cultivation of one kind or another. Yet only 3% of the working population is currently employed in agriculture, a figure that has declined drastically in recent years. Loss of rural populations has been an inevitable result of agricultural rationalization and improvements in farming methods. Those who deplore this trend might reflect that, though English farming formerly employed many more labourers, it supported them at little more than subsistence level.

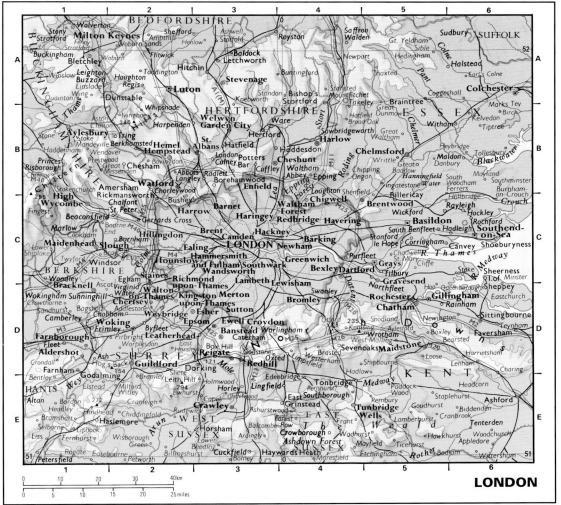

LONDON

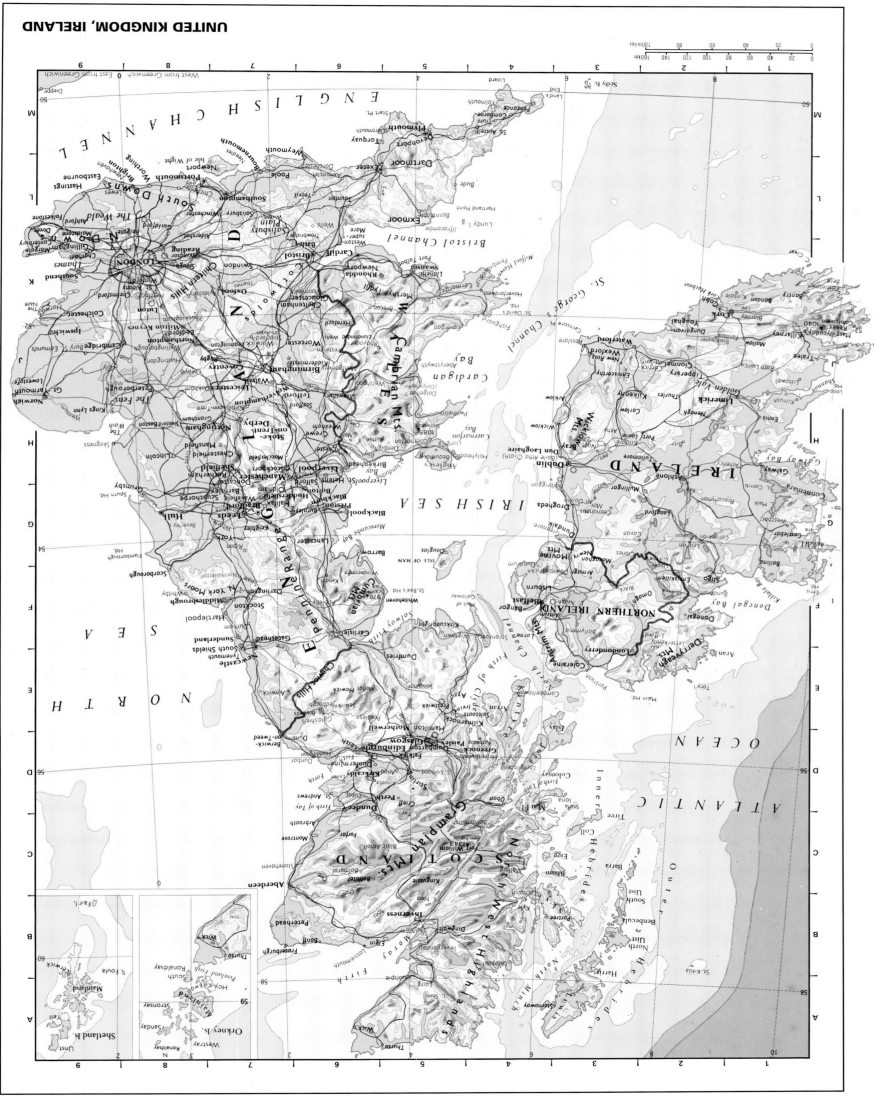

UNITED KINGDOM, IRELAND

Industry and urbanization: England had important reserves of coal, the major fields being on either side of the Pennines (Yorkshire, Lancashire, Northumberland and Durham), in the Midlands (Derbyshire and Nottinghamshire) and in South Wales. These coalfields and extensive reserves of iron ore – now largely defunct – were the basis of the Industrial Revolution of the 18th century and the industrial growth of the 19th century, which together resulted in major changes in the English landscape.

Although the coalfields of the north saw the greatest local expansion of population, London and England's other major ports, such as Liverpool and Bristol, also developed as export markets flourished. These developments were accompanied by enormous improvements in communications, including the building of an extensive canal network (with three canals over the Pennines by 1800) and, later, the spread of the railways.

From the 1840s town growth was rapid, and by the end of the 19th century 80% of the population was urban. While the working-class population was mainly housed in slums, the prosperity of the commercial and professional classes was reflected in the Victorian 'villas' that, in varying degrees of splendour, appeared in select areas of the towns.

The main areas of industrial growth since World War I have been around London and also in the West Midlands. A number of towns, for example Coventry, experienced extremely rapid growth. Conscious planning had the aim of controlling industrial expansion and preventing the indiscriminate growth of some towns, for example Oxford and Cambridge. By the early 1990s the old manufacturing-based economic structure had been dismantled, replaced by new technologies and service industries.

Planning: After World War II the need for replan-

The Atlantic rolls in near Porthtowan, in Cornwall. The scene is repeated everywhere on the Celtic fringes of the British Isles – Wales, Scotland and Ireland.

ning England to take account of the industrial areas was generally accepted. The existence of conurbations where towns had grown into one another was recognized by their listing in the 1951 census, when they included Greater London, the West Midlands (Birmingham and the Black Country), South-east Lancashire with North-east Cheshire (Greater Manchester), Merseyside and Tyneside. Prolonged discussion followed on the best form of new administrative structure needed in England, and ultimately, in 1974, the new scheme of local government emerged. Many county boundaries were changed but one alteration of particular significance was the definition of some new counties based on the major industrial areas.

In creating the new administrative units of Tyne and Wear, Cleveland, West Yorkshire, South Yorkshire, Greater Manchester and West Midlands, and in redefining Greater London on more generous lines, the planners at last recognized the realities of population distribution in England. However, the highly industrialized areas still cover only a small part of the country. Many towns are developing new industrial areas – the 'industrial estates', housing light industries on their outskirts – and since 1945 government-sponsored 'new towns' have arisen in many parts of the country in an attempt to stem the further growth of London and the existing conurbations.

WALES

United with England in 1535, Wales still preserves a sense of individuality – a separateness resting on history and sentiment rather than any clear boundary in the countryside. Although only 20% of the population speak Welsh, 75% of the inhabitants do so in the western counties of Gwynedd and Dyfed. The national sentiment is not only expressed through language, but also through literature, the arts (especially music), sport and political life. Cardiff, the capital, grew rapidly during the 19th century with the iron and steel industry and coal mining, but no Welsh

town is centrally placed for the whole country; meetings of the boards representing the colleges of the University of Wales – Cardiff, Swansea, Lampeter, Aberystwyth and Bangor – take place at Shrewsbury, an English border town.

Landscape: Wales is predominantly hilly and mountainous, although two-thirds of the rural area is farmland and one-third moorland. The most famous of the highland areas is Snowdonia, now a National Park covering 2,138 sq km [825 sq mls] from Snowdon to Cader Idris. But there are fine upland areas in central Wales, on both sides of the upper Severn Valley which cuts through them to the Dovey Valley and the coastal lowlands facing Cardigan Bay. South of the Severn, in the counties of Powys and Dyfed, the uplands dominate the landscape, and in the Brecon Beacons, south of the Usk Valley on which the old town of Brecon is situated, they provide another National Park, of 1,303 sq km [500 sq mls]. Many of the uplands and high lakes are sources of water for English towns, including Liverpool and Birmingham.

Mining and industry: Some writers on Wales regard the uplands as the country's real heartland, with their sheep pastures and forested valleys, interspersed by farming villages and small towns. But over half the population live in the industrialized area of South Wales, which includes the mining valleys of Gwent, Mid Glamorgan and West Glamorgan – all of which ceased to extract coal by the 1990s – and the towns of Newport, Cardiff and Swansea with their traditional heavy-metal industries and newer factories for light industry. All are ports, and Cardiff now has many central buildings for the whole of Wales, including the National Museum and the Welsh Office.

Tourism: Just as the railways stimulated economic growth in South Wales from the 1840s, so on the North Wales coast they stimulated the growth of holiday and residential towns, notably Rhyl, Colwyn Bay and Llandudno. These attracted English residents, many of them retired people from Lancashire, and the holiday industry boomed. In the motoring age it

developed further, so that almost every beach and coastal village had its guest houses, holiday cottages, caravan parks and camping sites. Now tourism has spread to virtually the whole of Wales. In Anglesey, many small places have devoted visitors who favour sailing as well as walking and sea bathing, while this is true also of many ports of the Welsh mainland coast.

The south-west, formerly Pembrokeshire but now part of Dyfed, has fine scenery, forming the Pembrokeshire National Park with a coast path 268 km [167 mls] long. Wales is rich in scenic attractions. The landscape is predominantly agricultural, with mixed farming, notably for dairying, cattle and sheep. Many upland farmers combine agriculture with the tourist trade. Forestry plantations exist in many upland valleys but the main characteristic of the countryside is farmland, with towns placed 20 km [12 mls] or so apart.

SCOTLAND

Scotland is a generally cool, hilly and, in the west, wet country occupying about a third of Great Britain. Physically it can be divided into three parts: the Highlands and Islands, bounded by the edge of the mountains from Stonehaven to the mouth of the Clyde; Central Scotland – sometimes called the Central Lowlands, though it is interspersed by a number of hill ranges; and the Southern Uplands, defined in the north by a geological fault extending from Dunbar to Girvan, and in the south by the border with England.

The Highlands and Islands: More than half of Scotland's area is in the Highlands and Islands. These are divided by the Great Glen, from Fort William to Inverness, with its three lochs – Lochy, Oich and Ness – linked by the Caledonian Canal. Much of the whisky for which Scotland is famous is produced in the Highlands, notably near the River Spey.

The north-western part of the Highlands has splendid scenery – deep, glaciated valleys dominated by mountains, and only limited areas of farmland, much of it now abandoned.

The financial returns from crofting (small-scale tenant farming) were meagre, and many old croft cottages have become holiday homes. Forests now cover many of the valleys; some of the mountains are deer parks, owned by landlords and let to visitors for seasonal shooting. Railways reach the western coast at Mallaig and Kyle of Lochalsh, from which there are boat services to Skye – to be augmented by a controversial bridge – and the Outer Hebrides. Roads are in part single track with passing places, although they are gradually being improved. At the various villages there are hotels, guest houses and other accommodation for visitors, and the main commercial occupations are fishing and home weaving.

The traditional weaving of Harris tweeds in the Hebrides is now industrially organized, with much of the work done in workshops. Skye has splendid climbing in the Cuillin Hills, and the numerous rivers and lakes are favoured by fishermen. Here, as in the rest of the Highlands, efforts to improve local industries have had some success.

The highland area east of the Great Glen is a richer country, flanked on the east by the lowlands around Aberdeen, which extend into Buchan and then westwards to Moray Firth around Inverness. This is sound farming country, famous for pedigree cattle, and from these lowlands tongues of farmland extend into the valleys of the Dee, Don, Spey and others. Aberdeen and Fraserburgh are major fishing centres. Aberdeen has become increasingly prosperous with the oil extraction from the North Sea.

Ben Nevis, at 1,343 m [4,406 ft] dominating the town of Fort William, is the highest summit in the British Isles (and one of the dullest to climb), and a number of peaks in the Cairngorms, including Ben Macdhui (1,311 m [4,300 ft]), are of almost equal height. Little known in the past, the Cairngorms have now been developed for winter skiing and summer climbing and fishing. There are still deer forests in the uplands but much of the country is used for sheep farming and tourism. Fort William and a few other centres have industry based on local hydroelectricity – aluminium smelting, for example – but Oban is the main holiday centre on the west coast.

In the north, the Orkney Islands are connected to Thurso (Scrabster) by boat and also to Aberdeen. Fishing and farming are the main support of the population, with a successful specialization in egg production. The Shetlands have a far harder environment, with craggy hills and limited areas suited to farming, though fishing is prominent, notably at Lerwick. The oil industry has brought great, if temporary, prosperity to some places in these islands.

The Central Lowlands: Scotland's economic heartland includes several ranges of rolling uplands – the Sidlaw Hills north of Dundee, the Ochils south of Perth, and the Pentlands extending in a south-westerly direction from the suburbs of Edinburgh. Most of Scotland's population and industrial activity occurs in this central area, and here too are its two largest cities – Glasgow on innumerable small glacial hills (drumlins) in the Clyde Valley, and the capital Edinburgh on splendid volcanic ridges, dominated by Arthur's Seat.

Clydeside is still the greatest industrial area of Scotland. Textile industries, engineering and shipbuilding were the basis of the prosperity of Glasgow and its neighbouring towns, which in time grew into one another and held more than a third of Scotland's total population. There is now a wide range of industries in Central Scotland including electronics, printing, brewing and carpet-making.

Edinburgh, with its port of Leith, remained much smaller than Glasgow, with only half its population, but is still the administrative centre, and the seat of the main law courts and the National Museum and Library, as well as of many cultural organizations. A favoured centre for retirement in Scotland, it has an increasing tourist trade, particularly during the Festival in the summer. Much of the central area is rich farmland, especially to the east of Edinburgh.

The Southern Uplands: Though less spectacular than the Highlands, these include many fine hills, rolling moorlands and rich valleys. From the summit of Merrick (843 m [2,764 ft]) in Galloway can be seen the Highlands to the north, the plateau of Northern Ireland to the west, and the Lake District, the Pennines and the Isle of Man to the south. The Tweed with its numerous tributaries and – further west – the Esk, Annan, Nith, Ken and Cree provide sheltered valleys for farming, and there is splendid agricultural country in Galloway, where dairying has been particularly successful. Cattle rearing with crop production is more general in the drier east, where many farms specialize in beasts for slaughter. The hills are used for sheep rearing. Some of the towns, notably Hawick and Galashiels, are prominent in the textile industry and have a large export trade.

Although tourism is relatively less important than in the Highlands, many people come to see the historic centres, such as Melrose and Dryburgh Abbey. To the west, in Galloway, there has been a policy of afforestation on the poorer soils, and several centres have been opened as small museums and educational sites. The coast attracts tourists and Forest Parks have been well laid out for visitors. In the west the towns are small, though there is heavy traffic to Stranraer, the packet station for the shortest sea crossing to Larne in Northern Ireland. ∎

[For geography of Northern Ireland see page 17.]

Although it has been without a resident monarch since 1603 and a Scottish parliament since 1707, Edinburgh still boasts some splendid and majestic buildings.

IRELAND

Geographically, Ireland is the whole island west of Britain; the Republic of Ireland (Eire, or the Irish Free State until 1949) comprises the 26 counties governed from Dublin, and Northern Ireland (Ulster) is the six counties that remained part of the United Kingdom from 1921, when the Free State was granted dominion status within the British Commonwealth. Today, the word 'Ireland' is used as political shorthand for the Republic – which occupies some 80% of the island of Ireland.

The original four provinces of Ireland gradually emerged as major divisions from Norman times. Three counties of the present Republic (Donegal, Cavan and Monaghan), together with the six counties which now make up Northern Ireland, formed the old province of Ulster; Connacht, in effect the land beyond the River Shannon, includes the five counties of Leitrim, Sligo, Roscommon, Galway and Mayo; Munster comprises Clare, Limerick, Tipperary, Kilkenny, Waterford, Cork and Kerry; and Leinster consists of the heart of the central lowland and the counties of the south-east (Wicklow, Wexford and Carlow) between Dublin and Waterford harbour.

The provinces never had any corporate government, and today have little significance except on the sports field. In the Republic local government is administered through the counties, which developed from Norman times and commonly coincide with diocesan boundaries.

Landscape

Physically the main outlines of Ireland are simple. In the western peninsulas of Donegal and Connacht ancient rocks were folded to form mountain chains running north-east to south-west; good examples are the fine Derryveagh range of Co. Donegal and the Ox Mountains of Co. Sligo. The highest peaks, for example Errigal, 752 m [2,466 ft], are generally of quartzite, a metamorphosed sandstone. The same trend is seen also in the long range, including the Wicklow Mountains, between Dublin Bay and Waterford harbour in the south-east, and in the Slieve Bloom of the central lowland. The fine east-west ranges of the south, extending from Waterford to the western peninsulas, and the islands of Kerry and West Cork, were formed at a later period. Much of lowland Ireland is floored by rocks contemporary with the coal-bearing measures in England, and these also form some uplands like those around Sligo. Unfortunately these rocks contain little coal; some is mined on a small scale in the Castlecomer area of Co. Kilkenny, and near Lough Allen in the upper Shannon Valley.

The basalt lavas that poured out in the north-east of Ireland, forming the desolate Antrim Plateau with its fine scenic cliffs on the famous Coast Road, and the Giant's Causeway, are more recent. Irish soils, however, are largely derived from glacial deposits, and the famous peat bogs result from the drainage patterns that emerged as the ice-sheets of the Ice Age dispersed. Peat remains the main indigenous fuel source, but reserves may not last long into the 21st century.

Horse-racing is not merely a passionate pursuit for many Irishmen: bloodstock sales also provide valuable revenue for the Republic's limited economy.

Economy

Agriculture has been the traditional support of the Irish people, though fishing, home crafts and local labouring have been extra sources of livelihood in the poorer western areas. There is a marked contrast between the richest and the poorest agricultural areas. In the eastern central lowland and the south-east, particularly the lowland areas of Wicklow and Wexford, there are splendid large farms, with pastures supporting fine-quality cattle, sheep and in some areas racehorses. From Wexford, too, rich farmlands extend through the valleys and lowlands westwards to the counties of Tipperary and Limerick, and from Waterford to Cork and Killarney. Many of the farms specialize in dairying; milk is taken daily to the creameries, or collected in vans which separate out the cream and return the 'skim' for pig feeding.

North of the Shannon, in Clare and east Galway, there is intensive sheep and some cattle production; here the glacial deposits are thin and the soils derived from limestones. To the north farming is mixed, with dairying, meat production, and in some cases specialization on crops such as potatoes and barley. Little wheat is grown; oats are better suited to the damp summer climate.

Farming in much of Ireland is now relatively prosperous, aided by EC grants. The number of people working on the land continues to decline, but that is due to the introduction of machinery, the union of small farms into larger holdings, and the increased opportunities of finding employment in the towns, with overseas emigration still an alternative if not a choice for many Irish workers or families. The tradition of emigration dates back to the great famine of 1846–51, when over a million people fled to Britain and the United States.

Ireland is economically far more prosperous than it was in 1845, when the population of the island numbered 8.5 million. Industrialization only really happened in the north-east, especially Belfast, leaving the Free State an agrarian country from the 1920s. As a result, it has something of a 'Third World' profile: rural (though 25% of the population lives in Dublin and its suburbs), dependent on tourism and, increasingly, high-tech industries such as electronics and pharmaceuticals. Prosperity in the 1960s was followed by a slowdown in growth – when government spending was high; however the 1980s appeared

to have successfully reversed the trend.

The poorer western areas have been aided by government grants and the development of local industries, including the tourist industry. Electricity is universally available. Home industries flourish, especially tweed manufacture, and the fishing industry is increasingly prosperous. The poor west, known from 1891 as the 'congested areas', is not depopulated as in some comparable areas of Scotland, though discarded houses are taken over as holiday cottages, sometimes by people from continental Europe. Many problems have been at least partially solved and the EU has been a source of help, giving the Republic the feeling of belonging to a wider world than the British Isles ■

NETHERLANDS

O ften, and inaccurately, called Holland – this refers only to the two north-western provinces, where less than 40% of the population lives – the Netherlands is the most crowded country of any size in Europe. Yet the daunting figures for density are only an average: the east and south are relatively sparsely populated, while the figure for the province of Zuid-Holland is 1,080 people per sq km [2,800 per sq ml].

The greatest concentration of population is in the towns and cities of Randstad Holland, a 50 km [31 ml] diameter horseshoe of urban areas, with Dordrecht at the centre of the loop. This area, dominant in the Dutch economy, includes most of the major cities, including (clockwise) Hilversum, Utrecht, Dordrecht, Rotterdam, The Hague (home of the International Court of Justice), Leiden, Haarlem and Amsterdam, the last still the centre of Dutch cultural life despite being overtaken in size by Rotterdam. Nearly all of this crucial area, rich in history and culture, lies well below sea level.

Landscape and agriculture

To anyone travelling westwards from Germany, the Netherlands' density of people is obvious in the landscape, for the fields are smaller, the villages more tightly concentrated with small neat houses, and the land is cultivated more intensively. Over much of the countryside rivers are higher than the surrounding land, with villages sited above the flood level.

Seen from the air, most of the Netherlands is made up of richly cultivated fields, mainly rectangular in shape, with water-filled ditches between them along which farmers travel by boat. Control of water is a major problem, for much of the best farmland lies at or below sea level.

Without the protection of dykes and sand dunes along the coast, more than two-fifths of the Netherlands (the 'Low Countries') would be flooded. Constant pumping – formerly by windpumps (as most picturesque 'windmills' were) and steam-pumps, but now by automated motor-pumps – lifts surplus water from ditches to canals at a higher level, and from canals to the rivers, particularly the Lek and Waal, which take the waters of the Rhine to the sea, and the Maas (Meuse in France and Belgium).

The dunes that line much of the coast are carefully guarded against erosion by planting marram grass and, where possible, trees. There are massive dykes to guard the farmland and towns, but in 1953 the exceptionally high tides at the end of January broke through coastal dykes and sand dunes, causing widespread devastation.

For over a thousand years the Dutch have wrested land from the unforgiving North Sea and the process still continues; only in the last 60 years, however, has the balance between reclamation and flooding, between gain and loss of land, swung permanently in the people's favour. Since 1900 almost 3,000 sq km [1,160 sq mls] have been added to the territory. The largest and most famous project has been the

Tending tulips near Lisse. The Dutch grow and sell more than 3 billion flowers each year.

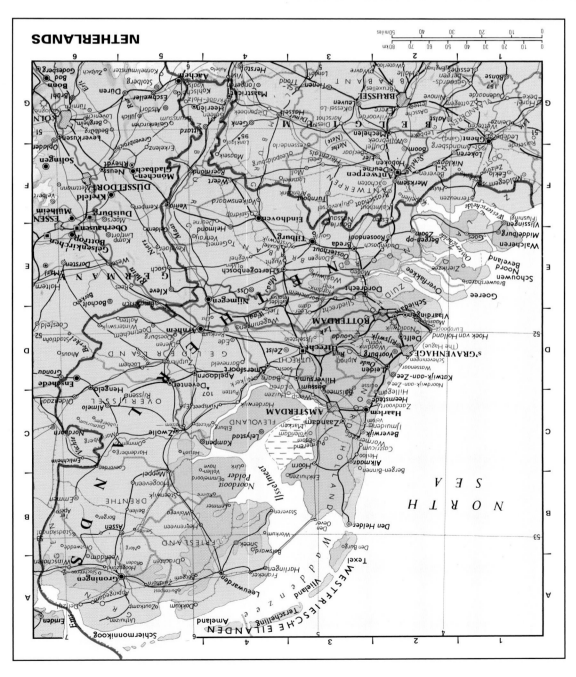

NETHERLANDS

reclamation of the Zuiderzee, begun in 1920. The major sea barrage of 32 km [21 mls] was completed in 1932, and by 1967 four large 'island' areas were finished, providing some 1,814 sq km [700 sq mls] of former seabed not only for cultivation but also for planned towns and villages. A controversial fifth area, Markerwaard, is under way, leaving the IJsselmeer, a freshwater lake, the only remnant of the original inlet.

The use of land in the Netherlands varies. In the west the concentration on bulb farming is marked near Haarlem in soils of clay mixed with sand. There, too, glasshouse cultivation, combined on many holdings with the growing of flowers and vegetables out-of-doors, is widespread.

Much of the produce is exported, some of it by air to London and other north European cities. Some soils are better suited to pastoral farming, with milk, cheese and butter production. In the areas above sea level farming is varied, with a combination of cattle and crops, including fruit. Gouda has a famous cheese market, and the well-known round red-coated Edam cheeses come from northern areas.

Industry and commerce

Industry and commerce provide support for the greater part of the Dutch population. Mineral resources include china clay, which is abundant, natural gas from the North Sea, and coal, though commercial mining ceased in 1965. The emphasis of modern industry is on oil, steel, electrical engineering and chemicals.

In the area south of Rotterdam a vast port and industrial area, Europoort, has been developed since 1958. Together with Rotterdam's own facilities, the complex is the largest and busiest in the world. The Dutch are skilled at languages, to which a considerable part of the teaching time is given even in primary schools. This is considered essential to the country's prosperity. The main export markets are the EU partners – Germany, Belgium, the UK and France – while strong trade links with Indonesia recall the Dutch colonial age ■

THE DUTCH POLDERS

Polders are artificial farmlands reclaimed from water. The first were formed in Holland and Zeeland about a thousand years ago, when settlers on marshlands found that they could protect their land by building dykes of earth, brushwood (around which mud would accumulate) and stones. The effort was vast, but dry land was created and protected against floods from rivers and high tides. Sluices were made in the dykes to let out surplus water; marshes and peat bogs were gradually drained and the water pumped out to major rivers and canals by windpumps. These were largely replaced in the mid-19th century by steam-pumps.

Today some of the most profitable farmland in the Netherlands is polderland, much of it 6 to 7 m [about 20 ft] below sea level. Within some of the polders the farmland is divided into hundreds of strips separated by water channels and accessible only by boat. Modern polders, including those of the Zuiderzee, have large fields of great fertility. With modern technology the level of water in each polder can be controlled from central pumping stations. Many older settlements are on dykes, or land above the highest flood levels.

The Dutch engineers have, over the centuries, exported their expertise to many areas, notably the Fens in eastern England.

BELGIUM

Throughout a chequered and stormy history as the 'cockpit of Europe', Belgium's fine cities, including Brussels, Ghent and Bruges, have maintained their churches and public buildings, though some have been rebuilt after wars. Following the Napoleonic Wars, from 1815, Belgium and the Netherlands were united as the 'Low Countries', but in 1830, a famous year of ferment in Europe, a National Congress proclaimed independence from the Dutch and in 1831 Prince Leopold of Saxe-Coburg was 'imported from Germany' to become king. At the Treaty of London in 1839 (which the Netherlands also signed), Britain, France and Russia guaranteed the independence of Belgium – and the famous 'scrap of paper' was upheld when Germany invaded Belgium in August 1914. For nearly four weary years the fields of Flanders became the battlefield of Europe.

The division between Belgium and the Netherlands rests on history and sentiment rather than on any physical features. Belgium is predominantly a Roman Catholic country, while the Netherlands is traditionally Protestant (though about 36% of the population are Roman Catholic). Both were neutral in foreign policy, but in 1940 they were invaded by Nazi Germany and remained under occupation until September 1944.

Since the end of World War II economic progress has been marked, for the geographical advantages Belgium possesses have given it a position of significance in Europe, especially in the EEC. The unity of the people, however, is less secure, and in the early 1990s there were growing signs that the fragile alliance which had preserved the nation for so long – and under such arduous circumstances – was beginning to crack.

Of the country's universities, Louvain (Catholic and Belgium's oldest, dating from 1426) provides courses in both Flemish and French; of the universities founded in the 19th century, Ghent (1816) is Flemish and Liège (1817) is French-speaking. At Brussels' Free University (founded in 1834) the courses are mainly in French, but provision is made for Flemish speakers. Gradually the grievances of the Flemish speakers have been removed and in 1974 regional councils were established for Flanders, Wallonia and the Brussels district.

Landscape and agriculture

Physically Belgium may be divided into the uplands of the Ardennes and the lowland plains, which are drained by the Meuse to the Rhine through the Netherlands, and by the Schelde through Antwerp to the North Sea. The Ardennes, rising in Belgium to about 700 m [2,296 ft] at the highest point, is an area predominantly of moorland, peat bogs and woodland.

Lowland Belgium has varied soils, including some poor-quality sands in the Campine (Kempenland) area near the Dutch frontier, supporting only heaths and woodland. But, in general, careful cultivation, sound husbandry and attention to drainage have provided good soils; lowland farming is prosperous, with a strong emphasis on grain crops, potatoes and other vegetables, hops, sugar and fodder beet, with hay.

Few hedges exist in the farmed landscape and the holdings are small with intensive cultivation.

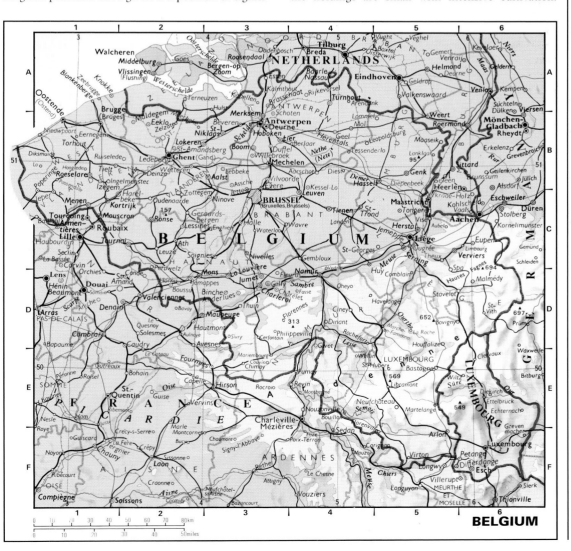

BELGIUM

The centre of Bruges, capital of West Flanders, from the belfry of the City Hall. Prosperity was founded on the wool trade and, later, on lace.

Traditionally many factory workers of the towns also had a smallholding. There is a small area of polders near the coast, in all less than 500 sq km [200 sq mls], which is rich agricultural land. Outside the towns the density of rural settlement is high.

Industry and commerce

No minerals other than coal exist in significant quantities and the Belgian emphasis on manufacturing is based on the import of raw materials. The Ardennes includes the country's most productive coalfield (the Campine) in the Sambre-Meuse Valley, centred on the cities of Charleroi and Liège. Charleroi is a coal-mining and metallurgical city while Liège is the centre of the iron industry. The Campine coalfield continues into the Netherlands and Germany, but production has declined in recent years as uneconomic mines have been closed.

Still of major importance, however, is the textile industry, which has existed in the towns of Flanders from medieval times and in its modern form includes a wide range of products. It is associated particularly with Ghent and Bruges, though these are equally renowned for their medieval architecture. Industry has been diversified and some manufactures, such as glass, are well known in the international market.

It is this part of the country that makes Belgium not only one of Europe's most crowded nations – 328 people per sq km [849 per sq ml] – but the most 'urban' of any reasonably sized independent state, with an official figure of 96.9%.

Belgium's main port is Antwerp, much modernized since 1956. The main industrial centres are served by ship canals, including one of 29 km [18 mls] from Ghent to Terneuzen. Constructed in 1825–7, it can take ships as large as 61,000 tonnes.

Now, as in past centuries, the lowlands of Belgium, and particularly the city of Brussels (headquarters of the EEC, of which Belgium was a founder member), remain a major focus of commercial and political life in Europe ∎

THE GREAT DIVIDE

Belgium has always been an uneasy marriage of two peoples: the majority Flemings, speaking a very close relative of Dutch, and the Walloons, who speak French (rather than the old Walloon variation of French). The dividing line between the two communities runs east-west, just south of Brussels, with the capital itself officially bilingual.

Since the inception of the country the Flemings have caught up and overtaken the Walloons in cultural influence as well as in numbers. In 1932 the Belgian government was designated bilingual, and in 1970 the country was effectively splintered into four parts. In the far eastern frontier areas German is the official language; Brussels remained bilingual but its province of Brabant divided; and the other eight provinces were split into four Fleming and four Walloon – with only the dominant language being official.

Belgium has three governments: the national authority in Brussels, and regional assemblies for Flanders and Wallonia. During the 1980s, as power gradually devolved from the centre to the regions in crucial aspects of education, transport and the economy, the tension between the 'Germanic' Flemings and the 'Latin' Walloons increased in government. The various coalitions of Dutch- and French-speaking Christian Democrats and Socialists – which had held together for more than a decade under the astute stewardship of Prime Minister Wilfried Martens – was seriously undermined by the results of the emergency election of November 1991, with many experts predicting the break-up of the national state into two virtually independent nations before the end of the century – leaving Brussels (ironically the focal point of European integration) as a political island.

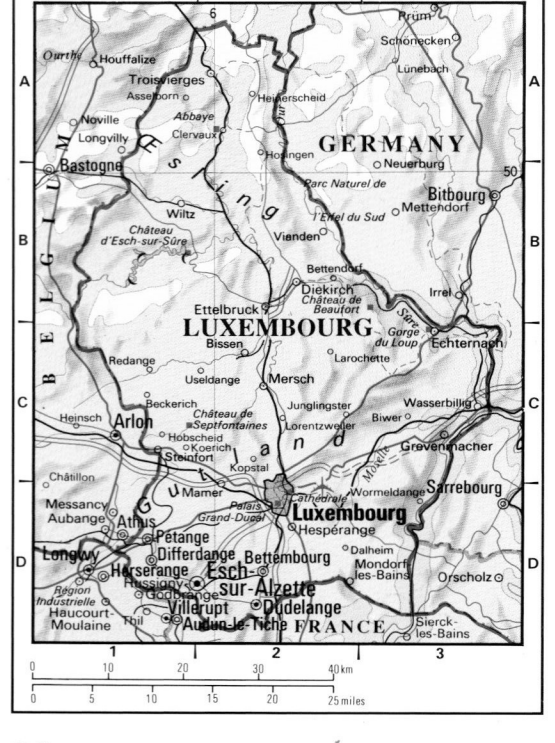

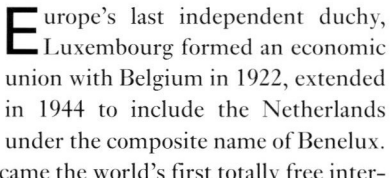

LUXEMBOURG

Europe's last independent duchy, Luxembourg formed an economic union with Belgium in 1922, extended in 1944 to include the Netherlands under the composite name of Benelux. In 1960 this became the world's first totally free international market for goods and labour.

Luxembourg is a founder member of NATO (1949) and the EEC (1957), and is perhaps best known to Europeans as the host for the Court of the European Communities, the Secretariat of the European Parliament, the European Investment Bank and the European Monetary Co-operation Fund.

Luxembourg consists partly of the Ardennes, well wooded and famed for its deer and wild boar, but the more prosperous agricultural areas are in the scarplands of Lorraine. Stock-rearing, especially of dairy cattle, is important, and crops include grains, potatoes, roots and fruit, and vines in the Moselle Valley.

There is also a prosperous iron and steel industry based on rich iron-ore deposits and this, together with its financial services industry (there are 114 different banks), provides most of its income.

Declaring itself a Grand Duchy in 1354, Luxembourg is the only one out of hundreds of independent duchies, which once comprised much of continental Europe, to survive and become a full member of the United Nations. Most Luxembourgers speak both German and French, but the main language is their own Germanic dialect.

In 1940, during World War II, Germany overran Luxembourg and incorporated it into the Third Reich. Over 10,000 of the inhabitants were forced to fight for Hitler, while others joined the Resistance against the occupying forces.

With its suburbs, the capital accounts for nearly a third of the country's population. A similar proportion are foreign workers, attracted by opportunities in industry and the many international organizations. Although Luxembourg's population is barely a thousandth of the EU total, it remains a relatively important player in Western European commerce and politics ∎

FRANCE

Although replaced by the Ukraine as Europe's biggest 'country' in 1991, France remains a handsomely proportioned runner-up, well ahead of Spain and more than twice the area of the entire United Kingdom. Yet the nation possesses space as well as size, and while the growth of cities in the years since World War II has been spoken of in terms of crisis (*la crise urbaine*), urban expansion is a problem only in a few special areas, notably Paris and its immediate surroundings. In general, France has stayed predominantly rural.

Many French towns show traces of the country's long history. In the south, for example, at Arles and Carcassonne, there are famous Roman remains. Medieval churches are abundant with splendid cathedrals such as Reims, Amiens and Notre-Dame in Paris. Traces of the period before the 1789 Revolution include the famous châteaux, many of them built or rebuilt in the 18th century, when rich landlords were patrons of the arts.

Frontiers

Frontiers are a natural concern of continental European countries, but of France's 5,500 km [3,440 mls] almost half consists of sea coast and another 1,000 km [620 mls] winds through the mountains of the Pyrenees and the Alps. In general the Pyrenees frontier follows the crest line of the major hills, rather than the watershed between rivers flowing north into France or south into Spain. There are few easy crossings through the Pyrenees into Spain, but good coastal routes exist on the west from Bayonne into the Basque country, and on the east from Perpignan to Gerona.

In the south-east of France, Savoie and the county of Nice were ceded by Italy at the Treaty of Turin in 1860 and in the following year the Prince of Monaco gave Menton and a neighbouring area to France. The cession of Savoie meant that France's territory extended to the summit of Mont Blanc, the highest mountain in Europe outside the Caucasus.

It also gave France part of the shores of Lake Geneva. Geneva itself is Swiss, but French territory lies within walking distance, and special customs arrangements exist so that people from the French countryside may use the city's trading facilities. North of Geneva the frontier runs through the Jura Mountains to Basle on the Rhine where France, Germany and Switzerland meet. Though Basle itself is in Switzerland, its airport is in France.

North of Basle, for 160 km [100 mls] the border between France and Germany follows the Rhine. Alsace and Lorraine, west of the river, were sought by both countries for centuries, and after the Franco-Prussian War in 1870–1 the whole of Alsace and part of Lorraine were returned to Prussia. This frontier remained until the Treaty of Versailles following World War I, but in World War II it was violated again by the Germans – their third invasion of France in 70 years. The frontiers from the Rhine to the North Sea were defined in their present form during the 18th century.

Local government in France was reorganized during the French Revolution. In 1790 Turgot defined the *départements* as areas in which everyone could reach the central town within one day.

Landscape

Highland France: Most of France lies less than 300 m [1,000 ft] above sea level, but there are several distinctive upland areas. The most impressive are the Alps and the Pyrenees, but they also include the ancient massifs of Brittany and the Central Plateau, the Vosges and that part of the Ardennes which is within France.

The Alps are formed of complex folded rocks of intricate structure, with relief made even more complicated by the successive glaciations of the Ice Age. Areas of permanent snow exist on Mont Blanc and many other high peaks, and visitors to the upper Arve Valley at Chamonix, St-Gervais and other holiday centres have easy access to glaciers. The Alps are visited by tourists throughout the year – in winter for skiing, and in summer for walking on the upland pastures (the original 'alps'). In the French Alps, as in the other alpine areas, hydroelectricity has become universal both for general home use and for industry. The Pyrenees, though comparable to the Alps, lack arterial routes.

The Breton massif includes part of Normandy and extends southwards to the neighbourhood of La Rochelle. In general physical character it is a much dissected hilly area. The Massif Central is more dramatic: it covers one-sixth of France between the Rhône-Saône Valley and the basin of Aquitaine, and its highest summits rise to more than 1,800 m [5,900 ft]; striking examples are Mont du Cantal and Mont Dore (1,866 m [6,200 ft]). Volcanic activity of 10–30 million years ago appears in old volcanic plugs. Earlier rocks include limestones, providing poor soils for agriculture, and coal measures which have been mined for more than a century at St-Étienne and Le Creusot. The Vosges and the Ardennes are areas of poor soil, largely forested.

Organic tomatoes being sold in Brittany. The French have jealously protected their farmers with the EU's Common Agricultural Policy since the 1950s.

Lowland France: Although France has striking mountain areas, 60% of the country is less than 250 m [800 ft] above sea level. Fine rivers, including the Rhône, Garonne, Loire and Seine, along with their many tributaries, drain large lowland areas. From the Mediterranean there is a historic route northwards through the Rhône-Saône Valley to Lyons and Dijon. North-westwards there is the famous route through the old towns of Carcassonne and Toulouse to Bordeaux on the Gironde estuary, into which the Garonne and the Dordogne flow. This is the basin of Aquitaine, bordered by the Massif Central to the north and the Pyrenees to the south. It is not a uniform lowland – there are several hilly areas and on the coast

a belt of sand dunes, the Landes, extending for 200 km [125 mls] from Bayonne to the Gironde estuary.

From Aquitaine there is an easy route to the north, followed by the major railway from Bordeaux to Poitiers, Tours, Orléans and Paris. This lowland is called the Gate of Poitou, though in place of the word 'gate' the French say *seuil* or 'threshold', which is perhaps more appropriate. Crossing the threshold brings the traveller to the Paris basin, in the heart of which is the great city itself.

The ancient centre of Paris lies on the Île de la Cité, where the Seine was easily crossed. The Paris basin is a vast area floored by sedimentary rocks. Those that are resistant to erosion, including some limestones and chalks, form upland areas. The Loire, with its many tributaries in the south-west of the basin, and the Seine, with its numerous affluents (notably the Yonne, Aube, Marne, Aisne and Oise), offer easy routes between the upland areas.

Agriculture

The lowlands of France are warmer than those of England in summer; the cooler winters of the north, with more frost and snow than on the lowlands of England, have little adverse effect on agriculture. Rainfall is moderate, with a summer maximum in the north and a winter maximum in the areas of Mediterranean climate to the south.

Modern improvements in agriculture include the provision of irrigation during the summer in the south. This has transformed many areas in the Rhône and Durance valleys, and also the coastal lands such as the Crau, south-east of Arles. Without irrigation this was a stony, steppe-like area; now it supports vast flocks of sheep and has fine hay crops, cut three times a year. Further west in the Camargue, on the Rhône delta, rice is grown with the help of irrigation and there are other areas of rice production close to the Mediterranean. Water comes either from canals, lead-ing into ditches through the fields, or by sprinkler systems from a network of underground pumps; one water point can supply 4 hectares [10 acres].

France's agricultural revolution is far from complete. There are areas where modern technology has made large reclamation schemes possible, but there are still many independent peasant farmers, making a living that is a meagre reward for the labour expended, even with the generous terms of the EU's Common Agricultural Policy (CAP). The younger generation tend to regard emigration to the towns as a more promising way of life.

Alpine areas: In the alpine areas of France, including the Pyrenees, farms are far more numerous on hill slopes having good exposure to sunlight (the *adret*) than on those less favoured (the *ubac*). There are fine upland pastures, apparently retaining their fertility through centuries of use, which provide summer feed for cattle. Although there is still much traditional farming in these areas, many people have diversified or emigrated. Some find work in tourist resorts, and many of the old timber-built houses have been bought by people from the cities as holiday homes. The future of peasant farming in mountain areas is a problem that France shares with Switzerland, Austria and Spain.

Mediterranean France: From the French Riviera lowlands extend northwards through the Rhône and Saône valleys and westwards through Languedoc to the neighbourhood of Narbonne. This is the area of Mediterranean climate, having most rain in winter, with wheat, vines and olives as the traditional crops. Wheat is well suited to a Mediterranean climate, for it grows best with a cool, moist period followed by one that is warm and dry. Vines need summer warmth – with temperatures of at least 18°C [64°F] for the greater part of the growing season – and dryness, but not to an excessive degree, during the 70 days from the opening of the buds to maturity. The olive is the

traditional tree of the true Mediterranean climate. Originally a native of Egypt, through the centuries it was planted first in the eastern and later in the western Mediterranean. The ripe, dark purple fruits contain oil, used for cooking; green, unripe olives are commonly used as appetizers.

These three crops are familiar in the south but with them are many more, including maize (the country is the world's fifth largest producer) and a wide range of vegetables. Mediterranean France is not everywhere a land of continuous agriculture, for in places it is interspersed with rocky outcrops unsuited to cultivation but covered with maquis or pines. Farmers have made fertile the patches of good soil and adequate moisture, and the general landscape is a mixture of rough hills and limestone pavements surrounding rich areas of cultivation.

Aquitaine: To the west, Aquitaine is not a uniform lowland; the agricultural land is interspersed by hills and plateaus that are generally wooded or left as heathland. It is nevertheless a richly productive area, with arable farming for cereal crops, maize and vegetables, and also pastures for cattle. Aquitaine is also a celebrated wine-producing area, with enormous fields laid out as vineyards. Many of the old farms have disappeared, and even whole villages have been abandoned, for example in the Dordogne, as vines have replaced other, less remunerative crops. Much of the wine is consumed on the home market as the normal *vin ordinaire*, mostly red but including some less favoured whites.

Around Bordeaux the famous claret-producing area includes the Médoc, between the Gironde estuary and the sea: here also are the districts that produce white table wines, such as graves and sauternes. Aquitaine can in fact boast a wide range of red and white wines; several of them, though well known locally, are not exported because the quantity produced is small, and possibly because they do not travel well. Cognac and Armagnac wines are suited to brandy distillation.

Northern France: Northwards from Aquitaine through the lowland Gate (*seuil*) of Poitou, the winters become cooler, with rain in the winter as well as the winter months. Though the summers are cooler in the Paris basin than in Aquitaine, vines flourish on favoured slopes facing south, and many fine French wines come from these northern areas.

As a whole the Paris basin is agriculturally rich, with varied soils. The last Ice Age has left many areas of drifts and wind-blown soils, here as elsewhere in Europe providing land of great fertility. Between the valleys of the Paris basin lie the *pays*, low plateaus, each with its own characteristic. Some, such as the Beauce, with fertile soils, are suited to crops; others, such as the Sologne, have poor, sandy soils, hard to cultivate and best suited to forest. Local farmers have for centuries adjusted their activity to the qualities of the soil, and now use their specialized production as a basis both for trade with other areas, and for sale in the towns. Despite all the profound changes in French life, the variety of agriculture and land use in the Paris basin remains clear – few areas of the world have so neat a division into units as the *pays* of France.

Finally, to the west of the Paris basin there is the area of ancient rocks covering Brittany and its margins. This area, regarded as archaic but

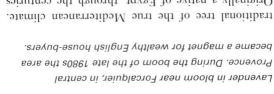

Lavender in bloom near Forcalquier, in central Provence. During the boom of the late 1980s the area became a magnet for wealthy English house-buyers.

picturesque, has small farms with fields divided by wooded hedges to give a sheltered *bocage* landscape. Rich in medieval churches, old customs and even costumes, it was never of great economic significance. Like Cornwall, in the far south-west of England, it had its own language (still used) and is part of the traditional Celtic west of Europe. There is now increasing pressure for local autonomy in Brittany, expressed particularly in efforts to improve agriculture by upgrading pastures, removing hedges to enlarge fields for animals and cultivation, developing market gardening, and encouraging industrial growth in the towns. Fishing remains a valued resource, while tourism (both from France and neighbouring Europe) brings additional prosperity to Brittany.

Agriculture remains a valued resource in the French economy – France accounts for almost 6% of the world's barley and wheat, for example (more of the latter than Canada), and agriculture contributes 17% of export earnings – and politicians make this

clear both in Paris and outside France. But there are many changes. In general these appear to reflect the opinion of the American geographer, Isaiah Bowman, that 'man takes the best and lets the rest go'. Poor land is abandoned, perhaps for forest, but promising areas are made rich through investment. Improvements such as drainage, irrigation and scientific fertilization in some areas counterbalance the decline in agriculture elsewhere, such as in the Alps and the Pyrenees. Loss of people from the land does not indicate a decline in agricultural production but rather an improvement in agricultural efficiency, and the freedom of people, no longer tied to the land, to seek, and generally to find, alternative and more satisfying employment.

Forests

Forests cover one-fifth of France. Most of them are on soils of poor quality, including the sands in parts of the Paris basin, the Vosges and the Landes between

Bordeaux and the Spanish frontier, the poor limestones of Lorraine and the clay-with-flints of Normandy. Some of the great forests were planted by landowners as parts of their estates, like those of Fontainebleau and Rambouillet near Paris; others were planted as barriers between former kingdoms, such as those between Normandy and Picardy.

The greatest single forested area in France is the Landes, covering 10,000 sq km [3,860 sq mls]. This is mainly coniferous forest, interspersed only here and there by farms. Since 1956 attempts have been made to reclaim and replant the extensive areas devastated by fire, and to substitute a more varied rural economy for the exclusive exploitation of the pine forests. In the Alps and the Pyrenees about a quarter of the land is covered with forest.

In France some two-thirds of all the woodlands are of deciduous trees, compared with less than a third in Germany, and about 60% of the country's timber requirements, especially for paper pulp-making, has to

FRANCE, MONACO

be imported. Since World War II various laws have been passed to encourage softwood production.

Farms revert to waste when they are no longer cultivated, and become impenetrable thickets of vegetation. Through most of France this vegetation is known as *maquis*, from the shelter it gives to fugitives: the term *maquis* was given in World War II to the resistance forces in hiding. In dry summers the risk of fire is considerable, especially in the south.

Resources and industry

France is a declining but still significant producer of iron ore (mostly from Lorraine), and several other minerals are also mined, including bauxite, potash, salt and sulphur. There are old coalfields in the northeast, but the output of these does not meet the country's needs. France instead switched to new sources of energy, including experiments with solar power in the Pyrenees and the world's first major tidal power station on the Rance estuary in Brittany, but more significantly utilizing the water of the mountains for hydroelectric power (24% of output) and mined uranium – almost 10% of world production – to create the most nuclear-based output of any nation (approaching 70% by the end of the 1980s).

Since World War II the marked industrial expansion in France has been accompanied by a change in the distribution of population. Before the war France was regarded as a country with a fairly even distribution of population between town and country, but from the late 1940s there was a spectacular increase in the urban population. In the first postwar planning

---

CORSICA

Annexed by France from Genoa in 1768 – just months before the birth of Napoleon Bonaparte, its most famous son – Corsica is 168 km [105 mls] from France and just 11 km [7 mls] from Sardinia, which is Italian territory. Corsica is divided into two *départements* of France, with its administrative centre at Ajaccio on the west coast. Roughly oval in shape, it is 190 km [118 mls] long and half as wide.

Most of the island is formed of rugged mountains, with more than 40 peaks over 2,000 m [6,500 ft] and some reaching over 2,900 m [9,500 ft]. Varied ancient rocks, much metamorphosed, make up these mountains. Only a quarter of Corsica provides rough grazing for sheep and goats; another quarter is in forests with evergreen oak and cork oak to 650 m [2,000 ft], then chestnuts with beech followed by pines to the treeline, between 1,600 and 2,000 m [5,000–6,000 ft]. In winter there is heavy snow on the mountains, causing severe flooding in the numerous short rivers.

---

period, 1947–53, industrial production rose by 70%, agricultural production by 21% and the standard of living by 30%.

During the following three years there was further expansion, particularly in the chemical and electrical industries. In the period of the third plan, 1958-61, the success of export industries became notable, especially in such products as automobiles, aircraft and electrical goods. In this period, too,

natural gas was discovered at Lacq, and such industries as chemicals and aluminium smelting prospered. However, traditional industries, such as textiles and porcelain, are still important, and despite technological innovation and success, France is still weak in 'high-tech' areas compared to Japan, the USA and several European rivals.

Nevertheless, the country's postwar transition to a prosperous, dynamic society with more relaxed attitudes has been rapid and pronounced. French life has been, and still is, focused to a remarkable degree on Paris, where traditional luxury industries, such as perfumes, thrive alongside commerce, light industry, heavy industry and services of all kinds. Virtually all the major commercial enterprises of France have their headquarters in Paris – and Paris and district now has almost a fifth of the total population.

The other important industrial centres are on and around the mining areas, and at or near the major ports where imported raw materials are used: Fos, west of Marseilles, for example, and the steel complex at Dunkerque. The aims of modern planning include the development of regional prosperity, based on such centres as Lyons, Marseilles, Toulouse, Nantes, Lille, Nancy and Strasbourg, home to the European parliament. While the industrial attraction of the Paris area remains powerful and population growth continues to exceed that of the second largest urban area, the district around Lyons, the traditional centralization of France is showing signs of weakening and governments of both complexions have sought to reduce state power both in local affairs and the economy ■

MONACO

The world's smallest nation outside Rome, and by far its most crowded, the tiny principality of Monaco – comprising a rocky peninsula and a narrow stretch of coast – has increased in size by 20% since its land reclamation programme began in 1958. A densely populated

modern city-state, it derives its considerable income almost entirely from services: banking finance, and above all, tourism; this is based not just on its Riviera Mediterranean climate but also on the famous casino. Monégasques are not allowed to gamble there, but there is ample compensation in paying no state taxes.

Monaco has been ruled by the Grimaldi dynasty since 1297, though in 1815 (with the Treaty of Vienna) it came under the protection of the kingdom of Sardinia; the greater part, including Menton, was annexed by France in 1848 and the remainder came under its protection in 1861 – a situation that essen-

tially survives today within a customs union. The present monarch, Prince Rainer III (ascended 1949), drew up a new liberalizing constitution in 1962.

Monaco falls into four districts: vacation-oriented Monte Carlo; the old town of Monaco-Ville, with royal palace and cathedral; the shops, banks and smart houses of La Condamine; and the light industries and marinas of Fontvieille ■

Expensive yachts moored in the spectacular setting of Monte Carlo – a gambling mecca with few rivals as 'the pleasure palace of the Mediterranean'.

GERMANY

The German Empire that was created under Prussian dominance in 1871, comprising four kingdoms, six grand duchies, five duchies and seven principalities, and centred on the great imperial capital of Berlin, was to last for fewer than 75 years. Even at its greatest extent it left large areas of Europe's German-speaking population outside its boundaries, notably in Austria and large parts of Switzerland. Following the fall of Hitler in 1945, a defeated Germany was obliged to transfer to Poland and the Soviet Union 114,500 sq km [44,200 sq mls] situated east of the Oder and Neisse rivers, nearly a quarter of the country's pre-war area. The German-speaking inhabitants were expelled – as were most German-speaking minorities in the countries of Eastern Europe – and the remainder of Germany was occupied by the four victorious Allied powers.

The dividing line between the zones occupied by the three Western Allies (USA, UK and France) and that occupied by the USSR rapidly hardened into a political boundary dividing the country. In 1948 West Germany was proclaimed as the independent Federal Republic of Germany (FRG), with a capital at Bonn (deemed 'provisional' pending hoped-for German reunification), and measuring 248,000 sq km [96,000 sq mls]. East Germany became the German Democratic Republic (GDR), a Soviet satellite of 108,000 sq km [41,700 sq mls]. Berlin was similarly divided, the three western sectors of an enclave of occupation becoming 480 sq km [186 sq mls] embedded in the territory of the GDR, of which the Soviet-occupied East Berlin was deemed to be capital.

On reunification, West and East Germany moved from the ninth and 15th biggest countries in Europe to a combined fourth – still much smaller than France, Spain and Sweden – but with the independence of the Ukraine the following year dropped back to fifth. It is, nevertheless, 12th in the world in terms of population.

Landscape

Germany extends from the North Sea and Baltic coasts in the north to the flanks of the central Alps in the south. The country includes only a narrow fringe of Alpine mountains, with the Zugspitze (2,963 m [9,721 ft]) the country's highest peak. There is, however, a wide section of the associated Alpine foreland bordering Switzerland and Austria, stretching northwards from the foothills of the Alps to the Danube. The foreland is largely covered by moraines and outwash plains which, with many lakes, including the Bodensee (shared with Switzerland), are relics of the glacial age, and reminders of the many glaciers that once emerged from the Alpine valleys.

The central uplands of Europe are more amply represented, occupying a broad swathe of Germany. Four types of terrain are found. Block mountains are remnants of pre-Alpine fold mountains shattered and reshaped by the later earth movements. The Harz, Thüringer Wald and Erzgebirge (Ore Mountains) massifs rise above a varied scarpland terrain, notably the Thüringian basin, which has the fertile Erfurt lowland at its heart.

Uplift was greatest in the south, close to the Alps, producing the Schwarzwald (Black Forest) and Böhmerwald. Between these great blocks of forested mountains are open basins of sedimentary rocks, their resistant bands picked out by erosion as in the magnificent scarp of the Schwäbische Alb, overlooking the Neckar basin.

A third kind of country is provided by down-faulted basins filled with softer deposits of more recent age, notably the Upper Rhine plain between Basle and Mainz. Earth movement and eruptions produced a fourth element, such volcanic mountains as the Vogelsberg and the hot and mineral springs that gave rise to the famous spas. Here is Germany at its most picturesque, with baronial castles on wooded heights, looking down over vineyards to clustered villages of half-timbered houses, whose occupants still cultivate open-field strips as they have done for centuries.

The northern lowlands, part of the great North European Plain, owe their topography mainly to the retreat of the ice-sheets. The most recent moraines, marked by forested ridges that may include good boulder-clay soils, are restricted to Schleswig-Holstein. The rest of the lowland is covered with leached older moraine and sandy outwash, so that in many places soils are poor. The glacial period also left behind loess,

Heidelberg's 18th-century 'Old Bridge' is overlooked by the ruins of its 13th-century castle. The town has Germany's oldest university, founded in 1386.

windblown dust deposited along the northern edge of the central uplands and in basins within them, providing some of the country's best soils for wheat, malting barley and sugar beet. This belt broadens in the lowland of Saxony around Halle and Leipzig.

The coast is also the product of glaciation and subsequent changes. The low Baltic shore is diversified by long, branching inlets, formed beneath the ice of the glacial period and now beloved by yachtsmen, while inland the most recent moraines have left behind a confused terrain of hills and lakes, but also areas of good soil developed on glacial till. The movement of water around the edge of the ice-sheets carved stream trenches (*Urstromtäler*), south-east to north-west; these are now in part occupied by the present rivers, and have also proved convenient for canal construction. The North Sea is fringed by sandy offshore islands, the products of a beach bar now breached by the sea.

THE REUNIFICATION OF GERMANY

In 1945, a devastated Germany was divided into four zones, each occupied by one of the victorious powers: Britain, France, the USA and the Soviet Union. The division was originally a temporary expedient (the Allies had formally agreed to maintain German unity), but the Russians published a constitution for the German Democratic Republic in 1946. The split solidified when the Russians rejected a currency reform common to all three Western zones. The German Federal Republic – 'West Germany' – was created in 1949.

Throughout the years of the Cold War, as NATO troops faced Warsaw Pact tanks across the barbed wire and minefields of the new frontier, the partition seemed irrevocable. Although both German constitutions maintained hopes of reunification, it seemed that nothing short of the total war both sides dreaded could bring it about. The West, with three-quarters of the population, rebuilt war damage and prospered. The East was hailed as the industrial jewel of the Soviet European empire, though some of its people were prepared to risk being shot to escape westwards.

By the late 1980s it was clear that the Soviet empire was crumbling. In the autumn of 1989, thousands of East Germans migrated illegally to the West across the newly open Hungarian border and mass demonstrations in East German cities followed. At first, the government issued a stream of threats, but when it became clear that there would be no Soviet tanks to enforce its rule, it simply packed up. With the frontiers open, it was obvious that the 'successful' East German economy was a catastrophic shambles, a scrapyard poisoned by uncontrolled pollution, with bankruptcy imminent. The choice facing German leaders in 1990 was starkly simple: either unite East and West, or accept virtually the entire Eastern population as penniless refugees.

The West German government acted quickly, often bullying the weaker Easterners. The Western Deutschmark became the common currency and on 3 October 1990 the country was formally reunited. But financial costs of bringing the East up to the standards of the West are high, and Germans will be paying them for years to come.

Agriculture

Over a quarter of Germany is forested, with particular concentration in the Alps, the massifs of the central uplands, and the poorer areas of the northern lowland. It is amazing that this economically most advanced country has some of Europe's smallest farms, particularly characteristic of southern Germany. Most are used for arable-based mixed farming, with minor livestock enterprises. In the warmer basins tobacco, vegetables and, increasingly, maize are grown. Vineyards and orchards clothe the slopes of the Rhine and its tributaries. Much larger wheat and sugar-beet farms with important livestock enterprises are characteristic of the loess soils on the northern edge of the central uplands. The Bavarian Alpine foreland in the south, and Schleswig-Holstein in the north, are other areas of above-average farm size. The sandy northern lowland, which used to support a poor agriculture based on rye, potatoes and pigs, increasingly specializes in intensive meat and poultry production. Dairy specialization is typical of the milder north-west and the Alpine fringes.

Because of the generally small size of holdings many farmers seek a supplementary income outside agriculture – often a halfway stage to giving up agriculture. Persons employed in agriculture, who were a quarter of the employed population of the FRG in 1950, accounted for well below 10% on reunification four decades later. With this movement out of agriculture, the average size of holding is steadily but all too slowly rising.

In the GDR, by contrast, all agricultural holdings were brought into 'co-operatives', many of over 500 hectares [1,236 acres]; and some up to ten times that size. The East German government's version of the collective farm proved much more efficient than the equivalent in many other Communist states, however, and the economic outlook was quite promising prior to reunification.

Minerals and energy

Germany is the most important coal producer of continental Western Europe, though output from the Ruhr, Saar and Aachen fields has dropped since the mid-1950s, owing mainly to competition from oil. Some oil and gas is home-produced, mainly extracted from fields beneath the northern lowland, but most of the oil consumed in Germany is delivered by pipeline from Wilhelmshaven, Europoort and the Mediterranean to refineries in the Rhineland and on the Danube.

Brown coal (lignite) is excavated between Cologne and Aachen, but the former GDR (East Germany) was unique in depending for energy supply on this source of low calorific value, economically mined in vast open pits. The older centre of mining was in the lowland of Saxony, between Halle and Leipzig, but the main area of expansion is now in Niederlausitz, south of Cottbus. Brown coal is increasingly reserved for electricity generation, although atomic plants built on the coast and principal rivers are expected to be of increasing importance (at present 34% of the total for the former FRG), with hydroelectric stations concentrated in the Bavarian Alps. Energy needs and feedstock for the important chemical industry around Halle are met by oil brought by pipeline from the former Soviet republics or by tanker through

Church and castle gaze down on the commercial traffic on the Rhine. Crucial to Germany and its neighbours, Western Europe's longest river is increasingly in danger from pollution as far up-river as Basel.

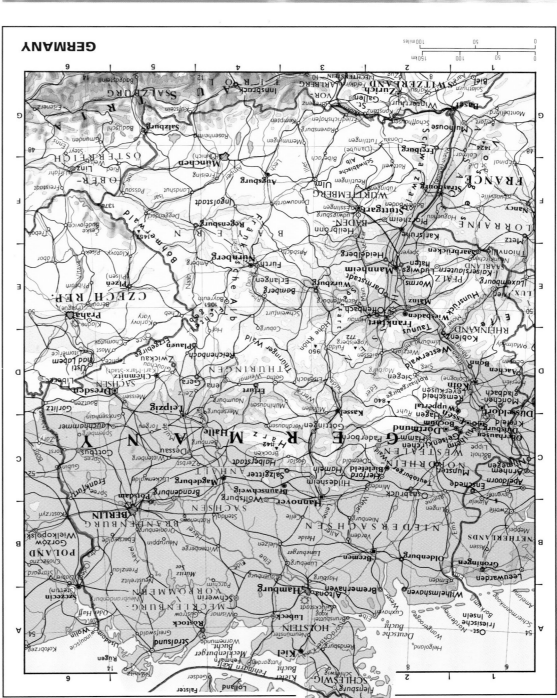

GERMANY

Rostock. The other mineral resource of value is potash, mined south of the Harz; Germany is the world's third largest producer. The non-ferrous metallic ores of the Harz and other massifs of the central uplands are no longer of great significance, while high-grade imported iron ores have proved more economic than the home ores of the Siegen and Peine-Salzgitter districts.

Settlement and industry

From Neolithic times the core settlement areas of Germany were the fertile lowlands – areas like the northern edge of the central uplands in Lower Saxony and Westphalia, the Upper Rhine plain, the Main and Neckar basins, and the Alpine foreland. From these core areas land-hungry medieval peasants advanced to clear large areas of forest in the uplands, and also streamed eastwards to settle beyond the Elbe.

The fragmentation of the Holy Roman Empire into a swarm of competing states had a positive side in the founding and fostering by local rulers, large and small, of a dense system of towns, among them future regional capitals like Hanover, Stuttgart or Munich (München). The contrast with the 'French desert' created by Parisian centralization is striking.

When industrial growth came in the 19th century, heavy industry naturally concentrated in the Ruhr and Saar coalfields, but thanks to the railways other production could disperse widely to these existing towns. Since 1945 the Ruhr and Saar coalfields have been undergoing a difficult period of conversion, owing to the problems of the now declining coal, steel and heavy engineering industries. Western Europe's largest industrial region, stretching from Duisburg to Dortmund, the Ruhr ('the forge of Germany') has seen its mines for top-grade coking coal cut from 145 to less than 20 and has been forced to diversify – the western end into petrochemicals based on the Rhine ports and pipelines, the eastern part into lighter and computer-based industry.

By contrast, towns away from the coalfields, especially the great regional capitals of southern Germany, have flourished with the inauguration of modern industries (motor vehicles, electrical equipment, electronics), the growth of administrative and office work, and the division among a number of cities of capital functions formerly concentrated in Berlin.

As an advanced industrial country of western type, the role of East Germany within the Communist-bloc states was to provide technically advanced equipment, receiving in return supplies of raw materials and semi-finished products such as steel. Because of industrial inertia, the location of the important machine-building industry had not greatly changed since capitalist times, being heavily concentrated in and around the southern cities of Leipzig, Chemnitz (then Karl-Marx-Stadt) and Dresden. Other centres were Magdeburg and East Berlin, which was also the leading producer of electrical equipment.

The GDR inherited a traditional strength in precision and optical industries, mostly located in Thüringia (such as the famous Zeiss works at Jena), the base for important developments in industrial instrumentation and electronics. The government tried to steer some major new developments into the rural north and east of the country, including ship-building at Rostock, also the site of a new ocean port, to avoid the use of facilities in the FRG, oil refining and chemicals at Schwedt, and iron smelting and steel rolling at Eisenhüttenstadt.

While the inner parts of the greatest cities have tended to lose population, their suburbs and satellites have exploded across the surrounding countrysides, forming vast urban areas of expanding population. In the west and south of the country, an axis of high population growth and high density stretches from the Rhine-Ruhr region (largest of all but checked in expansion by the problems of Ruhr industry) through the Rhine-Main (Frankfurt), Rhine-Neckar (Mannheim-Ludwigshafen) and Stuttgart regions to Munich. In the east and north the densely populated areas are more isolated, centred on the cities of Nuremberg, Hanover, Bremen, Hamburg, Dresden, Leipzig and of course Berlin.

Since 1950 there has been a tendency for the West's population to drift towards the more attractive south. Urban population losses have in part been made up by immigrant workers (nearly 2.5 million at their peak in the early 1970s, with Turkey the principal source), increasingly joined by their families to supplement a German native population – which at the end of the 1960s entered a period of negative growth.

Germany's wary neighbours, fearing that a nation suddenly swollen to nearly 80 million through reunification could swamp Europe, could rest easy. According to a report from the Institute of German Economy, published in 1992, there will be 20 million fewer Germans alive than today by the year 2030, and on current trends the number of young people below the age of 15 will drop from 13.7 million in 1990 to 10 million in 2010. The findings suggested that, as a result, the country would need at least 300,000 new immigrants a year to fill the gap in its labour market.

Communications

Germany has the advantage of the superb Rhine waterway, which from its Alpine sources cuts right across the central uplands to the North Sea. A combination of summer snow-melt from the Alps and autumn-spring rainfall in the central uplands gives it a powerful and remarkably even flow – if increasingly polluted. Although traffic is at its most intensive between Rotterdam and the Rhine-Ruhr region, where Duisburg is the largest inland harbour of Europe, standard 1,250-tonne self-propelled barges can reach Basle. The Rhine-Main-Danube waterway has also opened a through route to Eastern Europe and the Black Sea, while for north German traffic the Mittelland Canal, following the northern edge of the central uplands, opens up links to the north German ports and Berlin. Unusually for Europe, Germany's rivers and canals carry as much freight as its roads.

Hamburg is Germany's biggest seaport, followed by Bremen with its outport, Bremerhaven. All German ports suffer by being too far from the main centre of European population and economic activity in the Rhinelands; the Belgian and Dutch ports are at a great advantage being closer.

Germany was the first European country to build motorways (Hitler's *Autobahns*, centred on Berlin), and also enjoys an efficient if highly subsidized railway network. Both are crucial to a country which, on reunification, increased its land borders from nine to ten countries. Air travel, too, is important.

Administration

The system of powerful federal states (*Länder*) created in the FRG after World War II remained remarkably stable, though huge disparities of size have remained in spite of various reform proposals. Bavaria has by far the largest area, and North Rhine-Westphalia, with the Rhine-Ruhr region at its heart, has the largest population, over a fifth of the German total. At the other extreme are the 'city states' of Bremen and Hamburg, though Saarland is also small.

In 1990 the ten *Länder* of the FRG (excluding the enclave of West Berlin) were joined by the five rejuvenated old states of the GDR – Brandenburg, Mecklenburg-West Pomerania, Saxony, Saxony-Anhalt and Thüringia – plus the new 'united' Berlin. The East German organization had been very different, the country politically divided into 15 administrative districts (*Bezirke*) under the control of the central government in East Berlin. On reunification, Berlin became once more the formal capital – though a few ministries remained in Bonn ∎

SWITZERLAND

Nearly 60% of Swiss territory is in the Alps, of which two notable peaks are on the Italian border: the Matterhorn (4,478 m [14,700 ft]) and the Monte Rosa (4,634 m [15,200 ft]). The Alps are drained by the upper Rhine tributaries and by the Rhône Valley via Lac Léman (Lake Geneva). Numerous lakes add to the scenic attraction of high mountains with permanent snow, and the Alps have become one of the great tourist attractions of the world. As a result, around 200,000 people work in the hotel and catering industries. Nationally, unemployment is very low by world standards.

Despite its lingering image as predominantly pastoral, Switzerland is a very advanced country, providing its citizens with a per capita income which is by far the highest of the reasonably sized economies, and is outstripped only by neighbouring Liechtenstein. The reasons for Switzerland's high standard of living include neutrality in two world wars, plentiful hydroelectric power, a central geographical position and rich mineral deposits, including uranium (37% of the electricity is now nuclear-derived) and iron ore. It would also be unfair, however – as in the case of Germany and Japan – not to include hard work, a sense of purpose and organizational ability in the list of attributes.

Agriculture is efficient, with both arable and pastoral farming; a wide range of produce is grown throughout the country, including maize and other cereals, fruits, vegetables, and grapes for a local wine industry. The mountain pastures are still used for summer grazing, though most of the famous migrations of herds and herders up the mountains in summer no longer take place. Industry is progressive and prosperous, in particular engineering, both mechanical and electrical, metallurgy, chemicals and textiles. Watch- and clock-making is perhaps the most famed of all Swiss industries, and is still very important for the national economy.

In addition to agricultural and industrial strength Switzerland also has a world trade in banking and insurance, concentrated particularly in Zürich, while its revenues are boosted both by tourism and its position as the headquarters for numerous international bodies. Geneva alone hosts EFTA, GATT and the International Red Cross (which was first formed there in 1864), as well as ten UN agencies that include WHO, ILO and the High Commission for Refugees, while there are over 140 others: Basle, for example, is home to the Bank for International Settlements (the central banks' bank). Ironically, Switzerland has remained stubbornly outside the UN – a policy reiterated by a referendum held in 1986. As Europe started moving towards greater economic and political union, Switzerland announced in May 1992 that it would be applying to join the EEC; but a December 1992 referendum rejected this proposal. However, in June 1993 Switzerland decided to establish by 1995 a 600-man battalion for use in the UN peacekeeping force.

Switzerland is a multilingual patchwork of 26 cantons, each of which has control over housing and economic policy. Six of the cantons are French-speaking, one Italian-speaking, one with a significant Romansch-speaking community (Graubünden), and the rest speak German ∎

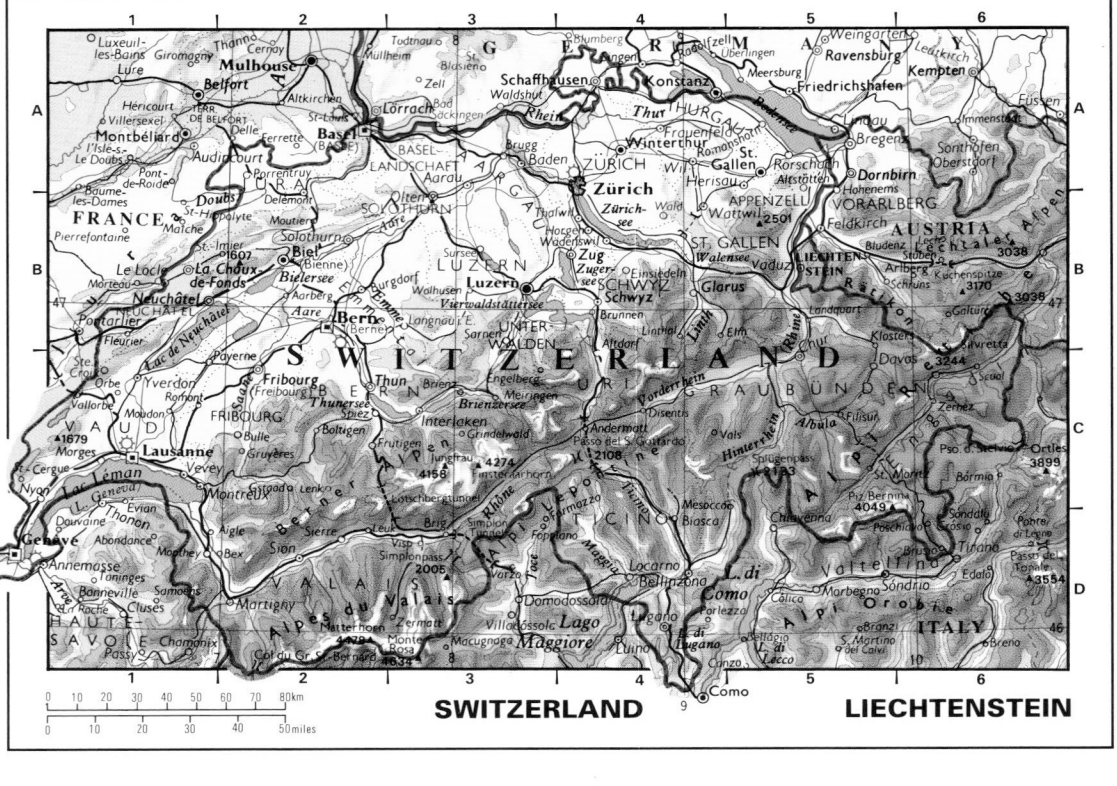

SWITZERLAND   **LIECHTENSTEIN**

THE ALPS

Thrust upwards by continental collision 25 or 30 million years ago, the Alps are Europe's principal mountain range: between north-eastern Italy and eastern Austria, they stretch for over 1,000 km [600 mls] and include Europe's highest mountain, Mont Blanc (4,807 m [15,771 ft]). The Alpine watershed is the source of many great European rivers, including the Rhine and the Po.

Nine major passes and six tunnels, including one under Mont Blanc, now make access very easy, and tourism has become a mass industry.

Alpine agriculture, once the mainstay of mountain life, is currently in decline, but skiing and summer tourism have brought new prosperity. Throughout the 1980s, the Alps attracted up to 50 million visitors a year, most intent on skiing some of the 40,000 runs that have been created for them. But the impact on the fragile environment is serious: thousands of hectares of high forest have been bulldozed to create smooth pistes, denuding the slopes of scarce topsoil and creating perfect conditions for huge avalanches.

The remaining Alpine forests are also under severe threat from acid rain.

AUSTRIA

A federal republic comprising nine states (*Länder*) – including the capital, Vienna – Austria's present boundaries derive from the Versailles Treaty of 1919, which dissolved the Austro-Hungarian Empire. It was absorbed by the German Reich in 1938, occupied by the Allies in 1945 and recovered its full independence in 1955.

A mountainous country, more Alpine even than Switzerland and with over 35% forested, Austria has two-thirds of its territory and rather less than a third of the population within the eastern Alps, which extend in a series of longitudinal ridges from the Swiss border in the west almost to Vienna in the east. The longitudinal valleys between the ridges accommodate much of the Alpine population, but are less effective than might be expected as routes of internal communication. Transverse routes, for example the Linz-Klagenfurt and Vienna-Semmering, are vital internal links across the eastern Alps to the valleys and basins of Steiermark and Kärnten. The rail and motorway routes over the 1,371 m [4,500 ft] Brenner Pass are more intensively used, but these benefit neighbours rather than Austria.

Austria's lowlands include a section of the northern Alpine foreland, which narrows eastwards towards Vienna and contains the Danube basin. This is Austria's most important east-west route with rail, motorway and river navigation leading through Vienna to Budapest and beyond. Another important lowland is the Burgenland, a rich farming area bordering the eastern Alps and facing south-east towards Hungary.

Unlike Switzerland, Austria has important heavy industries based largely on indigenous resources. The mountains are a major source of hydroelectric power. Oil and natural gas occur predominantly in the Vienna basin and are supplemented by imports from the former Soviet republics and from German refineries. Germany, sharing many cultural links as well as language, remains by far the most important trading partner. Minerals occur in the eastern Alps, notably iron ore in Steiermark (Styria); iron and steel production is located both at Donawitz (near Leoben)

Hallstatt nestles beneath the Dachstein Mountains south-east of Salzburg. The Austrians have exploited such timeless beauty to stimulate a thriving tourist industry of some 16 million foreign visitors a year.

in the mountains, and also in the Alpine foreland which has become a major centre of metal, chemical engineering and vehicle manufacturing industries.

The capital stands at a major European crossroads where the Danube is joined by the Moravian Gate route from the northern lowlands of Europe, and by the Alpine route through the Semmering Pass. A city of political as well as cultural and artistic importance, Vienna is home to OPEC and the International Atomic Energy Agency, among others, and contains one-fifth of Austria's population.

Austria's neutrality was enshrined in the constitution in 1955, but unlike Switzerland it has not been frightened to take sides on certain issues. Though a member of EFTA since 1960, the government led the group of nations that applied for membership of the EEC with the approval of the single market by the end of 1993, hoping for admission in 1995 ■

LIECHTENSTEIN

Standing at the end of the eastern Alps between Austria and Switzerland, where the Rhine cuts its way northwards out of the Alpine chains, tiny Liechtenstein became an independent principality within the Holy Roman Empire in 1719 and since then has always managed to escape incorporation into any of Europe's larger states. Liechtenstein has been in customs and currency union with Switzerland since 1923, which also provides overseas representation; and although many Swiss regard it as their 27th canton, it retains full sovereignty in other spheres.

The capital, Vaduz, is situated on the Oberland plateau above the fields and meadows of the Rhine Valley, and rising numbers of tourists (there were as many as 72,000 overnight visitors in 1988) are arriving at its royal castle, intrigued by the notion of this miniature state.

Liechtenstein's head of state, Prince Hans Adam II, is Europe's last hereditary ruler with real powers: he can call and dismiss the 25-member parliament, appoint the prime minister and cabinet, and conduct foreign affairs. Since taking over most duties from his father in 1984 (he succeeded him five years later), the Prince has pursued a cautiously assertive independent policy with Europe, trying to wean his nation off overdependence on Switzerland and applying to join the new EU-EFTA European Economic Area.

While Liechtenstein is best known abroad for its postage stamps – an important source of income – it is as a haven for international companies, attracted by extremely low taxation and the strictest (most secretive) banking codes in the world, that the state has generated the revenue to produce the highest GDP per capita figure on record. Since World War II there has also been an impressive growth in specialized manufacturing – the product of a judicious mixture of Swiss engineers, Austrian technicians, Italian workers and international capital ■

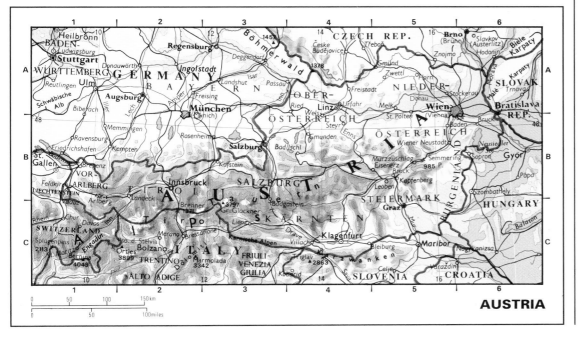

AUSTRIA

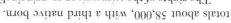

ANDORRA

Perched near the eastern end of the high central Pyrenees, Andorra consists mainly of six valleys (the Valls) that drain to the River Valira.

The population of this new 'nation' totals about 58,000, with a third native-born.

The rights of the *seigneurie* or co-principality were shared from 1278 between the Spanish Bishop of Urgel and the French Comte de Foix. The latter's lordship rights passed to the French government, represented by the prefect of the adjoining *départe-ment* of the Eastern Pyrenees. Andorrans paid a small annual sum to the bishop and prefect, and each co-prince was represented in their Council by a *viguier*, but in most other respects the co-principality governed itself – with no armed forces. In March 1993 the country voted for independence, and on 29 April a new constitution was signed to make Andorra Europe's youngest sovereign state.

Physically the country consists of deep glaciated valleys lying at altitudes of 1,000–2,900 m [3,280–9,500 ft]. In the north a lofty watershed forms the frontier with France and is crossed by a road over the Envalira Pass at 2,400 m [7,870 ft]; to the south the land falls away down the Valira Valley to the Segre Valley in Spain, again followed by the same vital high-way. In the colder months the Envalira Pass often becomes snowbound and land communications are then only with Spain.

The climate is severe in winter and pleasantly cool in summer when, because the valleys lie in a rain-shadow, slopes above 1,400 m [4,600 ft] often suffer from drought and need irrigation. Some agriculture is possible on the slopes: sheep and cattle are grazed, and crops grow in terraced fields.

Andorra has five main sources of income: stock rearing and agriculture, especially tobacco; the sale of water and hydroelectricity to Catalonia; fees from radio transmission services; tourism, based in winter on skiing; and the sale of duty-free goods and of postage stamps. Of these, tourism and duty-free sales are by far the most important – every year up to 10 million visitors come to Andorra to shop ∎

PORTUGAL

The most westerly of Europe's 'mainland' countries, Portugal occupies an oblong coastland in the south-west of the Iberian peninsula, facing the Atlantic Ocean. Here the Meseta edge has splintered and in part foundered to leave upstanding mountain ranges, particularly in the Serra da Estrela and its continuation just north of the River Tagus (Tejo), and in the Serra de Monchique.

Agriculture and fishing

The mild, moist airflow from the Atlantic encourages good tree growth. Forests reach a height of at least 1,300 m [4,260 ft] in the north and over a quarter of the country is forested. Pines form the most common species, especially on the sandy 'littoral', near the coast, where large plantations provide timber as well as resin and turpentine. Cork oaks abound in the Tagus Valley and further south; Portugal is the world's leading producer of the cork that is derived from their bark.

A wide variety of fruits is cultivated, including olives, figs and grapes. Portugal is home to some of the world's greatest vineyards and once ranked fifth in wine production. However, harvests have fallen dramatically from a peak of over a million tonnes to just 368,000 in 1988.

Most of the grapes are grown north of the Tagus, where the most celebrated speciality is port wine from the Douro Valley near the Portuguese–Spanish fron-tier. The grape juice is transported by boat down the Douro to Vila Nova, where it is fortified and stored for export. The lower parts of the Douro and Minho basins produce famous sparkling *vinhos verdes*, while the vineyards near the Tagus estuary are noted for white table wines and brandy. In the south the Algarve, with its greater sunshine and aridity, special-izes more in liqueurs and muscatels.

The Portuguese economy relies heavily on agri-culture and fishing, which together employ over a quarter of the national workforce. These industries are mostly undercapitalized and still rather primitive by European standards, although they provide valu-able exports. In the rainy north the pressure of over-population causes fragmented and tiny agricultural holdings (*minifundia*); in the drier south large hold-ings (*latifundia*) tend to create monoculture with below-average yields and seasonal unemployment.

Recently there has been some investment in irrigation.

The main general crops are food cereals and vegetables, including a wide variety of the beans that form a frequent and favourite item of the Portuguese diet. Maize and rye predominate in the north, and wheat, barley and oats in the south. Of the many farm animals the pig deserves special mention as the forager of the heavy yield of acorns from the cork and evergreen oaks.

Portugal's long coastline provides an important supplementary source of livelihood and of foreign tourist currency; the shallow lagoons yield shellfish, especially oysters; the coastal waters supply sardines, anchovy and tunny; the deep-sea fisheries, long frequented by Portuguese sailors, bring hake, mack-erel, halibut and, above all, cod.

Industry

While much of Portuguese industry is concerned with the products of farming, fishing and forestry, the manufacture of textiles and ceramics is also wide-spread. Modern engineering, associated with a complete iron and steel plant, has been established at Seixal near Lisbon. There is some small-scale mining for copper ores and wolfram (a tungstate of iron and manganese, from which tungsten is obtained), but a relative shortage of power resources is a problem. A small quantity of poor-quality coal is mined annually, and this is supplemented with foreign imports. Great efforts have been made to develop hydroelectric stations in the north, but Portugal remains the poor-est member of the EU since switching economic alle-giance from EFTA on 1 January 1986. Nevertheless, it compares more favourably than Spain on several scales: unemployment, for example, remained steady in the early 1990s at about 6%.

Portugal has two conurbations with over a million inhabitants. Lisbon, the capital, is the chief centre of the country's financial, commercial and industrial concerns and has a fine sheltered harbour in the large Tagus estuary. Porto, the main centre for the densely-populated north, has an ocean outport. These two cities still dominate the nation, but during recent decades tourism and rapid residential growth have transformed the subtropical coast of the Algarve and have led to a substantial increase in its population ∎

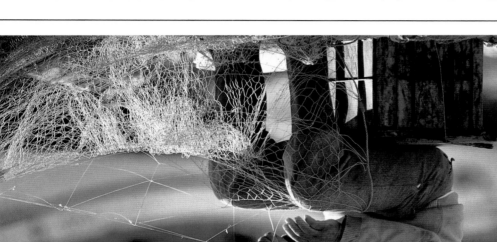

An Algarve fisherman patiently repairs his nets – as generations before him have done. Today a majority of Portugal's tourists head for his region.

SPAIN

A global position between coastal north-west Europe and Africa, and between the Mediterranean countries of the Old World and the Americas, made Spain a great crossroads. Yet the lofty Pyrenean barrier in the north weakened land contacts with the rest of Europe, while the narrow Strait of Gibraltar in the south encouraged African contacts, lending truth to the cliché that 'Africa begins at the Pyrenees'.

Landscape

The chief physical feature of Spain is the vast central plateau, the Meseta, which tilts gently towards Portugal. A harsh and often barren area, the plateau is crossed by the Central Sierras, a mountain chain running north-west to south-east. This central divide separates two mountain basins: Old Castile in the north and New Castile in the south.

On the north-eastern and southern edges of the Meseta are large triangular lowlands. That on the north drains to the Ebro, that in the south to the Guadalquivir, the largest river wholly in Spain. Beyond the Ebro trough the land rises to the Pyrenees, which form the Franco-Spanish border, and continue westwards in the Cantabrian Mountains. Similarly, the Mediterranean flank of Andalusia rises to a lofty *cordillera* (mountain chain) that culminates in the snowy Sierra Nevada (peaking at 3,478 m [11,400 ft]). The Mediterranean side of the Meseta has summits of about 2,000 m [6,560 ft] and drops sharply to narrow coastal plains.

Spain has perhaps the widest range of climate of any country in Western Europe. The most striking contrast is between the humid north and north-west and the mainly arid remainder of the country. Large areas of the country are barren or steppeland, and about a fifth is covered by *matorral*, a Mediterranean scrub like the French *maquis*.

A large part of the farmland is used for pastoral purposes, but there are rich soils in some of the major river valleys, such as the Ebro and the Guadalquivir, and areas of very productive agriculture, especially where there are *huertas* (irrigated market gardens) and *vegas* (irrigated orchards).

Vegetation

Spain is unique in Europe for the quantity and variety of her plant species, a reflection of varied local environments, a position as a land bridge between Africa and Europe, and a long colonial history during which many foreign plants were introduced. Generally, moisture-loving plants flourish north of the Central Sierras and drought-enduring species south of them.

The vegetation falls into three broad categories: forest, *matorral* and steppe. Forests (almost 10% of the land surface) are today mainly confined to the

rainier north and north-west, with beech and deciduous oak common. Towards the drier south and east,
Mediterranean pines and evergreen oaks take over,
and forests resemble open parkland. Widespread
clearance for fuel and cultivation and grazing by
sheep, goats and cattle have turned large areas into
matorral or scrub.

This low bush growth, often of aromatic evergreen plants, may be dominated over large tracts by
one species: thus *romillares* consist predominantly of
rosemary, *tomillares* of thyme, *retamales* of broom.
Where soils are thin and drought prevalent, *matorral*
gives way to steppe, mainly of alfalfa and *esparto*
grasses. This clothes considerable areas of La Mancha
and the Ebro trough.

Agriculture

Despite the problems of aridity and poor soils, agriculture occupies nearly a third of the national workforce. Irregular river regimes and deeply incised
valleys make irrigation difficult and expensive and, on
the higher and drier regions, tracts favourable for
cultivation are often isolated by expanses of low fertility where only a meagre livelihood can be wrested
from the soil. There are, too, problems connected
with the size of farms. In semi-arid Spain large estates
(*latifundios*) abound with much seasonal employment
or share-cropping, while in the rainy north-west and
north excessive fragmentation of small farms (*mini-
fundios*) has proved uneconomic.

It is against this picture of difficulties that the
great progress made since 1939 by the *Instituto
Nacional de Colonización* (INC) must be viewed. The
institute, by means of irrigation, co-operative farming schemes, concentration of landholdings, agricultural credit schemes and technical training, has
resettled over a quarter of the land needing reorgani-
zation and reclamation. But, generally, crop yields are
still comparatively modest and agricultural techniques remain backward.

Stock rearing: Large areas of farmland are used
solely or partly for pastoral purposes, which are of
great economic importance. Spain has about 20
million sheep, mainly of the native merino type which
produces a fine fleece. The Mesta, an old confederation of sheep-owners, controls the seasonal migrations on to the summer pastures on the high sierras.
Areas too rocky and steep for sheep are given over to
goats while cattle, apart from working oxen, are
mostly restricted to regions with ample grass and
water – for example the north and north-west. Pigs
are bred in the cattle districts of the north, and are
also kept to forage the acorns in the large tracts of
evergreen oaks in the south. Many working animals
are kept, and fighting bulls are bred on the marshes
(*marismas*) at the mouth of the Guadalquivir.

Arable crops: The typical arable crops are the classical Mediterranean trio of wheat, olive and vine, with
maize important in rainier districts and vegetables
and citrus fruits where there is irrigation water.
Wheat occupies a third of the cropland and is usually
followed in rotation by leguminous pulses or fallow,
grazed and so manured by sheep.

In dry areas barley, oats and rye, grown for fodder,
replace wheat, and in the wetter north maize dominates both for grain and feed. Rice is harvested in
Murcia, Valencia and the Ebro Valley and Spain
follows Italy for rice production in Europe.

Fruit-growing: Fruits occupy a high and honoured
place in Spain's agricultural economy. The olive crop,
mainly from large estates in Andalusia, makes Spain
the world's chief producer of olive oil. Vines cover
about 10% of the cultivated land and only Italy and
France exceed the Spanish output of wine. Sherry
(from Jerez) is renowned and there are other fine
wines such as the vintages of Rioja.

For citrus fruit Spain easily outstrips other
European producers, the bulk of the crop being Seville
oranges destined largely for Britain for making
marmalade. Large quantities of other fruits, especially
apricots and peaches, are grown with vegetables as a
ground crop in irrigated market gardens and orchards.
Some of the *huertas* are devoted to industrial
crops such as cotton, hemp, flax and sugar beet, while
most richer soils in Andalusia are entirely given over
to cotton. The poorer steppes yield *esparto* (a strong
grass) for paper-making.

Maps of modern Spain clearly indicate the
tremendous progress made recently in water reserva-
tion and river regulation on all the major rivers. Large
new reservoirs have been constructed on the Miño,
Duero, Tajo, Guadiana, Guadalquivir and other main
rivers as well as numerous dams on the lesser watercourses. The INC, which directs this work, aims
at bringing 70,000 hectares [173,000 acres] a year
under irrigation as well as undertaking all kinds of
land reclamation, drainage, reforestation, settlement
schemes and farm co-operative planning.

Mining and industry

Spain is lamentably short of its own supplies of solid
and liquid fuels and in an average year produces only
small quantities of poor-quality coal (mainly from
Asturias at Oviedo near Gijón), and some lignite from
a field south of Barcelona. Small deposits of petroleum found near Burgos and at the mouth of the Ebro
have not yet proved economic to develop. Some use
is made of nuclear power but the main developments
have been in hydroelectricity, especially in Catalonia
and the northern coastlands.

In contrast to fossil fuels, workable mineral
ores are widespread. High-quality iron ores, with
substantial reserves, occur in Vizcaya, Santander and
Granada. Bilbao, the chief ore-exporting port, has an
important integrated iron and steel plant, so have
Oviedo, Gijón and several other towns on the north
coast.

Many localities yield non-ferrous ores in sufficient quantity to broaden the base of Spain's metallurgical industries. The chief workings are for copper
at Rio Tinto, lead and silver at Linares and Peñarroya
(near Pueblonovo), and mercury at Almadén in addition, manganese, titanium and sulphur are produced
in small quantities and considerable amounts of
potassium salts come from Catalonia. The country is
also Europe's leading producer (and third in the
world) of mercury.

*Gaudí's Casa Batlló (1905), part of the rich architecture
boasted by Barcelona, capital of Catalonia and Spain's
second largest city.*

GIBRALTAR

Local rock carvings demonstrate that Gibraltar
has been inhabited since Neolithic times. Greeks
and Romans also settled here, but the first sure
date for colonization is AD 711 when Tariq ibn
Zaid, a Berber chieftain, occupied it. Although
taken over by Spaniards for a short while in the
14th century, it remained Moorish until 1462. An
Anglo-Dutch naval force captured it in 1704 and
it was formally recognized as a British possession at the Treaty of Utrecht in 1713. In spite of
long siege and assaults – not to mention pressure from Spain – it has remained British ever
since, becoming a strategically vital naval dockyard and base for reconnaissance aircraft.

The Rock, as it is popularly known, guards
the north-eastern end of the Strait of Gibraltar
and lies directly opposite the very similar peninsula of Ceuta, one of two remaining Spanish
enclaves in Morocco (the other is Melilla). The
Rock, 6.5 sq km [2.5 sq mls] in area, consists
largely of a narrow ridge thrusting south for 7 km
[4.4 mls] along the eastern side of Algeciras Bay,
rising to 426 m [1,400 ft] at Europa Point. It shelters a spacious anchorage and harbour from
east winds with long artificial breakwaters and
quays constructed of stone tunnelled from the
ridge. On the north there is a low, flat sandy plain
used for an airport.

Shrubs, partly wild olives, clothe the steeper
slopes and provide shelter for the only wild
monkeys in Europe. Considerable areas of
the summit are used as catchments for drinking
water, supplemented by diesel-powered sea-
water distillation.

The built-up area has an excellent road
network but the topography prohibits cultivation and the Gibraltarians rely on the port, the
ship-repairing yards, the military and air bases,
and on tourism for their livelihood. About 2,400
merchant ships and many pleasure craft call at
Gibraltar annually and the low import duties,
tourist facilities and almost rainless summers
make it a popular shopping and holiday centre.
The 30,000 Gibraltarians are of British,
Spanish, Maltese, Portuguese and Genoan
descent. Though bilingual in Spanish and
English, they remain staunchly pro-British. In
1966, following a long-standing claim, the
Spanish government called on Britain to give
'substantial sovereignty' of Gibraltar to Spain
and closed the border (1.2 km [0.74 mls]) to all
but pedestrian traffic. In a 1967 referendum
the residents voted overwhelmingly to remain
under British control, and in 1969 were granted
the status of a self-governing dependency.
Spain closed the frontier completely, preventing thousands of Spaniards from reaching
their daily work. The border was reopened fully
by Spain in 1985 following British agreement
that, for the first time, they would discuss the
sovereignty of Gibraltar; but there has been no
progress towards British compliance with the
UN resolution for an end to Gibraltar's colonial
status', by 1 October 1996.

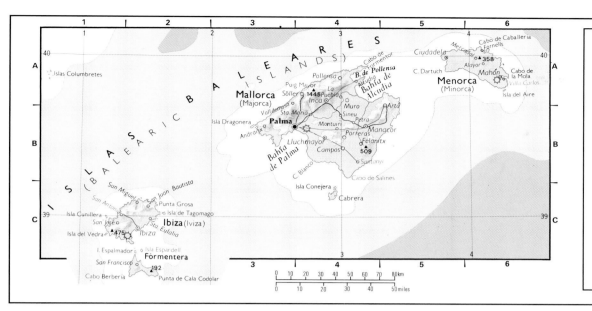

BALEARIC ISLANDS

The Islas Baleares group contains five larger islands (Majorca, Minorca, Ibiza, Formentera, Cabrera) and 11 rocky islets, together covering 5,014 sq km [1,936 sq mls] and spread over 350 km [218 mls].

The sunny Mediterranean climate supports typical vegetation. Shrub-growth still clothes the highest areas and is grazed by sheep and goats. Olives, carobs and vines are grown on the hill slopes, while the lowlands are planted with wheat and barley, usually in rotation with beans.

Power resources and raw materials for manufacture are scarce, apart from agricultural products; textile manufacture and food processing are the main factory occupations. Tourism is very important.

But the major Spanish manufacturing industries are based on agriculture rather than minerals. Textiles, including cotton, wool, silk, jute and linen lead the industrial sector. Barcelona, Catalonia's great industrial, financial and commercial centre, is surrounded by a ring of satellite textile towns, some of which specialize in spinning, as at Manresa and Ribas, and others in weaving, as at Sabadell and Granollers.

Cotton fabrics form the chief single product and supply a wide market, especially at home and in Latin America. However, Barcelona has a wide variety of light industries, including engineering, while the heavy metallurgical sectors are located mainly at Bilbao and other north-coast cities. Madrid has become an important centre for consumer goods, particularly electric appliances.

Food-processing industries are concentrated in the north-east, the chief being flour-milling, sugar refining and oil-pressing. Fish canning and processing are widespread in the coastal towns and Spain is fortunate in having a long coastline on the Atlantic, where the Galicians and Basques are skilled fishermen.

Tourism and communications

The relative absence of closely-packed industrial plants and industrial pollution, the historical attractions of the relics of a long history dating from the Greeks and Arabs, and the dry warm sunny climate of the Mediterranean south and east have fostered tourism, the greatest of all Spain's non-agricultural industries. In recent years over 30 million tourists have visited Spain annually and the Costa Brava and Costa del Sol are internationally famous.

Equally significant is the great increase in the number of those who came to live permanently or for most of the year in these picturesque coastlands with warm winters and subtropical vegetation. However, the economic recession that affected Western Europe into the 1990s substantially reduced Spain's tourist trade, leaving many resorts on the Mediterranean coast uncertain about a future almost wholly dependent on visitors in search of sun and fun on 'package' holidays.

The prime communication routes in Spain focus on Madrid, which has radial links to the peripheral cities. First-class highways radiate to the main ports and good roads connect all the major towns; but minor roads are still seldom tarred and for so large

The seaport of San Sebastian, on the northern coast of Spain near the French border. It is the capital of Guipúzcoa, one of Spain's three Basque provinces.

a country relatively few vehicles are registered.

Railways likewise converge on Madrid with minor networks round the regional capitals and main ports. The tracks are not of standard European gauge, about 75% being broad gauge and the remainder narrow. The chief land communications with France run at either end of the Pyrenees and are supplemented by several high-level transmontane rail and road routes. Air travel focuses on Madrid airport and, particularly for tourism, on 40 other civil airports.

Demography

The population of Spain is most dense on the coastlands and lowlands around the Meseta. Madrid, in the heart of the tableland, forms a grand exception. The capital stands on the small Manzanares River, a tributary of the Tagus, and has a long history dating from early Roman times. The Moors first provided it with clean drinking water and Philip II made it the seat of the national government in 1561. A fine metropolis, it has flourished during the decades since the Civil War (1936–9) and now accommodates about 10% of the total population of continental Spain. The second Spanish city, Barcelona, is a great commercial and industrial centre; in all ways the core of Catalonia, it was given a huge boost by the staging of the summer Olympics in 1992.

The other major cities include Bilbao, the Basque capital and chief urban area of the north coast, long noted for its metallurgy; Cádiz, an important naval centre; Seville, the river port and regional capital of Andalusia; Valencia and Murcia, the largest of the Mediterranean *huerta* cities; Zaragoza, the expanding centre for the Ebro lowland, noted for food processing and engineering; and Málaga, the fast-growing nucleus of the Costa del Sol. Toledo, which was the national capital before Madrid, ranks far below these conurbations in size – but, protected as a national monument, is the finest medieval city that survives almost intact from the golden age of Spain ■

ITALY

In 1800 present-day Italy was made up of several political units, including the Papal States, and a substantial part of the north-east was occupied by Austria. The struggle for unification – the *Risorgimento* – began early in the century, but little progress was made until an alliance between France and Piedmont (then part of the kingdom of Sardinia) drove Austria from Lombardy in 1859. Tuscany, Parma and Modena joined Piedmont-Lombardy in 1860, and the Papal States, Sicily, Naples (including most of the southern peninsula) and Romagna were brought into the alliance. King Victor Emmanuel II was proclaimed ruler of a united Italy in Turin the following year, Venetia was acquired from Austria in 1866, and Rome was finally annexed in 1871. Since that time Italy has been a single state, becoming a republic following the abolition of the monarchy by popular referendum in 1946.

North and south

Since unification the population has doubled, and though the rate of increase is notoriously slow today, the rapid growth of population, in a poor country attempting to develop its resources, forced millions of Italians to emigrate during the first quarter of the 20th century. Italy's short-lived African Empire enabled some Italians to settle overseas, but it did not substantially relieve the population pressure. Now there are immigrant Italians to be found on all the inhabited continents. Particularly large numbers settled in the USA, South America and Australia, and more recently large numbers of southern Italians have moved for similar reasons into northern Europe.

Almost all Italians are brought up as Roman Catholics; since a 1985 agreement between church and state, Catholic religious teaching is offered, but not compulsory, in schools. The Vatican, in theory an independent state, is in fact an enclave of Rome.

Despite more than a century of common language, religion and cultural traditions, great differences remain in the ways of life of people in different parts of Italy. These can partly be explained in terms of geography. The long, narrow, boot-shaped peninsula, with coastal lowlands on either side of the central Apennines, extends so far south that its toe, and the neighbouring island of Sicily, are in the latitudes of North Africa. Southern Sicily is as far south (36°N) as Tunis and Algiers, while the northern industrial city of Milan (45½°N) is nearer to London than it is to Reggio in Calabria, the extreme south of peninsular Italy. Given their markedly disparate social and historical backgrounds, the long period of isolation that preceded the unification and widely differing climates, it is hardly surprising that northern and southern Italy retain their independence of character and culture.

The Alps and Apennines

Italy's topographical structure is determined mainly by the events of the Alpine period of mountain building, when the main ranges of the Alps and the Apennines were uplifted together. There are traces of earlier periods in the central Alps, between Mont Blanc (4,807 m [15,771 ft]) on the French border and Monte Rosa (4,634 m [15,203 ft]) on the Swiss border, and in the Carnic Alps in the north-east. Here ancient crystalline rocks predominate, although many of the higher peaks are formed from limestone. The Dolomite Alps, famous for their climbing and skiing resorts, have given their name to a particular form of magnesian limestone.

Generally lower than the Alps, the Apennines reach their highest peaks – almost 3,000 m [9,800 ft]

– in the Gran Sasso range overlooking the central Adriatic Sea near Pescara. The most frequently occurring rocks are various types of limestone. The slopes are covered by thin soils and have been subjected to severe erosion, so that in many areas they are suitable only for poor pasture. Between the mountains, however, are long narrow basins, some of which contain lakes. Others have good soils and drainage and provide a basis for arable farming.

Italy is well known for volcanic activity and earthquakes. Three volcanoes are still active – Vesuvius, near Naples, renowned for its burial of Pompeii in AD 79, Etna in Sicily, and Stromboli on an island in the south Tyrrhenian Sea. Traces of earlier vulcanism are to be found throughout the country. Ancient lava flows cover large areas, and where they have weathered they produce fertile soils. Mineral deposits, such as the iron ores of Elba and the tin ores of the Mt Annata area, are often associated with earlier volcanic intrusions. Italy is still subject to earthquakes and volcanic eruptions. During the 20th century disasters have occurred at Messina (1908 – the worst in Europe in recent times, with more than 80,000 deaths), Avezzano (1915), Irpinia (1930), Friuli (1976) and Naples (1980).

ITALY, SAN MARINO, VATICAN CITY

Lombardy

The great triangular plain of Lombardy, lying between the northern Alps and the Apennines, is drained by the River Po, which flows west to east, rising in the Ligurian Alps near the French frontier and flowing across a delta into the Gulf of Venice.

The Lombardy plains are the most productive area of Italy, both agriculturally and industrially. There is no shortage of water, as in the areas further south, although some places are served by irrigation canals. Crops include maize, wheat, potatoes, tomatoes, rice and mulberries – these associated with the development of the silk industry. In the Alpine valleys above the Lombardy plain, vines are cultivated.

Industry and urban life in Lombardy is long established. Textiles – silk, cotton, flax and wool – metal-working and food processing all began long before the modern industrial period. Large-scale Italian industry was slower to develop than in Britain and Germany, partly because of the lack of coal, but in Lombardy this has been offset by the availability of hydroelectric power from the Alpine rivers, and by the development of a natural gas field in the area of the Po delta. Oil and gas are also imported by pipeline from Austria. Italy is more dependent on imported energy than any European country, nearly 60% of it oil, though Algeria remains a major supplier of gas through the Transmed pipeline via Tunisia.

Engineering and metal-working are now the most important industries, centred on Milan and, in Piedmont, on Turin. Lombardy remains dominant, however: the most densely populated region, it accounts for a third of Italy's GDP and some 30% of

Dawn over the undulating Tuscan landscape near Siena, on the southern flank of the Chianti area. Italy produces more grapes – and wine – than France.

export earnings, and in the 1992 election the separatist party made huge gains at the expense of established rivals.

Central Italy

Central Italy, between the Po Valley and the River Tiber, is a transitional zone between the industrially developed north and the poor, agrarian south. It contains Rome, which has survived as a capital city for over 2,000 years, Florence and Bologna.

The area has a glorious history of artistic and literary achievement, but with its limited resources, steep slopes and difficult communications it has been left behind in economic development by the more favoured lowlands of the north, and relies heavily on tourism for regional income.

Regions like Tuscany, Umbria and Lazio have considerable autonomy from Rome, with control over health and education, for example, and other devolved powers. Indeed five regions enjoy more autonomy than the rest: French-speaking Valle d'Aosta, in the north-west; Trentino-Alto Adige, the largely German-speaking area in the far north; Friuli-Venézia Giulia in the north-east; and the two island provinces of Sardinia and Sicily.

The Mezzogiorno

The south of Italy, known as the Mezzogiorno, is the least developed part of the country. It displays, in less severe form, many of the characteristics of the developing countries of the Third World. Its people depend for their livelihood on Mediterranean crops produced on small peasant farms too small to lend themselves to modern techniques, although there are some large estates.

Over a third of the people are still in agriculture, with unemployment three or more times that of the north. Though the eight regions of the Mezzogiorno cover some 40% of the land area (including Sicily and

---

SICILY

The triangular-shaped island of Sicily lies in a strategic position between the two basins of the Mediterranean, and has had a stormy history as successive powers wishing to dominate the Mediterranean have sought to conquer it. A beautiful island, it is however in a low state of economic development and its people are among the poorest in Europe.

There is some industrial development around the ports of Palermo, Catania, Messina and Syracuse, based on imported materials or on oil and natural gas found offshore in the 1960s. The only other local industrial materials are potash, sulphur and salt. However, many of the inhabitants still live by peasant farming, supplemented by fishing and work in the tourist industry.

There are few permanent streams on Sicily, as the island experiences an almost total drought in summer, and agriculture is severely restricted by the availability of water. Citrus fruits, vines and olives are the chief crops. On coastal lowlands such as those around Catania, Marsala and Palermo, wheat and early vegetables are grown. But the rapid growth in the population and strong family ties which exist among Sicilians have led to a situation in which too many people are trying to make a living from tiny areas of land.

VESUVIUS

Rising steeply from the Plain of Campania, behind the Bay of Naples, Vesuvius forms one of a family of southern Italian volcanoes. Others include the nearby island of Ischia, Stromboli and Vulcano of the Lipari Islands, and Etna in eastern Sicily. Ischia's volcanoes last erupted in the 14th century. Stromboli and Vulcano are currently active, emitting lava and gases, and Etna has a long record of eruptions from 475 BC to the present day: in April 1992 an eruption threatened to destroy a village on Etna's slopes.

Vesuvius, which probably arose from the waters of the bay some 200,000 years ago, has been intermittently active ever since; over 30 major eruptions have been recorded since Roman times. However, its slopes are forested or farmed, the fertile soils producing good crops during the quiescent periods.

The most famous eruption occurred in AD 79, when the Roman port of Pompeii (*left*, excavated since 1748) and town of Stabiae were engulfed in ash. Many artefacts of Roman times have been revealed.

Sardinia) and contain more than a third of the country's population, they contribute only about a quarter of the GDP.

The birth rate is much higher than in the north, and there is a serious problem of overpopulation which is partly eased by large-scale, often temporary, migration to the cities of the north and to Italy's more developed partners in the EEC, as well as more permanent migration overseas mostly of young people.

The problems of the Mezzogiorno, including especially those of the Naples area and Sicily, arise partly from geographical limitations and partly from historical circumstances. They are no longer a problem only for Italy, for the stability and prosperity of Italy is a matter of concern for the rest of Europe, and in particular for the countries of the EEC, of which Italy was a founder member. The continuing gulf between north and south has a disturbing effect on the economic and political health of Italy, a country whose people have contributed so much to the civilization of Europe.

Overall, however, Italy has made enormous progress since the devastation of World War II, particularly given its few natural resources and what outsiders have seen as a permanent state of near anarchy presided over by a succession of fragile coalition governments. In fact, Italy's government has always been more stable than it appeared: until the 1990s, coalitions were dominated by the Christian Democrats. A referendum in April 1993 saw 82% voting to replace the system of proportional representation for the Senate with one of majority voting and within a year the election had been won by an uneasy right-wing alliance of Silvio Berlusconi's 'Go Italy' party and the federalist Northern League ■

SAN MARINO

Surrounded by Italy, the tiny independent state of San Marino – the world's smallest republic – lies 20 km [12 mls] south-west of the Adriatic port of Rimini. Most of the territory consists of the limestone mass of Monte Titano (725 m [2,382 ft]), around which are clustered wooded mountains, pastures, fortresses and medieval villages. The republic is named after St Marinus, the stonemason saint who is said to have first established a community here in the 4th century AD.

Nearly all the inhabitants live in the medieval fortified city of San Marino, which is visited by over 2 million tourists a year. The chief occupations are tourism (which accounts for 60% of total revenues), limestone quarrying and the making of wine, textiles and ceramics. San Marino has a friendship and co-operation treaty with Italy dating back to 1862; the ancient republic uses Italian currency, but issues its own stamps, which contribute a further 10% to state revenues. The *de facto* customs union with Italy makes San Marino an easy conduit for the illegal export of lira and certain kinds of tax evasion for Italians.

The state is governed by an elected council and has its own legal system. In 1957 a bloodless takeover replaced the Communist-Socialist regime that had been in power from 1945. It has no army, and police are 'hired' from Italy's force ■

VATICAN CITY

The world's smallest nation – a walled enclave on the west bank of the River Tiber in the city of Rome – the Vatican City State exists to provide an independent base for the Holy See, governing body of the Roman Catholic Church and its 950 million adherents round the world. Sustained by investment income and voluntary contribution, it is all that remains of the extensive Papal States which, until 1870, occupied most of central Italy. In 1929 Benito Mussolini recognized the independence of the Vatican City in return for papal recognition of the kingdom of Italy.

The Vatican consists of 44 hectares [109 acres], including St Peter's Square, with a resident population of about 1,000 – including the country's only armed force of 100 Swiss Guards. The population is made up entirely of unmarried males – and the birth rate is zero.

The Commission appointed by the Pope to administer the affairs of the Vatican also has control over a radio station, the Pope's summer palace at Castel Gandolfo and several churches in Rome. The Vatican City has its own newspaper and radio station, police and railway station and issues its own stamps and coins, while the Papacy has since the 1960s played an important role in some areas of international diplomacy. In 1978 the present Pope, John Paul II, became the first non-Italian pope for 400 years.

The popes have been prominent patrons of the arts, and the treasures of the Vatican, including Michelangelo's frescoes in the Sistine Chapel, attract tourists from all over the world. Similarly, the Vatican library contains a priceless collection of manuscripts from both pre-Christian and Christian eras. The popes have lived in the Vatican since the 5th century, apart from a brief period at Avignon in the 14th century ■

A bemedalled Swiss Guard stands at ease outside the entrance to the Vatican – in a uniform designed originally by Michelangelo. He and his fellow Papal protectors form 10% of the city-state's population.

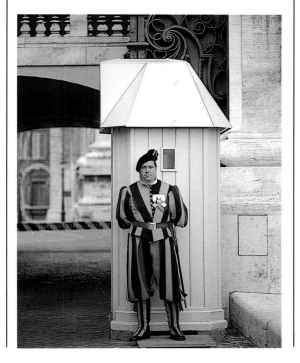

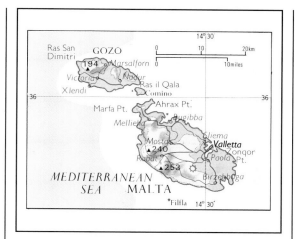

MALTA

A former British colony and now an independent, non-aligned parliamentary republic within the Commonwealth, Malta lies in the centre of the Mediterranean, roughly halfway between Gibraltar and Suez, 93 km [58 mls] south of Sicily and 290 km [180 mls] from North Africa. Its strategic importance arises from its position, and from its possession of magnificent natural harbours – notable among them Grand Harbour and Marsamxett; these lie on either side of the rocky peninsula on which stands the capital, Valletta.

Malta and the neighbouring islands of Comino and Gozo have few natural resources (apart from splendid building stone), and with no rivers and sparse rainfall there are only limited possibilities for agriculture. Yet they constitute one of the world's most densely populated states, with two-thirds of the people living in the 'conurbation' of districts around Valletta. The native islanders are of mixed Arab, Sicilian, Norman, Spanish, English and Italian origin. Maltese and English are spoken, the former universally, although it was not written until the present century.

From the Napoleonic period until after World War II, the Maltese economy depended on agriculture (which still involves nearly half the workforce), and the existence of British military bases. Before the last garrison left in 1979 Malta had already obtained independence, and was developing export-oriented industries and 'offshore' business facilities that would replace the income from the military and naval connections. Germany became its chief trading partner ahead of the UK and Italy, though Libya supplies most of its oil.

Year-round tourism, taking advantage of the mild Mediterranean winters and the hot, dry summers, brings over 360,000 visitors annually, of whom two-thirds are British. The skill of the dockyard workers is still world-famous, however, and with help from overseas, Malta is developing a new port, wharf and storage facilities. The country's other main industries include electronic appliances, textiles, foodstuffs and clothing. Malta applied in 1990 for full membership of the European Community, aiming at admission in 1993, but while larger countries jumped the queue the Maltese are now unlikely to join the European Union before 1998–9 ■

ALBANIA

By far Europe's poorest country, Albania is also one of the most isolated, separated physically and culturally even from its closest neighbours, Greece and Yugoslavia. The Albanian language has no close affinities with other European languages, and until 1990 the political system, priding itself on being the last fortress of true Marxism-Leninism, emphasized the country's remoteness.

Albania declared independence in 1912, after five centuries under the rule of the Ottoman Turks. A legacy of this period is the fact that, until the government closed all religious establishments in 1967, some 70% of Albanians were Muslims. Though still not official, the figure is likely to be the same today.

At the end of World War II, an Albanian People's Republic was formed under the Communist leadership which had led the partisans against the Germans. Pursuing a modernization programme on rigid Stalinist lines, the regime of Enver Hoxha has at various times associated politically and often economically with Yugoslavia (up to 1948), the USSR (1948–61) and China (1961–77) before following a fiercely independent policy.

Geographical obstacles have reinforced Albania's linguistic and political isolation. The mountainous interior forms a barrier to penetration from the east. The main ranges are continuations of the Dinaric Alps and rise to almost 2,000 m [6,500 ft]; they run from north-west to south-east, rising steeply from the coastal lowlands. Limestone is the most common type of rock, although in the central area there are igneous masses rich in mineral ores, including copper, iron, nickel and chrome. Albania relies heavily on exports of chrome for foreign exchange, and is the world's fifth largest producer, contributing 5.5% of the total in 1989.

Although the country has adequate energy resources – including petroleum, brown coal and hydroelectric potential as well as useful minerals – Albania remains one of the least industrialized countries in Europe, and transport is poorly developed. Horses and mules are widely used in rural areas, and there are no rail links with other countries. Most people still live by farming, with maize, wheat, barley, sugar beet and fruits predominant, though the country has always found it a difficult task feeding a population with a growth rate of 2.1% – the highest in Europe.

Hoxha's successor, Ramiz Alia, continued the dictator's austere policies after his death in 1985, but by the end of the decade even Albania was affected by the sweeping changes in Eastern Europe, and in 1990 the more progressive wing of the Communist Party (led by Alia) won the struggle for power. They instituted, somewhat reluctantly, a wide programme of reform, including the legalization of religion, the encouragement of foreign investment, the introduction of a free market for peasants' produce, and the establishment of pluralist democracy. In the elections of April 1991 the Communists comfortably retained their majority, but two months later the government was brought down by a general strike and an interim coalition 'national salvation committee' took over; this fragile 'government of stability' in turn collapsed after six months, when the Democrats withdrew their support. Elections in the spring of 1992 brought to an end the last Communist regime in Europe.

Meanwhile, the country had descended into chaos and violence, triggered by food shortages. Tens of thousands of unwelcome refugees fled the civil unrest to Greece and Italy, and in some places control rested with local bandits and brigands. In neighbouring Yugoslavia (itself in the throes of disintegration), the large Albanian population in the 'autonomous province' of Kosovo were in conflict with the Serbian authorities.

After a lifetime of Orwellian state control, a backward country was being catapulted without real government into modern industrialized Europe – and towards a Western world preoccupied with recession. At the end of 1991, a UN report put the annual income per capita figure for Albania at around $US1,000 – alongside many a struggling nation in what is still called the 'Third World'. ■

An Albanian shepherd and his flock on a tarred road outside Krujë, north of the capital Tirana.

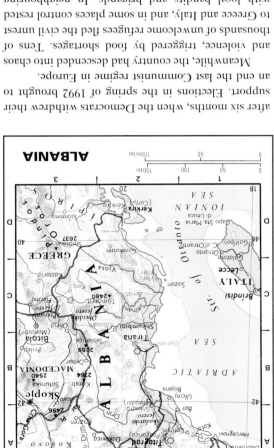

ALBANIA

GREECE

Mainland Greece consists of a mountainous peninsula which projects 500 km [312 mls] into the Mediterranean from the south-west corner of the Balkans, and an 80 km [50 ml] coastal belt along the northern shore of the Aegean Sea. Nearly a fifth of the total land area of Greece is made up of its 2,000 or so islands, mainly in the Aegean Sea to the east of the main peninsula but also in the Ionian Sea to the west; only 154 are inhabited, but they account for over 11% of the population. Some of the islands of the Dodecanese group in the eastern Aegean lie just 16 km [10 mls] off the coast of Turkey, and northern Corfu in the Ionian Islands is separated from the Albanian coast by a narrow channel.

The principal structural feature of Greece are the Pindos Mountains, which extend south-eastwards from the Albanian border to cover most of the peninsula. The island of Crete is also structurally related to the main Alpine fold mountain system to which the Pindos range belongs. Its highest peak, Mt Ida, is 2,456 m [8,057 ft] high. In these ranges limestone rocks predominate, though many of the Aegean Islands are of similar formation to the Rhodopi Massif in the north and made up of crystalline rocks.

With so much of Greece covered by rugged mountains, only about a third of the area is suitable for cultivation, yet 40% of the population depend for their living on agriculture. The average farm size is under 4 hectares [10 acres], though on a few areas of flat land, mostly around the Aegean coasts in Macedonia and Thrace, large estates are found. Wheat, olives, vines, tobacco and citrus fruits are the chief crops. Most villagers keep a few domestic animals, particularly sheep and goats. The mountain pastures are poor, mainly consisting of scrubland, and many areas have been stripped of what tree cover they once had by goats (notoriously destructive of growing trees), and by the need for wood for ships, house building and charcoal burning.

Greece has been described as a land of mountains and of the sea. Nowhere in Greece is more than

Houses designed to stay cool clustered on the island of Thíra (Santorini) in the southern Aegean.

opportunities for employment in Western Europe.

Greece is poorly endowed with industrial raw materials. There are deposits of iron ore, bauxite, nickel and manganese, but no coal and very small amounts of oil. The possibilities for hydroelectric development are severely limited because of the irregularity of the streams, many of which dry up entirely during the long summer drought. Thus Greece must import most of its sources of energy – mainly oil and coal. Industrial activity is largely concerned with the processing of agricultural produce – fruit and vegetables, canning, the production of wine and olive oil, cigarette manufacture, textiles and leather processing.

The tourist industry is vital. Overseas visitors are attracted by the warm climate, the beautiful scenery, especially on the islands, and also by the historical sites which survive from the days of classical Greece. However, a number of factors have combined to limit the importance of tourism in recent years, including the emergence of cheaper rivals like Turkey and Tunisia, the recession in Western countries and the appalling pollution in Athens.

The gap in economic strength and performance between Greece and most of its EU partners remains wide, but the prospect of a single market may help to overcome the traditional obstacles of partisan, often volatile politics, an inflated, slow-moving government bureaucracy, and a notorious 'black economy' ■

80 km [50 mls] from the sea, and most of the towns are situated on the coast. Greater Athens, which consists of the capital city and its seaport, Piraeus, has a third of the total population and has grown six-fold since 1945. Thessaloniki (Salonica), the second city, is also a seaport, serving northern Greece and southern Yugoslavia. Greece's mountainous terrain makes communication on land difficult, but the country has the world's largest merchant fleet (measured by ownership, not national registry), and shipbuilding and repairs are still important industries.

In the great days of classical Greece, during the thousand years before Christ, Greek colonies were established all round the shores of the Mediterranean and Black Seas. For a brief period in the 4th century BC, Alexander the Great built an empire which extended from the Danube, through Turkey and the Middle East to the Indus Valley of northern India. Even more important were the great contributions to culture made by the early Greeks.

The great epic poems of Greece – the *Iliad* and the *Odyssey* – speak of the exploits of ancient Greek seafarers who travelled around the Mediterranean.

Today Greeks are still great seamen and wanderers, and large communities are to be found in the USA, Australia, Canada and Latin America. Since 1960 many Greek migrants have found work in Germany, and the admission of Greece to the European Community (on 1 January 1981) has given further

CRETE

The island of Crete was the home of the seafaring Minoan civilization, which flourished in the period 3500–1100 BC and left behind a wealth of archaeological sites and artefacts. Most southerly and by far the largest of the Greek islands, Crete has a milder, more maritime climate than the mainland. The rugged, harbourless south coast, backed by steep limestone mountains, is the more inhospitable side, with winter gales adding to the hazards of navigation.

Most of the population of 502,000 live in the lowlands of the north, about a quarter of them in Iráklion (the capital) and Khania. About a quarter of the island is under crops; agriculture, tourism and small-scale mining are the main sources of income. Though Greek-speaking, Cretans differ in outlook and culture from the mainlanders; they suffered long occupation by Venetians and then by Turks, remaining under Turkish rule until 1898, 70 years after mainland Greece had been liberated.

GREECE

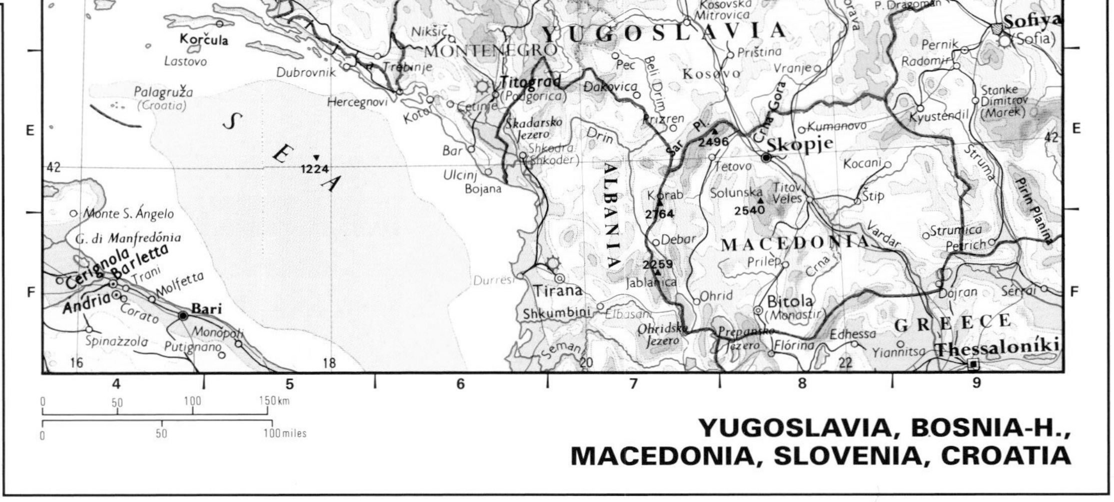

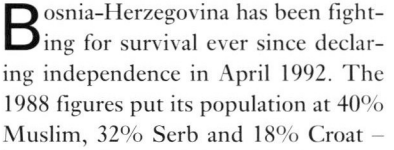

YUGOSLAVIA, BOSNIA-H., MACEDONIA, SLOVENIA, CROATIA

YUGOSLAVIA

Yugoslavia by 1992 was an almost figmentary state, the discredited and politically impotent rump of the southern Slav union created under Allied pressure after World War I. Known from 1918 as the State of the Serbs, Croats and Slovenes, and from 1929 as Yugoslavia ('land of the south Slavs'), the unity of the state was always under threat from nationalist and ethnic tensions. The most serious friction was between the Serbs, with 35% of the population the largest single group, and the neighbouring Croats with 20%; but Muslims, Slovenes, Macedonians, Montenegrins, Albanians and Hungarians also chafed against each other.

In the interwar period the country was virtually a 'Greater Serbia', and after Hitler invaded in 1941 Yugoslavs fought both the Germans and each other. The Communist-led Partisans of 'Tito' (Josip Broz, a Croat) emerged victorious in 1945, re-forming Yugoslavia as a republic on the Soviet model. The postwar Tito dictatorship kept antagonisms out of sight, but in 1990, a decade after his death, the first free elections since the war saw nationalist victories in four out of the six republics that made up the Yugoslav federation.

The formal secession of Slovenia and Croatia in June 1991 began an irreversible process of disintegration. Slovenia, the most ethnically homogeneous of Yugoslavia's component republics, made the transition almost bloodlessly; but the Serbian-dominated federal army launched a brutal campaign against the Croats, whose territory included a large and vociferous Serbian minority. The most destructive conflict in Europe since 1945 continued until January 1992, when the ceasefire finally held. The fighting simply moved to Bosnia-Herzegovina. Expelled from the UN in 1992, 'Yugoslavia' thereafter comprised only Montenegro and Serbia, the latter accounting for almost 90% of the republic's area and more than 90% of its population. Bolstered by successes in Croatia and Bosnia, Serbia controlled most remaining federal resources but had mounting problems of its own: for example, international sanctions struck at an already war-ravaged economy. Further and final dissolution seems inevitable ■

BOSNIA-HERZEGOVINA

Bosnia-Herzegovina has been fighting for survival ever since declaring independence in April 1992. The 1988 figures put its population at 40% Muslim, 32% Serb and 18% Croat – a mixture that has proved unworkable. The Muslim-dominated government, allied uneasily at first with the Croat minority, was at once under attack from local Serbs, heavily supported by their co-nationals beyond Bosnia's pre-war borders. In their 'ethnic cleansing' campaign, heavily-equipped Serbian militias drove Muslims from towns they had long inhabited. By early 1993, the Muslims controlled less than a third of the former federal republic, and even the capital, Sarajevo, was disputed territory under constant shellfire. The Muslim-Croat alliance disintegrated and refugees approached the million mark.

Tougher economic sanctions on Serbia were applied and a small UN force attempted to deliver relief supplies to civilian populations and maintain 'safe' Muslim areas. The UN, through the offices of NATO and with Russian support, intervened to create a precarious stalemate early in 1994, and in March 1994 the Muslims and Croats agreed a draft constitution. The country's future remains uncertain, however, and partition into three states (Serb, Croat and Muslim) may be the eventual, and only possible, outcome for a wartorn nation ■

MACEDONIA

Landlocked between Albania, Greece and Bulgaria, its northern frontier dangerously contiguous with Serbia's troubled Kosovo region, Macedonia has so far avoided the civil war that has marked the passing of Yugoslavia. International recognition has proved difficult to obtain, notably from the EU, without whose aid the republic (67% Macedonian and 20% Albanian, many of them Muslim) may have difficulty surviving. Despite pressure from Brussels, the Greek government, worried by the consequences for its own Macedonian region, has persistently vetoed any acknowledgement of an independent Macedonia on its borders. Macedonia was recognized by the UN in June 1993, under the temporary name of 'Former Yugoslav Republic of Macedonia', and 1,000 troops stayed in the new country. In February 1994 recognition came from the US, but the Greeks imposed a crippling trade embargo.

Historically, present-day Macedonia was once part of the Ottoman Empire, freeing itself from Turkish control only in the early part of the 20th century. Geologically, most of the country forms part of the Balkan Mountains, a well-wooded region of ancient, rounded crystalline rocks. Like the rest of the Balkan area, it is no more stable than its local politics: the capital, Skopje, was devastated by an earthquake as recently as 1963 ■

SLOVENIA

Part of the Austro-Hungarian Empire until 1918, Slovenia's Roman Catholic population found ready support from neighbours Italy and Austria (with Slovene populations of about 100,000 and 80,000 respectively) as well as Germany during its fight for recognition in 1991. The most ethnically homogeneous of Yugoslavia's component republics, it stayed relatively free of the violence that plagued Croatia. A mountainous state with access to the Adriatic through the port of Koper, near the Italian border – giving it a flourishing transit trade from landlocked central Europe – it has both strong agricultural sectors (wheat, maize, root crops, livestock) and industry (timber, textiles, steel, vehicles), with mineral resources that include coal, lignite, lead, zinc and mercury. Other important sources of income are wine-making and Alpine tourism. Along with Croatia, Slovenia went furthest in developing a market economy from 1988 before declaring independence from Belgrade in June 1991 ∎

CROATIA

Formerly Yugoslavia's second largest and second most populous republic, Croatia bore the brunt of the Serbian-dominated Yugoslav Army's campaign to resist the break-up of the federation in the autumn war of 1991. Most of the deaths and much of the destruction occurred in this 'U'-shaped new state, and most of the 650,000 or more refugees were Croats.

A massive reconstruction programme would be needed to return many towns to anything like normality; the vital tourist industry (Croatia accounted for 80% of the Yugoslav total in 1990) was also devastated, with the fine medieval city of Dubrovnik on the Dalmatian coast the prime casualty.

Rivalry between Croats and Serbs goes back centuries – Croatia was politically linked with Hungary, and therefore with Western Europe and the Catholic Church, from 1102 to 1918 – but was fuelled by the Croat position in World War II, when a puppet Fascist regime was set up (including much of Bosnia-Herzegovina) by Germany with the support of the Croatian Catholics. The split of 1991, however, left many questions unanswered, not least the final dimensions and population of the emergent Croat state: sizeable minority enclaves both complicated peacekeeping and ensured that the existing federal frontiers could not hope to endure. Mainly rural until 1945, Croatia now has industries based on timber, oil and gas (from Slavonia), bauxite, limestone deposits, hydroelectricity and iron ore ∎

The picturesque town of Korcula, on the Croatian island of the same name, is one of many innocent economic casualties of the Yugoslav wars. The growth of tourism along the Dalmatian coast, so strong in the 1970s and 1980s, was suddenly reversed with the onset of the tragic conflict in 1991.

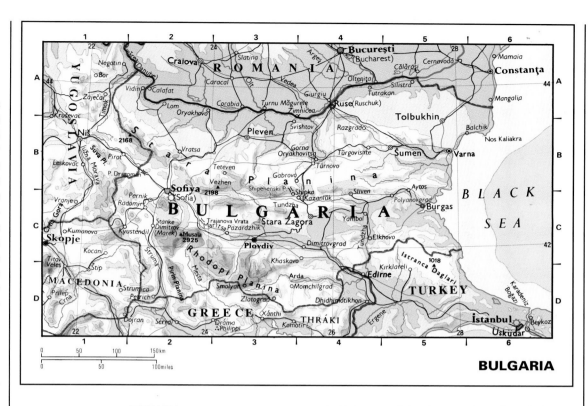

BULGARIA

BULGARIA

The most subservient of the former Eastern bloc satellites, Bulgaria's links with Russia date back to 1878, when the Tsar's forces liberated the country from five centuries of Ottoman (Turkish) rule. In the period after World War II, Bulgaria became all too dependent on its overseer, the USSR.

Predictably, Bulgaria was the last and least publicized of the Eastern European countries to fall. In 1990 the Communist Party held on to power, but with better organization the Union of Democratic Forces defeated the old guard the following year and began the unenviable task of making the transition from central planning to a free-market economy.

The new government inherited a host of problems – inflation, food shortages, rising unemployment, strikes, large foreign debt, limited Western interest, a declining traditional manufacturing industry, reduced demand at home and abroad and increased prices for vital raw materials.

With fertile soils but few natural resources, Bulgaria's economy has a distinct agricultural bias, with half the population still earning their living from the land. The most productive agriculture occurs in two lowland areas – the Danubian lowlands of the north, where wheat, barley and maize are the chief crops, and the warmer central valley of the River Maritsa, where grains, cotton, rice, tobacco, fruits and vines are grown.

Separating the two lowland areas are the Balkan Mountains (Stara Planina), which rise to heights of over 2,000 m [6,500 ft]. In the south-facing valleys overlooking the Maritsa plains, plums, vines and tobacco are grown. A particular feature of this area is the rose fields of Kazanluk, from which attar of roses is exported worldwide to the cosmetics industry.

South and west of the Maritsa Valley are the Rhodopi Mountains, containing lead, zinc and copper. There are also mineral veins of iron and non-ferrous metals in the Stara Planina, north of Sofia ∎

HUNGARY

As a large part of the Austro-Hungarian Empire, Hungary enjoyed an almost autonomous position within the Dual Monarchy from 1867, but defeat in World War I saw nearly 70% of its territory apportioned by the Treaty of Versailles to Czechoslovakia, Yugoslavia and Romania. Some 2.6 million Hungarians live in these countries today. The government hoped to regain lost land by siding with Hitler's Germany in World War II, but the result was the occupation of the Red Army and, in 1949, the establishment of a Communist state. The heroic Uprising of 1956 was put down by Soviet troops and its leader, Imre Nagy, was executed.

President János Kádár came to power in the wake of the suppression, but his was a relatively progressive leadership, introducing an element of political freedom and a measure of economic liberalism. Before the great upheavals of 1989 Hungary had gone further than any Eastern European Soviet satellite in decentralization and deregulation.

However, failure to tackle the underlying economic problems led in 1988 to some of his own Socialist Workers Party members exerting pressure for change. In 1989 the central committee agreed to a pluralist system and the parliament, previously little more than a rubber-stamp assembly, formally ended the party's 'leading role in society'. In 1990, in the first free elections since the war, Hungarians voted into office a centre-right coalition headed by the Democratic Forum.

Landscape and agriculture
Hungary has two large lowland areas – the aptly-named Great Plain (Nagyalföld) which occupies the south-eastern half of the country and is dissected by the country's two main rivers, the Danube and the Tisa, and the Little Plain (Kisalföld) in the north-west. Between them a line of hills runs south-west to north-east from Lake Balaton to the Slovak border. Balaton (72 km [45 mls] long), the largest lake in central Europe, is a favourite holiday resort.

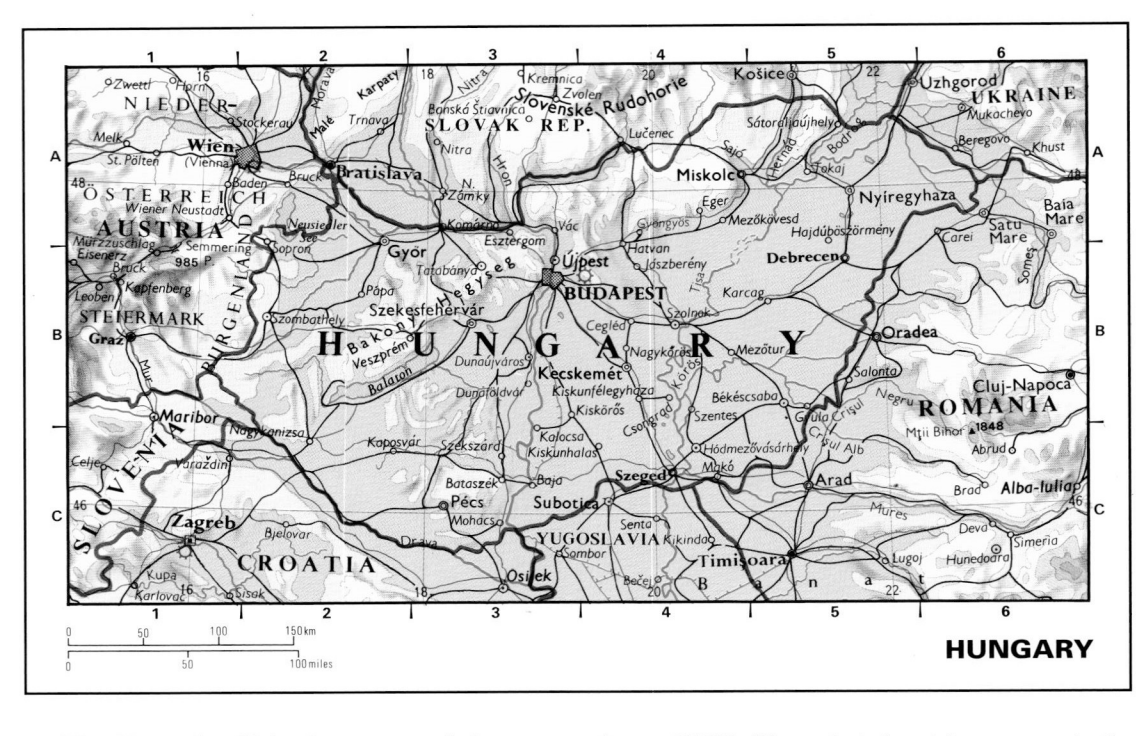

HUNGARY

The Hungarian Plains have some of the most fertile agricultural land in Europe, especially in the areas covered by a mantle of loess (a windblown deposit dating from the Ice Age), but there are also infertile areas of marsh, sand and dry steppeland, where crop growing gives way to grazing. In the region to the north-west of the Great Plain, known as Hortobagy and the only remaining steppe in Europe outside the former USSR, it is still possible to see Europe's last remaining cowboys – the *gulyas* – riding on horseback to round up their cattle. But the expanse of dry steppeland where this way of life is practised is dwindling as irrigation schemes are introduced, and ranching gives way to wheat, tobacco and rice.

The continental climate, with its spring rains, long, hot summers and cold winters, favours crops such as wheat, maize, sunflowers and vines. Rainfall is around 63 cm [25 in] in the west, but falls to under 50 cm [20 in] in the east.

Industry and economy
Hungary has reserves of gas, but is poorly endowed with natural resources, bauxite being one of the few plentiful minerals. Industries have been built up on the basis of imported raw materials, mainly from the former USSR. The main industrial centres are in the north, around Miskolc and Budapest (home to a fifth of the population) where iron and steel, engineering and chemicals predominate. Aluminium is manufactured north of Lake Balaton.

Unlike its more static neighbours, the new government of Prime Minister Jozsef Antall was able to press on with a rapid transition to a full market economy. The region's first stock market was set up, Budapest was chosen as the European Community's first regional office and Hungary – a founder member of the now defunct Warsaw Pact – applied to join NATO.

Hungary's move away from the classic Eastern European reliance on heavy industry and agriculture would be easier than, say, that of Poland, and many joint ventures with Western capital were inaugurated in the first months of the new democracy, bringing in not only high-tech expertise but also much-needed managerial skills. Hungary has the edge in tourism, too – by the late 1980s the number of annual visitors was already outstripping its own population.

But in May 1994, with unemployment at over 12% and a contraction of economic output by 20% since 1990, elections saw the Socialists, the former Communists, gain the largest number of votes ∎

THE DANUBE
With around 300 tributaries and a length of 2,850 km [1,750 mls], the Danube is Europe's second longest river. Rising from a source in the Black Forest in southwest Germany, it flows east and south through Austria, Slovakia, Hungary and Yugoslavia, and forms a large part of the Romanian-Bulgarian frontier before entering the Black Sea through a wide, swampy delta on the border between Romania and the Ukraine. Navigable as far upstream as Ulm in Bavaria, the Danube links the three capitals of Vienna, Budapest (*left*, the Chain Bridge) and Belgrade. Long one of Europe's main commercial waterways, with the ending of the Cold War and the consequent divisions between East and West, it is likely to be of growing importance – and conflict, as between Hungary and Slovakia.

ROMANIA

On three sides Romania has clearly defined natural boundaries – the Danube in the south, the 200 km [125 ml] Black Sea coast in the east, and the River Prut in the north-east – but in the west the frontier with Hungary crosses the Hungarian Plain, cutting across several tributaries of the River Tisa. This area has a mixed population of Romanians and Hungarians – the western province of Transylvania once belonged to Hungary – and it was here, following the suppression of demonstrations in Timisoara by the secret police (the Securitate), that the army-backed revolt of 1989 began, culminating only days later in the execution of the dictator Nicolae Ceausescu and his wife on Christmas Day, on charges of genocide and corruption.

Landscape

Romania is dominated by a great arc of high fold mountains, the Carpathians, which curve round the plateaus of Transylvania in the heart of the country. South and east of the Carpathians are the plains of the lower Danube. The southern arm of the fold mountains, rising to 2,538 m [8,327 ft], is known as the Transylvanian Alps, the legendary home of Count Dracula. Where these meet the Danube, on the border with Yugoslavia, the river has cut a deep gorge – the Iron Gate (Portile de Fier) – whose rapids over 160 km [100 mls] long have been tamed by the construction of a huge barrage. In the east the Danube delta area has more than 3,000 glaciated lakes and some of Europe's most celebrated expanses of wetland.

There is a great contrast between the fairy-tale landscape of wooded hills in Transylvania and the Carpathians, and the wheat and maize fields of the Danubian lowlands. Despite Ceausescu's manic programmes Romania is still a strong agricultural country, with an export surplus of cereals, timber, fruits and wine, though the agrarian workforce shrank from 75% in 1950 to less than 30% in 1984. In 1988 the country ranked fourth in maize production and seventh in wine.

Economy and politics

Under Ceausescu there was a great drive to develop industries, based on the abundant oil and gas resources of areas on the flanks of the Transylvanian Alps; in 1988 Romania was the world's sixth biggest producer of natural gas. The copper, lead, zinc and aluminium industries use domestic supplies, mainly found in the Bihor Massif in Transylvania, but the iron and steel industry, especially the new plant at Galati at the head of the Danubian delta, relies on imported ores.

Bucharest, the capital, lies between the Danube and the Carpathians. An important industrial centre, its manufactures include vehicles, textiles and foodstuffs.

Ceausescu's 24-year rule had been one of the Communist world's most odious. Corrupt and self-seeking, he had nevertheless won plaudits from the West for his independent stance against Soviet control – including a knighthood from Queen Elizabeth II. Coming to power in 1965, he accelerated the party policy of distancing the country from Moscow's foreign aims while pursuing a strict Stalinist approach on the domestic front.

The remorseless industrialization and urbanization programmes of the 1970s caused a severe debt problem, and in the 1980s he switched economic tack, cutting imports and diverting output to exports. But while Romania achieved the enviable status of a net creditor, its people – brainwashed by incessant propaganda – were reduced from sufficiency to subsidence to shortage, with food and energy both savagely rationed. Meanwhile, with many of his relatives in positions of power, Ceausescu built ghetto-like 'agro-industrial' housing complexes, desecrating some of the country's finest architecture and demolishing thousands of villages in the process.

After his death, a provisional government of the National Salvation Front (founded only on 22 December) took control; much of the old administrative apparatus was dismantled, the Communist Party was dissolved and religion was re-legalized. In May 1990, under Ion Iliescu, the NSF won Romania's first free elections since the war by a huge majority – a result judged flawed but not fraudulent by international observers.

The NSF, however, contained many old-guard Communists, and its credibility sank further when Iliescu used miners to curb anti-government demonstrations. Strikes and protests continued, not only against the new authorities but also against the effects of a gradual but nevertheless marked switch to a market economy: food shortages, rampant inflation and rising unemployment. In addition, foreign investment was sluggish, deterred by the political instability. During 1991 the struggle between the two factions of the NSF – conservative President Iliescu (a former Ceausescu Politburo member) and reformist Prime Minister Petre Roman – personified the split that existed right across a country in desperate need of unity.

Another problem appeared with the new independent status of Moldavia. The republic has a vociferous Romanian minority in the large area of Bessarabia, handed over to the USSR as part of the

Grim and imposing, Bran Castle clings to its crag deep in the heart of Transylvania, 120 km [74 mls] north of Bucharest. Built in 1377, it is associated with the 15th-century ruler, Vlad Tepes, 'the impaler' on whom Bram Stoker based the fictional vampire Count Dracula.

Hitler-Stalin pact of 1940 and not returned by the Red Army in 1945. The new mood in the former Soviet Union rekindled the concept of Romania Mare ('Greater Romania').

In November 1991 the parliament in Bucharest overwhelmingly voted for a new constitution enshrining pluralist democracy, human rights and a market economy, with elections set for the spring of 1992. It was not special by the standards of contemporary Eastern European events – many of the old guard remained in power – but it was a far cry from the oppression of Ceausescu's hideous despotism ∎

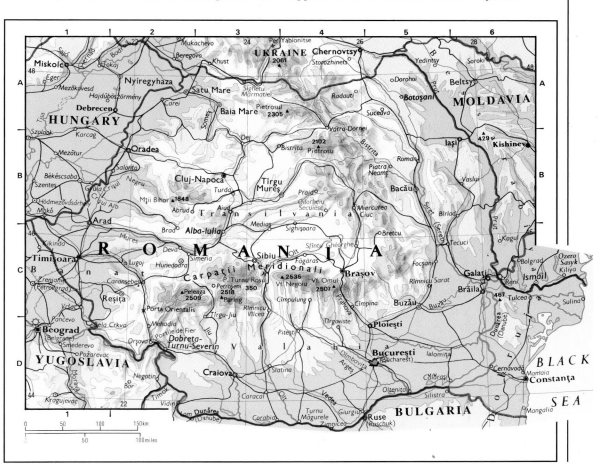

CZECH REPUBLIC

With 61% of the total land area of the former Czechoslovakia, the Czech Republic is the larger of its two successor states. Created after World War I and reorganized as a federation in 1969, Czechoslovakia was formally broken up on 1 January 1993, when the eastern Slovak Republic became independent in its own right. The Czech Republic is itself composed of two units, both Czech-speaking, mainly Protestant in religion and with a common history as provinces of the Austrian part of the Austro-Hungarian Empire, ruled from Vienna.

In the west, Bohemia is a diamond-shaped area, surrounded by ranges of mountains that enclose a basin drained by the River Elbe and its tributaries. In the centre lies Prague, the historic capital city. The mountains are rich in minerals, including iron ore, lead, zinc and uranium, while in western Bohemia there are also reserves of hard coal and lignite.

Moravia, in the middle of the country, is divided from Bohemia by plateau land known as the Moravian Heights. Central Moravia is a lowland, with the industrial city of Brno, home of the Bren gun, at its heart.

The Czech Republic is the most highly industrialized of the former Soviet satellites, but agriculture remains strong and well developed, with high yields of most crops suited to the continental climate. Food-processing industries, including brewing, are important in the western provinces.

Politics and economy

Czechoslovakia's 'velvet revolution' of 1989 was Eastern Europe's smoothest transition, toppling the old Communist regime by 'people power' and soon replacing it with a multiparty system that elected a government headed by President Václav Havel, the country's best-known playwright and noted dissident (with Charter 77, part of the coalition Civic Forum). It was all very different from 1968, when in the 'Prague Spring' Soviet forces suppressed an uprising supporting Alexander Dubcek's brave attempts at rekindling democracy and breaking the stranglehold of the party bosses.

As elsewhere in Central and Eastern Europe, the road to a free-market economy was not easy. The

St Nicholas Church dominates the Mala Strana in Prague's 'Lesser Town', a maze of winding streets on the west bank of the Vltava linked to the 'Old Town' by the famous Charles Bridge (1357). Like Rome, the Czech capital covers seven hills.

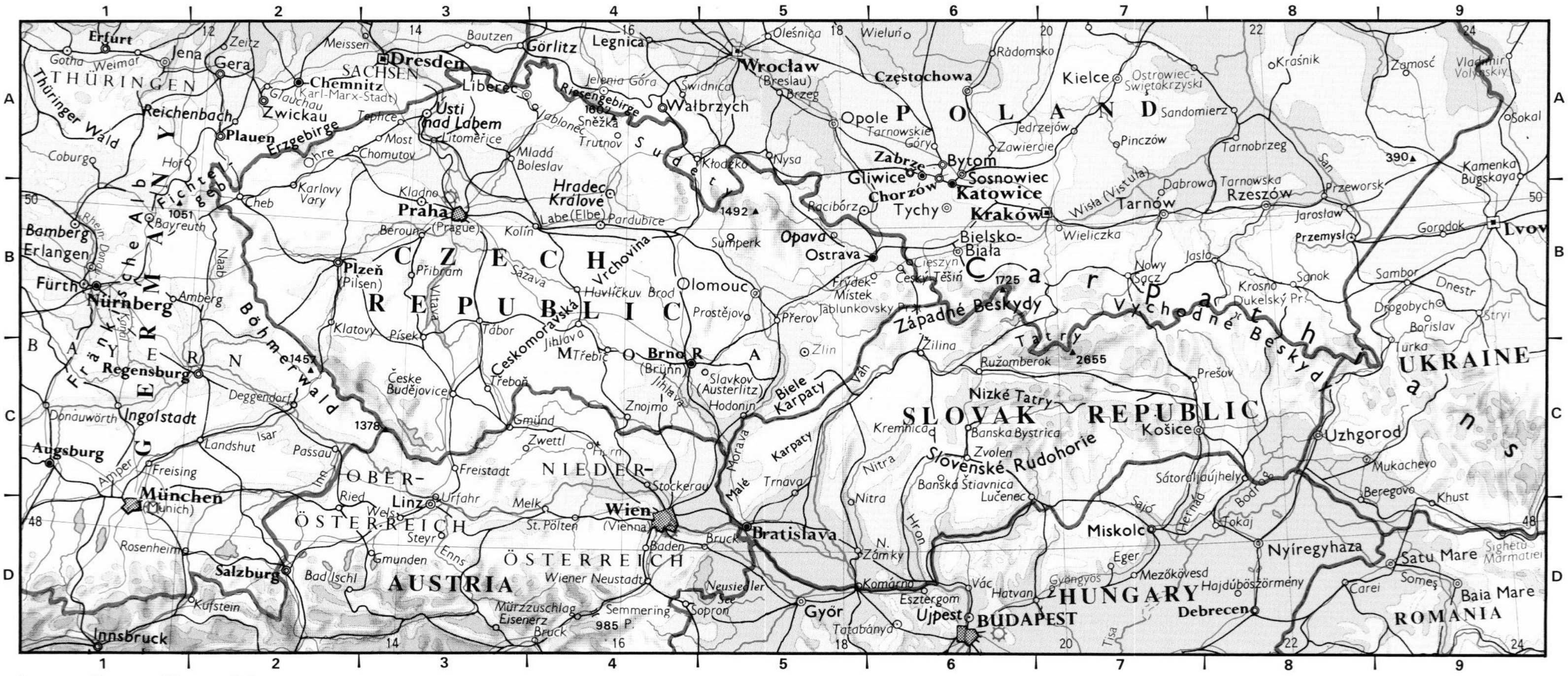

CZECH REPUBLIC, SLOVAK REPUBLIC

burdens that plagued the former Soviet satellites were all too obvious – large budget deficit, over-reliance on other Communist countries for trade, increasingly obsolete industrial capacity – and so were the immediate results: inflation, falling production, strikes and unemployment.

Politically, too, there were difficulties. Pragmatic concerns soon dulled the euphoria of democratization and indeed Civic Forum split over the pace of economic reform. Principles of the new constitution were still the subject of controversy in 1992, when resurgent Slovak nationalism forced the parliamentary vote that ended the old Czechoslovak federation – unnecessarily, according to most Czechs and a substantial minority of Slovaks.

But the Czech economy, with a serviceable foreign debt and a skilled and adaptable workforce, was in far better shape than that of, say, Poland, while the break-up was, for the most part, amicable. Border adjustments were negligible and negotiated calmly; after the separation, Czechs and Slovaks maintained a customs union and other economic ties, and there was no sign of the bitter hatreds that were causing so much bloodshed in Yugoslavia ∎

SLOVAK REPUBLIC

The other heir to Czechoslovakia, the Slovak Republic consists of a mountainous region in the north, part of the Carpathian system that divides Slovakia from Poland, and a southern lowland area drained by the River Danube. Bratislava, the new nation's chief city, lies in the south, and has become the fourth European capital (Vienna, Budapest and Belgrade are the others) to lie on the river, which forms Slovakia's border with Hungary.

Culturally as well as linguistically distinct from their Czech neighbours, the relatively agrarian Slovaks are mainly Roman Catholics. While the Czechs prospered and flourished under Austrian rule, Slovakia was subject to Hungarian authority for centuries. Its people suffered from enforced 'Magyarization' and their development was stifled. Divisions were exacerbated from 1939 when, after the proclamation of a pro-German Fascist regime in Slovakia, Hitler's troops invaded the Czech lands of Bohemia and Moravia. But, even in Communist Czechoslovakia, the Slovaks were in no sense a persecuted minority; their post-1989 independence movement was driven more by the desire to revive their distinct culture than by serious ethnic grievances.

As a result, newly-independent Slovakia still maintains close links with its former partner: around 400,000 Slovak workers cross the frontier to work each week, while about 200,000 are still resident in the Czech Republic. Conversely, 60,000 Czechs live in Slovakia; but at between 500,000 and 600,000, the nation's most substantial minority is Hungarian. Predictably, Slovak independence has raised national aspirations among its Magyar-speaking community, mostly in its southern regions; such ethnic tensions as exist, though, are likely to be settled pragmatically and not by violence. Conflict may arise, however, with Hungary, whose government claims Slovakia has diverted the Danube to feed its hydroelectric scheme at Gabcikovo ∎

POLAND

The geographical location of Poland has had a strong influence on the country's stormy history. On many occasions powerful neighbours – notably Russia and Germany – have found it all too easy to invade and occupy the land. The most recent frontier changes came at the end of World War II – in which the country lost 6 million people, or a massive 17% of the total population – when Poland gave up territory to the USSR, and in compensation gained parts of Germany as far as the River Oder.

As a result of these changes Poland lost poor agricultural land in the east and gained an important industrial region in the west, including in the south-west Silesia and the former German city of Breslau (now called Wroclaw), in the north-west the Baltic port of Stettin (now Szczecin), and in the north the other port of Danzig (now Gdansk). Acquisition of a length of Baltic coastline (there was only a narrow access corridor where the Poles developed the port of Gdynia as a competitor with Danzig) gave Poland a chance to develop maritime interests. Now a major fishing nation, Poland's fleets operate worldwide.

Before World War II Poland was primarily an agricultural country, with 65% of the population dependent on farming, but the postwar industrialization drive under Communism reduced this propor-

A dock worker makes his way home from the Gdansk shipyards – cradle of the pioneering trade union movement Solidarity, whose actions in 1980 signalled the massive changes to be wrought right across Eastern Europe by the end of the decade.

tion to about 30%, most of them still on privately owned farms. Poland is still, however, a major supplier of agricultural produce: nearly two-thirds of the land surface is farmed, about half of this area supporting crops of rye and potatoes. Oats, sugar

POLAND

beet, fodder crops, pigs and dairy produce are also important.

Poland's industrial development since World War II has been striking. Coal, lignite, sulphur, lead and zinc are the main mineral products, though Poland is also Europe's top producer of copper and silver. Underground salt deposits form the basis of important chemical industries. Most of Poland's industrial energy is derived from coal, but oil and natural gas are being developed, and hydroelectric power is being produced in increasing amounts from the Carpathians. Heavy industries include manufacture of steel and cement, and many secondary products. Many of Poland's newer industries are still almost wholly reliant on Russian gas and oil from various parts of the former Soviet Union – a difficult position in a changing world.

Politics and economy

Poland's reliance on heavy industry, much of it state-controlled and unprofitable, proved to be a major obstacle in the country's 'fast-track' route from Communism to capitalism that followed the pioneering triumph of democratic forces in 1989. The old industries needed drastic measures – re-equipping, restructuring and diversifying – but this could be achieved only with huge assistance from the West; Poland received nearly 70% of all Western credits to Eastern Europe between 1989 and 1991, adding to an already unserviceable foreign debt. Meanwhile, rising inflation (1,000% at one stage) and unemployment, coupled with a drastic drop in living standards (the economy shrank by 10% in 1991), led to a resurgence of militant unionism – the very movement that had set Poland on the path to democratization back in 1980.

Under the banner of the independent trade union Solidarity, based originally in the Gdansk shipyards and led by Lech Walesa, Poland was the first of the Soviet satellites to challenge and bring down its Communist regime. The example set by the Poles (even though they were to be the last Eastern European country to implement full democratic processes, in October 1991), proved an inspiration not only to the other European Socialist states but also to the peoples of the Baltic republics, with neighbouring Lithuania the most persistent irritant to Moscow.

Elected national president a year earlier, Lech Walesa found it a tough task to form a stable government after the 1991 elections – the country's first truly democratic ballot since before World War II – with the new constitution producing a parliament representing no less than 29 different parties. Solidarity itself had not lived up to its name, dividing in 1990 over personality clashes and the speed of political and economic reform, seemingly unable to reconcile an innate conflict between its two roles – on the one hand forming 35% of a government implementing severe economic measures and, on the other, a trade union trying to protect the livelihood and interests of its millions of members.

Poland's transition to a free market has proved more painful than that of more flexible societies and economies such as Czechoslovakia and Hungary. Despite being the pioneer of the process it seemed weighed down by its very size, a prisoner of its postwar past. One long-term legacy of the past is a colossal and wide-ranging environmental problem. The Communist government's obsession with heavy industry has given Poland perhaps the worst pollution in Europe – hardly a priority for a nation struggling to survive ∎

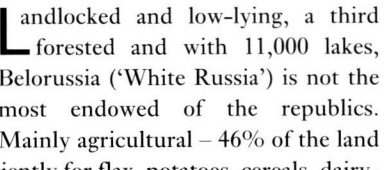

BELORUSSIA

Landlocked and low-lying, a third forested and with 11,000 lakes, Belorussia ('White Russia') is not the most endowed of the republics. Mainly agricultural – 46% of the land being used efficiently for flax, potatoes, cereals, dairying, pigs and peat-digging – it also has the largest petrochemical complex in Europe and the giant Belaz heavy-truck plants; these, however, like its many light industries, are heavily reliant on Russia for electricity and raw materials, including steel. More relentlessly integrated into the Soviet economy than any republic, Belorussia was also the most dependent on trade, at nearly 70%. Large areas of its land were contaminated by fallout from Chernobyl in 1986.

Most observers were surprised when this most conservative and Communist-dominated of parliaments declared independence on 25 August 1991, forcing the Party president to stand down. The quiet state of the European Soviet Union, it played a big supporting role in its deconstruction and the creation of the CIS; the latter's first meeting was in Minsk – subsequently chosen as its capital. Like the Ukraine, Belorussia has been a separate UN member since 1945, the end of World War II, during which it bore much of the force of the German invasion; one in four of its population died ∎

MOLDAVIA

The most densely populated of the former Soviet republics, Moldavia is also ethnically complex. Created by Stalin in his 1940 pact with Hitler by combining the Moldavian part of Ukraine with the larger Bessarabia – the section of Romania between the Prut and Dnestr rivers – its majority 'Moldavian' population is ethnically Romanian, and people on both sides of the border favour reunification. This is opposed by Russians, Ukrainians, and, in the south, the Gagauz, the Christian

Selling honey in Kishinev. Like all former Soviet citizens, Moldavians had to adjust rapidly to free-market reforms after independence in 1991.

Orthodox Turks. The last two groups both pronounced their sovereignty before the republic declared independence from Moscow on 27 August 1991. However, elections held in March 1994 suggested that the threat of civil conflict had at least receded.

Though barred from the Black Sea by an arm of the Ukraine, Moldavia is well off. Fertile lands and a tolerant climate provide vines, tobacco and honey as well as more conventional produce, while light industry – based mainly on food processing and household appliances – is expanding ∎

UKRAINE

The Ukraine became the largest complete nation in Europe with its declaration of independence on 24 August 1991 and the subsequent disintegration of the Soviet Union. It is also a well-populated state: fourth in Europe, discounting Russia, and 22nd in the world. More significantly, it was the world's third nuclear power.

The western Ukraine comprises the fertile uplands of Volhynia, with the Carpathians cutting across the far western corner of the country. The north is mostly lowlands, with the Dnepr River at its heart, which include marshes and the state capital of Kiev in addition to arable land. This area, however, suffered most from the Chernobyl nuclear disaster of April 1986, with huge tracts of land contaminated by radioactive fallout.

In the centre of the republic, south of Kiev and west of Kirovograd (Yelizavetgrad), are the rich lands of chernozem, fertile black earth. In the south are dry lowlands bordering the Black Sea and the Sea of Azov, with Odessa the main port. There can be frequent droughts in these areas. Further south still is the Crimean peninsula, a favourite tourist area for Russians as well as Ukrainians. In the east are the main industrial cities, clustered round the coalfields and iron-ore mines of the vital Donetsk Basin.

Ukraine's main industries are coal mining, iron and steel, agricultural machinery, petrochemicals and plastics, but there are also numerous food-processing plants based on agricultural output that includes wheat, rye, oats, maize, barley, flax, sugar beet, hops, soya, sunflower seeds, potatoes and other vegetables, meat, dairy produce and cotton.

Though traditionally 'the granary of the Soviet Union', the Ukraine is neither the largest nor the most efficient producer of grain; Russia accounted for more than 53% of the total in 1988 (Ukraine 24%), while Belorussia's agricultural output per capita was some 65% higher than that of its southern neighbour. Indeed the conventional image of the mutual dependency of Russia and the Ukraine is something of a myth, with the latter producing a quarter of all USSR coal and 35% of steel. Not blessed with huge reserves of oil, the Kiev government signed an agreement in February 1992 to secure future supplies from Iran.

The Ukraine's declaration of independence from Moscow was ratified by referendum on 1 December 1991, when Leonid Kravchuk, the former Communist Party ideological secretary, was voted president by direct poll over five rivals. A week later, in Minsk, Kravchuk helped Boris Yeltsin create the basis for the Commonwealth of Independent States, and in the early months of 1992 the Ukraine and Russia reached agreement on a number of potentially explosive issues, not least in the military field, with resolutions on nuclear weapons, the Red Army and the distribution of the Black Sea fleet.

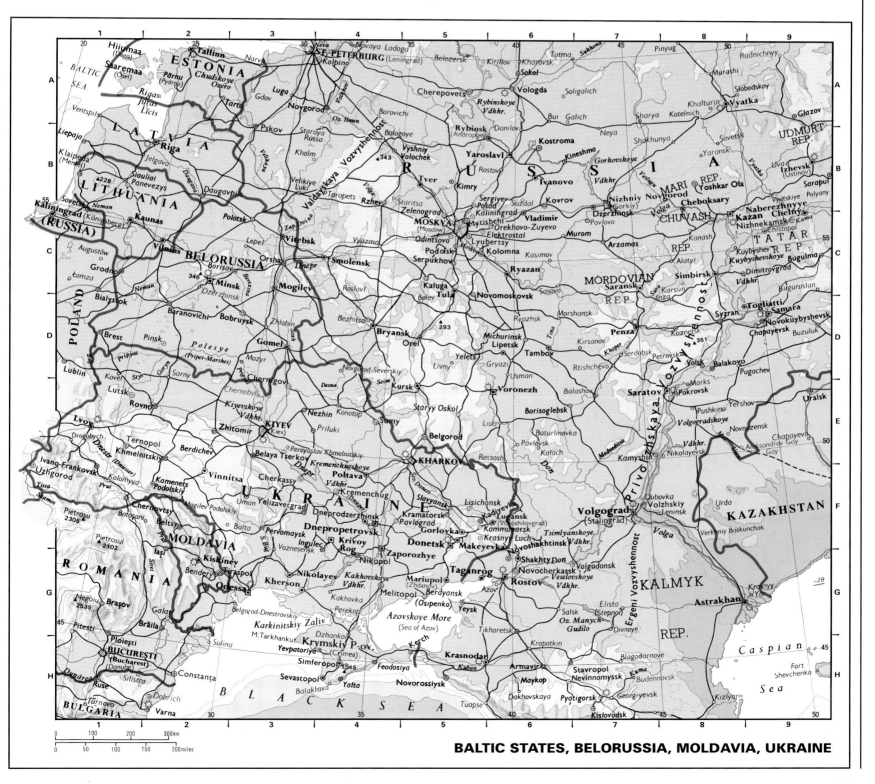

The Convent of Percherskaia in Kiev. Despite 74 years of Communist harassment, the Ukrainian Orthodox Church has survived to celebrate the arrival of religious as well as political freedom.

The Ukraine, however, will not be seen as Russia's sidekick. While it suffered many of the economic agonies endured by its massive neighbour – notably chronic food shortages and the hyperinflation that followed the abolition of price controls – it set out from the beginning to be a fully-fledged and large independent nation. While Russia assumed the diplomatic powers of the Soviet Union, the Ukraine already had a seat at the UN – a reward granted in 1945 for the appalling devastation caused by the German invasion in 1941 and its aftermath – and would seek separate representation on bodies such as the CSCE and OECD.

Co-operation with Russia remains crucial, and early in 1994 there were signs of a pragmatic approach, Ukraine transferring nuclear warheads in return for essential supplies of foodstuffs and fuel ■

ESTONIA

Smallest of the three Baltic states, and the least populous of any of the 15 former Soviet republics, Estonia is bounded on the north by the Gulf of Finland and on the west by the Baltic Sea. The country comprises mostly flat, rock-strewn, glaciated lowland, with over 1,500 lakes, and has more than 800 offshore islands, by far the biggest being Saaremaa and Hiiumaa. The largest lake, Chudskoye Ozero, forms much of the border with Russia in the east.

Over a third of the land is forested, and the timber industry is among the country's most important industries, alongside metal-working, shipbuilding, clothing, textiles, chemicals and food processing. The last is based primarily on extremely efficient dairy farming and pig breeding, but oats, barley and potatoes suit the cool climate and average soils. Fishing is also a major occupation. Like the other two Baltic states, Estonia is not endowed with natural resources, though its shale is an important mineral deposit: enough gas is extracted by processing to supply St Petersburg, Russia's second largest city.

Related ethnically and linguistically to the Finns, the Estonians have managed to retain their cultural identity and now look to increasing their links with Europe, and with Scandinavia in particular. But despite having the highest standard of living of any of the 15 former Soviet republics, it has found the free market hard going. In January 1992 the combination of food shortages and an energy crisis forced the resignation of Prime Minister Edgar Savissar, who enjoyed widespread popular and parliamentary support. A co-founder of the Popular Front, the country's pro-democracy movement, he was held responsible for a recession which appeared to have hit Estonia far harder than its two neighbours ■

LATVIA

Its Baltic coast heavily indented by the Gulf of Riga, Latvia is a small country of flat glaciated lowland, with natural vegetation and agriculture virtually mirroring that of Estonia. So, too, does much of its commerce; like its Baltic neighbours it contains much of the Soviet Union's less traditional, 'clever' industries, while Ventspils is an important conduit for the export of Russian oil and gas. Latvia is the most urbanized of the Baltic states, with over 70% of the population living in cities and towns.

Although forming only a slender majority today, the native Latvians (Letts) have a highly developed folklore, their sense of identity honed during the nationalist drive in the late 19th century and rekindled in the quest for separation from the Soviet Union more than 100 years later. Latvia declared independence in May 1990, two months after Lithuania, and despite a large 'foreign' population the subsequent referendum indicated a substantial majority in favour of a break with Moscow.

Strong ties remain, however. Like its neighbours, Latvia is (in the medium term at least) almost totally reliant on the network of Russian and Ukrainian energy supply, while Russia will not simply surrender the 'Soviet' investments in the country, most obviously in the ports ■

LITHUANIA

Largest and most populous of the Baltic states, Lithuania is also the most homogeneous, some 80% of its population being staunch Catholics who speak the native language and are proud of their history and culture. From 1988 it was Lithuania which led the 'Balts' in their drive to shed Communism and regain their nationhood; in March 1990 it became the first of the 15 constituent Soviet republics to declare itself an independent, non-Communist country, resulting in the occupation of much of its capital by Soviet troops and an economic blockade not suffered by the other states of the Union.

The successful crusade was led by the emotional president, Vytautas Landsbergis, whose crucial role in the process of 'deconstruction' – and that of his people – was somewhat overshadowed by the figure of Boris Yeltsin and the Russian Federation.

The country consists mostly of a low, glaciated but fairly fertile central lowland used primarily for cattle, pigs and poultry – livestock rearing having been highly intensified under the Soviet collective system. Crops grown are very similar to those of Estonia, while there are also widespread forests and significant peat reserves, though Lithuania remains pitifully short of natural resources. In the east, towards the border with Belorussia, is an area of forested sandy ridges, dotted with lakes.

A range of industries, among them many of the most advanced programmes in the former Soviet Union, include timber, metal-working, textiles, building materials, fertilizers, fibres and plastics, computers and instruments, and food processing.

While Lithuania, in concert with the other Baltic states, seeks to establish closer ties with the rest of Europe – a US$2.5 billion highway is planned, linking the three capitals with Warsaw – it also has simmering ethnic problems of its own. Its significant Polish population, largely self-governing under the Soviets, now fear 'Lithuanization', while the majority who took on Moscow and won resent the pro-Union stance taken by Poles and Russians during their fight for freedom ■

THE BALTIC STATES

The three Baltic republics have always found it hard to establish their nationhood, though their cultures have proved resilient. Estonia and Latvia survived 1,000 years of rule by Danes, Swedes, Lithuanians and Poles before becoming part of the Russian Empire in 1721; Lithuania, once a powerful medieval empire, was united with Poland in 1385 but also came under Russian control in 1795.

Nationalist movements grew in all three countries in the late 19th century, and in 1920, following German occupation, the Soviet Union granted them the status of independent democratic republics. However, all had Fascist coups by the time Hitler assigned them to Stalin in the notorious secret pact of 1939.

After three years of occupation by (Nazi) Germany, incorporation into the USSR was confirmed by plebiscite in 1944. On declaring independence in 1990, the Baltic states claimed this was fraudulent and that their countries were never legally part of the Soviet Union. Referenda supported this view, and on 6 September 1991 the transitional States Council of the Soviet Union recognized them as independent sovereign states. All three were UN members by the end of the year – but all three have found the economic going tough in the post-Cold War world.

GEORGIA

Positioned between Russia and Turkey, Georgia comprises four main areas: the Caucasus Mountains in the north, including Mt Elbrus (5,633 m [18,841 ft]) on the Russian border; the Black Sea coastal plain in the west; the eastern end of the mountains of Asia Minor to the south; and a low plateau in the east, protruding into Azerbaijan. Separating the two mountain sections is the crucial Kura Valley, in which the capital Tbilisi stands.

The largest of the three Transcaucasian republics, Georgia is rich in citrus fruits and wine (notably in the Kakhetia region), tea (the main crop), tobacco, wheat, barley and vegetables, while perfumes are made from flowers and herbs and, in Imeretia, silk is a flourishing industry. Almost 40% forested, it also has a significant stake in timber. It has large deposits of manganese ore, but despite reserves of coal and huge hydroelectric potential, most of its electricity is generated in Russia and the Ukraine.

Always a maverick among the Soviet republics, Georgia was the first to declare independence after the Baltic states (April 1991), and the only one not to join the Commonwealth of Independent States. When Gorbachev resigned, the democratically elected leader of Georgia, Zviad Gamsakhurdia, found himself holed up in Tbilisi's KGB headquarters, under seige from rebel forces representing widespread disapproval of his policies, from the economy to the imprisonment of political opponents. In January he fled the country (now ruled by a military council), returning to lead resistance from his home territory in the west, though to little effect. A charismatic, highly individual president, Gamsakhurdia had also been in conflict with the Ossetian minority in one of the republic's three autonomous regions, who feared being swamped in a new independent nation. In March 1992 former Soviet foreign minister Eduard Shevardnadze agreed to become chairman of the ruling council. In 1993 Abkhaz separatist militancy almost brought about the fall of Shevardnadze, at one stage forcing the former Georgian Communist Party head into hiding. The Abkhazians were subordinated to Georgia by Stalin in 1931, and like the South Ossetians, they do not relish rule from Tblisi. Shevardnadze and his council were forced to turn to Russia's President Yeltsin, whose condition for armed intervention – and continued economic support – was Georgia's belated membership of the CIS.

Mostly Orthodox Christians, Georgians have a strong national culture and a long literary tradition based on their own language and alphabet. Land of the legendary Golden Fleece of Greek mythology, the area was conquered by the Romans, Persians and Arabs before establishing autonomy in the 10th century, but Tartars, Persians and Turks invaded before it came under Russian domination around 1800. Renowned for their longevity, the population's most famous product was Josef Stalin, born in Gori, 65 km [40 mls] north-west of Tbilisi ■

Harvest time on the plains of Georgia. While the country has a wide-ranging agricultural base, from flowers and fruit to tea and tobacco, it relies heavily on Russia for its sources of energy.

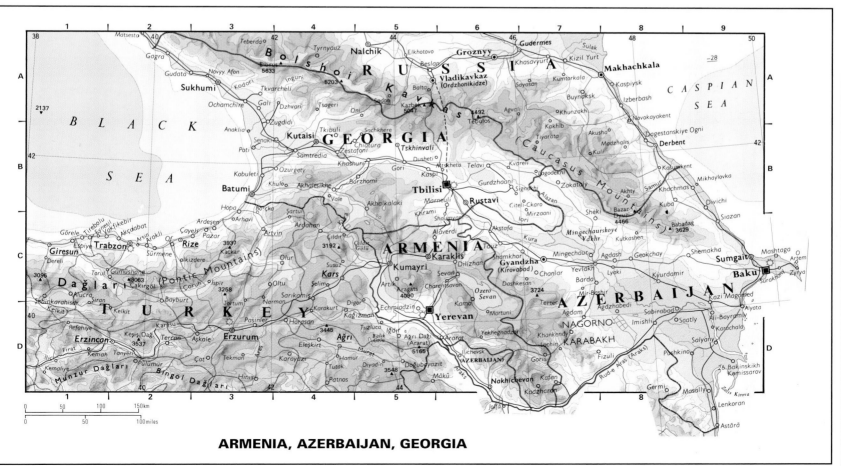

ARMENIA, AZERBAIJAN, GEORGIA

ARMENIA

The smallest of the 15 republics of the former Soviet Union, Armenia was also one of the weakest. A rugged, mountainous country land-locked between traditionally hostile neighbours, it has few natural resources (though lead, copper and zinc are mined), limited industry, and registered the poorest agricultural output per head in the Union; the main products are wine, tobacco, olives and rice, the main occupation the raising of livestock. Much of the west is recovering from the devastating earthquake of 1988, in which some 55,000 people died. Its vulnerability is heightened by the lack of support for its conflict with Azerbaijan over Nagorno-Karabakh, its heavy reliance for energy on other republics, and a crippling economic blockade imposed by Azerbaijan.

Originally a larger independent kingdom centred on Mt Ararat, Armenia had already been established for more than 1,000 years when it became the first country in the world to make Christianity (Armenian Apostolic) the official state religion in the 4th century. Ever since, its people have been subject to war, occupation and massacre – the most documented example being the genocide by Turks in World War I ■

AZERBAIJAN

Now in relative decline (3% of the Soviet total in 1989), oil is still the mainstay of Azerbaijan's revenue. It was being collected by the Caspian Sea near Baku over 1,000 years ago, and burning natural gas leaking from the ground gave the area its name: 'Land of eternal fire'. Today, along with industries both traditional (carpets, timber, iron) and modern (cement, aluminium, chemicals), it makes the country's economy a viable one. Though much of Azerbaijan is semi-arid – with a large tract below sea level – it still grows crops such as cotton, grains, rice and grapes, with fishing also important.

As the Azerbaijanis look to their fellow Shiite Muslims in Iran after independence (declared in August 1991), their biggest problem remains that of their western neighbour, Armenia, and the intractable problem of Nagorno-Karabakh, the predominantly Armenian 'oblast' enclave of 177,000 people in the south-west, scene of bitter fighting and appalling atrocities since 1988. Soviet troops went in early in 1990, and two years later it became a real test for the new Commonwealth. Ironically, Azerbaijan has itself an enclave, the autonomous republic of Nakhichevan (population 270,000), completely isolated from the main part of the country on the border of Armenia and Turkey. Nearly three times the size of Armenia, with more than twice the population, more wealthy and with help from its fellow Muslims, Azerbaijan is in theory equipped to defend Nagorno-Karabakh ■

An Armenian view of Mt Ararat, legendary resting place of Noah's Ark now in north-east Turkey. Most of Armenia, too, comprises mountainous terrain.

Asia

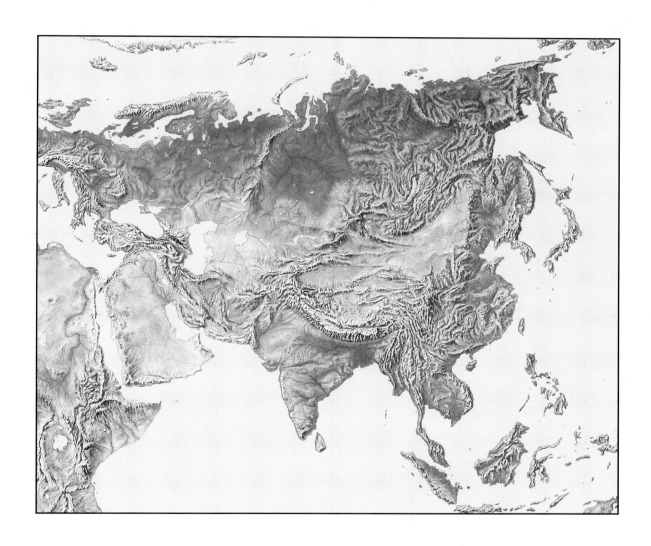

ASIA

The largest continent, accounting for a third of the world's land surface — and well over half its population — Asia extends from the Mediterranean Sea to the Pacific Ocean and from the tropical islands of the East Indies to the frozen shores of the Arctic. Most of its boundary is shoreline, but the boundary with Europe is the subject of some debate.

Geologically, Asia is made up of two vast sets of rock platforms — the Russian and Siberian in the north, and the Arabian, Indian and Chinese platforms in the south, which for aeons have converged on each other, squashing between them an enormous extent of sedimentary rocks that were laid down in ancient seas. The platforms provide the great, stable plateaus on the periphery; the sediments have been squeezed and folded into the massive mountain ranges that spread across the continent from Turkey ('Asia Minor') in the west to the Pacific seaboard in the east.

Climatically Asia includes almost every known combination of temperature, precipitation and wind, from the searing heat of Arabia in summer to the

Cherry blossom graces a hillside in Japan. Stretching from here by the Pacific to the Red Sea, and from the Arctic to the Equator, Asia's vast land mass experiences almost every type of climate and vegetation.

biting chill of north-eastern Siberia in Winter. Similarly, almost every pattern of vegetation from polar desert and tundra to tropical rainforest can be found within the bounds of this vast continent.

Asia comprises a 'heartland' centred on Siberia, and a series of peripheral areas of widely different character. The heartland includes the tundra wastes of the north, the coniferous forests ('taiga'), and the vast, thinly-populated interior deserts of Mongolia, north-west China and Tibet. Not entirely desert, some of the heartland was traditionally pastoral and is now responding to new agricultural techniques, while the wealth of its minerals is slowly being developed. To the west lie the plains of Russia, homeland of the 16th- and 17th-century invaders who, unlike their many predecessors, finally came to settle in the heartland and organize its massive resources. To the south-west lies the 'fertile crescent' of the Tigris and Euphrates valleys, possibly the world's first centre of agriculture, and beyond it the Mediterranean coastlands of Turkey, Syria, Lebanon and Israel.

From Iran eastwards, right around the shores of the continent and its off-lying islands as far as eastern Siberia, lie the coastlands that contain and support the main masses of Asia's populations. Isolated by the northern mountain barrier, India has traditionally formed a subcontinent in its own right. China, the second great civilization of Asia, centred

on the 'Middle Kingdom' of 18 historic provinces, has expanded steadily over the centuries and is a great influence on neighbouring states. Beyond the mainland coasts lie the mountainous but mostly highly fertile islands of the volcanic arcs that skirt the eastern edge of the continental shelf. The population of these islands, already high, are among the fastest growing in the world – though only Japan provides a standard of living comparable to those in the West.

The Indian subcontinent, though a relatively small part of Asia as a whole, is almost continental in its impact on the traveller and in its share (nearly one-fifth) of the world's population. It extends from sub-equatorial coral beaches in the south to icy mountains overlooking the Vale of Kashmir in the north – approximately in the latitude of Greece.

South Asia is a subcontinent of unity and diversity. Binding it in unity is the annually occurring rhythm of human activities caused by the seasonal reversal of winds in the monsoon. Yet diversity arises from the same cause – the annual vagaries of the monsoon that bring drought and near-famine to one region, flood and disease to another, in apparently

RIGHT While desert is readily associated with Africa, Asia hosts five of the world's ten largest: Arabian, Gobi, Takla Makan, Turkestan and Thar. This self dune is in the 'Empty Quarter' of the Arabian Desert.

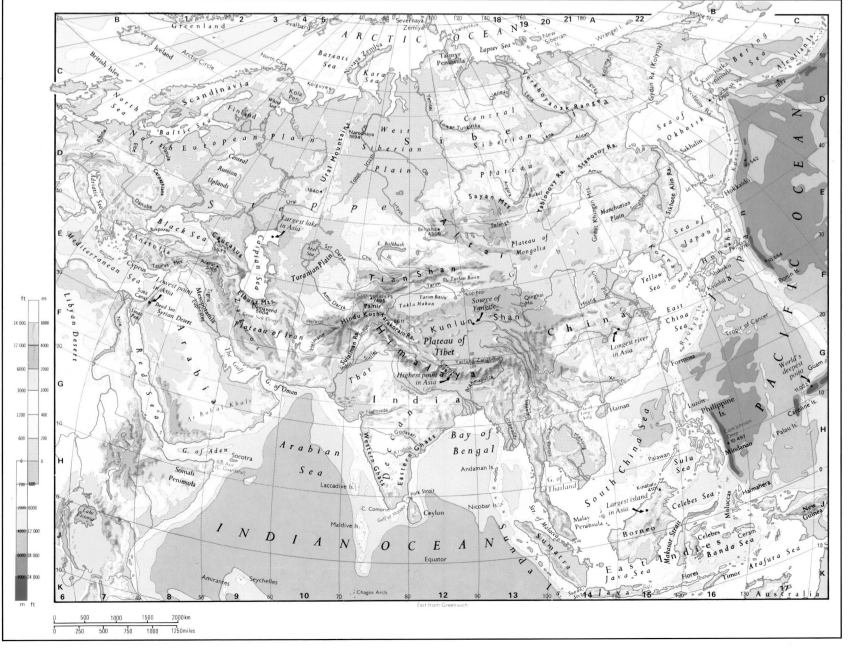

The highest place on Earth, Mt Everest (centre right) is only one of 18 peaks in the Himalayas over 8,000 m [26,247 ft]. With the Pamirs, Hindu Kush and Karakorams, they were pushed up when the Indian and Asian continental plates 'collided' 25 million years ago.

random patterns. There is a cultural unity, too, to which the sensitive traveller reacts, from Kashmir to Cape Comorin (Kanya Kumari). Yet here again is the paradox of extraordinary diversity. Variety of race, language and religion all contribute, often related to invasions, trading connections or a colonial past. At the root of the culture of this subcontinent lies South Asia's millennial role as the cradle of Hinduism and Buddhism.

East Asia comprises the lands to the east of the great mountain barrier which runs from south-west China, through the Himalayas, the Karakoram and the Tian Shan, to the Altai range on the borders of Mongolia, China and Russia. It occupies roughly 9% of the land area of the globe, and exhibits a very great diversity of relief and climate. Altitudes vary from the high Tibetan plateau, where the average elevation is over 4,500 m [14,670 ft], to the floor of the Turfan (Turpan Hami) depression to the north, 154 m [505 ft] below sea level. East Asian climates range from the cold continental of northern Mongolia to the warm humid tropical of southern China.

The area contains well over a quarter of mankind. This population is unevenly distributed with the main concentrations in lowland areas open to the influence of the summer monsoon in eastern China, Korea, and Japan. Until recent times the whole area has been strongly dominated by the Chinese civilization.

Only since World War II has the term 'South-east Asia' become widely used to describe the series of peninsulas and islands which lie east of India and south of China. The name was first employed around 1900 to designate a particular trade and shipping area, but the concept of a South-east Asian region goes back a long way. This was recognized by both the Chinese and the Japanese, who respectively called it the Nan Yang and the Nanyo, both meaning the 'southern seas'. Today the region includes Burma, Thailand, Laos, Vietnam, Cambodia, Malaysia, Singapore, Brunei and the islands of Indonesia and the Philippines.

South-east Asia, which lies almost wholly in the humid tropics, is an area of rivers and seas. Each of the mainland states is focused on one major river, with the Irrawaddy in Burma, the Chao Phraya in Thailand, the Mekong in Cambodia and South Vietnam and the Hongha in North Vietnam. The maritime states, however, revolve around a series of

seas and straits, from the highly strategic Strait of Malacca in the west to the Sulu, Celebes and Banda Seas in the east.

The evergreen rainforest of the ever-wet, ever-hot tropics is a very complex community. In 20 hectares [49 acres] there can be as many as 350 different species of trees. In the forest, climbing and strangling plants are abundant. Many of the trunks are buttressed, and certain trees bear their flowers and fruits directly on the trunks and branches. The canopy is the home of a wide range of birds, bats and other mammals, including the orang-utan.

Much of the rainforest has now been completely destroyed by shifting cultivators or felled for timber by extracting companies, and the remaining tracts are also under pressure from mining concerns, rubber companies, hydroelectric developments and tourism.

The peaks and high plateaus of the Himalayas and central Asia are forested up to about 4,000 m [13,000 ft] with an open woodland of pines, cedars, bamboos and rhododendrons. Above lies a zone of dwarf shrubs – willows, birches and junipers that spend half their year in swirling snow. This grades into a rough, semi-frozen tundra of coarse sedges and grasses, dotted with cushions of brightly coloured alpine flowers; primulas, edelweiss and gentians become prominent as the snow retreats in early summer. In the thin, cool air at 4,500 to 5,500 m [15,000 to 18,000 ft] insects are surprisingly plentiful. At 6,000 m [19,500 ft] tundra turns to dry desert and both plants and animals become rare.

Larger grazing animals – yaks, hangul deer and blue sheep, for example – emerge from the forest to feed on the high plateaus in summer, and mountain goats and ibex find a living among the high, snow-encrusted crags. Wolves, snow leopards and high-flying eagles are their chief predators ∎

Siberia is colossal. Provideniya Bay on the Chukotskoye Peninsula, home to one of its most easterly settlements, is closer to Los Angeles, near the border with Mexico, than it is to the Russian national capital in Moscow.

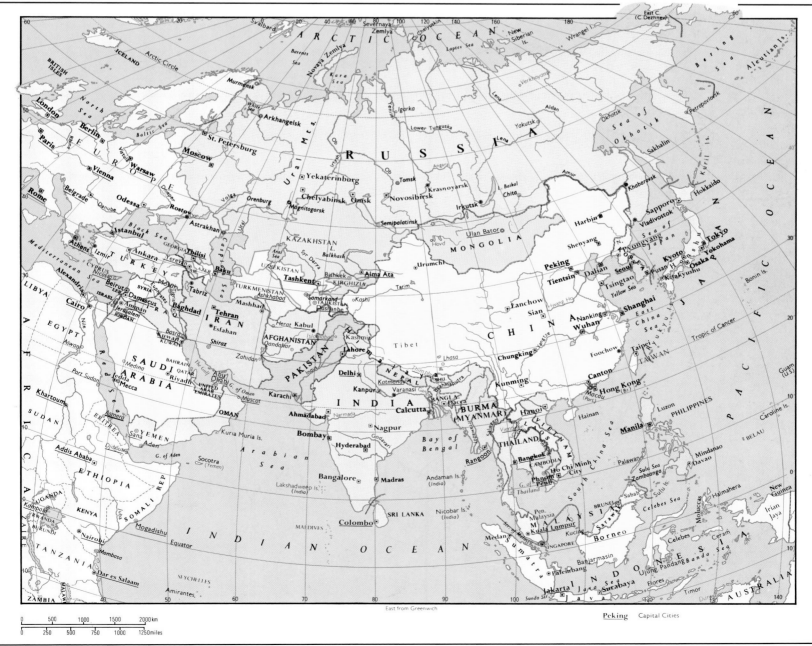

Peking   Capital Cities

RUSSIA

I t is an indication of the sheer size of the former Soviet Union that, having shed very nearly a quarter of its area with the departure of the 14 repu- blics in 1991, its Russian Federation remains by far the largest country in the world, still almost twice the size of Canada, China or the USA. This territorial immensity brings a number of disad- vantages – it is awkward to administer, large invest- ments have to be made in the transport system and the long borders are difficult to defend – but set against these are the benefits that derive from the diversity of environments and cultures and the abun- dance of resources in the country's vast expanses, many of which are relatively untouched.

Landscape

Diversity certainly characterizes Russia's landforms, for within the country's borders are to be found rugged peaks and salt flats, glaciers and deserts, marshes and rolling hills as well as broad level plains.

In the west the North European Plain, underlain by the ancient peneplained rocks of the Russian plat- form, occupies the greater part of European Russia as well as much of Ukraine and all of Belorussia and the Baltic nations. On the eastern side of the plain are the Ural Mountains; popularly seen as the divide between Europe and Asia, the Urals are low and rounded with few peaks rising above 1,600 m [5,248 ft]. The east- ern slopes of the Urals merge into the West Siberian lowland, the largest plain in the world, with extensive low-lying marshes. Still further to the east the Siber- ian platform, similar in origin to the Russian plat- form, underlies the Central Siberian Plateau. The relief of this plateau is a good example of a peneplain, with its rolling uplands rising 500 to 700 m [1,640 to 2,300 ft] and deeply incised river valleys.

The extensive plains of Russia are surrounded on the south and east by mountain ranges of geologically recent origin: the Caucasus, rising to over 5,000 m [16,400 ft] on the borders of Georgia and Azerbaijan; the Altai and Sayan, extending into Mongolia; and, beyond Lake Baykal and the Lena River, the East Siberian ranges at the easternmost tip of the Asian land mass. The Kamchatka peninsula is still geolog- ically unstable – part of the 'Pacific Rim' – and volcanic eruptions and earthquakes occur fairly often.

Much of Russia's landscape bears the imprint of the last Ice Age in the form of chaotic drainage systems, extensive marshlands, lakes and moraines in the lowland areas and cirques and 'U'-shaped valleys in the mountains. Today large areas remain ice-bound, while more than half the total area has permafrost – perma- nently frozen ground which may extend hundreds of metres in depth. In the permafrost of East Siberia prehistoric woolly mammoths have been found in near- perfect condition.

The rivers that flow across the Russian plains are among the longest and most languid in the world. Drainage in European Russia forms a radial pattern with the hub in the Central Uplands west of Moscow. The Volga flows from this area for 3,700 km [2,300 mls] south to the landlocked Caspian Sea, the world's largest inland body of water. In Siberia the main rivers flow north to the Arctic – among them the Yenisey-Angara, the Ob-Irtysh and the Lena, respectively the fifth, sixth and 11th longest in the world. Shifting channels and irregular flow make these rivers difficult to navigate and they are ice- bound in winter. In the east Lake Baykal (Oz Baykal) acts as a holding reservoir for the Yenisey.

Natural regions

Extending latitudinally across Russia, and corre- sponding to the major climatic belts, are a series of sharply differentiated natural zones – from north to south the tundra, the taiga, the mixed forests and the steppe. The dominant natural zones can also be seen as vertical bands in the mountainous regions.

Tundra: This zone forms a continuous strip north of the Arctic Circle from the Norwegian border to Kamchatka. Climatic conditions here restrict plant growth and soil formation so that the region will deserves its name 'bald mountain top', the meaning of the word 'tundra' in Lapp. Stunted shrubs, mosses, lichens and berry-bearing bushes growing in thin, infertile soils form the vegetation cover, supporting various hardy creatures – including the herds of reindeer which for centuries have formed the basis of the local tribes' economy.

Taiga: Extending south from the boundary with the tundra and occupying about 60% of the country are the coniferous forests that make up the taiga – larger than the Amazonian rainforest. Different species of tree dominate in different parts of the taiga, but throughout the most common are firs, pines and the silver birch. Soils under the forest are podzols, a Russian term meaning 'ashy-grey underneath'. These soils are acidic and usually unsuitable for cultivation unless fertilized. A major source of wealth in the taiga has always been its large population of fur-bearing animals such as ermine, sable and beaver – and it was the quest for furs that first lured man into this inhos- pitable environment.

Mixed forest: In the west and east the coniferous forests merge into zones of mixed forest – wide in European Russia but contracting towards the east to form a narrow finger which peters out beyond the Urals. The mixed forest contains both coniferous species and broadleaves such as oak, beech, ash, horn- beam and maple. Today much of the natural vegeta- tion has been cleared for farming, despite the fact that the soils require heavy application of fertilizers to be productive. From early times the mixed forest has been the focus of settlement for the Russians.

Steppe: Sandwiched between the forests to the north and the semi-deserts and deserts of the Central Asian republics to the south is the steppe zone. Hardly any natural vegetation remains in the steppe today as vast expanses have been brought under the plough. The soils of the steppe are chernozems, black-earths, and they are among the most fertile in the world. Before conversion into farmland the steppe consisted of extensive grasslands which in the north were inter- spersed with trees. The vast majority of the steppe- land of the former Soviet Union, however, falls in the Ukraine and Kazakhstan.

LAKE BAYKAL

With a lowest point of 1,620 m [5,315 ft], Oz Baykal in southern Siberia is the world's deepest lake. Also the largest by Eurasia – at 636 km [395 mls] long by an average width of 48 km [30 mls] it measures 31,500 sq km [12,160 sq mls] – it is the world's largest body of fresh water and contains a fifth of the fresh water contained in all the world's lakes. Its volume of 23,000 cu km [5,520 cu mls] is as much as the five Great Lakes of North America combined; and it drains an area 13% larger.

Situated in a deep tectonic basin, and fed by 336 rivers and streams, it acts as a reservoir for only one river: the Angara, which flows north (left, with Baykal in the background) to join the Yenisey. Though renowned for the purity of its water and its endemic lifeforms (65% of its 1,500 animal species and 35% of its plant species are unique to Baykal), industrial plants, includ- ing mining but notably cellulose factories at the southern end, have caused increas- ing pollution since the 1960s.

Natural resources

Russia's physical environment offers varied opportunities for exploitation. The vast stretches of forest make it the world's largest possessor of softwoods, but although the most extensive stands are found in Siberia, felling has been concentrated in the European part of the country, where the wood is of high quality and is more readily accessible.

The rivers, lakes and seas have yielded marine and freshwater products from early days. In the 11th century fishing villages were already established on the northern coast of European Russia for whaling, sealing and fishing. Today fish catches are large on the Pacific coast while, among the freshwater varieties, the sturgeon continues to be valued for its caviare.

Because of the widespread occurrence of poor soils and harsh climatic conditions, agriculture is confined to a relatively small area of the country. Most of the arable is in the steppe and forest-steppe and from the time this was first ploughed it has been used for grains. More than half of the output that made the USSR the world's top producer of barley, oats and

East meets West on Red Square in the nine chapels of St Basil's Cathedral, now a museum. Moscow has been the centre of the Russian Orthodox Church since 1326.

rye, and second in wheat, came from Russian land. On the Black Sea coast, subtropical conditions allow the cultivation of crops exotic to the rest of the country, including wines, tea and citrus fruits.

While agriculture is limited, mineral and energy resources are abundant and have formed the basis of the former USSR's powerful industrial economy. The most notable mineral deposits are found on the Kola peninsula by the Barents Sea, in eastern Siberia and the far east where spectacular discoveries of gold, lead, zinc, copper and diamonds have been made. Iron ore is found in most regions – the Soviet Union produced a quarter of the world total – but the most recently opened field is at Kursk, south of Moscow.

Energy resources are varied. Estimates show Russia to have sufficient coal to last several hundred years, while oil and natural gas deposits are projected to last for several decades, with the main fields in the Volga-Urals region and western Siberia. Before 'deconstruction' the USSR was by far the world's leading producer, and Russia was responsible for over 90% of oil output and nearly 80% of gas. Large hydropower complexes have also been built on many rivers, though the development of nuclear energy was under review following the disaster of Chernobyl (in the Ukraine) in 1986.

History

The present size of Russia is the product of a long period of evolution. In early medieval times the first Slavic state, Kievan Rus, was formed at the junction of the forest and steppe in what is now the Ukraine. As the centuries wore on other states were formed further to the north. All were eventually united under the principality of Muscovy. In the 13th century Mongol hordes from the east penetrated the forests and held sway over the Slavic people there, extracting tribute from them.

It was only in the 16th century that the Mongol yoke was thrown off as the Slavs, under Ivan the Terrible, began to advance across the steppes. This signalled the beginning of a period of expansion from the core area of Slavic settlement to the south, east and west. Expansion across Siberia was rapid and the first Russian settlement on the Pacific, Okhotsk, was established in 1649. Progress across the open steppe, the realm of tribal horsemen, was slower but by 1696 Azov, the key to the Black Sea, was secured. A series of struggles in the 17th and 18th centuries against the Swedes and Poles resulted in the addition of the Gulf of Finland, the Baltic coast and part of Poland to the growing Russian Empire, and in the 19th century the Caucasus, Central Asia and new territories in the Far East were added. In the 20th century the gains and losses of area through war, treaties and secret deals have been comparatively small, if at times dramatic.

Russia has been a centralized state throughout its history. A major landmark in the country's history, and indeed in the history of the world, was the 1917 Revolution, when the Tsarist order was overthrown and a Communist government established under Lenin – replacing one form of totalitarianism with another. The years from 1917 witnessed colossal changes in the political, social and economic structure of the country, the most dramatic and far-reaching of which took place from the 1930s when Stalin instituted central planning of the economy, collectivized agriculture and began a period of rapid industrialization. After Stalin's death in 1953, Soviet leaders modified some policies but they remained true to the general principles of Communism until the rad-

A bright shuttered window brings welcome colour to a traditional small wooden house (izba) in the vastness of the Russian taiga – the world's largest forest.

ical approach of Mikhail Gorbachev changed the face of Russia – and in the process most of the Communist world.

A new country

Russia held most of the economic trumps on the break-up of the Soviet Union, in terms of both natural resources and production; in 1989, for example, the Federation accounted for nearly 60% of crude steel output. But despite Gorbachev's best and at times brave efforts, the Russian President Boris Yeltsin inherited an economy in crisis, bogged down by lumbering and often obstructive bureaucracy, inept use of resources and a cumbersome, inefficient transport system, of which the state airline Aeroflot (the world's largest) was a prime example. Though the West preferred aid, the impressive-sounding amounts were relatively small, and the final solution would lie with the Russians themselves.

After the abolition of price controls sent the cost of basic commodities rocketing, 1992 and 1993 saw food shortages worsen and unemployment rise. Like

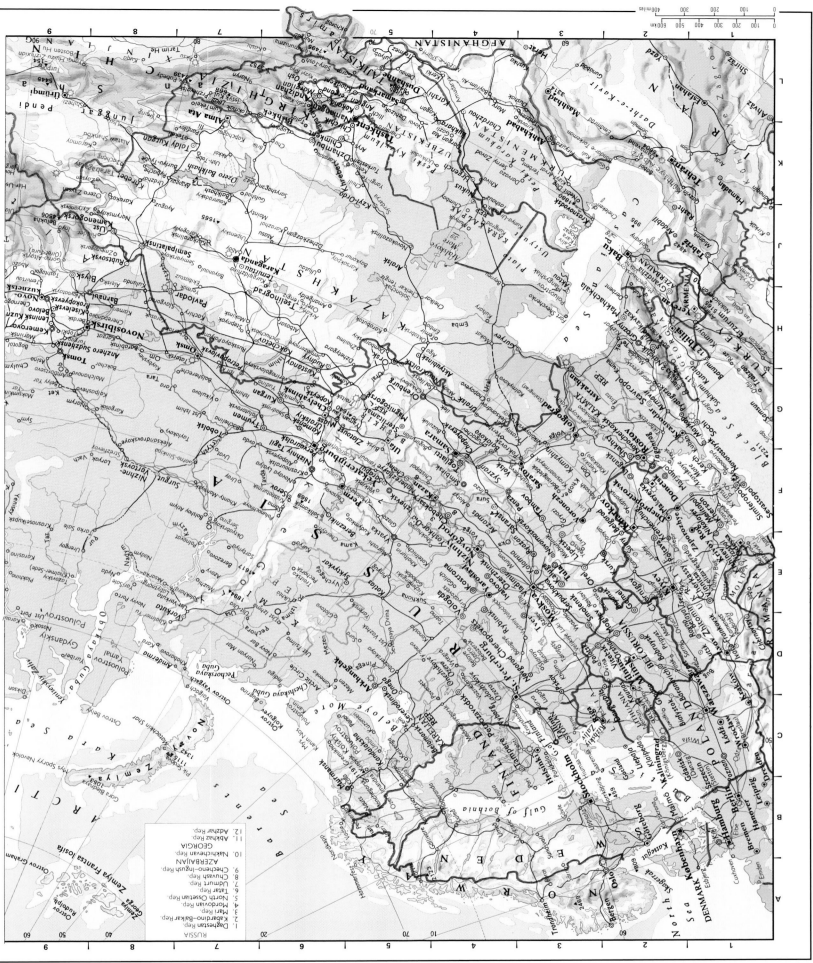

Eastern Europe, the Russians found it difficult to stabilize their economy, its citizens paying a high social as well as financial price for the introduction of Western-style democratic capitalism. While the people backed Yeltsin's programme of reforms in a referendum in April 1993, his increasingly dictatorial style – suspending an obstructive parliament in September, calling in the army and special forces to crush a revolt in October – contributed to a rejection of his policies when the country's first multiparty elections were held at the end of the year. The results gave over a quarter of the seats to the new right-wing Liberal Democratic Party of Vladimir Zhirinovsky, whose ultra-nationalist stance stirred dreams of a 'Greater Russia', incorporating the willing Russian populations of neighbouring states. The mood was mirrored there, too: Ukraine's Crimea and eastern regions, for example, both voted for similar sentiments in the spring of 1994.

Yet neither is the nation homogeneous. Several autonomous regions – including Karelia, Komi, North Ossetia, Tartarsian, Bashkiria, Gorny-Altay, Buryatia and the vast Yakutia – declared independence in the last months of Soviet control. They could well pursue their policy, seeing Russia shrink further in size and influence in the region.

It may be thought that Russia would not need the CIS, its economic strength (properly managed) making it more than viable as a major nation and a natural successor internationally to the Soviet Union; it inherited the USSR's mantle on the UN Security Council and its diplomatic missions worldwide, while

applying for membership of CSCE and even NATO.

But Russia, despite its size, fears isolation. With the Eastern European countries and the Baltic states now fully independent, the three Caucasus republics unstable, the Asian republics (whose fast-growing populations suggest that by 2000 Russia will lose its majority in the CIS) looking increasingly to their Islamic neighbours, and even Mongolia converting to

democracy and the free market, Russia has little control of the former 'buffer zones'. Though large and powerful, it has always felt under siege, and better that the buffers were partners rather than opponents. In any case the Commonwealth states had once to live with the structure created by the Soviet system – and that meant interdependency ■

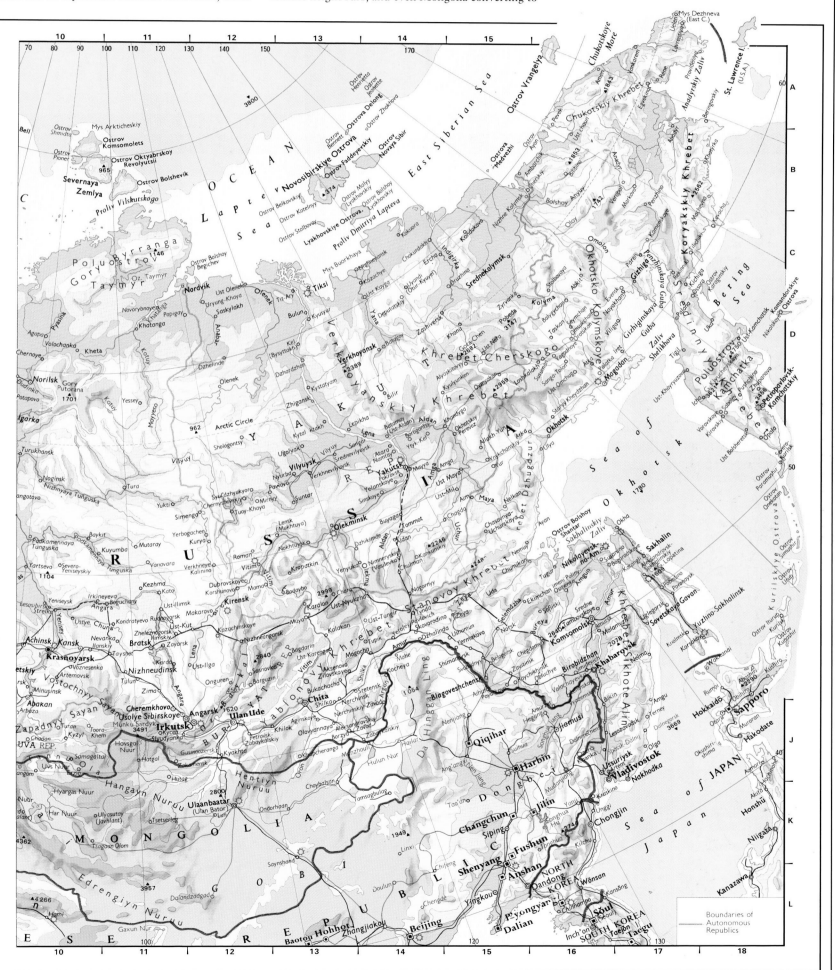

KAZAKHSTAN

Although a modest second in size behind Russia among the former Soviet republics, Kazakhstan is a colossal country – more than two and a half times the combined area of the other four Central Asian states, over four times the size of Ukraine (Europe's largest 'whole' state), bigger than any nation in Africa and indeed ninth in the world.

This massive new nation, stretching from near the Volga River in the west to the Altai Mountains in the east, comprises mainly vast plains with a (mineral-rich) central plateau. North to south, the steppe gradually gives way to desert, though irrigation schemes have led to the fertilization of large areas between the Aral Sea and Lake Balkhash, a rich fishing ground. Though its agriculture is traditionally associated with livestock rearing, Kazakhstan accounted for 20% of the cultivated area of the Soviet Union and some 12% of its grain output in 1989.

The first extension of the Russian Empire in Central Asia, the area's 'khanates' were gradually subdued or bought off from the 18th century, though rural resistance persisted well into the Soviet era. It was Kazakhstan that gave Mikhail Gorbachev his first ethnic problem, when in 1986 nationalist riots erupted after a Russian replaced a Kazakh as the republic's Party leader, and in 1991 it led the Central Asian states into the new Commonwealth; indeed, the meeting that finally buried the Soviet Union was held in Alma Ata, testimony to Kazakhstan's rank as number three in the hierarchy – an estimate helped by its 1,800 nuclear warheads.

It was not always so. Successive Soviet regimes used the huge republic as a dumping-ground and test-bed. Stalin exiled Germans and other 'undesirables' there, and Khrushchev experimented with his (largely catastrophic) Virgin Lands Programme; the Soviet missile- and rocket-launching site was located at Baykonur, north-east of the Aral Sea (shrunk by 70% after disastrous Soviet irrigation projects dried up its two feeder rivers), and the USSR's first fast-breeder nuclear reactor was built at Mangyshlak, on the Caspian Sea.

Kazakhstan has nevertheless emerged as a powerful entity, wealthier and more diversified than the other Asian republics. Well endowed with oil and gas, it also has good deposits of coal, iron ore, bauxite, copper, nickel, tungsten, zinc, silver, and gold (70% of the Soviet total). Though not industrialized by Western standards, it is growing in oil refining (notably for aviation fuel), metallurgy, engineering, chemicals, footwear, food processing and textiles, the last mostly dependent on home-grown cotton and, increasingly, high-quality native wool.

Kazakhstan could provide the 'new order' with a valuable bridge between East and West, between Islam and Christianity; it is the only former Soviet republic where its ethnic population is actually outnumbered by another group (the Russians), and its (Sunni) Muslim revival is relatively muted. Such divisions can of course have the opposite effect, leading to ethnic tensions and cruelties that have cursed the Caucasus. In March 1994 the country's first genuine multiparty elections were described by accredited Western observers as 'unfair' ∎

Courtyard of the Tila-Kari mosque in Samarkand. A stop on the 'Silk Road' to China which was the capital of the Tartar warlord Tamurlane in the 14th century. The city is now a strange mix of Islamic and ex-Soviet influences.

UZBEKISTAN

Only a fraction of Kazakhstan's size, but with a larger population, Uzbekistan stretches from the shores of the shrinking Aral Sea, through desert and increasingly fertile semi-arid lands, to the peaks of the Western Pamirs and the mountainous border with Afghanistan, with a populous eastern spur jutting into Kirghizia.

The fertile sections comprise an intensely irrigated zone that made Uzbekistan the world's third largest cotton producer, contributing 67% of the Soviet total; the republic was also responsible in 1989 for half the rice, a third of astrakhan and 85% of the hemp produced. However, oil and gas (especially in the desert of Kyzylkum), coal and copper are important, while industries other than textiles – fertilizers, engineering, food processing – are slowly gaining ground.

The Uzbeks were the ruling race in southern Central Asia before the Russians took over in the 19th century. Today the Russians are a vulnerable minority in the republic noted for ethnic violence, most dangerously between Uzbeks, a Turkic people speaking Jagatai Turkish, and the Tajiks, a Persian people who speak an Iranian dialect. This problem, added to a suspect economy overdependent on one commodity and a deserved, enduring reputation for government corruption, could well see Uzbekistan – with 21,627,000 people the most populous of the five Asian republics – struggle as an independent nation.

As with many former Soviet republics, the Communist Party has changed its name but the same old-guard élite has continued in power – a well-organized alliance of local Russian technocrats and wealthy regional clans.

The new ideologies the regimes propound are little more than decorative versions of the tired Communist model, but with subtle shifts – increased Turkish influence (and investment) in business and education, for example, or an independent currency from the Russian rouble. In November 1993 Uzbekistan launched (like Kazakhstan, Turkmenistan and Kirghizia) its own monetary system ∎

TURKMENISTAN

More than 90% of Turkmenistan is arid, with over half the country covered by the Karakum, Asia's largest sand desert. As much Middle Eastern as Central Asian, its scant population is found mainly around irrigated oases, growing cereals, cotton and fruit, and rearing karakul lambs. Apart from astrakhan rugs and food processing, industry is largely confined to mining sulphur and salt and the production of natural gas. The latter is crucial to the economy: Turkmenistan is the second biggest producer in the CIS after Russia, accounting for almost 11% of the total output.

Dependent on trade with other former Soviet republics for more than 75% of its GDP – and much of that subsidized – Turkmenistan is still a one-party state and ill-equipped for democratic nationhood. Since declaring independence in October 1991 it has looked south to the Muslim countries rather than to the CIS for support – like its Turkic associates, Azerbaijan and Uzbekistan, it has joined the Economic Co-operation Organization formed by Turkey, Iran and Pakistan in 1985 – and its future links with Iran would appear strong; Ashkhabad, the capital, lies only 40 km [25 mls] from the frontier.

Projects on exporting gas through pipelines to Turkey are mooted, with Iran and Russia vying for alternative routes. But while Western multinational companies were winning contracts exploiting natural resources, Turkish entrepreneurs (often with help from Ankara) were building sugar factories, bakeries and trading centres to broaden the economic base and increase purchasing power ∎

KIRGHIZIA

Despite its geographical isolation on the borders of China's Xinjiang province, its mainly mountainous terrain and its conventionally strong links with Moscow, Kirghizia has pursued very aggressive, 'European' policies towards Western-style capitalist democracy in the period since independence was declared in August 1991. It has also established good relations with China, a suspicious neighbour and potential foe. However, the large Russian minority (in positions of power under the Soviet regime), disenchanted Uzbeks and an influx of Chinese Muslims have the potential for an ethnic tinderbox.

Kirghizia has a strong agricultural economy. Much of the lower land is pasture for sheep, pigs, cattle, goats, horses and yaks – pastoralism is the traditional livelihood of the Mongoloid Kirghiz, though few nomads remain – while irrigated land produces a wide range of crops from sugar beet and vegetables to rice, cotton, tobacco, grapes and mulberry trees (for silkworms). The main manufacturing industry is textiles ■

TAJIKISTAN

The smallest of the five Central Asian CIS republics, Tajikistan lies on the borders of Afghanistan and China. Only 7% of the country is below 1,000 m [3,280 ft] and the eastern half is almost all above 3,000 m [9,840 ft]. In the north-west the limited agricultural land is irrigated for wheat, cotton, fruit, vegetables and mulberry trees (for silkworms), and there is a thriving electro-chemical industry.

Tajikistan, however, was the poorest of the Soviet republics, heavily subsidized by Moscow, and independence (declared in September 1991) brought huge economic problems. The Tajiks are a Persian people, and with a population 95% Muslim the country was the most likely of the Central Asian republics to follow the Islamic fundamentalism of Iran rather than the secular, pro-Western model proffered by Turkey. Judged by the ethnic violence of 1990, the large Uzbek and Russian minorities are unlikely to agree; some 20,000 people died in the civil war that followed an Islamic insurrection in 1992, and Russian troops guard an uneasy state of emergency ■

A Tajik peasant passes a pond, its guardian trees whitewashed to reduce traffic accidents. His newly independent country is the highest, poorest and most Islamic of the 15 former republics of the Soviet Union.

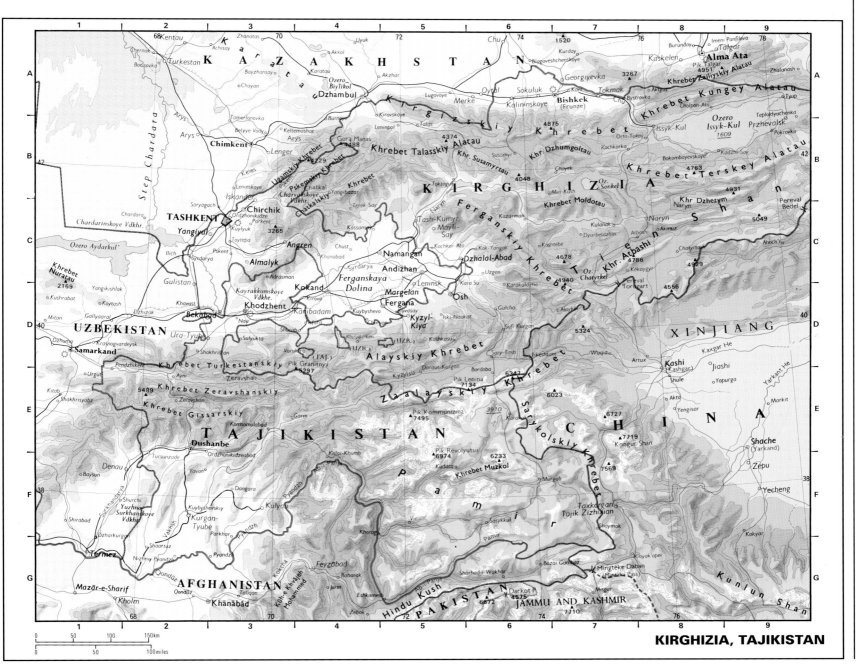

KIRGHIZIA, TAJIKISTAN

TURKEY

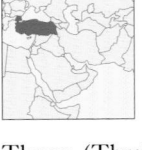

The most populous country in south-west Asia, Turkey comprises the broad peninsula of Asia Minor, together with its 'roots' around Lake Van, and in Europe that part of Thrace (Thraki) which lies to the east of the lower Maritsa River. The straits separating the European (5%) and Asiatic parts of Turkey have been of strategic importance for thousands of years. The Dardanelles, joining the Aegean Sea to the Sea of Marmara, are 1.6 km [1 ml] wide at their narrowest point; the Bosphorus, linking the Sea of Marmara to the Black Sea, measures just 640 m [2,100 ft] at one point and is spanned by a suspension bridge at Istanbul.

The heart of the country is the high karst plateau of Anatolia, semi-desert around the central salt lake, but mainly sheep country. The Taurus ranges afford summer grazing for the plateau flocks, and also timber. The northern Pontic ranges are better wooded, with fertile plains.

The valleys of the Gediz and Cürüksu, which open westwards from the plateau to the Aegean, export tobacco and figs, while the deltaic plain around Adana grows abundant cotton. The very high and thinly-peopled plateaus and ranges to the east of the Euphrates produce chrome, copper and oil. The small but populous district of the Hatay, including Antakya and Iskenderun, was transferred from Syria to Turkey in 1939.

Istanbul, the former imperial capital of Byzantium and Constantinople, which controls the straits between the Black Sea and the Mediterranean, is the country's chief port and commercial city, but the function of capital has been transferred to the more centrally-placed town of Ankara. Turkey, with a rapidly growing population, now has one of the best railway networks in the Middle East, and though lacking in large resources of mineral oil has built up a thriving industrial economy based on imported oil, on coal (from Zonguldak), and above all on hydro-electric power. Though still important, agriculture has been overtaken by manufacturing, particularly textiles and clothing.

History and politics

Constantinople's huge Ottoman Empire had been in decline for centuries when alliance with Germany in World War I ended in the loss of all non-Turkish areas. Nationalists led by Mustafa Kemal – known later as Atatürk ('father of the Turks') – rejected peace proposals favouring Greece and after a civil war set up a republic. Turkey's present frontiers were established in 1923, when Atatürk became president, and until 1938 he ruled as a virtual dictator, secularizing and modernizing the traditional Islamic state.

Between 1960 and 1970 the government was overthrown three times by military coups; civilian rule returned in 1983 and since then democracy has been relatively stable, though the country's human rights record remained more Third World than Western European. In June 1993, Turkey's first woman prime minister, Tansu Ciller, was elected.

The economic progress that partnered political stability in the mid-1980s – growth averaged more than 7% a year – encouraged Turkey to apply for EEC membership in 1987, but the response from Brussels was unenthusiastic. Turkey's disputes with Greece – notably over Ankara's invasion of northern Cyprus in 1974, but also over claims to territory and mineral rights in the Aegean – plus the country's poor human rights record, policy over the Kurdish rebels and still-low standard of living were all factors. While Turkey has been a NATO member since 1952, this was likely to remain the EU's position.

Situated at one of the world's great geopolitical crossroads, the nation seemed destined to remain sandwiched between Europe and the Middle East. Turkey nevertheless has a two-way traffic in people with Western Europe: while tourism was a boom industry in the late 1980s (often at the expense of Greece), with 2.5 million visitors a year visiting the country, these were outnumbered by Turkish men working (or seeking work) in EU cities, the majority of them in Germany ∎

The view across Halic (the Golden Horn) to the Mosque of Suleiman the Magnificent on one of Istanbul's seven hills. The city is the only one to lie in two continents.

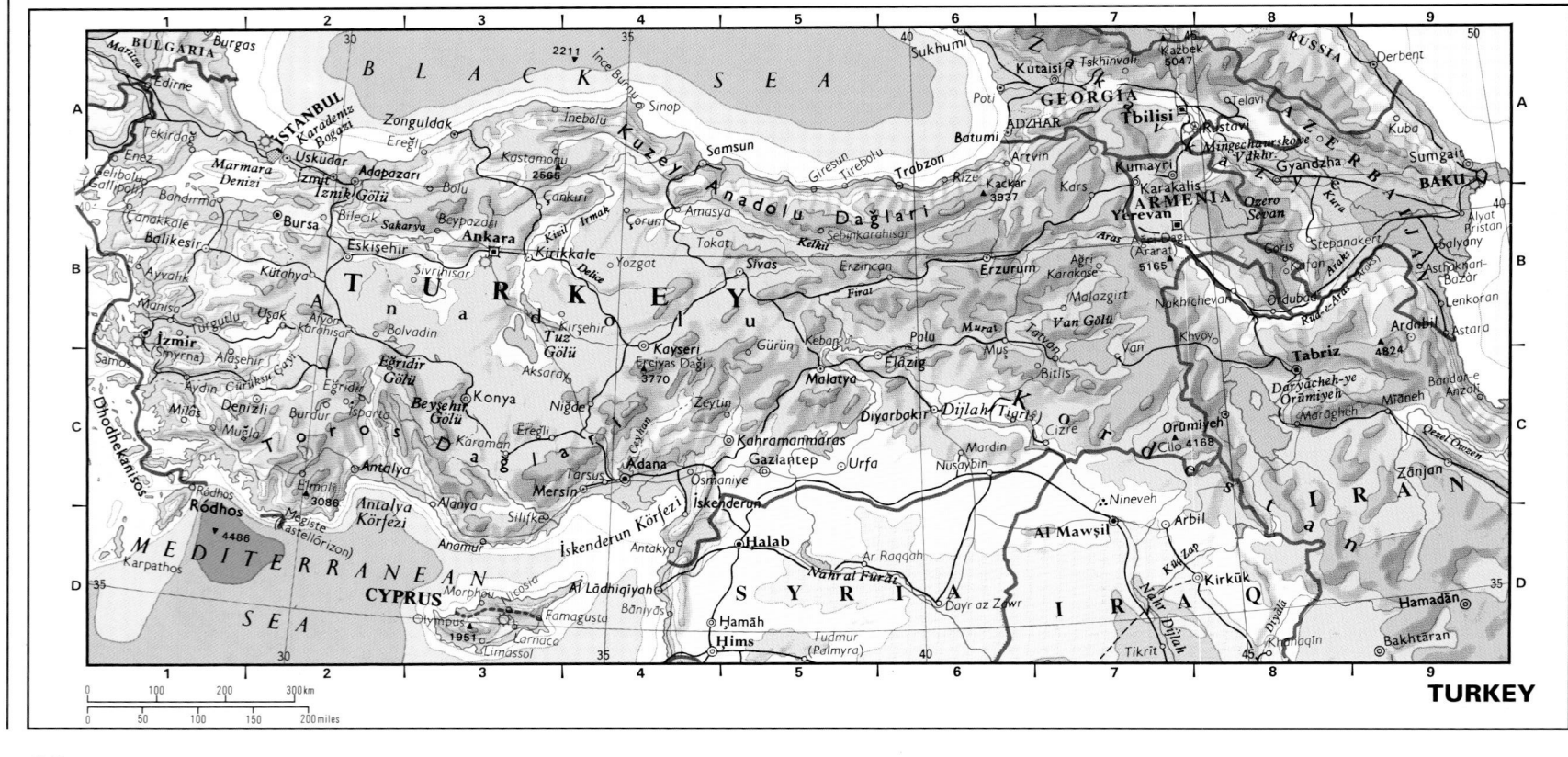

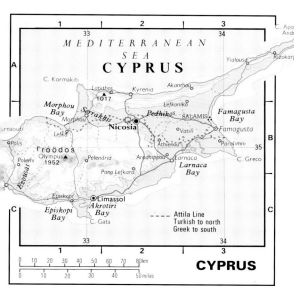

CYPRUS

CYPRUS

A small but strategically situated Mediterranean island, Cyprus is a detached fragment of the mainland mountains to the east. In the south, the broad massif of Troödos, rich in minerals, is a classic example of an ophiolite, or intrusive dome of ancient suboceanic rocks. The northern coast is backed by the long limestone range of Kyrenia. The central plain between Morphou and Famagusta is fertile and well irrigated and grows fruits, flowers and early vegetables. The former forests were cut mainly in classical times to fuel the copper smelteries; 'Kypros' is the Greek for copper.

Turks settled in the north of the island during Ottoman rule, from 1571 to 1878, when Cyprus came under British administration. In the 1950s Greek Cypriots, led by Archbishop Makarios (later President), campaigned for union with Greece (Enosis), while the Turks favoured partition. After a guerrilla campaign by EOKA a power-sharing compromise was reached and in 1960 the island became a republic.

This fragile arrangement broke down in 1963, however, and the following year the UN sent in forces to prevent more intercommunal fighting. In 1968 the Turkish Cypriots set up an 'autonomous administration' in the north, but in 1974, following a coup by Greek-born army officers that deposed Makarios, Turkey invaded the mainland and took control of the northern 40% of the country, displacing 200,000 Greek Cypriots. The UN has since supervised an uneasy partition of the island.

During nearly two decades when all attempts at federation have failed, the Greek Cypriot sector has prospered from tourism, British bases, invisible earnings and specialized agriculture, as well as increased manufacturing. The more agriculturally based north has done rather less well: the 'Turkish Republic of Northern Cyprus' is recognized only by Ankara and relies heavily on financial aid from Turkey.

In return the north has welcomed immigrants to the point where Turks outnumber Turkish Cypriots, fuelling Greek Cypriot fears of domination. The two communities remain bitterly split and mutually suspicious, and a UN plan for federation – moving the existing 190 km [118 ml] 'green line' further north in places – was rejected in 1992 by the Turkish Cypriot leader Rauf Denktash. With the fall of the Berlin Wall, Nicosia and its UN-patrolled buffer zone retained the dubious distinction of being the world's last divided capital ∎

Plastic sheeting and rubber gloves aid the harvest on the fertile central plain of Cyprus near Famagusta, close to the partition line which since 1974 has divided the Greek and Turkish communities – but south of the border proposed by the UN in 1992.

LEBANON

For three decades after its independence from the French mandate in 1944 Lebanon was a relatively peaceful and prosperous country by Middle East standards. An association with France going back a century – before that the country was part of the Ottoman Empire – had bequeathed a distinct Gallic flavour, though with so many racial and religious groups the population was truly cosmopolitan; Beirut, the dominant city, was both a centre of international commerce (the Lebanese are descendants of the Phoenicians, legendary traders and businessmen) and an elegant playground of the wealthy.

All that changed suddenly after March 1975 when this beautiful country saw sporadic conflict spiral into violent civil war between Christians, Muslims and Druses. The complex politics of the next 14 years proved almost unfathomable as Lebanon sank into a seemingly permanent state of ungovernable chaos. Bombing, assassination and kidnapping became routine as numerous factions and private militias –

Maronite, Druse, Sunni and Shia groups (including fundamentalists backed by Iran) – fought for control. The situation was complicated by a succession of interventions by Palestinian liberation organizations, Israeli troops, the Syrian Army, Western and then UN forces, as the country became a patchwork of occupied zones and 'no-go' areas.

The core religious confrontation has deep roots: in 1860 thousands of Maronites (aligned to the Catholic Church) were murdered by Druses (so tangential to other Islamic sects that they are now not regarded as Muslims), and Muslim tolerance of Christian power after independence lasted only until 1958. Though not directly involved, Lebanon was destabilized by the Arab-Israeli War of 1967, and the exile of the PLO leadership to Beirut in 1970. By 1990 the Syrian Army had crushed the two-year revolt of Christian rebels against the Lebanese government, but peace proved fragile and a solution elusive: at the start of 1994 Israel still occupied the south of the country (claimed to be a base for Palestinian terrorists and garrisoned by the proxy South Lebanese Army), while the fundamentalist Hezbollah still controlled much of the Beqaa Valley in the north – and with it the lucrative crops of opium and marijuana that fund their operations ∎

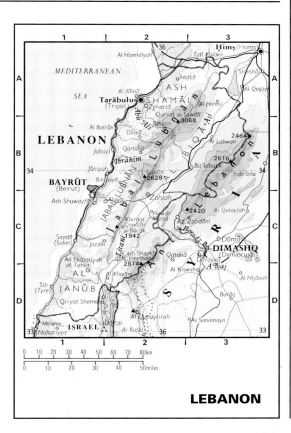

LEBANON

ISRAEL

In 1948 the new Jewish state of Israel comprised the coastal plain, the vale of Esdraelon (Jezreel) behind Haifa, the foothills in the south, most of the hill country of Samaria, and half of Jerusalem with a corridor to the west. It was also the intention of the UN that Israel should acquire either Galilee in the north or the Negev Desert in the south, but in the event both were included.

In general, the country is most fertile in the north, and becomes progressively more desert-like towards the south. The object of the Jordan–Western Negev scheme, the most ambitious of Israel's irrigation enterprises, has been to direct through canals and culverts all the water that can be spared from the Upper Jordan and the streams and drainage channels of the coastal plain southwards to the deserts of the Negev.

In the north of Israel, Galilee is rolling hill country with good rainfall and a rich black soil weathered from basalt. Both here and in the hills of Judaea, new pine-woods have been established to fix the soil and hold the water. The Upper Jordan Valley is excellent farmland, reclaimed from the swamps of Lake Huleh. The valley of Jezreel, with a deep alluvial soil washed down from Galilee, is intensively tilled with market gardens. South of the promontory of Carmel, the coastal plain of Sharon is excellent fruit-growing country, but needs irrigation, especially in its southern stretches. Here the drifting dunes have been fixed with grass and tamarisk and reclaimed for pasture.

Israel has become the most industrialized country in the Near East. Iron is smelted at Haifa and converted to steel at the foundries of Acre. Chemicals are manufactured at Haifa and at plants by the Dead Sea. With the aid of a national electricity grid, factories for textiles, ceramics and other products have been widely established in country towns, including the new foundations of Dimona and Mizpe Ramon in the Negev.

Elat on the Gulf of Aqaba is an increasingly successful tourist town and Israel's sea outlet to Africa and most of Asia. From here, a pipeline takes imported oil to the refinery at Haifa. To supplement the facilities of Haifa, Israel built a deep-sea port at Ashdod to replace the old anchorage at Jaffa (Yafo). Despite the 1993 accord with the PLO, Israel remains vulnerable on many fronts: reliance on US aid, continued terrorism over Palestine, huge defence spending, lack of natural resources, and a massive influx of immigrants, often overqualified and notably now from the former Soviet republics. For the Jewish state, however, little of this is anything new. ■

The inhospitable environment of the Negev Desert has not deterred Jewish settlers from searching for their own promised land. South of the Be'er Sheva, new towns mine oil, copper and phosphates, factories use the potash and salt of the Dead Sea, and experimental farms explore methods of raising hot-weather crops.

JERUSALEM

Although it is held sacred by all three great monotheisms, Jerusalem's religious importance has brought the city little peace. King David's capital in the 11th century BC, with the building of the Temple of Solomon, it became the cult centre of Judaism. The Temple was destroyed by the Assyrians and rebuilt in the 6th century, reassuming its importance until AD 70, when Jerusalem was destroyed by Roman legions during the Jewish Revolt against the Empire. Later, a rebuilt Jerusalem became a centre of Christian pilgrimage. In the 7th century it was captured by the armies of Islam, and for Muslims, too, Jerusalem (al-Quds in Arabic) is also a holy place: it was visited by Mohammed during the 'Night Journey', as told in the Koran, and Muslims believe that it was from Jerusalem that the Prophet ascended to paradise. The mosque known as the Dome of the Rock was built on the site of the Jewish Temple.

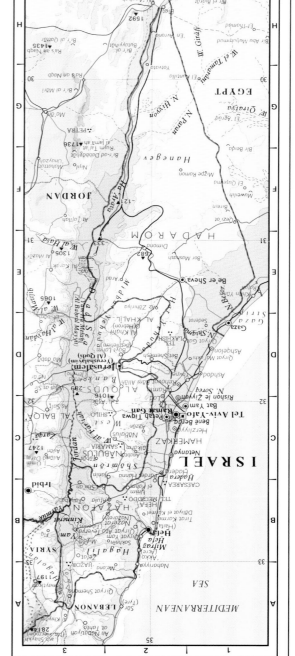

THE MIDDLE EAST CONFLICT

Modern Arab-Jewish hostility in the Middle East dates from the so-called Balfour Declaration of 1917, when an embattled British government proposed a 'Jewish national home' in the then Turkish imperial province of Palestine without prejudicing the 'existing rights' of the overwhelmingly Arab (Christian and Muslim) population. After World War I, Palestine became a League of Nations mandate under British control; throughout the 1920s, a trickle of Jewish immigrants inspired rioting without noticeably affecting the population balance. But the rise of Nazism in Europe brought floods of Jewish refugees, and Arab-Jewish violence became endemic.

In 1947 the recently formed United Nations proposed a formal partition of the land, accepted by the Jews and rejected by the Palestinians. Even before the British announced they would withdraw in May 1948, 150,000 Arab refugees had already fled.

On 14 May, the day the British quit, the independence of a new State of Israel was declared. Egypt, Lebanon, Syria, Transjordan and Iraq at once launched an invasion, later joined by Yemen and Saudi Arabia. By the 1949 ceasefire, however, Israel controlled more territory than the UN partition plan had allocated the Jews. Jerusalem remained a divided city, half controlled by Israel,

half by the armies of Trans-jordan, later the kingdom of Jordan.

An uneasy peace descended, with sporadic border clashes; hundreds of thousands of Palestinians lost their homes. In 1956, full-scale war erupted once more when Israel joined with Britain and France in an attack on Egypt. Egypt's armies were badly mauled, but Israel's borders remained unchanged. In 1967, Israel responded to an Egyptian maritime blockade – and public threats from Syria and Egypt – with a pre-emptive strike that left it in control of the Sinai peninsula and the Gaza Strip (Egypt), the 'West Bank' of the Jordan and all of Jerusalem (Jordan), and the Golan Heights (Syria). But Israeli battle skills brought real peace no nearer: instead, Israel had acquired (along with the newly occupied territories) an Arab population of several million. Palestinian freedom fighters – 'terrorists' to their enemies – began a worldwide campaign, including aircraft hijacking and mostly counter-productive, to broadcast their people's plight.

A 1973 Egyptian attack across the Suez Canal, backed by Syria, came close to over-running Sinai, but Israeli counter-attacks recovered much of the lost territory. Egypt's partial victory eventually led to the Camp David accord of 1979, by which Israel returned Sinai in exchange for Egyptian recogni-

tion of Israel's right to exist. Egypt was excoriated by its former Arab allies, and Palestinian terrorism continued. Between 1982 and 1985 Israeli forces were heavily engaged in Lebanon, seeking to destroy Palestinian bases at heavy cost to the Lebanese people. Israeli settlements began to proliferate in the occupied territories, provoking, from 1987 onwards, a low-intensity Palestinian uprising – the *intifada* – which Israel repressed by increasingly brutal methods. Meanwhile, Israel (backed by US aid) continued to flaunt UN resolutions over withdrawal.

The situation changed dramatically in August 1993 with a peace agreement brokered by Norway. The PLO would recognize Israel's right to exist in return for autonomy in Gaza and Jericho, with a view to ultimate self-rule in all the occupied territories. The deal, sealed in Washington on 13 September by PLO chairman Yasser Arafat and Israeli Prime Minister Yitzhak Rabin, received support from almost all Arab states, but opposition from extremists was inevitable, whether Palestinian terrorist organizations like Hamas or Zionist hardliners, including many settlers. In May 1994, however, the two leaders finally signed the pact granting self-rule to Palestinians in Gaza and Jericho, thereby implementing the first step in the complex accord.

SYRIA

The northern part of the former Ottoman province of the same name, Syria stretches from the Mediterranean to the Tigris, and from the southern edge of the Kurdish plateau in the north to the heart of the Hamad or stony desert in the south. The northern border for most of its length follows the railway from Aleppo to Mosul (part of the old Berlin-Baghdad line). Syria has only one large harbour, at Latakia, though the country usually enjoys privileged access to the ports of Lebanon.

The Orontes River flows northwards along the great rift valley, through alternating gorges and wide valleys which have been reclaimed by drainage and irrigation. Near Hamā and Hims the ranges of Lebanon and Anti-Lebanon, which flank the valley to west and east, are relatively low, but further south the Anti-Lebanon rises to the Heights of Hermon, whose snows water the gardens of the capital, Damascus, on the eastern or desert side. In the far south, by the frontier with Jordan, the volcanic mass of Mount Hauran supports a group of oases around the town of Suwayda. The Golan Heights, in the south-west, are occupied by Israel.

Aleppo, the second city of Syria, is set in a well-watered agricultural area. Further east the steppe becomes progressively drier. This was traditionally winter pasture for the nomads who moved in from their summer homes in the mountains of Lebanon, but in recent years, thanks to techniques of dry-farming with machinery, it has become a prosperous farming zone, devoted almost exclusively to cotton and cereals. The water from the Euphrates barrage, which produces 70% of the country's electricity, will extend agriculture in this region.

Syria has struck oil in the 'panhandle' by the

Tigris in the far north-east, and a pipeline has been laid from there to the Mediterranean. Another pipeline crosses the desert further south from the Kirkuk fields in Iraq to the sea-terminal at Baniyas.

President Assad's repressive but stable regime, in power since 1970, was heavily reliant on Arab aid, but Syria's anti-Iraq stance in the 1991 Gulf War will almost certainly result in greater Western assistance to the improving economy. Though small compared to Egypt or Saudi Arabia, Syria's position (both historical and geographical) makes the country a key player in the complicated power game of Middle East politics ■

A selection of spices on sale at Hamā. While Syria's exports are industrial (oil, gas, chemicals, textiles), its agriculture is still crucial – but Turkey controls the vital flow of the Euphrates with the Ataturk Dam.

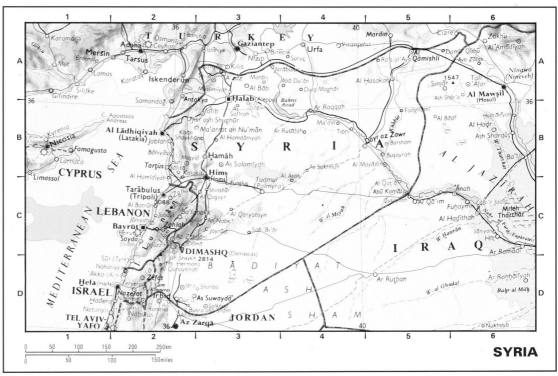

SYRIA

JORDAN

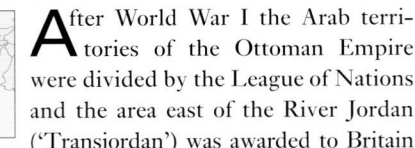

After World War I the Arab territories of the Ottoman Empire were divided by the League of Nations and the area east of the River Jordan ('Transjordan') was awarded to Britain as part of Palestine, becoming a separate emirate in 1923. When the mandate ended in 1946 the kingdom became independent, as Jordan, and two years later (in the first Arab-Israeli War) it acquired the West Bank, which was officially incorporated into the state in 1950.

This crucial area, including Arab Jerusalem, was lost to Israel in the 1967 war, and Jordan has since carried the burden of Palestinian refugees on its own limited territory. In the 1970s the guerrillas using Jordan as a base became a challenge to the authority of King Hussein's government, and after a short civil war the Palestinian leadership fled the country. In 1988 Hussein renounced all responsibility for the West Bank – a recognition that the PLO and not Jordan was the legitimate Palestinian representative.

Palestinians nevertheless still formed a majority of the population; Jordan sustains some 900,000 refugees (nearly half the total), a figure which puts an intolerable burden on an already weak economy. Jordan is not blessed with the natural resources enjoyed by some Middle East countries – whether oil or water – and a limited agricultural base is supported by mining of phosphates and potash, the main exports.

The country's position was further undermined by the 1991 Gulf War, when despite official neutrality the pro-Iraq, anti-Western stance of the Palestinians did nothing to improve prospects of trade and aid deals with Europe and the US, Jordan's vital economic links with Iraq having already been severed. Another factor was the expulsion and return of large numbers of Palestinians and Jordanians from crucial jobs in Kuwait, Saudi Arabia and other wealthy Gulf states.

There were, however, signs of political progress: in 1991 the ban on political parties was removed and martial law was lifted after 21 years; and November 1994 saw the first multiparty elections since 1956 ∎

The spectacular sandstone remains of Petra, the 'rose-red city' founded around 1000 BC, constitute Jordan's most important tourist attraction.

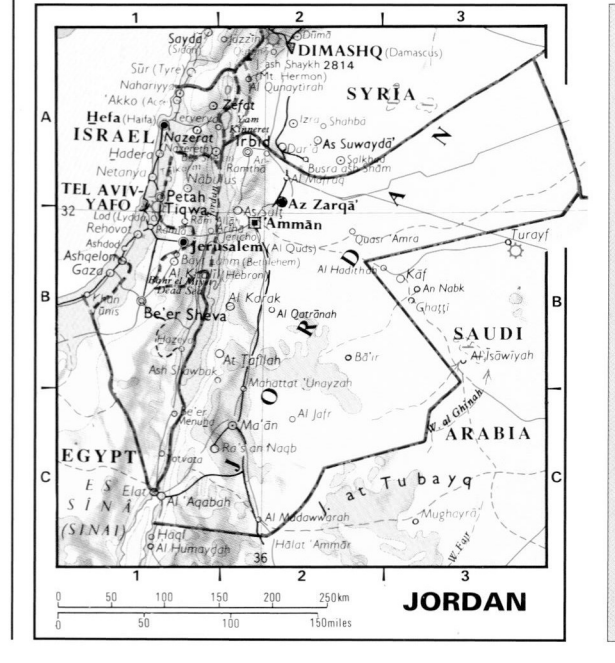

JORDAN

THE PALESTINIANS
The modern history of the Palestinians began in 1948, when the birth of Israel transformed most of their former territory into a foreign state; some 700,000 fled, most to refugee camps in Jordan, Lebanon and Egypt's Gaza Strip. After the 'Six Day War' in 1967, most Palestinians not already refugees found themselves living under enemy occupation. Since 1964, the Palestine Liberation Organization has existed to free them by 'armed struggle', but the PLO's adoption of international terrorism as a tactic alienated many potential allies, as did their alliance with Saddam Hussein during the 1991 Gulf War. It was not until the unexpected peace agreement between the PLO and Israel was signed in September 1993 that long-term autonomy became a future possibility. These hopes were strengthened by the granting of Palestinian self-rule in Gaza and Jericho by Israel in May 1994. Millions of Palestinian refugees do still remain in camps.

SAUDI ARABIA

During and shortly after World War I, the Saudis of Najd (central Arabia) extended their territory at the expense of the Rashidis and Hashemites, and consolidated their control over the greater part of the Arabian peninsula, including the holy cities of Mecca (Makkah) and Medina (Al Madinah). The frontiers with neighbours to the south and east remained ill-defined, but this mattered little until its vast reserves of oil (the world's largest) were tapped after World War II; since then some disputes have been settled, notably the division of the Gulf-shore Neutral Zone with Kuwait.

The heart of the state – the largest in the Middle East but over 95% desert – consists of the province of Najd, within which are three main groups of oases. Najd is enclosed on its east side by a vast arc of sandy desert which broadens out into the two great dune-seas of Arabia, the Nafud in the north, and in the south the Rub 'al Khali, or 'Empty Quarter', the largest expanse of sand in the world. Here are found most of the country's Bedouin nomads, still deriving a living as traders and herdsmen.

To the west, Najd is separated from the border hills of the Red Sea by fields of rough basaltic lava. Particularly in its southern section towards the border with Yemen, this coastal strip is quite well supplied with water, and a high storage dam has been built inland from Jizan. The hills of Asir which back the plain here benefit from the summer monsoon, and are extensively terraced to grow grain and orchard trees. For the most part, however, lack of water is a big problem. Saudi Arabia relies heavily on desalination and has the world's biggest plants on the Gulf.

The eastern province, by the shores of the Gulf, is known as the Hasa. Near its chief city of Hufuf in particular, the long underground seepage of water from the Hijaz, the western mountains, breaks out in the artesian springs of the oases. This region contains the country's great oilfields including Ghawar, the world's largest. The oil port of Az Zahran is linked with Riyadh by the only railway; asphalt roads and air travel are the country's main means of transport.

The world's third largest producer and biggest exporter of oil – a position extended by the limits on Kuwait and Iraq from 1991 – Saudi Arabia used the enormous revenues (peaking at more than US$100 billion a year after the 400% price hikes of 1973) to launch a colossal industrial and domestic development programme: some $250 billion was spent on the plan for 1980–5, requiring over a million foreign workers. A strictly Muslim society suddenly boasted some of the most advanced architecture and cultural facilities in the world, as well as introducing an array of social and educational benefits.

Progress has not always been smooth. In the mid-1980s world oil prices slumped dramatically, disrupting many of the projects begun in the boom years. Meanwhile, expenditure on defence is high even by the profligate standards of the region. The country's position as the West's staunchest Middle East ally has often conflicted with its role as the guardian of Islam's most holy places and despite large donations to the poorer Arab nations, its commitment to their cherished cause of a Palestinian state has at times appeared relatively weak ∎

MECCA

The holiest city of Islam, Mecca was an important centre of pilgrimage long before the Prophet Mohammed was born. Its chief sanctuary, then as now, was the Ka'ba, a square building housing a remarkable and much venerated black stone of probable meteoric origin, said to have been given to the patriarch Abraham by the Archangel Gabriel.

In 632, shortly before his death, the Prophet undertook his own final pilgrimage to the city; the pilgrimage to Mecca – the Hajj – remains the fifth of the Five Pillars of Islam, and every Muslim is expected to make it at least once in a lifetime. Mecca is also part of the Second Pillar, the duty of prayer, for it is towards the Ka'ba (*left*, now enclosed by Mecca's Great Mosque) that the world's Muslims face five times daily when they pray.

Mecca's chief business remains the Hajj, with upwards of 1.5 million pilgrims visiting annually. Non-Muslims (infidels) are to this day excluded from the city.

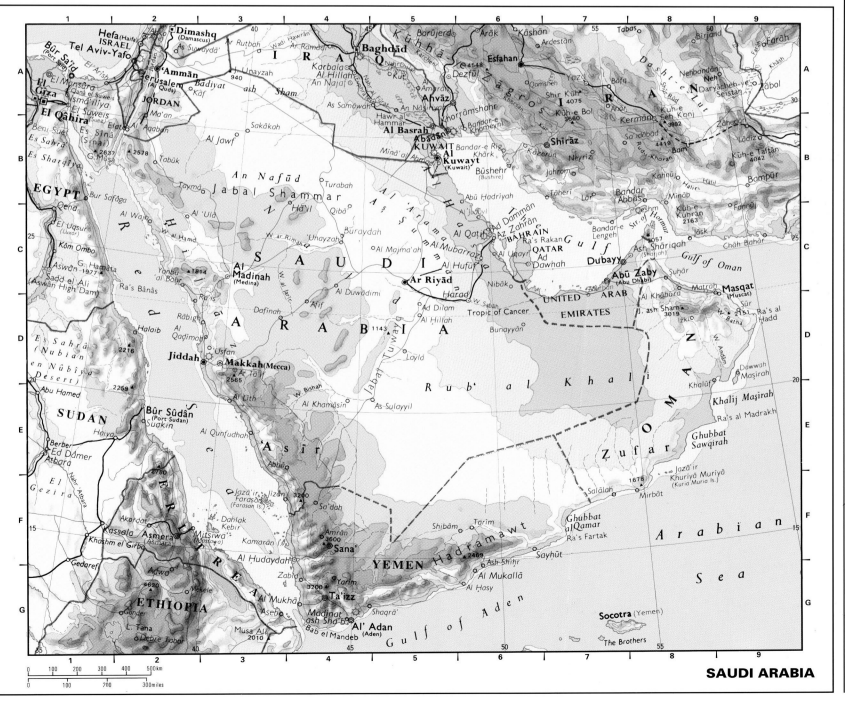

KUWAIT

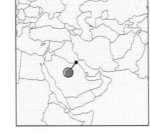

The impressive if unevenly distributed prosperity built by the ruling Sabah family in Kuwait since oil was first commercially produced in 1946 was suddenly and brutally undermined by the Iraqi invasion of 1990. Occupying troops were soon expelled by a US-led multinational force – but not before they had set fire to more than 500 oil-wells (causing unprecedented pollution) and destroyed almost all industrial and commercial installations.

Kuwait's revenge over the devastation was directed mainly at the many Palestinian, Jordanian and Yemeni immigrant workers (seen as pro-Iraq) on whom the economic progress of the country had been founded since independence in 1961. Reconstruction for this former British protectorate was expected to cost hundreds of billions of dollars, using chiefly American rather than European companies. Predictably, in a country with virtually no meaningful agricultural activity, oil would be the key to recovery ∎

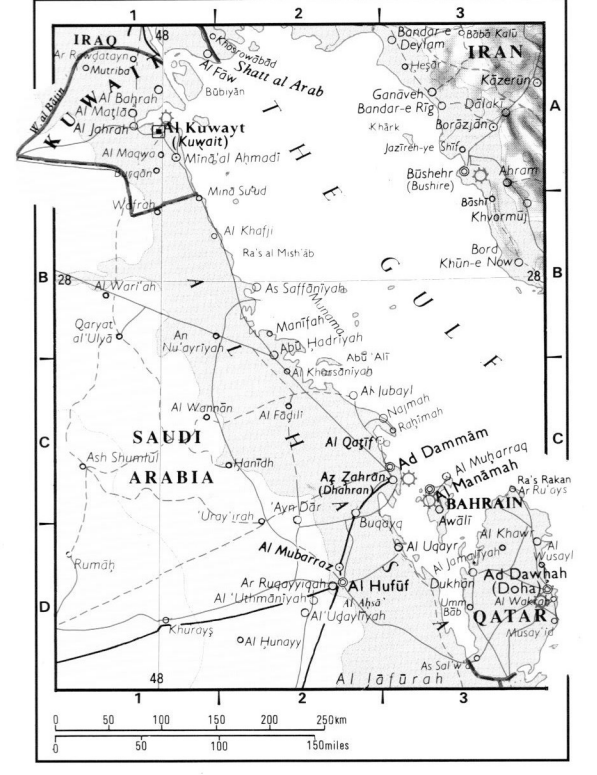

BAHRAIN

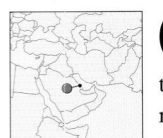

Comprising 35 small islands, by far the largest of them called Bahrain, this relatively liberal state led the region in developing oil production after discovery in 1932. When production waned in the 1970s it diversified into other sectors: its aluminium-smelting plant is the Gulf's largest non-oil industrial complex, and the moves into banking, communications and leisure came when the cosmopolitan centre of Beirut was plunging into chaos. Banking now accounts for some 15% of GDP, while oil takes as much as 20% – though far more of government revenues. Most of the land is barren, but soil imports have created some fertile areas.

Bahrain does have problems, however. Tension between the Sunni and majority Shiite population (the latter favouring an Islamic republic) has been apparent since before independence, and during the First Gulf War Iran responded to Bahrain's support for Iraq by reiterating its claims to the territory ∎

QATAR

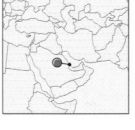

Occupying a low, barren peninsula on the Persian Gulf, the former British protectorate of Qatar derives its high standard of living from oil and gas. Despite diversification into cement, steel and fertilizers, these still account for over 80% of revenues, and gas reserves are enormous.

The economy of the country (and many institutions) is heavily dependent on the immigrant workforce, notably from the Indian subcontinent and poorer Middle East states ∎

Kuwaiti dhows proudly fly the national flag. Fishing provides a crucial food supplement for the poor of the arid states bordering the Gulf.

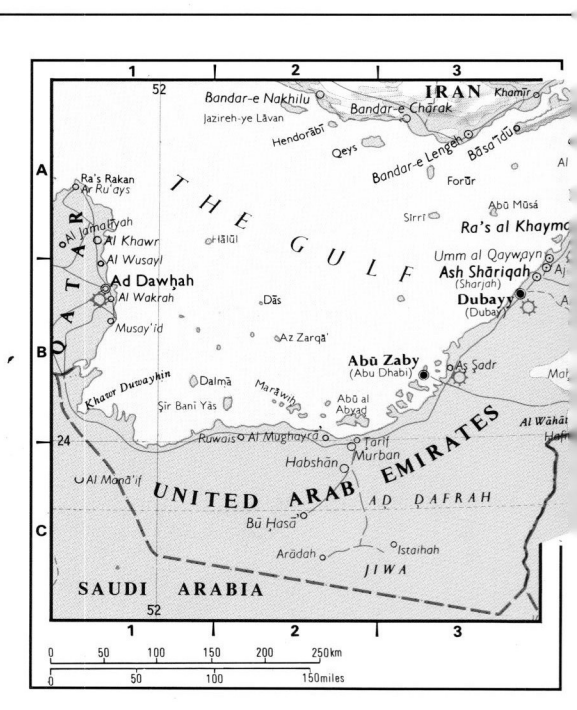

The wealthy élites of the Gulf states wager vast sums on camel races. This one is in Dubai, hub of the UAE.

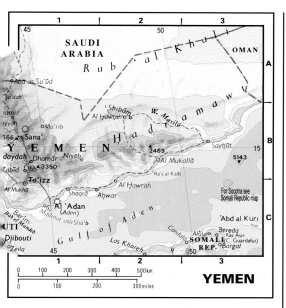

YEMEN

The optimism that greeted unification of the two Yemeni countries – the Yemen Arab Republic and the People's Democratic Republic of Yemen – in May 1990 proved short-lived; support for Iraq in the Gulf War wrought swift revenge from Iraq's Arab enemies on the ending of hostilities, with Kuwait and Saudi Arabia expelling vast numbers of Yemeni workers. This not only removed the main source of earnings for a homeland already struggling with a weak economy, but it also jeopardized hopes of much-needed foreign aid from wealthy Gulf nations and the West.

The process of marrying the disparate needs of a traditional state (an independent kingdom since 1918 and backed by the Saudis) and the failed Marxist regime based in the South Yemen capital of Aden proved difficult. In May 1994 a civil war erupted between the north and south, with President Saleh (a northerner) attempting to remove the Vice-President Ali Salem al-Beidh (a southerner) ∎

UNITED ARAB EMIRATES

In 1971 six of the seven British-run Trucial States of the Gulf – Abu Dhabi, Ajman, Dubai, Fujairah, Sharjah and Umm al-Qaiwain – opted to form the United Arab Emirates (UAE), with Ras al-Khaimah joining in 1972. It could have been a federation of nine, but Bahrain and Qatar chose independence. The country could well have been named Abu Dhabi, since it is more than six times the size of the rest put together, has the largest population and is easily the biggest oil producer. Nevertheless, the capitals of Dubai and Sharjah also contain over 250,000 people.

The UAE's oil and gas have provided the highest GNP per capita figure in Asia after Japan. However, only 20% of the population are citizens – the rest are expatriate workers – and traditional values, sustained by the control of the emirs, remain strong ∎

OMAN

Backward compared to its oil-rich Persian Gulf neighbours to the west until 1970 – when with British collusion Sultan Said was deposed by his son Qaboos – Oman has since made substantial strides, seeing an end to the civil war against Yemen-backed left-wing separatist guerrillas in the southern province of Dhofar (Zufar) and enjoying an expanding economy based on oil reserves far larger than expected when production began modestly in 1967. Petroleum now accounts for more than 90% of government revenues – and because of Oman's detached situation the industry was not hit by the lack of confidence that afflicted the Gulf states in the 1991 war. In addition, huge natural gas reserves were discovered the same year that were equal in size to all the finds of the previous two decades. There are also some copper deposits.

An absolute ruler – as his family heads have been since 1749 – Qaboos has tended to forego the usual prestigious projects so favoured by wealthy Arab leaders, in favour of social programmes. Even so, by 1989 only one in five adults of this arid, inhospitable country were literate (less than 1% of the land is cultivated), and defence and internal security were taking a large proportion of the annual budget ∎

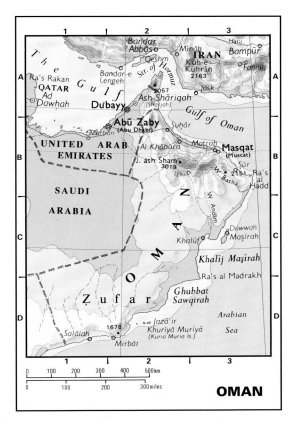

The Sultan's Palace in Muscat shines out against the old fortifications of the city. Generally, however, Oman has targeted social programmes rather than the architectural extravagances of some oil-rich emirates.

IRAQ

Absorbed into the Ottoman (Turkish) Empire in the 16th century, Iraq was captured by British forces in 1916 and after World War I became a virtual colony as a League of Nations mandated territory run by Britain. The Hashemite dynasty ruled an independent kingdom from 1932 (British occupation 1941-5), but in 1958 the royal family and premier were murdered in a military coup that set up a republic. Ten years later, after struggles between Communists and Pan-Arab Baathists, officers for the latter seized control. From 1969 the vice-president of this single-party government was Saddam Hussein, who in a peaceful transfer of power became president in 1979. The next year he invaded neighbouring Iran.

Landscape

The country includes a hilly district in the north-east, and in the west a substantial slice of the Hamad or Syrian Desert; but essentially it comprises the lower valleys and combined deltas of the Tigris and Euphrates. Rainfall is meagre, but the alluvium is fertile and productive when supplied with water. The western desert is nomad country, with good winter grazing, and from here the tribes move in summer with their flocks to the banks of the Euphrates.

The north-east of Iraq includes part of the Zagros Mountains, where fruits and grains grow without the help of irrigation. The Kirkuk oilfield is the country's oldest and largest, and nearby the Lesser Zab River has been impounded behind a high dam. The population here includes many Turks, settled in the times of Ottoman rule, and Kurdish tribes akin to those in Iran.

Upstream of Ramadi and Sāmarrā, Jazirah stands too high for irrigation, though the swamp of Tharthar is used to store the excess flow of the Euphrates through a diversionary channel from Sāmarrā. This is dry-farming country or pasture. In the north near the Syrian frontier the block mountain of Sinjar is an oasis of fertility, with an unorthodox Yezidi population (a religious sect).

Downstream of the Jazirah lies Iraq proper, the deltaic plains which, with skill and effort, can be drained and irrigated. The rivers rise rapidly in spring as the snows melt around their sources in Turkey, and are full enough for irrigation throughout the summer. Lower down, a barrage on the Euphrates at Hindiyah and another on the Tigris at Kut control canals which irrigate land reclaimed from the great swamp.

In addition to the Kirkuk oilfield, which exports by pipeline through Syria and Lebanon, there are reserves of oil near Mosul, Khanaqin and Basra. The main seaport, Basra, is connected to the Gulf by the crucial Shatt-al-Arab Waterway, shared with Iran and the ostensible cause of the First Gulf War (Iran-Iraq War).

The Gulf Wars

Supplied with financial help and arms by the West, the Soviets and conservative Arab countries, all of whom shared a fear of the new Islamic fundamentalism in Iran, Saddam amassed the fourth largest army in the world by 1980. His attack on Iran was meant to be a quick, land-grabbing, morale-boosting victory. Instead it led to an eight-year modern version of Flanders which drained Iraqi resolve (over a million men were killed or wounded, many of them fighting fellow Shiites), and nearly crippled a healthy if oil-dependent economy that had, despite colossal defence spending, financed a huge development programme in the 1970s. Even then, Iraq was still the world's sixth biggest oil producer in 1988, and Saddam's repellent regime continued to enjoy widespread support from Western countries.

If Iraq was hit by this long war, it was decimated by the Second Gulf War. In August 1990 Saddam, having accused Kuwait of wrecking Baghdad's economy by exceeding its oil quota and forcing prices

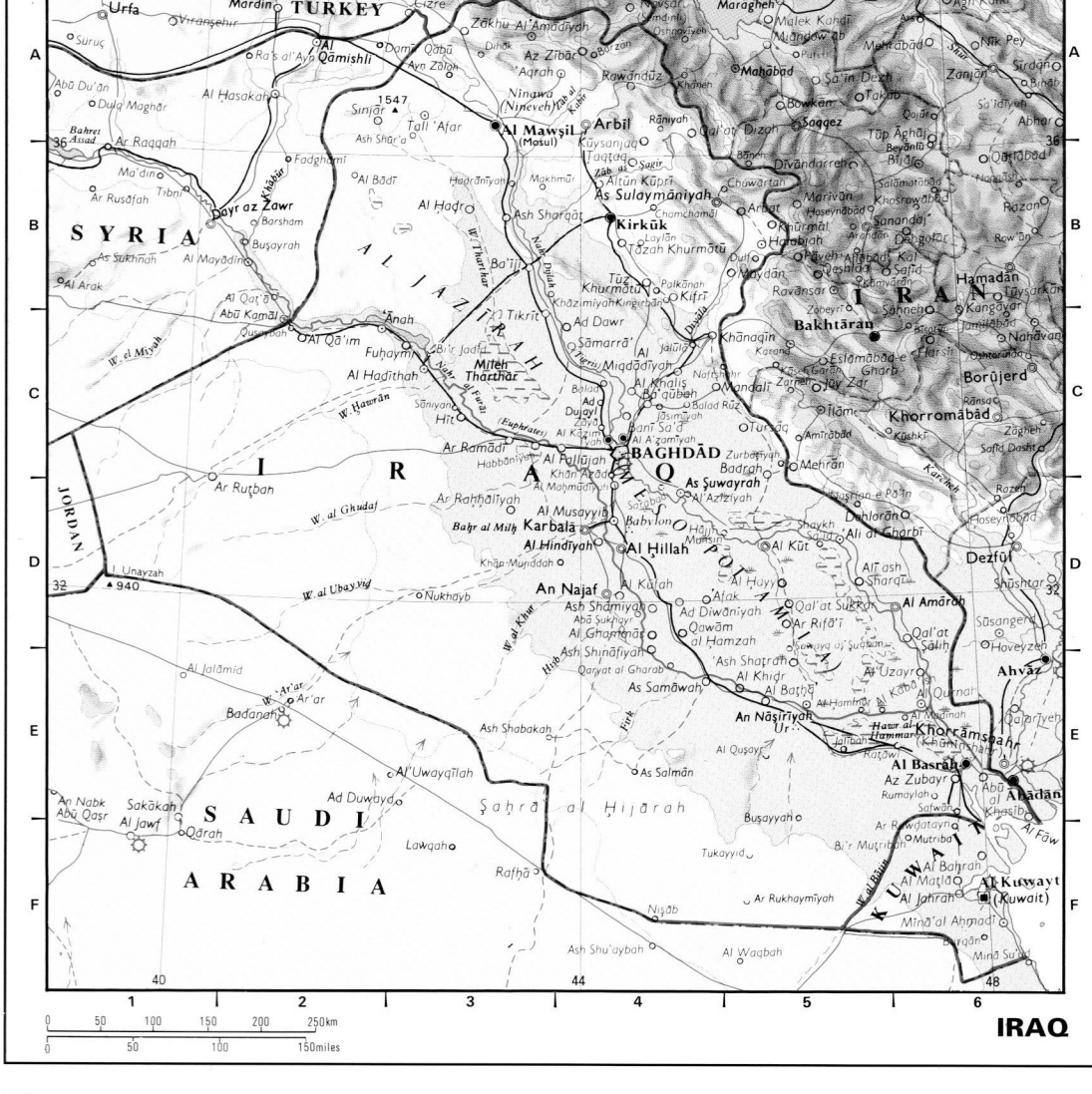

IRAQ

Shiite Marsh A'rabs have negotiated the wetlands near the Tigris for thousands of years; now the area has been systematically drained by Saddam Hussein's regime.

down, ordered the invasion of Kuwait, then annexed it as an Iraqi province. It gave him more oil and far better access to the Gulf. Unlike a decade before, the international community were almost unanimous in their condemnation of the invasion, and following the imposition of sanctions a multinational force – led by the USA but backed primarily by Britain, France and Saudi Arabia – was dispatched to the Gulf to head off possible Iraqi moves on to Saudi oilfields.

After Saddam failed to accede to repeated UN demands to withdraw his troops, the Second Gulf War began on 16 January 1991 with an Anglo-American air attack on Baghdad, and in late February a land-sea-air campaign freed Kuwait after just 100 hours, Iraq accepting all the terms of the UN ceasefire and Coalition troops occupying much of southern Iraq. This did not, however, prevent the brutal suppression of West-inspired revolts by Shiites in the south and Kurds in the north, millions of whom fled their homes. International efforts were made to help these refugees, some of whom had fled to Iran and, less successfully, to south-east Turkey.

Saddam Hussein, though surviving in power, was left an international leper in charge of a pitiful country. Much of the infrastructure had been destroyed in the war, disease was rife and food scarce, trade had virtually ceased and oil production was near a standstill. Sanctions, war damage and mismanagement have combined to cause economic chaos and personal hardship, and normal life is unlikely to return until the establishment of a regime acceptable to the rest of the international community; that, in turn, means the end of Saddam's dictatorship ■

IRAN

The most populous and productive parts of Iran lie at the four extremities – the fisheries, rice fields and tea gardens of the Caspian shore in the foothills of the earthquake zone to the north, the sugar plantations and oilfields of Khuzestan to the south (target of the Iraqi invasion in 1980), the wheat fields of Azarbayjan in the west, and the fruit groves of the oases of Khorasan and Seistan in the east. In between are the deserts of Kavir and Lut, and the border ranges which broaden in the west into the high plateaus of the Zagros, the summer retreats of the tribes of Bakhtiars and Kurds.

The cities of the interior depend on ingenious arrangements of tunnels and channels for tapping underground water, and these have been supplemented by high dams, notably at Dezful. The burgeoning capital of Tehran is the crossing-point of the country's two great railways, the Trans-Iranian from the Gulf to the Caspian and the east-west track from Mashhad to Tabriz.

Called Persia until 1935, the country retained its Shah – thanks first to British and later American support – until 1979, when the emperor's extravagantly corrupt regime (a single-party affair from 1975) was toppled by a combination of students, middle-class professionals and, above all, clerics offended by the style and pace of Westernization.

The despotism was replaced with another: that of a radical fundamentalist Islamic republic inspired by the return of exiled leader Ayatollah Khomeini. The revolution created a new threat to the conservative

Metal engravers at work in Esfahan, Iran's third largest city, in the Zagros Mountains south of Tehran.

Arabs of the Gulf and beyond, who saw it as a dangerous call to challenge the flimsy legitimacy of their own oil-rich governments.

The war with Iraq from 1980–8, when hundreds of thousands of young Shiite men died defending their homeland, left Iran's vital oil production at less than half the level of 1979 (though still seventh highest in the world and supported by the largest known gas reserves outside Russia), and the government began to court the Western powers. Its stance during the Second Gulf War and a tempering of the militant position to one of peace-broker on international issues – led by President Rafsanjani – encouraged many powers to re-establish closer links with a country whose role took on even greater significance with the Muslim republics of the former Soviet Union to the north gaining independence from Moscow in 1991 ■

THE KURDS

With between 15 and 17 million people dispersed across the territories of five countries – Turkey (8 million), Iran, Iraq, Syria and Armenia – the Kurds form the world's largest stateless nation. The 1920 Treaty of Sävres, designed to dismember the old Ottoman Empire, proposed a scheme for Kurdish independence, but it was never implemented.

Neither Arab nor Turk, the Kurds are predominantly Sunni Muslims, and in the past have provided more than their fair share of Islam's leaders: indeed, Saladin, the near-legendary nemesis of the Crusaders, was a Kurd. Now, as in the past, the Kurds are an agricultural people; many earn their living by pastoralism, a way of life that pays little attention to borders or the governments that attempt to control them. Since World War II, they have suffered consistent repression by most of their titular overlords. Turkey has regularly used armed force against the PKK Kurdish nationalists; an uprising in Iran was put down in 1979–80; and during the Iran-Iraq war of the 1980s, Iraqi forces regularly used chemical weapons – as well as more orthodox brutality – against Kurdish settlements.

The defeat of Iraqi dictator Saddam Hussein by Coalition forces in 1991 inspired another massive uprising; but Saddam's badly weakened army still proved capable of murdering Kurdish women and children on a scale that provoked a limited Western intervention and promises from Baghdad. The outcome, though, was upwards of 1.5 million Kurds living in refugee camps, with the dream of Kurdistan no nearer realization.

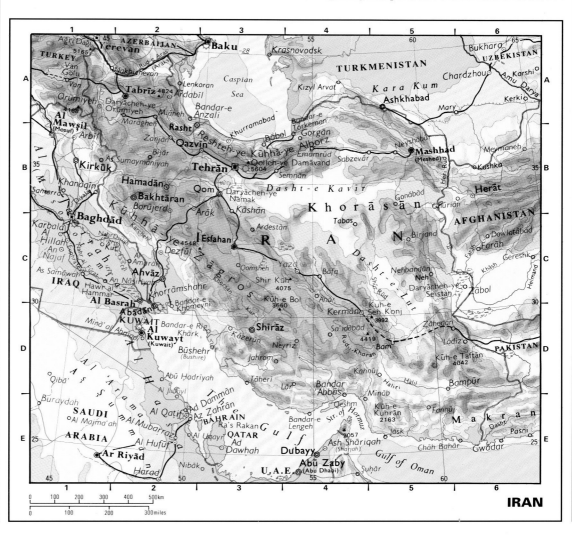

IRAN

AFGHANISTAN

Nearly three-quarters of Afghanistan is mountainous, comprising most of the Hindu Kush and its foothills, with several peaks over 6,400 m [21,000 ft], and much of the rest is desert or semi-desert. However, the restoration of the Helmand canals has brought fertility to the far south-west, and the sweet waters of the Hamun support fish and cattle; the plains of the north, near the borders with Turkmenistan, Uzbekistan and Tajikistan, yield most of the country's limited agriculture.

The most profitable crop may well be opium, from poppies grown in the hills of the Pathans adjoining Pakistan's North-West Frontier province. With the Islamic Revolution in Iran and the crackdown in the 'Golden Triangle' of Laos, Burma and Thailand, Pakistan became the world's biggest source of heroin (the derivative drug); but while US pressure saw the Pakistani government start to control production on its side of the border, it could do little to stem the flow from Afghanistan – a prime source of revenue for the Mujaheddin's fight against occupying Soviet forces in the 1980s.

Landlocked Afghanistan has always been in a critical position in Asia: the Khyber Pass was both the gateway to India and the back door to Russia. Since earliest times it has been invaded by Persians, Greeks, Arabs, Mongols, Tartars and the British, who finally failed in their attempts to create a buffer state between India and Russia and bowed to Afghan independence after the 'Third Afghan War' in 1921. The latest invaders, entering the country on Christmas Day 1979, were 80,000 men of the Soviet army.

The Russian forces were sent in support of a Kremlin-inspired coup that removed a revolutionary council set up after the ousting of the pro-Soviet government of Mohammed Daud Khan. Killed in that 1978 coup – the Saur Revolution – Daud Khan had been in power since 1953, first as prime minister and then, after he toppled the monarchy in 1972, as founder, president and prime minister of a fiercely pro-Soviet single-party republic.

The Saur Revolution and subsequent Soviet occupation led to a bitter and protracted civil war, the disparate Muslim tribes uniting behind the banner of the Mujaheddin ('holy warriors') to wage an unrelenting guerrilla war financed by the US and oiled with the co-operation of Pakistan. Despite their vastly superior weaponry and resources, the Soviet forces found it impossible to control the mountain-based rebels in a country the size of Texas, and Afghanistan quickly threatened to turn into an unwinnable war.

President Gorbachev began moves to end the conflict soon after coming to power in 1985, and in 1988 a ceasefire was agreed involving both Afghanistan and Pakistan, its main overt ally. In February 1989 the Soviet troops withdrew, leaving the cities in the hands of the pro-Moscow government and the countryside under the control of the Mujeheddin; the civil war intensified, however, fuelled by internecine and traditional feuds as well as the battle for the country's government, before a fragile ceasefire was agreed in 1991 with a view to talks the following year. The chances were, nevertheless, that the divisions would remain, that the nation would return to its familiar patchwork pattern of feuding tribal fiefdoms, with little control over the countryside being exercised from Kabul.

The war, which cost over a million Afghanis their lives, left what was an already impoverished state almost totally crippled. Before the Soviet invasion Afghanistan had one of the world's poorest records for infant mortality, literacy, women's rights and a host of other measurements, but the occupation also reduced the economy to ruins. Before the 1978 Marxist revolution Afghans abroad sent home remittances worth some US$125 million, and tourism brought in about US$50 million; now all that had gone. Based on natural gas, exports were not helped by the decision of the USSR to cap the wells in 1989.

The greatest problem, however, was the one of refugees. Some 2 million people had moved into crowded cities and towns to avoid the Russian shelling, but far more – somewhere between 3 million and 5 million by most accounts, but nearer 6 million altogether, predominantly to Pakistan. This latter estimate, the UN stated in 1990, was around 42% of the entire world total of displaced persons. In the spring of 1992, after a prolonged onslaught by the Mujaheddin, the government in Kabul finally surrendered, bequeathing an uncertain future.

The continuing factional fighting took on an ethnic dimension in January 1994 as it spread north from Kabul to envelop Uzbeks and Tajiks as well as the majority Pathans (82%), claiming over 10,000 lives in two months ∎

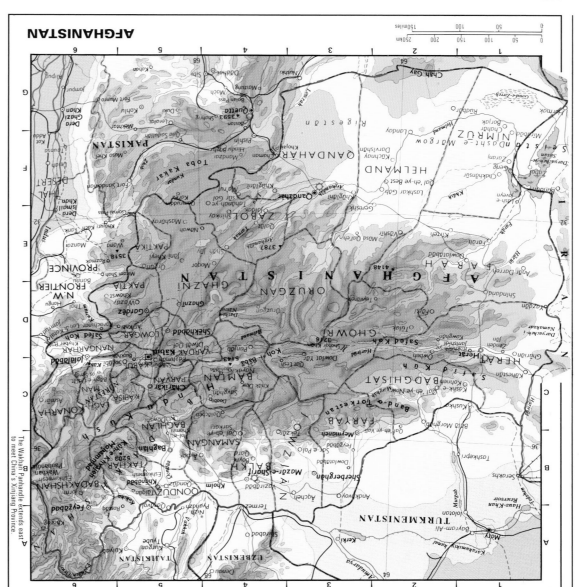

AFGHANISTAN

The Wakhan Panhandle extends east to meet China's Xinjiang Province.

LEFT *The Karakoram Highway heads through Azad (Free) Kashmir towards K2 (or Chogori), the world's second highest mountain, near the Chinese border.*

Colourful cushions and covers on sale at Quetta, capital of Baluchistan. The trader standing up wears the traditional clothes of the Pathans, the Pushto-speaking tribes who dominate the border areas with Afghanistan.

population ruled by a Hindu maharaja who acceded to India – but there was also an underlying strategic issue: five rivers rising in or passing through Kashmir or the neighbouring Indian state of Himachal Pradesh are vital to Pakistan's economy, and could not be left in the hands of possible enemies.

Like most developing countries, Pakistan has increased both mineral exploitation and manufacturing industry. To the small oil- and coalfield near Rawalpindi has now been added a major resource of natural gas between Sukkur and Multan. Karachi, formerly the capital and developed in the colonial period as a wheat port, is now a considerable manufacturing centre, principally textiles; so is the cultural centre, Lahore, in the north. The well-planned national capital of Islamabad, begun in the 1960s, is still growing to the north-east of Rawalpindi, with the serrated outline of the Murree Hills – refuge for the wealthier citizens on weekends – as a backdrop to the architecture of the new city.

The world's ninth most populous country, Pakistan is likely to be overtaken by Bangladesh – its former partner separated by 1,600 km [1,000 mls] of India – by the end of the century. Then East Pakistan, Bangladesh broke away from the western wing of the nation in 1971, following a bitter civil war and Indian military intervention, but neither country has enjoyed political stability or sound government – a dangerous scenario in the case of Pakistan, a nuclear power.

Pakistan has been subject to military rule and martial law for much of its short life, interspersed with periods of fragile democracy resting on army consent. During one such, in 1988, Benazir Bhutto – daughter of the president executed after his government was overthrown by the army in 1977 – was freely elected prime minister, the first female premier in the Muslim world. Two years later she was dismissed by the president following accusations of nepotism and corruption, but returned in 1993 as only the second democratically elected leader in the country's 46-year history; the first had been her father.

'West' Pakistan's economy has also done better than poor Bangladesh, while reserves of some minerals (notably bauxite, copper and phosphates) have yet to be exploited. Yet there are huge problems: dependence on textiles, an increasingly competitive area, and on remittances from Pakistani workers abroad, especially in the Middle East (the main source of foreign income); a chronic trade deficit and debt burden; massive spending on defence and security; growing drug traffic through the North-West Frontier; and the added pressure of some 5 million Afghan refugees who fled the civil war in their homeland ■

PAKISTAN

As Egypt is the gift of the Nile, so Pakistan is the gift of the Indus and its tributaries. Despite modern industrialization, irrigated farming is vital to this Islamic state, both in Punjab, the 'land of the five rivers' – Indus, Jhelum, Beas, Ravi and Sutlej – and downstream on the dry plains flanking the Indus between Khairpur and Hyderabad. The stations at Tarbela (on the Indus) and Mangla (on the Jhelum) are among the world's biggest earth- and rock-filled dams.

West of the Indus delta the arid coastal plain of Makran rises first to the Coast Range, then in successive ridges to the north – stark, arid, deforested and eroded. Between the ridges lie desert basins like that containing the saltmarsh of Hamun-i-Mashkel on the Iranian border. Ridge and basin alternate through Baluchistan and the earthquake zone round Quetta, the *daman-i-koh* ('skirts of the hills') still irrigated by the ancient tunnels called *karez* or *qanats*, for growing cereals and fruit.

North again stretches the famous North-West Frontier province, pushing up between the towering Hindu Kush and Karakoram, with K2 on the border with China the world's second highest mountain at 8,611 m [28,251 ft]. East of Peshawar lies Kashmir, which Pakistan controls to the west of the 1947 ceasefire line, and India to the east. The ceasefire ended war and appalling internecine slaughter that followed the grant of independence from Britain, when the old Indian Empire was divided between India and Pakistan – Hindu and Muslim states. The Kashmir problem was partly religious – a mainly Muslim

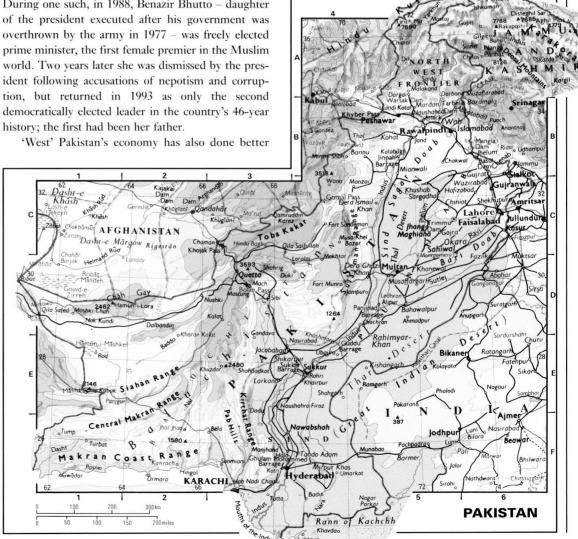

PAKISTAN

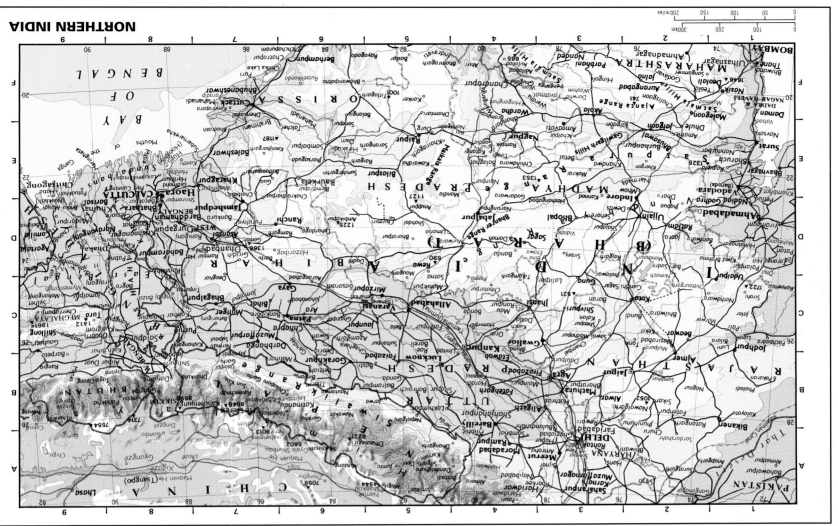

74

NORTHERN INDIA

INDIA

A diamond-shaped country – the world's seventh largest – India extends from high in the Himalayas through the Tropic of Cancer to the warm waters of the Indian Ocean at 8°N. More than 850 million people live here in the world's second most populous state – and its largest multiparty democracy.

Landscape and agriculture

Geographically India can be divided into three parts – the mountainous north, the great alluvial plains of the Brahmaputra and Ganges, and the plateaus and lowlands that occupy the southern area, including the Deccan and most of the peninsula. Each provides an astonishing range of scenery – a picture intensified by the variety of peoples, cultures and activities to be found within them.

The mountainous north: The Himalayan foothills make a stunning backdrop for northern India, rising abruptly from the plains in towering ranks. Harsh dry highlands, sparsely occupied by herdsmen, stretch northwards to the everlasting snows of the Karako-ram. Below lie alpine meadows, lakes and woodlands, often grazed in summer by seasonally migrant flocks from lower villages. The fertile Vale of Kashmir has emerald-green rice-terraces, walnut and plane trees, and apple and apricot orchards around half-timbered villages. It is crossed by ancient trackways once used as trade routes by mule and yak trains, now military roads to the garrisons of the north.

The wet, forested eastern Himalayas of Assam are ablaze with rhododendrons and magnolias, and terraced for buckwheat, barley and rice-growing. The high plateau of Meghalaya ('abode of the clouds') is damp and cool; nearby Cherrapunji has one of the highest rainfalls in the world. Tropical oaks and teaks on the forest ridges of Nagaland, Manipur and Mizo-ram, bordering Burma, alternate with rice-patches and small towns; on the hilltops dry cultivation of rice is practised, in plots cleared for a few years' cultiva-tion and then left fallow.

The plains: The great plains form a continuous strip from the Punjab eastwards. Heavily irrigated by canals engineered in the late 19th century, the rich alluvial soils have provided prosperity for Sikh and Jat farmers of the Punjab and Haryana. Here are grown winter wheat and summer rice, cotton and sugar cane with sorghum in the drier areas, the successful agriculture forming a foundation for linked industrial development. Many small market towns are thriving and the fine plans for the joint state capital of Chandigarh, devised by Le Corbusier, have been fully realized.

Somewhat similar landscapes extend east to the plains surrounding Delhi, India's third largest city on the west bank of the Jumna (Yamuna) River. An ancient site, occupied for over 3,000 years, it now includes the Indian capital New Delhi, designed by Sir Edwin Lutyens and built from 1912. Old city and new lie at a focal point of road and rail links, and like many Indian cities became rapidly overcrowded. To the east again are the lowlands of Uttar Pradesh, criss-crossed by the Ganges and Jumna rivers and their many tributaries. Slightly wetter, but less irri-gated, these plains are farmed less for wheat and rice than for spiked millet and sorghum, though maize

and rice cultivation increase again in the wetter areas towards Bihar.

Among the most densely populated areas of India (the state of Uttar Pradesh has a population larger than Nigeria, Pakistan or Bangladesh), these lowlands support dozens of cities and smaller settlements – notably Agra, with its Red Fort and Taj Mahal, and the sacred cities of Allahabad and Varanasi (Benares). Along the Nepal border the *terai* or *tarai* plains, formerly malaria-infested swamp forest, have now

Dyeing cloth by the Sabarmati in the Gujarat capital of Ahmadabad, India's sixth largest city (2,550,000) and centre of India's cotton trade since the 15th century.

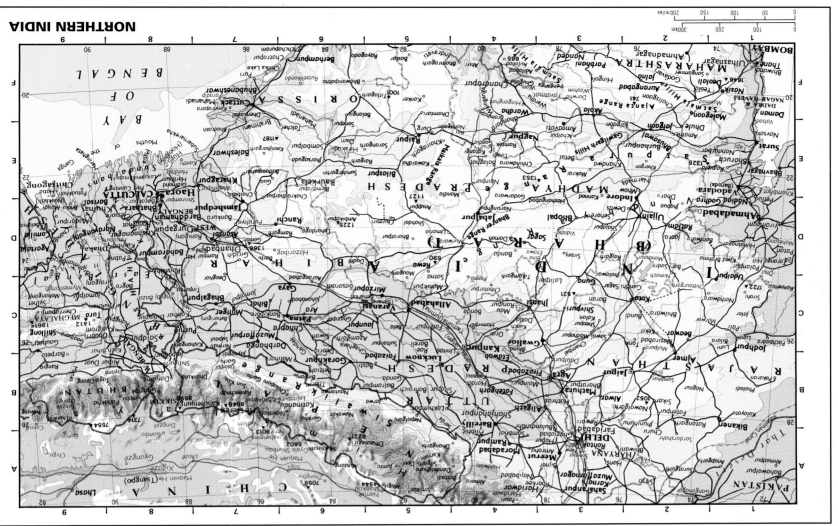

ASIA

THE HIMALAYAS

The Earth's highest mountain range, with an average height of 6,100 m [20,000 ft], the Himalayas are structurally part of the high plateau of Central Asia. The range stretches over 2,400 km [1,500 mls] from the Pamirs in the north-west to the Chinese border in the east. There are three main ranges: Outer, Middle and Inner; in Kashmir, the Inner Himalayas divide into five more ranges, including the Ladakh Range and the Karakorams. The world's highest mountain, Mt Everest (8,848 m [29,029 ft]) is on the Tibet-Nepal border; next is K2 (8,611 m [28,251 ft]) in the Karakorams, and there are a further 17 peaks over 8,000 m [26,247 ft].

The name comes from the Nepalese words *him* ('snows') and *alya* ('home of'), and the mountains are revered in Hindu mythology as the abode of gods. Recently, the hydro-electric potential of the range has inspired more secular reverence: enormous quantities of energy could be tapped, although at some cost to one of the world's pristine environments. Over 100,000 trekkers visit Everest's base camp each year, and more than 400 climbers have reached the summit since 1953.

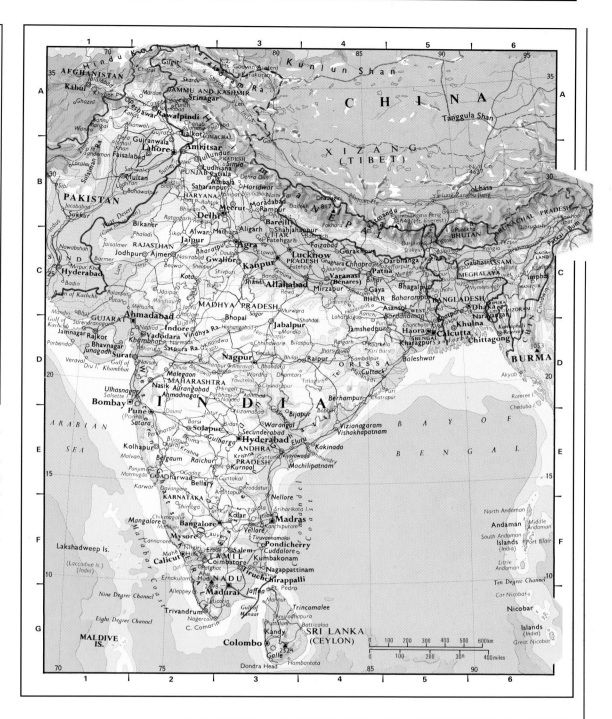

been cleared and made healthy for prosperous farming settlements.

Downstream from Tinpahar ('three hills'), near the Bangladeshi border, the Ganges begins its deltaic splitting into distributary streams, while still receiving tributaries from the north and west. West Bengal consists largely of the rice- and jute-growing lands flanking the distributary streams that flow south to become the Hooghly, on which Calcutta is built. The Ganges-Kobadak barrage now provides irrigation for the north of this tract, while improving both water supply and navigation lower down the Hooghly. The Sundarbans – mangrove and swamp forests at the seaward margin of the Ganges delta – extend eastwards into Bangladesh.

South-west from the Punjab plains lies the Thar or Great Indian Desert, its western fringes in Pakistan but with a broad tract of dunes in the north-eastern lowlands in Rajasthan, India's largest state. The desert ranges from perenially dry wastelands of shifting sand to areas capable of cultivation in wet years. As the name Rajasthan implies, this state was once (until 1950) a land of rajahs and princes, palaces and temples; some of the buildings – including universities – endowed by these private benefactors remain important in Jodhpur, Jaipur, Ajmer, Udaipur and other cities. Rajasthan rises in a series of steps to a jagged, bare range of brightly-coloured sandstone ridges, the Aravallis, that extend north-eastwards and end at Delhi.

South and west of the Aravallis lie the cotton-growing lands of tropical Gujarat; Ahmadabad is its chief city. Between the Gulfs of Khambhat and Kachchh is the low peninsular plateau of Kathiawar, whose declining deciduous forests still harbour small groups of tribal peoples, and indeed the last of India's native lions. Between this and the Pakistan border stretches the desert saltmarsh of the Rann of Kachchh, once an arm of the Arabian Sea and still occasionally flooded by exceptionally heavy rains.

The Palace of the Winds (Hawa Mahal) in the 'pink city' of Jaipur, capital of Rajasthan. In the 1980s, the hottest decade on record, a series of droughts in the state devastated crops and destroyed 30% of livestock.

Women harvesting a variety of crops in the foothills of north India. Despite its image of perpetual poverty, the country has a rich and diverse agricultural base.

South-east of the Aravallis is an area of transition between the great plains of the north and the uplands and plateaus of peninsular India. First come the Chambal badlands (wastelands south of Agra, now partly reclaimed), then rough hill country extending south-eastwards to Rewa. The River Sone provides a lowland corridor through the hills south of Rewa, and an irrigation barrage provides water for previously arid lands west of Gaya. Eastwards again the hills are forested around Ambikapur and Lohardaga. Industrial development becomes important around the coalfields of the Damodar Valley, centred on Asansol and the developing steel town of Jamshedpur.

Peninsular India: South of the Chambal River and south of Indore (a princely capital until 1950), the sandy plateau of the north gives way to forested hills, split by the broad corridors of the Narmada and Tapi rivers. Tribal lands persist in the Satpura Range, and the Ajanta Range to the south is noted for primitive cave paintings near Aurangabad. From here to the south volcanic soils predominate.

Bombay, India's second largest city, lies on the coastal lowlands by a broad estuary, among rice-fields dotted with low lava ridges. Fishing villages with coconut palms line the shore, while inland rise the stepped, forested slopes and pinnacles of peninsular India's longest mountain chain, the Western Ghats (Sahyadri).

East of the Ghats, on rich black soils well watered by the monsoons, stretch seemingly endless expanses of cotton and sorghum cultivation. Arid in late winter and spring, and parched by May, they spring to life when the rains break in late May or June. The sleepy market towns follow a similar rhythm, full of activity when the agricultural cycle demands, and relaxing under the broiling sun when the time for activity is past.

South from the holiday beaches of Goa (formerly a Portuguese enclave, still Portuguese in flavour), past busy Mangalore, Calicut and Cochin to the state capital of Kerala, Trivandrum, the coast becomes a kaleidoscope of coconut groves and fishing villages, rice-fields, scrublands, cashew orchards and tapioca plantations. Here the Ghats are edged with granite, gneiss, sandstone and schist, and clad in heavy rain-forest. To the east the peninsula is drier, with rolling plateaus given over to the production of millet, pulses and other dry crops. Sugar, rice and spices are grown where simple engineering provides tanks, stopped

with earth or masonry dams, to save the summer rains; now canals perform the same task. Bangalore and Hyderabad, once sleepy capitals of princely states, are now bustling cities, respectively capitals of Karnataka and Andhra Pradesh.

History

India's earliest settlers were widely scattered across the subcontinent in Stone Age times. The first of its many civilizations developed in the Indus Valley about 2600 BC, and in the Ganges Valley from about 1500 BC. By the 4th and 3rd centuries BC Pataliputra (modern Patna) formed the centre of a loosely-held empire that extended across the peninsula and beyond into Afghanistan. This first Indian empire broke up after the death of the Emperor Asoka in 232 BC, to be replaced by many others, both transient and lasting, during the centuries that followed. The Portuguese who crossed the Indian Ocean in the late 15th century, and the British, Danes, French and Dutch who soon followed them, found a subcontinent divided in itself and ripe for plundering.

As a result of battles fought both in Europe and in India itself, Britain gradually gained ascendancy over both European rivals and local factions within the subcontinent; by 1805 the British East India Company was virtually in control, and the British Indian Empire (which included, however, many autonomous states) was gradually consolidated throughout the 19th and early 20th centuries. Organized opposition to Britain's rule began before World War I and reached a climax after the end of World War II. In August 1947 the Indian subcontinent became independent, but divided into the separate states of India, a mainly Hindu community, and Pakistan, where Muslims formed the vast majority. In the boundary disputes and reshuffling of minority populations that followed perhaps a million lives were lost – and events since then have done little to promote good relations between the two states.

A country of diversity

India is a vast country with enormous problems of organization. It has over a dozen major languages, each with a rich literature, as well as many minor languages. Hindi, the national language, and the Dravidian languages of the south (Tamil, Telugu and Malayalam) are Indo-European; in the north and east occur Sino-Tibetan tongues, and in forested hill refuges are found residual Austric languages. Racial stocks too are mixed, with dark tribal folk in forest remnants, Mongoloids in the north and east, and

often lighter-coloured skins and eyes in the north-west – and in higher castes throughout the country.

The mosaic of religion also adds variety – and potential conflict. Hinduism is all-pervasive (though the state is officially secular), and Buddhism is slowly reviving in its country of origin (the Buddha was born on the border of India and Nepal about 563 BC). Buddhism's near-contemporary Mahavira and Jainism, with common elements including stress against destruction of any form of life, are strong in the merchant towns around Mt Abu in the Aravalli hills north of Ahmadabad. Islam contributes many mosques and tombs to the Indian scene; the Taj Mahal is the most famous, but there are many more. The forts of Delhi, Agra and many other northern cities, and the ghost city of Fatehpur Sikri, near Agra, are also Islamic relics of the Mogul period (1556–1707). Despite the formation of Pakistan, India retains a large Muslim minority of about 76 million and violence erupts sporadically to threaten the fragile co-existence – for example in the autumn of 1992 following the destruction of the mosque at Ayodya by Hindu zealots. Before that it had been the turn of the Punjab's militant Sikhs, claiming to represent their population of 13 million, who sought separation.

Christian influences range from the elaborate Catholic churches and shrines remaining from Portuguese and French settlement, to the many schools and colleges set up by Christian denominations and still actively teaching; there are also notable church unions in both south and north India. The British period of rule left its own monuments; Bombay and Calcutta both have some notable Victoriana, and New Delhi is a planned city of the Edwardian period.

A more vital memorial is the railway network – a strategic broad-gauge system fed by metre-gauge subsidiaries, with additional light railways, for example to the hill-stations of Simla (in Himachal Pradesh), Darjeeling (between Nepal and Bhutan) and Ootacamund (in Tamil Nadu). Among developments since independence are the intercity diesel-electric trains, but steam-engines remain the main workhorses in a coal-rich country.

However, despite its complexities and disadvantages, and annual predictions of collapse, India still remains in one piece ∎

KASHMIR

Until Indian independence in August 1947, Kashmir's mainly Muslim population was ruled, under British supervision, by a Hindu maharaja. Independence obliged the maharaja to choose between Pakistan or India; hoping to preserve his own independence, he refused to make a decision. In October, an army of Pathan tribesmen invaded from Pakistan. The Pathans advanced slowly, and India had time to rush troops to the region. The first Indo-Pakistan war resulted in a partition that satisfied neither side, with Pakistan holding one-third and India the remainder, with a 60% Muslim population. Despite promises, India has refused to allow a plebiscite to decide the province's fate. Two subsequent wars, in 1965 and 1972, failed to alter significantly the 1948 UN ceasefire lines.

In the late 1980s, Kashmiri nationalists in the Indian-controlled area began a violent campaign in favour of either secession to Pakistan or local independence. India responded by flooding Kashmir with troops. By 1994, at least 3,500 Kashmiris had died.

NEPAL

Over three-quarters of Nepal lies in a mountain heartland located between the towering Himalayas, the subject of an inconclusive boundary negotiation with China in 1961, and the far lower Siwalik Range overlooking the Ganges plain. Its innumerable valleys are home to a mosaic of peoples, of Indo-European and Tibetan stock, with a wide range of cultures and religions, and exercising fierce clan loyalties.

This heartland, some 800 km [500 mls] from west to east, is divided between the basins of three main rivers – the Ghaghara, Gandak and Kosi. Between the last two, on a smaller river flanked by lake deposits, stands Katmandu, the royal and parliamentary capital, surrounded by emerald rice-fields and orchards. The provincial centre of Pokhara is in a similar valley tributary to the Gandak, north of Nuwakot.

South of the Siwalik Range, the formerly swampy and malarious *terai*, or hillfoot plain, is now an economic mainstay, with new farming settlements growing rice, wheat, maize, jute and sugar. Development is encouraged by the *terai* section of the Asian Highway. There are two short railways from India, Jaynagar-Janakpur and Raxaul-Amlekganj, where the railhead from the south meets the road that takes goods up to Katmandu. As well as general development aid from the West, China has built a road from Tibet to Katmandu, India one from near Nautanwa to Pokhara. Nepal's most famous assets are the mountains, now an increasing tourist attraction bringing vital revenue to the country. Everest (8,848 m [29,029 ft]) and Kanchenjunga (8,598 m [28,208 ft]) are the tallest peaks of a magnificent range, giving a backdrop that dominates every vista in Nepal.

The authorities now hope for more than increased tourism. Today's plan is for the Himalayas to be tapped for their colossal hydroelectric potential, to supply the factories of industrial India; Nepal's goal is to become the powerhouse of the region. If the scheme envisaged by the government and the World Bank proceeds, the first stage would be under way by the mid-1990s at Chisapani Gorge. Once completed, the 267 m [878 ft] dam would house the second-largest HEP plant in the world, generating more than the total of Britain's nuclear stations combined. There would be environmental costs, including the displacement of 70,000 people, but the result would be valuable and renewable 'clean' power.

Financing such schemes – at $6 billion Chisapani alone is nearly twice the total gross national product – is a huge problem for a country which ranks alongside Laos as the poorest in Asia. With Chinese Tibet to the north and India to the south, the nation is already very reliant on Indian trade and co-operation – a fact emphasized when border restrictions operated in the late 1980s. Devoid of coast, independent trade links and mineral resources, Nepal has remained an undeveloped rural country, with more than 90% of the adult population (only one in four of whom can read) working as subsistence farmers. In addition, indiscriminate farming techniques have led to deforestation – in turn causing the erosion of precious soils. The situation deteriorated further in July 1993 when Nepal was hardest hit by torrential monsoon rains

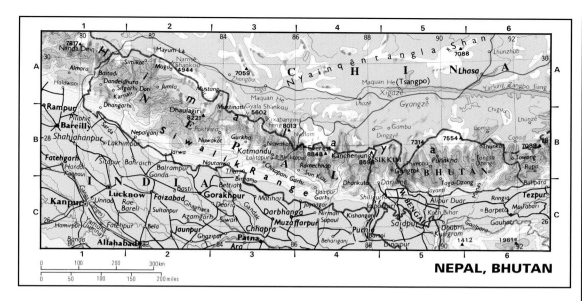

NEPAL, BHUTAN

that swept the subcontinent – the country's worst natural disaster for more than 60 years.

While tourism is now encouraged, it was only in 1951 that Nepal was opened up to foreigners. Before that it had been a patchwork of feudal valley kingdoms, and though these were conquered by the Gurkhas in the 18th century – forming the present country – local leaders always displayed more allegiance to their clans than to the state. From the mid-19th century these families (notably the powerful Rana) reduced the power of the central king, but in 1951 the monarchy was re-established. A brief period of democracy ended with the return of autocratic royal rule in 1960 under King Mahendra, but after mass demonstrations and riots his son Birendra, despite attempts at stalling, was forced to concede a new constitution incorporating pluralism and basic human rights in 1990 and the hierarchical system of *panchayats* (local councils) was over. In May 1991 the first democratic elections for 32 years took place with 10 million voters, and were won by the left-of-centre Nepali Congress Party. Though the birthplace of Buddha (Prince Siddhartha Gautama, *c.* 563 BC), Nepal remains a predominantly Hindu country ■

A Nepalese peasant makes his way to market at Sarangot. In many parts of his beautiful country walking is still the only viable means of moving goods.

BHUTAN

Geographically a smaller and even more isolated version of Nepal, the remote mountain kingdom of Bhutan faces many of the same problems and hopes for many of the same solutions – notably the harnessing of hydroelectric power from the Himalayas: India has already built one plant and commissioned two more from King Jigme Singye Wangchuk. The monarch is head of both state and government, though foreign affairs are under Indian guidance following a treaty of 1949.

The world's most 'rural' country (less than 6% of the population live in towns and over 90% are dependent on agriculture), Bhutan produces mainly rice and maize as staple crops and fruit and cardamom as cash crops. Timber is important, too, though outweighed by cement (25% of exports) and talcum (10%) in earning foreign exchange. Despite these activities, plus tourism and stamps, the World Bank in 1989 ranked Bhutan the world's ninth poorest country, ahead only of Laos, Nepal and Bangladesh in Asia. Aircraft and diesel fuels are its main imports, supplying crucial contacts ■

SRI LANKA

Known as Ceylon until 1972, when it became a Socialist republic, Sri Lanka has been described as 'the pearl of the Indian Ocean'; the island is also its crossroads. First inhabited by forest-dwelling negroid Veddas, it was settled later by brown-skinned Aryans from India. These are now dominant in the population, though diluted by successive waves of incomers. Long-resident Tamils farm in the northern limestone peninsula of Jaffna, and Arab dhow sailors and merchants settled in the ports. After Vasco da Gama's contact with India in the 15th century came new traders and colonists – first Portuguese, then Dutch, then British (in control from 1796 to 1948) –

and new immigrant Tamils were brought in from south-east India to farm the plantations.

From mountain core to coral strand stretches the 'wet zone' of south-western Sri Lanka, supporting cool, grassy downs, rainforests and tea-gardens near the ancient religious centre of Kandy, and evergreen forest and palm-fringed beaches in the lowlands from Colombo to east of Galle. White Buddhist shrines and peasant cottages dot the cultivated land among coconut palms, rice-paddies, sugar-cane plantations and spice gardens. In contrast are the much drier zones of the north and east.

While light industry has gone some way to diversifying an agricultural base dependent on tea, rubber and coconuts, Sri Lanka's economic progress since independence – when it was a relatively prosperous state – has been plagued by civil war and communal violence. The main conflict, between the Sinhalese Buddhist majority and the Tamil Hindu minority, led

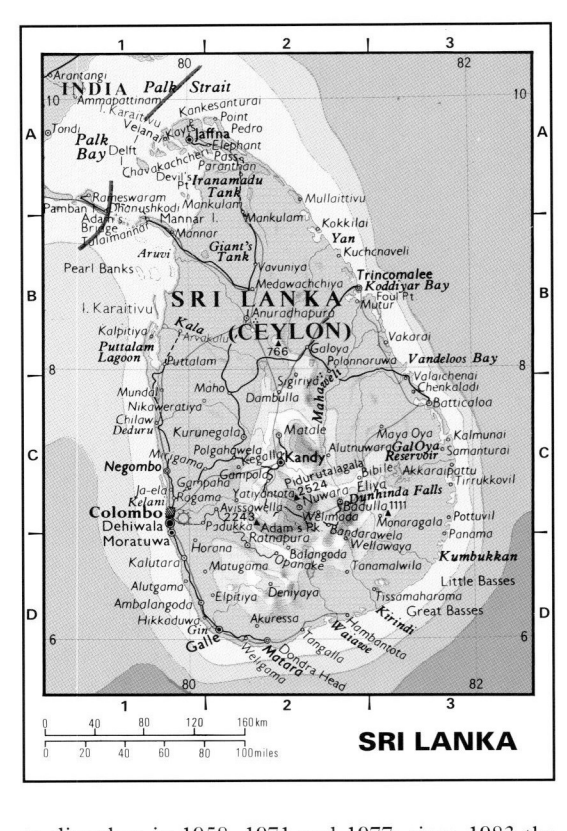

SRI LANKA

to disorders in 1958, 1971 and 1977; since 1983 the conflict has been virtually continuous as Tamil guerrillas have fought for an independent homeland in the north (Eelam), with Jaffna the capital.

An Indian-brokered ceasefire in 1987 allowed an Indian peacekeeping force in, but it failed to subdue the main terrorist group, the Tamil Tigers, and withdrew in March 1990. Between then and the start of 1994 more than 15,000 people died in renewed clashes between the predominantly Sinhalese government forces and the rebels, despite an agreement on autonomy for the 2.5 million Tamils ■

Picking tea on Sri Lanka, which means 'the resplendent island' in Sinhalese. The country is the world's third largest tea producer after India and China.

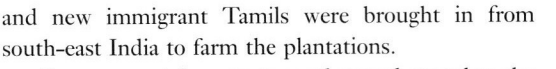

MALDIVES

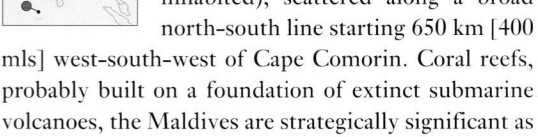

The archipelago of the Maldives comprises over 1,190 small low-lying islands and atolls (202 of them inhabited), scattered along a broad north-south line starting 650 km [400 mls] west-south-west of Cape Comorin. Coral reefs, probably built on a foundation of extinct submarine volcanoes, the Maldives are strategically significant as mid-ocean islands.

The islands were settled from Sri Lanka about 500 BC. For a time under Portuguese and later Dutch rule, they became a British protectorate in 1887, administered from Ceylon but retaining local sultanates. They achieved independence in 1965, and the last sultan was deposed three years later.

Adequately watered and covered with tropical vegetation, the islands' crops are coconuts, bananas, mangoes, sweet potatoes and spices, but much food is imported – as are nearly all capital and consumer goods. Fish are plentiful in lagoons and open sea; bonito and tuna are leading exports together with copra and coir. Tourism, however, has now displaced

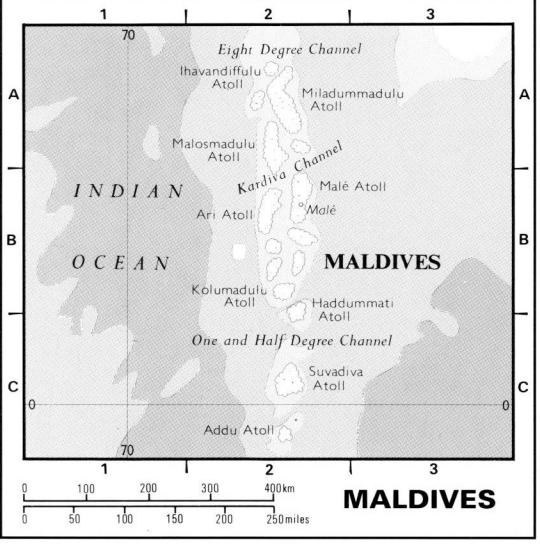

MALDIVES

fishing as the mainstay of the economy, though its future depends much on political stability; the 1988 coup against the authoritarian nationalist government was put down with Indian troops ■

These Maldive fishermen may be the last; with a high point of just 1.5 m [5 ft], their island could disappear early next century with the effects of global warming.

BANGLADESH

Battered by a relentless cycle of flood and famine, and plagued by political corruption and a succession of military coups, Bangladesh is perhaps Asia's most pitiful country, once known as Golden Bengal (Sonar Bangla) for its treasures but gradually plundered and now pushed near to the bottom of the Third World pile. It is – apart from statistically irrelevant city-states and small island countries – the most crowded nation on Earth: the 1990 figure was a density of some 803 people per sq km [2,080 per sq ml], well ahead of the next realistic rival Taiwan (554 per sq km [1,435 per sq ml]) and far greater than Europe's contender Belgium (323 per sq km [837 per sq ml]), which in any case has a much larger urban proportion. The world's tenth biggest population – a figure expected to increase by another 36 million or more between 1988 and 2000 – lives on an area of precarious flat lowlands smaller than the US states of Illinois or Iowa.

Landscape

Apart from a south-eastern fringe of forested ridges east of Chittagong, Bangladesh consists almost entirely of lowlands – mainly the (greater) eastern part of the large delta formed jointly by the Ganges and Brahmaputra. The western part (now West Bengal, in India) is largely the 'dying delta' – its land a little higher and less often flooded, its deltaic channels seldom flushed by flood-waters. In contrast, the heart of Bangladesh, following the main Ganges channel and the wide Brahmaputra, is the 'active delta'. Frequently flooded, with changing channels that are hazardous to life, health and property, the

Crowded river traffic at Khulna illustrates Bangladesh's twin problems – too many people and not enough land. Over 60% of internal trade is carried by boat.

rivers also renew soil fertility with silt washed down from as far away as the mountains of Nepal and Tibet. Indeed, while deforestation in the Himalayan foothills has caused enough silt to form new 'islands' for the burgeoning Bangladeshi population, it has also led to the blocking of some waterways – 60% of the country's internal trade is carried by boat – and danger to fish stocks, as well as increased risk of flooding.

The alluvial silts of the 'active delta' yield up to three rice crops a year as well as the world's best jute, and though Bangladesh is now only the third largest producer in a declining market, high-quality fibre is exported to India; jute and cotton are processed also in post-independence mills, for example at Narayanganj. There is a large hydroelectric plant at Karnaphuli reservoir, and a modern paper industry using bamboo from the hills. Substantial reserves of coal await exploitation, but a more realistic development may be the construction of a 320 km [200 ml] canal to transfer water from the flooding Brahmaputra to the Ganges, in order to increase supplies to India's drought-affected areas.

History and politics

Bangladesh was until 1971 East Pakistan, the oriental wing of the Muslim state set up by the partition of British India in 1947. Separated by 1,600 km [1,000 mls] of India from the politically-dominant, Urdu- and Punjabi-speaking western province, the easterners felt the victims of ethnic and economic discrimination. In 1971 resentment turned to war when Bengali irregulars, considerably aided and abetted by Indian troops, convened the independent state of 'Free Bengal', with Sheikh Mujibur Rahman as head of state.

From 1992 the country faced the increasing prospect of war with Burma, triggered by Rangoon's treatment of the Rohingyas, its Muslim minority. In 1978 Bangladesh took in some 300,000 Rohingyas fleeing persecution, and while most went back, the emigrants of the 1990s are unlikely to follow suit – exacerbating the problem of overpopulation ∎

BANGLADESH

THE DELTA CYCLONES

Most of Bangladesh is almost unbelievably low and flat, and the people of the coastal fringes are all too familiar with the cyclones from the Bay of Bengal. Even so, 1991 brought the worst in memory: the official death toll was a staggering 132,000 (or possibly higher), and more than 5 million people, almost all of them poor peasants already living on or below the poverty line, were made homeless.

The cyclone caused inestimable damage to the area around Chittagong: crops and fields were inundated with sea water; herds of cattle and goats and flocks of poultry were decimated; dykes were breached and trees ripped up; wells filled up with salt water. The struggling survivors were victims of dysentery and cholera, dehydration and malnutrition. However generous, aid rarely reached the most needy, as it was sifted and filtered down the line despite the efforts of charity administrators. Corrupt practices, like the cyclones, are endemic to Bangladesh; funds allocated for concrete cyclone-proof shelters, for example, were appropriated by individuals and government officials. As with most natural disasters – earthquakes, volcanic eruptions, tidal waves, landslips – the cyclones usually affect countries least equipped to deal with them and least able to withstand the losses.

Nor does it relent: in the torrential monsoons of July 1993 half of Bangladesh's land area was flooded.

MONGOLIA

Worthy of its harsh, isolated reputation, Mongolia is the world's largest landlocked country and the most sparsely populated. Despite its traditional nomads, more than half the population live in towns, a quarter of them in Ulan Bator, a modern city built in the postwar Soviet mould. Geographically Mongolia divides into two contrasting regions, north and south of a line joining the mountains of the Altai, Hangayn and Hentiyn ranges.

In the north, high mountains alternate with river valleys and lake basins. Pastures are watered enough to support herds of cattle and wheat is grown, especially where black earth soils occur. In the far north-west, where the Altai rise to over 4,000 m [13,120 ft], boreal forests blanket the slopes.

The southern half of the country, still averaging 1,500 m [4,900 ft], has a strong continental climate with meagre, variable rainfall. In these semi-desert steppelands, salt lakes and pans occupy shallow depressions, poor scrub eventually giving way to the arid wastes of the Gobi Desert.

Mongolia is still a land of nomadic pastoralists – less than 1% of the land is cultivated – and a huge herds of sheep, goats, yaks, camels and horses form the mainstay of the traditional economy. Herdsmen's families inhabit gers (yurts), circular tents covered in felt, and subsist on a diet of milk, cheese and mutton.

Politics and economy

Outer Mongolia broke away from China following the collapse of the Ch'ing dynasty in 1911, but full independence was not gained until 1921 – with Soviet support in what was the world's second Socialist revolution. In 1924 a Communist People's Republic was proclaimed and the country fell increasingly under Soviet influence, the last example being a 20-year friendship and mutual assistance pact signed in 1966.

Textiles and food processing were developed, with aid from the USSR and Comecon also helping to open up mineral deposits such as copper, molybdenum and coking coal; in addition, Mongolia is the world's third biggest fluorspar producer. In the late 1980s minerals overtook the agricultural sector as the country's main source of income.

In recent years Mongolia has followed the path of other less remote Soviet satellites, reducing the presence of Soviet troops (1987–9), introducing pluralism (the country's first multiparty elections were held in 1990), launching into privatization and a free-market economy (1991), and early in 1992 adopting a new constitution eschewing Communism and enshrining democracy. In June 1993, Mongolians voted in their first direct presidential election, electing Pun Salmaagiyn Ochirbat as president. The pace of change was frantic after seven decades of authoritarian rule – Mongolia still owes Moscow $15 billion – and, like the newly independent republics of the former Soviet empire, the Mongolians will not find the transition easy. ■

ABOVE Mongolians sit outside the Temple of the Living Buddha in Ulan Bator. Meaning 'Red Hero', the capital's name was coined by the old Communist regime in 1924.

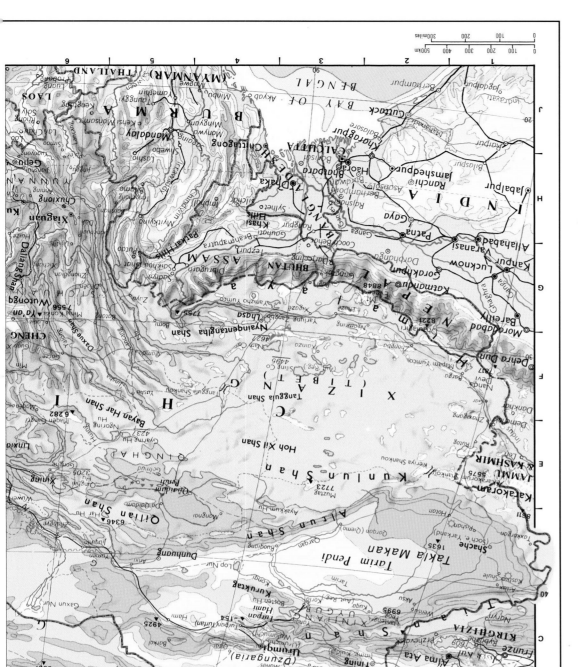

CHINA

By far the most populous country in the world – one in every five people is a citizen – the People's Republic of China also ranks as the third largest country after Russia and Canada, being marginally bigger than the USA. Before the development of modern forms of transport, the vast size of China often hampered efficient communication between the centre of the country and the peripheries. Distances are huge: by rail, the distance from Peking (Beijing) to Canton (Guangzhou) is 2,324 km [1,450 mls].

One of the main determining influences on the evolution of Chinese civilization had been the geographical isolation of China from the rest of the world. Surrounded to the north, west and south by forests, deserts and formidable mountain ranges, and separated from the Americas by the vast expanse of the Pacific Ocean, China until modern times was insulated from frequent contact with other civilizations, and its culture and society developed along highly individual lines. In the 1990s China again finds itself an enigma – the great giant of Communism in an era when the creed is experiencing a global and perhaps terminal collapse.

Landscape and relief

The Chinese landscape is like a chequerboard in which mountains and plateaus alternate with basins and alluvial plains. There are two intersecting systems of mountain chains, one trending from north-north-east to south-south-west, the other from east to west. Many mountain areas have been devastated by soil erosion through indiscriminate tree-felling. The agricultural wealth of China is all in the lowlands of the east – where the vast majority of the population lives.

The chequerboard pattern includes an extraordinary variety of landscapes. Manchuria, in the far north, comprises a wide area of gently undulating country, originally grassland, but now an important agricultural area. The loess lands of the north-west occupy a broad belt from the great loop of the Hwang Ho (Huang He) into Shanxi and Henan provinces. Here, valley sides, hills and mountains are blanketed in loess – a fine-grained unstratified soil deposited by wind during the last glaciation. Within this region, loess deposits occur widely in the form of plateaus which are deeply incised by spectacular gorges and ravines.

By contrast with the loess lands, the landscape of the densely populated North China Plain is flat and monotonous. Settlement is concentrated in walled villages while large fields are the product of post-1949 land consolidation schemes. Further south the Yangtze delta is a land of large lakes. Water is a predominant element of the landscape – the low-lying alluvial land with its irrigated rice-fields is traversed by intricate networks of canals and other man-made works, many of which date back several centuries.

Far inland in the Yangtze basin, and separated from the middle Yangtze Valley by precipitous river gorges, lies the Red Basin of Szechwan (Sichuan). To the north, west and south, the basin is surrounded by high mountain ranges. The mountains of the Qin Ling ranges, in particular, protect the basin from cold winter winds. With its mild climate and fertile soils, the Red Basin is one of the most productive and densely populated regions of China. Rice-fields, often arranged in elaborate terraces, dominate the landscape.

Other distinctive landscapes of southern China include those of north-eastern Guizhou province, where limestone spires and pinnacles rise vertically above small, intensively cultivated plains, and the Guangdong coastal lowlands, with their villages in groves of citrus, bananas, mangoes and palms.

The Hwang Ho and the Yangtze

The two major rivers of China are the Hwang Ho (Huang He) and the Yangtze (Chang Jiang), the world's seventh and third longest. The Hwang Ho, or Yellow River (so called from the large quantities of silt which it transports), is 4,840 km [3,005 mls] long. Also known as 'China's Sorrow', it has throughout history been the source of frequent and disastrous floods. In 1938, dykes along the Hwang Ho were demolished in order to hamper the advance of the Japanese army into northern China, and the river was diverted so as to enter the sea to the south of the Shandong peninsula. In the catastrophic floods which followed, nearly 900,000 lives were lost and 54,000 sq km [21,000 sq mls] of land was inundated. Since 1949, the incidence of flooding has declined sharply, largely as a result of state investment in flood prevention schemes.

The Yangtze, China's largest and most important river, is 6,380 km [3,960 mls] long, and its catchment

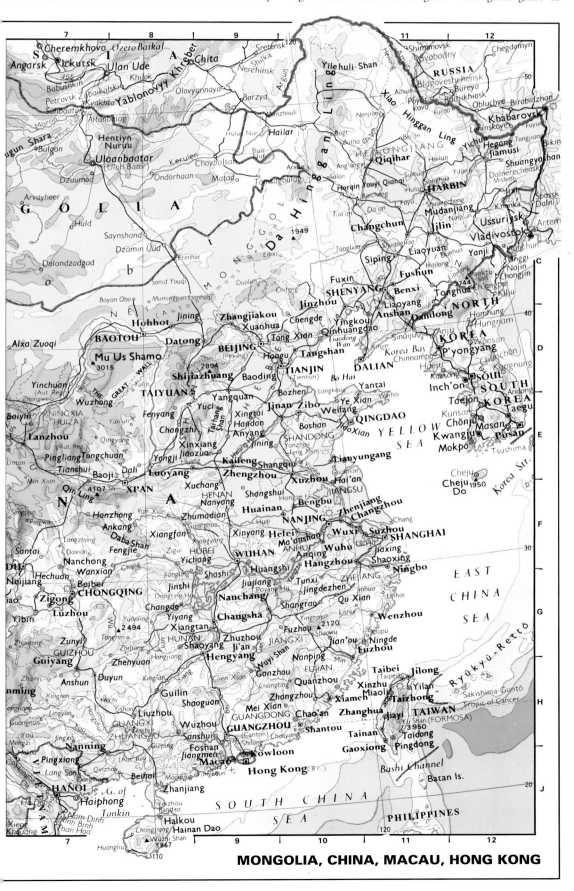

MONGOLIA, CHINA, MACAU, HONG KONG

Soldiers extricate their bicycles in Nanjing. With a population of 2,290,000, the city – capital of Chiang Kai-shek's Nationalist government from 1928 to 1937 – is still only the 12th largest in China.

TIBET

With an average elevation of 4,500 m [14,750 ft] – almost as high as Europe's Mont Blanc – and an area of 1.2 million sq km [460,000 sq mls], Tibet (Xizang) is the highest and most extensive plateau in the world. It is a harsh and hostile place, and most of its population of just over 2 million people live in the relatively sheltered south of the country, where the capital, Lhasa, is situated.

Since the 7th century, Tibet has been deeply influenced by Buddhist beliefs, and for much of its history was ruled by Buddhist priests – lamas – as a theocracy. The Dalai Lama, a title passed on in successive incarnations from a dying elder to a newborn junior, usually dominated from Lhasa. Between 1720 and 1911 Tibet was under Chinese control, and in 1950 Tibet was reabsorbed by a resurgent Red China; after an unsuccessful uprising in 1959, the Dalai Lama fled to Delhi and a brutal process of forced Chinese acculturation began: in 1961, a report of the International Commission of Jurists accused China of genocide. An 'Autonomous Region of Tibet' was proclaimed in 1965, but during the 1966–76 Cultural Revolution, many Tibetan shrines and monasteries were destroyed. Some 330,000 people were executed or died in labour camps.

basin is over twice as extensive as that of the Hwang Ho. Unlike the Hwang Ho, the Yangtze is navigable. During the summer months, ocean-going vessels of 10,000 tonnes may reach Wuhan, and 1,000-tonne barges can go as far upstream as Chongqing. Despite the post-1949 improvement of roads and railways, the Yangtze remains an important transport artery.

Climate and agriculture

Although the Chinese subcontinent includes a wide variety of relief and climate, it can be divided into three broad regions. Eastern China is divided into two contrasting halves, north and south of the Qin Ling ranges, while the third region comprises the mountains and arid steppes of the interior.

Northern China: Throughout northern China, rainfall is light and variable, and is generally insufficient for irrigated agriculture. In winter, temperatures fall to between –1°C and –8°C [30°F and 18°F] and bitterly cold winds blow eastwards across the North China Plain from the steppes of Mongolia. Summer temperatures, by contrast, are little different from those of southern China, and may reach a daily average of 28°C [82°F]. The growing season diminishes northwards and in northern Manchuria only 90 days a year are free of frost. Despite advances in water conservation since World War II, aridity and unreliability of rainfall restrict the range of crops that can be grown. Millet, maize and winter wheat are the staple crops of the North China Plain, while coarse grains and soya beans are cultivated in Manchuria.

Southern China: The area to the south of the Qin Ling ranges receives heavier and more reliable rainfall than the north, and winter temperatures are generally above freezing point. Summer weather, especially in the central Yangtze Valley, is hot and humid. At Nanjing, temperatures as high as 44°C [111°F] have been recorded. Inland, the mild climate and fertile soils of the Red Basin make this an important agricultural region. Rice production is dominant but at lower altitudes the climate is warm enough to allow the cultivation of citrus fruits, cotton, sugar cane and tobacco, of which China is the world's biggest producer.

The far south of China, including Guangdong province and the island of Hainan, lies within the tropics and enjoys a year-round growing season. Irrigated rice cultivation is the economic mainstay of southern China. Double cropping (rice as a main crop followed by winter wheat) is characteristic of the Yangtze Valley; along the coast of Guangdong province two crops of rice can be grown each year, and in parts of Hainan Island the annual cultivation of three crops of rice is possible; the country produces more than 35% of the world total. Crops such as tea, mulberry and sweet potato are also cultivated, and in the far south sugar cane, bananas and other tropical crops are grown.

The interior: While the Qin Ling ranges are an important boundary between the relatively harsh environments of the north and the more productive lands of the south, a second major line, which follows the Da Hinggan mountains and the eastern edge of the high Tibetan plateau, divides the intensively cultivated lands of eastern China from the mountains and arid steppes of the interior. In the north, this boundary line is marked by the Great Wall of China. Western China includes the Dzungarian basin, the Turfan depression, the arid wastes of the Takla Makan desert, and the high plateau of Tibet.

Although aridity of climate has hampered the development of agriculture throughout most of western China, oasis crops are grown around the rim of the Takla Makan desert, and farming settlements also exist in the Gansu corridor to the north of the Qilian mountains.

Early history

Early Chinese civilization arose along the inland margins of the North China Plain, in a physical setting markedly harsher (especially in terms of winter temperatures) than the environments of the other great civilizations of the Old World. The Shang dynasty, noted for its fine craftsmanship in bronze, flourished in northern China from 1630 to 1122 BC. Shang civilization was followed by many centuries of political fragmentation, and it was not until the 3rd century BC that China was unified into a centrally administered empire. Under the Ch'in dynasty (221 to 206 BC) the Great Wall of China was completed, while Chinese armies pushed southwards beyond the Yangtze, reaching the southern Chinese coast in the vicinity of Canton.

In succeeding centuries there was a gradual movement of population from the north to the warmer

Seven Star Lake in the prosperous southern Chinese province of Guangdong, where the growing season in the fertile valleys and lowlands lasts all year.

moister, and more productive lands of the south. This slow migration was greatly accelerated by incursions of barbarian nomads into north China, especially during the Sung dynasty (AD 960 to 1279). By the late 13th century the southern lands, including the Yangtze Valley, probably contained somewhere between 70% and 80% of the Chinese population.

During the Han, T'ang and Sung dynasties, a remarkably stable political and social order evolved within China. The major distinguishing features of Chinese civilization came to include Confucianism, whereby the individual was subordinated to family obligations and to state service, the state bureaucracy, members of which were recruited by public examination, and the benign rule of the emperor – the 'Son of Heaven'. Great advances were made in the manufacture of porcelain, silk, metals and lacquerware, while gunpowder, the compass, and printing were among several Chinese inventions which found their way to the West in medieval times. Nevertheless, the economy was overwhelmingly agricultural.

Despite the geographical diversity and great size of its territory, China during pre-modern times experienced long periods of unity and cohesion rarely disturbed by invasion from outside. Two important dynasties, the Yuan (1279–1368) and the Ch'ing (1644–1912), were established by the Mongols and Manchus respectively, but, almost invariably, alien rulers found it necessary to adopt Chinese methods of government, and the Chinese cultural tradition was preserved intact.

The birth of the Republic

In the 18th century, China experienced a rapid acceleration in the rate of population growth, and living standards began to fall. By the early 19th century, the government was weak and corrupt, and the country suffered frequent famines and political unrest. British victory in the Opium War (1839–42) was followed by the division of China into spheres of influence for the major Western imperialist powers, and by the establishment of treaty ports, controlled by Western countries, along the Chinese coast and the Yangtze.

Meanwhile, the disintegration of imperial China was hastened by peasant uprisings such as the Taiping rebellion (1850–64), and by the defeat of China in the Sino-Japanese War of 1894–5. Belated attempts were made to arrest the decline of the Chinese empire, but in 1912, and following an uprising in Wuhan, the last of the Chinese emperors abdicated and a republic was proclaimed.

Although the republican administration in Peking was regarded as the legitimate government, real power rested with army generals and provincial governors. Rival generals, or warlords, raised private armies and plunged China into a long and disastrous period of internal disorder. Alternative solutions were offered by two political parties – the Kuomintang (or Chinese Nationalist Party) formed by Sun Yat-sen and later led by Chiang Kai-shek, and the Communist Party. In 1931, Japan seized Manchuria, and in 1937 full-scale war broke out between the two countries. In the bitter fighting which followed, the Communists, under Mao Tse-tung, gained the support of the peasantry and proved adept practitioners of guerrilla warfare.

The defeat of Japan in 1945 was followed by a civil war which cost 12 million lives: the Communists routed the Kuomintang armies, forcing them to take refuge on the island of Taiwan, and the People's Republic of China was officially proclaimed on 1 October 1949.

Communist China

Under Communist rule the mass starvation, malnutrition and disease which afflicted China before World War II were virtually eliminated, and living standards greatly improved, especially in the countryside.

One of the salient features of the centrally planned economy was the organization of the rural population into 50,000 communes – self-sufficient units of varying size which farm the land collectively. Communes also run rural industries, and are responsible for the administration of schools and clinics. Through the communes, labour has been organized on a vast scale to tackle public works schemes such as water conservation, flood control and land reclamation.

Living standards improved markedly, with life expectancy doubling and education improving, though the GNP per capita figure remained that of a poor Third World nation – some 1.5% that of Japan. The agricultural communes were not notably

At times as unfathomable as its human compatriots, the panda's role of reluctant Cold War icebreaker was superseded by that of cuddly endangered species.

successful, and since peasants have been freed from petty bureaucracy, harvests of the major grain crops went up by over 40% in the decade from 1976.

Although food supply has generally kept abreast of population growth, the size and growth rate of the Chinese population has always been a problem. By the early 1980s, the population was growing at 1.3% per year, a net annual increase of about 13 million people; government penalties and incentives over the size of family have met with some success, but between 1988 and 2000 it was expected to grow by 187 million – less than the prediction for India, but above the 1988 totals for Indonesia or Brazil. Hong Kong will add more in 1997.

THE GREAT WALL OF CHINA

The world's longest fortification, the Great Wall was begun in the 3rd century BC and extended throughout Chinese history; most of the present wall was constructed during the Ming Dynasty, between 1368 and 1644. Its main purpose was to protect the Chinese Empire from northern nomadic raiders, though (like Egypt's pyramids) it was also a make-work project for hundreds of thousands of otherwise unemployed labourers.

The total length of the wall is at least 6,400 km [4,000 mls]; recently, archaeologists discovered what may be another 1,000 km [600 mls]. Only a few small sections, renovated largely as tourist attractions, remain in good repair; the best-preserved section is at Nankou Pass, 80 km [50 mls] north of Beijing. Contrary to legend, the Great Wall is not visible from the Moon, nor even from very high altitudes. Despite its great length, its flat top is no more than 4 m [13 ft] wide.

Only 10% of the land area of China is cultivable, but environmental constraints are such that there is little prospect of meeting increased food demand by reclaiming land for agriculture. Future growth in food supply must come from continued intensification of land use and gains in yields.

Although China is an agricultural country, government planners, especially since the death of Mao Tse-tung in 1976, have emphasized the need to industrialize. China has sufficient resources in coal, iron ore and oil to support an industrial economy, but it is deficient in capital and industrial technology. While ignoring the wave of political reform sweeping through world socialism in 1990 and 1991 – the country's record on human rights is appalling – the Chinese leadership has now allowed certain market forces to operate, encouraging further foreign investment and begun to promote the enormous potential

of tourism. In 1992 and 1993, it had the fastest growing major economy in the world (12–13%), aided by its precarious 'Most Favored Trading' status with the USA, which takes a third of its exports.

Peking, the capital city of China, is a governmental and administrative centre of prime importance. Several buildings of outstanding architectural interest, such as the former imperial palace complex (once known as the Forbidden City) and the Temple and Altar of Heaven, have been carefully preserved and are now open to the public. In the 19th and early 20th centuries, Shanghai grew rapidly as a major banking and trading centre. Since 1949, the city has lost its former commercial importance, but it remained China's largest and has emerged as a major centre for the manufacture of iron and steel, ships, textiles and a wide range of engineering products ∎

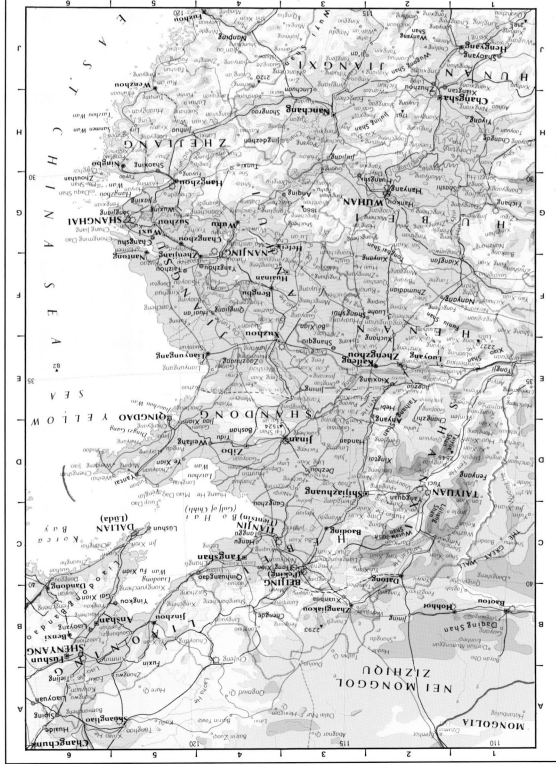

TAIWAN

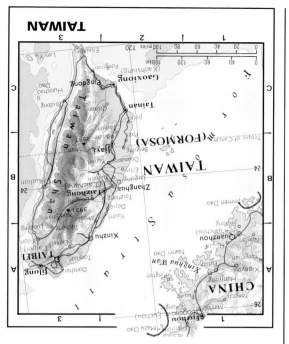

Ceded by the Chinese Empire to Japan in 1895, Taiwan was surrendered by the Japanese Army to General Chiang Kai-shek's Nationalist Chinese government in 1945. Beaten by Mao Tse-tung's Communists, some 2 million Nationalists and their leader fled the mainland to the island in the two years before 1949. The influx was met with hostility by the 8 million Taiwanese, and the new regime was imposed with force.

Boosted by US help, Chiang's government set about ambitious programmes for land reform and industrial expansion, the latter taking Taiwan into the world's top 20 nations by 1980 and providing high living standards. The island nevertheless remained politically isolated, losing its UN seat to Communist China in 1971, and being diplomatically abandoned by the US in 1979, when Washington switched recognition to Peking. Though few countries take seriously Taipei's claim to be the sole legitimate government of China, the country administers a number of islands, notably Quemoy (Jinmen) and Matsu (Mazu).

High mountain ranges, which extend for the entire length of the island, occupy the central and eastern parts of Taiwan, and only a quarter of the island's surface is cultivated. The central ranges rise to altitudes of over 3,000 m [10,000 ft], and carry dense forests of broadleaved evergreen trees such as camphor and Chinese cork oak. Above 1,500 m [5,000 ft], conifers such as pine and cedar dominate. With its warm, moist climate – the island sits astride the Tropic of Cancer – Taiwan provides a highly favourable environment for agriculture, and the well-watered lands of the western coastal plain produce heavy rice crops. Sugar cane, sweet potatoes, tea, bananas and pineapples are also grown.

Taiwan produces a wide range of manufactured goods, including colour television sets, electronic calculators, footwear and ready-made clothing, and is the world's leading shipbreaker.

Less than half the size of Tasmania or Ireland, but supporting more than 20 million people, Taiwan has been a remarkable success story, averaging nearly 9% growth every year from 1953 to the 1990s ∎

MACAU

Portuguese colony from 1557 and for 200 years one of the great trading centres for silk, gold, spices and opium, Macau was overtaken in importance by Hong Kong in the 19th century. When China re-established diplomatic relations with the colonial power in 1979, the coastal enclave was redefined as 'Chinese territory under Portuguese administration', and in 1987 the powers agreed that the territory will return to China in 1999 as a Special Administrative Region of that country – an agreement based on the 'one country, two systems' principle used by China and Britain to settle the future of Hong Kong in 1984.

Macau is a peninsula at the head of the Canton (Pearl) River, 64 km [40 mls] west of Hong Kong and connected to China by a narrow isthmus. The main industries are textiles and tourism, but there is no airport – most visitors arrive via jetfoil from Hong Kong – and the territory, with a population of 446,000 that is 98% Chinese, is heavily reliant on the Chinese mainland for food, water and raw materials.

From the first Sino-British treaty of 1842 Macau was never able to cope with the commercial dynamism of Hong Kong and the enclave degenerated into something of a seedy Far East backwater, known mainly for its gambling, vice and crime. Since the 1970s, however, it has emerged as an industrial centre, concentrating on the export of textiles and light goods, notably toys and artificial flowers ■

A Macau rickshaw rider takes a break in front of a building typical of the Portuguese colonial style. The territory will revert to full Chinese rule in 1999 – almost certainly without the acrimony which seems likely to plague Hong Kong's scheduled return to control from Beijing (Peking) two years earlier.

HONG KONG

On 1 July 1997 the British Crown Colony of Hong Kong will pass into the hands of the Chinese government. What Peking will receive is Hong Kong Island, 235 smaller islands, the Kowloon peninsula on their province of Guangdong and the 'New Territories' adjoining it.

More important, they will inherit the world's biggest container port, its biggest exporter of clothes and its tenth biggest trader. Hong Kong's economy has been so successful since World War II that its huge neighbour will be increasing its export earnings by more than a quarter; in return, under a 1984 accord, China agrees to allow the territory to enjoy economic autonomy for at least another 50 years.

Certainly, the entrepreneurial spirit was still abroad as time ticked away to the changeover: in 1992 Hong Kong embarked on its scheme for a controversial new airport to replace the dangerous Kai Tak – the world's largest civil engineering project and due for opening in 1997, with final completion in 2040. Nevertheless, in the early 1990s, with the future uncertain and the spectre of Tiananmen Square still fresh, the economy began to slow as some businessmen drifted elsewhere and some services shifted to rivals such as Singapore; while relations between Peking and London become increasingly strained.

Hong Kong was acquired by Britain in three stages. The island itself, containing the city of Victoria, was ceded in 1842; Kowloon, on the mainland, came under its control in 1860; and the New Territories, between Kowloon and the Chinese border, were leased in 1898. Today the fortunes of this dynamic and densely populated community are based on manufacturing, banking and commerce, with the sheltered waters providing one of the finest natural deep-water harbours in the world.

Yet the colony has little else, and most of its food, water and raw materials have to be brought in, principally from China ■

A traditional Chinese junk contrasts vividly with the skyscrapers of Hong Kong's modern business district.

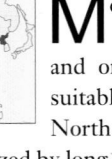

NORTH KOREA

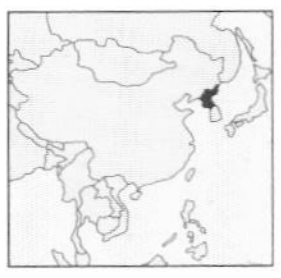

Mountains and rugged hills occupy most of the Korean peninsula, and only 20% of the surface area is suitable for cultivation. The interior of North Korea is a harsh environment, characterized by long and severe winters, during which lakes and rivers regularly freeze over. High forested mountains, cut by river gorges, lie along the borders of North Korea and Manchuria. Further south, a chain of bare, eroded mountains runs for almost the entire length of the peninsula, parallel with and close to the eastern coast.

The most productive land in the peninsula occurs along the southern coast, where winters are relatively mild. While South Korea contains the best rice lands in the peninsula, most mineral resources, including coal – which supplies 70% of the country's energy needs – and iron ore, are concentrated in North Korea. Though the North has nearly 55% of the land area, it has only just over a third of the total Korean population.

The Stalinist regime of North Korea installed by the Soviet Union after World War II – and supported by China during the Korean War of 1950–3 – has long been a total dictatorship revolving around the dynastic Kim Il Sung and his nominated heir, Kim Jong Il, whom the president also designated his successor as supreme commander of the army. The world's most durable Communist ruler until his sudden death on 8 July 1994 – he came to power in 1948 as a former partisan fighter against the Japanese, who ruled the peninsula between 1910 and 1945 – Kim Il Sung imposed on North Korea his own unique brand of Marxism-Leninism, resting on the principles of self-reliance and party supremacy, and created a forbidding society virtually closed to foreigners and with few international friends.

Enormous sums had been pumped into promoting the personality cult of Kim Il Sung, the 'Great Leader', in recent years. The Museum of the Living Revolution in Pyongyang has 95 halls and 5 km [3 mls] of exhibits glorifying his achievements, and the celebrations for his 80th birthday in 1992 cost over £500 million.

As the Cold War ended and the Soviet satellites strived for a new age, North Korea remained isolated from the momentous events taking place outside. In 1991, however, there were quite sudden signs of progress (*see South Korea*), with various and unexpected breakthroughs.

While the Communist regime's collectivist agriculture programme has been reasonably successful – around 90% of cultivated land is under the control of co-operative farms – most of its effort went into the development of heavy industry, a decision which, after initial success, left the economy lagging well behind the 'sunrise' countries of the region, which moved into light engineering manufactures, specializing in electronics and, later, computers. Defence, too, continues to be a significant drag on the economy – another reason for healing the rift with South Korea and taking on a more open stance in international relations.

While China has not followed most of the Second World in forsaking Communism, it has adopted key elements of capitalism – and in 1992 it further isolated North Korea by normalizing diplomatic relations with Seoul. But the North's alleged nuclear capacity remained a problem for the West: in 1990 Kim Il Sung had agreed to the inspection of his weapons programme by the UN's Atomic Energy Agency but, after rescinding the decision, it withdrew from the Nuclear Non-Proliferation Treaty in April 1993.

Over a year later Kim Il Sung was still refusing access to his installations, a course of action which prompted the US, backed by Japan and South Korea, to pursue UN economic sanctions. With Pyongyang warning that this would be regarded as an act of war, and experts believing that North Korea could manufacture a dozen or more nuclear bombs a year, the Cold War was far from over in the Far East ∎

THE KOREAN WAR

Hastily divided in 1945 between a Soviet-occupied North and an American-occupied South, Korea was considered by most Western strategists an irrelevance to the developing Cold War. But when the heavily-armed North invaded the South in June 1950, US President Truman decided to make a stand against what he saw (mistakenly) as Moscow-organized aggression. A Soviet boycott of the UN allowed American troops – assisted by contingents from Britain, Canada, France and other allies – to fight under the UN flag, and under General Douglas MacArthur they went on the offensive. American seapower permitted a landing far behind North Korean lines.

With some misgivings, Truman ordered his forces north of the 38th parallel, the former partition line. But as US troops neared the Chinese frontier in November 1950, hundreds of thousands of Chinese 'volunteers' surged across the Yalu River and threatened to overwhelm them. They retreated far southwards in disarray, until a 1951 counterattack slowly pushed back up the country and the combatants became entrenched along the 38th parallel in a bitter war of attrition that endured until an armistice was negotiated in 1953.

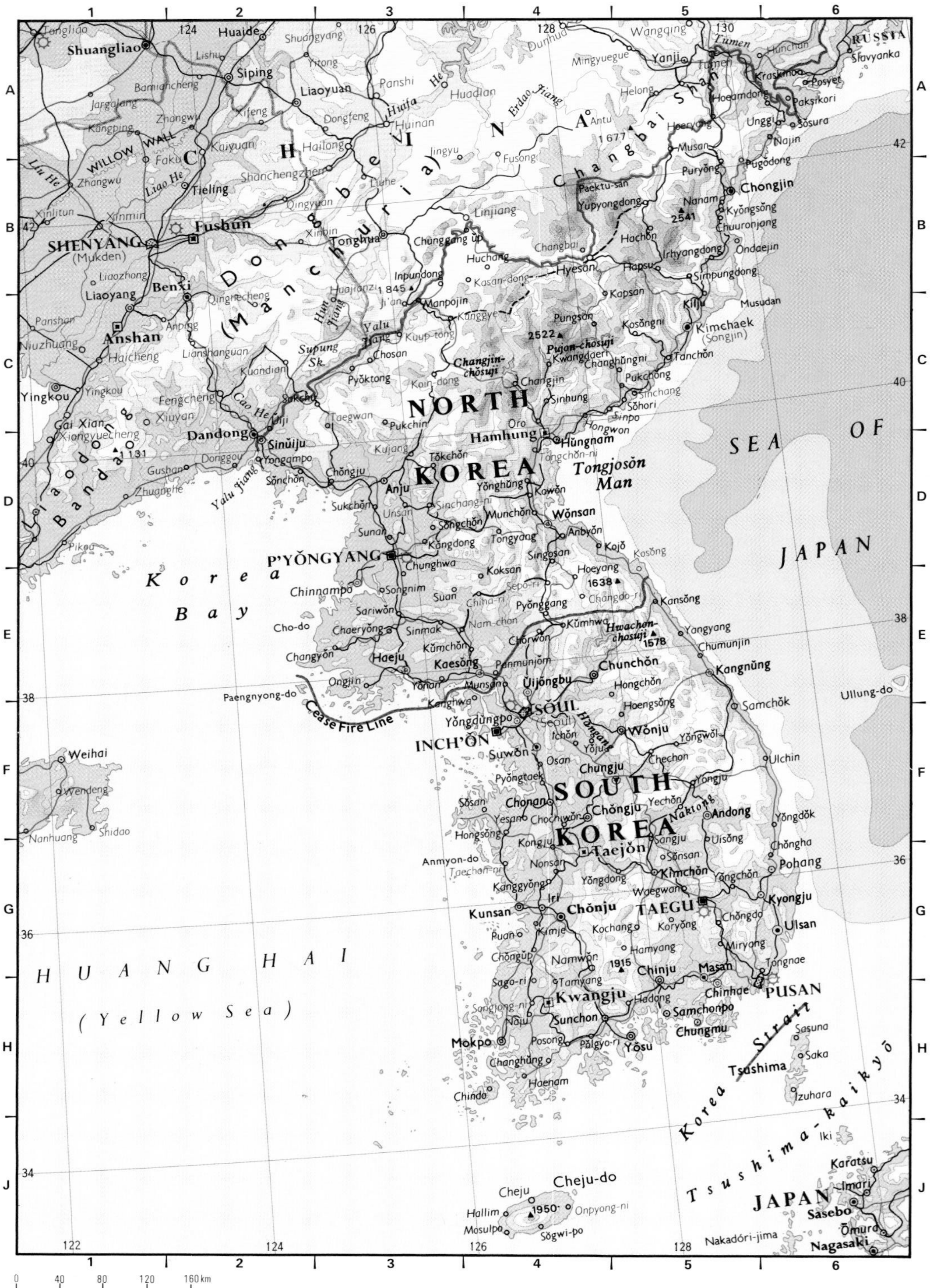

NORTH KOREA, SOUTH KOREA

SOUTH KOREA

For centuries the Koreans were very much a united people, an independent kingdom – 'Land of the Morning Calm' – knitted together by race, language and culture. Then, in 1910, came annexation by Japan and its harsh colonial rule, followed after World War II with division by the Allied powers into the Soviet (North) and American (South) zones of occupation each side of the 38th parallel. In 1948 the Soviets established a Communist regime in the North, the Americans a republic in the South, and the country – especially after the civil war of 1950–3 – seemed permanently partitioned. With a handful of interruptions, the two governments retained their hostile positions on the artificial frontier for nearly four decades; then, in 1991, the sides began to talk.

They first came together over a combined table-tennis team, yet only ten months later they had signed a full-blown non-aggression pact. In January 1992, following New Year messages from both presidents talking of unification, they signed a nuclear weapons agreement, setting up a joint control committee. However, with North Korea still refusing access to its installations by the middle of 1994, relations between the two countries have deteriorated. South Korea has the support of the US and Japan and economic sanctions have been imposed against North Korea. The possibility of reunification now seems remote.

The story of South Korea since the civil war had been a very different one from the North, though it was hardly a Far Eastern oasis of liberalism. While land reform based on smallholdings worked well enough to produce some of the world's highest rice yields (and self-sufficiency in food grains), the real economic miracle came in industrial expansion from the early 1960s. Initiated by a military government – one of several bouts of army rule since the inaugur-

ation of the republic – and based on slender natural resources, the schemes utilized cheap, plentiful but well-educated labour to transform the economy and make South Korea one of the strongest countries in Asia. The original manufacturing base of textiles remains important, but South Korea is now a world leader in footwear, shipbuilding and a host of other activities, including consumer electronics, toys and vehicles.

Seoul, hiding its pollution and housing shortages as best it could, celebrated the country's growth by hosting the 1988 Olympic Games: from a population of 1.4 million in 1950, it had reached 10.5 million by 1985. The dynamism of the country must now

A detail from the busy shipyards of Hyundai, a major contributor to South Korea's economic success.

be linked to more liberal policies – and less spending on defence.

The economy was growing, too: at nearly 9% a year from 1960 to 1990. South Korea has now opened up the possibility of trade links with China – which, though Communist, is desperate to broaden its economic possibilities – while approaches are being made to bodies to recognize the country's achievements and net status. A major breakthrough occurred in 1991 when both North and South Korea were admitted as full members of the United Nations ■

JAPAN

The Japanese archipelago lies off the Asian mainland in an arc extending from 45°N to 30°N, occupying a latitudinal range comparable to the Atlantic seaboard of the USA from Maine to Florida. Four large and closely grouped islands (Hokkaido, Honshu, Shikoku and Kyushu) constitute 98% of the nation's territory, the remainder being made up of some 4,000 smaller islands, including the Ryukyus, which lie between Kyushu and Taiwan. Japan is a medium-sized country, smaller than France but slightly larger than Italy.

Japan is a predominantly mountainous country and only 16% of the land is cultivable. Although Japan lacks extensive habitable areas, the population is nevertheless the sixth largest in the world. A limited area of agricultural land must therefore support many people, and Japan is now one of the most densely populated countries in the world – with an ever-ageing profile.

The Japanese islands occupy a zone of instability

in the Earth's crust, and earthquakes and volcanic eruptions are frequent. Throughout Japan, complex folding and faulting has produced an intricate mosaic of landforms, in which mountains and forested hills alternate with small inland basins and coastal plains. The pattern of landforms is further complicated by the presence of several volcanic cones and calderas. The highest mountain in Japan, the majestic cone of Fuji-san (3,776 m [12,388 ft]), is a long-dormant volcano which last erupted in 1707.

In the mountains, fast-flowing torrents, fed by snow-melt in the spring and by heavy rainfall during the summer, have carved out a landscape of deep valleys and sharp ridges. In central Japan, dense mixed forests of oak, beech and maple blanket mountain slopes to an altitude of 1,800 m [5,900 ft]; further north in Hokkaido, boreal forests of fir and spruce predominate. In central Honshu, the Japan Alps with their snow-capped ridges provide spectacular mountain scenery.

Small intensively cultivated coastal plains, separated from one another by rugged mountain spurs, make up most of Japan's lowlands. None of the plains

Unusual body decoration is revealed with the back view of a geisha girl. Postwar Japanese society has evolved into a strange blend of traditional and modern values.

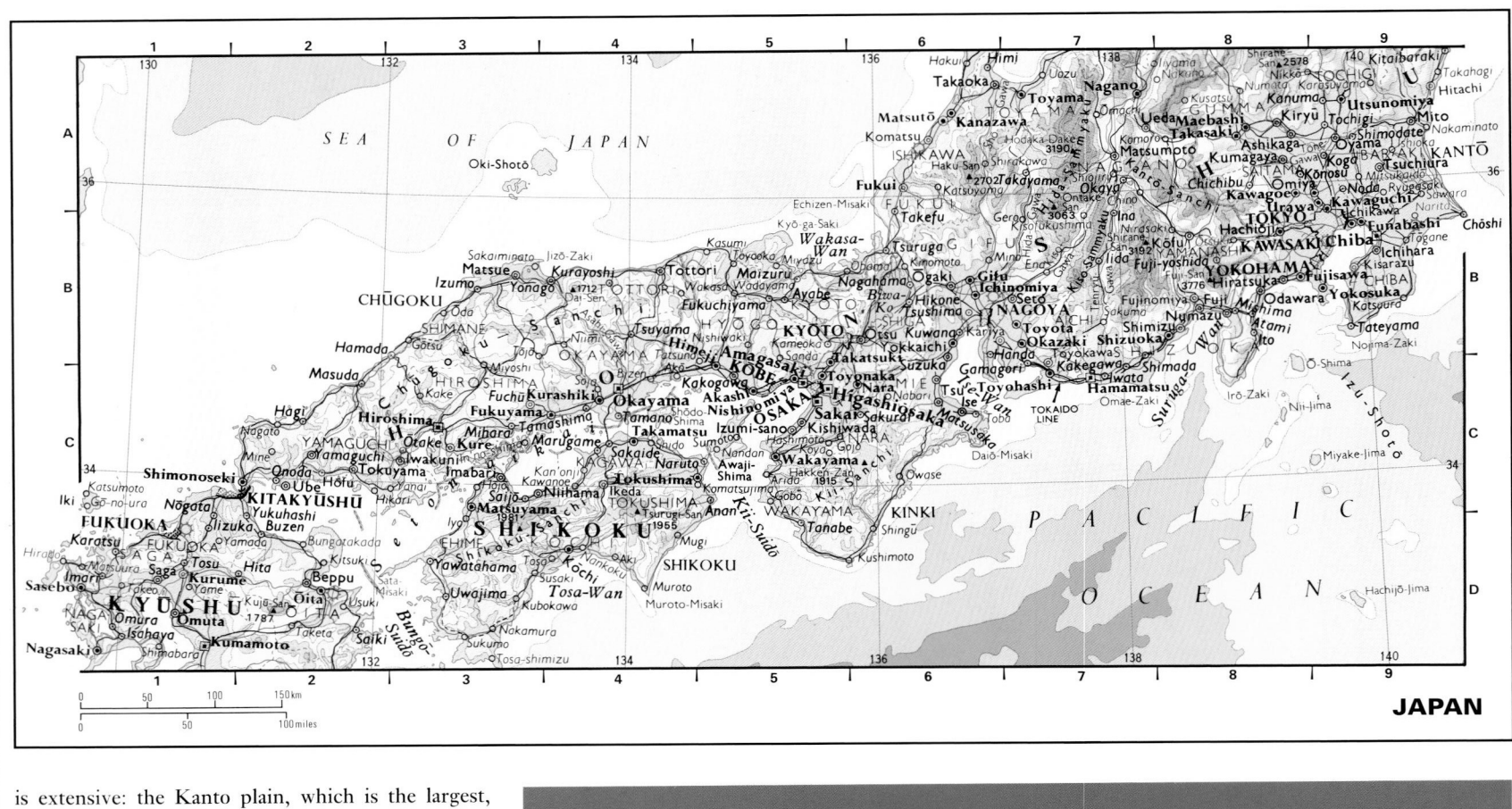

JAPAN

is extensive: the Kanto plain, which is the largest, covers an area of only 13,000 sq km [5,000 sq mls]. Most of the coastal plains are formed of material deposited by rivers, but their soils have been altered and improved by centuries of careful cultivation.

Early Japan was peopled by immigrants arriving in successive waves from Korea and elsewhere on the Asian mainland. The earliest zone of settlement included northern Kyushu and the coastlands of the Setonaikai (Inland Sea). By the 5th century AD, Japan was divided amongst numerous clans, of which the largest and most powerful was the Yamato. Shinto, a polytheistic religion based on nature worship, had already emerged, as had the Japanese imperial dynasty.

During the next three centuries Chinese cultural and political influences entered Japan. These included Buddhism, the Chinese script, and Chinese methods of government and administration. At a later stage, Confucianism was also imported. Early cities, modelled on the capital of T'ang-dynasty China, were built at Nara (710) and at Kyoto (794); the latter city remained the seat of the imperial court until 1868.

The adoption of the Chinese system of centralized, bureaucratic government was relatively short-lived. From the early 12th century onwards, political power passed increasingly to military aristocrats, and government was conducted in the name of the emperor by warrior leaders known as *shoguns*. Civil warfare between rival groups of feudal lords was endemic over long periods, but under the rule of the Tokugawa *shoguns* (1603–1867), Japan enjoyed a great period of peace and prosperity; society was feudal and rigidly stratified, with military families (the feudal lords and their retainers, or *samurai*) forming a powerful élite. In the 1630s, Japan embarked on a lengthy phase of enforced isolation from the rest of the world.

The pioneering 'bullet train' speeds past Mt Fuji en route from Nagoya to Tokyo. Dormant since 1707, Fuji-san is sacred to the Japanese and has been celebrated in poems and paintings for centuries.

This policy of seclusion could not be maintained indefinitely. In 1853, Commodore Perry of the US Navy arrived in Japan and demanded that ports be opened to Western trade. The capitulation of the *shogun* to Perry's demands prepared the way for the overthrow of the Tokugawa government, and with the Meiji Restoration of 1868 imperial rule was resumed.

Under Western-style government, a programme of modernization was set in train. Industrialization proceeded swiftly, and after victories in the Sino-Japanese War (1894–5) and the Russo-Japanese War (1904–5), Japan began to build up an overseas empire which included the colonies of Taiwan and Korea. The growing strength of the Japanese military was demonstrated by the army's seizure of Manchuria in 1931. During the 1930s, and especially after the outbreak of war between Japan and China in 1937, militarist control of the government of Japan grew steadily. In 1941, the launching of a surprise attack on the American naval base of Pearl Harbor took Japan – and drew the USA – into World War II.

From its defeat in 1945 to 1952, Japan was administered by US forces. Many liberal reforms were enacted, and under the new constitution the power of the emperor was much reduced, with sovereignty formally vested in the people. The following decades saw an economic success story, all the more remarkable since – especially in the 1980s and 1990s – leaders in government were almost consistently corrupt.

The main centres of population and industry are concentrated within a narrow corridor stretching from the Kanto plain, through the coastlands of the Setonaikai, to northern Kyushu. This heavily urbanized zone contains nine cities with populations of over a million and three great industrial regions, centring respectively on Tokyo, Osaka and Nagoya. The capital Tokyo, soon to be overtaken by Mexico City and São Paulo as the world's most populous metropolis, forms the nucleus of a congested conurbation ■

THE JAPANESE BOOM

In 1945 Japan lay in ruins, with its major cities in ashes – two of them dangerously radioactive. Its smouldering ports were choked with the sunken remnants of its merchant marine, and its people were demoralized. Less than two generations later, the Japanese economy was second only to that of the US. Its high-technology products dominated world markets, while Japanese banks and private investors owned huge slices of industry and real estate on every continent.

The far-sighted American Occupation authorities deserve some of the credit. Realizing that industrial recovery could only go hand in hand with political development, they wrote Japan a new constitution. As a link with the past, the Emperor kept his place, but as a constitutional monarch answerable to a democratically elected Diet, with women given full voting rights for the first time. Trade unions were established, land reform eliminated subservient tenants and education was expanded.

The Korean War in 1950 gave the slowly recovering Japanese economy a tremendous boost. Japanese factories, well paid in American dollars, provided much of the steel, vehicles and other equipment the war demanded. When the Occupation formally ended in 1952, Japan was clearly on the way up.

The Japanese owed the first stage of their transformation to the Americans; the rest, they did themselves. Carefully planned economic policies, organized by the Ministry of Trade and Industry directed investment to key industries. First, the metal, engineering and chemical industries were rationalized and modernized. In the 1950s and 1960s efficient Japanese steelmakers consistently undersold European and American rivals, while producing better quality steel.

Japan's major weakness was its near-total lack of natural resources; but foresight and planning made up for them. After the 1970s oil crisis, it was clear that the costs of heavy industry were going to rise unprofitably high, and MITI switched resources to automobiles and electronics. Soon, Japan began to capture and dominate these markets, too.

By the 1980s, Japan's trading partners were becoming seriously alarmed. Noting that trade with Japan was largely a one-way traffic – Japan's home market is still notoriously hard to penetrate – they built protective walls of tariffs and duties. Japan responded with its usual flexibility: it bought factories within its rivals' walls, and traded from there.

BURMA (MYANMAR)

Once a green and gentle land, rich in agriculture and timber and blessed with many natural resources from precious stones to oil, Burma has become one of the three poorest countries in Asia, run by a regime whose record on human rights is among the world's worst. A change of name – the title Union of Myanmar was officially adopted in 1989 – has not changed the political complexion of a desperate nation.

Geographically, the country has three main regions. The core area is a great structural depression, largely drained by the Chindwin and Irrawaddy rivers. Its coastal zone has a wet climate, but the inner region between Prome and Mandalay constitutes a 'dry zone', sheltered from the south-west monsoon and with an annual rainfall of less than 1,000 mm [40 in]. In this dry zone, which was the original nucleus of the Burmese state, small-scale irrigation has long been practised in the narrow valleys, and rice, cotton, jute and sugar cane are important crops. Until 1964 Burma was the world's leading exporter of rice, and the crop still accounts for more than 40% of Burma's meagre export earnings. This central area was also the base of Burmah Oil, hosting the small fields that once made the country the British Empire's second largest producer. Even today it has sufficient oil and gas to meet most of Burma's needs.

To the west lie the fold mountains of the Arakan Yoma, while to the east rises the great Shan Plateau. In the south-east, running down the isthmus that takes Burma on to the Malay Peninsula, are the uplands of the Tenasserim, with hundreds of islands dotted along the coast of the Andaman Sea. More than 60% of the country is forested, rubber plantations augmenting the indigenous teak.

British since 1895, Burma was separate from India as a Crown Colony in 1937. A battleground for Japanese and British troops in World War II, it became an independent republic in 1948 and left the Commonwealth. Military dictatorship came in 1962 and a one-party state in 1974, both headed by General Ne Win, leader of the Burma Socialist Programme Party.

'The Burmese Way to Socialism'

The party's rigid combination of state control, Buddhism and isolation, under the banner 'The Burmese Way to Socialism', had disastrous results, the country plunging quickly from prosperity to poverty. Politically, too, Burma was in a perilous state, with over a third of the country in rebel hands.

In the south-east the guerrillas of two Karen liberation movements control large tracts of mountains near the Thai border; in the north and east the Burmese Communist Party holds sway in most of Kachin and a good deal of Shan; here also, at the western end of the 'Golden Triangle', the authorities try to contain the local warlords' trafficking in opium. Another flashpoint is in the west, where Rohingya, the Muslim minority, have been persecuted by the army and repeatedly pushed over the border with Bangladesh in tens of thousands.

Burma spends more than 35% of its budget on 'defence' – much of it on the brutal suppression of political opposition and of human rights. In 1990, the coalition NLD won over 80% of the votes in a multi-party election conceded by the regime following violent demonstrations, but the ruling junta simply refused to accept the result – keeping its leader, Nobel Peace Prize winner Aung San Suu Kyi, under house arrest. The powerless opposition were forced to renounce the result and agree to a new and no doubt again ineffective agenda for a return to democracy.

Meanwhile, the country continued to crumble, if with great charm; despite the hideous regime a black market flourishes behind the crumbling colonial façade of Rangoon, once a rival to Bangkok and Singapore. Though some visitors make the trips round the attractions of Rangoon, Mandalay and Pagan, tourism is hardly encouraged by the suspicious government, and most of the country is still closed to foreigners.

By 1994 there were tentative signs of the authorities opening their doors a little wider, due mainly to economic pressures. And there is much for tourists to admire. Deeply Buddhist, the Burmese keep faith with their festivals and boast some of the most marvellous temples, pagodas and statues in the world. Many of the numerous *stupas* – dome-shaped monuments both large and small – are coated with pure gold.

Tenth biggest nation in Asia, in both area and population, Burma remains an anomaly, holding out almost friendless against the tide of democratic and diplomatic changes that swept the world in the late 1980s and early 1990s. It seems that, even with some form of conciliation, it will not long survive as a geopolitical entity ∎

The Dhamma Yangyi Temple at Pagan, capital of Burma from 1044 to 1287, when it was sacked by Kublai Khan's Mongol hordes. Though devastated by an earthquake in 1975, the sprawling city of ruined Buddhist temples and monuments is still impressive.

THAILAND

Meaning 'Land of the Free' (*Muang Thai*), and known as Siam until 1939, Thailand is the only South-east Asian country that has not been colonized, or occupied by foreign powers, except in war. Comparable in size to France or Spain, Thailand is centred on the valley of the Chao Phraya River that flows across the central plain extending from the Gulf of Siam to the foothills of the northern mountains. Bounded in the west by the narrow mountain range that borders Burma, and in the east by lower hills separating the plain from the higher Khorat Plateau (Cao Nguyen Khorat), the central plain is Thailand's rice-bowl; it presents long vistas, with extensive rice-fields, canals and rivers that provide the main routeways, with villages raised on stilts.

The capital city Bangkok stands at the southern edge of the plain, near the mouth of the Chao Phraya; with a seaport and international airport it is the transport centre of the country. Ornate Buddhist temples stand side by side with modern concrete buildings, and the growing population is already over a tenth of the total. Extraordinarily, the country's next largest city is less than 200,000.

Northern Thailand is a region of fold mountains, with agriculturally rich intermontane basins. The hill forests produce teak and other valuable timbers. Thailand's highest mountain, Doi Inthanon (2,576 m [8,451 ft]), and the high hills surrounding it are the home of many hill tribes who live by shifting cultivation of dry rice and opium poppies; Chiang Mai, the beautiful northern capital, lies in this area. The Khorat Plateau to the east is a sandstone region of poor

Women sell fruit and vegetables on the Chao Phraya, north of Bangkok. Much of the transport in Thailand's fertile central plain is carried by rivers and canals, though the capital itself is sinking a little each year.

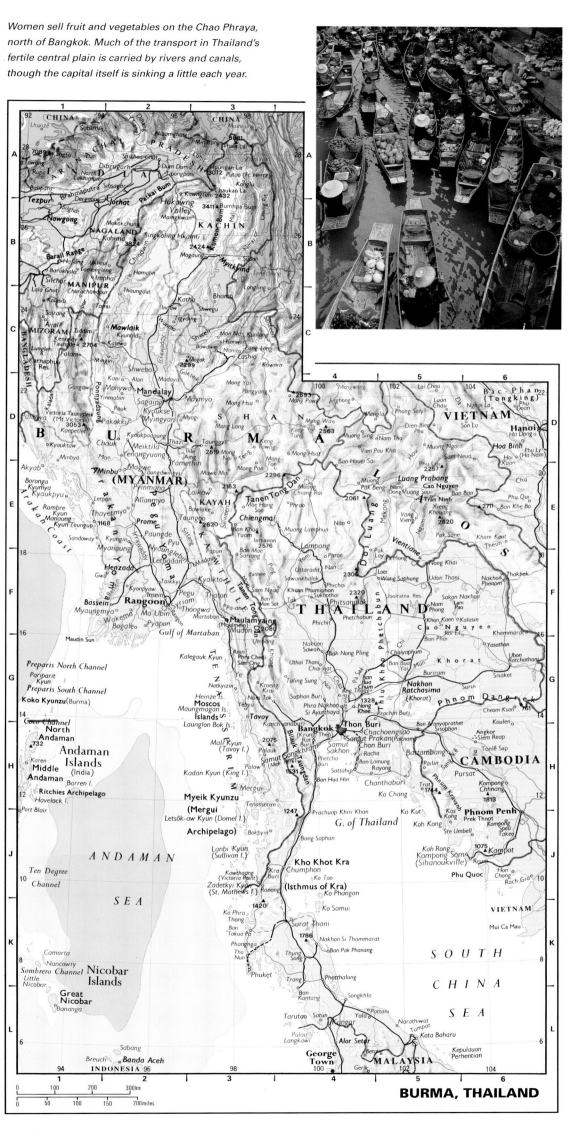

BURMA, THAILAND

soils supporting savanna woodlands; glutinous rice and cassava (the country has overtaken Brazil as the world's leading producer) are its main crops. The long southern part of Thailand, linked to the Malay Peninsula by the Isthmus of Kra, is a forested region of rolling hills, producing tin ore and plantation rubber.

Economy and politics

Thailand has long been famous for rice production; though fifth in the world league, it is the biggest exporter and it is still the country's best agricultural earner, despite the increasing importance of several other commodities including rubber, tapioca products and sugar. Wolfram, forest products and fisheries are also being exploited. Industries remain largely underdeveloped, but manufacturing based on cheap labour is expanding rapidly in textiles, clothing, electrical goods and food processing, contributing more to GDP than agriculture since 1984, while local crafts in the villages help to provide overseas income, as does tourism. In 1987 Thailand received nearly 3.5 million visitors – compared with Burma's 47,000.

An absolute monarchy until 1932, when the king graciously surrendered to a bloodless coup that set up a provisional constitution, Thailand has seen a more stable recent history than most of its unfortunate neighbours, though for most of the next 40 years it was dominated by military rulers. Forced into alliance with Japan in World War II, the Thais aligned themselves firmly to the USA after 1945 – a policy that has brought much military, technical and financial aid.

Despite continuing army involvements and interventions – the bloodless coup of 1991, claimed to be protecting King Rama IX and promising a swift return to civilian democracy, was the 17th takeover in half a century – and despite the presence of Cambodian refugees and its use by various camps as a political conduit and military springboard for intentions in South-east Asia, Thailand's subtle and pragmatic approach to life has seen the country prosper. In a system often referred to as 'semi-democracy', constitutional rule propped up by the pillars of military, monarch, bureaucracy and religion, Thailand has managed to avoid the dreadful events that have afflicted the rest of mainland South-east Asia since the end of World War II – though in May 1992 the unelected leadership found itself under serious pressure. Hundreds died in protests against the takeover as prime minister by the head of the army, and an uneasy peace was restored only after his removal and an appeal for order from the King.

While their religion borrows from Hinduism and other creeds, 95% of Thais are Buddhists. There are huge festivals, nearly 30,000 *wats* (temples) and about 250,000 monks.

Situated about 30 km [20 mls] from the Gulf of Thailand, Bangkok is perhaps more dominant in its country's life than any other Asian capital. A city of over 5 million people, it is a remarkable mixture of ancient and modern, subtle and gauche. The old city is a place of more than 300 temples and monasteries (*wats*) dotted near canals (*klongs*). Founded as a royal capital in 1782, this 'Venice of the East' is rich in examples of Thai culture, including fantastic statues of Buddha.

The name Bangkok is in fact incorrect: it means 'village of the wild plum' and refers only to the Thon Buri side of the Chao Phraya River; the proper term is Krung Thep ('city of angels' – like Los Angeles). Today, however, it is a sprawling metropolis struggling to absorb the waves of migrants who pour in from rural areas in search of work ■

LAOS

Designated Asia's poorest country by the World Bank in 1989, Laos is a narrow, landlocked, largely mountainous country with no railways – the Mekong River is the main artery – where 85% of the sparse population work on collective farms at subsistence level, growing mainly rice. The hilly terrain broadens in the north to a wide plateau, 2,000 m [6,500 ft] above sea level, which includes the Plain of Jars, named after prehistoric stone funerary jars found by early French colonialists. The Communists took power in 1975 after two decades of chaotic civil war following the departure of the colonial French, their policies bringing isolation and stagnation under the dominance of the Vietnamese government in Hanoi, who had used the country as a great supply line during their war with the US.

In 1986 the politburo embarked on their own version of perestroika, opening up trade links with neighbours (notably China and Japan), but most crucially developing the export of hydroelectric power from the Mekong to Thailand. Most enterprises are now outside state control, while alternative crops to opium (Laos was estimated the world's third biggest source in the late 1980s) are being tried. Political reform towards a multiparty democracy, however, remains a forlorn hope ∎

Waterfall on the Laotian section of the Mekong, South Asia's longest river and main artery of Indo-China.

CAMBODIA

The heartland of Cambodia is a wide basin drained by the Mekong River, in the centre of which lies the Tonlé Sap ('Great Lake'), a former arm of the sea surrounded by a broad plain. From November to June, when rains are meagre and the Mekong low, the lake drains to the south and away to the sea. During the rainy season and period of high river water in June to October the flow reverses, and the lake more than doubles its area to become the largest freshwater lake in Asia.

The Tonlé Sap lowlands were the cradle of the great Khmer Empire, which lasted from 802 to 1432; its zenith came in the reign of Suryavarman II (1113–50), who built the great funerary temple of Angkor Wat; together with Angkor Thom, the 600 Hindu temples form the world's largest group of religious buildings. The wealth of 'the gentle kingdom' rested on abundant fish from the lake and rice from the flooded lowlands, for which an extensive system of irrigation channels and storage reservoirs was developed

To the south-west stand low mountain chains, while the northern rim of the country is bounded by the Phanom Dangrek uplands, with a prominent sandstone escarpment. Three-quarters of the country is forested, and 90% of the population live on the fertile plains, mostly in small village settlements; Phnom Penh, the capital, is the only major city.

Cambodia was under French rule from 1863 as part of French Indo-China, achieving independence in 1954. In a short period of stability during the late 1950s and 1960s the country developed its small-scale agricultural resources and rubber plantations – it has few workable minerals or sources of power – remaining predominantly rural but achieving self-sufficiency in food, with some exports. However, following years of internal political struggles, involvement in the Vietnam War, a destructive civil war and a four-year period of ruthless Khmer Rouge dictatorship – under which Pol Pot ordered the genocide of somewhere between 1 million and 2.5 million people – Cambodia was left devastated.

After the overthrow of Pol Pot in 1979 by Vietnam, there was civil war between Vietnam's puppet government of the People's Republic of Kampuchea (Cambodia) and the government of Democratic Kampuchea, which was a coalition of Prince Sihanouk – deposed by a US-backed coup in 1970 – Son Sann's Khmer People's Liberation Front and the Khmer Rouge, who from 1982 claimed to have abandoned their Communist ideology. It was this strange tripartite government in exile that was recognized by the United Nations.

Denied almost any aid, Cambodia continued to decline, but it was only the withdrawal of Vietnamese troops in 1989, sparking a fear of a Khmer Rouge revival, that forced a settlement. In October 1991, following numerous failures, a UN-brokered peace plan for elections by 1993 was accepted by all parties concerned, and a glimmer of real hope returned to the beleaguered people of Cambodia. However, peace was fragile following the vote in May, with the Khmer Rouge still running 20% of the country, and there was the massive problem of hundreds of thousands of refugees camped over the border in Thailand ∎

LAOS, CAMBODIA, VIETNAM

CONFLICT IN INDO-CHINA

Vietnamese conflict dates back at least to 1939, when the Viet Minh coalition of nationalists, including Communists, began agitating for independence from France; by 1945 they would not accept a quiet return to colonial administration. Within months of proclaiming the Democratic Republic of Vietnam they were fighting French troops, but gradually the Viet Minh, increasingly dominated by a Communist leadership under Ho Chi Minh, began to overwhelm the French. The US provided weaponry and logistical support, but Presidents Truman and Eisenhower both refused military aid. The climax came in May 1954, when a French army surrendered at Dien Bien Phu. At a peace conference at Geneva, the French abandoned their colony. The country was partitioned on a provisional basis between a Communist north, its capital in Hanoi, and a non-Communist south, administered from Saigon.

The US poured aid into the South, the supposedly Democratic Republic of Vietnam; then President Kennedy decided to make a stand against Communism. American aid was backed up by military advisers, then combat units. The Viet Cong, heirs to the Viet Minh tradition, continued to make progress. In 1963 President Johnson increased the military commitment, but American casualties began to rise – more than 50,000 would die – and with them the tide of anti-war sentiment back home. Johnson stood down from power in 1968, convinced that the war could not be won. Under his successor, Richard Nixon, the war continued, drawing neighbouring Cambodia into the cauldron.

Finally, in 1972, a peace treaty was signed. The Americans withdrew; in 1975 North Vietnamese troops rolled across the 'provisional' border, and the country was reunited.

Mobile street traders sell their meagre wares by the roadside in Hanoi, capital of the reunified Vietnam since 1975.

VIETNAM

A land of mountains, coastal plains and deltas, Vietnam is perhaps Asia's most strangely shaped country. In the north the coastal lands widen into the valley and delta of the Hongha (Red) River and the valley of the Da. This region has long been the main cultural focus of the country, and it was the original core of the Annamite Empire which came into being with the revolt against Chinese rule in AD 939. In the south of the country, the coastal plains open out into the great delta of the Mekong, the world's tenth longest river.

For most of their length the coastal lowlands are backed in the west by the steep and deeply dissected mountains of the Annamite chain, and to the north the country is dominated by the plateaus of Laos and Tongking, often characterized by an intensely craggy, inhospitable karstic (limestone) landscape. The mountain areas are the home of many different hill peoples.

Vietnam already had a long and turbulent history before the French, following decades of missionary involvement and a military campaign lasting 25 years, made it a French protectorate in 1883, later joined by Laos and Cambodia in the French Indo-Chinese Union. Freedom movements starting early in the 20th century made little headway until the end of World War II, when Communist-led guerrillas under Ho Chi Minh, having fought the Japanese occupation, declared Vietnam once again united and free. There then followed a long war against the French (1946–54), which resulted in a Communist-dominated north centred on Hanoi and a non-Communist south, divided at the 17th parallel of latitude. A second and more ferocious conflict between the north and south, involving heavy deployment of US troops – the 'Vietnam War' – began in the early 1960s and engulfed the whole region before the ceasefire in 1973. In 1975, after a relatively brief campaign between north and south, Vietnam was united under a Communist government. Vietnamese forces then invaded Cambodia in 1978 and were involved in a border war with China in 1979.

Such a recent history left Vietnam exhausted – 2 million of its people died in the American war alone and the countryside was devastated – and the problems facing the reunified nation's Communist government in 1976 were enormous. Doctrinaire policies and further aggravation of the Western powers in Cambodia did not help its economic and political isolation, and in 1978 there started the sad saga of the 'Boat People' – peasants fleeing hardship and perhaps persecution in Vietnam to find a new life in Hong Kong and elsewhere; after being put into camps, many were forcibly repatriated years later.

The Hanoi regime softened its position in many ways from the late 1980s, efforts being made to establish diplomatic and trading ties with important international clients and aid donors, Soviet assistance having dwindled with the events in the USSR. However, Vietnam's huge standing army of 1.2 million (plus reserves of 3 million) remained a great drain on a desperately poor nation subsisting on agriculture: rice, cassava, maize, sweet potatoes and the world's largest population of ducks. Despite the industries of the north, based on natural resources, the economy needed to diversify along the pattern of the 'sunrise' countries of eastern Asia. The lifting of the US trade ban by President Clinton in February 1994 was a promising starting point in that process ∎

MALAYSIA

The new country of Malaysia was born in 1963 by the joining of the Federation of Malaya (independent from Britain since 1957), the island state of Singapore and the colonies of Sarawak and North Borneo (renamed Sabah). In 1965 Singapore seceded to become an independent nation, and the present federation comprises 11 states and a federal territory (Kuala Lumpur) on the Malay Peninsula, and two states and a federal territory (Labuan) in northern Borneo. The regions are separated by some 650 km [400 mls] of the South China Sea.

The Malay Peninsula is dominated by fold mountains with a north-south axis. There are seven or eight ranges, with frequently exposed granite cores. The most important is the so-called Main Range, which runs from the Thai border to the south-east of Kuala

Lumpur, attaining 2,182 m [7,159 ft] at its highest point, Gunong Kerbau. South of the Main Range lies the flat and poorly drained lowland of Johor, which is punctuated by isolated hills, often rising over 1,060 m [3,500 ft]. The small rivers of Malaya have built up a margin of lowland around the coasts.

Northern Borneo has a mangrove-fringed coastal plain, up to 65 km [40 mls] wide, backed by hill country averaging 300 m [1,000 ft] in height. This is dominated by the east-west fold mountains of the interior, which rise from 1,400 m to 2,300 m [4,500 to 7,500 ft]; the most striking is the granite peak of Mt Kinabalu (4,101 m [13,455 ft]) in Sabah, Malaysia's highest mountain.

The natural vegetation of most of Malaysia is lowland rainforest and its montane variants. The Malaysian forests, which are dominated by the dipterocarp family of trees, are the richest in species of all the world's forests. Unfortunately, few undisturbed areas remain, mostly in such national parks as the Gunong Mulu in Sarawak and the Kinabalu in Sabah.

In 1414, the ruler of Malacca accepted the Islamic faith, which remains the official religion of Malaysia today. The country is, however, characterized by great ethnic, religious and cultural diversity, with Malays of many different origins, Chinese and Indians (mainly brought in by the British to work the tin mines and rubber plantations), Eurasians, Europeans and a number of aboriginal peoples, notably in Sabah and Sarawak.

This patchwork has, understandably, caused tensions, particularly between the politically dominant Muslim Malays and the economically dominant, mainly Buddhist, Chinese, but while riots did break out in 1969, it has never escalated into serious armed conflict; nor has it prevented remarkable economic growth that has, according to the World Bank ratings, made Malaysia an upper middle-income country.

The traditional mainstays of the economy – rice, plus exports of rubber, palm oil and tin (Malaysia is the world's biggest producer of all three) – have been supplemented by exploitation of other natural resources, notably oil and timber, though the pace of the latter is causing widespread unrest among environmentalists. Exports are now safely diverse, from Sarawak's pepper to the new Proton 'national car', and with a growing tourist industry in support Malaysia seems set to join Japan and the four 'little dragons' as a success story of postwar eastern Asia ∎

SINGAPORE

When Sir Stamford Raffles established British influence in 1819, leasing the island and its muddy Malay fishing village for the East India Company, there were only 150 inhabitants. This had not always been so; 'Singapura' (the city of the lion) was an important settlement in the 14th century, but had been destroyed in the rivalry between the great kingdoms of Madjapahit (Java) and Siam. The modern city, originally planned by Raffles, remained under British rule until self-government in 1959. In 1963, Singapore became part of the Federation of Malaysia, but seceded in 1965 to become a fully independent nation.

The republic comprises the main island itself and an additional 54 much smaller islands lying within its territorial waters. The highest point on the main island is Bukit Tiamah (177 m [581 ft]). The position of Singapore at the southernmost point of the Malay Peninsula, controlling the Strait of Malacca, has throughout history been one of enormous strategic importance.

Singapore is one of the world's most remarkable commercial and industrial experiments. It is, in effect, a city-state, its downtown thick with skyscrapers, the most densely populated country in South-east Asia and an economy based on its vast port, manufacturing and commercial and financial services.

The port began its modern expansion as a conduit for shipping out tin and rubber from Malaya. Today, easily the world's busiest, it handles nearly 70 million tonnes a year, much of it entrepôt (re-export) trade but also involving significant amounts of materials for and from its own thriving industries.

With an area of just over 618 sq km [239 sq mls] and a population of just over 3 million, Singapore is a very crowded state; when Hong Kong reverts to Chinese rule in 1997 it will become the world's most densely populated independent country. Yet it has few natural resources, growing little food and reliant on the causeway from Malaysia for most of its water.

The success of Singapore owes much to the vision and dynamism of Lee Kuan Yew, prime minister from independence in 1959 to 1990, who despite having a

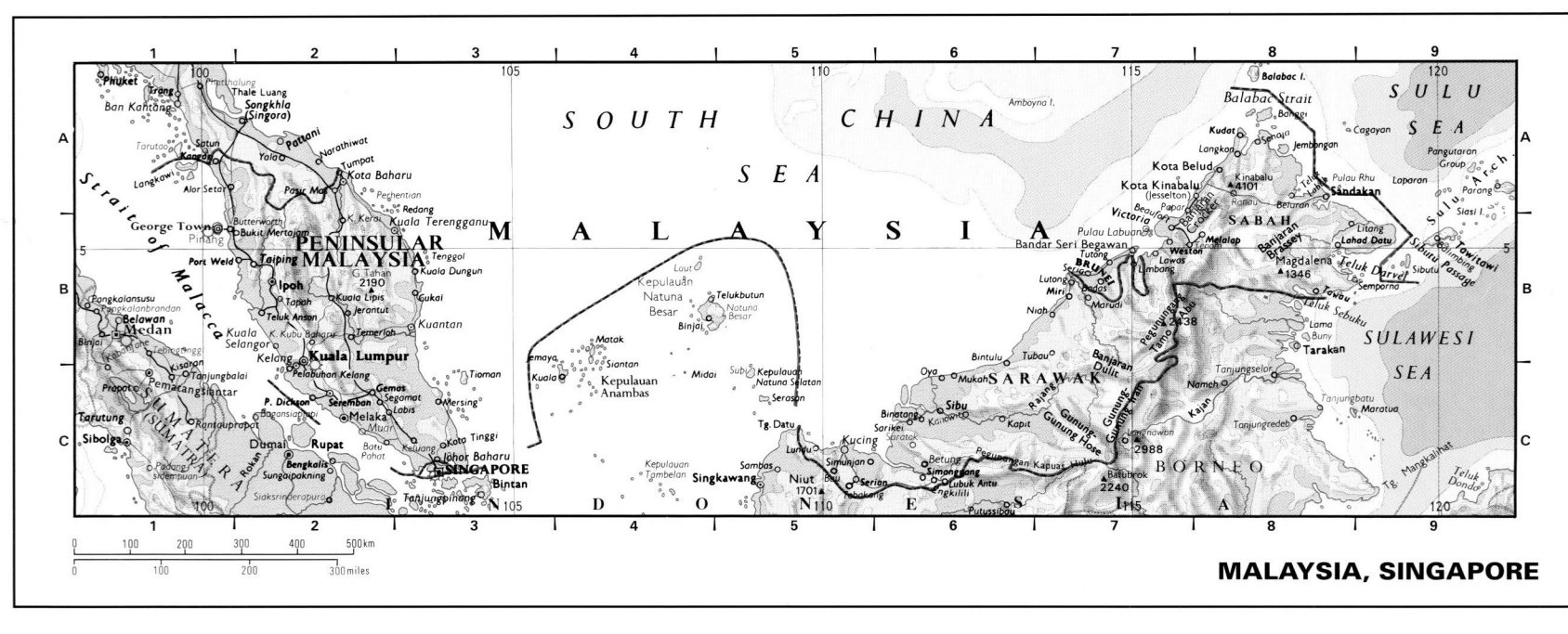

MALAYSIA, SINGAPORE

predominantly Chinese population in a Malay region made his ambitious policies work. The strategy of industrialization, first labour- and later skill-intensive, gave Singapore an average growth of 7% a year and made it the richest of Asia's four 'little dragons'.

The cost, however, was a lack of genuine democracy, his regime increasingly bordering on a one-party dictatorship; his attitude, essentially, was that Singapore could not afford the luxury – or danger – of political debate. Impressive though the new city may be, most Singaporeans live in massive apartment blocks reminiscent of postwar Eastern Europe, with most aspects of their lives rigidly controlled and much of their former culture buried forever beneath a Western façade.

Lee's groomed successor, Goh Chok Tong, seemed set to continue his policies with equal vigour, turning Singapore into the hub of an expanding region. Despite its political stance, it was in the vanguard of nations opening up links with the reticent Communist countries of Laos, Vietnam and North Korea in the post-perestroika era.

The future of his party's wealthy establishment appeared secure, with the island state setting its sights on replacing Hong Kong as eastern Asia's second financial and commercial centre after Tokyo. The feeling nevertheless persisted that Singapore's crucial tertiary activity would give it little to fall back on in the face of a really deep and lasting world recession ■

The central business district of Singapore masks part of the city's vast harbour complex. The world's busiest port is being expanded by using rock and earth capped from the modest hills of the island's centre and reclaiming land from the sea.

BRUNEI

Comprising two small enclaves on the coast of northern Borneo, Brunei rises from humid plains to forested mountains over 1,800 m [6,000 ft] high along the Malaysian border. Formerly a British protectorate, and still a close ally of the UK, the country was already rich from oil (discovered by Shell in 1929) when it became independent in 1983. Today oil and gas account for 70% of GDP and even more of export earnings – oil 41%, gas 53% – though income from the resultant investments overseas exceeds both. Imports are dominated by machinery, transport equipment,

Floating palace: the Sultan of Brunei's fanciful home, one of his many residences, reflects the massive wealth of the world's richest man.

manufactures and foodstuffs. Brunei is, however, currently undergoing a major drive towards agricultural self-sufficiency.

The revenues have made Sultan Hassanal Bolkiah (crowned 1968) allegedly the world's richest man, and given his people the second highest income per capita in Asia after Japan. There is no income tax system in Brunei and citizens enjoy free cradle-to-the-grave welfare. All government employees (two-thirds of the workforce) are banned from political activity, and the Sultan and his family retain complete control ■

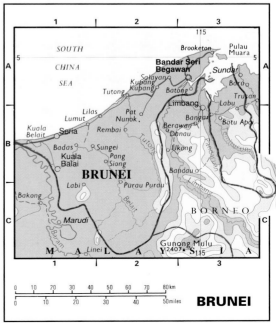

BRUNEI

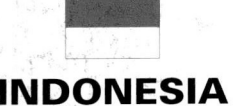

INDONESIA

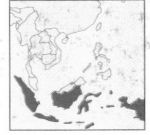

With the break-up of the Soviet Union in late 1991, Indonesia moved up from the fifth to the fourth most populous nation on Earth. It is also the world's largest archipelago, with 13,677 islands (less than 6,000 of which are inhabited) scattered over an enormous area of tropical sea. However, three-quarters of the area is included in the five main centres of Sumatra, Java, Kalimantan (southern Borneo), Sulawesi (Celebes) and Irian Jaya (the western end of New Guinea), which also include over 80% of the people; more than half the population live on Java alone, despite its being only 7% of the land area.

Most of the big islands stand on continental shelves and have extensive coastal lowlands, though Sulawesi and the chain of islands between Java and Irian Jaya rise from deep water. All are mountainous, for this is an area of great crustal activity. Along the arc formed by Sumatra, Java and the Lesser Sunda Islands stand over 200 volcanoes, about 70 of which – including Krakatoa (Pulau Rakata) in the Sunda Strait – have erupted within the last two centuries, usually with memorable violence. Java alone has over 120 volcanoes, 14 of which exceed 3,000 m [10,000 ft].

The natural vegetation of the tropical lowlands is rainforest, which also spreads up into the hills. Much of this has now been cleared by shifting cultivators and replaced by secondary growth, though forest is still the dominant vegetation on most of the less populated islands. About a tenth of the land area is under permanent cultivation, mostly rice, maize, cassava and sweet potato, and Indonesia remains essentially an agricultural nation. There are also large plantations of rubber, sugar cane, coffee and tea. Accessible parts of the rainforest are being exploited at an alarming rate for their valuable timber; native forest in Sumatra is now virtually restricted to reserves and national parks, though mountain forests, less vulnerable because they are more isolated, still remain over wide areas. Many of the coasts are lined with mangrove swamps, and several accessible islands are stunningly beautiful; tourism is one of the country's fastest growing sectors.

The population of Indonesia is complex and varied. There is a wide range of indigenous peoples, speaking some 25 different languages and over 250 dialects. Four of the world's major religions – Islam, Hinduism, Christianity and Buddhism – are well represented, though followers of Islam are in the great majority and Indonesia is the world's most populous Muslim nation.

The first important empire in the region was centred at Palembang in south-eastern Sumatra. This was the great maritime power of Sri Vijaya, which held sway from the 8th to 13th centuries over the important trade routes of the Malacca and Sunda Straits. During the 14th century it was replaced by the kingdom of Madjapahit, centred on the fertile lands of east-central Java. From the 16th century onwards, European influences grew, the area coming progressively under the domination and ruthless exploitation of the Dutch East India Company. Freedom movements starting in the early 20th century found their full expression under Japanese occupation in World War II, and Indonesia declared its independence on the surrender of Japan in 1945. After four years of intermittent but brutal fighting, the Dutch finally recognized the country as a sovereign state in 1949 under Achmed Sukarno, leader of the nationalist party since 1927.

Sukarno's anti-Western stance and repressive policies plunged his country into chaos, while costly military adventures drained the treasury. In 1962 he invaded Dutch New Guinea (Irian Jaya) and between 1963 and 1966 he attempted to destabilize the fledgling Federation of Malaysia by incursions into northern Borneo. Throughout his dictatorship Indonesia seemed to be permanently on the edge of disintegration, government forces fighting separatist movements in various parts of the island chain.

In 1967 Sukarno was toppled by General Suharto, following the latter's suppression of a two-year allegedly Communist-inspired uprising that cost 80,000 lives. However, his military regime, with US technical and financial assistance, brought a period of relatively rapid economic growth, supported by an oil boom that by 1970 accounted for 70% of export earnings – a figure that shrank to less than 50% by 1990. Self-sufficiency in rice and a degree of population control also helped raise living standards, though

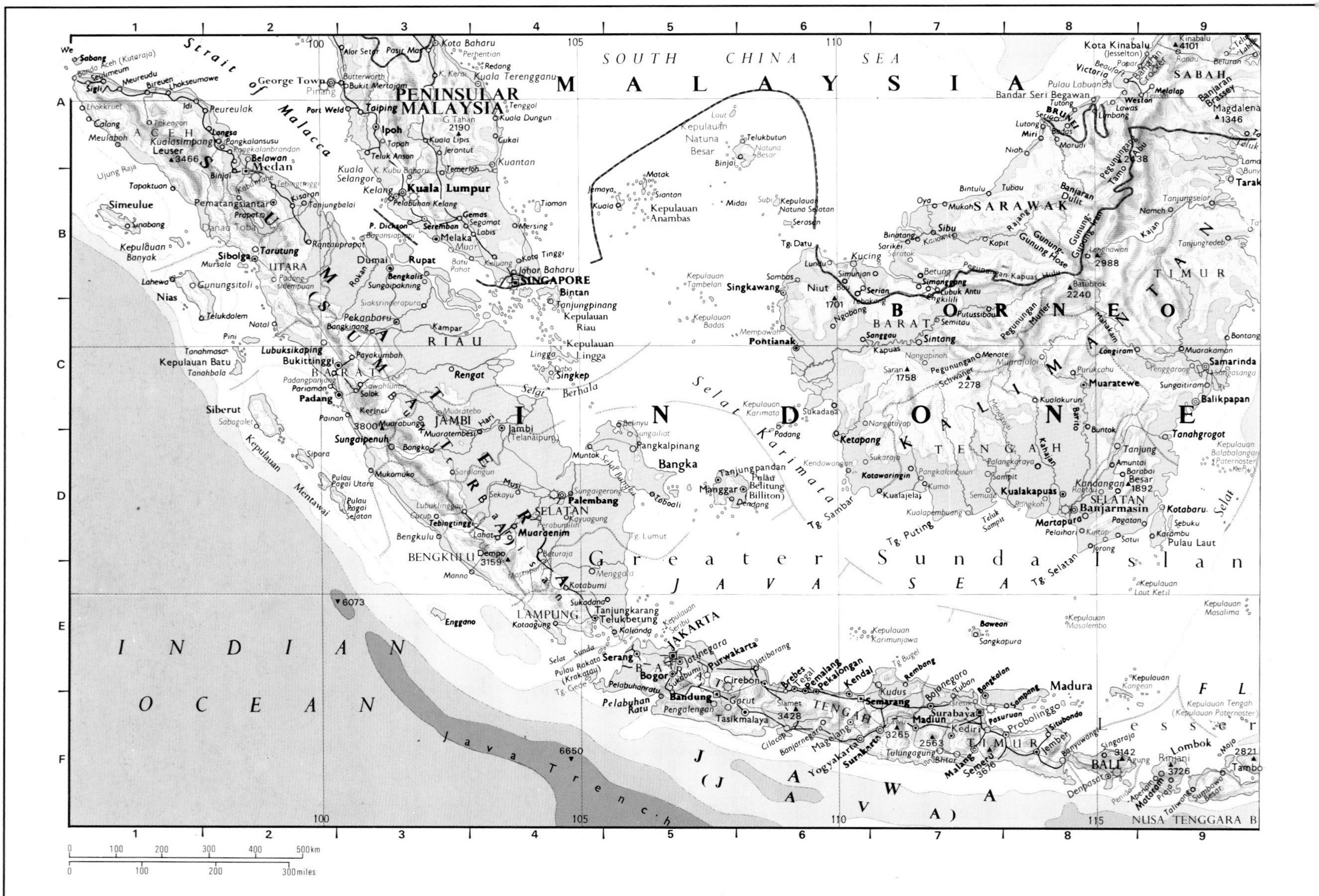

Sculptured terracing for rice on the slopes of Bali. The intricate irrigation system, refined over centuries, represents a complex social structure among the landowners and tenants.

Java's overcrowding remained a problem, and in 1986 a 'transmigration programme' was initiated to settle large numbers of Javanese on sparsely populated islands, notably (and notoriously) on Irian Jaya.

While the Javanese dominate Indonesian affairs, most of the country's wealth – oil, timber, minerals and plantation crops – come from other islands. Establishing better relations with the West and its ASEAN (Association of South-east Asian Nations) neighbours, the government has now deregulated much of the economy, but corruption and nepotism remain rife and power is firmly in the hands of Golkar, the military-backed coalition which thwarts the aspirations of the two permitted political parties. The army, perhaps correctly, continues to regard itself as the only protector of stability in a country that has proved almost impossible to govern ■

EAST TIMOR

Invaded by Indonesian troops in 1975, East Timor has effectively remained its 21st state despite numerous UN condemnatory resolutions. The end of the Cold War has done little to ease the people's plight; Australia still does not recognize their right to self-determination, while the Western powers leave the problem to the ineffectual UN.

East Timor was a neglected, coffee-growing Portuguese colony for 300 years before Lisbon promised independence in 1974. The 1975 free elections were won by Fretilin, the left-wing nationalists who had fought the empire for years, but the following month Indonesia occupied the territory. Their policies of deportation, resettlement, harassment, torture, bombings, executions and massacres – including one filmed by a British film crew in 1991 – have resulted in the deaths of a third of the population (still officially 630,000) and the encampment of 150,000 or more, according to Amnesty International. At the same time, 100,000 Indonesians have been settled in a country rich in sandalwood, marble and coffee, with oil reserves estimated at some 5 billion barrels.

Fretilin's fighters, who returned to the hills in 1975, have since kept up a sporadic and dispersed campaign, while the population – mostly devout Roman Catholic – await international help. In practice, however, East Timor stays closed to the world, its people effectively ignored by Western nations keen not to de-stabilize the regime in Jakarta.

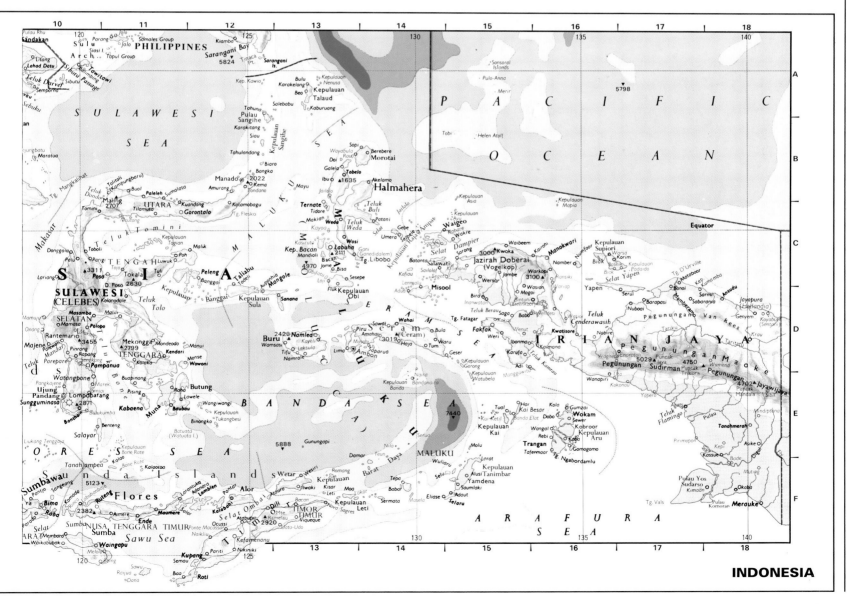

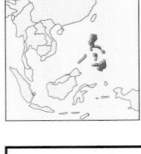

PHILIPPINES

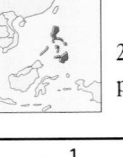

The Republic of the Philippines consists of 7,107 islands, of which, 2,770 are named and about 1,000 permanently inhabited, with the two

A water buffalo grazes near the volcanic cone of Mt Mayon, the highest point in southern Luzon.

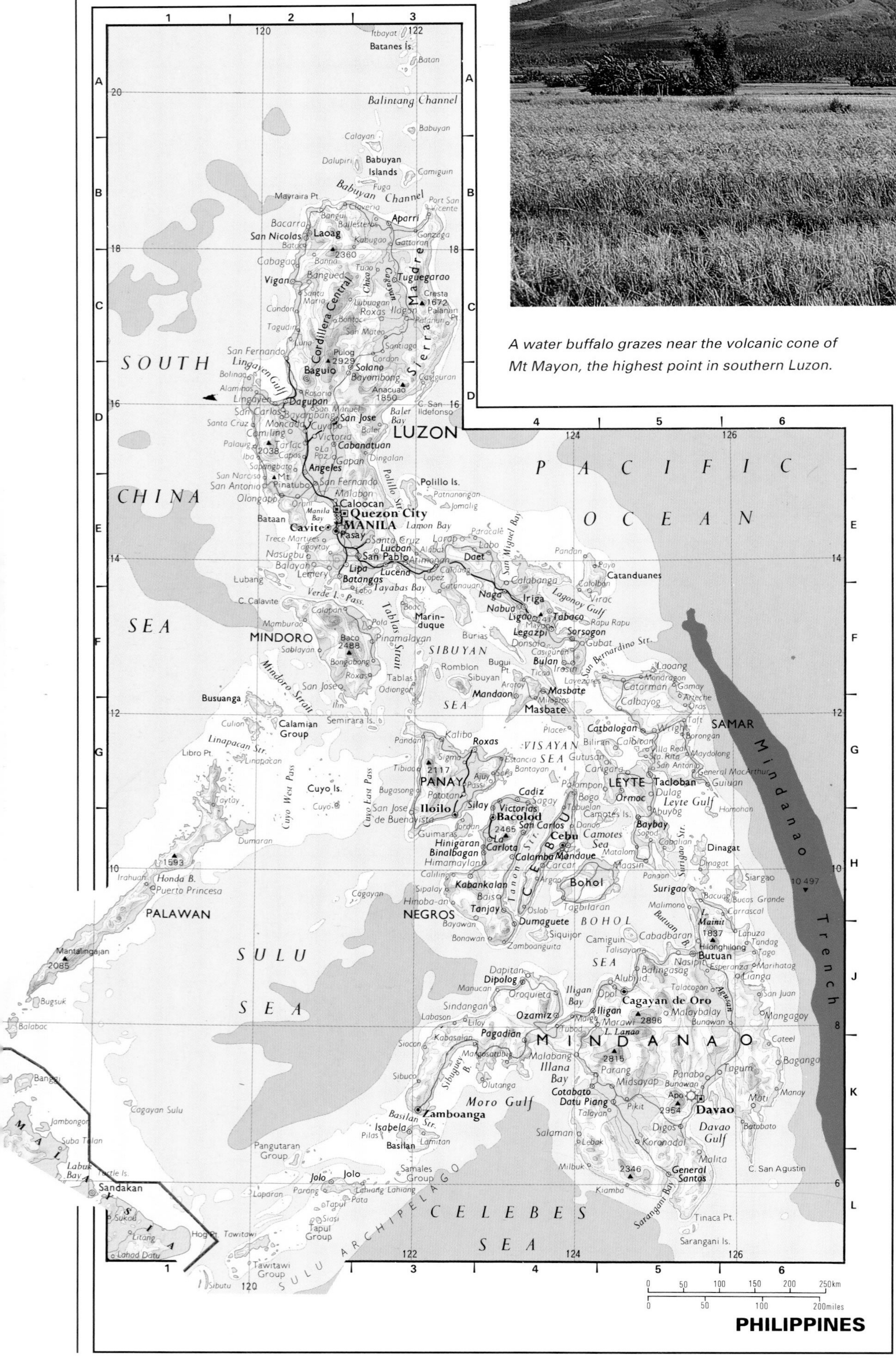

largest, Luzon and Mindanao, taking up over two-thirds of the total area. The country lacks extensive areas of lowland and most of the islands are characterized by rugged interior mountains, the highest of which are Mt Apo (2,954 m [9,691 ft]) in Mindanao and Mt Pulog (2,929 m [9,610 ft]) in Luzon. There are over 20 active volcanoes in the islands, including Mt Apo and Mt Pinatubo, which erupted violently in 1991. The most important lowland region is the central plain of Luzon, a key rice-producing area and a major zone of population concentration, including the Manila Bay area.

The most impressive man-made sight, however, is the spectacular series of irrigated rice terraces that contour the mountain slopes in the northern interior of Luzon. These have been constructed by Igorot tribesmen, descendants of some of the earliest people to colonize the Philippines. Elsewhere in the islands, and especially on Cebu, Leyte and Negros, maize is the staple foodstuff, reflecting the Philippines' former contacts with Spanish America. Another link is Roman Catholicism; over 80% Catholic, and named after King Philip II of Spain, the country is the only predominantly Christian nation of any size in Asia.

Following three centuries of harsh Spanish rule the islands were ceded to the US in 1898 after the Spanish-American War. Though the Philippines gained independence from the USA in 1946, ties with the US have remained strong, notably during the corrupt regime of President Ferdinand Marcos (1965–86), though in 1991 the Philippines government announced the closure of Subic Bay US naval base, the largest in Asia, by the end of 1992.

Marcos was overthrown by the 'people power' revolution that brought to office Cory Aquino, wife of the opposition leader assassinated in 1983, but the political situation remained volatile, with Communist New People's Army guerillas and Muslim Nationalist extremist rebels and Muslim separatists in southern Mindanao all undermining stability. Mrs Aquino was subsequently defeated by former defence secretary Fidel V. Ramos in the May 1992 presidential elections. The economy, lacking any real natural resources is unable to imitate its successful 'sunrise' neighbours and remains weak; levels of unemployment and emigration among Filipinos are high ∎

PHILIPPINES

Africa

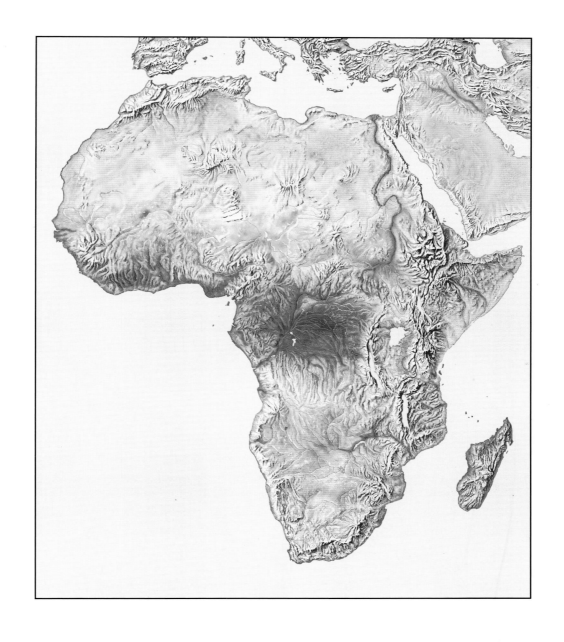

AFRICA

Extending to some 35° north and south of the Equator, the vast continent of Africa covers a wide range of environments. Mediterranean Africa, lying north of the Sahara, includes the sharply folded and eroded Atlas Mountains; the coastal and Nile valley lands were the home of the ancient civilization of Egypt, with rich evidence of early Phoenician, Greek, Roman and Muslim contacts. The Sahara

Desert stretches across northern Africa from west to east, containing the mountain massifs of Hoggar and Tibesti; lowlands to the east are threaded from south to north by the Nile Valley.

South of the Sahara, Africa may be divided by the 1,000 m [3,000 ft] contour line running from south-west (Angola) to north-east (Ethiopia). North of this line the low plateaus of Central and West Africa surround the great river basins of the Zaire (Congo) and Niger rivers and the inland basin of Lake Chad. Here are Africa's major areas of tropical rainforest, with savanna dominant on the inner and higher ground. East and south of this contour lie Africa's high-est plateaus and mountains, and the complex rift

valley systems of north-eastern and East Africa.

The rift valleys of East Africa are part of the most extensive fissure in the Earth's crust, extending south from the Dead Sea, down the Red Sea, across the Ethiopian Highlands, through Kenya to reach the sea again near the mouth of the Zambezi. Both this main rift and its principal branch to the west of Lake Victoria contain deep long lakes of which Tanganyika, Turkana (formerly Rudolf) and Nyasa are the largest. Here also are the high, open and grassy savanna plains

RIGHT A view across Tanzania's Arusha National Park towards the Kenyan border and Mt Kilimanjaro, at 5,895 m [19,340 ft] Africa's highest mountain.

Africa's most precious commodity, water, too often arrives in the wrong places. These falls are a modest pipeline away from arid areas in Ethiopia.

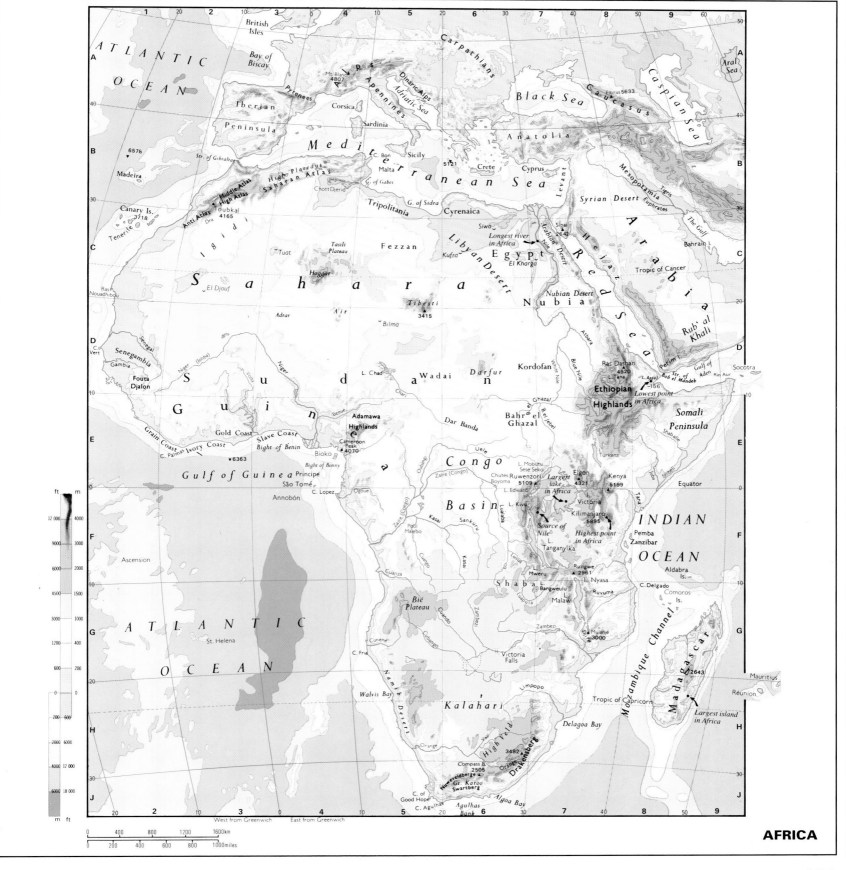

AFRICA

with most of Africa's famous wildlife game parks and great snow-capped peaks, notably Kilimanjaro. South and west of the Zambezi River system lie the arid uplands of the Kalahari and Namib deserts, and the dry highlands of Namibia. In the far south a damper climate brings the Mediterranean conditions to the plains of South Africa, and to the Drakensberg and Cape Ranges.

The Sahara Desert formed a barrier that was at least partly responsible for delaying European penetration; Africa south of the Sahara remained the 'Dark Continent' for Europeans until well into the 19th century. The last 15 years of the century saw the final stages of the European 'scramble for Africa' that

resulted in most of the continent being partitioned between and colonized by Britain, France, Germany, Belgium, Portugal and Spain. Today, almost all the states of Africa are independent, though traces of their recent colonial history are still evident in their official languages, administrative institutions, legal and educational systems, architecture, transport networks and economics.

The colonial pattern, and the current political pattern succeeding it, were superimposed on a very complex and fluid system of indigenous tribal states and cultures, many of which have proved to be remarkably resilient. There are many hundreds of ethnic groups, languages and religions; indeed, the

peoples of Africa themselves are of many physical types, at many different levels of economic, social and political development, and they have reacted in differing ways to European colonial rule ∎

RIGHT *Shifting sands in southern Morocco, on the eastern fringes of the Sahara. The world's largest desert was not always a wasteland: as recently as 15,000 years ago, during the last Ice Age, areas like this were green and fertile.*

BELOW RIGHT *Traditional settlements on rich red earth in Kenya, at the southern end of the Rift Valley that governs the topography of eastern Africa.*

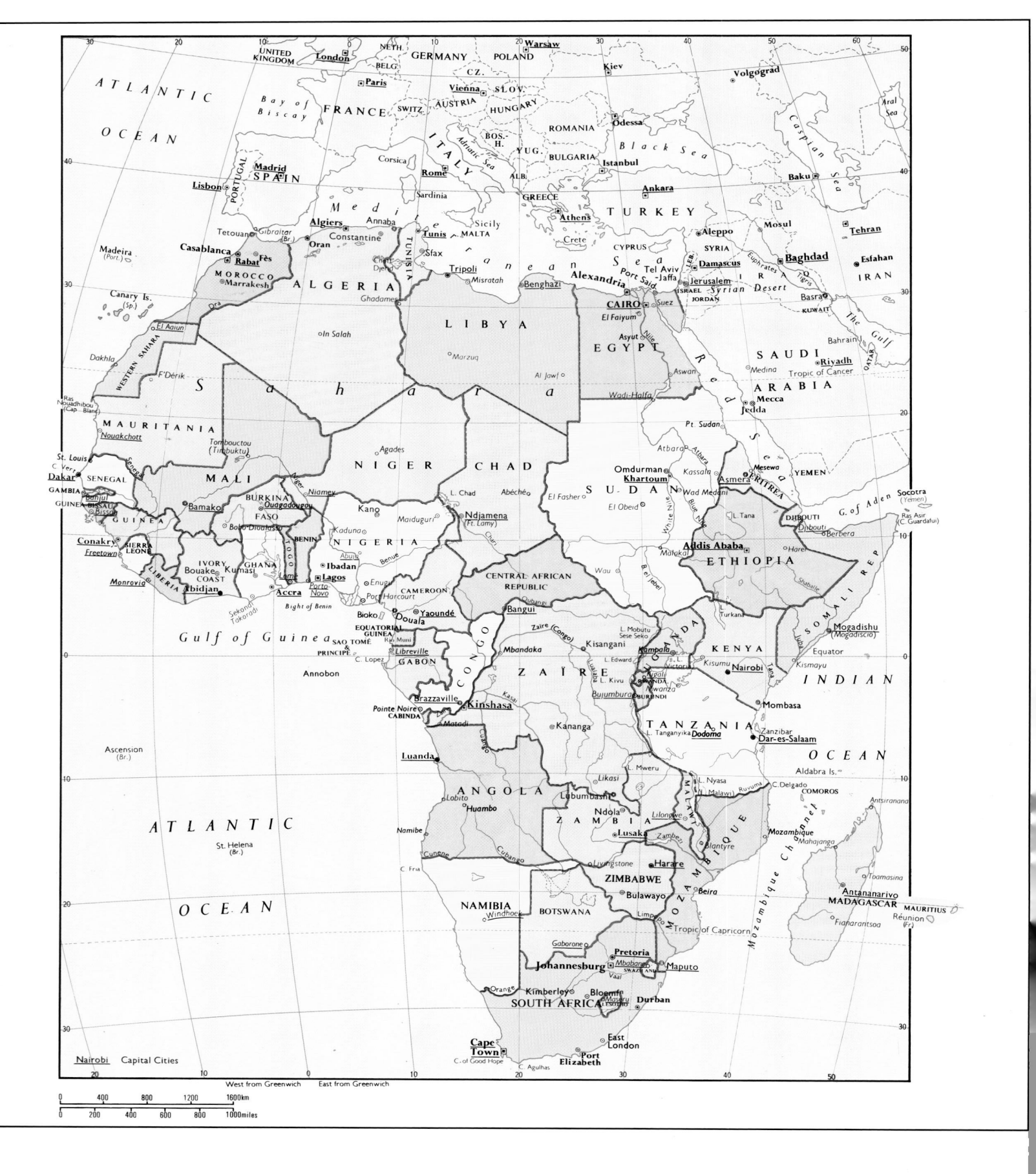

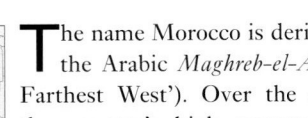

MOROCCO

The name Morocco is derived from the Arabic *Maghreb-el-Aksa* ('the Farthest West'). Over the centuries the country's high mountains have acted as a barrier to penetration, so that Morocco has been much less affected by outside influences than Algeria and Tunisia. Morocco was the last North African territory to succumb to European colonialism; not until 1912 did the Sultan of Morocco accept the French protectorate, in a settlement that gave Spain control of the Rif Mountains and several enclaves along the coast (of which Ceuta and Melilla remain under Spanish administration).

In 1956 France and Spain gave up their protectorate as Morocco became independent, and in 1958 the international zone of Tangier was incorporated in a unified Morocco, which became an independent kingdom. Ruled since 1961 by the authoritarian and nationalistic regime of King Hassan II, Morocco is today one of only three kingdoms left on the continent of Africa, though the king's grip was showing signs of slipping during the unsettled 1980s.

Since independence a large proportion of the once-important European and Jewish communities have departed. To the difficulties accompanying reunification were added the burdens of a fast-growing population – nearly half the people are under 15 – high unemployment and lack of trained personnel and capital. Yet Morocco has considerable potential for economic development: the country possesses large cultivable areas, abundant water supplies for irrigation and hydroelectric power, and diverse mineral resources including deposits of iron ore, lead and zinc.

Agriculture and industry

More than a third of Morocco is mountainous. The main uplands are the High, Middle and Anti 'arms' of the Atlas Mountains in the west and north, and a plateau in the east. Peasant cultivation and semi-nomadic pastoralism are the main ways of life.

In contrast to these, modern economic development is found in the Atlantic plains and plateaus. The major irrigation schemes created during the colonial period are situated here, as well as the majority of Morocco's agricultural production – citrus fruits, grapes, vegetables, wheat and barley. More than half of the population is involved in agriculture.

A Berber tribesman, a descendant of the original inhabitants of Morocco, tends his camels in the Middle Atlas mountains.

Phosphates, of which Morocco is the world's leading exporter and third largest producer, are mined around Khouribga as well as in Western Sahara. These are the vital raw material for fertilizers. But the country's modern industry is concentrated in the Atlantic ports, particularly in Casablanca, which is the largest city, chief port and major manufacturing centre.

The biggest growth industry, however, is tourism, based on the Atlantic beaches, the Atlas Mountains and the rich, international history of cities like Casablanca, Tangier, Agadir, Marrakech, Rabat and Fès (Fez), famed not only for its hat but also as the home of the University of Kairaouin – founded in 859 and the oldest educational institution in the world. Morocco is Africa's biggest tourist destination, the only one attracting more than 2 million visitors a year. Tunisia and Egypt are its nearest rivals.

Western Sahara is a former Spanish possession (and the province of Spanish Sahara from 1960) occupying the desert lands between Mauritania and the Atlantic coast; with an area of 266,000 sq km [102,700 sq mls] it is more than half the size of Morocco. Most of the indigenous population are Sahrawis, a mixture of Berber and Arab, almost all of whom are Muslims. The capital is El Aaiún, which has a population of 97,000.

Rich in phosphates – it has the world's largest known deposits of phosphate rock – the country has since the mid-1970s been the subject of considerable conflict, with the Rabat government claiming the northern two-thirds as part of 'Greater Morocco'.

In 1991, more than 170,000 Sahrawi refugees were living in camps around Tindouf, in western Algeria, when a ceasefire was brokered between the Rabat government and the Polisario Front, the Sahrawi liberation movement, but three years later King Hassan had still not implemented the referendum agreed at the UN ∎

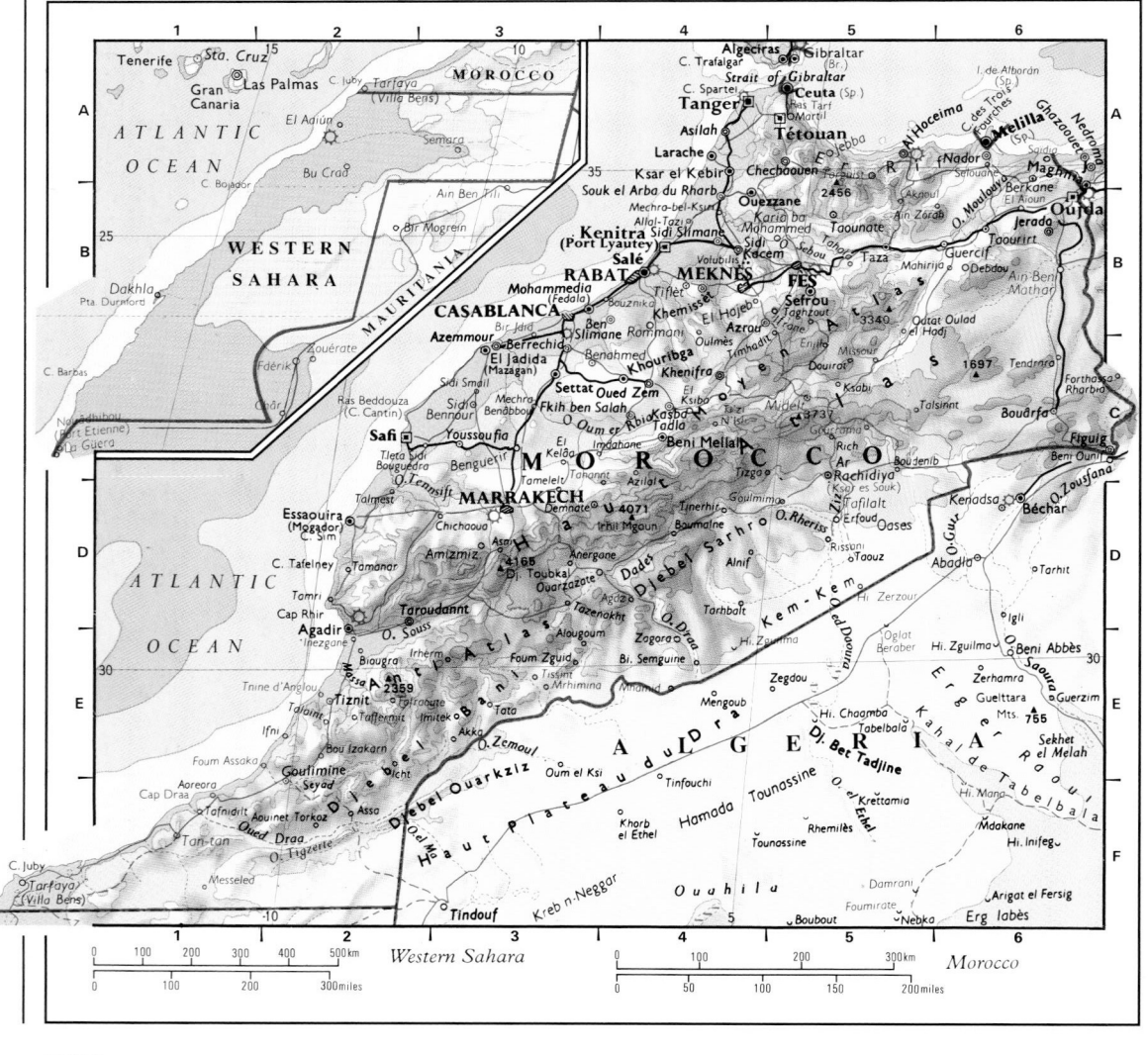

ALGERIA

After Sudan, Algeria is the biggest political unit in the Middle East and Africa, and the world's 10th largest nation. However, over 90% of the country's 25.7 million inhabitants live in the Mediterranean coastlands. The vast Saharan territories, covering over 2 million sq km [772,200 sq mls], or about 85% of the total area, are very sparsely populated; most of the inhabitants are concentrated in the oases, which form densely-populated 'islands' separated by vast empty areas. The majority of the population speak Arabic, but there is a significant Berber-speaking indigenous minority in the mountainous north-east.

Like its neighbours Morocco and Tunisia, Algeria experienced French colonial rule and settler colonization. Algeria was the first Maghreb country to be conquered by France and the last to receive independence, following years of bitter warfare between nationalist guerrillas and the French armed forces.

Oil was discovered in the Algerian Sahara in 1956 and Algeria's natural gas reserves are among the largest in the world. The country's crude-oil refining capacity is the biggest in Africa. Since independence in 1962 revenues from oil and gas, which provide 65% of all revenue and account for over 90% of exports, have enabled the government to embark on an ambitious economic development programme, with rapid industrialization.

Industrial developments include iron and steel plants, food processing, chemicals and textiles, while Algeria is one of the few African nations to have its own car-manufacturing facility, producing about a third of its commercial vehicles. In addition there is a variety of industry allied to the oil and gas reserves, including oil refineries and petrochemical plants.

Though agriculture has suffered by comparison, about 30% of Algerians are farmers. Arable land accounts for only 3% of the total land area, but the rich northern coastlands produce wheat, barley, vines and olives – as well as early fruit and vegetables for the European markets, notably France and Italy. Further south the primary occupation of the Berber population is the rearing of sheep, cattle and goats.

In January 1992, with the Islamic fundamentalist FIS on course for electoral victory, the government cancelled the second round and declared a state of emergency, with Western approval ending Algeria's four-year flirtation with Western-style democracy ■

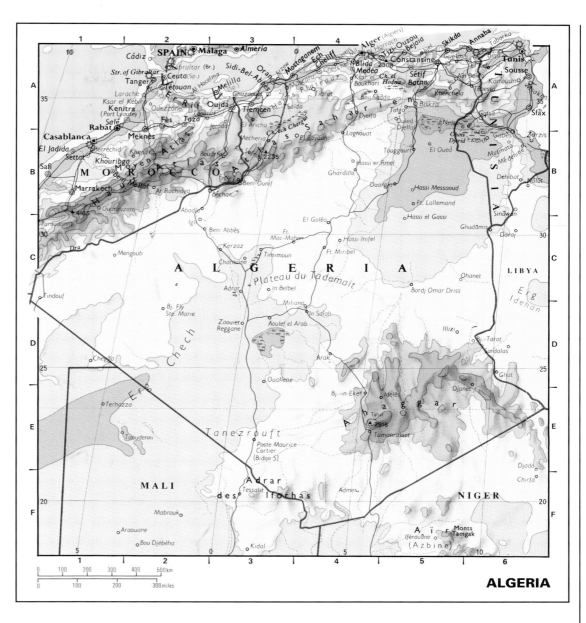

ALGERIA

THE ATLAS MOUNTAINS

Extending from Morocco into northern Algeria and Tunisia, the Atlas is a prominent range of fold mountains. Its highest peak and the highest in North Africa, Jebel Toubkal (4,165 m [13,670 ft]), is one of a jagged row – the High Atlas – in central Morocco; the lesser ranges cluster on either side and to the east, generally with a north-east to south-west trend.

In Morocco there are the Anti-Atlas in the south-west, the Middle Atlas in the centre of the country (*left*) and the Er Rif mountains near the Mediterranean coast. In Algeria the range includes the Saharan Atlas and, further north, the Tell or Maritime Atlas. Heavily glaciated during the Ice Age, the highest Atlas ranges are now capped with alpine tundra and patches of permanent snow. North-facing slopes receive good winter rainfall, and are forested with pines, cedars, and evergreen and cork oaks. Tablelands between the ranges provide high pastures and rich soils for farming. The southern and eastern ranges are drier and covered with semi-desert scrub.

LIBYA

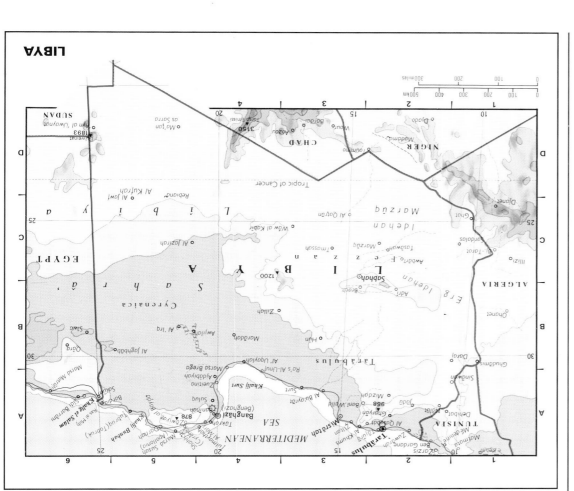

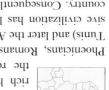

W hen the Kingdom of Libya gained independence from British and French military adminis-tration in 1951, the former Turkish possession and Italian colony was one of the poorest countries in the world, with a predomi-nantly desert environment, few known natural re-sources and a largely nomadic, poor and backward population. This bleak picture changed dramatically after 1959 with the discovery of vast reserves of oil and natural gas.

With growing revenues from petroleum and gas exports, important highways were built to link the different regions across the desert, and considerable investment was made in housing, education and health. Today the country's income per head is twice that of its nearest rivals on the African continent – Algeria, Gabon and South Africa. But despite a high population growth rate (6.5%), the process of agri-cultural development and industrialization still relies heavily on immigrant specialists and workers.

In 1969 a group of 12 army officers overthrew King Idris in a coup and control of all matters has since been in the hands of the Revolutionary Command Council, chaired in dictatorial style by Colonel Muammar Gaddafi. While this includes a violently pro-Palestinian and anti-Western stance, Gaddafi also has long-running disputes with his neighbours, notably Chad – where he suffered hum-iliating defeat in 1987 – and Sudan ∎

A Moorish backstreet in the old part of Tripoli. Heavily bombed during World War II, the Libyan capital was attacked by US aircraft in 1986 – a vain attempt to mollify the regime's hardline anti-Western attitude.

TUNISIA

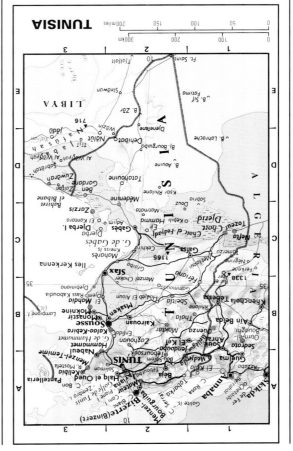

S mallest of the three Maghreb countries that comprise north-west Africa, Tunisia has a long and rich history. It was the first part of the region to be conquered by the Phoenicians, Romans, (Carthage is now a suburb of Tunis) and later the Arabs and Turks, and each succes-sive civilization has left a marked impression on the country. Consequently Tunisia has acquired a distinct national identity, with a long tradition of urban life. Close contacts with Europe have always existed – France established a protectorate in 1881 – and the majority of today's 2 million tourists a year are European, many of them French.

Tunisia consists of the eastern end of the Atlas Mountains together with the central steppelands to the south, which are separated from the country's Saharan sector by the vast low-lying saltpans of Chott Djerid. In the north the lower Medjerda Valley and the low-lying plains of Bizerte and Tunis were densely colonized. Major irrigation schemes have been carried out in recent years and these lowlands, which produce cereals, vines, citrus fruits, olives and vegetables, represent the country's most important agricultural area. New industries, sometimes coupled with tourism, have transformed a number of coastal towns, including Sfax, Monastir and Sousse. By comparison the interior has been neglected, except to produce the main exports of oil and gas.

Although Tunisia has introduced the elements of democracy since the removal of Habib Bourguiba in 1987, it remains effectively a one-party (RCD) dicta-torship. In 1992 the government also clamped down heavily on the already outlawed Islamic fundamen-talist movement, the latest threat to its supremacy, but six opposition parties were allowed in 1994 ∎

EGYPT

But for the River Nile, which brings the waters of the East African and Ethiopian Highlands north to the Mediterranean, Egypt would scarcely be populated, for 96% of the present population lives in the Nile Valley and its rich delta.

The vast majority of the country, away from the Nile, is desert and semi-desert. Egypt's deserts are not uniform, but offer varied landscapes. Beyond the Gulf of Suez and the Suez Canal, the Sinai Peninsula in the south is mountainous and rugged; it contains the highest of Egypt's mountains – Gebel Katherina (2,637 m [8,650 ft]) – and is almost entirely uninhabited. The Eastern Desert, between the Nile and the Red Sea, is a much dissected area and parts of the Red Sea Hills are over 2,000 m [6,560 ft]; water is obtained from the light rainfall, from occasional springs, and from beneath dry stream beds. Except for a few mining settlements along the coast, this area is not suitable for permanent settlement and is occupied mostly by nomads.

The Western Desert includes almost three-quarters of Egypt and consists of low vales and scarps, mainly of limestones. Over its stony and sandy surfaces great tank battles were fought in World War II. A number of depressions in the desert surface fall below sea level, the most notable being the Qattâra Depression (–133 m [–435 ft]) – a waste of salt lakes and marshes.

The Nile Valley was one of the cradles of civilization, and Egypt has the longest-known history of any African country. The dependable annual flooding of the river each summer and the discovery of the art of cultivating wheat and barley fostered simple irrigation techniques and favoured co-operation between the farmers. Stability and leisure developed arts and crafts, city life began and the foundations were laid of writing, arithmetic and astronomy. Great temples and pyramid tombs within the valley remain as memorials to this early civilization – and a magnet for nearly 2 million tourists every year.

Today, even more than in the past, the Egyptian

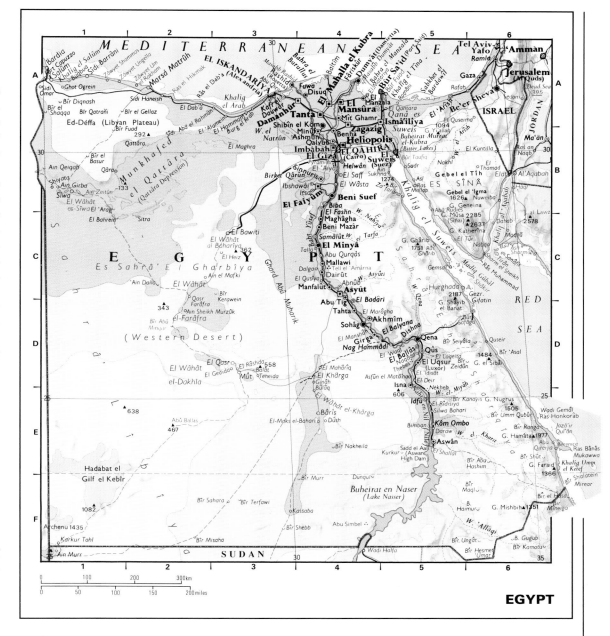

EGYPT

people, living within a desert, depend almost entirely on the waters of the Nile. These are extremely seasonal, and control and storage have become essential during this century. For seasonal storage the Aswan Dam (1902) and the Jebel Awliya Dam in Sudan (1936) were built. The Aswan High Dam (1970), sited 6.4 km [4 mls] above the Aswan Dam, is the greatest of all. Built with massive Soviet aid, it holds back 25 times as much as the older dam and permits year-round storage. Through this dam the Egyptian Nile is now regulated to an even flow throughout the year. The water that has accumulated behind the dam in Lake Nasser (about 5,000 sq km [1,930 sq mls]) is making possible the reclamation of more desert land, the intensification of agriculture and the cultivation of crops that need more water, such as rice for export. The dam is also a source of hydroelectric power and aids the expansion of industry. However, 50,000 Nubians had to be resettled and the regulation of the river's flow has led to some unforeseen environmental problems.

Egypt's industrial development has come about since World War II. Textiles, including the spinning, weaving, dyeing and printing of cotton, wool, silk and artificial fibres, form by far the largest industry. Other manufactures derive from local agricultural and mineral raw materials.

The Suez Canal, opened in 1869 and 173 km [107 mls] long, is still an important trading route. Though it cannot take the large modern cargo-vessels, oil-tankers and liners, it still carries 20,000 vessels a year between the Mediterranean and the Red Sea ■

Harvesting sugar cane near the Nile at Luxor. The name derives from the Arabic for palaces, and temples and cenotaphs to the pharoahs pepper the area.

MAURITANIA

O ver two-thirds of Mauritania – twice the size of France but just over 2 million people – consists of rocky and sandy desert wastes, much of it in the Sahara. Apart from the main north-south highway and routes associated with mineral developments, land communications consist of rough tracks.

Only in the southern third of the country and along the Atlantic coast is precipitation sufficient to support Sahelian thorn-bush and grassland. Apart from oasis settlements such as Atar and Tidjikja, the only permanent arable agriculture is in the south, concentrated in a narrow strip along the Senegal River. Crops of millet, sorghum, beans, peanuts and rice are grown, often using the natural late-summer floods for irrigation. When the Senegal River Project is complete, large areas should be developed for irrigated crops of rice, cotton and sugar cane.

Many people are still cattle-herders who drive their herds from the Senegal River through the Sahel steppelands in tandem with the seasonal rains. In good years the country's livestock outnumber the human population by about five to one, but the ravages of drought and the development of the mining industries in the 1980s – allied to traditional overgrazing – have reduced the nomadic population from three-quarters to less than a third of the national total.

Off the Atlantic coast the cold Canaries Current is associated with some of the richest fishing grounds in the world. The national fishing industry is still evolving and over 100,000 tonnes of fish are landed and processed each year, mainly at the major fishing port of Nouadhibou (Port Etienne); the potential catch is estimated at 600,000 tonnes.

As the Atlantic coast in the south of the country lacks good harbours, a port and capital city have been constructed at Nouakchott. This now handles a growing proportion of the country's trade, including exports of copper mined near Akjoujt. Exported minerals, particularly high-grade iron ores, worked from the vast reserves around Fdérik, provide the country with most revenue, though animal products, gum arabic and dates are also among the exports.

The rulers in Nouakchott surrendered their claims to the southern part of the Western Sahara in 1979. The following year slavery was formally abolished – though some estimates put the number of 'Haratines' (descendants of black slaves) still in bondage as high as 100,000 and the Moor (Arab-Berber) elite effectively practise apartheid by denying any political say to the black minorities. Unlike several of the former colonial territories of West and Central Africa, Mauritania was not affected by the wave of democratization that toppled military and single-party regimes from the late 1980s, though multiparty elections were announced in 1991. An opposition boycott, however, allowed Moaouia Taya, president since 1984, to stay in power ∎

Originally 14th century, the Grand Mosque in Djenne, Mali, was rebuilt in the traditional Afro-Arab style by the French in 1907. North-east of the capital of Bamako, the market town is noted for Islamic teaching, thriving crafts and remarkable archaeological finds, including jewellery, preserved in sand.

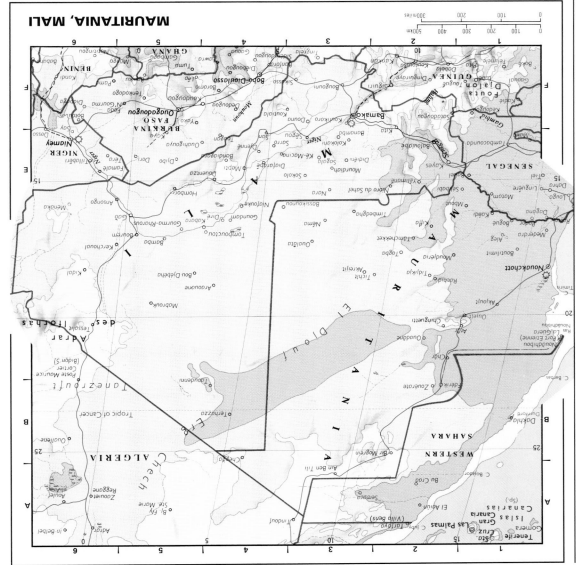

MAURITANIA, MALI

MALI

In the 14th century the centre of a huge West African Malinka empire based on the legendary city of Tim-buktu (Tombouctou), Mali is today a poor, landlocked, butterfly-shaped country consisting mainly of lifeless Saharan desert plains. Water (or the lack of it) dominates the life of the people and most of the country's population is concentrated along the Senegal and Niger rivers, which provide water for stock and irrigation and serve as much-needed communication routes. The Niger and its tributaries support a fishing industry that exports dried fish to neighbouring Ivory Coast, Burkina Faso and Ghana.

With the exception of small areas in the south of the country, irrigation is necessary for all arable crops. The savanna grasslands and highland areas in the Sahelian south-east are free of tsetse fly (carrier of sleeping sickness), and large numbers of sheep and cattle are traditionally kept in the area, though grazing lands have been decimated by a series of catastrophic droughts. Northern Mali is entirely poor desert, inhabited only by Tuareg and Fulani nomads.

Millet, cotton and groundnuts are important crops on the unirrigated lands of the south, while rice is intensively grown with irrigation. A large irrigation scheme has been developed near Ségou which produces rice, cotton and sugar cane, and there are many other smaller schemes. Industry is confined mainly to one commercial gold mine, salt production and embryonic manufacturing – shoes, textiles, beer and matches. More than 70% of the labour force, however, remain in the agricultural sector, with cotton, the leading if modest export.

Mali – a French colony between 1893 and 1960 – was governed by a radical Socialist government for the first eight years of independence, before this was overthrown by a bloodless coup under General Moussa Traoré. His repressive military, single-party regime did little for the country – despite successful pressure from aid donor nations to liberalize the planned economy – and in 1987 the World Bank classified Mali as the world's fourth poorest country; they were still in the bottom 20 in 1989. In 1985 the government had been involved in a border dispute with neighbouring Burkina Faso; the International Court of Justice finally granted Mali 40% of its claimed land.

Student-led protests finally ended Traoré's 23-year reign in 1991. Following a referendum in 1992, elections were held, in which Alphar Oumar Konare became Mali's first democratically elected president. However, in April 1993 Prime Minister Younoussi Toure, appointed the previous August to head the country's first democratic government, resigned after student protests mushroomed into widespread riots about the grinding poverty afflicting the nation.

Nomadic Tuareg tribesmen were also destabilizing the situation, though a 1994 agreement – helped by aid from France – should help. Mali is a member of the 'franc zone', and with six other nations forms the Union Monétaire Ouest-Africaine. Their freely convertible currency, the CFA franc, is linked to the French franc at a fixed rate and backed by the Treasury in Paris ∎

NIGER

The title Niger, derived from the Tuareg word *n'eghirren* ('flowing water'), is something of a misnomer for the country that bears the river's name. West Africa's great waterway runs through only the extreme south-west of what is, apart from its fertile southern strip, a desolate territory of hot, arid sandy and stony basins.

The monotony of the northern 60% of the country is broken by the jagged peaks of the Aïr Mountains, rising to 1,900 m [6,230 ft] from the desert plains; here rainfall is sometimes sufficient to permit the growth of thorny scrub. However, severe droughts since the 1970s have crippled the traditional lifestyle of the nomads in the area, grazing their camels, horses, cattle and goats, and whole clans have been wiped out as the Sahara slowly makes its way south.

The same period has seen the growth of uranium mining in the mountains by the government in conjunction with the French Atomic Energy Commission, and this has now overtaken groundnuts as Niger's chief export, despite the drop in world demand during the 1980s. Tin and tungsten are also mined here, but reserves of other minerals, including iron ore, manganese and molybdenum, remain largely untouched. Over 95% of Niger's population still derive their living from agriculture and trading.

The southern part of the country, including the most fertile areas of the Niger basin and around Lake Chad, have also been affected by drought; but here desertification, linked to overgrazing, climbing temperatures as well as water shortage, is a wider problem. The crucial millet and sorghum crops – often grown by slash-and-burn techniques – have repeatedly failed, and migration to the already crowded market towns and neighbouring countries is widespread. The capital of Niamey, a mixture of traditional African, European colonial and modern Third World, is the prime destination for migrants travelling in search of food and work.

South of Niamey is the impressive 'W' national park, shared with Burkina Faso and Benin. The wooded savanna – protecting elephants, buffaloes, crocodiles, cheetahs, lions and antelopes – is intended to attract growing numbers of tourists in the 1990s.

Niger comes close to the bottom of all the world tables measuring aspects of poverty, along with its Sahara/Sahel neighbours Mali and Chad. French colonial rule came to an end in 1960, and the original post-independence government was overthrown in 1974, in the wake of a prolonged drought, and military rule followed. Civilian control was reinstated in 1989 (with army backing) and in 1990, after student protests, a route to democracy was mapped out; after a 90-day conference in the autumn of 1991, the last pillars of military dictatorship were abolished. In 1992 a multiparty constitution was adopted, and fair elections followed in March 1993 ∎

THE SAHARA DESERT

The world's biggest desert, the Sahara's 9,065,000 sq km [3,500,000 sq mls] stretch from the Atlantic to the Red Sea and amount to almost a third of the African continent. To the north, it is bordered by the Mediterranean; to the south, it merges with the Sahel, a zone of sparse vegetation and irregular rainfall. On average, the Sahara receives less than 100 mm [4 in] of rain annually, though a scattering of oases fed by underground water support small communities and nomadic herdsmen; the region has only around a million inhabitants.

Over 70% of the Sahara's area is covered with coarse gravel and rock, rising in its high central plateau to mountains of 3,000 m [10,000 ft] or more, mostly of volcanic origin. About 15% is made up of plains of shifting sand, including the Great Western Erg, a sand sea of more than 78,000 sq km [30,000 sq mls] in Algeria.

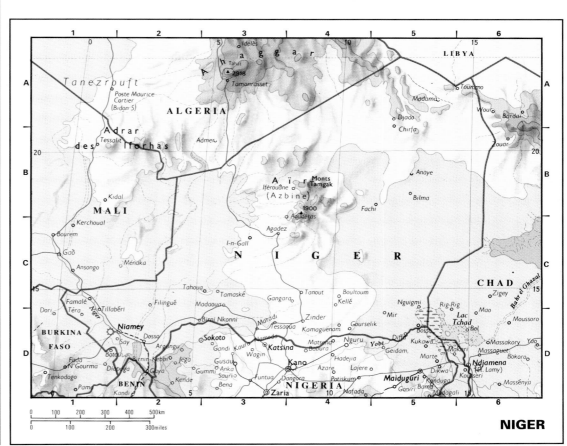

NIGER

CHAD

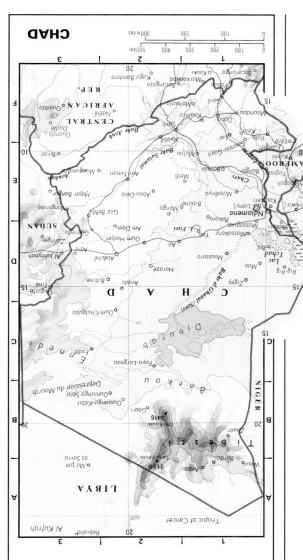

CHAD

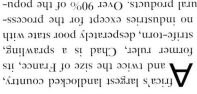

Africa's largest landlocked country, and twice the size of France, its former ruler, Chad is a sprawling, strife-torn, desperately poor state with no industries except for the processing of agricultural products. Over 90% of the population make a living from crop cultivation, notably cotton, or by herding animals.

In the Saharan northern third of the country, a sparse nomadic Arabic population lives in a harsh desert containing large tracts of mobile dunes (Erg du Djourab), and the volcanic Tibesti Mountains.

The wetter southern portions of the country are covered by wooded savanna and crops of cotton, groundnuts, millet and sorghum are grown – drought permitting – by settled black cultivators. A central bank of thorn bush (Sahel) provides pasturage for migratory cattle and herds of game, though drought and desertification have combined to wreak havoc here in recent years.

Lake Chad is the focal point of much of the country's drainage, affecting two-thirds of the country. However, most water feeding the lake comes from the rivers Chari and Logone, the only large perennial watercourses in the country and now only streams. Agriculture and population are concentrated along their valleys and in the vicinity of Lake Chad, now shrinking fast; some estimates state that the water area is only 20% of its size in 1970, and the levels much lower – so while fishing is locally important, catches are less each year. Dried fish is still exported.

Since independence Chad has been plagued by almost continuous civil wars, primarily between the Muslim Arab north and the Christian and animist black south, but also with many subsidiary ethnic conflicts. In 1973 Colonel Gaddafi's Libya, supporters of the Arab faction, occupied the mineral-rich Aozou Strip in the far north and has held it virtually ever since.

Libya tried incursions further south in 1983 – to back the forces of the previously separate state of Bourkou-Ennedi-Tibesti – and in 1987, to support one of many abortive coups against a succession of repressive governments in Ndjamena; the latter ended in agreement on 'joint withdrawal', the former in crushing victory for French and Chadian forces. The French (and some American) forces were present at least in part because of the prospect of uranium – but the mineral never materialized.

Diplomatic relations were restored with Libya in 1988, but Chad's massive commitments in maintaining control in the drought-afflicted country as well as on several of its borders – in addition to an impossible foreign debt – make it one of the terminally ill nations of Africa.

In theory a multiparty democracy for some time, Chad's politics are in reality wretched, its parties little more than legitimized warring tribal factions. When Idriss Deby overthrew the murderous eight-year reign of Hissène Habré in 1990 he pronounced himself shocked at Amnesty International assertions of 40,000 politically linked deaths, but after promises of a fresh start the new regime proved as proficient as its predecessor in removing opponents, and Deby survived an attempted coup in October 1993 ■

but sales of cotton, meat and other animal products provide most exports.

CENTRAL AFRICAN REPUBLIC

Declared independent in 1960, this former French colony hit the headlines briefly in 1976 when the ex-French Army sergeant Jean-Bédel Bokassa crowned himself head of the 'Central African Empire' in a lavish ceremony. His extravagance and repressive methods were ended in 1979 with the help of French paratroops, and the self-styled emperor was sentenced to death – later commuted to life imprisonment – and released in 1993.

The Central African Republic could ill-afford Bokassa's obscenely expensive tastes. This poor, landlocked country lies on an undulating plateau between the Chad and Congo basins; the numerous rivers drain to both, and natural erosion has been accentuated by the planting of trees in rows on foreign plantations. Rainforest is confined to the south-west. The rest of the country is savanna, much de-populated for the European and Arab slave trades and later for forced labour. Most farming is for subsistence, but coffee, cotton and groundnuts are exported, as well as significant amounts of timber and uranium. But the main earner is gem diamonds, while CAR is France's chief military base in Africa ■

ABOVE A bush fire feeds on precious shrubs on a roadside in the Central African Republic.

SUDAN

The Sudan, formerly an Anglo-Egyptian Condominium, is the largest state of Africa. It consists essentially of vast clay plains and sandy areas, parts of the Nile basin and the Sahara, but it presents two very different landscapes. The extreme north is virtually uninhabited desert; to the south, where the desert gives way to semi-desert, nomads move over age-old tribal areas.

The belt across the centre of the country holds most of the population. Here low rainfall, supplemented by wells and small reservoirs for irrigation, allows subsistence farming, but the bulk of the population lives by or near the Blue and White Niles. This is the predominantly Arab part of the Sudan, where 70% of the population live. Near these rivers, and relying on them for irrigation, are a number of modern mechanized farming schemes, headed by the famous if fallible Gezira Scheme, one of the first of its kind in the world. Crops grown are cotton and oilseed for export, sugar cane and sorghum for local consumption. Despite once being 'the bread-basket of Africa', schemes like Gezira have failed to realize agricultural potential.

Southern Sudan presents a very different landscape. Much of it is a great clay plain, fringed by uplands and experiencing a heavy annual rainfall. During the rainy season the plain becomes a vast reed-covered swamp and the Nilotic cattle-rearing tribes (Shilluk and Dinka) move to the dry ridges and islands until the floods abate.

The Sudan suffers from an awesome amalgam of the plagues which, in various combinations, afflict much of post-colonial Africa: ethnic, religious and ideological division; political repression and instability; intermittent civil war, with high spending on 'defence'; economic crisis and massive foreign debt which, to service, would cost three times as much as export earnings; prolonged drought (punctuated by flash floods such as those in 1988, which left 1.5 million people homeless); and an influx of famine-stricken refugees from Ethiopia since the 1980s.

The 17-year-old civil war that ended in 1972 was rekindled in 1983 by the (largely effective) pressure from extremists for the reinstatement of fundamental Sharic law. The renewed rivalries of the Arab north and the non-Muslim south – a pattern mirrored in neighbouring Chad, which shares many of Sudan's problems – have caused the deaths of hundreds of thousands of people and the decimation of a traditional way of life in an area already prone to drought and severe food shortages.

While the power in the land rests in the north with the military council in Khartoum – a city laid out in the pattern of the British flag at the confluence of the White Nile and Blue Nile – there seems little hope of a return to democracy, and the possibility of the south seceding remains a distinct if distant one. The regime has remained unmoved by international actions, such as expulsion from the IMF, and by the beginning of 1994, fuelled by splits in the rebel movements, the situation had worsened further ■

Sudanese fishermen on the lake behind the White Nile Dam at Jabal el-Awliyâ, south of Khartoum. This famous river is as important to Sudan as it is to Egypt.

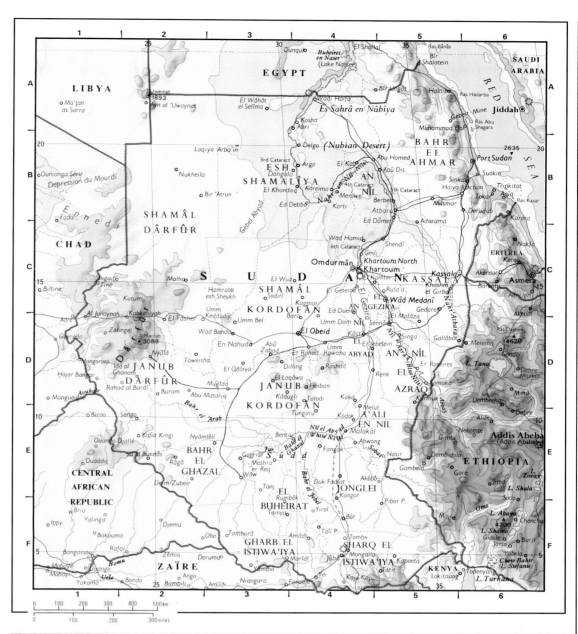

Corrugated roofs on block bases are replacing the traditional thatched wooden dwellings in much of Africa. This settlement is in Tigray, northern Ethiopia.

ETHIOPIA

Previously known as Abyssinia, Ethiopia was thrust before the attention of the world late in 1984 by unprecedented television pictures of starving millions – victims not only of famine but also of more than two decades of civil war and a Marxist government determined to enforce hardline economic and social policies. While that regime was finally toppled in 1991, and aid continued to pour in from the richer nations, the accumulative effects of drought (beginning in 1972, but with three merciless ones in the 1980s) combined with administrative mismanagement had left the nation destitute. By 1989, stated the World Bank, only Mozambique was worse off in terms of income per head.

Ethiopia's main feature is a massive block of volcanic mountains, rising to 4,620 m [15,150 ft] and divided into Eastern and Western Highlands by the Great Rift Valley. Steep escarpments face each other across the rift, opening northwards to form the southern and eastern boundaries of the high Welo plateau. The Eastern Highlands fall away gently to the south and east. The Western Highlands, generally higher and far more extensive and deeply trenched, are the sources of the Blue Nile and its tributaries. Off their north-eastern flank, close to the Red Sea, lies the Danakil Depression, an extensive desert that falls to 116 m [380 ft] below sea level.

In the lower areas of both highlands tropical cereals, oil seeds, coffee and cotton were the dominant crops before the wrecking of the rural economy, while at higher altitudes temperate cereals, pulses and fruits are produced. Giant thistles, red-hot pokers and lobelia are characteristic of the montane vegetation. In the desert of the Rift Valley the Danakil tend their diminishing herds, as do the Somali pastoralists on the dry Ogaden plain to the south-east.

Coptic Christianity reached the northern kingdom of Aksum in the 4th century, surviving there and in the south when Islam spread through the rest of north-east Africa. These core areas also survived colonial conquest; indeed Ethiopia (Abyssinia) itself became a colonial power between 1897 and 1908, taking Somali and other peoples into its feudal Empire. Invaded by Italy in 1935, Ethiopia became independent again six years later when British troops forced the Italians out.

Emperor Haile Selassie ('the Lion of Judah'), despite promising economic and social reforms following a two-year drought, was deposed after his 44-year rule by a revolutionary military government in 1974. A month later Ethiopia was declared a socialist state: foreign investments and most industries were nationalized and a programme of land collectivization was started, sweeping away the feudal aristocracy. Though the ideology changed, it was still centralized, bureaucratic despotism: neo-Communism proved just as corrupt and inefficient as the old system.

By 1977 President Mengistu was in control, and with Soviet military and financial aid pursued interlocking policies of eliminating rival left-wing groups, suppressing secessionist movements (in Eritrea, Tigray, Wollo, Gondar and Ogaden) and instituting land reform, including the forced resettlement of millions from their drought-afflicted homelands. His period of 'Red Terror' killed tens of thousands of innocent people. Collectivist agriculture failed to cope with deforestation, overgrazing and the effects of drought, while for 14 years more than 60% of the national budget was spent on defence and 'security'.

After a decade of unparalleled disaster driven by drought, Mengistu was finally put to flight in 1991 as Addis Ababa was taken by forces of the EPRDF – an unstable alliance of six separate rebel organizations. The EPRDF announced a caretaker coalition government and plans for multiparty elections ■

ETHIOPIA, ERITREA

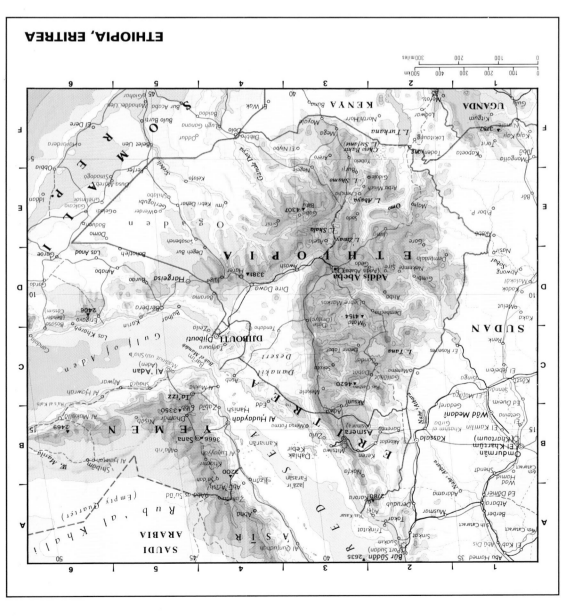

ERITREA

The far northern province of Ethiopia bordering the Red Sea, Eritrea was an Italian colony until 1941, when it passed to British military administration. In accordance with a UN resolution, it was given to Ethiopia in 1952, becoming an autonomous region within the Federation of Ethiopia and Eritrea. This became a unitary state ten years later, when the region was effectively annexed by Haile Selassie.

The Eritrean People's Liberation Front (EPLF) then pressed for independence with an unrelenting guerrilla campaign in what became Africa's longest war. Like their counterparts in Tigray and the Oromo movement in Wollo and Gondar, they held large tracts of the countryside for years while government forces occupied the towns. With the fall of the Mengistu regime in 1991 the EPLF gained agreement on independence for Eritrea, guaranteeing access to the Red Sea by making Aseb (Assab) a free port. Independence was formally declared on 24 May 1993.

Eritrea was Ethiopia's third largest province but, with 2.6 million, only seventh in terms of population. However, the capital, Asmara, was easily the country's second city (319,000) after Addis Ababa.

Africa's 52nd state was expected to do better than most fledgling nations, despite the dreadful legacy of 75% of the population dependent on aid and 750,000 or more refugees to be repatriated. Practical, experienced leaders and a surprisingly skilled labour force should enable Eritrea to steal ahead of local rivals – though its position makes it a natural target for the forces of Islamic fundamentalism ∎

DJIBOUTI

This small state lies in the Afro-Asian rift valley system, forming a hinterland to the Gulf of Tadjoura. Part of Djibouti lies below sea level; much of the low ground is hot, arid and unproductive basalt plain. Mt Goudah, the principal mountain, rises to 1,783 m [5,848 ft], and is covered with juniper and box forest.

Djibouti is important because of the railway link with Addis Ababa, which forms Ethiopia's main artery for overseas trade and was vital to an Ethiopian

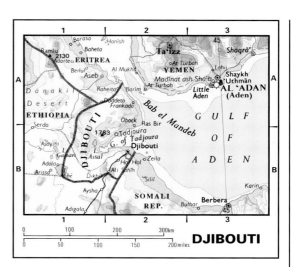

government whose only other access to the sea was through rebel-held Eritrea. Its town grew from 1862 around a French naval base, which is being redeveloped as a container port, thanks to its important position as a staging post between the Indian Ocean and the Red Sea. The French still maintain a garrison there and offer support to the authoritarian one-party regime of Hassan Ghouled Aptidon, president since independence in 1977, who was re-elected to a fourth six-year term of office in 1993.

Djibouti was previously the French territory of the Afars and Issas. The majority of Afars, most of whom are nomadic, live in Ethiopia and are better known by the Arabic word 'Danakil', while the Issas (or Ishaak) are Somali. This majority dominates the struggling economy, and there is periodic unrest among the underprivileged Afars ∎

Salt crusts on the shores of Lake Assal. With most land too poor for cultivation and few natural resources, Djibouti's prospects depend largely on overseas aid.

SOMALIA

More than twice as large as Italy (which formerly ruled the southern part), the Somali Republic became independent in 1960. The northern section, formerly British Somaliland and the literal 'Horn of Africa', is the highest and most arid, rising to 2,408 m [7,900 ft]; the mountains are an easterly projection of the Ethiopian Highlands, wooded with box and cedar. The east and south have some 500 mm [20 in] rainfall on the coast. Dunes have diverted one of the country's two rivers, the Scebeli, to the south, making it available for irrigation, and bananas are a major export from this area, especially to Italy.

The Somali, though belonging to separate tribes or clans, are members of one of Africa's rare nation states. Expatriate Somali living in southern Djibouti, Ogaden (eastern Ethiopia) and north-east Kenya are mostly pastoralists, who move across borders in an increasingly desperate search for pasture and water. The quest for a reunification of all the Somali peoples led to conflict with neighbouring countries, notably Ethiopia and the Ogaden war of 1978.

Somalia relied heavily on Soviet aid until Ethiopia went Marxist and sought massive help from Moscow; the revolutionary socialist government of President

Siyad Barre, which had seized power and suspended the constitution in 1969, then became increasingly reliant on Italian support and, most important, US aid.

Grievances against the repressive regime, spearheaded by secessionist guerrillas in the north, reached their peak in 1991 with the capture of Mogadishu. Free elections and the independence of the north-east part of the country, as the Somaliland Republic, were promised after the ceasefire and Barre's fall from power, but vicious factional fighting continued not only in the capital but also in many parts of the countryside. The Western nations virtually abandoned Somalia to its fate, with thousands dying every week in interclan bloodletting. One of the world's poorest countries was plunged into anarchy. The situation deteriorated further into 1992, despite UN attempts at mediation and several ceasefires. Much of Mogadishu was reduced to rubble, violence spread to country areas, and hundreds of thousands of refugees fled to northern Kenya and eastern Ethiopia.

In 1993 the UN intervened, sending in a task force of US Marines to protect and oversee the distribution of food aid, but the Americans and their UN allies proved poor peacekeepers before pulling out their troops in March 1994.

Somaliland, the north-western part of the country once called British Somaliland, broke away in May 1991 and from the devastation of civil war (and with little outside aid) appeared to be progressing towards genuine stability ∎

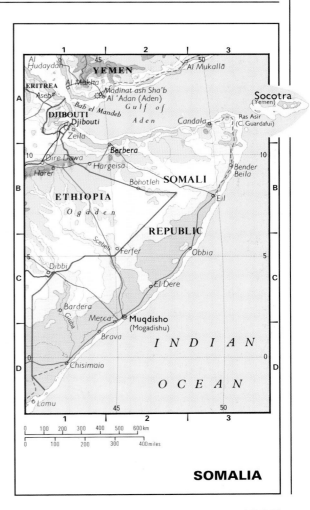

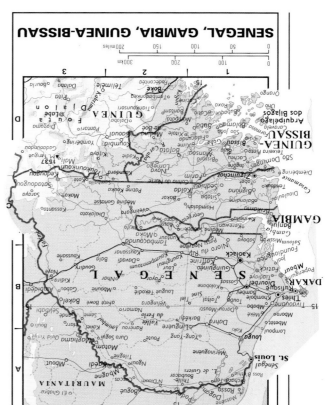

SENEGAL, GAMBIA, GUINEA-BISSAU

SENEGAL

On gaining independence in 1960 Senegal had a well-planned capital, a good road network and a top-heavy administration, all legacies from its role as the administrative centre for French West Africa. One-fifth of the country's population lives in Dakar and the area around volcanic Cape Verde (Cap Vert), the most westerly point on mainland Africa. The name derives from the Zenega Berbers, who invaded from Mauritania in the 14th century, bringing Islam with them.

Dakar, once the administrative centre for France's federation of West African colonies, has large modern docks with bunkering and ship-repair facilities and is the nation's major industrial centre. In the north-east of the country Fulani tribesmen eke out a spartan existence by keeping herds of cattle on the scrub and semi-desert vegetation. In contrast, in the wetter and more fertile south the savanna bushlands are cultivated and cassava, sorghum and rice are grown. About half of the cultivated land produces groundnuts, a crop that still dominates the country's economy and exports.

In an attempt to diversify and stabilize the economy the government is encouraging fishing and tourism, and is involved with Mali and Mauritania in a major scheme to increase irrigated crop production. One of the few African countries to remain stable and democratic through the 1980s, Senegal nevertheless struggles economically, is prone to drought and reliant on aid. Federations with Mali (1959–60) and Gambia (1981–9) were unsuccessful, and since 1989 there have been some violent clashes with Mauritania.

Senegal was the only African colony where French citizenship was granted to the people, and indeed the Senegalese were encouraged to become 'black Frenchmen'. As a result many of the Wolof – the largest tribe group and traditionally savanna farmers – are now city dwellers in Dakar, dominating the political, economic and cultural life of the country. Strangely, today's quality of life is for most Senegalese little better than their neighbours'.

Something of a model for African democracy, enjoying a multiparty system since 1973, Senegal's economic progress under Leopold Senghor has not been extended by Abdou Diouf. As well as droughts and riots over devaluation of the CFA franc, separatists in the south-western province of Casamance were in 1994 becoming increasingly violent ∎

A phosphates plant creates white dunes near Thiès, east of Dakar. Though Senegal slipped from the list of the world's top ten producers in the early 1990s, phosphates remain the country's second biggest export.

GAMBIA, THE

Britain's first (1765) and last colony in Africa, this small low-lying state forms a narrow strip on either side of the River Gambia, almost an enclave of the French-oriented Senegal.

Except for the capital Banjul, which is also the major port, no town has a population of more than 10,000, and all the large settlements are on the river, which provides the principal means of communication.

Rice is grown in swamps and on the floodplains of the river (though not enough to feed the country's modest population), with millet, sorghum and cassava on the higher ground. Groundnuts still dominate the economy and provide nine-tenths of export earnings, but a successful tourist industry has now been developed: whether northern Europeans looking for sunshine or black Americans tracing their ancestry, the number of visitors rose from a few hundred at independence to more than 90,000 a year in 1990. Though much poorer than its larger neighbour, The Gambia is determined to go it alone and continues to reject suggestions of unification with francophone Senegal ∎

GUINEA

The first independent state of French-speaking Africa, Guinea is a country of varied landscapes, ranging from the grasslands and scattered woodland of the interior highlands and Upper Niger plains, to the swampy mangrove-fringed plains of the Atlantic coast. Dense forests occupy the western foothills of the Fouta Djalon.

Two-thirds of the population are employed in agriculture and food processing. Bananas, palm oil, pineapples and rice are important crops on the wet Atlantic coastal plain, where swamps and forests have been cleared for agricultural development, while in the drier interior cattle are kept by nomadic herdsmen.

France granted the troublesome territory independence after a referendum in 1958, and for more than a quarter of a century Guinea was ruled by the repressive regime of President Ahmed Sekou Touré, who isolated Guinea from the West and leaned towards the Eastern bloc for support. Though reconciled with France in 1978, it was not until after the military coup following Touré's death in 1984 that economic reforms began to work. It is estimated that up to a quarter of the population left for neighbouring countries during Touré's presidency.

Guinea's natural resources are considerable: it has some of the world's largest reserves of high-grade bauxite, and the three large mines account for some 80% of export earnings. The Aredor diamond mine has also been very profitable since opening in 1984, and there is great potential for iron-ore mining and hydroelectric power.

Touré's successor, General Lansana Conté, ruled from 1984 – though his election victory was not helped by an attempted coup against him in 1985 and tumbling world prices for bauxite and its derivative, aluminium ∎

GUINEA-BISSAU

Guinea-Bissau is a land largely composed of swamps and riverine estuaries. On gaining independence from Portugal in 1974 the country possessed few basic services and agriculture had been severely dislocated by the guerrilla war. There appeared to be no mineral deposits and industrial output was negligible.

About 85% of the active population are subsistence farmers, and a small surplus of groundnuts is exported. Large numbers of livestock are kept on the grasslands in the east, and there is considerable potential for growing irrigated rice and sugar cane. A fishing industry and cash crops such as tropical fruits, cotton and tobacco are being developed, and there are untapped reserves of bauxite and phosphates as well as offshore oil – hampered by disputes with Guinea and Senegal.

In December 1991 the Supreme Court ended 17 years of Socialist one-party rule by legalizing the opposition group, the Democratic Front. However, rivalry between black Guineans (especially predominant Balante) and the mestizo élite remained strong ■

GUINEA, SIERRA LEONE

SIERRA LEONE

Freetown, the capital of Sierra Leone ('lion mountain'), has the best natural harbour in West Africa, and was established as a settlement for freed slaves at the end of the 18th century. At independence from Britain in 1961, three-quarters of the population were employed in subsistence agriculture, yet rice had to be imported, and only small surpluses of palm kernel, coffee and ginger were produced. Revenues from diamond and iron-ore mining, of major importance since the 1930s, plus other minerals, provide the country with funds for education and agricultural developments. Sierra Leone is also one of the few producers of rutile (titanium ore), now its most important export.

The main centres for the production of coffee, cocoa and timber products are in the south-east of the country near Kenema. Rice and palm oil are produced throughout Sierra Leone, except in the drier north, where groundnuts and cattle herding are more important. The government has established large-scale mechanized rice cultivation in the bolilands of the north-west, the seasonally-flooded riverine grasslands of the south-east and the mangrove swamps near Port Loko. Apart from mills processing palm oil and rice, most factories are in or near Freetown.

A military government ruled a one-party state after the coup of 1968, but in 1991 the regime claimed to 'welcome' multiparty democracy. Junior officers took power in a 1992 coup, and after a purge promised a return to civilian rule; but corruption is rife and the country's prospect – it ranked second poorest in the world in 1993 – looked bleak indeed. Tourism, attracting visitors who may go instead to the Caribbean, may be a short-term solution ■

Toke Beach near Freetown, one of many beautiful beaches the government hopes will attract more overseas visitors – and foreign exchange.

LIBERIA

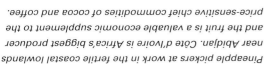

West Africa's oldest independent state, Liberia lacks a legacy of colonial administration. A sparsely populated country with large tracts of inaccessible tropical rainforest, Liberia is popularly known for its 'flag of convenience' (used by about one-sixth of the world's commercial shipping), and for large American-owned rubber plantations. The country was founded in the early 19th century as an American colony for freed black slaves wanting to return to Africa from the United States.

There has been an open-door policy towards foreign entrepreneurs, and the economy has developed rapidly following the exploitation of large iron-ore deposits by foreign companies, mainly American. Though diamonds and gold have long been worked, iron ore accounts for about half the value of all exports. The economy is a mixture of large foreign-owned corporations operating mines and plantations, and of various indigenous peoples who still exist largely as very poor shifting subsistence cultivators.

In 1989 Liberia was plunged into vicious civil war when a force led by Charles Taylor invaded from the Ivory Coast. The president, Samuel Doe, who had seized power in a coup in 1980, was later assassinated and a jigsaw of conflicts developed between his successor, Amos Sawyer, Taylor and other rebel forces, including those led by Prince Johnson. Peacekeeping troops from five West African countries arrived in October 1990 but despite several agreements fighting continued. Estimates put the number of civilian deaths at more than 13,000 and some 800,000 people – nearly a third of the population – fled to neighbouring countries, leaving the nation and its devastated capital in chaos even after elections were agreed for 1995. ■

IVORY COAST

Except for Nigeria, the Ivory Coast is the largest Guinea coastal land – a little larger than Italy. Formally known as Côte d'Ivoire since 1986, it has substantial forests in the south where the basic resources of coffee, cocoa and timber are produced, as well as the lesser crops of bananas and pineapple. The depletion of the rainforest, as in much of West Africa, is rapid.

The Guinea savanna lands of the centre and north are much less fertile, producing small amounts of sugar, cotton and tobacco that now support developing industries, and food crops important to a rapidly growing market in the capital, Abidjan. Like Kenya, which is economically comparable, the Ivory Coast has few worked minerals, but manufacturing industries are developing.

In terms of such indices as GNP and international trade figures, the relatively stable Ivory Coast is one of Africa's most prosperous countries. This show of prosperity was initiated by the Vridi Canal, opened in 1950, which made Abidjan a spacious and sheltered deep-water port – a rarity in an area of Africa renowned for barrier reefs. The Ivory Coast's free-market economy has proved attractive to foreign investors, especially French firms, and France has given much aid, particularly for basic services and education. It has also attracted millions of migrant West African workers. On achieving independence in 1960, the Ivory Coast freed itself economically from support of seven other countries in the French West African Federation. The country is the world's largest exporter of cocoa and Africa's biggest producer of coffee. It has few worked minerals, but its manufacturing industries are developing.

Outward prosperity is visually expressed in Abidjan, whose skyline is a minor Manhattan, and where most of the 44,000 French live. However, the cost of living for Ivoriens is high; almost everything is centralized in Abidjan – which is due to be replaced as the country's capital by Yamoussoukro (120,000), site of the world's biggest church (consecrated by Pope John Paul II in 1990) – and there are great social and regional inequalities. Nevertheless, a second port has been developed since 1971 at San Pedro, and efforts are being made to develop other towns and the relatively backward north.

In 1990 the country's first multiparty presidential election returned to power Félix Houphouët-Boigny, leader since 1960, but his death in December 1993, adding to problems caused by falling cocoa prices, suggested a period of instability ahead. ■

Pineapple pickers at work in the fertile coastal lowlands near Abidjan. Côte d'Ivoire is Africa's biggest producer and the fruit is a valuable economic supplement to the price-sensitive chief commodities of cocoa and coffee.

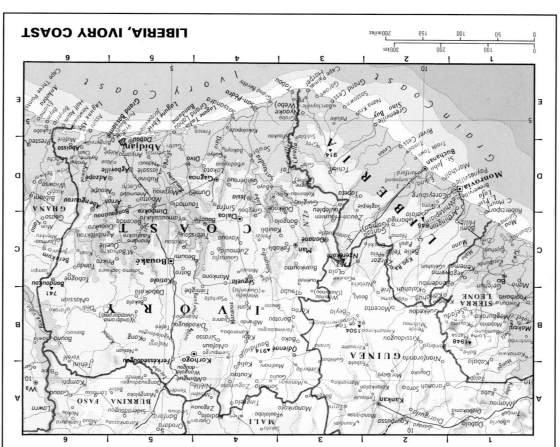

LIBERIA, IVORY COAST

BURKINA FASO

Landlocked Burkina Faso ('land of upright men') is the successor to Mossi, an early West African state dating from 1100. As large as Italy, and with just over 9 million inhabitants, it is nevertheless overpopulated: low, seasonal and erratic rainfall, thin, eroded soils, desertification and a dearth of other natural resources combine to keep Burkina Faso one of the poorest and most agrarian states in the world, heavily reliant on aid.

The Mossi people, who are the majority tribe, live around Ouagadougou, the capital; another major group, the Bobo, dwell around the second city of Bobo Dioulasso. Both grow cotton and millet, guinea corn (sorghum) and groundnuts for food, and collect shea nuts for cooking oil. Nomadic Fulani keep cattle. Though small surpluses of all these products are sold overseas and to the better-off countries to the south, especially the Ivory Coast, remittances sent home by migrants working in those countries probably provide most of Burkina Faso's foreign income. Manganese mining could be developed in the far north-east, though this would necessitate a 340 km [210 ml] extension to the railway from Abidjan already 1,145 km [715 mls] long. Another hope lies in eliminating the simulium fly, whose bite causes blindness. This would permit settlement and farming of the valleys, which have the most fertile and best watered lands.

Plagued by numerous coups and political assassinations, Burkina Faso (known until 1984 as Upper Volta) tasted democracy in December 1991 for the first time in more than a decade when the military regime of Blaise Compaore, who had come to power in 1987 following the death of his friend Thomas Sankara, granted elections. However, 20 opposition parties combined to produce a boycott involving 76% of the electorate (claiming that it was a ploy to legitimize the military rule), and the government registered a hollow victory.

Among these is the 'W' national park, shared with Niger and Benin. Named after the shape made by the River Niger there, this multinational wildlife reserve comprises a 10,230 sq km [3,950 sq ml] area of savanna and hosts a vast range of animals and birds. Though accessible at present only in the dry season (between January and June) and less developed than neighbouring Benin's Pindjara National Park, 'W' promises much over the next few decades ■

BURKINA FASO

GHANA

Formerly known appropriately as the Gold Coast, Ghana's post-colonial name recalls the state which lay north of the upper Niger from the 8th to the 13th centuries. In 1957 Ghana was the first tropical African country to become independent of colonial rule, and until 1966 was led by Dr Kwame Nkrumah, a prominent Third World spokesman and pioneer of Pan-African Socialism. Under him the Akosombo Dam was completed below Lake Volta (one of the world's largest artificial lakes), providing power to smelt imported alumina into aluminium, and for the main towns, mines and industries in the Takoradi-Kumasi-Tema triangle, the most developed part of the country. To build the dam, a second deep-water port was built at Tema, east of Accra, the capital. Tema is now Ghana's main port for imports and for cocoa export.

Cocoa has been the leading export since 1924, and until the late 1970s Ghana was the world's leading producer. However, neighbouring Ivory Coast has now overtaken Ghana both in this and in forestry production. In turn, Ghana has attempted to expand the fishing, tourism and agricultural industries.

Unlike the Ivory Coast, Ghana has long been a producer of minerals – gold has been exploited for a thousand years. However, production of most minerals is currently static or declining. The few remaining gold mines, with the notable exception of Obuasi, are now scarcely economic. Manganese production was recently revived to meet a new demand in battery manufacture, but the country's substantial reserves of bauxite remain undeveloped while imported alumina is used in the Tema aluminium smelter. Industrial diamonds contribute modestly to Ghana's economy.

Nkrumah's overthrow in 1966 was followed by a

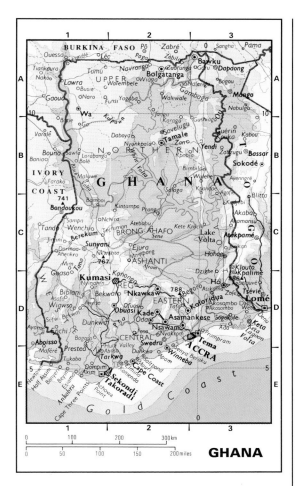

GHANA

succession of coups and military governments, with Flight-Lieutenant Jerry Rawlings establishing himself as undoubted leader in 1981. While his hardline regime has steadied the economy, with IMF support, political progress has been slow. Rawlings won the election of 1993 but he faced fierce opposition from many non-military quarters ■

Rocky breakwaters protect Ghanaian fishing boats from Atlantic waves at Elmina, centre of the 'Gold Coast'.

TOGO

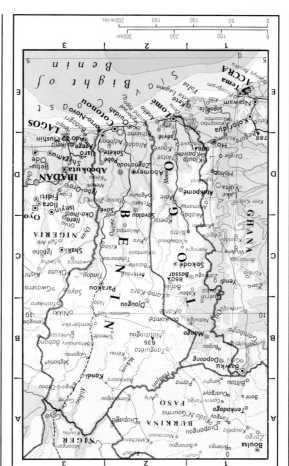

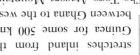

A small country nowhere more than 120 km [75 mls] wide, Togo stretches inland from the Gulf of Guinea for some 500 km [312 mls] between Ghana to the west and Benin to the east. The Togo-Atacora Mountains cross the country from south-west to north-east, and the major forests and cash crops are in the south-west.

The railway inland from the coast stops at Blitta, in central Togo, and the road is the only means of keeping the poorer, drier northern parts of this awkwardly shaped country in touch with the more developed areas of the south, including the capital and main port of Lomé and the important phosphate mining area, with its port of Kpémé. Phosphates, coffee and cocoa are the important exports, but major food crops are cassava, yams and maize.

As Togoland the country was colonized by Germany in 1884 and then occupied by Franco-British troops during World War I. It was partitioned between the two powers under a League of Nations mandate in 1922, with British Togoland later becoming part of Ghana and the larger eastern French section eventually gaining independence as Togo in 1960.

From 1967 Togo was ruled by the military regime of General Gnassingbé Eyadéma, whose government took a pro-Western stance and pioneered privatization in Africa. Following strikes and protests, the principle of multiparty elections was conceded in March 1991, but by the end of the year old rivalries between Eyadéma's northern Kabye people and the dominant Ewe tribe re-emerged to block the path to stable democratization. Eyadéma won the 1993 election – but so rigged the system that all opposition withdrew ■

BENIN

Previously called Dahomey (the name of an old cultured kingdom centred on Abomey), Benin, one of Africa's smallest countries, extends some 620 km [390 mls] north to south, although the coastline is a mere 100 km [62 mls] long.

Rival tribal kingdoms flourished in this part of Africa for centuries until the French began establishing their presence from around 1850, creating a colony (Dahomey) in 1892 and formally making the country part of French West Africa in 1904. Before that, from the 13th century, the area had been the western part of the kingdom (or empire) of Benin, centred on the Nigerian city of that name and famous for its life-size brass heads and plaques and for its ruler, the Oba, from the 15th century. Situated east of Lagos, Benin City is now capital of the Nigerian state of Bendel.

Today's dominant tribe in Benin is the Fon, who (with the Yoruba) occupy the more populous and fertile south, mostly as subsistence farmers, growing yams, cassava, sweet potatoes and vegetables. In the central parts and some of the north are the Bariba, renowned for their horsemanship, and the Somba, while some Fulani still follow the increasingly precar-

Benin has little to sell, its main exports being palm-oil produce, cotton and groundnuts, with the timber from the central rainforest belt depleting rapidly. Fees from Niger's transit trade through Cotonou are an important additional source of revenue, but illegal trade with Nigeria is also rife. Offshore oil began production in 1982, but output peaked three years later and the industry has since been hampered by low prices.

Following independence from France in 1960, the country experienced a series of coups and power struggles, going through 11 changes of government in 12 years. Then, during the military single-party regime of General Mathieu Kerekou, who in 1974 introduced 'scientific socialism' (and the following year dropped the name Dahomey), Benin found itself sitting awkwardly as a Marxist state between the market-oriented economies of Togo and Nigeria. Kerekou officially abandoned his path in 1989, and in 1990 he was forced to concede multiparty elections in a referendum. He was roundly beaten in March 1991, when the country enjoyed a remarkably peaceful transition from one-party rule to democracy ■

...ious nomadic lifestyle in the far north, the least populated of the regions.

Okra, pimentoes and red chillies add colour to a market scene in Benin. As in most of Africa, the majority of people eke out a living by trading with each other – not exporting to First World countries.

NIGERIA

Four times the size of the United Kingdom, whose influence dates from 1861, Nigeria is tropical Africa's most important country. Ranking seventh as a world producer of oil, there are many other resources (albeit dwarfed in exports by oil), including cocoa in the south-west, timber, rubber and palm oil in the south-centre and east, and cotton and groundnuts in the north. The variety of these resources reflects the latitudinal (4–14°N) and altitudinal extent of the country: highlands rise to over 1,830 m [6,000 ft].

There are nearly 89 million Nigerians, making it by far the most populous African state; one in every six Africans is Nigerian. It is also the second most populated country of the Commonwealth, and eighth in the world. Natural wealth and substantial armed forces give Nigeria a commanding position in Africa, and its oil and gas reserves are a focus of worldwide interest.

Nigeria's landscape varies from the savanna of the north – much of it under threat of desertification – through mountains and tropical rainforests to the coastal lands on the Gulf of Guinea. The coast has huge expanses of fine sandy beaches, interspersed with mangrove swamps where rivers join the ocean. Much of the country's coast is formed by the Niger delta, behind which lie thousands of creeks and lagoons.

Before roads were constructed, these inland waterways provided crucial transport, and boats and canoes still carry both people and cargoes between

Fulani women carry their pots to market. Decreasingly nomadic, theirs is the smallest (9%) of Nigeria's four largest tribes: the Hausa (21%), Yoruba (20%) and Ibo (17%, mostly in former Biafra) are more numerous.

NIGERIA

DEMOCRACY IN AFRICA

The great flush of liberty that followed decolonization in the 1950s and 1960s did not bring the rewards of peace, prosperity and self-government that many early African nationalists had envisaged. Instead, within a few years, most of the newly-independent African nations had been transformed into corrupt and incompetent dictatorships, at best authoritarian one-party states, usually heavily reliant on Western or Soviet subsidies and often plagued by guerrilla fighting and banditry. Governments were changed, if at all, by means of a coup d'état.

In the late 1980s, however, new hope reached the world's poorest continent. Everywhere, it seemed, dictators were succumbing peacefully to popular demands for multiparty elections and many long-running civil wars were coming to an end. By the early 1990s, some form of democracy was in place in 80% of African nations.

Few survived. Ethnic and religious conflict, natural disasters and overpopulation created pressures that saw many return to military rule or, even worse, descend into the anarchy of gang warfare.

While several determined exceptions – Gambia, Benin, Botswana and others – continued to buck the trend, it may be that Western-style democracy cannot simply be grafted on to the political bodies of Africa.

Though blessed with many natural resources, Nigeria has had an uneasy path since independence in 1960 (becoming a full republic in 1963). Democratically elected governments have found it an impossible task to unify and stabilize an unruly jigsaw of more than 250 ethnic and linguistic groups, and civilian administrations have held sway for only ten years since the departure of the British.

An unwieldy tripartite federal structure first introduced in 1954 proved unable to contain rivalries after independence and in 1966 the first Prime Minister, Abubaka Tafawa Balewa, and many other leaders were assassinated in a military coup. A

A federation of 30 states, many of which are larger than most independent African states, Nigeria includes many tribal groups, the largest being the Yoruba of the south-west, the Ibo of the east, and the Hausa, Fulani and Kanuri of the north. The north is predominantly Muslim, and the Islamic influence is increasing in the south, where most people are pagan or Christian. With so many diversities, including those of religion and a developing social system, national unity is often strained.

counter-coup brought General Yakubu Gowon to power, but a vicious civil war ensued from 1967 when the Eastern Region, dominated by the Christian Ibo and known as Biafra, attempted to secede from the union after the slaughter of thousands of members of their tribe in the north by Muslim Hausa – and wrangles over increasing oil revenues.

Hundreds of thousands died (most from starvation) before Biafra admitted defeat early in 1971. The federation was gradually splintered from three to 21 full states (now 30) to try to prevent one area becoming dominant. Gowon was overthrown in 1975, but another attempt at civilian rule (1979–83) also ended in a military takeover. The latest coup, a bloodless affair in 1985, brought General Ibrahim Babangida to office, and he immediately faced the crucial problems of falling oil prices and mounting foreign debts.

Nigeria's foreign exchange earnings from oil, the country's prime source of income, were halved in a year. Oil production had begun in the 1950s and risen steadily to a peak of 2.4 million barrels a day in the early 1980s. Foreign exchange earnings peaked in 1980 at $26 billion, but by the end of the decade this figure had shrunk to $9 billion. At the same time the foreign debt, constantly shuffled and rescheduled, had blossomed to some $36 billion, easily Africa's largest. In seven years the annual income of the average Nigerian has shrunk from $1,120 (among the top three on the continent) to a meagre $270, a figure below even that of some poor neighbours. In 1991 the World Bank officially reclassified Nigeria as a low-income rather than middle-income country.

In the early 1990s there were, nevertheless, signs of a recovery, with agriculture (50% of the population still rely on farming) and some areas of manufacturing growing quickly. The political scene was changing too, with Babangida's promise of civilian rule (made in 1989) fulfilled for only a few months before General Sani Abacha's bloodless coup restored military rule in November 1993 ∎

---

rubber, hardwoods and palm oil. North of the Jos Plateau, parkland gives way to grassland, but the savanna becomes increasingly dry and some areas are now little more than semi-arid scrub.

Northern Nigeria is reliant on one precarious wet season, while the south enjoys two. Poor-quality millet and sorghum are the staples, with cotton and groundnuts the main cash crops. Where desertification has not taken hold, livestock are still important – enjoying the absence of the tsetse fly that afflicts the area of moist vegetation in the south.

Nigeria is unique in Africa south of the Sahara for the numerous pre-colonial towns of the south-west (such as Ibadan) and the north (such as Kano). Domestic trade between these and Nigeria's very varied regions was developed in pre-colonial days, and is now intense.

---

towns and villages in the area. Here the heavy rains produce yams, cassava, maize and vegetables, with rice grown on the patches of land beside rivers and creeks and on large stretches of irrigated land where streams do not flood in the wet seasons.

Further north, in the forest belt, the hills rise towards the Jos Plateau – famous for its holiday resorts – and in the east towards the steep valleys and wooded slopes of the Cameroon Highlands. These areas produce Nigeria's important tree crops – cocoa,

DESERTIFICATION OF THE SAHEL

The Sahel is a wide band of scrub and savanna grassland stretching from Mauritania and northern Senegal in the west through parts of Mali, Burkina Faso, Benin and Niger to southern Chad in the east, and including much of northern Nigeria. To the north is the Sahara, the world's largest desert; to the south are the rainforests of tropical West and Central Africa. Though used mainly for pasture, the whole area has irregular rainfall and suffers frequently from drought and the resultant famine. The desperate plight of the region was highlighted by the Sahelian famine of 1973, when hundreds of thousands died, and the problem has since became virtually permanent.

Over the past 30 years, the Sahara has gradually encroached southwards. The causes are many and interwoven. As well as declining rainfall, there are the pressures of a growing population; herdsmen overgrazing the land with their cattle, sheep and goats (left); overcultivation by uneducated farmers; cutting of ground cover, mainly for fuelwood; and poor or faulty irrigation techniques, where limited water supplies are wasted and the land left too saline or alkaline to support crops.

SÃO TOMÉ AND PRÍNCIPE

These mountainous, volcanic and heavily forested Atlantic islands, some 145 km [90 mls] apart, comprise little more than twice the area of Andorra, with São Tomé the larger and more developed of the two. A Portuguese colony since 1522, the islands were suddenly granted independence in 1975, and the cocoa plantations that formed the platform for the economy quickly deteriorated under a one-party hardline Marxist state.

Reliance on the Soviet Union was lessened from the mid-1980s and the cocoa industry revived – as well as diversification into palm oil, pepper and coffee and the encouragement of tourism. In 1991 there was a smooth transition to multiparty democracy ■

EQUATORIAL GUINEA

In 1778 the Portuguese ceded the islands of Fernando Poó (Bioko) and Annobon (Pagalu) to Spain, together with rights on the mainland, Mbini (Rio Muni), against Spanish agreement to Portuguese advance west of 50°W in Brazil. Plantations of coffee and cocoa were established on these mountainous and volcanic islands.

Mainland Mbini, which accounts for over 90% of the country's land area, is very different, lower and thinly peopled, less developed, and with fewer foreign enterprises, except in forestry (especially okoume and mahogany production) and palm oil.

Guinea was once used to describe the whole coastal region of West Africa. Equatorial Guinea was granted partial autonomy from Spain in 1963, and gained full independence in 1968. Thanks to its cocoa plantations, Equatorial Guinea once had the highest per capita income in West Africa. But after independence, the 11-year dictatorship of President Nguema left the economy in ruins, and the one-party rule of his nephew Obiang has since survived several coup attempts. Some 100,000 Equatorial Guineans are thought to have fled both regimes ■

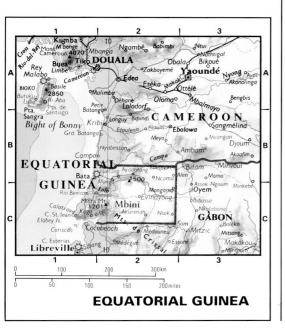

EQUATORIAL GUINEA

CAMEROON

Though half the size of neighbouring Nigeria, Cameroon has only a tenth of the population. It is, nevertheless, a remarkably diverse country, stemming from more than 160 ethnic groups (each with their own language) and a colonial past involving several European countries. The mountainous borderlands between Nigeria and Cameroon lie on a line of crustal weakness dating from the break-up of the supercontinent, Gondwanaland. Mostly volcanic, the mountains include Mt Cameroon (4,070 m [13,350 ft]) which is occasionally active. There is desert to the north, dense tropical rainforest in the south and dry savanna in the intermediate area.

The word Cameroon is derived from the Portuguese *camarões* – prawns fished by Portuguese explorers' seamen in coastal estuaries – but European contact dates mainly from German rule as a protectorate after 1884. After World War I the country was divided according to League of Nations mandates between France (mainly) and Britain. The French Cameroons became independent in 1960, while following a 1961 plebiscite the north of the British Cameroons voted to merge with Nigeria and the south federated with the new independent state; this became unitary in 1972 and a republic in 1984. Though Cameroon is officially bilingual, the government and public sector are dominated by French-speakers – a fact that continues to upset the rest.

Despite oil production passing its peak in the 1980s and likely to stop before the end of the century, and despite patchy industrial development, Cameroon is one of tropical Africa's better-off nations, with an annual income per person of nearly $1,000 and rare self-sufficiency in food. This relative prosperity rests partly on diverse but well-managed agriculture, with extensive plantations of palm, rubber, bananas and other crops in the south-west dating from colonial times. Douala is Cameroon's main port for exports of cocoa, coffee (the chief cash crops) and aluminium, and for the transit trade of neighbours, while Kribi exports timber. Aluminium is produced at Edéa, using hydroelectric power generated from the Sanaga River, and a railway is being built to the north.

One of Cameroon's many cocoa plantations. The country's equatorial climate – high rainfall, high temperatures, high humidity with no prolonged dry season – is ideally suited to the crop.

The austerity programme of President Paul Buja, initiated in 1987, appeared to reap rewards by the end of the decade, but there was widespread unrest at the repressive regime; one-party politics was introduced in 1966 by Buja's mentor and predecessor Ahmadou Ahidjo, who had been president since independence. Elections were held in October 1992, but Buja was forced to declare a state of emergency after his corrupt tribalist regime rigged the results. The riots that followed split the country ethnically between the French and non-French parts; with the oil revenues going to the francophone élite and the opposition repressed, the gulf between the two communities began to grow dangerously wide ■

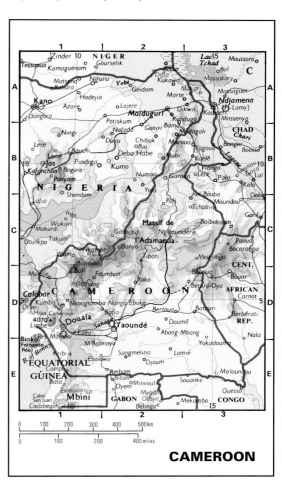

CAMEROON

GABON, CONGO

GABON

The name Gabon is derived from one given by a Portuguese explorer in the 16th century to an estuary which he thought resembled a hooded and sleeved cloak, *gabão* in Portuguese. In the 19th century the French Navy suppressed the local slave trade, and landed freed slaves at the base called Libreville – where, as in the British counterpart (Freetown, in Sierra Leone), an educated élite arose.

Most of the country is densely forested, and valuable timbers were the main export until 1962. Since then minerals have been developed, as so often in Africa, by foreign companies whose profits leave the country. First came oil and gas from near Port Gentil (oil still provides over 65% of export earnings). Then the world's largest deposit of manganese was mined at Mouanda, near Franceville, although originally the ore had to be exported through the Congo by a branch of the Congo-Ocean railway. Gabon is the world's fourth biggest producer of manganese and has about a quarter of the world's known reserves. Lastly, there is uranium from nearby Mounana; Gabon, Niger and the Central African Republic are France's main sources of uranium. The Trans-Gabon railway was completed in 1987 to provide the country's own outlet for the manganese and uranium, and to open new areas to forestry. Apart from cocoa and coffee grown in the north near Mbini, farming of all kinds is rare and engages only 1% of the land area, the Gabonese preferring to work in other economic activities and the towns. Most food is imported.

Independent in 1960, Gabon became a one-party state in 1967 and has since been ruled by Omar Bongo. Oil revenues have created a francophone elite, and though multiparty elections were held in 1990 – following widespread demonstrations that required French military intervention – and again in 1993, these were deeply flawed. Resentment among the poor classes grew, and in March 1994 a state of emergency was imposed ■

CONGO

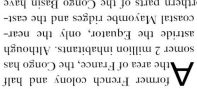

A former French colony and half the area of France, the Congo has somer 2 million inhabitants. Although astride the Equator, only the near-coastal Mayombe ridges and the eastern, central and northern parts of the Congo Basin have truly equatorial climate and vegetation, and these are the sources of valuable exports of timber and palm-oil produce. The areas around Brazzaville, the capital, and those north and west of it are drier, with savanna vegetation except where tributaries of the Congo flood widely.

In 1970 the Congo became Africa's first declared Communist state, but Marxist-Leninist ideology did not prevent the government seeking Western help in exploiting the vast deposits of offshore oil, soon by far the country's main source of income (as Africa's fifth largest producer). The timber industry, in relative decline, has always been hampered by poor trans-port – despite the spectacular Congo-Ocean railway from Brazzaville (formerly capital of French Equatorial Africa) to Pointe Noire, the nation's only significant port. Almost half the country remains covered in rainforest.

Marxism was officially abandoned in 1990 and the regime announced the planned introduction of a multiparty system. Following a referendum over-whelmingly in favour of a new constitution, multi-party elections were held in June and July 1992. From 1979 to that point the country had been ruled by Colonel Denis Sassou-Nguesso, who despite his Marxist pronouncements lived a very capitalist lifestyle on oil revenues, 60% of which came from the USA. His successor, Pascal Lissouba, introduced stringent economic reforms to rectify the sliding economy – including, on the instructions of the International Monetary Fund, massive cutbacks in the civil service.

Because of the huge areas of dense forest more than half the population live in towns – a high proportion for Africa – though subsistence agriculture, mainly for cassava, occupies a third of the still fast-growing workforce ■

ZAIRE

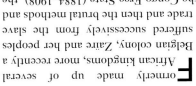

Formerly made up of several African kingdoms, more recently a Belgian colony, Zaire and her peoples suffered successively from the slave trade and then the brutal methods and corruption of the Congo Free State (1884–1908), the personal possession of King Leopold II, before Belgium assumed administration until independence was granted in 1960. The country's huge size and small population stretched Belgium's modest resources. Africa's third biggest and the world's 11th biggest country, Zaire is no less than 77 times the size of its former master: the distance between the two largest cities, Kinshasa and Lubumbashi, is as great as between Paris and Moscow.

In colonial days, palm and rubber plantations were developed in the equatorial Congo Basin (the world's second largest river drainage system), with mining on the Congo-Zambezi watershed and coffee-growing on the Congo-Nile watershed in the north-east. The Congo (Zaire) River was developed as a major artery, its rapids and falls by-passed by railways – including the Boyoma (Stanley), the world's most voluminous, and an important railway built from the river port of Kinshasa to the coastal port of Matadi. Despite its vast size, Zaire's Atlantic coastline consists of only 27 km [17 mls].

Minerals from the 'Copperbelt' in the far south-eastern province of Shaba (formerly Katanga), refined on the spot, provide much of Zaire's export income, though shortages of skilled workers and spare parts, gross misgovernment, illegal trade, and dislocation of railway links through Angola, Zimbabwe and Mozambique because of war have all affected revenues. Most outstanding of many minerals are copper and cobalt, with copper accounting for more than half the country's export earnings, but manganese, tin, gold and diamonds are also important. 'Strategic minerals', including cadmium, also emanate from Shaba. Industry was already substantial at indepen-

A crowded ferry-boat on the Congo (Zaire) River at Kisangani, formerly Stanleyville. Though the ninth longest river in the world, its drainage basin and flow both rank second only to the Amazon.

dence, and the massive hydroelectric developments at Inga, below Kinshasa, which supplies power to the mining town of Kolwezi in Shaba, some 1,725 km [1,800 mls] to the south-east, should provide for further expansion under new government policies.

With its massive mineral reserves Zaïre should be among the wealthiest of African states, but it remains a low-income nation and well inside the world's bottom 20 according to World Bank figures. While transport and communications are difficult in a huge country still dominated by dense rainforest, the reasons for Zaïre's plight are largely man-made.

Belgium left the country politically unprepared for its sudden withdrawal, and within days of independence the army mutinied and the richest province, Katanga (Shaba), tried to secede. Then called the Congo, the country invited the UN to intervene, but the appallingly violent civil war lasted three years. In 1965 General Mobutu seized control in a period of sustained confusion and remained in power into the 1990s, declaring a one-party state in 1967 and renaming the nation Zaïre in 1971 as part of a wide-ranging Africanization policy that also brought conflict with the Christian churches.

His long dictatorship was a catalogue of repression, inefficiency and corruption in government and unrest, rebellion and poverty among the people, with impenetrably inconsistent policies wreaking havoc in the economy even during the various mineral booms of the 1970s and 1980s, and confused by alternating periods of nationalization and privatization. His reign was one of orchestrated chaos.

On the whole, he was supported by the West, notably France, Belgium and the USA, who valued his strategic minerals and his support to the UNITA rebels in Angola and wanted Zaïre outside the Soviet sphere of influence. But with the end of the Cold War that support evaporated: indeed, the US soon pushed hard for reform. This, combined with increasing protests, finally forced Mobutu in 1990 to concede limited multiparty elections for the summer of 1991. But the newly elected leaders faced complete chaos in Kinshasa as thousands rioted against inflation spiralling towards 2,000% a year. French and Belgian troops were sent in to restore order and evacuate European nationals (many of whom had done very well from the regime), while Mobutu – who, according to the US State Department, enjoyed a personal wealth of about $5 billion – consolidated what had become more a kingdom than a country. He was still in power in 1994, having conceded only cosmetic influence to his prime minister the previous year ∎

ZAÏRE

UGANDA

Extending from Lake Victoria to the western arm of the Great Rift Valley and beyond, Uganda is a land of lakes (sources of the White Nile) originating from the tilting and faulting associated with the rift valley system. On the western side of the country the Ruwenzori block has been uplifted to 5,109 m [16,762 ft], while the eastern frontier bisects the large extinct volcano of Mt Elgon.

In the south rainfall is abundant in two seasons, and patches of the original rainforest (25% of land area) remain. However, most of the forest has been cleared from the densely settled areas, notably in the historic kingdoms of Buganda and Busoga. Here the banana is a staple of diet, and coffee, tea and sugar are cash crops; Uganda is the world's sixth largest coffee producer. Here, too, are the capital Kampala, and the industrial centre of Jinja, adjacent to the huge Owen Falls hydroelectric plant. The western areas, the former kingdoms of Bunyoro, Toro and Ankole, depend more on cattle rearing.

To the north, one rainy season each year supports a savanna of trees and grassland. Population is generally less dense, and farmers grow finger-millet and sorghum, with cotton and tobacco as cash crops. Tsetse fly inhibits cattle-keeping in some areas, which have become game parks, but the dry north-east (Karamoja) supports nomadic pastoralists.

Blessed with an equable climate, fertile soils and varied resources, from freshwater fish to copper, Uganda could have lived up to Churchill's colonial description as 'the pearl of Africa'. Instead, independence soon brought two decades of disaster with almost ceaseless internal conflict and a shattered economy.

Between the break from Britain in 1962 and the takeover by Yoweri Museveni in 1986, the country suffered a succession of linked civil wars, violent coups, armed invasions and tribal massacres. The worst of several bad periods was the sordid regime of Idi Amin, who in 1971 ousted the first Prime Minister Milton Obote – then president of a one-party state – and in an eight-year reign of terror killed up to 300,000 people ∎

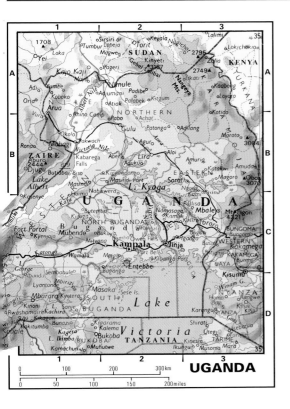

UGANDA

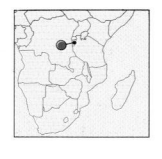

BURUNDI

From the capital of Bujumbura on Lake Tanganyika a great escarpment rises to the rift highlands – reaching 2,670 m [8,760 ft] – which make up most of Burundi. Cool and healthy, the highlands support a dense but dispersed farming population, the Hutu, and a minority of the unusually tall cattle-owning Tutsi. This is similar to

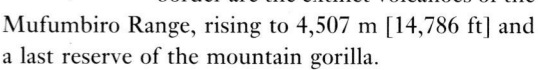

Pens and ponds: a pig farm and a fish farm in Burundi, a nation reliant on intensive agriculture.

Rwanda and being also a small country and overpopulated, employment is sought in neighbouring countries. Coffee is widely grown for export throughout the uplands (80% of total earnings), and cotton is grown on the rift valley floor in the Ruzizi Valley.

The enmity between the Hutu and Tutsi is centuries old. The worst recent manifestation was in 1972, when the murder of the deposed king led to the massacre of more than 100,000 Hutu, but tens of thousands were killed in 1988 and 1992 ∎

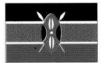

KENYA

Bisected by the Great Rift Valley, the Kenya Highlands were formed by volcanoes and lava flows rising from 1,500 m [4,900 ft] to the snow-capped peak of Mt Kenya at 5,199 m [17,000 ft]. The greater part of the country, however, comprises plains cut across old crystalline rocks, except where sedimentary strata extend across the Tana Basin and into the Somali Republic.

Some 80% of the people crowd into about 15% of the plains in the south-west of the country, where average rainfalls of over 750 mm [30 in] a year support dense farming populations. Corn meal is the staple diet, but Kenya is one of the few African nations also supporting a dairy industry. The Kikuyu and other tribes practise small-scale farming on the fertile volcanic soils on the eastern flanks of the Highlands from Limuru to Nyeri, Meru and Embu.

The western Highlands descend to the equally populous Lake Victoria basin around Kakamega and Kisii, focusing on Kisumu. Nakuru and Eldoret are farming centres originally settled by Europeans. The modern capital city of Nairobi is within this core area of Kenya, from which derive most of the exports of tea, coffee, pyrethrum and sisal, with soda ash from the Magadi alkaline lake.

A second concentration of population occurs along the coast adjacent to Mombasa, Kenya's second city and a port that also serves Uganda via Nairobi. There are ancient towns and ruins, and an Islamic Swahili culture. These now coexist with an international tourist industry that is Kenya's third biggest source of foreign exchange. By contrast, the extensive semi-arid interior plains contain widely scattered pastoral peoples such as the Masai, Turkana and Galla.

By the standards of tropical Africa, Kenya has a stable and safe economy, even allowing for the traditionally thriving black market and usual reliance on aid. The country could nevertheless be in danger from two explosions, one in AIDS and the other, by

RWANDA

Uplift on the flank of the western arm of the Great Rift Valley has raised much of Rwanda to well over 2,000 m [6,000 ft]. On the northern border are the extinct volcanoes of the Mufumbiro Range, rising to 4,507 m [14,786 ft] and a last reserve of the mountain gorilla.

A small, landlocked and poor rural country, Rwanda is by far Africa's most densely populated state and the steep slopes are intensively cultivated, with contour ploughing to prevent erosion. Exports include coffee, tea, pyrethrum and tungsten, but when conditions permit there is a large movement into neighbouring countries for employment.

Rwanda was merged with Burundi by German colonialism in 1899, making Ruanda-Urundi part of German East Africa. Belgium occupied it during World War I, and then administered the territory under a League of Nations mandate, later (1946) a

UN trusteeship. In 1959 it was again divided into two, Rwanda finally achieving full independence in 1962, the same year as Burundi.

As in Burundi, there are deep social and cultural divisons between the farming majority, the Hutu, and the traditional owners of cattle, the unusually tall Tutsi. Several decades of ethnic strife climaxed in 1990 when a rebel force of Tutsi 'refugees' invaded from Uganda and occupied much of the north before being repulsed by French, British and Zaïrian troops brought in by the Hutu-dominated Rwanda government. The problems stem from the revolution of 1959, when the Hutu overthrew the aristocratic Tutsi minority rulers in one of the most violent clashes in modern African history. In February 1991, in return for its neighbours granting Tutsi refugees citizenship, Rwandan leaders agreed to the principle of a return to democracy, but the violence continued.

Following the assassination of the Rwandan and Burundian prime ministers in April 1994, murderous Tutsi-led RPF forces wrought a violent response from Hutu-dominated militiamen. Hundreds of thousands were killed or forced to flee, many into a Tanzania ill-prepared for such a human flood ∎

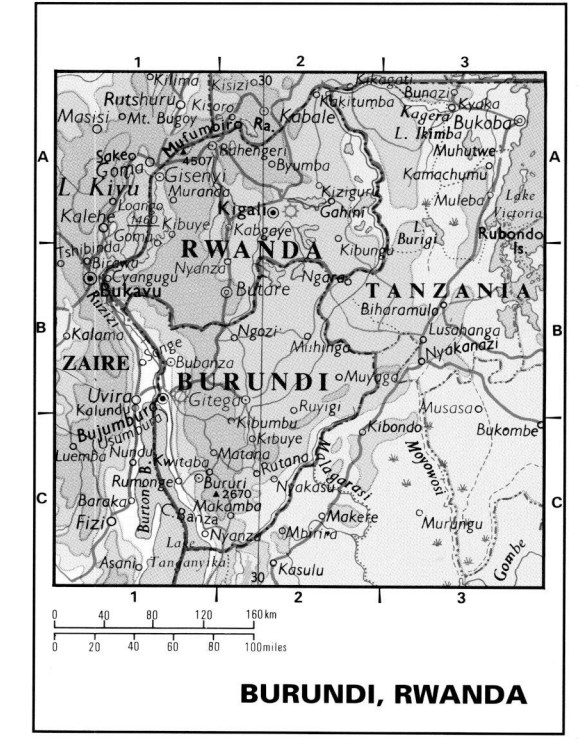

BURUNDI, RWANDA

Elephants on the move in Amboseli National Park, one of the many reserves that now help make tourism Kenya's most important source of foreign exchange.

contrast, in sheer numbers of people. Though relatively sparse in terms of density, Kenya's extraordinarily high birth rate of 4.2% is expected to produce an increase of 82% in its population between 1988 and 2000 – a figure exceeded only by Haiti.

The 1990s brought signs, too, of increasing political problems as Daniel arap Moi, president since 1978 and successor to the moderate Jomo Kenyatta, found his corrupt one-party regime under threat. In December 1991, after months of pressure and government defections, he was forced to concede the principle of pluralist democracy – not seen since 1969. The president (a Kalenjin in a country whose affairs have always been dominated by the Kikuyu) was re-elected in multiparty elections in December 1992, though there were many allegations of vote-rigging and unrest was growing ■

AIDS IN AFRICA

The Acquired Immune Deficiency Syndrome was first identified in 1981, when American doctors found otherwise healthy young men succumbing to rare infections. By 1984, the cause had been traced to the Human Immunodeficiency Virus (HIV), which can remain dormant for many years and perhaps indefinitely; only half of those known to carry the virus in 1981 had developed AIDS ten years later. By the early 1990s, AIDS was still largely restricted to male homosexuals or needle-sharing drug users in the West. However, here the disease is spreading fastest among heterosexual men and women, its usual vector in the Third World.

Africa is the most severely hit. In 1991, a World Health Organization conference in Dakar, Senegal, was told that AIDS would kill more than 6 million Africans in the coming decade. In the same period, 4 million children would be born with the disease, and millions more would be orphaned by it. In Uganda, an estimated million people are thought to be carrying the virus. The conference heard that Africa's educated élites were among the most at risk – trained people desperately needed to help the continent's future development. Africans are also more than usually vulnerable to HIV and AIDS infection, because of urbanization and sexual freedom. But most are poor, many are undernourished; many more suffer from various debilitating, non-fatal diseases such as parasitic infestations. Their immune systems are already weak, making them less likely to fight the HIV virus, and more likely to develop full-blown AIDS.

Yet AIDS is only the newest scourge in Africa. Malaria, measles, a host of water-borne infections, such as cholera and bilharzia, and simple malnutrition still kill far more people.

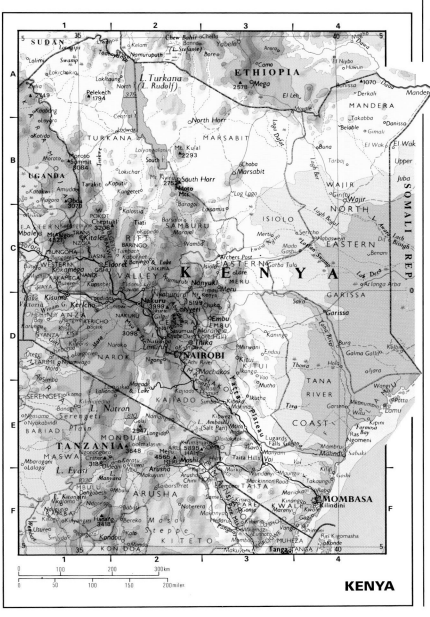

KENYA

TANZANIA

From the islands of Zanzibar and Pemba, Tanzania extends across the high plateau of eastern Africa, mostly above 1,000 m [3,000 ft], to the rift valleys filled by lakes Tanganyika and Nyasa (Malawi). The Northern Highlands flank branches of the eastern rift valley, containing the strongly alkaline Lake Natron and lakes Eyasi and Manyara, and dominated by the ice-capped extinct volcano of Kilimanjaro which, at 5,895 m [19,340 ft], is the highest mountain in Africa. The Southern Highlands overlook Lake Nyasa at the southern end of the rift system.

Tanzania's population is dispersed into several concentrations mostly on the margins of the country, separated by sparsely inhabited savanna woodland (*miombo*). Attempts to develop the *miombo* woodlands have been hindered by sleeping sickness, drought and poor soils, and traditional settlement is based on shifting cultivation.

Along the coast and on self-governing Muslim Zanzibar and other islands are old cities and ruins of the historic Swahili-Arab culture, and the major ports and railway termini of Dar es Salaam and Tanga. Rail connections enable Dar es Salaam to act as a port for Zambia and, by ferry across Lake Tanganyika, for eastern Zaire. Local products include sisal and cashew nuts with cloves from Zanzibar and Pemba, and there are some fine beach resorts.

The Northern Highlands centre on Moshi and support intensive agriculture, exporting coffee, tea and tobacco. This contrasts with the nomadic Masai pastoralists of the surrounding plains. Tea also comes from the Southern Highlands. South of Lake Victoria is an important cotton-growing and cattle-rearing area, focusing on Mwanza.

Tanzania was formed in 1964 when mainland Tanganyika – which had become independent from Britain in 1961 – was joined by the small island state of Zanzibar. For 20 years after independence Tanzania was run under the widely admired policies of self-help (*ujamaa*) and egalitarian socialism pioneered by President Julius Nyerere.

While his schemes produced relatively high levels of education and welfare for Africa, economic progress was stifled not only by lack of resources and falling world commodity prices but also by inefficient state corporations and corrupt bureaucracies. As a result the country ranks little better than wartorn

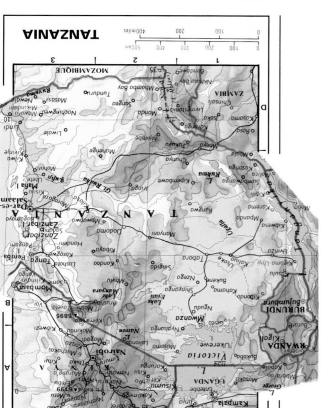

MALAWI

A small, hilly if not mountainous country, Malawi's strange shape (nowhere is it more than 160 km [100 mls] wide) derived from a 19th-century missionaries' and traders' route up the Zambezi, Shire and Lake Nyasa (Malawi). The country is relatively poor in natural resources, and a high population density places excessive pressure on the land. This problem was inflamed during the 1980s, when Malawi became the main host to nearly a million refugees from neighbouring Mozambique, putting an intolerable burden on an already weak economy, despite massive aid packages. Industrial and urban development are extremely limited. Most of the commercial activity centres on agriculture, which provides over 90% of Malawi's domestic exports. Tea and tobacco, mostly from large estates, are the principal export crops, while basic foodstuffs such as maize are largely derived from small, quasisubsistence peasant holdings which occupy most of the farmland. Malawi has a long history as an exporter of labour migrants, and large numbers of Malawians still work or seek work abroad.

Malawi's recent history has been dominated by one man: Dr Hastings Kamuzu Banda. Already 62 years old, he led the country (formerly Nyasaland) to independence in 1964, and two years later declared a one-party republic with himself as president – for life from 1971. His autocratic regime was different from most of black Africa in being conservative and pragmatic, hostile to socialist neighbours but friendly with South Africa. In 1993, 63% of voters chose a multi-party system in a referendum; elections in May 1994 saw Dr Banda and his Malawi Congress Party defeated and Bakili Muluzi elected president.

At first his austerity programme and agricultural policies seemed to have wrought an economic miracle, but the 1980s sealed a swift decline and a return to poverty. As well as a million refugees Malawi faced another immediate problem – the world's worst recorded national incidence of AIDS ■

Villagers in Malawi. Though the name means 'the land where the sun is reflected in the water of fire', the country's great beauty lies in savanna and woodland.

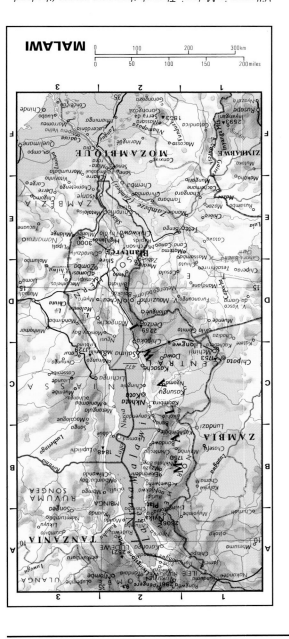

MOZAMBIQUE

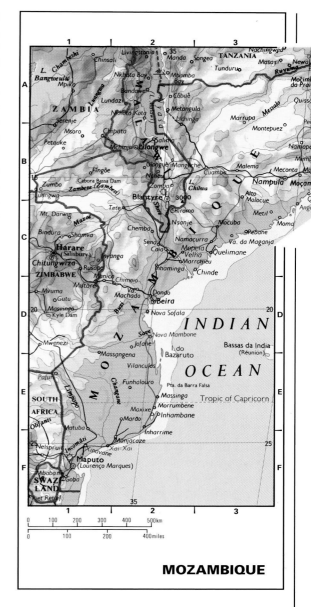

MOZAMBIQUE

Like other former ex-Portuguese African countries, Mozambique arose from the search for a route round Africa to the riches of Asia; Vasco da Gama and his successors established forts at Beira (Sofala), Quelimane and Moçambique Island. Dutch conquest of Portuguese Asia in the 17th century, and subsequent concentration by the Portuguese on the slave trade from West Africa to the Americas, resulted in decay of Mozambique settlements. However, being so little affected by the slave trade, and acting as a refuge in wars, Mozambique was never depopulated to the extent of Angola, and still maintains a higher population on a smaller area.

Because of the warm Mozambique (Agulhas) Current, all the country is tropical. Coral reefs lie offshore, and the only real natural harbour is Maputo (Lourenço Marques). Here is southern Africa's widest coastal plain, with plantations of coconut, sisal and sugar on the alluvial flats. As in the northern foothills, farmers grow maize, groundnuts, cotton and cashew. Only the inner borderlands are high; because of this and its remoteness from Portugal, Mozambique attracted few European settlers. At the limit of navigation on the Zambezi is Africa's biggest dam, Cabora Bassa, whose power goes largely to South Africa. Large deposits of coal, copper, bauxite and offshore gas have yet to be exploited. Prawns are the biggest export earner.

Despite the relentless civil war Mozambique forms a transit route for much of the overseas trade of Swaziland, the Transvaal, Zimbabwe and Zambia, involving mainly the ports of Maputo, Beira and Nacala-Velha, just north of Moçambique. Rail, port and handling services provide employment and substantial revenues.

Mozambique has been plagued by civil war since

well before Portugal abruptly relinquished control in 1975. Combined with frequent droughts and floods, this has caused tens of thousands of deaths and, by 1989, had reduced the country to the status of the world's poorest country.

When the Portuguese rulers and settlers abandoned Mozambique they left behind a country totally unprepared for organizing itself – the literacy rate, for example, was less than 1%. The Marxist-Leninist government of Samora Machel's Frelimo movement, which had been fighting the colonial regime for more than a decade, tried to implement ambitious social policies, but erratic administration, along with a series of natural disasters, reduced the economy to ruins by the mid-1980s.

From the 1970s the progress was also severely hampered by the widespread activities of the Mozambique National Resistance (MNR, or Renamo), backed first by Rhodesia and later by South Africa. Renamo soon controlled huge areas of the countryside – convoys could only cross the 'Tete Corridor' escorted by Zimbabwean and Malawian troops – forcing 1.5 million refugees to flee their land, the vast majority of them going to poor Malawi, and displacing almost double that figure from their homes; by 1988 almost half of all Mozambique's population was reliant on external aid.

Well before Machel was mysteriously killed in a plane crash inside South Africa in 1986, his government had been opening up the country to Western investment and influence – a policy continued by his successor, President Joaquim Chissano. In 1989 Frelimo formally abandoned its Marxist ideology, and the following year agreed to end one-party rule and hold talks with the rebels. Despite South Africa's withdrawal of official assistance, the talks dragged on without a permanent ceasefire and hostilities continued to dog the country until October 1992, when the UN finally brokered an agreement between the two parties and guaranteed 6,000 peacekeeping troops.

The UN authorities were faced with a massive refugee problem. By March 1994 some 800,000 had returned, with as many to follow, providing UNHCR with the biggest repatriation programme in Africa's history ■

---

states like Ethiopia and the Somali Republic in terms of income, and is almost as dependent on foreign financial aid.

Nyerere stepped down as president in 1985, but retained the (only) party leadership and considerable influence for another five years. In the meantime his successor, Ali Hassan Mwinyi, was attempting to liberalize the economy and agreed in 1992 to abolish the one-party system. Another target was tourism: Tanzania received 103,000 visitors in 1987; this is less than a sixth of Kenya's total, but there are hopes of a rise.

Certainly it has many of the prerequisites for a successful tourist industry. There are 17 national parks and reserves – among them the Selous, the largest game reserve in the world; the celebrated Serengeti; and the Ngorongoro Crater, renowned for its abundant wildlife. In addition, there are important archaeological sites such as Olduvia Gorge, west of the Serengeti, where in 1964 Louis Leakey, the famous British archaeologist and anthropologist, discovered the remains of humans some 2 million years old ■

Part of the Ngorongoro Crater in northern Tanzania: 18 km [11 mls] across, it fills with seasonal rains (April–May) to create a home for 30,000 animals. Masai tribesmen also herd their cattle across the crater's floor.

ANGOLA

More than 13 times the size of its former colonial ruler, Portugal, Angola is southern Africa's largest state, extending through 13° of latitude. There is a strong cooling effect from the cold offshore Benguela Current, and climate and vegetation vary from desert on the south coast to equatorial and montane conditions in the centre and north. Thus Angola has exceptionally varied agricultural output, while the coastal waters are rich in fish.

Portugal established Luanda in 1575, and Angola's capital is the oldest European-founded city in Africa south of the Sahara. As a centre of the slave trade, some 3 million captives from Angola passed through it to the Americas, and the depopulation dislocated local life for many generations. As a Portuguese colony and then overseas province, Angola's development was hampered by the small population, by Portugal's economic weakness, centralized rule and mercantilist theories, and more recently by years of persistent guerrilla warfare.

Potentially, Angola is one of Africa's richest countries. Oil reserves are important both on the coast and offshore near Luanda in the enclave of Cabinda, and hydroelectric power and irrigation developments are substantial. Diamonds, a major export (Angola is one of the world's largest producers), come from the north-east, and there are unexploited reserves of copper, manganese and phosphates.

Economic progress has been hampered by austere Marxist policies and vast spending on defence and security, but in 1991 the crippling 16-year war between the MPLA government and UNITA rebels ended in a peace accord. The election of 1992 was narrowly won by the MPLA (reborn as free marketeers) under President Eduardo de Santos, but Jonas Savimbi of UNITA refused to accept the result, and within days the war, ethnic now rather than ideological, had resumed. With the Cold War over the West took little interest in what became an increasingly appalling conflict – one in which deaths averaged a thousand every day and over 3 million people faced starvation ■

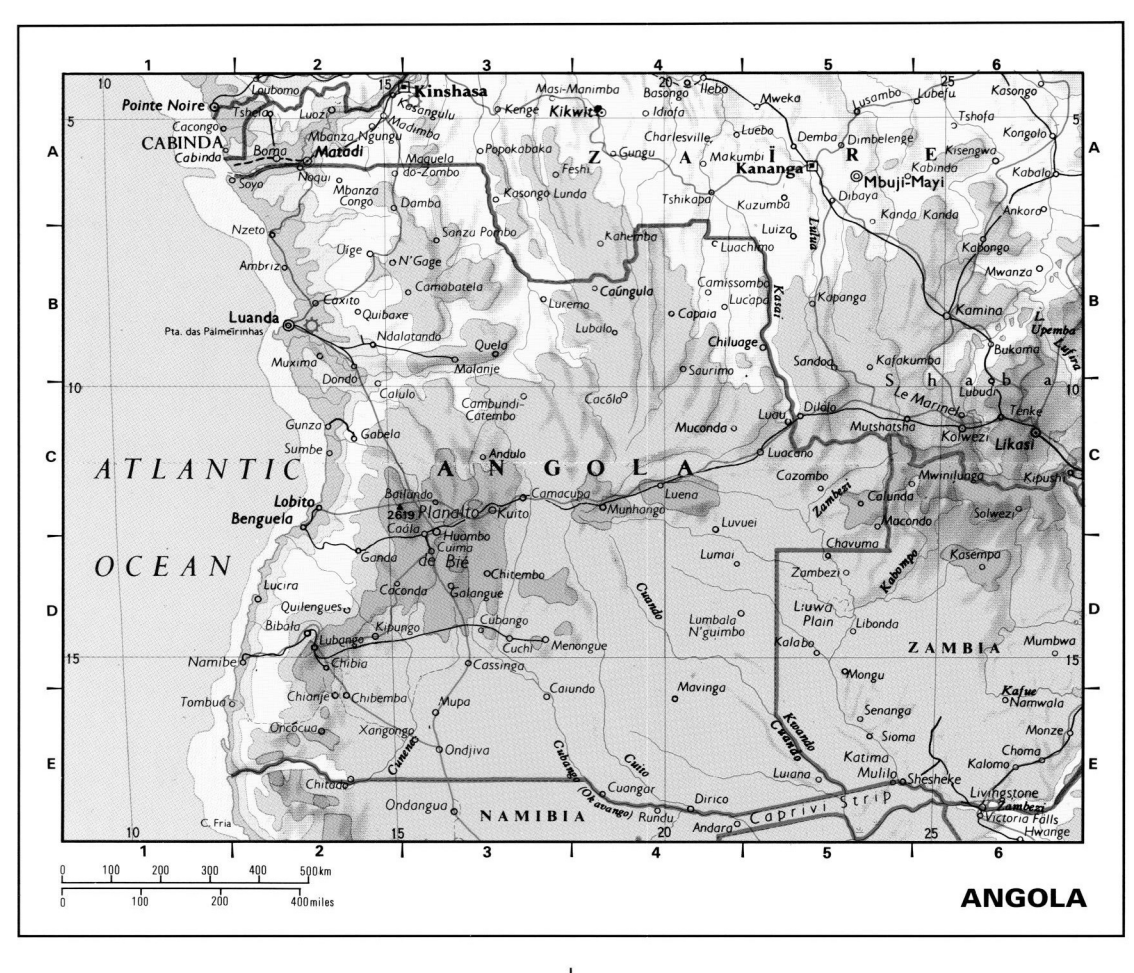

ANGOLA

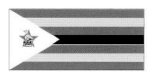

ZIMBABWE

Formerly Rhodesia (and Southern Rhodesia before 1965), Zimbabwe is a compact country lying astride the high plateaus between the Zambezi and Limpopo rivers. It was nurtured by Britain as a 'white man's country', and there were some 280,000 Europeans there when Ian Smith declared UDI in 1965. Guerrilla action against the Smith regime soon escalated into a full-scale civil war, eventually forcing a move to black majority rule in 1980. The rift that followed independence, between Robert Mugabe's ruling ZANU and Joshua Nkomo's ZAPU, was healed in 1989 when they finally merged after nearly three decades and Mugabe renounced his shallow Marxist-Leninist ideology. In 1990 the state of emergency that had lasted since 1965 was allowed to lapse – three months after Mugabe had secured a landslide election victory.

Zimbabwe's relatively strong economy – founded on gold and tobacco but now far more diverse – evolved its virtual self-sufficiency during the days of international sanctions against Smith's white minority regime. After 1980 there was a surge in most sectors, with successful agrarian policies enabling the nation to supply less endowed well-off neighbours with food in good years and the exploitation of the country's rich and varied mineral resources. Zimbabwe is not so dependent on one commodity as some southern African countries (Angola's oil, Zambia's copper, Botswana's diamonds), but a fast-growing population will exert pressure on both land and resources in the 1990s. The economy was badly dented by drought in 1993, forcing Mugabe (whose own power base comprises small farmers) to seize white-owned land in what was largely a display of gesture politics ■

ZIMBABWE

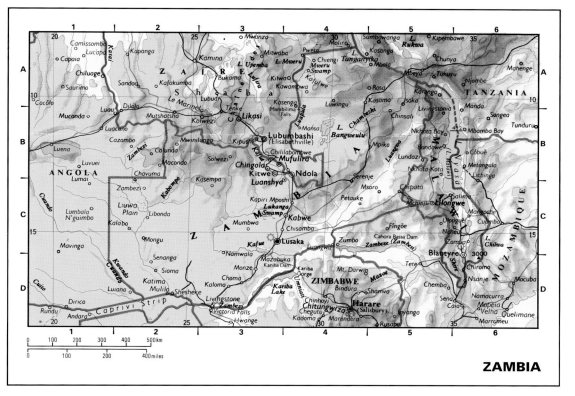

ZAMBIA

ZAMBIA

A vast expanse of high plateaus in the interior of south-central Africa, most of Zambia (formerly Northern Rhodesia) is drained by the Zambezi and two of its major tributaries, the Kafue and the Luangwa. The latter and the central section of the Zambezi occupy a low-lying rift valley bounded by rugged escarpments. Lake Kariba, formed by damming in 1961 and the second largest artificial lake in Africa, occupies part of the floor of this valley; like the hydroelectric power it generates, the lake is shared with Zimbabwe, though power from the Kafue River now supplements supplies from Kariba. The magnificent Victoria Falls are similarly shared between the two countries. Much of northern Zambia is drained to the Atlantic Ocean by headwaters of the Zaïre (Congo), including the Chambeshi, which loses itself within the vast swamps of the Bangweulu Depression.

Zambia is one of the world's largest producers of copper, but despite efforts to diversify, the economy remains stubbornly dependent (95% of export earnings in 1989) on this one mineral. The Copperbelt, centred on Kitwe, is the dominant urban region while the capital, Lusaka, provides the other major growth pole. Rural-urban migration has increased markedly since independence in 1964 – Zambia has 'black' southern Africa's highest proportion of town dwellers – but work is scarce.

Commercial farming, concentrated in central regions astride the railway, and mostly maize, frequently fails to meet the needs of the growing urban population, but as a landlocked country heavily dependent on international trade, Zambia relies on its neighbours for access to ports via Zimbabwe, Mozambique and South Africa. Alternatives, notably a railway, highway and oil pipeline to Dar es Salaam, have been developed, but Zambia continues to have serious transport problems.

President Kenneth Kaunda's government enjoyed reasonable income until the copper crash of the mid-1970s, but his collectivist policies failed to diversify the economy (before or after) and neglected agriculture. In 1972 he declared UNIP the only legal party, and it was nearly 20 years before democracy returned: then, in the 1991 elections (conceded by Kaunda after intense foreign pressure), he was trounced by union leader Frederick Chiluba of the Movement for Multiparty Democracy – Kaunda's first challenger in 27 years of post-colonial rule. Chiluba inherited a foreign debt of $4.6 billion – one of the world's biggest per capita figures – and by 1994 opposition mounted as promises of more political freedoms and economic progress went unfulfilled ■

Spectators stand above the spray of the Victoria Falls on the Zambezi, the longest river in southern Africa and the border between Zimbabwe and Zambia. The Falls (actually three falls – Leaping Water, Main Fall and Rainbow Falls) are not spectacular in height and volume in statistical terms, but they are among the world's most beautiful and famous. The first European to see them, in 1855, was the Scottish missionary and explorer David Livingstone, who invoked his queen; but the local name – 'Mosi-oa-Toenja' – is a little more romantic, meaning 'the smoke that thunders'.

NAMIBIA

Born out of the late 19th-century scramble for Africa, Namibia is a country of enormous diversity, physically and socially. Fringing the south-ern Atlantic coastline is the arid Namib Desert, virtually uninhabited, separated by a major escarpment from a north-south spine of mountains which culminate in the Khomas Highlands near Windhoek. This rugged spine, built of thick schists and quartzites, rises to 2,483 m [8,150 ft] in the peak of Moltkeblik. To the east the country occupies the fringes of the Kalahari Desert.

Namibia was (as South West Africa) a German protectorate from 1884 before being occupied by the Union of South Africa at the request of the Allied powers in 1915. Granted a League of Nations mandate in 1920, South Africa refused to place the territory under UN trusteeship after World War II, and in 1966 the mandate was cancelled. The main nationalist movement, SWAPO, began a guerrilla campaign supported by Cuba and Angola, but it was not until 1990, following increasing international pressure, that it became independent. ∎

BOTSWANA

The British protectorate of Bechuanaland from 1885, Bots-wana became an independent state in 1966 after a peaceful six-year transi-tion. It was then one of the world's poorest countries, with cattle as the only significant export, and its physical environment hardly induced optimism: more than half of the land area is occupied by the Kalahari Desert, with much of the rest taken up by saltpans and swamps. Although the Kalahari extends into Namibia and South Africa, Botswana accounts for the greater part of this vast dry upland. It is, however, not a uniform desert: occasional rain-fall allows growth of grasses and thorny scrub, enabling the area's sparse human population of about 100,000 – mostly nomadic Bantu herdsmen – to graze their cattle.

Botswana was transformed by the mining of vast diamond resources, starting at Orapa in 1971, and, despite a protracted drought, expanding output in the 1980s made the economy the fastest growing in sub-Saharan Africa, paving the way for wide-ranging social programmes. By the end of the decade Botswana was producing some 16% of the world's total, behind Australia and Zaïre.

Politically stable under Seretse Khama, the coun-try's main target became diversification, not only to reduce dependence on diamonds (85% of export earnings) and on South African imports, but also to create jobs for a rapidly expanding – though still rela-tively sparse – population. Copper has been mined at Selebi-Pikwe since 1974, but the emphasis in the 1980s was put on tourism: 17% of Botswana's huge area (the world's highest figure) is assigned to wildlife conservation and game reserves, and more than half a million visitors a year are drawn to them, mostly from South Africa. ∎

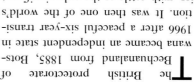

Gemsbok on the savanna of Botswana, the world leader in percentage of land dedicated to wildlife conservation.

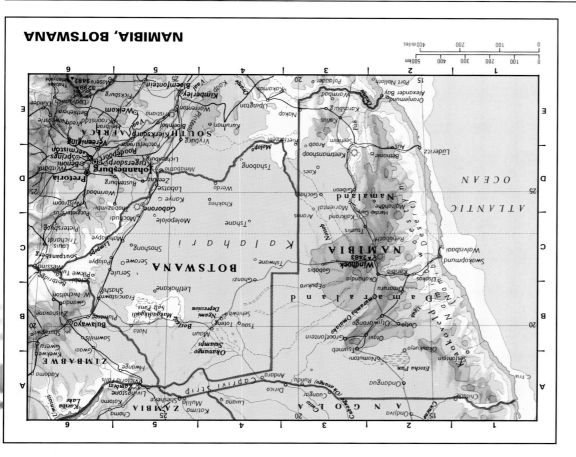

NAMIBIA, BOTSWANA

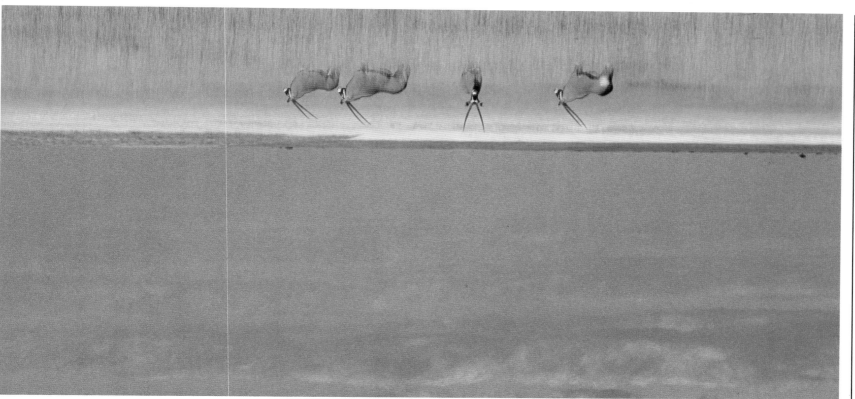

SOUTH AFRICA

Geologically very ancient, South Africa has only scant superficial deposits of sediments less than 600 million years lod. Geological history has had a great effect on all aspects of the country's development – on its landforms, patterns of population, industrial growth and agricultural potential.

The country is divisible into two major natural zones – the interior and the coastal fringe – the interior in turn consisting of two major parts. Most of Cape Province, the Transvaal and the Orange Free State are drained by the Orange River and its important right-bank tributaries which flow with gentle gradients over level plateaus, varying in height from 1,200–2,000 m [4,000–6,000 ft]. The northern

Shrouded in cloud, Table Mountain forms a dramatic backdrop to Cape Town.

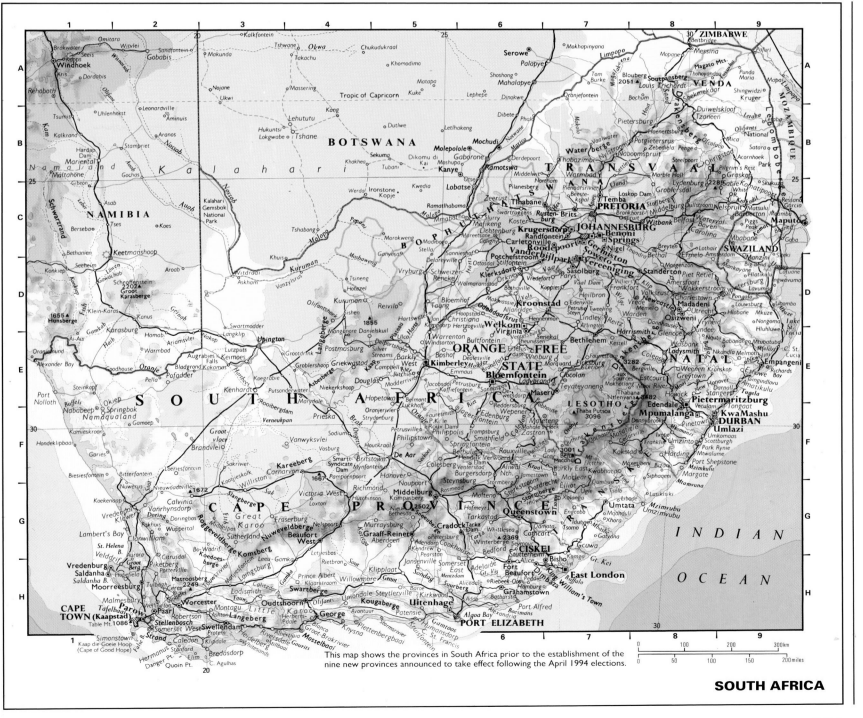

This map shows the provinces in South Africa prior to the establishment of the nine new provinces announced to take effect following the April 1994 elections.

SOUTH AFRICA

THE END OF APARTHEID

From its 1948 institution, apartheid – 'separate development' – meant not only racial segregation but also massive racial discrimination. Over the next generation, a whole body of apartheid law was created, denying Africans, Indians and 'coloureds' the most basic of human rights.

The African National Congress, the main black political organization, was banned, and black opposition was brutally suppressed. South Africa's racial policies led to increasing isolation from the civilized world, and by the 1980s the country was considered a pariah.

Changing demographic patterns – the blacks were increasingly outnumbering the whites by more and more every year – combined with international sanctions to make apartheid unsupportable. The 1989 election of liberal Nationalist President F.W. de Klerk brought dramatic change: veteran ANC leader Nelson Mandela was released from jail, and in 1991 de Klerk announced his intention to dismantle the entire structure of apartheid. In 1992, an all-white referendum gave him a mandate to move towards a multiracial democratic system.

Though intertribal violence became almost endemic (some 6,000 have been killed since 1986), and armed white extremists constantly threatened a polygonous civil war, non-racial elections with universal suffrage did take place in April 1994. The ANC won 62%, the Nationalists 20%, the mainly Zulu Inkatha 10%, and on 10 May Nelson Mandela was inaugurated as President of South Africa, leading a coalition that included six former cabinet ministers, notably de Klerk (who became second Deputy President). The world's last white empire had fallen – but the real challenge was just beginning.

Transvaal is occupied by the Bushveld, an area of granites and igneous intrusions, drained by rivers which flow northwards to the Limpopo.

The coastal fringe is divided from the interior by the Fringing Escarpment, a feature that makes communication within the country very difficult. In the east the massive basalt-capped rock wall of the Drakensberg, at its most majestic near Mont-aux-Sources and rising to over 3,000 m [over 10,000 ft], overlooks the Natal and Transkei coastlands. In the west there is a similar divide between the interior plateau and the coastlands, though this is less well developed. The Fringing Escarpment also runs along

the south coast, where it is fronted by many independent mountain ranges with an east-west alignment.

South Africa's economic and political development is closely related to these physical components. The country was first peopled by negroids from the north, who introduced a cattle-keeping, grain-growing culture. Entering by the plateaus of the north-east, they continued southwards into the well-watered zones below the Fringing Escarpment of present-day Natal and Transkei. Moving into country occupied by Bushmanoid peoples they absorbed some of the latter's cultural features, especially the 'clicks' so characteristic of the modern Zulu and Xhosa languages. By the 18th century these Bantu-speaking groups had penetrated to the south-east in the region of the Kei and Fish rivers.

Simultaneously with this advance, a group of Europeans was establishing a victualling point for the Dutch East India Company on the site of modern Cape Town. These Company employees, augmented by Huguenot refugees, eventually spread out from Cape Town, beginning a movement of European farmers throughout southern Africa and bringing about the development of the Afrikaners. Their advance was channelled in the south by the parallel coastal ranges, so that eventually black and white met near the Kei River. From this colonizing process, aided by an implanting of British people in the south-east and near Durban, the present disposition of black-dominated and white-dominated lands arose.

Not surprisingly, conflict arose from the juxtapositioning of the two groups, and with the discovery of valuable minerals – gold in the Banket deposits of the Witwatersrand, diamonds in the Kimberlite pipes of the Cape, platinum in the Bushveld and coal in the Transvaal and Natal – both were drastically affected. South Africa still produces 30% of the world's gold, and today we can add chrome, uranium, nickel and many others to the list.

Exploitation of southern Africa's minerals led to trade with overseas markets and the development of major urban complexes. Johannesburg grew the fastest; its growth encouraged the expansion of Durban and to a large extent caused Cape Town and Port Elizabeth to flourish. The appearance of a capitalist, market-oriented economy caused even greater divergence between white and black. The politically-dominant whites reproduced a European economy and, after the transfer of political power, developed strong links with Britain ■

LESOTHO

Consisting mainly of a high mountainous plateau deeply fretted by the headwaters of the Orange (Oranje) River, Lesotho declines altitudinally from east to west, with the highest ridges, over 3,000 m [9–10,000 ft], developed on basaltic lavas. This treeless zone with its steep valleys has an excess of water, making it boggy in summer, frozen in winter. It is nevertheless overpopulated. All of this contrasts with the lower narrow western belts of the sandstone foothills and lowlands, stretching southwards from Butha-Buthe to Mohale's Hoek.

The physical environment and being surrounded on all sides by South Africa provide major economic and political problems for the country. Most of the population are involved in subsistence agriculture, battling for a living against steep slopes and thin soils. The only urban and industrial development lies at Maseru, but the trend is still for people to drift to the small towns or to find employment in the gold and coal mines of South Africa. The country's scenery is conducive to tourism and the altitude allows winter sports, but huge capital investment, especially in roads, is necessary to develop this potential ■

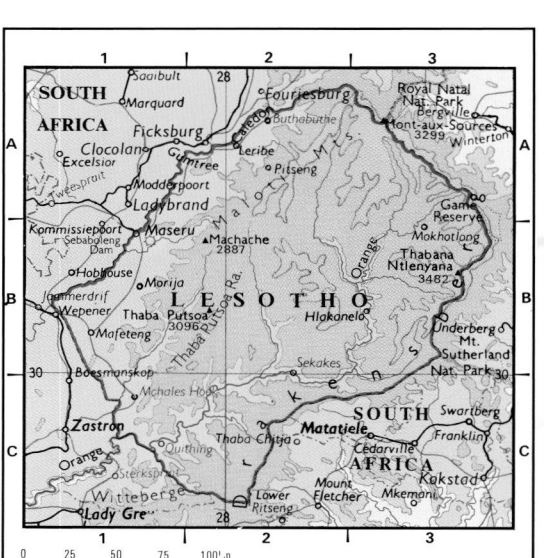

LESOTHO

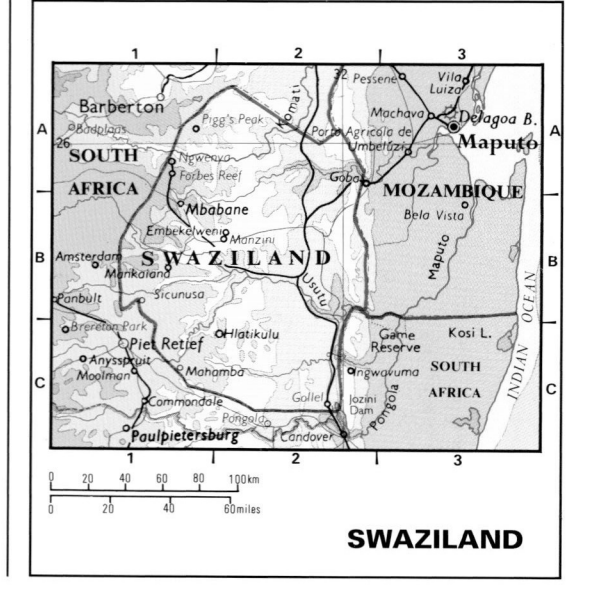

SWAZILAND

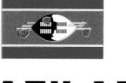

SWAZILAND

Although the smallest country in sub-Saharan Africa, Swaziland nevertheless reveals strong scenic contrasts. From west to east the country descends in three altitudinal steps: the Highveld, average altitude 1,200 m [4,000 ft], and the Middleveld, lying between 350 and 1,000 m [1,000 and 3,500 ft], are made of old, hard rocks; the Lowveld, average height 270 m [900 ft], is of softer shales and sandstones in the west, and basalts in the east. Shutting the country in on the east are the Lebombo Mountains (800 m [2,600 ft]). Rivers rising in South Africa completely traverse these belts; their valleys provide communication lines and are vital

sources of perennial water, important for irrigation.

In the late 19th century European colonists settled and today the main economic features result from basic differences in occupational structures between 'black' and 'white' Swazi. Those derived from European stock are involved in commerce, industry and, predominantly, production of exports such as sugar, citrus fruits and wood pulp as well as farming cereals and cattle. The majority indigenous Swazi are still mostly engaged in subsistence farming based on maize, with fragmented landholdings and a dispersed settlement pattern. Potentially fertile, Swaziland was hit by a series of droughts in the early 1990s – a fact hindering the young king, Mswati III, in attempts to modernize the country.

Swaziland, which gained independence from Britain in 1968, is part of a customs union which includes South Africa, but for overseas trade the country relies largely on the port of Maputo ■

MADAGASCAR

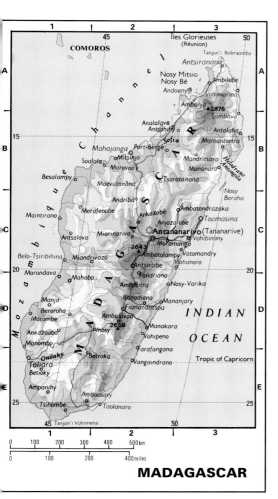

The world's fourth largest island, Madagascar is virtually a semi-continent, bigger than France and immensely varied, physically, ecologically and culturally. Almost all geological eras are represented, and made more vivid by steep faulting, volcanic outpourings and deeply-trenched valleys. There are extensive rugged areas, so that soils are often poor and farming unrewarding, and the coasts are hostile, with little natural shelter. The north and east are hot and wet, and subject to cyclones. The west is drier, and the south and south-west are arid.

MADAGASCAR

Separated from the African mainland for more than 50 million years, Madagascar developed a distinct flora and fauna – over 150,000 plant and animal species are unique to the islands. Before the coming of people some 3,000 years ago, nearly all the island was variously forested, and though much of it was cleared for agriculture a strange collection of animals survived in the remnants – among them 40 species of chameleons, pygmy hippos, elephant birds and the renowned lemurs.

Also unique to the island is its mixture of peoples, derived from several continents. Those on the west side are of Bantu origin, drawn from southern Africa via the Comoros Islands 'bridge'. Those of the centre and east (the Merina or Hova people) came first from Indonesia, as early as 2,000 years ago, with later waves arriving during the 7th to 15th centuries. Other Asians followed, all rice-growers, reverent to cattle, with language and funeral rites similar to those in South-east Asia. They had a monarchy until French occupation in 1895. In the south, the Betsileo are more mixed Bantu-Indonesian, as are other groups, yet all feel 'Malagasy' rather than African or Asian. Many other immigrant groups, including Europeans, Chinese and Indians, have also settled.

Both landscapes and agriculture (dominantly rice with cattle and pigs) in the central highlands are south Asian in character; the east coast and northern highlands are more African, with fallow-farming of food crops and cultivation of coffee, sugar, essential oil plants and spices for export – the country produces two-thirds of the world's vanilla. In the dry west and south nomadic pastoralism is important, and rice is grown by irrigation. Significant minerals are graphite, chromite and mica. Because of the combination of rough terrain, wet season and size of the country, air transport is important, with a network of over 60 airports and airstrips.

The government which took power on independence in 1960 continued Madagascar's links with France, but a resurgence of nationalism in the 1970s was followed by the emergence of Didier Ratsiraka, who seized power in 1975 and established a dictatorial one-party socialist state. Under a new constitution approved in 1992 Ratsiraka, whose incompetence had plunged Madagascar into poverty, was defeated in elections in 1993. The new government of Albert Zafy tried to reassert authority, but he found both the environment and the economy in spiral decline.

With 90% of the forest gone, Madagascar is today

A pair of ring-tailed lemurs, one of the many animal species unique to Madagascar. More a small isolated continent than a large country, the island has evolved its own special habitat.

one of the most eroded places in the world, its coasts clogged with red lateritic soils. Free-market policies had served only to plunder resources further, and despite electoral reform the island seemed destined for a decade of despair as its population burgeoned. One helpful approach, however, has been the pioneering 'debt-for-nature' schemes, which have increased funding for crucial conservation work while offering the chance to pay off huge debts to foreign governments and international organizations ∎

RÉUNION

Réunion is the largest of the Mascarene islands, lying east of Madagascar and south-west of Mauritius and composed of a rugged, mountainous forested centre surrounded by a fertile coastal plain. The volcanic mountains rise to the peak of Piton des Neiges (3,070 m [10,076 ft]), which is sporadically active. Réunion receives heavy rainfall from the cool south-east trade winds in winter, while the summers can be oppressively hot and humid. The lowlands are intensely cultivated with huge plantations of sugar cane; providing 75% of exports, this remains the island's only significant industry, though vanilla, perfume oils

and tea also produce revenue. Local consumption revolves around vegetables, maize and livestock.

Tourism is a big hope for the future following the success of Mauritius, but unemployment is high and France still subsidizes the islands heavily in return for its use as its main military base in the area. The people of the island – which has a very varied and potentially explosive ethnic mix – are divided on its status; as in the other Overseas Departments (Guadeloupe, Martinique and French Guiana), there is increasing pressure on Paris for independence, especially from the young underprivileged population. Though several people were killed in outbreaks of civil unrest in 1991, the majority continue to vote against complete autonomy. This may be as much from financial insecurity as lack of nationalist passion since, like all modern dependencies, Réunion does well from its relationship with France and the risks of independence are great ∎

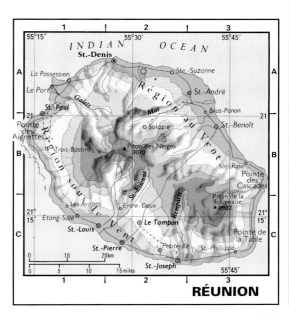

RÉUNION

COMOROS

The Comoros are three large mountainous islands and several smaller coral islands, lying at the northern end of the Mozambique Channel. Njazidja (formerly Grande Comoro) rises to an active volcano; Nzwami (Anjouan) is a heavily eroded volcanic massif; Mwali (Moheli) is a forested plateau. With fertile though porous soils, the islands were originally forested; now they are mostly under subsis-tence agriculture and produce cash crops such as coconuts, coffee, cocoa and spices, vanilla accounting for 78% of exports. Formerly French, the Federal Islamic Republic of the Comoros became indepen-dent (without the agreement of France) following a referendum in 1974. One of the world's poorest coun-tries, it is plagued by lack of resources and political turmoil. French mercenary and Muslim convert Bob Denard effectively ruled until 1989, but his successor Said Djohar then led seven governments in two years.

Mayotte, the easternmost of the large islands, voted to remain French in the 1974 referendum, and in 1976 became a Territorial Collectivity ■

SEYCHELLES

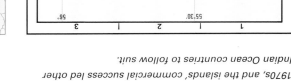

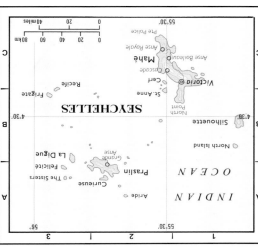

The Seychelles are a compact group of four large and 36 small granitic islands, plus a wide scattering of coralline islands (14 of them inhab-ited) lying mainly to the south and west; 82% of the land area is composed of the four main islands which host 98% of the population, the vast majority on lush and mountainous Mahé.

With a beautiful tropical oceanic climate the Seychelles produce copra, cinnamon and tea, though rice is imported. Fishing and luxury tourism (50% of revenue and growing) are the two main industries. French from 1756 and British from 1814, the islands gained independence in 1976. A year later a political coup set up a one-party Socialist state that lasted until multiparty democracy was restored in 1992 ■

The Seychelles suddenly became a playground paradise with the building of the international airport in the 1970s, and the islands' commercial success led other Indian Ocean countries to follow suit.

MAURITIUS

Mauritius consists of the main island, situated 800 km [500 mls] to the east of Madagascar, Rodrigues (formerly a dependency), 20 nearby islets and the dependencies of the Agalega Islands and the tiny Cargados Carajas shoals (St Brandon). French from 1715 and British from 1810, the colony gained independence within the Commonwealth in 1968.

The beautiful main island, fringed with coral reefs, rises to a high lava plateau. Good rainfall (up to 5,000 mm [200 in] a year) and steep slopes have combined to give fast-flowing rivers, now harnessed for limited hydroelectric power. Similar to Réunion in climate and soils, its vast plantations produce sugar cane (now declining but with derivatives like molasses still accounting for over 40% of exports), tea and tobacco, while home consumption centres around livestock and vegetables. To some extent the decline in sugar has been offset by the growth in tourism (239,000 visitors in 1988) and the expansion of textiles and clothing (nearly half of exports), though Mauritius remains badly in debt – having been a Third World success story in the 1970s.

The islands also suffer from increasing tensions between the Indian majority – descended from contract workers brought in to tend the plantations after the end of slavery in 1834 – and the Creole (mixed Afro-French) minority ■

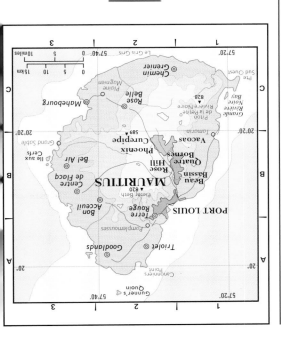

Australia and Oceania

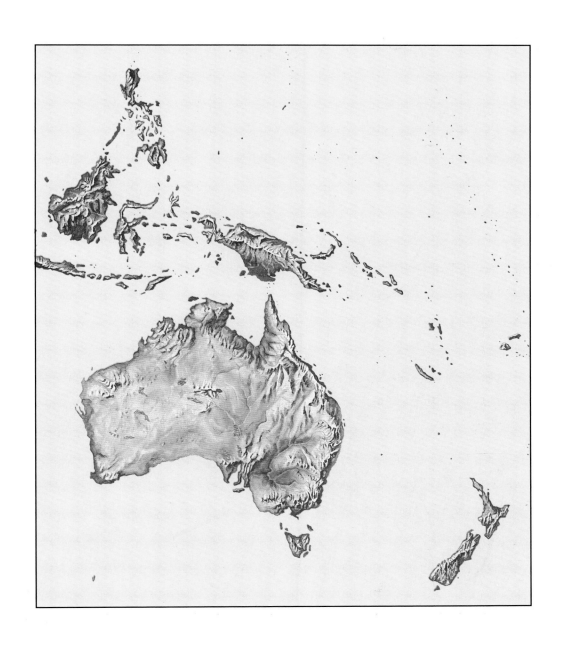

AUSTRALIA AND OCEANIA

A somewhat awkward geographical label, 'Oceania' is a collective term for Australia, New Zealand, most of the Pacific islands and New Guinea. It is characterized by a seemingly bewildering array of islands, of varying origins; some are coral islands, others volcanic, and yet others, such as New Guinea, 'continental' islands. Only about 3,000 of the tens of thousands scattered from Belau to Easter Island and from Midway to Macquarie are large enough even to merit names. Despite the Pacific's vast size, nearly all its islands are tiny and, even with Australia, 'Oceania' is still far smaller than Europe.

The islands of the south and western Pacific divide into three groups, based as much on ethnic differences as on geography. Melanesia ('black islands') comprises New Guinea and the larger groups close to Australia. The name refers to the dark complexion of the fine-featured people with black, frizzy hair who are today the many indigenous coastal dwellers of the South-west Pacific. Polynesia ('many islands') includes numerous islands in the central Pacific. The basically Caucasoid Polynesians, skilled in navigation, are sometimes termed the 'supreme navigators of history'. Micronesia ('small islands') includes the many minute coral atolls north of Melanesia and a narrow Polynesian 'corridor' linking the Society Islands with South-east Asia. Micronesians today are often markedly Polynesian, but in the west are more Malay or Mongoloid ■

The symmetrical cone of dormant Mt Egmont rises to 2,518 m [8,261 ft] on New Zealand's North Island. Maori legend says that 'Taranaki' stands aloof above the other volcanoes in the area following a lover's tiff with Mt Tongariro, far to the east.

RIGHT *Silt discolours a river in the rainforest of New Guinea. The island is the world's third largest after Australia and Greenland, and the border that dissects it is a political division between Asia and Australasia.*

FAR RIGHT *Aerial view of the Olgas, a cluster of 28 domed peaks to the west of Ayers Rock, in the inhospitable heart of Australia. The Aboriginal name for them is 'Katajuta', – 'Many Heads'.*

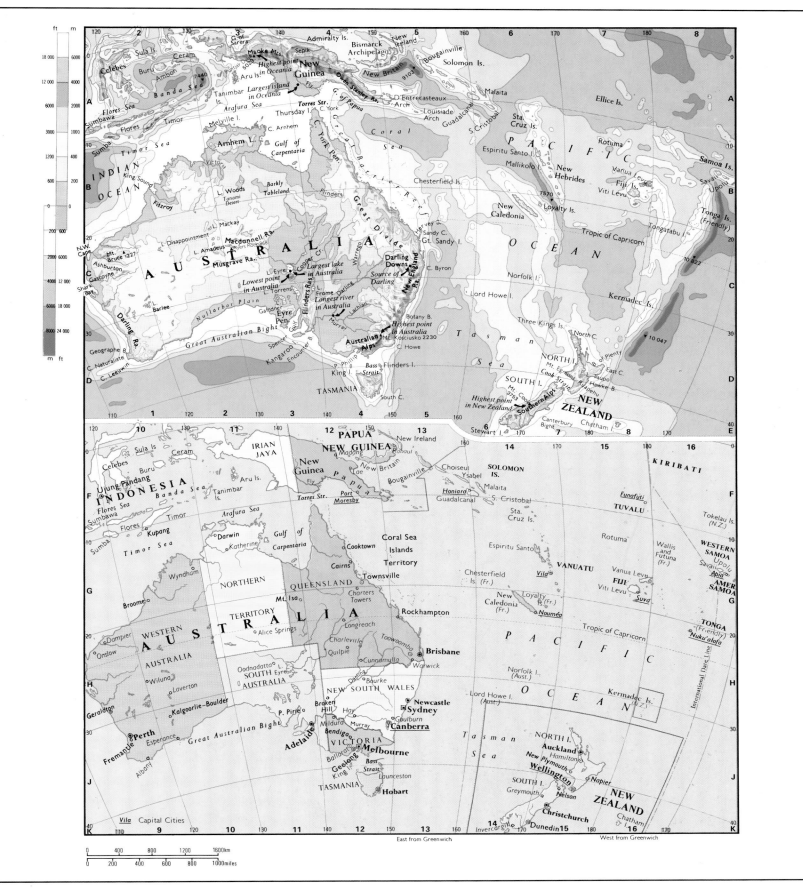

ft m
18 000 6000
12 000 4000
6000 2000
1200 1000
1200 400
600 200
0 0
200 600
2000 6000
4000 12 000
6000 18 000
8000 24 000
m ft

Map labels (upper map — Australia & Oceania physical)

INDIAN OCEAN
Celebes
Sula Is.
Ceram
Buru
Ambon
Banda Sea
Aru Is.
Tanimbar
Arafura Sea
Flores Sea
Sumbawa
Flores
Timor
Sumba
Timor Sea
King Sound
Fitzroy
Ashburton
Mt. Bruce 1227
Gascoyne
Shark Bay
N.W. Cape
Darling Ra.
Geographe B.
C. Naturaliste
C. Leeuwin
Barlee
Nullarbor Plain
Great Australian Bight
Musgrave Ra.
Macdonnell Ra.
L. Amadeus
L. Disappointment
L. Mackay
Tanami Desert
L. Woods
Barkly Tableland
Arnhem L.
Melville I.
C. Arnhem
Gulf of Carpentaria
C. York
C. York Pen.
Thursday I.
Torres Str.
AUSTRALIA
Lowest point in Australia
Largest lake in Australia
L. Eyre
L. Torrens
L. Frome
L. Gairdner
Eyre Pen.
Spencer
Kangaroo I.
Encounter B.
Flinders Ra.
Cooper
Warrego
Source of Darling
Longest river in Australia
Murray
Lachlan
Darling
Darling Downs
New England Ra.
C. Byron
Botany B.
Highest point in Australia Mt. Kosciusko 2230
Australian Alps
C. Howe
TASMANIA
King I.
Flinders I.
Bass Strait
P. Phillip
South C.
Maoke Mts. 5029
Highest point in Oceania
7440
New Guinea
Largest island in Oceania
Sepik
Fly
Gt. of Papua
Owen Stanley Ra.
Great Dividing Ra.
Great Barrier Reef
Coral Sea
Admiralty Is.
Bismarck Archipelago
New Ireland
New Britain
Bougainville
Solomon Is.
9103
D'Entrecasteaux Arch.
Louisiade Arch.
Guadalcanal
S. Cristobal
Malaita
Sta. Cruz Is.
Ellice Is.
Rotuma
Espiritu Santo I.
Mallikolo I.
New Hebrides
7570
Loyalty Is.
New Caledonia
Vanua Levu
Fiji Is.
Viti Levu
Samoa Is.
Savaii
Upolu
Tonga Is. (Friendly)
Tongarabu
10 822
Tropic of Capricorn
Norfolk I.
Lord Howe I.
Kermadec Is.
Three Kings Is.
North C.
10 047
Bay of Plenty
Mt. Egmont
Cook Strait
L. Taupo
Ruapehu
Hawke B.
East C.
NORTH I.
Chesterfield Is.
Hervey B.
Sandy C.
Gt. Sandy I.
Tasman Sea
SOUTH I.
Mt. Cook 3763
Southern Alps
Highest point in New Zealand
Canterbury Bight
Chatham
Stewart I.
NEW ZEALAND
PACIFIC OCEAN

Map labels (lower map — political)

INDONESIA
Ujung Pandang
Celebes
Sula Is.
Ceram
Buru
Banda Sea
Aru Is.
Tanimbar
Flores Sea
Sumbawa
Flores
Timor
Sumba
Timor Sea
Kupang
IRIAN JAYA
PAPUA NEW GUINEA
New Guinea
Magang
New Britain
New Ireland
Rabaul
Lae
Papua
Fly
Torres Str.
Port Moresby
Darwin
Katherine
Gulf of Carpentaria
Wyndham
Broome
Dampier
Onslow
NORTHERN TERRITORY
WESTERN AUSTRALIA
Wiluna
Laverton
Kalgoorlie–Boulder
Geraldton
Perth
Fremantle
Esperance
Albany
Great Australian Bight
Alice Springs
Mt. Isa
QUEENSLAND
Cooktown
Cairns
Townsville
Charters Towers
Longreach
Rockhampton
Charleville
Quilpie
Cunnamulla
Toowoomba
Warwick
Brisbane
Bourke
Broken Hill
NEW SOUTH WALES
Hay
Darling
Murray
Mildura
Goulburn
Newcastle
Sydney
Canberra
Bendigo
Ballarat
Geelong
VICTORIA
Melbourne
King I.
Bass Strait
Launceston
TASMANIA
Hobart
Oodnadatta
L. Eyre
SOUTH AUSTRALIA
P. Pirie
Adelaide
AUSTRALIA
SOLOMON IS.
Choiseul
Ysabel
Malaita
Honiara
Guadalcanal
S. Cristobal
Sta. Cruz Is.
KIRIBATI
Funafuti
TUVALU
Tokelau Is. (N.Z.)
Rotuma
Espiritu Santo
VANUATU
Vila
Chesterfield Is. (Fr.)
Loyalty Is. (Fr.)
New Caledonia (Fr.)
Nouméa
Wallis and Futuna (Fr.)
WESTERN SAMOA
Upolu
Apia
AMER. SAMOA
Vanua Levu
FIJI
Viti Levu
Suva
TONGA (Fr. friendly)
Nuku'alofa
Tropic of Capricorn
Norfolk I. (Aust.)
Lord Howe I. (Aust.)
Kermadec Is. (N.Z.)
International Date Line
PACIFIC OCEAN
Tasman Sea
NORTH I.
Auckland
Hamilton
New Plymouth
Wellington
Napier
Nelson
Greymouth
SOUTH I.
Christchurch
Chatham
Dunedin
Invercargill
NEW ZEALAND

Vila Capital Cities

East from Greenwich   West from Greenwich

0 400 800 1200 1600km
0 200 400 600 800 1000miles

AUSTRALIA

Whether Australia is the world's largest island or its smallest continental land mass – or both, or neither, depending on the school of geography – it is primarily a land of low to medium altitude plateaus that form monotonous landscapes extending for hundreds of kilometres. The edges of the plateaus are more diverse, particularly in the east where deep gorges and waterfalls create rugged relief between the Great Divide and the coast. In the north-west, impressive gorge scenery is found in the Hamersley Range and Kimberley area.

The western half of Australia is formed of ancient rocks. Essentially an arid landscape of worn-down ridges and plateaus, with depressions occupied by sandy deserts and occasional salt lakes, this area has little surface water.

The eastern sixth of the continent, including Tasmania, forms the Eastern Highlands, the zone of greatest relief, greatest rainfall, most abundant vegetation and greatest population. Peaks in this region include Mt Kosciusko, at 2,230 m [7,316 ft] Australia's highest. Much of this area shows signs of volcanic activity in the relatively recent geological past, and these young basalts support nutrient-rich soils in contrast to the generally well-weathered, nutrient-poor soils of nearly all the remainder of Australia.

Between the western plateaus and Eastern Highlands lie the Carpentaria, central and Murray lowlands. The central lowlands drain to the great internal river systems supplying Lake Eyre, or to the Bulloo system, or through great inland deltas to the Darling River. The parallel dune ridges of this area

Surfer's Paradise, on the Queensland coast south of Brisbane. The majority of white Australians work and play on a relatively narrow Pacific coastal strip.

form part of a great continent-wide set of dune ridges extending in a huge anti-clockwise arc, eastwards through the Great Victoria Desert, northwards through the Simpson Desert and westwards in the Great Sandy Desert. All these, though inhospitable, are only moderately arid, allowing sparse cover.

Vegetation

On the humid margins of the continent are luxuriant forests. These include the great jarrah forests of tall eucalyptus hardwoods in the extreme south-west of Western Australia; the temperate rainforests with the Antarctic beech found in Tasmania and on humid upland sites north through New South Wales to the Queensland border; and the tropical and subtropical rainforests found in the wetter areas along the east coast, from the McIllwraith Range in the north to the vicinity of Mallacoota Inlet in the south. Some of these rainforest areas are maintained as managed forests, others are in national parks, but most of the original cover has been cleared for agriculture, particularly for dairying and cattle-fattening, and for sugar and banana cultivation north of Port Macquarie.

The most adaptable tree genus in Australia is the *Eucalyptus*, which ranges from the tall flooded gum trees found on the edges of the rainforest to the dry-living mallee species found on sand-plains and inter-dune areas. Acacia species, especially the bright-yellow flowered wattles, are also adapted to a wide range of environments. Associated with this adaptation of plants is the wide variety of animal adaptations, with 277 different mammals, about 400 species of reptiles and some 700 species of birds. Aborigines arriving from Asia over 40,000 years ago brought the dingo, which rapidly replaced the Tasmanian wolf, the largest marsupial predator, and preyed on smaller animals. Fires, lit for hunting and allowed to burn uncontrolled, altered much of the vegetation, probably allowing eucalyptus forests to expand at the expense of the rainforest. However, the Aborigines understood their environment, carefully protecting vital areas of natural food supply, restricting the use of certain desert waterholes which traditionally taught would be reliable in a drought, and developing a policy which was aimed at living with nature

European settlement after 1788 upset this ecological balance, through widespread clearing of coastal forests, overgrazing of inland pastures and introduction of exotic species, especially the destructive rabbit. But Europeans also brought the technology which enabled the mineral, water and soil resources of Australia to be developed.

Mineral resources

Much of Australia's growth since the beginning of European settlement has been closely related to the exploitation of mineral resources, which has led directly to the founding, growth and often eventual decline of the majority of inland towns. Broken Hill and Mount Isa are copper, lead, zinc and silver producing centres, while Kalgoorlie, Bendigo, Ballarat and Charters Towers all grew in the 19th-century gold rushes. Today, less glamorous minerals support the Australian economy. In Western Australia, the great iron-ore mines of Mount Tom Price, Mount Newman and Mount Goldsworthy are linked by new railways to special ports at Dampier and Port Hedland. Offshore are the oil and gas fields of the north-west shelf.

In the east, the coal mines of central Queensland and eastern New South Wales are linked by rail to bulk loading facilities at Sarina, Gladstone, Brisbane, Newcastle, Sydney and Port Kemble, which enable this high-grade coking coal to be shipped to worldwide markets and by 1986 had made Australia the biggest exporter (15% of export earnings). Bauxite mining has led to new settlements at Nhulunby and Weipa on the Gulf of Carpentaria, with associated refineries at Kwinana, Gladstone and Bell Bay.

Rum Jungle, south of Darwin, became well known as one of the first uranium mines, but now deposits further east in Arnhem Land are being developed. Meanwhile, new discoveries of ore bodies continue to be made in the ancient rocks of the western half of Australia. Natural gas from the Cooper Basin, just south of Innamincka on Cooper Creek, is piped to Adelaide and Sydney, while oil and gas from the Bass Strait and brown coal from the Yallourn-Morwell area have been vital to the industrial growth of Victoria. Fossil fuels are supplemented by hydroelectric power from major schemes in western Tasmania and the Snowy Mountains and smaller projects near Cairns and Tully in north Queensland.

Australia's mineral wealth is phenomenal. In 1989 it produced over a third of the world's diamonds and bauxite, 14% of lead, 11% of iron ore, uranium and zinc, 10% of gold, 9% of manganese, 7% of nickel and silver, and was the biggest exporter of mineral sands. Even this impressive array could not help Australia resist slumps in world demand, however, and in the early 1990s the country was experiencing its worst recession since the 1920s.

Agriculture

Apart from the empty desert areas in Western Australia and the Simpson Desert, extensive cattle or sheep production dominates all of Australia north and west of a line from Penong in South Australia, through Broken Hill in New South Wales to Bundaberg in Queensland, and east of a line from Geraldton to Esperance in Western Australia. Cattle and sheep populations in this zone are sparse while pastoral holdings are large, some over 400,000 hectares [1 million acres], and towns are far apart.

Some Aborigines retain limited tracts of land in Arnhem Land and on the fringes of the deserts where they live by hunting and gathering, but most now live close to government settlements or mission stations. Many are employed as stockmen and seasonal agricultural workers, while thousands of others have migrated to country towns and the major cities.

The intensive pastoral and agricultural zones support the bulk of the sheep and cattle of Australia, and wool, mutton and beef production is still the basic industry. The country is the world's largest producer of wool and third in lamb and mutton. Wheat is cultivated in combination with sheep raising over large tracts of the gentle inland slopes of the coastal ranges.

Along the east coast are important dairy, cattle-fattening and sugar-cane industries, the latter significant on the east coast from Brisbane to Cairns. Irrigated areas also support cotton, rice, fruit and vegetable crops, largely for consumption within Australia. Wine production around Perth, Adelaide, central Victoria and eastern New South Wales has expanded in recent decades, producing vintages of international renown.

Development

European settlement in Australia began in 1788 as a penal colony in New South Wales, spreading quickly to Queensland and Tasmania. During the 19th century the continent became divided into the states of New South Wales, Queensland (1859), South Australia (1836), Tasmania (1825), Victoria (1851) and Western Australia (1829), with the area now forming the Northern Territory being under the control of South Australia. During this colonial period the state seaport capitals of Sydney, Brisbane, Adelaide, Hobart, Melbourne and Perth became established as the dominant manufacturing, commercial, administrative and legislative centres of their respective states – a position they still retain.

In 1901 the states came together to create the Commonwealth of Australia with a federal constitution. Trade between the states became free, and external affairs, defence and immigration policy became federal responsibilities, though health, education, transport, agricultural and industrial development remained firmly in the hands of each state. Only gradually did powers of taxation give the federal government the opportunity to develop national policies.

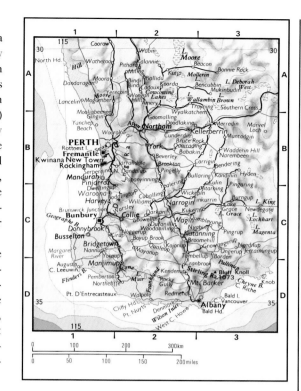

SOUTH-EASTERN AUSTRALIA

The federal capital established at Canberra, in the new Australian Capital Territory, grew from a tiny settlement in 1911 to become a great seat of administration and learning, and the largest inland regional commercial centre. The federal government's territorial responsibilities also include the Northern Territory, self-governing since 1978.

Immigration has changed the ethnic character of Australia since about 1960. Australian society now has Greek, Italian, Yugoslav, Turkish, Lebanese and South-east Asian communities alongside the longer-established Aboriginal, British, Irish, Chinese, Dutch and German communities, though the culture remains strongly British in flavour. Almost 60% of the total Australian population live in Sydney, Melbourne, Adelaide, Brisbane, Perth and Hobart. Migration within the states from inland rural areas to capital cities or coastal towns leaves many rural communities with an ageing population, while the new mining centres have young populations. The most rapid growth outside new mining centres is occurring in coastal towns.

Soon after 1788, small-scale manufacturing began to supply domestic goods and machinery to the colonial community. Manufacturing grew in the seaport capitals, especially Sydney and Melbourne, which now have over 60% of all manufacturing industry.

Under the Australian Constitution, the federal government has control over interstate and overseas transport, with the state governments responsible for regulation within their own borders. Seven railway systems thus exist, each state system focusing on its capital city, with the Commonwealth Railways responsible for the Trans-Australian, Central Australian and Northern Territory routes. The notorious differences in gauges between the states have been partially overcome by the construction of the standard-gauge links from Brisbane to Sydney, Sydney to Melbourne, and Sydney to Perth via Broken Hill. The completion of the Tarcoola-Alice Springs route provides the basic strategic standard-gauge rail network for Australia.

Railways are vital for bulk freight, especially mineral ores, coal and wheat. Among the busiest of the railways are the iron-ore lines in the north-west of Western Australia. Most cattle and sheep, however, are carried by 'road trains' – a powerful unit pulling several trailers.

A rapidly improving highway system links all major cities and towns, providing easy mobility for a largely car-owning population. Some journeys are still difficult, especially when floods wash away sections of road or sand-drifts bury highways. Although 90% of all passenger transport is by road, air services cope with much interstate travel.

Australia is also well served by local broadcasting and television. The radio remains a lifeline for remote settlements dependent on the flying doctor or aerial ambulance, and for many others when floods or bush fires threaten isolated communities ■

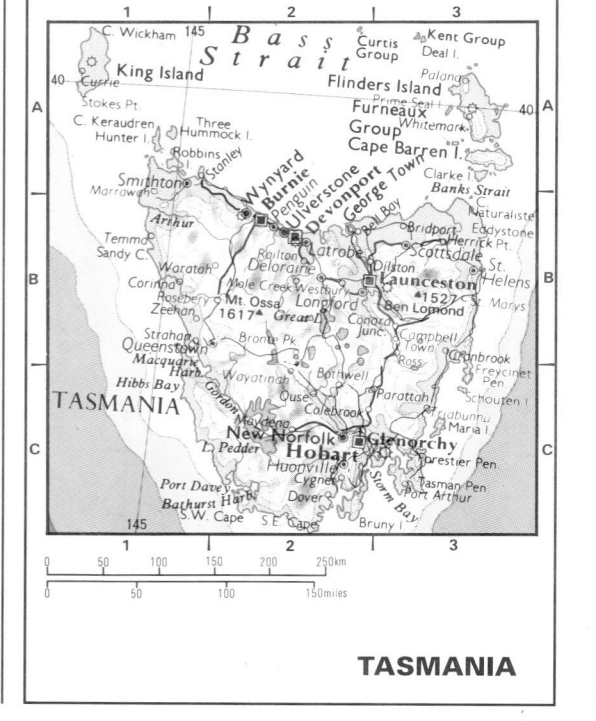

TASMANIA

PAPUA NEW GUINEA

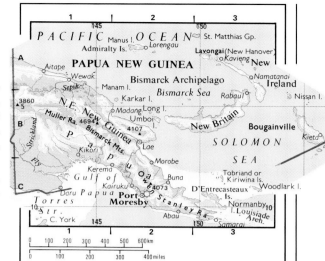

Forming part of Melanesia, Papua New Guinea is the eastern section of the island of New Guinea, plus the Bismarck Archipelago and the copper-rich island of Bougainville – geographically, though not politically, part of the Solomons. The backbone of the main island is a high cordillera of rugged fold mountains, averaging between 2,500 to 4,600 m [8,000 to 15,000 ft] in height and covered with tropical montane 'cloud' forest.

The traditional garden crops of the 'highlanders' include kaukau (sweet potato), sugar cane, bananas, maize, cassava and nut-bearing pandans. Pigs are kept mainly for status and ritual purposes. In the lowlands, taro is the staple food and the main cash crops are coconuts, coffee, cocoa and rubber.

Although the first European contact came as early

While Stone Age peoples still inhabit the highlands of 'PNG', sing-songs at Port Moresby are for tourists.

as 1526, it was only in the late 19th century that permanent German and British settlements were established. After World War II, the UN Trust Territory of New Guinea and the Territory of Papua were administered by Australia. Self-government came in 1973, with full independence in 1975 ■

SOLOMON ISLANDS

The double chain of islands forming the Solomons and Vanuatu extends for some 2,250 km [1,400 mls] and represents the drowned outermost crustal fold on the borders of the ancient Australian continent. New Caledonia lies on an inner fold, nearer the mainland. The main islands, all of volcanic origin, are Guadalcanal, Malaita, New Georgia, San Cristóbal, Santa Isabel and Choiseul.

The northern Solomons have a true hot and wet tropical oceanic climate, but further south there tends to be an increasingly long cool season. The coastal plains are used for the subsistence farming that

sustains about 90% of the population. While coconuts (giving copra and palm oil) and cocoa are important exports, tuna fish is the biggest earner and lumbering the main industry, with Japan the main market for both. Significant phosphate deposits are also mined on Bellona Island. Plagued by a population growth of 3.5% – half the total is under 20 – the Solomons' progress is faltering, with development hampered by the mountainous and densely forested environment of the six main islands; transport is often impossible between scattered settlements. The economy was also hit by a devastating cyclone in 1986.

Occupied by the Japanese during World War II, the islands were the scene of fierce fighting, notably the battle for Guadalcanal, on which the capital Honiara lies. Known as the British Solomons, the islands won full independence in 1978. Though a stable parliamentary monarchy, political activity is

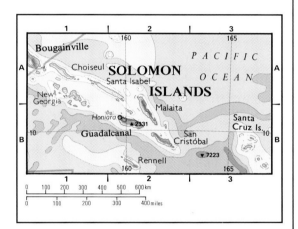

turbulent, and it is likely that a federal republican structure will be introduced to the country during the 1990s ■

NEW CALEDONIA

Most southerly of the Melanesian countries, New Caledonia comprises the main island of Grande Terre and the dependencies of the Loyalty Islands (Iles Loyauté), Ile des Pins and the Bélep archipelago. The other islands (many of them atolls) are small and uninhabited.

New Caledonia's economy is dominated by a single commodity, nickel, which accounts for over 83% of export earnings. The world's largest producer in the 1960s, it has now slipped to third place.

A French possession since 1853 and Overseas Territory from 1958, New Caledonia today has a fundamental split on independence from Paris. The Kanaks, the indigenous Melanesians, support it; the less numerous French settlers are against it ■

Colourful public gardens in Noumea, capital of the French Overseas Territory of 'Nouvelle Calédonie'.

FIJI

By far the most populous of the Pacific nations, Fiji comprises more than 800 Melanesian islands, the larger ones volcanic, mountainous and surrounded by coral reefs, the rest being low coral atolls. Easily the biggest are Viti Levu (10,430 sq km [4,027 sq mls]), with the capital of Suva on its south coast, and Vanua Levu, just over half the size of the main island, though a very different shape. The islands' economy is basically agricultural, with sugar cane (45% of exports), copra and ginger the main cash crops, and fish and timber also exported. However, 20% of revenues are generated by gold.

Fiji suffers today from its colonial past. The Indian workers brought in by the British for the sugar plantations in the late 19th century now outnumber the native Fijians, but have been until recently second-class citizens in terms of electoral representation. The constitution adopted on independence in 1970 was intended to ease racial tension, but two military coups in 1987 overthrew the recently elected (and first) Indian-majority government, suspended the constitution and set up a Fijian-dominated republic outside the British Commonwealth.

The country returned to full civilian rule in 1990, but with a new constitution guaranteeing Melanesian political supremacy, many Indians had emigrated before the elections of 1992, taking valuable skills with them. The turmoil of the late 1980s also had a disastrous effect on the growing tourist industry ∎

NEW ZEALAND

Geologically part of the Circum-Pacific Mobile Belt of tectonic activity, New Zealand is mountainous and partly volcanic. Many of the highest mountains – the Southern Alps and Kaikoura Range of the South Island, for example – were thrust up from the seabed in the past 10 to 15 million years, representing only the latest in a long series of orogenies. Much of the North Island was formed by volcanic action even more recently, mainly in the past 1 to 4 million years. Minor earthquakes are common, and there are several areas of volcanic and geothermal activity, especially in the North Island.

Its youth makes New Zealand a rugged country with mountains always in sight and about 75% of the total land area above the 200 m [650 ft] contour. The North Island has many spectacular but low ranges with peaks of 1,200 to 1,500 m [4,000 to 5,000 ft], made up of folded sedimentary rocks that form good soils. Folding and faulting give the eastern half of the island a strong north-east to south-west 'grain', especially in the south-east where the rivers have cut broad, fertile valleys between the ranges. The Coromandel Range and hilly Northland peninsula are softer and more worn, with few peaks over 800 m [12,600 ft].

Overlying these older rocks in the centre and north are massive spreads of lava, pumice and volcanic tuffs, formed during the past 1 to 3 million years. The great central plateau is dominated by three slumbering volcanoes – Ruapehu (2,797 m [9,176 ft], the North Island's highest peak), Ngauruhoe and Tongariro. Further north extensive fields of lava and ash cones lies across the base of the Northland peninsula, forming a firm, rolling site for the suburbs of Auckland, New Zealand's largest city.

The far larger South Island is also mainly mountainous, with an alpine backbone extending obliquely from north-east to south-west. The highest peaks form a central massif, the Southern Alps, clustered around Mt Cook, at 3,764 m [12,349 ft] New Zealand's highest mountain. From this massif, which is permanently ice-capped, glaciers descend on either flank, and on the east the outwash fans of glacier-fed rivers form the Canterbury Plains – South Island's only extensive lowland. The north end of the island has many high, rolling ranges rising to the steeply-folded and faulted Kaikoura Ranges of the north-east. In the far south-west (Fiordland), the coast is indented by deep, steeply-walled sounds that wind far into the forested mountains.

New Zealand was discovered by Abel Tasman in 1642 and charted thoroughly by James Cook in 1769-70. Both explorers recorded the presence of Maoris–Polynesians who hunted and farmed from well-defended coastal settlements, who were themselves relatively recent arrivals on the islands. Sealing gangs and whalers were New Zealand's first European inhabitants, closely followed by missionaries and farmers from Britain and Australia. By the early 1830s about 2,000 Europeans had settled there.

In 1840 Britain took possession, in a treaty which gave rights and privileges of British subjects to the Maori people. The following decades saw the arrival of thousands of new settlers from Britain, and by mid-century there were over 30,000. Though their relationships with the Maoris (who at this stage outnumbered them two to one) were generally good, difficulties over land ownership led to warfare in the 1860s. Thereafter, the Maori population declined while European numbers continued to increase. British settlers found a climate slightly warmer than their own, with longer growing seasons but variable rainfall, sometimes with crippling drought in the dry areas. From 1844, when the first Merinos were introduced from Australia, New Zealand became predominantly a land of sheep, the grassy lowlands (especially in the South Island) providing year-round forage. Huge flocks were built up, mainly for wool and tallow production. From the lowlands they expanded into the hills – the 'high country' which was cleared of native bush and sown with European grasses for pasture. More than half the country is still covered with evergreen forest. The North Island proved more difficult to turn into productive farmland, only later proving its value for dairying.

New Zealand's early prosperity was finally established when the export of frozen mutton and lamb carcasses began in 1882. Soon a steady stream of chilled meat and dairy products – and later of fruit – was crossing the oceans to established markets in Britain, and the country is still the world's second biggest producer of lamb. Wheat and other cereals

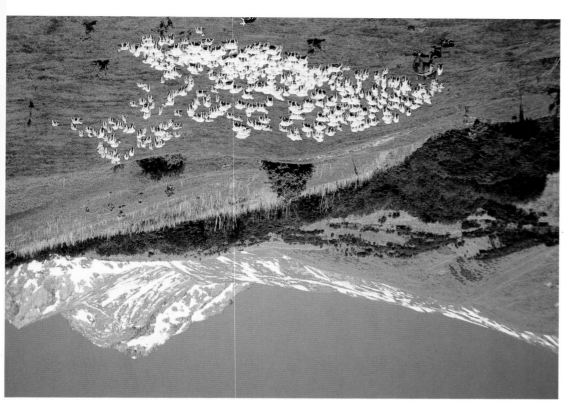

A mounted farmer polices his flock on South Island. Sheep outnumber people 20 to 1 in New Zealand, and wool and lamb remain the leading exports.

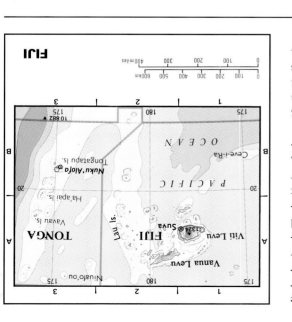

were also grown. High productivity was maintained by applications of fertilizers, mainly based on rock-phosphate mined on Nauru.

New Zealand is a prosperous country, with a high standard of living for a refreshingly harmonious multiracial population. Since 1907 a self-governing Dominion, it long relied on British markets for the export of agricultural produce, and has generally strong ties and affinities with Britain. Though agricultural products are still the main exports, the economy has diversified considerably since World War II, including fish, timber and wood pulp. Iron ores, coal and small amounts of gold are among the few valuable minerals, recently boosted by natural gas and

A geothermal electricity station at Taupo, North Island. Though lacking coal, New Zealand has several energy sources including oil, gas and hydroelectric power.

petroleum. Geothermal and hydroelectric power are well developed, and timber and forest products are finding valuable overseas markets. Despite the country's isolation, a promising tourist industry is also developing, based on the scenic beauty, abundance of game animals, and relatively unhurried way of life.

However, problems began to arise from the 1970s, beginning when the UK joined the EEC and New Zealand's exports to Britain shrank from 70% to 10%. Along with a re-evaluation of its defence position, the country has had to rethink its previous 'safe' economic strategy – cutting subsidies to farmers, privatization, seeking new markets in Asia – and, like most fellow members of the OECD, find a way to survive the recession of the 1980s and early 1990s. The new order was confirmed in March 1994 when Prime Minister Jim Bolgar called for his country to follow Australia and become a republic by 2000 ■

NEW ZEALAND TERRITORIES
New Zealand comprises not just the two main islands, Stewart Island, Chatham Island and a number of uninhabited outlying islands, but also territories further out in the Pacific, including the Kermadec Islands (with a meteorological station) and Tokelau (population 2,000); formerly part of the Gilbert and Ellice Islands (now called Kiribati) and transferred from Britain to New Zealand in 1926, the group became part of the country in 1949.

The Cook Islands (population 18,000) became an internally self-governing state in 'free association' with New Zealand in 1965; Niue (population 2,000) has had the same status since 1974. These islanders have full citizenship, while Wellington controls foreign affairs. The main exports are citrus fruits and juices, copra (coconut), bananas and honey.

THE MAORIS
'Strong, raw-boned, well-made, active people, rather above than under the common size ... of a very dark brown colour, with black hair, thin black beards, and ... in general very good features.' So Captain James Cook described the Maoris he met in New Zealand in 1770. Of Polynesian stock, the Maoris settled (mainly in North Island) from about AD 800 to 1350. Living in small fortified settlements, they cultivated sweet potatoes and other crops, hunted seals and moas (extinct flightless birds) and gathered seafoods.

The Maoris befriended the early European settlers; readily accepting British sovereignty, Christianity and pacification, they rebelled only as more and more of their communal land was bought for the settlers' use. Given parliamentary representation from 1876, they eventually integrated fully. Now Maoris form about 9% of New Zealand's population, living mostly in North Island. Though socially and politically equal to whites, they are still over-represented in the poorer, unskilled sections of the population, separated more by lack of opportunity than by colour from the mainstream of national life.

NEW ZEALAND

FEDERATED STATES OF MICRONESIA

The Federated States of Micronesia became a sovereign state in 1986, when after 17 years of negotiation entered into 'free association' with the USA, which had run them as a US Trust Territory since 1947 and will continue to control defence and security until 2001. They were formally admitted as an independent member of the UN in September 1991.

Comprising the bulk of the Carolines, the Federation – despite a land area of just 705 sq km [272 sq mls] – stretches across more than 3,200 km [2,000 mls] of Pacific, with the Equator as the southern boundary; the 607 islands divide into four groups and range from mountains to low atolls. Over half the area is contributed by the main island, Pohnpei, on which the former capital of Kolonia stands; Pohnpei also accounts for 52,000 out of a total population of 107,000 (Kolonia 7,000).

The cultures of the 'FSM', both Micronesian and Polynesian, are diverse, and four main languages are spoken in line with the four states of Yap, Truk, Pohnpei and Kosrae – though English is official. While some areas are highly Americanized, the traditional way of life has survived in others, based on subsistence farming and fishing. Copra is the main crop and phosphate is also exported, while the rich tuna-fishing grounds in territorial waters bring in revenue from American, Japanese and Korean fleets. Tourism is growing rapidly, but the FSM remains heavily dependent on US aid ■

MARSHALL ISLANDS

The Marshall Islands became a republic 'in free association' with the USA in 1986, moving from Trust Territory status to a sovereign state responsible for its own foreign policy but not (until 2001) for its defence and security. Self-governing since 1979, the country comprises over 1,250 islands and atolls – including the former US nuclear testing sites of Bikini and Enewetak – totalling just 181 sq km [70 sq mls]. The population, mainly Micronesian, Protestant and English-speaking, is 48,000 ■

NORTHERN MARIANAS

The Northern Marianas comprise all 17 Mariana Islands except Guam, the most southerly, forming a mountainous and volcanic chain extending northwards with a total land area of 477 sq km [184 sq mls]. Part of the US Trust Territory of the Pacific from 1947, its people voted in a 1975 UN plebiscite for Commonwealth status in union with the USA. The US approved the change in 1976, granting US citizenship, and internal self-government followed in 1978. The population of 22,000 is concentrated on three of the six inhabited islands, with Saipan and the capital of Susupe accounting for 19,000 ■

Almost half the population of 145,000 are Chamorro – of mixed Indonesian, Spanish and Filipino descent – and another quarter Filipino, but 20% of the total is composed of US military personnel and their families. In 1979 a referendum overwhelmingly backed a return of much of the military land to civilian use, and a 1982 vote showed clear support for the Commonwealth status enjoyed by the Northern Marianas ■

NAURU

A low-lying coral atoll of just 21 sq km [8 sq mls] located halfway between Australia and Hawaii, 40 km [25 mls] south of the Equator, Nauru is the world's smallest republic. The climate is hot and wet, though the rains can fail. Discovered by Britain in 1798, the island was under the control of Germany (1888), Australia (1914), Japan (1942) and Australia again (with a UN Trusteeship from 1946) before it gained independence in 1968.

A plateau rising to over 60 m [200 ft], surrounded by a belt of fertile, cultivated land, has provided the island with deposits of high-grade phosphate rock, exported to the Pacific Rim countries for fertilizer. The industry, nationalized in 1970, accounts for over 98% of exports, and though Nauru is only the 12th largest world producer this is enough to furnish the population with an average national income of US$20,000 – a similar figure to Canada or Denmark – giving them exemption from taxes and free education and welfare. The 7,000 native people – of mixed Micronesian and Polynesian origin, speaking a hybrid Nauruan language and predominantly Christian (mainly Protestant) – are supplemented by more than 3,000 migrant workers.

Nauru's economic future is uncertain, since the phosphates may be exhausted by the end of the century. Revenues from shipping and air services, as well as developing as a tax haven, are planned ■

KIRIBATI

Known as the Gilbert Islands until independence in 1979, the republic of Kiribati comprises three groups of coral atolls – 16 Gilbert Islands, eight Phoenix Islands and 11 of the Line Islands – plus the higher and volcanic Banaba. Though amounting to only 728 sq km [281 sq mls], they are scattered over 5 million sq km [2 million sq mls] of the Pacific, straddling both the Equator and the International Date Line. Together with the Ellice Islands (which broke away as Tuvalu in 1975), the Gilberts were a British protectorate from 1892 and a colony from 1916; they were occupied by the Japanese in World War II, and recaptured after the battle for Tarawa in 1943. Today the capital has 24,000 residents, out of a total population of 71,000. The people of the islands are almost exclusively Christian, with a slight Roman Catholic majority.

Little of the coral islands rises above 4 m [13 ft], though coconuts, bananas, papayas, and breadfruits are harvested, with taro (babai) laboriously cultivated in deep pits to provide the staple vegetable. Following the exhaustion of Banaba's phosphate deposits in 1980, the main exports are copra (65%), and fish and fish preparations (24%), but Kiribati remains heavily dependent on foreign aid. The future, both medium-term economic and long-term environmental (due to possible rising sea levels from global warming) is bleak, compounded by an overcrowding problem that has forced the resettlement of some 4,700 people in the early 1990s ■

BELAU

The last remaining member of the four states that comprised the US Trust Territory of the Pacific, established under UN mandate in 1947 – thanks to sustained American skulduggery – Belau (Palau) voted to break away from the Federated States of Micronesia in 1978, and a new self-governing constitution became effective in 1981. The territory then entered into 'free association' with the USA, providing sovereign-state status, but in 1983 a referendum rejected the proposal, since Washington refused to secede to a 92% vote in a 1979 referendum that declared the nation a nuclear-free zone. In a July 1993 vote 65% of the 11,000 voters agreed to end 'ward status', and the territory would no longer be the world's last under UN Trusteeship.

The republic comprises an archipelago of six Caroline groups, totalling 26 islands and over 300 islets varying in terrain from mountain to reef and measuring 458 sq km [177 sq mls]. Agriculture is still largely at subsistence level, with copra the main export crop, but luxury tourism is growing, based strongly on scuba-diving and sea fishing. The country relies heavily on US aid and the US government is the largest employer. Eight of the islands are permanently inhabited ■

GUAM

Largest of the Marianas, measuring 541 sq km [209 sq mls], Guam is composed mainly of a coralline limestone plateau, with mountains in the south, hills in the centre and narrow coastal lowlands in the north. Populated for over 3,000 years, charted by Magellan in 1521, colonized by Spain from 1668 but ceded to the US after the 1896-8 war and occupied by the Japanese 1941-4, it is today – as a 'self-governing unincorporated territory' – of huge strategic importance to Washington, and a third of its usable land is occupied by American naval and air force establishments and installations.

TUVALU

Tuvalu became an independent constitutional monarchy within the Commonwealth in 1978, three years after separation from the Gilbert Islands – a decision supported by a large majority in a referendum held in 1974. None of its nine coral atolls – total area 24 sq km [9 sq mls] – rises more than 4.6 m [15 ft] out of the Pacific, and though the climate is uniformly pleasant, poor soils restrict vegetation.

The population of 10,000 (a third of which lives on the main island of Funafuti) survive by subsistence farming, raising pigs and poultry, and by fishing. Copra is the only significant export crop, but most foreign exchange comes from the sale of elaborate postage stamps to the world's philatelists.

The population, once far higher, was reduced from about 20,000 to just 3,000 in the three decades after 1850 by Europeans abducting the inhabitants to work in the plantations of other Pacific island territories.

Today storms effectively submerge the islands at least twice a year, and despite the EEC-built barrier round the capital, Funafuti, global warming seems set to claim Tuvalu in the future ∎

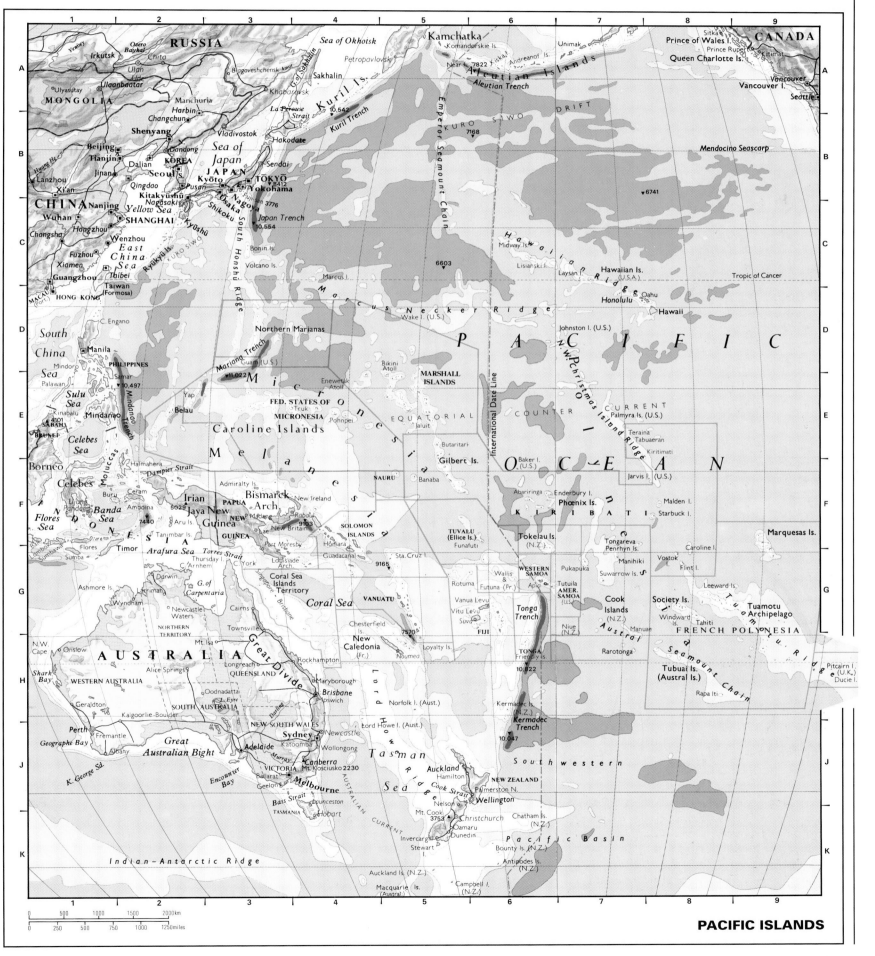

FRENCH POLYNESIA

French Polynesia consists of 130 islands, totalling only 4,000 sq km [1,544 sq mls] but scattered over 4 million sq km [1.5 million sq mls] of ocean halfway between Australia and South America in five groups. The Society Islands comprise the Leewards, of which the best known is Bora-Bora, and the Windwards, which include Moorea and Tahiti – the largest island and home to the capital of Papeete. Along with the Marquesas, most of the Tubuais and the smaller Gambier islands, these are of volcanic origin with steep-sided mountains; the Tuamotus are low-lying coralline atolls.

The tribal chiefs of Tahiti eventually agreed to a French protectorate in 1843, and by the end of the century France controlled all the present islands. They formed an Overseas Territory from 1958, sending two deputies and a senator to Paris, and in 1984 gained increased autonomy with a territorial assembly. There are sporadic calls for independence, but the high standard of living (the annual per capita income is US$8,000) derives from the links with France, including a substantial military presence ■

Palms ark skyward on the shores of Bora Bora, in French Polynesia. The territory shares the Pacific franc with New Caledonia and the Wallis and Futuna Islands.

WESTERN SAMOA

Western Samoa comprises two large islands, seven small islands (two of which are inhabited) and a number of islets, forming a land area of 2,840 sq km [1,097 sq mls]. The main islands of Upolu and Savai'i both have a central mountainous region, heavily forested and divided by fast-flowing rivers, surrounded by narrow coastal lowlands and coral reefs. Upolu contains two-thirds of the population of 161,000, including 33,000 in the capital of Apia.

The cradle of Polynesian civilization, Western Samoa first gained independence in 1889, but ten years later became a German protectorate. Administered by New Zealand from 1920 – first under a League of Nations mandate and later a UN Trusteeship – the island achieved independence as a parliamentary monarchy in 1962, following a plebiscite. Under a friendship treaty New Zealand handles relations outside the Pacific islands zone.

The population remains mainly Polynesian, with a Maori majority, and almost exclusively Christian (70% Protestant). The traditional lifestyle still thrives, with over 60% of the workforce engaged in agriculture, chiefly tropical fruits and vegetables, and in fishing. Many of the 50,000 tourists a year visit the home of Robert Louis Stevenson – now the official residence of King Malietoa Tanumafili II ■

VANUATU

An archipelago of 13 large islands and 70 islets, the majority of them mountainous and volcanic in origin, with coral beaches, reefs, forest cover and very limited coastal cultivation, Vanuatu totals 12,190 sq km [4,707 sq mls] in land area. Nearly two-thirds of the population of 154,000 lives on four islands, 18,000 of them in the capital of Port Vila, on Efate.

Formerly the New Hebrides and governed jointly by France and Britain from 1906, the islands became independent as a parliamentary republic in 1980. The francophone island of Espiritu Santó attempted separation from the English government, and politics have remained unstable. The Melanesian, Bislama-speaking people live largely by subsistence farming and fishing, with copra, beef and veal the main exports ■

WALLIS AND FUTUNA ISLANDS

The smallest, least populous and poorest of France's three Pacific Overseas Territories, the Wallis and Futuna Islands comprise three main islands and numerous islets, totalling 200 sq km [77 sq mls]. Futuna and uninhabited Alofi, main constituents of the Hoorn group, are mountainous; the much larger Uvea, the chief island of the Wallis group, is hilly with coral reefs. Uvea contains 60% of the 18,000 population, 800 of them in the capital of Mata-Utu. French aid remains crucial to a subsistence economy ■

TONGA

Tonga is an absolute monarchy. Since 1965 the ruler has been Taufa'ahau Tupou IV, latest in a line going back a thousand years, who presided over the islands' transition from British protectorate to independent Commonwealth state in 1970. His brother is prime minister on a council that has hereditary chiefs as well as elected representatives; there are no parties. The country has remained peaceful, enhancing the name given by Captain James Cook in the 1770s – the Friendly Islands.

The archipelago comprises over 170 islands, 36 of which are inhabited, covering 750 sq km [290 sq mls] in a mixture of low coralline and higher volcanic outcrops that fall into three distinct belts. Nearly two-thirds of the Polynesian population – over 100,000 and growing fast – live on the largest island of Tongatapu, 29,000 of them in the capital of Nuku'alofa, site of the royal palace. Vava'u (15,000) in the north is the second most populous. Predominantly Christian, the people speak Tongan, though English is also official.

Most Tongans live off their own produce, including yams, tapioca and fish. While the government owns all land, men are entitled to rent areas to grow food – a policy now under pressure with a burgeoning young population. The main exports are coconut oil products and bananas, with New Zealand the main trading partner. Tourism is starting, with 45,000 visitors to the islands in 1988.

This has not been enough to settle discontent over the king's authority. Economic stagnation, evidence of corruption and foreign influence have created pressure for much-needed power sharing in the 1990s ■

AMERICAN SAMOA

A self-governing 'unincorporated territory of the US', American Samoa is a group of five volcanic islands and two atolls covering a land area of 200 sq km [77 sq mls] in the South Pacific, with Tutuila the largest. Swain Island to the north also comes under its administration, taking the total population to 43,000.

The Samoan Islands were divided in 1899, with British consent, between Germany and the US along a line 171° west of Greenwich. American influence in the territory is still vital, giving substantial grants and taking 90% of exports, almost exclusively canned tuna. Most of the land is bush or jungle.

While Pago Pago is the capital, the seat of government is to the east at Fagatogo. There is little prospect of Samoan reunification: the American islands enjoy a standard of living some ten times as high as their neighbours in Western Samoa ■

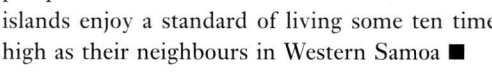

PITCAIRN ISLANDS

A British dependent territory of four islands (48 sq km [19 sq mls]), Pitcairn is situated halfway between New Zealand and Panama. Uninhabited until 1790, it was occupied by nine mutineers from HMS *Bounty* and some men and women from Tahiti. In 1856 some 194 of its people moved at their own request to Norfolk Island, though 43 of them returned between 1859 and 1864. The present population is 60, all living in Adamstown on Pitcairn ■

North and
Central America

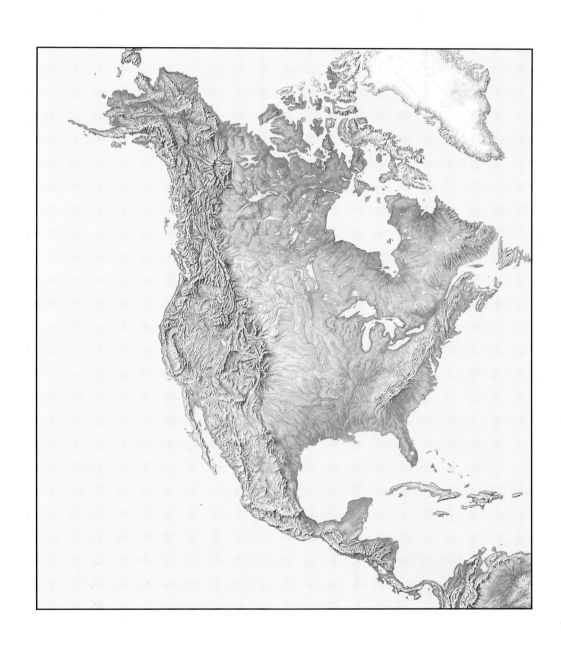

NORTH AND CENTRAL AMERICA

Third largest of the world's continents, North America spans 116° of longitude from Newfoundland to the Bering Strait – almost a third of the northern hemisphere; in latitude it extends from the tropical Gulf of Mexico in the south to the Arctic.

With a reputation for containing the biggest and the best of everything, North America tends towards superlatives and extremes. Its highest peak falls short of the highest in Asia and South America, but it includes the world's largest freshwater lake (Lake Superior) and the greatest canyon (Grand Canyon,

Arizona). Climatic extremes are common, though some of its world records reflect little more than good coverage by an unusually complete network of well-equipped weather stations.

Topography and climate combine to provide an immense range of natural habitats across North America, from mangrove swamps and tropical forests in the south, through hot deserts, prairie, temperate and boreal forests, taiga and tundra to polar deserts in the far north. North America can claim the largest and oldest known living organisms (giant redwood cedars and bristlecone pines), both found in the western USA.

Standing at the edge of the world's six great structural plates, North America has been subject to pres-

sure and uplift from its neighbouring Pacific plate, with results which show clearly on a physical map. Roughly a third of the continent, including the whole of the western flank, has been thrown into a spectacular complex of young mountains, valleys and plateaus – the Western Cordilleras. To the east lie the much older mountains, long-weathered and lower – the Appalachians in the south and the Laurentian Highlands in the north; these are separated from the

RIGHT *Tranquility among the Canadian Rockies: the scene near Kicking Horse Pass in Banff National Park, south-western Alberta – the country's oldest national park (1885) and probably the most spectacular.*

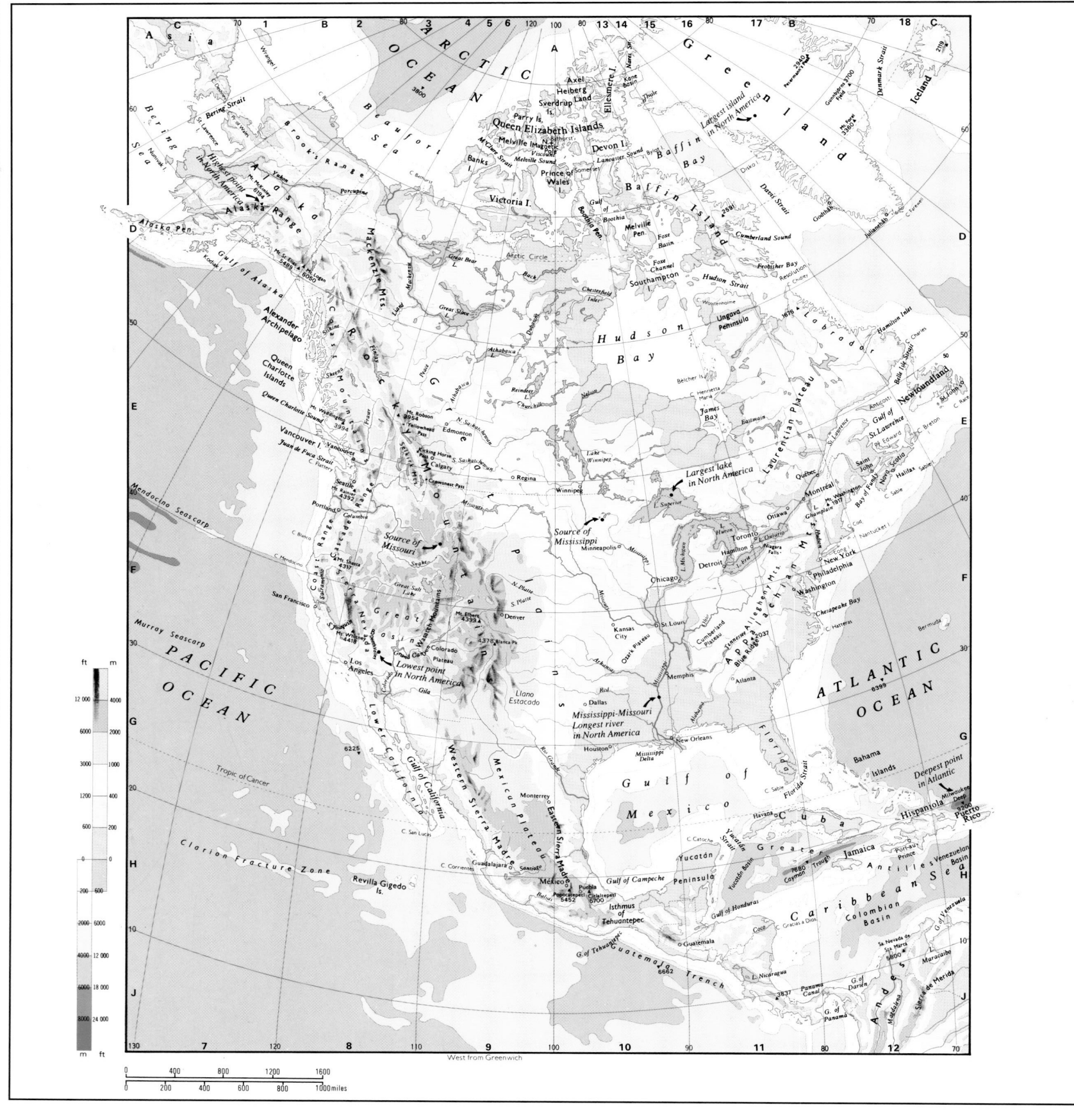

western ranges by broad interior lowlands drained by the Mississippi–Missouri system.

The bleak northern plains, centred about Hudson Bay, rest on a shield or platform of ancient rocks that underlies most of central and eastern Canada. This Laurentian Shield, though warped and split by crustal movements, was massive enough to resist folding through successive periods of mountain building that raised the Western Cordilleras. Planed by more than a million years of glaciation throughout the Ice Age, it is now free of permanent ice except on a few of the northern islands. Its surface remains littered with glacial debris that forms thin, waterlogged tundra or forest soils, and the once glaciated region is fringed by

a crescent of interlinked lakes and waterways, including the Great Bear Lake and the five Great Lakes.

From Stone Age times to the end of the 15th century, North America was thinly peopled with hunting or farming communities making little impact on the environment. It now supports a population of 360 million, with resources utilized on a grand scale.

Central America is the narrow waistline of the Americas, and the continent's southern limit is the narrow isthmus of Panama which has been cut by the canal connecting the two world oceans. The backbone of this southern finger of the continent is mountainous, many of the volcanic vertebrae reaching heights of over 4,000 m [13,000 ft]. It is the most tectonically

active zone in the Americas with over 100 large volcanoes and frequent earthquakes ■

RIGHT *Joshua trees (a species of yucca), cacti and granite outcrops are the main features of the Joshua Tree National Monument, 160 km [100 mls] east of Los Angeles. The US was a pioneer of conservation, its vast network of national parks beginning with Yellowstone in Wyoming in 1872.*

BELOW RIGHT *An idyllic beach on Trinidad, the far southeast corner of Central America. Though part of the Caribbean, the island is only 12 km [7.5 mls] from the coast of Venezuela.*

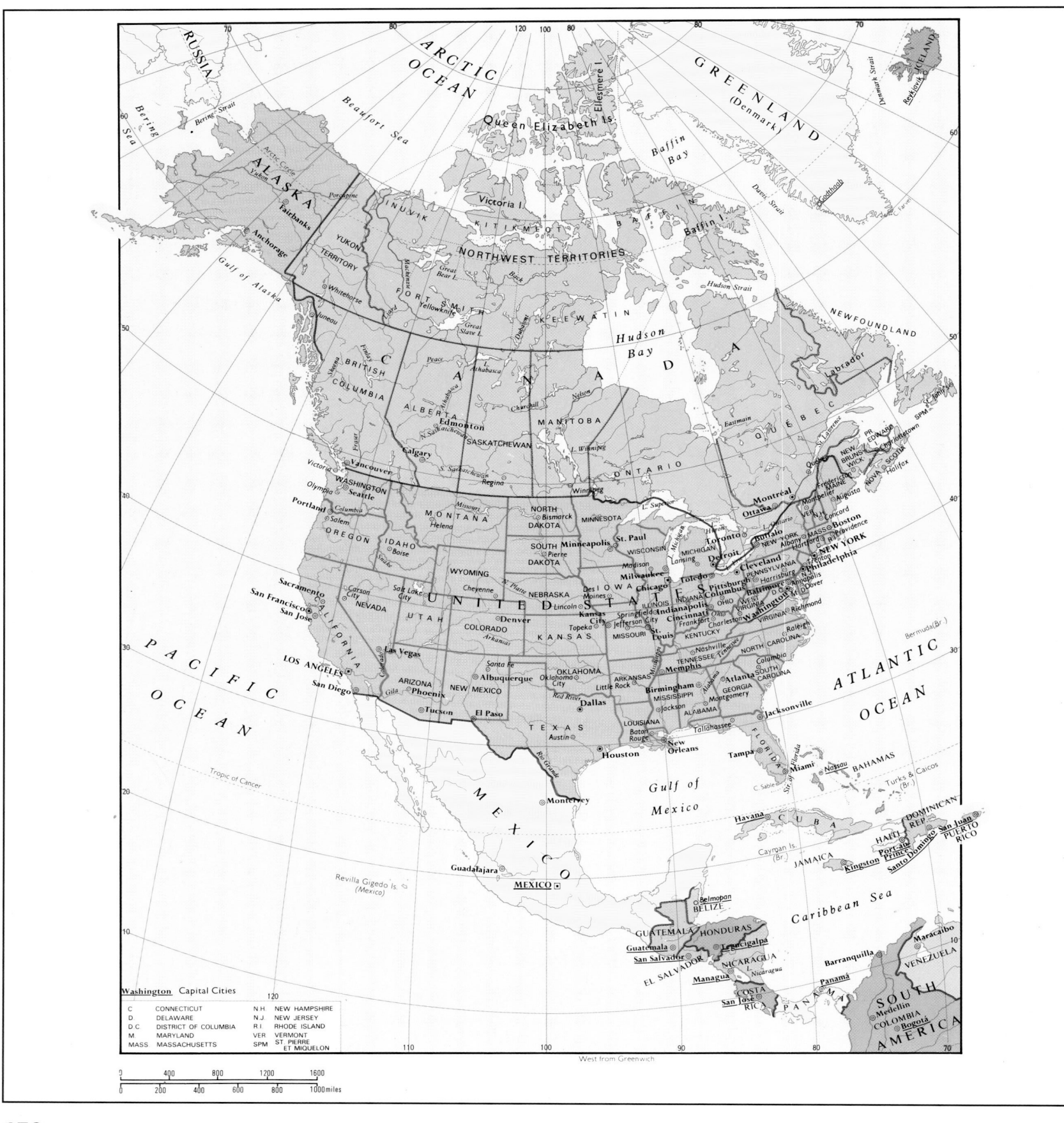

Washington	Capital Cities		
C	CONNECTICUT	N.H.	NEW HAMPSHIRE
D	DELAWARE	N.J.	NEW JERSEY
D.C	DISTRICT OF COLUMBIA	R.I.	RHODE ISLAND
M	MARYLAND	VER	VERMONT
MASS	MASSACHUSETTS	SPM	ST. PIERRE ET MIQUELON

CANADA

A vast confederation of ten provinces and two territories, Canada is the world's second largest country after Russia, and with an even longer coastline (250,000 km [155,000 mls]). Sparsely populated, it has huge areas of virtually unoccupied mountains, forests, tundra and polar desert in the north and west.

To the east lie the Maritime provinces of Newfoundland, Nova Scotia, New Brunswick and Prince Edward Island, and the predominantly French-speaking province of Québec; clustered about the Gulf of St Lawrence, they are based on ancient

The CN tower, at 553 m [1,841 ft] the world's tallest freestanding structure, dwarfs downtown Toronto.

worn-down mountains – the northern extension of the Appalachians – and the eastern uptilted edge of the even older Canadian Shield. The central province of Ontario borders the Great Lakes, extending north across the Shield to Hudson Bay. Further to the west come the prairie provinces of Manitoba, Saskatchewan and Alberta; like Québec and Ontario, these include fertile farmlands in the south, where most of the population is to be found, and lake-strewn forest on the subarctic wastelands to the north.

South-western Alberta includes a substantial block of the Rocky Mountains, with peaks rising to over 4,000 m [13,120 ft] in Banff, Yoho and Kootenay National Parks. The westernmost province of British Columbia is mountainous, a land of spectacular forests, lakes and fjords, with sheltered valleys harbouring rich farmland. The huge northern area includes the small and mountainous Yukon Territory in the west, bordering Alaska, and the much more extensive Northwest Territories stretching from the 60th parallel to the northern tip of Ellesmere Island.

Exploration and settlement

Norse voyagers and fishermen were probably the first Europeans briefly to visit Canada, but John Cabot's later discovery of North America, in 1497, began the race to annex lands and wealth, with France and Britain the main contenders.

Jacques Cartier's discovery of the St Lawrence River in 1534 gave France a head start; from their settlements near Québec explorers, trappers and missionaries pioneered routes deeply penetrating the northern half of North America. With possible routes to China and the Indies in mind, Frenchmen followed the St Lawrence and Niagara rivers deep into the heartland of the continent, hoping for the riches of another Eldorado.

Discovering the Great Lakes, they then moved north, west and south in their search for trade. From the fertile valley of the upper St Lawrence, French influence spread north beyond the coniferous forests and over the tundra. To the west and south they reached the prairies – potentially fertile farming country – exploring further to the Rockies and down the Ohio and Mississippi rivers.

By 1763, after the series of wars that gave Britain brief control of the whole of North America, French-speaking communities were already scattered widely across the interior. Many of the southern settlements became American after 1776, when the USA declared independence from Britain, and the northern ones became a British colony.

British settlers had long been established on the Atlantic coast, farming where possible, with supplementary fishing. In the 1780s a new wave of English-speaking settlers – the United Empire Loyalists – moved north from the USA into Nova Scotia, New Brunswick and Lower Canada. With further waves of immigration direct from Britain, English speakers came to dominate the fertile lands between Lakes Huron and Erie. From there they gradually spread westwards.

The birth of Canada

Restricted to the north by intractable coniferous forests and tundra, and to the south by the USA, the settlers spread through Québec into Upper Canada – now Ontario, the only province along the Canadian

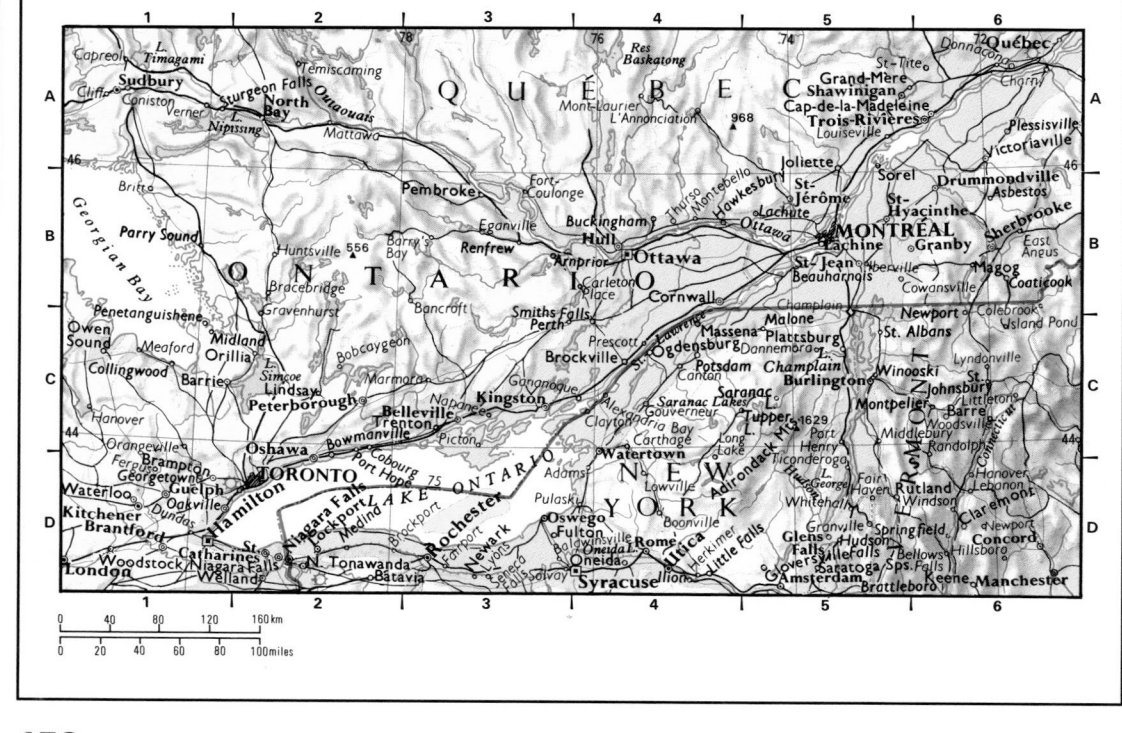

THE TUNDRA
Beyond their habitable southern rim, the northlands of Canada and Alaska are bleak and bare; in the subarctic zone conifers stretch across the continent, but northwards the boreal forest thins and dies out, replaced with tundra. Glaciation has scoured the rocks bare, and soils have had insufficient time to form; the surface thaws in summer, but subsoils remain frozen. Winters are long and bitterly cold, summers brief and cool. Even in the south the season of plant growth (*left*) is only 70–80 days. Precipitation is light – usually less than 250 mm [10 in] a year – and most of it snow; except where it drifts, the snow seldom lies deep, but it provides cover for vegetation and burrowing animals.

The tundra is covered with low grasses, lichens, mosses and spindly shrubs, providing food for migrating reindeer and resident hares, voles, lemmings and other small browsers and grazers. Their numbers are augmented each summer by hosts of migrant birds – such as ducks, geese, swans, waders – that fly in from temperate latitudes to feed on the vegetation and insects. Canada's best-known migrants are caribou, which travel vast distances each year.

shores of the Great Lakes. Mostly English-speaking and retaining British traditions, they continued westwards to establish settlements across the narrow wedge of the northern prairie, finally crossing the Rockies to link with embryo settlements along the Pacific coast. So the fertile lowlands of the St Lawrence basin and the pockets of settlement on the Shield alone remained French in language and culture. The bulk of Canada, to east and west, became predominantly British.

Canada's varied topography and immense scale inhibited the development of a single nation; to promote Canadian unity across so wide a continent has been the aim of successive governments for more than two centuries. The union of British Upper Canada and French Lower Canada was sealed by the Confederation of 1867, when as the newly-named Provinces of Ontario and Québec they were united with the Maritime core of Nova Scotia and New Brunswick. Three years later the settlement on the Red River entered the Confederation as Manitoba, and in the following year the Pacific colonies of Vancouver Island and British Columbia, now united as a single province, completed the link from sea to sea. Prince Edward Island joined in 1873, the prairie provinces of Alberta and Saskatchewan in 1905, and Newfoundland in 1949.

Though self-governing in most respects from the time of the Confederation, Canada remained technically subject to the British Imperial parliament until 1931, when the creation of the British Commonwealth made the country a sovereign nation under the crown.

With so much of the population spread out along a southern ribbon of settlement, 4,000 km [2,500 mls] long but rarely more than 480 km [300 mls] wide, Canada has struggled constantly to achieve unity. Transcontinental communications have played a critical role. From the eastern provinces the Canadian Pacific Railway crossed the Rockies to reach Vancouver in 1885. Later a second rail route, the Canadian National, was pieced together, and the Trans-Canada Highway links the extreme east and west of the country symbolically as well as in fact. Transcontinental air routes link the major centres, and local air traffic is especially important over trackless forests, mountains and tundra. With radio and telephone communications, all parts of the Confederation – even the most remote corners of the Arctic territories – are now firmly linked, though the vastness is intimidating and the country spans six time zones: at noon in Vancouver it is already 3 pm in Toronto, and 4.30 pm in St Johns, Newfoundland.

A constant hazard to Canadian nationhood is the proximity of the USA. Though benign, with shared if dwindling British traditions, the prosperous giant to the south has often seemed to threaten the very survival of Canada through economic dominance and cultural annexation. The two countries have the largest bilateral trade flow in the world.

A real and growing threat to unity is the persistence of French culture in Québec province – a lasting political wedge between the western prairie and mountain provinces and the eastern Maritimes. Urbanization and 'Americanization' have fuelled a separatist movement that seeks to turn the province into an independent French-speaking republic. This issue may obscure a wider and more fundamental division in Canadian politics, with the development of a Montréal-Toronto axis in the east, and a Vancouver-Winnipeg axis in the west.

Population and urbanization
Though the population of Canada expanded rapidly from Confederation onwards, it remained predominantly rural for many generations; only in recent decades have Canada's cities grown to match those of the USA. At Confederation in 1867 about 80% was rural, and only Montréal had passed the 100,000 population mark, with but six towns over 25,000. Not until the end of World War II did the rural and urban elements stand in balance, and today the situation is reversed: 76% of Canada's population is urban.

The metropolitan areas of Toronto and Montréal jointly contain a quarter of the total, and together with Vancouver account for over 30% of the entire population. By contrast the urban centres of Newfoundland and the Maritimes have been relatively stable.

Agriculture and industry
Although farming settlements still dominate the landscape, if not the economy, abandonment of farmland is a serious problem in the eastern provinces, where the agrarian economy – except in such favoured areas as the Annapolis Valley, Nova Scotia – has always been marginal. Through the St Lawrence lowlands and Ontario peninsula farms are more prosperous and rural populations are denser, thinning again along the north shores of the Great Lakes. On the prairies mechanization of grain farming long ago minimized the need for labour, so population densities remain low; the mixed farming communities on the forest margins are often denser. The Pacific coast population is generally concentrated in such rich farming areas as the Okanagan and lower Frazer River basins.

Industry, often dependent on local development of power resources, has transformed many remote and empty areas of Canada. Newfoundland's Labrador iron-ore workings around Schefferville are powered by the huge hydroelectric plant at Churchill Falls, one of the largest of its kind in the world. Cheap hydroelectric power throughout Québec and Ontario, coupled with improved transmission technology, has encouraged the further development of wood pulp and paper industries, even in distant parts of the northern forests, and stimulated industry and commerce in the south. Canada is by far the world's leading producer and exporter of paper and board. Mining, too, has helped in the development of these provinces; Sudbury, Ontario, supplies about 20% of the Western world's nickel, while Canada is one of the leading producers of zinc and uranium.

In the prairie provinces, small marketing, distribution and service centres have been transformed by the enormous expansion of the petrochemical industry; the mineral-rich province of Alberta produces 90% of the country's oil output, and the boom towns of Alberta, Edmonton and Calgary have far outpaced the growth of the eastern cities during recent decades.

By contrast – lacking hydrocarbons and depending mainly on farming, logging and pulping for their prosperity – the settlements of Pacific Canada have on the whole grown slowly, with the notable exception of Vancouver.

The northlands

Canada's northlands, virtually uninhabited apart from small Inuit communities, have an immense though localized potential for development. Though the soils are poor and the climate is unyielding, mineral wealth

is abundant under the permanently frozen subsoils. Already a major producer of uranium, zinc and nickel, the North also holds vast reserves of copper, molybdenum, iron, cadmium, and other metals of strategic importance; sulphur, potash and asbestos are currently being exploited, and natural gas and petroleum await development beyond the Mackenzie River delta.

Much of this immense mineral wealth will remain in the ground until the high costs of extraction and transportation can be justified. Also, pressure for legislation to protect the boreal forest and tundra against unnecessary or casual damage is rapidly growing – a trend which one day may also curb a massive timber industry, which at present generates 15% of Canadian exports ■

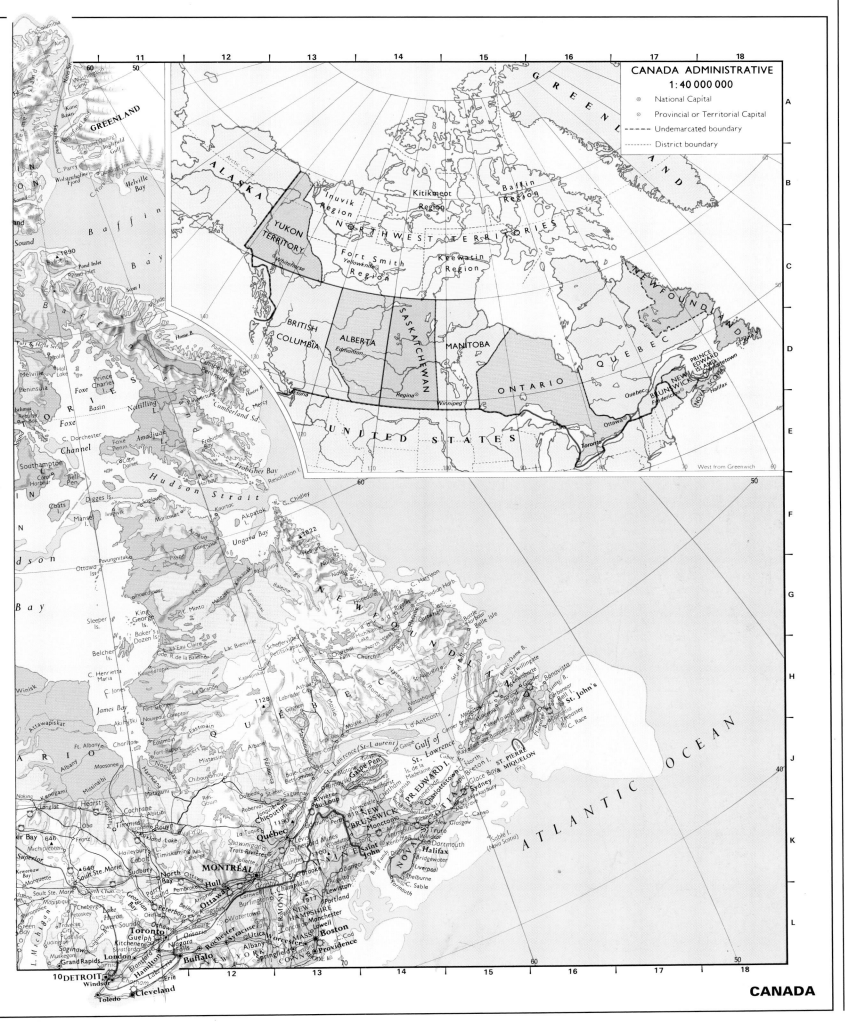

UNITED STATES OF AMERICA

The world's fourth largest country – and third most populous – the United States of America fills the North American continent between Canada and Mexico and also includes Alaska and the archipelago of Hawaii. Geographically, the main part (of 48 states) falls readily into an eastern section, including the Appalachian Mountains and eastern coastal plain; a central section, including the Mississippi basin and the broad prairie plains from the Dakotas to Texas; and a western section, including the Rocky Mountains and Pacific coastlands.

The East

Eastern North America is crossed by a band of folded mountains: though nowhere much above 2,000 m [6,500 ft], they long formed a barrier to settlers. In the north are the Adirondacks, rising to 1,629 m [5,344 ft], a southern extension of the ancient Canadian granite shield. From Maine to Alabama runs a broad range of sedimentary mountains, the Appalachians. Younger than the Adirondacks (though much older than the Rockies) the Appalachians separate the Atlantic coastlands of the east from the Great Lakes and low plateaus of Ohio, Kentucky and Tennessee.

North-east of New York City lie the six New England states – the fertile wooded country that, at least in summer, made the early settlers feel at home. To the south the coastal plain widens, to be split by the drowned estuaries of the Susquehanna and Potomac rivers, draining into Chesapeake Bay. From Virginia south to Florida smaller rivers drain eastwards, across a much broader plain, many of them entering coastal sounds with offshore sand-bars and islands.

In New York State a major spillway cuts through the mountains between the Adirondacks and the Appalachians, linking the Great Lakes with the Hudson Valley and the Atlantic Ocean. This is the line of the famous Erie Canal route, the most used of several that gave the early settlers access to the Ohio country beyond the mountains. Other routes led to Pittsburgh and, through the southern Appalachians,

into Tennessee. Central Ohio, Indiana and Illinois, which once formed America's Northwest Territory, are rolling uplands and plains, smoothed by glaciation in the north but more rugged in the south, and drained by the rambling Ohio River.

Vegetation: The original vegetation of eastern America, on either flank of the mountains, was broadleaf deciduous forest of oak, ash, beech and maple, merging northwards into yellow birch, hemlock and pine. In the drier Midwest these immense woodlands turned to open country. Patchy grasslands covered northern Indiana and southern Illinois; central Illinois was forested along most watercourses, with prairie blue-stem grasses on the drier land. Around the southern Appalachians mixed oak, pine and tulip-tree dominated; pines covered the coastal plains to the south and east with bald cypress in northern Florida. Spruce blanketed the highlands from northern Maine to the Adirondacks; spruce, tamarack and balsam fir covered the high Appalachians.

Most of this original forest is now gone, but there is still enough left – and some regenerating on abandoned farmland – to leave the mountains a blaze of colour each autumn. Despite more than 300 years of European settlement, the overall impression of eastern America, seen from the air, is still one of dense semi-continuous forests, except in the extensive farmlands north of the Ohio.

Settlement and development: The eastern USA is the heartland of many of America's rural and urban traditions. In the 19th century European immigrants poured through the ports of Boston, New York, Philadelphia and Baltimore. Many stayed to swell the cities, which grew enormously. Others moved across the mountains to populate the interior and start the farms that fed the city masses. As raw materials of industry – coal and iron ore especially – were discovered and exploited, new cities grew up in the interior. Some were based on old frontier forts: Fort Duquesne became Pittsburgh and Fort Dearborn became Chicago.

Railways spread over the booming farmlands, linking producer and consumer. Huge manufacturing cities, vast markets in their own right, developed along the Great Lakes as people continued to arrive – firstly from abroad, but latterly from the countryside, where mechanization threw people off the land

Space Age monument: the Trans-America Building looks set to take off from San Francisco.

into the cities and factories. In less than a hundred years between the late 18th and 19th centuries, the Ohio country passed from Indian-occupied forests and plains to mechanized farmlands of unparalleled efficiency, becoming virtually the granary of the Western world, and spawning some of its greatest and wealthiest industrial centres.

While the North boomed, the warmer southern states slipped into rural lethargy; becoming over-dependent on cotton cultivation, they remained backward and outside the mainstream of American prosperity. Though fortunes were made on the rich cotton estates of the south-east, Tennessee and the southern Appalachians spelled rural poverty for many generations of settlers.

Today the pattern is much the same, though prosperity has increased throughout the East. The densest concentrations of industry and population lie in the north-east, especially in central New England. New York remains an important financial hub, while Washington D.C., now part of a vast, sprawling megalopolis, loses none of its significance as the centre of federal government. The south-eastern states remain relatively rural and thinly populated, though they are increasingly popular with the retired, notably Florida.

The Central States

Within the 1,400 km [875 mls] from the Mississippi to the foothills of the Rockies, the land rises almost 3,000 m [9,850 ft], though the slope is often imperceptible to the traveller. From the Gulf of Mexico northwards to Minnesota and the Dakotas the rise is even less noticeable, though the flatness is occasionally relieved by the outcrops of uplands – the Ozarks of northern Arkansas, for example. In summer nothing bars the northwards movement of hot moist air from the Gulf of Mexico, nor in winter the southwards movement of dry, cold air from the Arctic. These air masses produce great seasonal contrasts of climate, exacerbated by storms, blizzards and tornadoes. Westwards from the Mississippi the climate grows progressively drier.

The plains are crossed by a series of long, wide rivers, often of irregular flow, that drain off the Rockies: the Missouri, the Platte, the Arkansas, the Canadian and the Red. In contrast to the Ohio, which enabled travellers to pass downstream and so westwards to the Mississippi, these rivers of the plains provided little help to settlers moving westwards, due to their seasonal variations in flow and the effort which was needed to move upstream when floods gave them depth.

Vegetation: West of the margins of the Mississippi tall blue-stem prairie grasses once extended from the Canadian border to southern Texas. Only along the watercourses were there trees – cottonwood and willow in the north, merging into oak and hickory further south. Westwards the prairie grasslands thinned to the bunch grass and needle grass of the Great Plains in a belt from central North Dakota to western Oklahoma; locally favoured areas such as western Nebraska had patches of broadleaf evergreens amidst shrubs and grasses.

West of about meridian 100°W a variety of short grasses stretched from Montana and the Dakotas southwards to north-west Texas: in the far south on the Mexican border low xerophytic shrubs indicated increasing aridity. Higher ground, for example the Black Hills of south-western South Dakota, supported stands of pine.

Settlement and development: Over 30 major tribes of native Indians used these vast and varied plains. Some – the Mandan, the Omaha and the Kansa along the Missouri River, for example – were settled farmers, while on the drier western plains the Blackfoot, Crow, Arapaho, Kiowa and Comanche were nomadic, following the buffalo, the game and the pasture.

European influences revolutionized their lives. By 1800 the horse, introduced from the south by the Spanish, made the Indian population of about 100,000 mobile as never before. Then English- and French-speaking trappers and traders from the east brought firearms: the mounted Indian with a gun became too efficient a hunter, and rapidly depleted his food supply. Behind the traders came white settlers, killing off the buffalo and crowding in other native peoples that they had driven from homelands in the south-east. As railways, cattle trails and the fences of the ranchers crossed the old hunting grounds, Indian farmers and hunters alike lost their traditional lands and livelihoods to the European intruders, and the plains settlement was virtually completed by the late 19th century.

The coming of the railways after the Civil War of the 1860s not only doomed the remnant Indian societies, but also introduced long and often bitter competition between different types of European farming. The dry grasslands that once supported the buffalo could just as well support herds of cattle on the open range, raised to feed the eastern cities. So

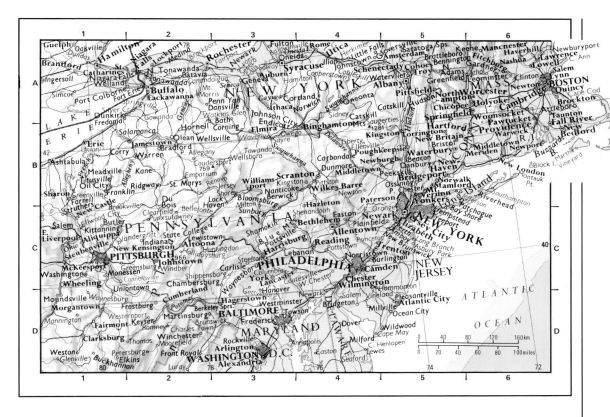

New England in the fall: turning leaves envelop a
whiteboarded church and clean streets in Vermont.

the range lands often became crop-farms. In the dry years that followed, soil deterioration and erosion began, becoming a major problem in the early decades of the present century.

With their markets in the cities of the East and in Europe, the plains farmers were caught in a vice between the desiccation of their farms and the boom and slump of their markets. By the 1930s agricultural depression led to massive foreclosing on mortgaged lands, and when the dust storms of eroded topsoil came the people were driven away – the 'Okies' of Woody Guthrie and John Steinbeck who fled to California. Much farmed land subsequently reverted to ranching.

Farming prospects improved during the later 1930s, when the New Deal brought better price structures. New approaches to farming practice, including dry farming (cropping only one year out of several), contour ploughing, diversification beyond basic grains, and widespread irrigation that was linked to the creation of a vast network of dams and reservoirs, all transformed the plains. However, these areas are marginal to semi-desert, remaining susceptible to periodic changes in precipitation over a wide area: thus a poor snowfall on the Rockies may mean insufficient water for irrigation the following summer. Coupled with worldwide fluctuations in the cereals market (on which Midwest farmers still depend heavily), farming

on the plains remains very risky.

The growth of industry: In the Gulf Coast states, petroleum provides a radically different basis for prosperity. Since the exploitation of oil reserves in the early years of the century, Oklahoma, Texas and Louisiana have shifted from a dependence on agriculture (notably wheat, cattle, rice and sugar production) to the refining and petrochemical industries. Oil has transformed Dallas-Fort Worth into a major US conurbation, now larger than the twin cities of Minneapolis-St Paul, which were once the chief urban focus of the agricultural economy of the upper Mississippi. At the meeting of the High Plains and the Rocky Mountains, Denver changed from a small elevated railhead town to a wealthy state capital (and further to a smog-ridden metropolis) in response to mineral wealth and the growth of aerospace industries.

Further north the cities of the central USA are great trading centres, dependent on local agriculture for their prosperity. The trans-shipment of produce has been crucial since the days of the railheads, but cities like St Louis, Kansas City and Chicago have been able to diversify far beyond their original role to become major manufacturing centres. Chicago, for example, is the main mid-western focus of the steel industries. Today the interstate freeway system supplements and has partly replaced the railway networks, and air passenger traffic has increased rapidly.

From the air the landscape between the Mississippi and the Rockies is one of quilted farmlands and vast reservoirs, blending into wheatlands with extensive grasslands. Almost all the original vegetation is long gone, and most people now live in the cities, but the landscape still reflects the critical importance of the type of agricultural activity past and present.

The West

The western USA is a complex mountain and plateau system, rich in scenic beauty and natural history, bordered by a rugged coast that starts in the semi-deserts of the south and ends in the rain-soaked forests of the north. Americans appreciate their far west; for long the final frontier of a youthful, expand-

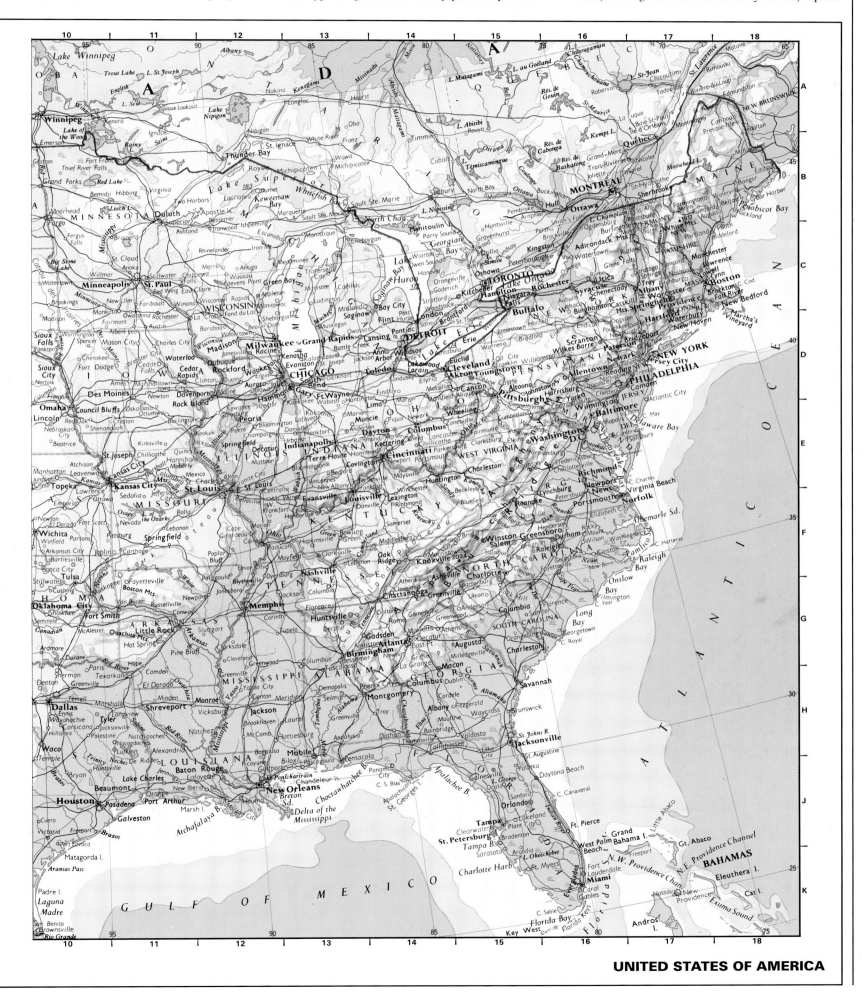

Latter-day cowboys, now toting only Raybans, at work on the wild side with horses in Colorado.

forests, grasslands, alpine tundras and marshes are ecologically fascinating, and the wild animals are reasonably accessible. There is every chance for tourists to see bison, wapiti, mule deer, moose, black and brown bears, beavers and a host of smaller mammals and birds.

West of the Rockies, beyond the dry plateau scrublands of Arizona, Utah and Nevada, a double chain of mountains runs parallel to the coast from Mexico to Canada. In the arid, sun-baked south they form the desert landscape on either side of the Gulf of California. At Los Angeles they merge, parting again to form the Sierra Nevada and the Coastal Ranges that face each other across the Great Valley of central California. They rejoin in the Klamath Mountains, then continue north on either side of a broad valley – to the west as a lowly coastal chain, to the east as the magnificently forested Cascade Range. By keeping rain away from the interior, these mountains create the arid landscapes of the central Cordilleras.

Climate and agriculture: In the damp winters and dry summers of southern California the coastal mountains support semi-desert scrub; the Sierra Nevada, rising far above them, is relatively well-watered and forested. In the early days of settlement the long, bone-dry summers made farming – even ranching – difficult in the central valley of California. But the peaks of Sierra Nevada, accumulating thick snow in winter, now provide a reservoir for summer irrigation. Damming and water channelling have made the semi-deserts and dry rangelands bloom all over southern and central California, which now grows temperate and tropical fruits, vegetables, cotton and other thirsty crops in abundance – despite experiencing severe drought from the late 1980s.

Through northern California and Oregon, where annual rainfall is higher and summer heat less intense, the coastal mountains are clothed in forests of tall cedars and firs; notable among them are stands of giant redwood cedars, towering well over 100 m [330 ft]. In coastal Washington Douglas firs, grand firs, Sitka spruce and giant arborvitae are the spectacular trees, rivalling the giant redwoods. Forests of giant

ing nation, it is still the goal of tens of thousands of immigrants each year and the vacation dream of many more: tourism is the most widespread industry.

Landscape and vegetation: Topographically the West is a land of high mountain ranges divided by high plateaus and deep valleys. The grain of the country runs north-west to south-east, at a right-angle to the crustal pressures that produced it, and the highest mountains – the Rocky Mountains of a thousand legends – form a spectacular eastern flank. The southern Rockies of Colorado and New Mexico, remnants of an ancient granite plateau, are carved by weathering into ranges of spectacular peaks; Colorado alone has over 1,000 mountains of 3,000 m [10,000 ft] or more. Rising from dry, sandy, cactus-and-sagebrush desert, their lower slopes carry grey piñon pines and juniper scrub, with darker spruce, firs and pines above. At the timberline grow gnarled bristlecone pines, some 3,000 and more years old. Between the ranges 'parks' of mixed forest and grassland support deer and other game in summer grazing. To the south-west are the dry, colourful sandstones of the Colorado

Plateau, dotted with cactus and deeply gouged by the Colorado River; to the north lies the Wyoming Basin, a rangeland of rich volcanic soil that once grazed herds of bison, and now supports sheep and cattle.

The central Rocky Mountains, towering over western Wyoming, Idaho and Montana, include a number of snow-capped peaks of more than 4,000 m [13,000 ft]; their eastern outliers, the Bighorn Mountains, rise 3,000 m [10,000 ft] almost sheer above the surrounding grasslands. These are the Rockies of the tourists; each year thousands of people visit the many national parks and reserves in the splendid heartland of the Cordilleras. The scenery is matchless, the

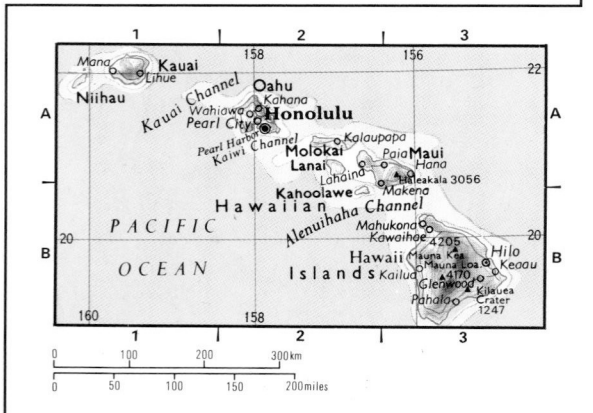

HAWAII
Most recent and most southerly of the United States, Hawaii is an archipelago of eight large and over 100 smaller volcanic islands in mid-Pacific, 3,850 km [2,400 mls] south-west of California. Only on the main island are there active volcanoes such as Kilavea (*left*). The high rainfall, warmth and rich soils combine to provide a wealth of year-round vegetation; originally forested, the islands are still well covered with trees and shrubs, but now provide commercial crops of sugar cane, cereals, forage for cattle, and a wide range of fruit and vegetables.

Originally settled by Polynesians and visited by James Cook in 1778, Hawaii became a port-of-call for trans-Pacific shipping and a wintering station for New England whalers, but retained its independent status until annexed by the USA in 1898. Only about 2% of its people are full-blooded Polynesians; the rest are of Chinese, Japanese, Korean, Philippine and Caucasian origins, including many immigrants from mainland USA.

ALASKA

In 1867 the USA bought Alaska from the Tsarist government of Russia for a mere $7 million. More extensive than the south-western lands acquired from Mexico, Alaska remained a territory for over 90 years, becoming America's largest state in 1959. Geographically it forms the north-western end of the Western Cordilleras; peaks in the main Alaska Range rise to over 6,000 m [20,000 ft], and the southern 'panhandle' region is a drowned fjordland backed by ice-capped mountains. A gold rush in the 1880s stimulated the later development of other mineral resources – notably copper and, especially, oil. Alaska is the first real test of the USA's resolve to balance economic development and conservation; the six largest US national parks are in Alaska. Some farming is possible on the southern coastal low-lands; the interior is tundra-covered and rich in migrant birds and mammals, like this brown bear at Brook Falls.

conifers cover the Cascade Range too, providing the enormous stocks of timber on which the wealth of the American north-west was originally based.

Settlement and development: The Indian cultures of western America included hunting, fishing, seed-gathering and primitive irrigation farming. Some were semi-nomadic, others settled, living mostly in small, scattered communities. The first European colonists, spreading northwards from New Spain (Mexico) in the 1760s, made little impact on the Indians. But their forts and missions (which included San Diego, Los Angeles and San Francisco) attracted later settlers who proved more exploitative. From the 1840s pressures increased with the arrival of land-hungry Americans, both by sea and along wagon trails from the east. After a brief struggle, the south-west was sold to the USA; almost immediately the gold rushes brought new waves of adventurers and immigrants.

The Oregon coast, though visited by Spanish, British and Russian mariners in search of furs from the 16th century onwards, was first settled by American fur traders in 1811. Immigration began during the 1830s, the famous Oregon Trail across Wyoming and Idaho from the Mississippi coming into full use during the 1840s. After the establishment of the 49th parallel as the boundary between Canada and the USA, Oregon Territory (including Washington, Idaho and part of Montana) became part of the USA. Here in the north-west the forests and rangelands were equally vital to Indians and to settlers, and many battles were fought before the Indians were subdued and confined in tribal reserves.

Now the wagon trails are major highways, the staging posts, mission stations and isolated forts transformed into cities. Gold mining, once the only kind of mining that mattered, has given way to the delving and processing of a dozen lesser metals, from copper to molybdenum. Fish canning, food processing, electronics and aerospace are major sources of employment. The movie industry is based in Los Angeles, but this urban cluster now has a broad economy based on high-technology industries. The mountain states – once far behind in economic development – have caught up with the rest of the USA. But the enduring beauty of the western mountains remains.

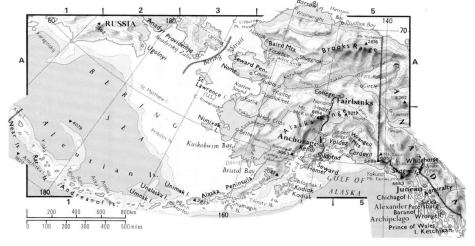

Resources and industry

The spread of prosperity throughout a very broad spectrum of the community generated new consumer industries, to satisfy the demands of a large middle class for ever-increasing standards of comfort and material welfare. America became the pioneer of massive-scale industrial production of everything from thumbtacks to automobiles. With almost every material needed for production available within its own boundaries, or readily gained through trading with neighbours, its mining and extractive industries have been heavily exploited from the start.

For several generations coal formed the main source of power and the basis of industrial prosperity. Anthracite from eastern Pennsylvania, good bituminous and coking coals from the Appalachians, Indiana, Illinois, Colorado and Utah are still in demand, and enormous reserves remain. Oil, first drilled in Pennsylvania in 1859, was subsequently found in several major fields underlying the Midwest, the eastern and central mountain states, the Gulf of Mexico, California and Alaska. Home consumption of petroleum products has grown steadily: though the US remains a major producer, it is also by far the world's greatest consumer, and has for long been a net importer of oil. Natural gas, too, is found in abundance, usually in association with oil, and is moved to the main consumer areas through an elaborate, transcontinental network of pipes.

Population

The USA has one of the most diverse populations of any nation in the world. Until about 1860, with the exception of the native Indians and the southern blacks, the population was largely made up by immigrants of British (and Irish) origin, with small numbers of Spanish and French. After the Civil War, however, there was increasing immigration from the countries of central and south-eastern Europe – such as Italy, Poland and Russia. This vast influx of Europeans, numbering about 30 million between 1860 and 1920, was markedly different in culture and language from the established population. More recently there have been lesser influxes of Japanese, Chinese, Filipinos, Cubans and Puerto Ricans, with large numbers of Mexicans (many of them illegal) from across the southern border. Although there are strong influences and pressures towards Americanization, these minority groups have tended to establish distinct social and cultural enclaves.

The major westwards movement of population through the last century was replaced after 1900 by more subtle but no less important shifts of population away from rural areas and into the cities. Today there is further movement from the old, industrial centres and the tired, outmoded cities that flourished early in the century, away from the ageing buildings and urban dereliction, especially in the north and east, to new centres elsewhere ■

MEXICO

The world's largest and most populous Spanish-speaking nation, Mexico has a faster growing population than any other big country: between 1960 and 1980 it doubled, growing at an unprecedented 3.5% a year. It is thus an astonishingly young society; the average Mexican is a 17-year-old, and 75% of the people are under 30.

The combination of a stable and very high birth rate (now about 32 per thousand) and a declining and now low death rate (about five per thousand) is the main cause of this population explosion. Mexico City (population 1 million in 1930, 8.7 million in 1970, 16.6 million in 1985) is already the most populous in the Americas and estimated to be the world's largest by 2000 (24.4 million), overtaking Tokyo and staying well ahead even of São Paulo.

Landscape and vegetation

Mexico is a land of great physical variety. The northern, emptier, half is open basin-and-range country of the Mesa Central. The land rises southwards from the Rio Grande (Rio Bravo del Norte) at the US border, averaging about 2,600 m [8,500 ft] above sea level in the middle, where it is crowned by many snow-capped volcanic cones, Orizaba (5,750 m [18,865 ft]) in the east being the highest. Though an active earthquake zone, this is the most densely settled part of the country. The Mesa Central ends equally dramatically in the west, where the Sierra Madre Occidental rise to over 4,000 m [13,120 ft], and in the east, where the Sierra Madre Oriental form a backcloth to the modest coastal plain bordering the Gulf of Mexico. In the far northwest is the isolated, 1,220 km [760 ml] mountain-cored peninsula of Baja California.

Mountains dominate southern Mexico, broken only by the low, narrow isthmus of Tehuantepec, which is crossed by railways and roads linking the Gulf ports with Salina Cruz on the Pacific. The flat, low-lying limestone Yucatan peninsula in the southeast is an exception in a country where half the land is over 1,000 m [3,280 ft] above sea level, and a quarter has slopes of over 25 degrees. Deserts characterize the north-west, and tropical rainforest is the natural vegetation of Tehuantepec; over 70% of the country is arid or semi-arid and irrigation is mandatory for agriculture.

Economy and politics

Agriculture occupies half the population but contributes less than a third of the economic product contributed by manufacturing, with metals also important. Fresh petroleum discoveries during the 1970s from huge reserves in Tabasco and Campeche have turned Mexico into the world's fourth biggest producer, much of it exported to the USA, but the economy is now very diverse with textiles, forestry and tourism all making significant progress. Only an estimated 15–20% of the nation's mineral wealth has been exploited, with precious metals comprising almost half the value of total known mineral reserves.

While the century after independence in 1821 was characterized by political chaos, climaxing in the violent revolution of 1910–21, the post-revolutionary period was steady by Latin American standards, with the PRI in power for more than six decades from 1929 and instituting crucial land reforms in the 1930s. The economy has been dominated by this regime since oil was nationalized in 1938, enjoying huge growth in the 1970s, when living standards rose considerably, but running into massive debt crises in the 1980s.

In June 1993, it was announced that Mexico would join the OECD, the first new member for some 20 years. Mexico pursued the idea of a trading area with Canada and the US – President Clinton finally steered the legislation for NAFTA (North American Free Trade Association) through Congress in November 1993 – but rural-urban migration and high unemployment remain the biggest domestic problems. Above all, there is the emigration across the world's busiest border: hundreds of thousands of Mexicans cross into the USA each year, many of them staying as illegal immigrants. At home, a peasants' revolt in Chiapas and political assassinations did not augur well for the elections in 1994 ■

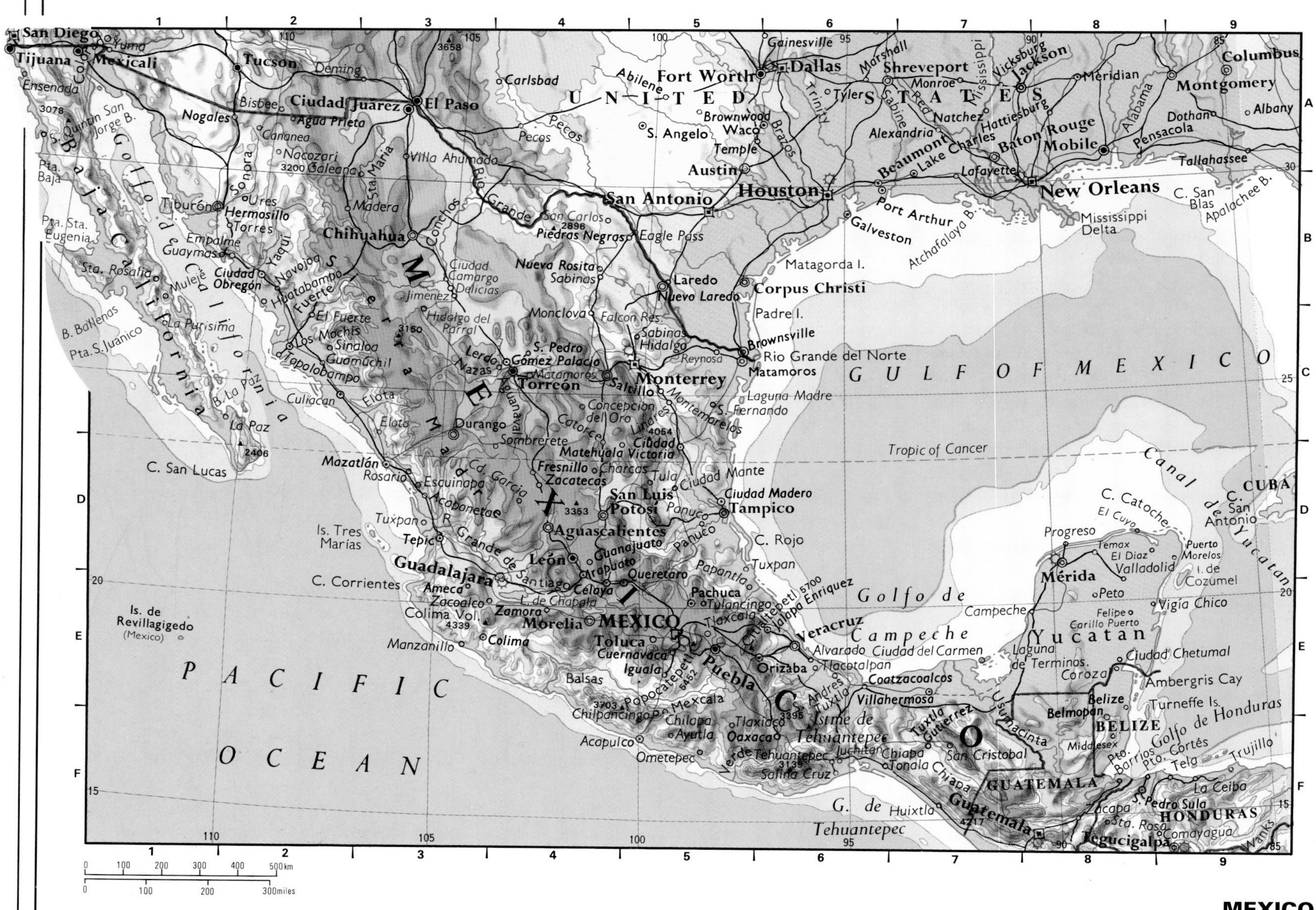

MEXICO

GUATEMALA

Most populous of the Central American countries, Guatemala's Pacific coastline, two and a half times longer than the Caribbean coast, is backed by broad alluvial plains, formed of material washed down from the towering volcanoes that front the ocean. These include extinct Tajumulco (4,217 m [13,830 ft]), the highest peak in Central America.

A heavily dissected plateau, the Altos, forms the core of the country; beautiful lakes such as the Atitlán mark its junction with the mountains. This area, with comfortable temperatures for living and maize cultivation, is both a focus of dense rural settlement and also the site of the capital – earthquake-prone Guatemala City. The north-eastern third of the country is the Petén, a flat, low-lying limestone wilderness on the Yucatan Peninsula and once a centre of Mayan civilization.

The plains have been used for commercial-scale agriculture only since the 1950s, when malaria was brought under control and roads were built; cattle and cotton are now more important than the traditional banana crop. Lower mountain slopes, up to about 1,500 m [5,000 ft], yield most of the country's best coffee.

While Indians are in the majority, society and government are run on autocratic, often repressive

Twice a week colourful Maya Indians descend on Chichicastenango, north-east of Guatemala City. They come not just for the market but also for religious ceremonies that are a typically Central American mixture of Christian and pre-Christian.

lines by the mestizos of mixed Indian and European stock. The Indians were the principal victims of the army's indiscriminate campaign against left-wing URNG guerrillas in the early 1980s – the acceleration of a policy in place since the 1950s. The 'low-intensity' civil war that followed was still smouldering when a ceasefire became operative in neighbouring El Salvador in February 1992. This influence, allied to the government's sudden recognition of Belizean independence in 1991 (Guatemala had claimed the entire territory), paved the way for a UN-sponsored peace accord in March 1993 – a welcome prospect for a nation whose 'defence' spending takes 15% of the budget, and whose human rights record is appalling. As in El Salvador, Washington's stance is vitally important: in keeping with all the Central American republics (except Nicaragua), the US is crucial to the economy – in Guatemala's case accounting for more than 40% of trade ■

BELIZE

Larger than El Salvador but with only 3.5% of its population, Belize is a sparsely populated enclave on the Caribbean coast of Central America. The northern half of the country is low-lying swamp, the south a high plateau.

Formerly British Honduras, it enjoyed a boom after independence, with processing of citrus fruits and tourism helping to allay the dependency on timber, bananas and, most notably, sugar.

The 50-year dispute with Guatemala ended in 1991 and British troops began withdrawal in 1994. Over a quarter of the population lives in Belize City, replaced as the capital by Belmopan in 1970 following the 1961 hurricane ■

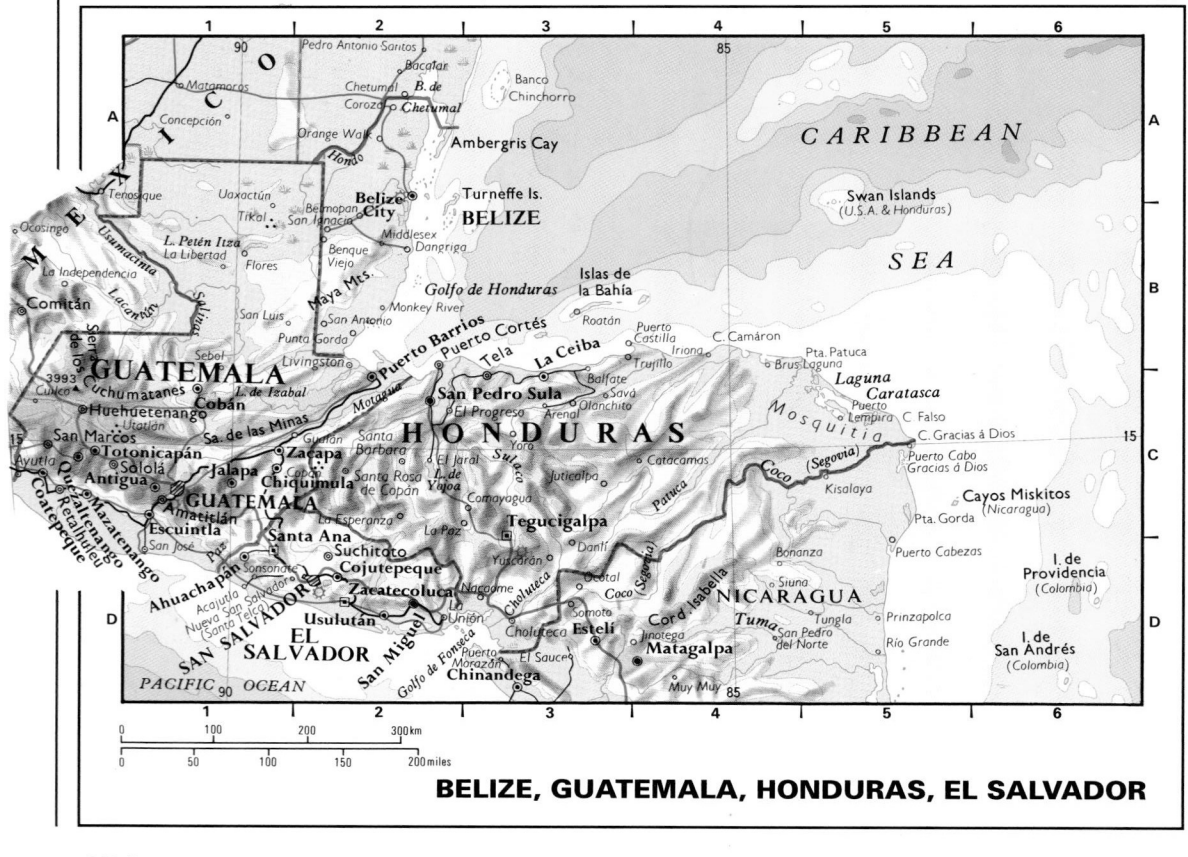

HONDURAS

Second largest of the Central American countries, Honduras has a small population: indeed, it is five times as large as neighbouring El Salvador – its opponent in the famous 'Soccer War' of 1969, triggered by illegal Salvadorean immigration – but has fewer people (5,105,000).

Some 80% of Honduras is mountainous, with peaks of more than 2,500 m [8,000 ft] in the west. The mountain ranges are highly metalliferous: lodes of gold drew the first Spanish *conquistadores* to found Tegucigalpa, the capital, in 1524, and silver is still an important export. Mining contributes more to the economy than it does in any other Central American state. However, the state has a short 124 km [80 ml] frontage on the Pacific in the Gulf of Fonseca, and the limited lowlands around the Gulf form some of the prime cotton lands of the country.

Most of Honduras has a seasonal climate, relatively dry between November and May. Traditional cattle ranching, employing cowboys, is as much in evidence as agriculture. The aromatic pine forests of the east are being consumed by new paper mills on the hot, rain-soaked Caribbean coast. The lower alluvium-filled valleys of the rivers draining into the Caribbean have been reclaimed and the forest replaced by orderly banana plantations.

Honduras was the original 'banana republic' – the world's leading exporter in the interwar years. Today it remains an important crop, accounting for nearly a quarter of exports, with production dominated by two US companies, though coffee is now the largest earner. Dependent on these cash crops, the country is the least industrialized in the region with shrimps and lobsters, timber and roundwood the other main earners of foreign exchange.

It is also the most reliant on the US for trade – quite a claim in Central America: 56% of its imports and 49% of its exports are with the Americans. Aid from the US is crucial, partly in return for services rendered; strategically important to Washington, Honduras allowed the US-backed 'Contra' rebels to operate from its territory against the Communist revolutionary Sandinista government in Nicaragua throughout the 1980s, and in 1990 – following the Sandinistas' defeat in the elections – signed a peace agreement with the pro-American government of Violeta Chamorro. Less enthusiastically, the Honduran Army also collaborated with US efforts to defeat left-wing guerrillas in El Salvador.

After a short civil war in the 1920s a series of military regimes ruled Honduras until 1980, when civilians took over; the country has since had a series of democratically elected pro-American centre-right governments, but with the military retaining considerable influence ■

BELIZE, GUATEMALA, HONDURAS, EL SALVADOR

EL SALVADOR

The only Central American country without a Caribbean coast, El Salvador is also the smallest and the most densely populated; pressure on agricultural land, combined with civil war, has led to widespread emigration. The Pacific coastal plain is narrow and backed by a volcanic range averaging about 1,200 m [4,000 ft] in altitude. El Salvador has over 20 volcanoes, some still active, and crater lakes occupying a fertile central plain 400 to 800 m [1,300 to 2,600 ft] above sea level. Urban and rural populations in this belt together account for 60% of the country's total.

This fertile zone also produces 90% of the coffee and tobacco, and most of the maize and sugar – the foundations of the agricultural economy, with coffee usually accounting for over half the total value of exports. The towns are centres of manufacturing for the domestic market. Inland the frontier with Honduras is marked by mountain ranges which reach heights of 2,000 m [6,560 ft]; previously forested and

An inland waterway on the narrow coastal plain near Jiquilisco, south-east of San Salvador – capital of the most densely populated country in Central America.

empty, they are now attracting migrants desperate for agricultural land – nearly all of which is owned by a tiny white élite in a country where 89% of the people are mestizo (mixed Spanish and Indian) and 9% are pure Indian. As a result there is massive emigration from this crowded country, and it was the underlying cause of the 'Soccer War' with Honduras – which still suspects El Salvador of looking to expand – in 1969.

El Salvador was plagued by conflict from the early 1970s and by full-blown civil war from 1980, when the political left joined revolutionary guerrillas against the US-backed extreme right-wing government. During the next 12 years, more than 75,000 people were killed (mostly civilians) and hundreds of thousands were made homeless as the regime received $4 billion in aid from the US in abetting the 55,000-strong Salvadorean Army and infamous death squads. After 19 months of UN-mediated talks the two sides agreed complicated terms at the end of 1991. A cease-fire took effect in February 1992, but the country remained in disarray, with unemployment, for example, standing at more than 50% of the workforce.

In April 1994, in the country's first peacetime elections in 64 years, the right-wing National Republican candidate (aided by widespread fraud) comfortably beat a left-wing coalition that included Marxists from the former FMLN. Armando Calderon Sól's task was daunting: he took over a country with its infrastructure all but destroyed, coffee prices at an all-time low and foreign aid dwindling ∎

COSTA RICA

In many ways the exception among the Central American republics, Costa Rica ('rich coast') has become the most European of the republics of the isthmus, with the best educational standards, a long life expectancy, the most democratic and stable system of government, the highest per capita gross domestic product, and the least disparity between the poor and the rich. The abolition of the armed forces in 1948 – it has only 750 civil guards – meant there has been no familiar military regime and its neutral stance has enabled the country to play the role of broker in many regional disputes.

Three mountain ranges form the skeleton of the country. In the south-east the Talamanca ranges rise to 3,837 m [12,585 ft] in Chirripo Grande; further north and west the Central Cordillera includes volcanic Irazú (3,432 m [11,260 ft]) and Poas (2,705 m [8,875 ft]), both active in recent decades; Miravalles (2,020 m [6,627 ft]) is one of four active volcanoes in the Cordillera de Guanacaste.

Coffee grown in the interior has been a cornerstone of the economy since 1850; in this century bananas have become a second, and together they supply nearly half of overseas earnings ∎

NICARAGUA

Largest and least densely populated of the Central American countries, Nicaragua's eastern half is almost empty. The Caribbean plain is extensive, and the coast is a mixture of lagoons, sandy beaches and river deltas with shallow water and sandbars offshore. With over 750 cm [300 in] of rain in some years, it is forested and rich in a tropical fauna including crocodiles, turtles, deer, pumas, jaguars and monkeys. Cut off from the populous west of Nicaragua, it was for two centuries the British protectorate of the Miskito Coast, with Bluefields (San Juan del Norte) as the largest settlement.

Inland the plain gives way gradually to mountain ranges broken by basins and fertile valleys. In the west and south they overlook a great depression which runs from the Gulf of Fonseca south-eastwards and contains lakes Managua and Nicaragua. Nicaragua (8,264 sq km [3,191 sq mls]) is the largest lake in Central America; though only 20 km [12.5 mls] from the Pacific, it drains to the Caribbean by the navi-gable San Juan River and formed an important route across the isthmus before the Panama Canal was built. The capital city, Managua, and other major centres are here, as is much of Nicaragua's industrial development; so, too, are the cotton fields and coffee plantations that provide the country's chief cash crops and exports (23% and 36% respectively).

Forty volcanoes, many active, rise above the lakes; San Cristobál (1,745 m [5,725 ft]) is the highest, still-smoking Momotombo the most spectacular. Earthquakes are common and Managua was virtually destroyed in 1931 and 1972.

Nicaragua has been in a state of civil war almost continuously since the 1960s. In 1979, after a 17-year campaign, the long domination of the corrupt Somoza family (who controlled 40% of the economy) was ended by a popular uprising led by the Sandinista National Liberation Front (FSLN), who went on to win democratic power in 1985. Meanwhile, the US trained and supplied Contra guerrillas from bases in Honduras and imposed a trade embargo, pushing Nicaragua into increasing reliance on Soviet aid.

A ceasefire agreed in 1989 was followed the next year by electoral defeat for Daniel Ortega's Sandinistas at the hands of the US-backed coalition of Violeta Chamorro. The win was due mainly to the state of the economy, reduced to crisis point by a combination of US sanctions and government incompetence; an uneasy alliance followed ∎

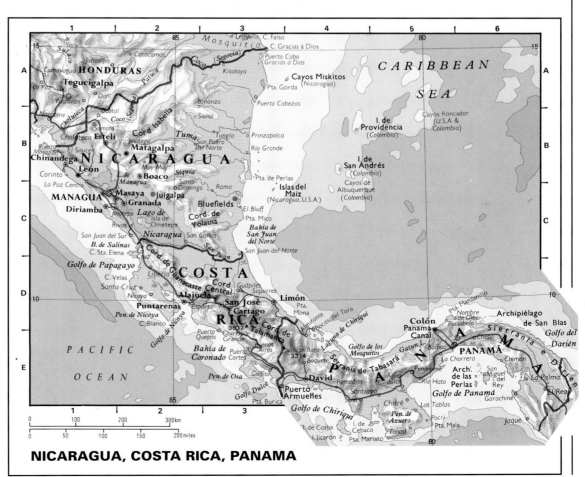

NICARAGUA, COSTA RICA, PANAMA

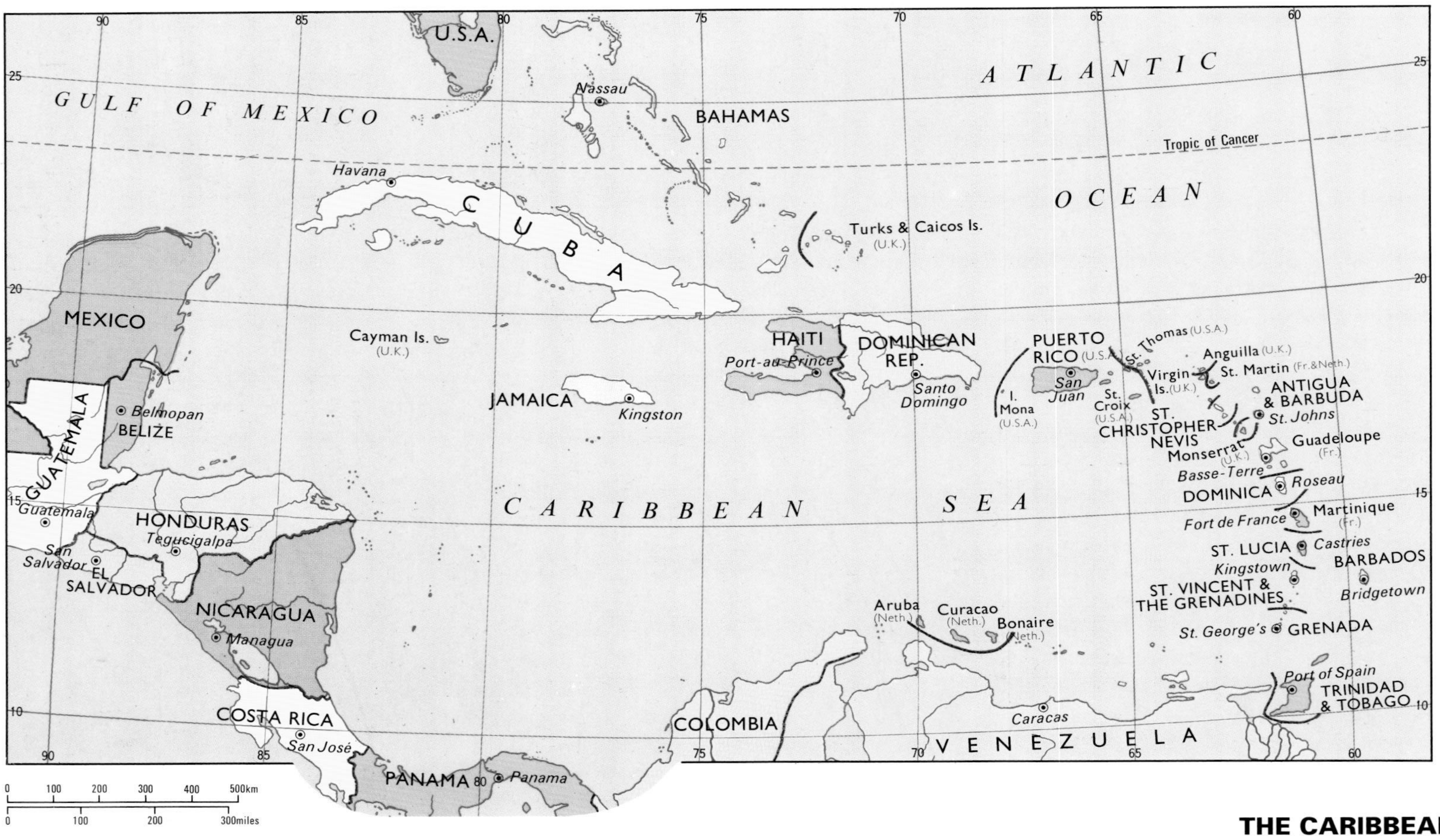

THE CARIBBEAN

PANAMA

Less than 60 km [37 mls] wide at its narrowest point, the isthmus of Panama not only links Central and South America but also, via its Canal, the Atlantic and Pacific Oceans. Most of the country, including some 750 offshore islands, lies below 700 m [2,300 ft], sweltering daily in tropical heat and high humidity, with heavy downpours marking the May-December rainy season.

The mountain ranges trend north-west to south-east slightly against the lie of the country, and fragment the lowlands. Basins and valleys between the ranges support pockets of agriculture, and rainforests have been cleared for production of bananas, coffee, cocoa and sugar cane, for cattle ranching and for subsistence crops of rice and maize. To the east, in Darien, the jungle remains largely undisturbed and still home to a few indigenous Indian tribes.

Many Panamanians live within about 20 km [12 mls] of the Canal Zone, a quarter of them in the capital city; and 80% of the country's GDP originates here. This includes revenues from free trade, the open-registry merchant fleet (some 12,000 ships), and 'offshore' finance facilities. With exports of bananas (25% of total), shrimps (19%) and mahogany, not to mention substantial US aid, these have given Panama the highest standard of living in Central America – though Western confidence in the economy took a dive after the crisis of 1989, when the US invaded to depose General Manuel Noriega, later put on trial in Miami for drug trafficking. Noriega's party, the PRD, returned to power in May 1994 in the new electoral system, despite winning only a third of the vote.

The Panama Canal is 82 km [51 mls] long from deep water at either end, 65 km [40 mls] long from coast to coast. Three sets of locks at each end lift vessels to the elevated central section 26 m [85 ft] above sea level, which includes Gatun Lake and the 13 km [8 ml] Gaillard Cut through the continental divide.

Though an American-built railway crossed the isthmus in 1855, it was a French company under Ferdinand de Lesseps that began cutting the Canal in 1880, but engineering problems and deaths from disease stopped operations after ten years. In 1903 the province of Panama declared independence from Colombia and granted the USA rights in perpetuity over a 16 km [10 ml] wide Canal Zone. Work on the present Canal began a year later, and it was finally opened for shipping in 1914.

In 1980 there were some 13,000 transits through the Canal – over 36 ships per day – carrying twice the total cargo of 1960. Now running close to capacity, the Canal cannot take fully-laden ships of over about 80,000 tonnes (thus excluding most large tankers) and an alternative Panama Seaway is under discussion. From 1979 sovereignty of the Canal Zone was restored to Panama, and the Canal itself reverts at the end of the century ∎

A freighter enters one of three sets of locks on the Panama Canal, used by up to 44 ships a day.

CUBA

As large as all the other Caribbean islands put together, Cuba is only 193 km [120 mls] across at its widest, but stretches for over 1,200 km [750 mls] from the Gulf of Mexico to the Windward Passage. Though large, it is the least mountainous of all the Greater Antilles. The plains run the length of the island from Cape San Antonio in the far west to Guantánamo Bay in the south-east (site of an anomalous US naval base), broken by three sets of mountains which occupy no more than a quarter of the country.

The undulating fringes of these areas provide some of the best tobacco lands, while the higher areas also produce coffee as a cash crop. Sugar cane, however, remains the outstandingly important cash crop, as it has done throughout the century, and Cuba is the world's third largest producer behind the giants of Brazil and India. It uses over 1 million hectares [2.5 million acres], more than half the island country's cultivated land, and accounts for more than 75% of exports.

Before the 1959 Revolution the cane was grown on large estates, many of them owned by US companies or individuals, but after these were nationalized the focus of production shifted eastwards to Guayabal, with the USSR and Eastern European countries replacing the USA as the main market. Cattle raising and rice cultivation have also been encouraged to help diversify the economy, while Cuba is also a significant exporter of minerals, notably nickel.

A colony until 1898, Cuba took on many Spanish immigrants during the early years of independence. Since the Revolution that deposed the right-wing dictator Fulgencio Batista and brought Fidel Castro to power in 1959 – when 600,000 people fled the island, many of them to Florida – rural development has been fostered in a relatively successful bid to make the quality of life more homogeneous throughout the island. Havana, the chief port and capital, was particularly depopulated.

Cuba's relationship with the US, which secured its independence from Spain but bolstered the corrupt regimes before the revolution, has always been crucial. In 1961, US-backed 'exiles' attempted to invade at the Bay of Pigs, and relations worsened still further in 1962 when the attempted installation of Soviet missiles on Cuban soil almost led to global war. A close ally of the USSR, Castro has encouraged left-wing revolutionary movements in Latin America and aided Marxist governments in Africa, notably in Angola, while emerging as a Third World leader.

The rapid changes in Eastern Europe and the USSR from 1989 to 1991 left Cuba isolated as a hardline Marxist state in the Western Hemisphere, and the disruption of trade has severely affected the economy of a country heavily dependent on subsidized Soviet oil and aid. This undermines Castro's considerable social achievements, but a new Cuba is almost inevitable given the collapse of Communism around the world – and his advancing years.

By 1993 the dual pressures of an aid drought and ruthless US trade embargo (imposed in 1962) were crippling Cuba's economy, and Castro's government allowed a limited degree of free enterprise. Aid and support agencies claimed that social conditions on the island, badly hit by March storms, were deteriorating rapidly, and called for the US to lift its blockade.

Meanwhile, restrictions on the access of hundreds of thousands of exiles waiting in the US were eased – though they would have to wait much longer for the counter-revolution and their permanent return ∎

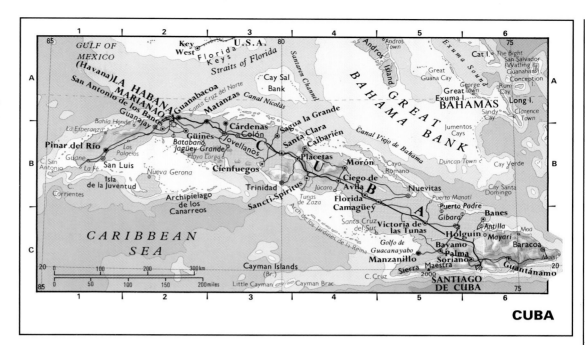

CUBA

JAMAICA

Third largest of the Caribbean islands and the most populous in the English-speaking 'West Indies', Jamaica has a central range culminating in Blue Mountain Peak (2,256 m [7,402 ft]), from which it declines westwards. Called Xaymaca ('land of wood and water') by the Arawak Indians, half the country lies above 300 m [1,000 ft] and moist south-east trade winds bring rain to the mountains, windward slopes receiving up to 500 cm [200 in] in a normal year; hurricanes may bring exceptionally heavy rains during the later part of the wet season, which extends from May to October – as well as devastation, as with Gilbert in 1988.

The 'cockpit country' in the north-west of the island is an inaccessible limestone area of steep broken ridges and isolated basins. These offered a refuge to escaped slaves prior to emancipation in 1838. Elsewhere the limestone has weathered to bauxite, an ore of aluminium. Bauxite overlies a quarter of the island; mined since 1952, most is exported as ore, about one-fifth as alumina, making Jamaica the world's third producer and accounting for nearly 40% of exports. Tourism and bauxite production, Jamaica's two most important industries, comprise almost two-thirds of foreign earnings. In 1988 the island had over a million visitors, spending more than US$500 million. Garment manufacture, bananas and illegal marijuana are also important elements of an economy hampered by large foreign debts.

Sugar, a staple product since the island became British in 1655, first made Jamaica a prized imperial possession, and the African slaves imported to work the plantations were the forefathers of much of the present population. But the plantations disappeared and the sugar market collapsed in the 19th century; today sugar contributes only about 10% of the country's foreign earnings.

Michael Manley's democratic socialist experiment in the 1970s was followed by a modest growth in the 1980s; but unemployment and underemployment are currently rife, and many Jamaicans leave their country each year to work abroad, mainly in the USA, Canada and the UK ∎

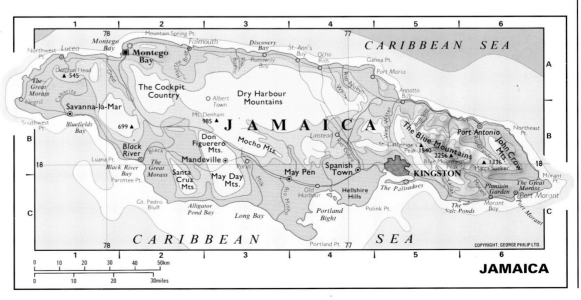

JAMAICA

HAITI

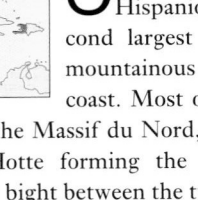

Occupying the western third of Hispaniola, the Caribbean's second largest island, Haiti is mainly mountainous with a long, indented coast. Most of the country is centred around the Massif du Nord, with the narrow Massif de la Hotte forming the southern peninsula. In the deep bight between the two lies the chief port and capital, Port-au-Prince. Haiti has few natural resources and most of the workforce is engaged on the land, with coffee the only significant cash crop. Two-thirds of the population, however, lives at or below the poverty line, subsisting on small-scale agriculture and fishing.

Ceded to France in 1697, a century before the rest of Hispaniola, Haiti developed as a sugar-producing colony. Once the richest part of the Caribbean, it is now the poorest nation in the Western Hemisphere. For nearly two centuries, since a slave revolt made it the world's first independent black state in 1804, it has been bedevilled by military coups, government corruption, ethnic violence and political instability, including a period of US control from 1915 to 1934.

The appalling regime of François Duvalier ('Papa Doc'), president from 1957 and declaring himself 'President for Life' in 1964, was especially brutal, but that of his son Jean-Claude ('Baby Doc'), president from 1971, was little better; both used their murderous private militia, the Tontons Macoutes, to conduct a reign of terror. In 1986 popular unrest finally forced Duvalier to flee the country, and the military took over. After another period of political chaos and economic disaster – not helped by the suspension of US aid between 1987 and 1989 – the country's first multiparty elections were held in December 1990, putting in office a radical Catholic priest, Father Jean-Bertrand Aristide, on a platform of sweeping reforms.

Haitians head for market down the steps of the Sans Souci Palace. The image of decadent post-colonialism could not be more apt for a country in chaotic decline.

But with the partisans of the old regime, including the Tontons Macoutes, still powerful, the military took control in September 1991, forcing Aristide to flee (to Venezuela) after only seven months of government. Tens of thousands of exiles followed in the ensuing weeks, heading mainly for the US naval base at Guantánamo Bay, in Cuba, in the face of a wave of savage repression, but the American government returned the 'boat people' to Port-au-Prince. Military intervention (as in Panama in 1989) was considered by the Organization of American States, but they instead imposed a trade embargo, inflicting further hardship on an impoverished Haitian population. Despite UN resolutions and an accord with the military rulers in July 1993 for the return of Aristide, the elected leader continued to languish in Washington ∎

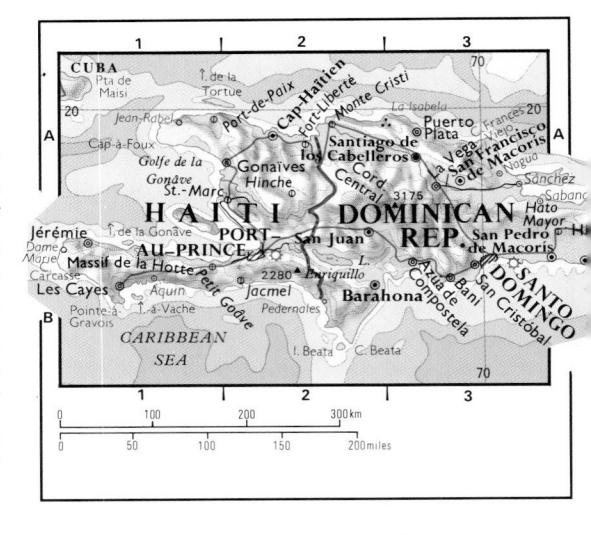

DOMINICAN REPUBLIC

Second largest of the Caribbean nations in both area and population, the Dominican Republic shares the island of Hispaniola with Haiti, occupying the eastern two-thirds. Of the steep-sided mountains that dominate the island, the country includes the northern Cordillera Septentrional, the huge Cordillera Central (rising to Pico Duarte, at 3,175 m [10,417 ft] the highest peak in the Caribbean), and the southern Sierra de Bahoruco. Between them and to the east lie fertile valleys and lowlands, including the Vega Real and the coastal plains where the main sugar plantations are found. Typical of the area, the Republic is hot and humid close to sea level, while cooler and fresher conditions prevail in the mountains; rainfall is heavy, especially in the north-east.

Columbus 'discovered' the island and its native Amerindian population (soon to be decimated) on 5 December 1492; the city of Santo Domingo, now the capital and chief port, was founded by his brother Bartholomew four years later and is the oldest in the Americas. For long a Spanish colony, Hispaniola was initially the centrepiece of their empire but later it was to become its poor relation. In 1795 it became French, then Spanish again in 1809, but in 1821 (then called Santo Domingo) it won independence. Haiti held the territory from 1822 to 1844, when on restoring sovereignty it became the Dominican Republic. Growing American influence culminated in occupation from 1916 to 1924, followed by a long period of corrupt dictatorship. Since a bitter war was ended by US military intervention in 1965, a precarious fledgling democracy has survived violent elections under the watchful eye of Washington.

In the 1980s, growth in industry (exploiting vast hydroelectric potential), mining (nickel, bauxite, gold and silver) and tourism have augmented the traditional agricultural economy based on sugar (still a fifth of exports), coffee, cocoa, tobacco and fruit. This highly Americanized Hispanic society is, however, far from stable; and only neighbouring Haiti has a lower GDP per head figure in the Caribbean ∎

TURKS AND CAICOS

A group of 30 islands (eight of them inhabited), lying at the eastern end of the Grand Bahama Bank, north of Haiti, the Turks and Caicos are composed of low, flat limestone terrain with scrub, marsh and swamp providing little agriculture. Previously claimed by France and Spain, they have been British since 1766, administered with Jamaica from 1873 to 1959 and a separate Crown Colony since 1973, with a governor representing the British monarch. A third of the 12,000 population, mainly of mixed Afro-European descent, lives in the capital of Cockburn Town on Grand Turk.

Tourism has recently overhauled fishing (chiefly lobsters) as the main industry, with direct flights from Miami feeding the new airport on the main tourist island of Providenciales. Offshore banking facilities are also expanding, though these were harmed in the mid-1980s by allegations of ministerial drug-trafficking and organized crime ∎

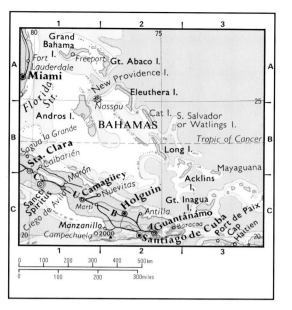

BAHAMAS

Acoral-limestone archipelago of 29 inhabited low-lying islands, plus over 3,000 uninhabited cays, reefs and rocks, centred on the Grand Bahama Bank off eastern Florida and Cuba, the Bahamas has developed close ties with the USA since independence from Britain in 1973.

Over 90% of its 3 million visitors per year are Americans, and tourism now accounts for more than half the nation's revenues, involving some 40% of the workforce. Offshore banking, financial services and a large 'open registry' merchant fleet also offset imports (including most foodstuffs), giving the country a relatively high standard of living. The remainder of the non-administrative population works mainly in traditional fishing and agriculture, notably citrus fruit production.

Though the Bahamas is an independent democracy, it is also élitist. Relations with the US were strained when it was used as a tax haven for drug traffickers in the 1980s, with government ministers implicated in drug-related corruption.

However, in the Caribbean only the Cayman Islands, Bermuda and Aruba have a higher GDP per head figure (US$10,280 in 1991) and the standard of living for most Bahamians is comfortable; compare that with the pitiful figure for Haiti (US$369).

While the climate is enviable, tempered by trade winds to give warm summers and mild winters, the Bahamas are also on the end of the curved hurricane path from the eastern Caribbean between July and November. Summer thunderstorms can also cause severe damage across the islands ■

CAYMAN ISLANDS

The Cayman Islands comprise three low-lying islands covering 259 sq km [100 sq mls], south of Cuba, with the capital Georgetown (population 12,000, in a total of 27,000) on the biggest, Grand Cayman. A dependent territory of Britain (Crown Colony since 1959), they were occupied mainly with farming and fishing until the 1960s, when an economic revolution transformed them into the world's biggest offshore financial centre, offering a secret tax haven to 18,000 companies and 450 banks. Drug trafficking has waned since 1986. The flourishing luxury tourist industry (predominantly from US sources) now accounts for more than 70% of its official GDP and foreign earnings, while a property boom has put beachfront prices on Grand Cayman among the world's highest. An immigrant labour force, chiefly Jamaican, constitutes about a fifth of the population – similar to European and black groups; the rest are of mixed descent ■

BRITISH VIRGIN ISLANDS

Like their larger American neighbours, the British Virgin Islands were 'discovered' by Columbus in 1493. Most northerly of the Lesser Antilles, they comprise four low-lying islands of note and 36 islets and cays, covering a total of 153 sq km [59 sq mls]. The largest island, Tortola, contains over three-quarters of the total population of 17,000, a third of whom live in the capital Road Town. Dutch from 1648 but British since 1666, they are now a British dependent territory enjoying (since 1977) a strong measure of self-government.

Though an increasing rival to the Caymans and the Turks and Caicos in offshore banking from 1985, with 6,000 companies already registered by 1988, tourism is the main source of income, agriculture being limited by the low rainfall and poor soils. Most food has to be imported, and rum is the chief export. The US, Puerto Rico and the neighbouring US Virgin Islands are the main trading partners ■

US VIRGIN ISLANDS

The US Virgin Islands were Spanish from 1553, Danish from 1672 and, for a sum of US$25 million, American from 1917 – Washington wishing to protect the approaches to the newly-built Panama Canal. As an 'unincorporated territory', the residents have been US citizens since 1927, and from 1973 have elected a delegate to the House of Representatives. The 68 islands (dominated by the three largest – St Thomas, St Croix and St John) total 340 sq km [130 sq mls] and host a population of 117,000, more than 100,000 of them split almost evenly between St Croix and St Thomas, home of the capital Charlotte Amalie. The ethnic breakdown is about 80% black and 15% white.

Tourism is now the main industry, notably cruise ships but also airborne day-trippers from the USA to the duty-free shops of St Thomas. Construction is continuing to grow, and the islands have the highest density of hotels and 'condominiums' (apartment buildings with private units) in the Caribbean ■

PUERTO RICO

Ceded by Spain to the USA in 1898, Puerto Rico ('rich port') became a self-governing commonwealth in free political association with the USA after a referendum in 1952. Though this gave the island a considerable measure of autonomy, American influence stretches well beyond its constitutional roles in defence and immigration. Full US citizens, Puerto Ricans pay no federal taxes – but nor do they vote in US elections. Debate over the exact status of the country subsided in the 1970s, the compromise apparently accepted as a sensible middle way between the extremes of being the 51st state of the US or completely independent, but resurfaced with the boom years, a referendum in December 1991 narrowly rejecting a proposal to guarantee 'the island's distinct cultural identity' – a result interpreted as a move towards statehood. Meanwhile, free access to the US has relieved the growing pressure created by one of the greatest population densities in the New World, with New York traditionally the most popular destination; the immigrants, however, are not always welcome.

Easternmost of the major Greater Antilles, Puerto Rico is mountainous, with a narrow coastal plain; Cerro de Punta (1,338 m [4,389 ft]) is the highest peak. Flat ground for agriculture is scarce, mainly devoted to cash crops like sugar, coffee, bananas and, since the arrival of Cuban refugees, tobacco, as well as tropical fruits, vegetables and various spices.

However, the island is now the most industrialized and urban nation in the Caribbean – nearly half the population lives in the San Juan area – with chemicals constituting 36% of exports and metal products (based on deposits of copper) a further 17%. Manufacturing, dominated by US companies attracted by tax exemptions, and tourism are now the two growth sectors in a country where the standard of living (while low in US terms) is nevertheless the highest in Latin America outside the island tax havens, and rising.

Washington's internal revenue code grants tax exemptions to American companies based on the island, provided they pay 10% of their profits into the Puerto Rican government's development bank. The Puerto Rican administration has offered to utilize US$840 of this fund – standing at a total of US$7 billion – to help the expansion of industry in countries involved with the CBI (Caribbean Basin Initiative), mainly by establishing plants for semi-manufactured goods. The scheme echoes 'Operation Bootstrap', begun in the late 1940s which changed Puerto Rico from 'the poorhouse of the Caribbean' to one of Latin America's strongest economies ■

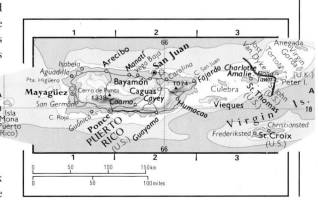

ANGUILLA

Deriving its name from its 'discovery' in 1493 by Columbus – *anguil* is Spanish for eel – Anguilla is indeed long and thin, a low coral atoll covered with poor soil and scrub, measuring 96 sq km [37 sq mls]. First colonized by Britain in 1690 and long administered with St Kitts and Nevis, the island was subject to intervention by British troops in 1969 to restore legal government following its secession from the self-governing federation in 1967. Its position as a separate UK dependent territory (colony) was confirmed in 1971 and formalized in 1980 ∎

ST CHRISTOPHER AND NEVIS

The first West Indian islands to be colonized by Britain (1623 and 1628), St Christopher and Nevis became independent in 1983. The federation comprises two well-watered volcanic islands, mountains rising on both to around 1,000 m [3,300 ft], and about 20% forested. St Christopher is usually shortened to St Kitts; Nevis derives its name from Columbus (1493), to whom the cloud-covered peaks were reminiscent of Spanish mountains (*nieves* meaning snow). Thanks to fine beaches tourism has replaced sugar, nationalized in 1975 and still producing 57% of exports, as the main exchange earner ∎

ANTIGUA AND BARBUDA

Antigua and Barbuda are strategcally situated islands linked by Britain after 1860; gaining internal self-government in 1967 and independence in 1981. They rely heavily on tourism, though some attempts at diversification (notably Sea Island cotton) have been successful. Run by the Antiguan Labour Party almost without break since 1956, its white-owned sugar industry – accounting for most of exports in the 1960s – was closed down in 1971 ∎

MONTSERRAT

Colonized from 1632 by Britain, which brought in Irish settlers, Montserrat (though still a UK dependent territory) has been self-governing since 1960. The island measures 102 sq km [39 sq mls] and has a population of 13,000, nearly a quarter living in the capital, Plymouth; 96% are of African descent.

Though tourism is the mainstay of the economy it is well supported by exports of electronic equipment, Sea Island cotton, fruit and vegetables; unusually for the Caribbean, it is almost self-sufficient in food. Traditional cotton was once the main industry, but new ones have moved in under generous tax concessions ∎

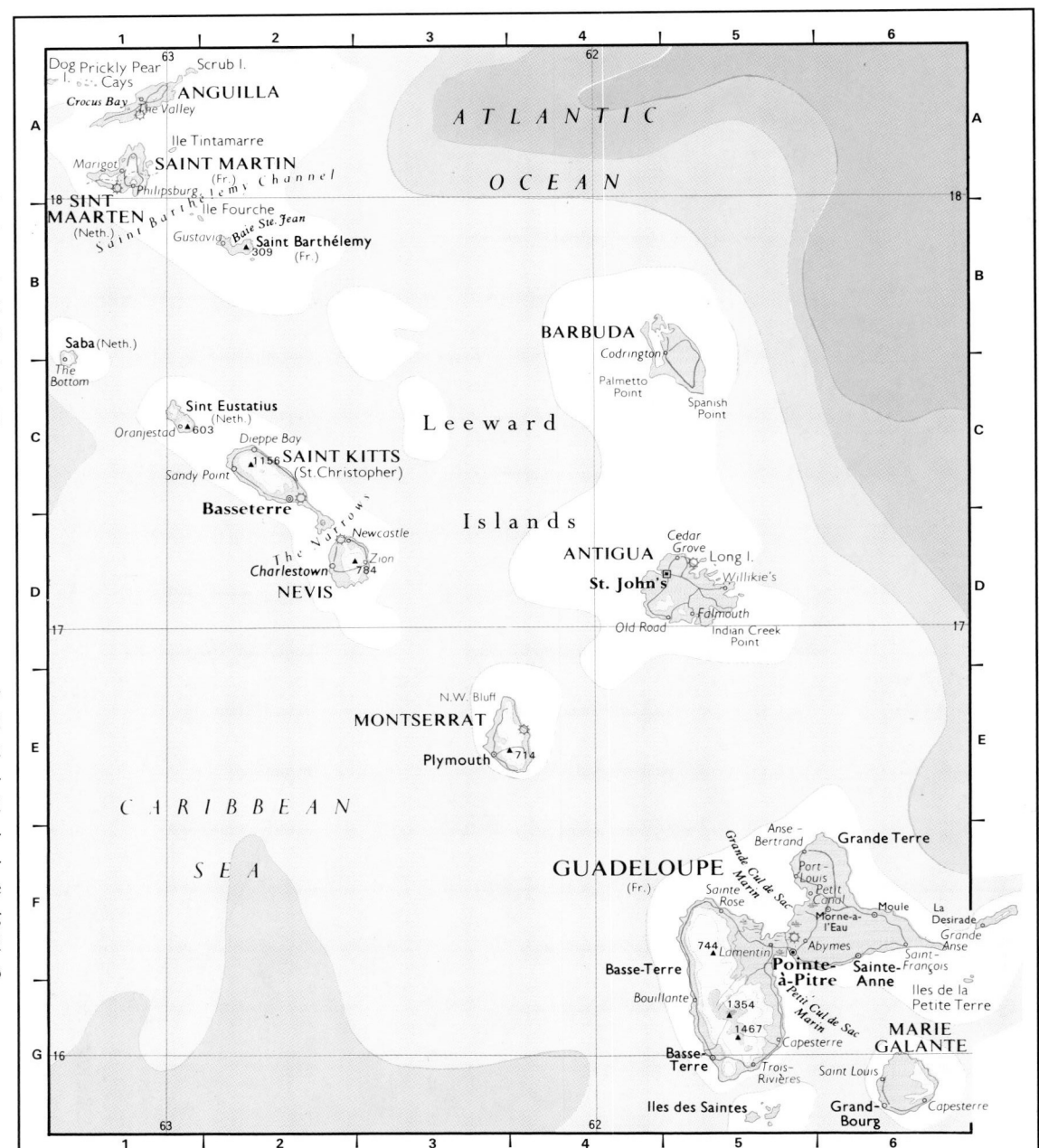

CARIBBEAN ISLANDS

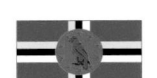

GUADELOUPE

Slightly the larger of France's two Caribbean overseas departments, Guadeloupe comprises seven islands including Saint-Martin and Saint-Barthélemy to the north-west, with a total population of 345,000. Over 90% of the area, however, is taken up by Basse-Terre, which is volcanic – La Soufrière (1,467 m [4,813 ft]) is the highest point in the Lesser Antilles – and the smaller Grande-Terre, made of low limestone; the two are separated by a narrow sea channel called Rivière-Salée (Salt River). The commercial centre of Pointe-à-Pitre (population 25,000) is on Grande-Terre.

Food is the biggest import (much of it from France), bananas the biggest export, followed by wheat flour, sugar, rum and aubergines. French aid has helped create a reasonable standard of living, but despite this and thriving tourism – the majority of it from France and the USA – unemployment is high. Though sharing an identical history to Martinique, Guadeloupe has a far stronger separatist movement, which sporadically resorts to acts of terrorism ∎

DOMINICA

Dominica has been an independent republic (the Commonwealth of Dominica) since 1978, after 11 years as a self-governing UK colony; Britain and France fought long over the island, ownership decided in 1805 by a ransom of £12,000 (then US$53,000). The population of 83,000 is over 90% African and 6% mixed, with small Asian and white minorities and a settlement of about 500 mainly mixed-blood Carib Indians. Predominantly Christian (80% Catholic), most people speak the local French patois, though English is the official language. Nearly 25% of the islanders live in the capital, Rosseau, and its suburbs.

Dominica is a mountainous, forested island of 751 sq km [290 sq mls], its indented coast edged with steep cliffs. Though rich soils support dense vegetation, less than 10% is cultivated; bananas and coconut-based soaps are the chief exports. Much food is imported, and future prospects for a relatively poor Caribbean island depend a good deal on the development of luxury tourism ∎

ST LUCIA

First settled by the British in 1605, St Lucia changed hands between Britain and France 14 times before finally being ceded formally in 1814. Internally self-governing as 'Associated State of the UK' from 1967, it gained full independence in 1979. A mountainous, forested island of extinct volcanoes – graphically represented on its flag – St Lucia boasts a huge variety of plant and animal life. To the south of its highest point of Mt Gimie (949 m [3,114 ft]) lies the Qualibou, an area containing 18 lava domes and seven craters. In the west are the dramatic Pitons.

Though not poor, St Lucia is still dependent on bananas, a crop easily hit by hurricane and disease ■

The dramatic Pitons rise to over 750 m [2,460 ft] behind the town of Soufrière on St Lucia's west coast.

ST VINCENT AND THE GRENADINES

St Vincent and the Grenadines comprise the main island (constituting 89% of the area and 95% of the population) and the Northern Grenadines, of which the largest are Bequia, Mustique and Canouan, with Union the furthest south. 'Discovered' in 1498, St Vincent was settled in the 16th century and became a British colony with the Treaty of Versailles in 1783, after a century of conflict with France, often supported by the Caribs – the last of whom were deported to Honduras after the Indian War of 1795-7. The colony became self-governing in 1969 and independent in 1979.

St Vincent is a mountainous, volcanic island that boasts luxuriant vegetation. Soufrière (1,178 m [3,866 ft]), which last erupted in 1979, is one of two active volcanoes in the eastern Caribbean – Mt Pelée is the other. Bananas account for 38% of exports, but the island is also the world's biggest producer of arrowroot (for medicines and computer paper). It remains, however, less prosperous than its neighbours ■

MARTINIQUE

Martinique was 'discovered' by Columbus in 1493, colonized by France from 1635 and, apart from brief British interludes, has been French ever since. It became an overseas department in 1946 – enjoying the same status and representation as *départements* – and, like Guadeloupe, was made an administrative region in 1974. Despite a more homogeneous population than its neighbour, the island has a less vociferous independence movement – though in the 1991 elections the separatists made substantial gains, winning 19 of the 41 seats in the provincial assembly.

Martinique comprises three groups of volcanic hills and the intervening lowlands. The highest peak is Mt Pelée, notorious for its eruption of 1902, when in minutes it killed all the inhabitants of St Pierre

GRENADA

The most southern of the Windward Islands, the country of Grenada also includes the Southern Grenadines, principally Carriacou. Formally British since 1783, a self-governing colony from 1967 and independent in 1974, it went Communist after a bloodless coup in 1979 when Maurice Bishop established links with Cuba. After Bishop was executed by other Marxists in 1983, the US (supported by some Caribbean countries) sent in troops to restore democracy, and since the invasion the ailing economy has been heavily reliant on American aid.

Mainly mountainous and lush, Grenada is known as 'the spice island of the Caribbean' and is the world's leading producer of nutmeg, its main crop. Cocoa, bananas and mace also contribute to exports, but attempts to diversify the economy from an agricultural base have been largely unsuccessful. In the early 1990s there were signs that the tourist industry was finally making a recovery after the debilitating events of 1983 ■

(estimated at about 28,000) except one – a prisoner saved by the thickness of his cell.

Bananas, rum and pineapples are the main agricultural exports, but tourism (mainly French and American) is the biggest earner; transport equipment and food, chiefly from France, are the main imports. The industrial sector includes cement, food processing and oil refining, using Venezuelan crude ■

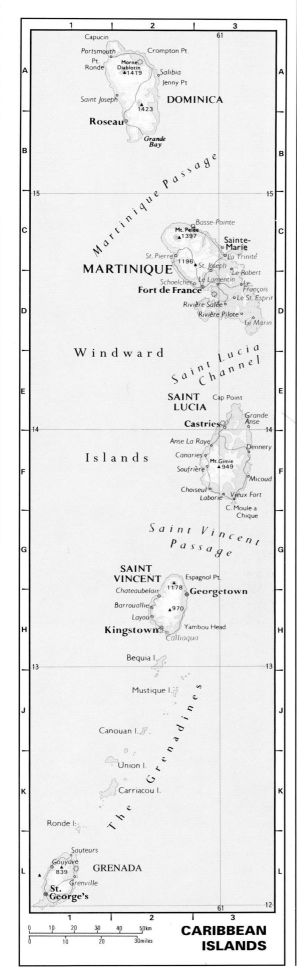

CARIBBEAN ISLANDS

NETHERLANDS ANTILLES

The Netherlands Antilles consists of two very different island groups – Curaçao and Bonaire, off the coast of Venezuela, and Saba, St Eustacius and the southern part of St Maarten, at the northern end of the Leeward Islands, some 800 km [500 mls] away. With Aruba, they formed part of the Dutch East Indies, in 1954 attaining internal self-government as constitutional equals with the Netherlands and Surinam. Curaçao is politically dominant in the federation; it is the largest island, accounting for nearly 45% of the total of 993 sq km [383 sq mls] and 80% of the population of 191,000, almost half of it in the capital Willemstad. The people – mainly mulatto, Creole-speaking and Catholic – are well off by Caribbean standards, enjoying the benefits of an economy buoyed by tourism, offshore banking and oil refining (from Venezuela), mostly for export to the Netherlands, more than the traditional orange liqueur. Curaçao may eventually follow Aruba's path, reducing the federation from five islands to four, hoping to stimulate the economy with its own currency ∎

BARBADOS

The most eastern Caribbean country, and first in line for the region's seasonal hurricanes, Barbados is underlain with limestone and capped with coral. Mt Hillaby (340 m [1,115 ft]), the highest point, is fringed by marine terraces marking stages in the island's emergence from the sea. Soils are fertile and deep, easily cultivated except in the north-east.

Barbados became British in 1627 and sugar production, using African slave labour, began soon afterwards. Cane plantations take up most of the cropped land (over half the total), but at 17% now contributes far less than previously to exports. Manufactures now constitute the largest exports, though tourism is the growth sector and the leading industry (430,000 visitors in 1988), and is the most likely future for this relatively prosperous but extremely overcrowded island; at 593 per sq km [1,536 per sq ml], it is one of the most densely populated 'rural' societies in the world (42% urban) ∎

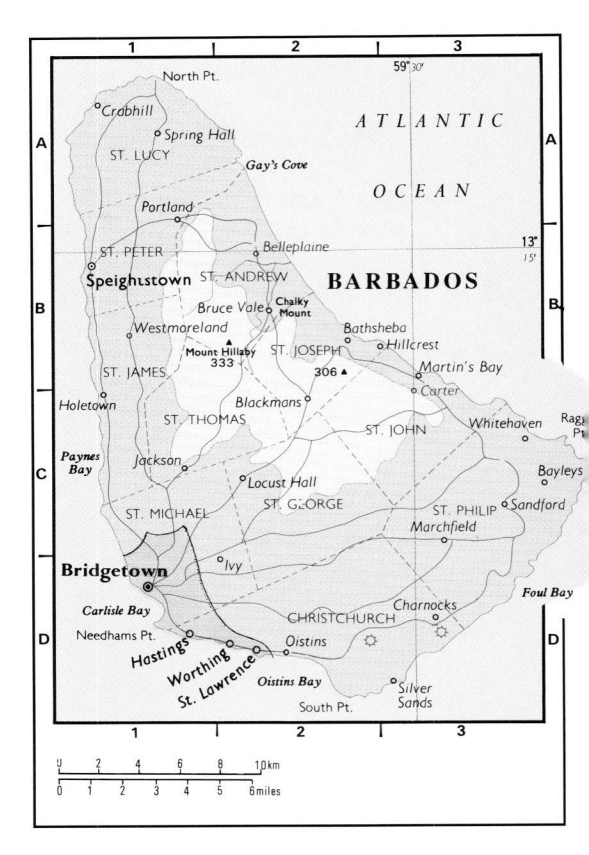

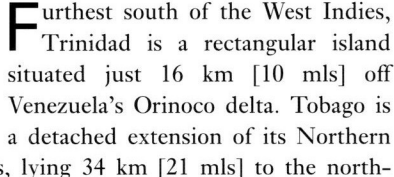

TRINIDAD AND TOBAGO

Furthest south of the West Indies, Trinidad is a rectangular island situated just 16 km [10 mls] off Venezuela's Orinoco delta. Tobago is a detached extension of its Northern Range of hills, lying 34 km [21 mls] to the north-east. Trinidad's highest point is Cerro Aripe (940 m [3,085 ft]) in the rugged, forested Northern Range; the capital, Port of Spain, nestles behind the hills on the sheltered west coast.

'Discovered' by Columbus in 1498, Trinidad was later planted for sugar production by Spanish and French settlers before becoming British in 1797. Black slaves worked the plantations until emancipation in 1834, when Indian and some Chinese indentured labourers were brought in. Indian influence is

Wooded slopes fringe Charlotteville on the far north-east coast of Tobago. Linked with Trinidad since 1899, the island (population 45,000 to Trinidad's 1.18 million) is now pushing for internal self-government.

still strong in many villages, with African in others. Tobago was competed for by Spain, Holland and France before coming under British control in 1814, joining Trinidad to form a single colony in 1899. Independence came in 1962 and a republic was established in 1976.

Both islands are valued for their agricultural produce, including sugar, coffee, cocoa, rubber and citrus fruits, but the main source of income is oil. First exploited in 1867, it has been the lifeblood of the nation's economy throughout the 20th century, giving the island a relatively high standard of living, and (with petrochemicals) still accounts for over 70% of exports, much of it now from offshore rigs. Falling prices in the 1980s had a severe effect, however, only partly offset by the growth of tourism and asphalt ∎

ARUBA

A dry, flat limestone island and the most western of the Lesser Antilles, Aruba measures 193 sq km [75 sq mls]. Incorporated into the Netherlands Antilles in 1845, and part of the self-governing federation from 1954, Aruba held a referendum in 1977, which supported autonomy. With Dutch agreement (in 1981) it separated from the Antilles on 1 January 1986, and full independence is due in 1996.

The country has a population of 62,400, a third living in the capital of Oranjestad. About half the people are of Arawak Indian stock; on most Caribbean islands the Amerindian population was extirpated by genocide, disease or transportation. While petrochemicals, fertilizers and tourism are important, over half of export earnings still come from beverages and tobacco, while foodstuffs account for over half of imports ∎

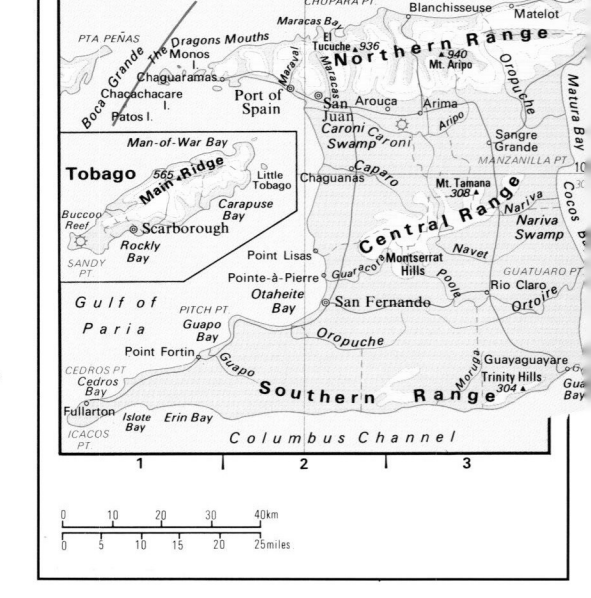

South America

SOUTH AMERICA

Occupying 12% of the Earth's land surface, South America has three structural parts – the Andes Mountains, the river basins and plains, and the ancient eastern highlands. The Andes run almost the entire length of the continent for about 8,000 km [5,000 mls]. Glaciers and snowfields grace many of

The Andes run almost the entire length of western South America, rising steeply from the coastal plains. Huascarán, in Peru, is 6,768 m [22,205 ft] high, yet only just over 100 km [62 mls] from the Pacific.

the peaks, some of which rise to over 6,550 m [21,000 ft]; Aconcagua (6,960 m [22834 ft]), in Argentina, is the highest mountain outside Asia. West of the Andes lies a narrow coastal strip, except in the far south and on Tierra del Fuego ('Land of Fire').

Three vast river basins lie to the east of the Andes: the *llanos* of Venezuela, drained by the Orinoco, the Amazon Basin (occupying 40% of the continent), and the great Paraguay-Parana-Uruguay Basin that empties into the River Plate estuary. The highlands are the rolling Guiana Highlands of the north, and the more extensive Brazilian plateau that fills and gives shape to South America's eastern

RIGHT *Argentino is the most southern of several large lakes on the windswept plateaus of Patagonia. Sheep rearing has been the main occupation here ever since Welsh immigrants arrived in the early 19th century.*

bulge. Both are of hard crystalline rock, geologically much older than the Andes, and their presence helps to explain the wanderings and meanderings of the great river systems.

South America has great climatic variety, due partly to the wide latitudinal extent of the continent but also to the great range of altitude; 80% falls within the tropics, but height may temper the tropical

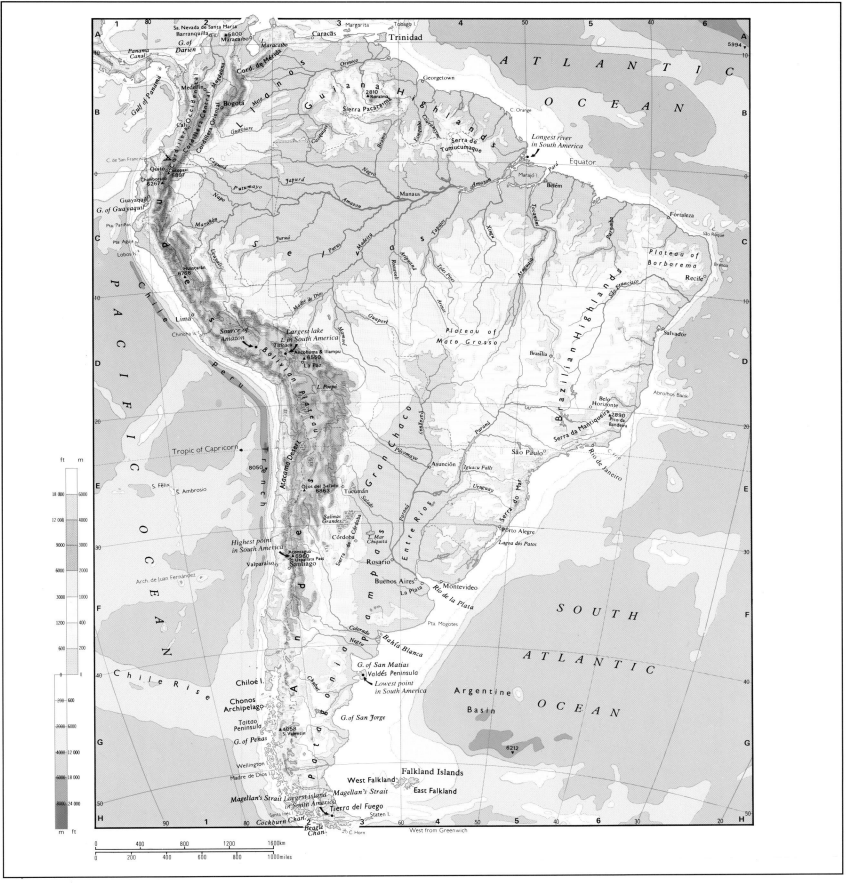

A 1 80 2 3 Margarita Tobago I. 4 50 5 40 6 A
5994

Sa. Nevada de Santa Marta
Barranquilla 5800 Caracas Trinidad
Maracaibo Margarita
Panamá Canal G. of Darien Maracaibo A T L A N T I C
Cord. de Mérida Orinoco Georgetown
Medellín Guaviare Sierra Pacaraima Serra de O C E A N B
Cali Bogotá 2810 Roraima Tumucumaque
C. Orange Longest river
in South America

C. de San Francisco Equator
Quito Cotopaxi 5897 Amazon Pará
Chimborazo Napo Marajó I.
6267 Putumayo Japurá Manaus Belém Fortaleza
Guayaquil Negro São Roque C
G. of Guayaquil Marañón Amazon Tocantins
Pta. Parinas Juruá Purus Madeira Tapajós Xingú Araguaia C. Branco
Pta. Aguja Ucayali Plateau of
Lobos Is. Huascarán Borborema
6768 Recife

Lima Madre de Dios Guaporé Plateau of São Francisco 10
Source of Mato Grosso
Amazon Largest lake Salvador
L. in South America Mamoré Brasília
Titicaca Ancohuma & Illampu Abrolhos Bank D
6550 Belo
L. Poopó La Paz Horizonte 2890
Pico da
Bandeira
Serra da Mantiqueira

Tropic of Capricorn Paraná São Paulo
8050 Pilcomayo Rio de Janeiro
Ojos del Salado Asunción Iguaçu Falls
6863 Tucumán Uruguay E
S. Félix Salado Serra do Mar
S. Ambrosio Salinas Paraná Pôrto Alegre
Grandes Córdoba L. Mar Lagoa dos Patos
Chiquita

Highest point Sierra de Córdoba Rosario
in South America Entre Rios
Aconcagua 6960 Buenos Aires
Valparaíso Uspallata Pass La Plata Montevideo
Santiago Río de la Plata
S O U T H
Arch. de Juan Fernández Pta. Mogotes F
A T L A N T I C
Colorado Bahía Blanca
Negro O C E A N

G. of San Matias Argentine
Chiloé I. Valdés Peninsula Basin
Lowest point
Chonos in South America
Archipelago G
Taitao G. of San Jorge 6212
Peninsula 4058
G. of Peñas S. Valentín

Wellington Falkland Islands
Madre de Dios West Falkland
Magellan's Strait Largest island Magellan's Strait East Falkland H
in South America Tierra del Fuego
Santa Inés I. Staten I.
Cockburn Chan. West from Greenwich
Beagle Chan.
C. Horn
90 1 80 2 3 4 50 5 6 40 20

0 400 800 1200 1600km
0 200 400 600 800 1000miles

ft m
18 000 6000
12 000 4000
9000 3000
6000 2000
3000 1000
1200 400
600 200
0 0
200 600
2000 6000
4000 12 000
6000 18 000
8000 24 000
m ft

175

climate considerably – for example, in the Altiplano of Bolivia. The natural flora and fauna are equally varied. Long isolation from the rest of the world allowed a great variety of plants and animals to evolve, and this natural variety has not yet been reduced significantly by human pressures. Electric eels, carnivorous piranha fish, manatees, river dolphins, amphibious boa constrictors, sloths, anteaters, armadillos, several kinds of marsupials, camel-like guanacos and llamas, rheas, Andean condors and humming birds are some of the many indigenous animals.

Many of the plants found useful to man – potato, cassava, quinoa, squashes, sweet potato, cacao, pine-apple and rubber, for example – were originally South American, and the vast forests of the Amazon and Andes may yet contain more. Pressures on the natural fauna and flora are growing, however, in a continent that is, so far, weak on conservation.

South America is prodigal, too, with mineral wealth. Silver and gold were the first attractions but petroleum, iron, copper, and tin are also plentiful, and many reserves have yet to be exploited. The people – who could still prove Latin America's greatest resource – include a rich mix of original Amerindians, Spanish and Portuguese colonial immigrants, African slaves, and a later generation of immigrants and refugees from the turmoils of Europe. Though large and growing fast, the population is still small compared with the vast potential of the continent ■

RIGHT *Flooded plains in Surinam. Over 90% of the country is covered in dense tropical rainforest – the world's highest figure.*

BELOW RIGHT *Despite being sandwiched between the Pacific Ocean and the Andes, the Atacama Desert in northern Chile is the world's driest habitat: Calama, for example, received no recorded rainfall in the four centuries to 1971.*

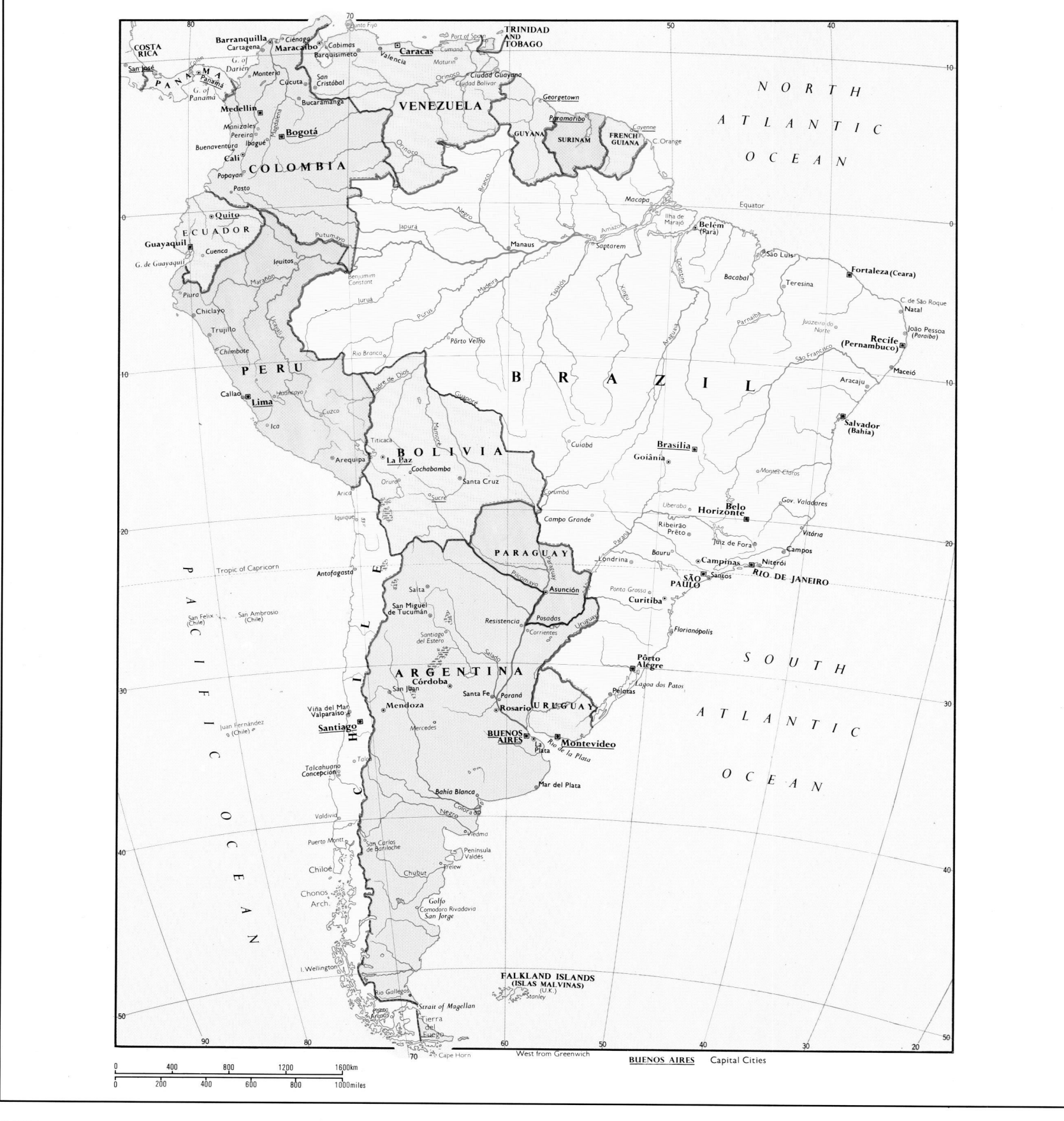

COLOMBIA

Christopher Columbus sighted the country that would bear his name in 1499, and the Spanish conquest of the territory began ten years later. The nation gained independence from Spain following a decade of conflict in 1819, and since the 19th century the two political parties, the pro-clerical, centralizing Conservatives and the anti-clerical, federal-oriented Liberals, have regularly alternated in power. Their rivalry led to two brutal civil wars (1899–1902 and 1949–57), in which some 400,000 people lost their lives: the 1950s conflict, known as 'La Violencia', claimed 280,000 of them. In 1957 the two parties agreed to form a coalition, and this fragile arrangement – threatened by right-wing death squads, left-wing guerillas and powerful drug cartels – lasted until the Liberal President Virgilio Barco Vargas was elected by a record margin in 1986. Even by the violent standards of South America, however, Colombia remains politically unstable.

The Andes cross Colombia from south to north, fanning out into three ranges with two intervening valleys. In the west the low Cordillera Occidental rises from the hot, forested Pacific coastal plain. Almost parallel to it, and separated by the Cauca Valley, is the much higher Cordillera Central; the high peaks of this range, many of them volcanic, rise to over 5,000 m [16,400 ft].

To the east, across the broad valley of the Magdalena River, lies the more complex Cordillera Oriental, which includes high plateaus, plains, lakes and basins; the capital city, Bogotá, is situated on one of the plateaus, at a height of 2,610 m [8,563 ft]. North-west of the mountains lies the broad Atlantic plain, crossed by many rivers. The Andean foothills to the east, falling away into the Orinoco and Amazon basins and densely covered with rainforest (albeit rapidly diminishing), occupy about two-thirds of the total area of the country. Less than 2% of the population, mainly cattle-rangers and Indians, live east of the mountains.

Little of the country is under cultivation, but much of the land is very fertile and is coming into use as roads improve. The range of climate for crops is extraordinary and the agricultural colleges have different courses for 'cold-climate farming' and 'warm-climate farming'. The rubber tree grows wild and fibres are being exploited, notably the 'fique', which provides all the country's requirements for sacks and cordage. Colombia is the world's second biggest producer of coffee, which grows mainly in the Andean uplands, while bananas, cotton, sugar and rice are important lowland products. Colombia imports some food, though the country has the capacity to be self-sufficient. Drugs, however, may be the biggest industry: it was reported in 1987 that cocaine exports earn Colombia more than its main export, coffee.

Colombia was the home of El Dorado, the legendary 'gilded one' of the Chibcha Indians, but today the wealth is more likely to be coal or oil. The country has the largest proven reserves of coal in Latin America (18 billion tonnes) and is South America's biggest exporter. Gold, silver, iron ore, lead, emeralds (90% of world production) and other minerals are plentiful, and hydroelectric power is increasingly being developed. Petroleum is an important export and source of foreign exchange; large

THE DRUGS TRADE

Colombia is notorious for its illegal export of cocaine, and several reliable estimates class the drug as the country's most lucrative source of foreign exchange. US agencies estimated that in 1987 retail sales of South American cocaine totalled $22 billion – earning about $2 billion in foreign exchange for the producers to reinvest in their own countries, often in property.

Violence, though focused on the drug capitals of Medellín and Cali, is endemic, with warfare between both rival gangs and between producers and the authorities an almost daily occurrence. Assassinations of civil servants, judicial officials, police officers or anyone attempting to investigate, control or end the rule of the multimillionaire drug barons are commonplace.

In February 1990, as part of President George Bush's $10.6 billion 'war on drugs', the governments of three Andean states – Colombia, Bolivia and Peru – joined forces with the US Drug Enforcement Agency in a concentrated attempt to clamp down on the production and distribution of cocaine – a virtually impossible task given the demand for cocaine and 'crack', its major derivative.

reserves have been found in the north-eastern areas of Arauca and Vichada and in 1991 proven reserves were put at 1.3 billion barrels. In 1992 BP increased its exploration programme amid speculation that new finds were among the world's biggest ∎

A coffee plantation in the Cordillera Central. Colombia is the world's leading exporter of the crop – though Brazil remains the world's leading producer.

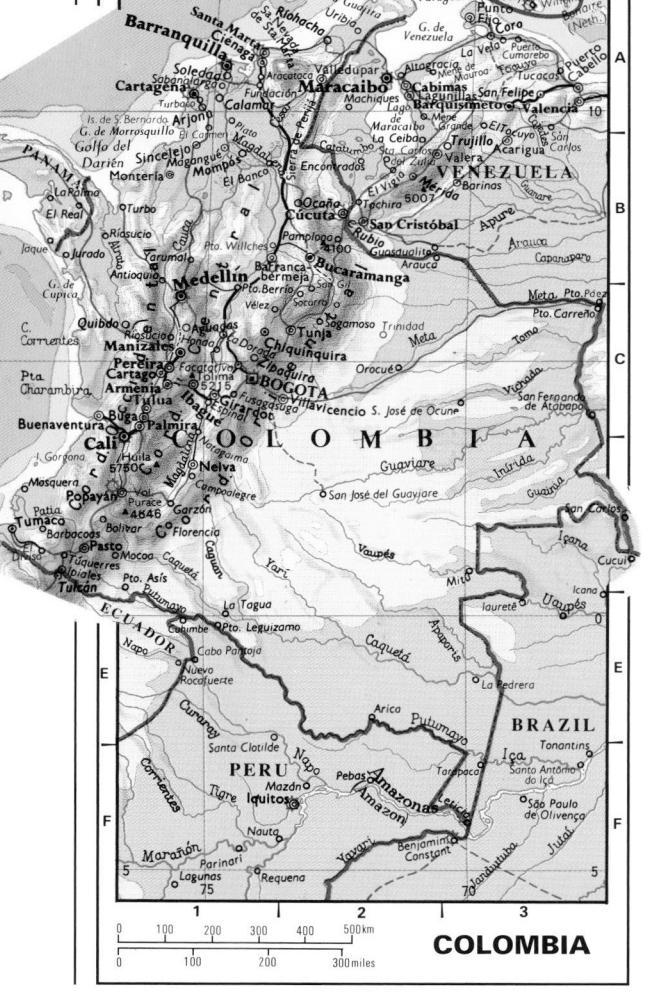

COLOMBIA

VENEZUELA

Sighted by Columbus in 1498, the country was visited by Alonzo de Ojeda and Amerigo Vespucci in 1499, when they named it Venezuela ('Little Venice'). It was part of the Spanish colony of New Granada until 1821 when it became independent, first in federation with Colombia and Ecuador and then, from 1830, as a separate independent republic under the leadership of Simón Bolívar. Between 1830 and 1945 the country was governed mainly by dictators; after frequent changes of president, a new constitution came into force in 1961 and since then a fragile civilian-rule democracy has been enjoyed, resting on widespread repression and corruption, with all presidents completing their term of office, despite periodic violence.

Landscape

In the north and north-west of Venezuela, where 90% of the population lives, the Andes split to form two ranges separated from each other by the Maracaibo basin. At 5,007 m [16,427 ft], snow-capped Merida is the highest of several tall peaks in the area. Above 3,000 m [10,000 ft] are the *paramos* – regions of grassland vegetation where Indian villagers live; temperatures are mild and the land is fertile. By contrast, Maracaibo swelters in tropical heat alongside the oilfields that for half a century have produced Venezuela's wealth.

The mountains running west to east behind the coast from Valencia to Trinidad have a separate geological history and gentler topography. Between the ranges are fertile alluvial basins, with many long-established market towns. Caracas, the teeming capital, was one such town before being expanded and modernized on the back of the 1970s oil boom. It now has to take a rapidly swelling population and is fringed with the shanties of hopeful immigrants from poor rural areas.

South of the mountains are the *llanos* of the Orinoco – mostly a vast savanna of trees and grasslands that floods, especially in the west, during the April-to-October rains. This is now cattle-raising country. The Orinoco itself rises on the western rim in the Guiana Highlands, a region of high dissected plateaus made famous as the site of Arthur Conan Doyle's *Lost World*, and dense tropical forest makes this still a little-known area. Mount Roraima, the highest peak, rises to 2,810 m [9,217 ft] at the conjunction of the border with Guyana (with whom Venezuela has a grumbling territorial dispute – as it does with Colombia) and Brazil.

Not far to the north, however, lies Cerro Bolívar, where iron ore is mined and fed to the steel mills of Ciudad Guayana, a new industrial city built on the Orinoco since 1960. The smelting is powered by hydroelectricity from the nearby Caroni River, and a new deep-water port allows 60,000-tonne carriers to take surplus ore to world markets. Modern developments in a primeval setting typify the changes that Venezuela is undergoing.

Industry

Oil made Venezuela a rich country, but the wealth was always distributed very unevenly and concentrated in the cities – hence the rapid urbanization that made 17

out of every 20 Venezuelans a city dweller and left enormous areas of the country unpopulated.

Commercially-viable reserves of oil were found in Venezuela in 1914, and by the 1930s the country had become the world's first major oil exporter – the largest producer after the USA. The industry was nationalized in 1976 but by 1990 there were signs of dangerous dependence on a single commodity controlled by OPEC and in plentiful supply, while the large foreign debt saw austerity measures that triggered a violent reaction from many Venezuelans. The oil-producing region around Maracaibo covers an area of 77,700 sq km [30,000 sq mls] and is thought to contain South America's largest known oil reserves, while producing three-quarters of the nation's total. Exploration for oil is also being carried on offshore in the Caribbean.

Before the development of the oil industry Venezuela was predominantly an agricultural country, but 85% of export earnings are now from oil and some of the profits from the industry help to fund developments in agriculture and other industries, including the exploitation of natural gas. Gold, nickel, iron ore, copper and manganese are also found and aluminium production has increased following further discoveries of bauxite; aluminium has now replaced iron ore as the second most important export earner. Manufactures include cement, steel, chemicals, food processing, shipbuilding and vehicles.

Agriculture can supply only 70% of the country's needs. Only 5% of the arable land is cultivated and much of that is pasture. The chief crops are sugar cane, coffee, bananas, maize and oranges; there is also substantial dairy and beef production ■

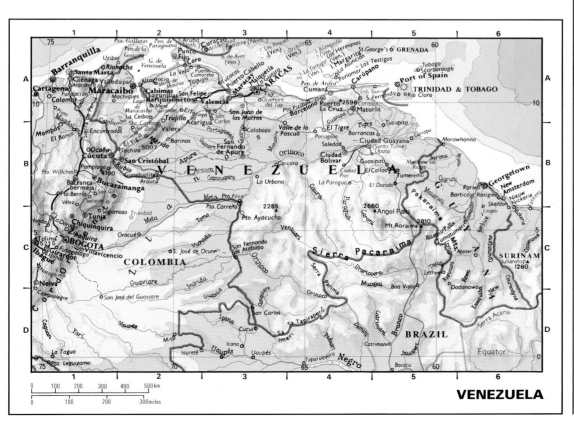

VENEZUELA

PERU

Largest of the Andean states, Peru is spread over coastal plain, mountains and forested Amazon lowlands in the interior. It was formerly the homeland of Inca and other ancient civilizations, and has a history of human settlement stretching back over 10,500 years. The last Inca empire ended in the 16th century with the arrival of the Spaniards, who made Peru the most important of their viceroyalties in South America.

The coastal plain is narrow and mainly arid, cooled by sea breezes from the offshore Humboldt Current. Occasionally it suffers violent rainstorms, associated with shifts in the pattern of surface waters. Rivers that cut through the foothills provide water for irrigated agriculture, mainly of cotton, rice and sugar cane. The middle slopes of the Andes – the Quechua, at heights of 2,000 to 3,500 m [6,500 to 11,500 ft] – are warm-temperate and fairly well watered. These areas supported the main centres of Indian population in the Inca empire, and are just as well suited to densely populated rural settlements today.

Above stand the higher reaches of the Andes, extending westwards in cold inhospitable tablelands at 4,000 to 4,800 m [13,000 to 15,700 ft], cultivated up to 4,200 m [13,700 ft] by peasant farmers and grazed by their sheep, alpacas, llamas and vicuñas. The snowy peaks of the high Andes rise to over 6,000 m [19,500 ft]. Though close to the Pacific Ocean, most of the rivers that rise here eventually drain into the Amazon. Their descent to the lowlands is through the *montaña*, a near-impenetrable maze of valleys, ridges and plains, permanently soaked by rain and thickly timbered. Beyond extend the Amazon lowlands – hot, wet and clad mainly in dense tropical rainforest. Occupying half the country, they are thinly inhabited by Indians.

Lima was developed as the Spanish colonial capital, and through its port of Callao passed much of the trade of Spanish settlers; 19th-century exports included guano (bird-droppings, valuable as an agri-

Alpacas in the arid Andes, near Lake Titicaca. Like the llama bred from the wild guanaco, the alpaca is sheared every two years for up to 5 kg [111 lb] of long, fine, silky wool.

PERU

cultural fertilizer) from the offshore islands, and wild rubber. Peru gained independence from Spain in 1824, but difficulties of communication, political strife, earthquakes and other disasters (including the worst cholera outbreak in the Americas this century), and a chronically unbalanced economy have dogged the country's development.

Today Peru faces many economic, social and political problems. Agricultural production has failed to keep up with population, so wheat, rice, meat and other staple foods are imported. Cotton, coffee and sugar are exported. Peru is the leading producer of coca, the shrub used in the illegal production of

cocaine, and earnings were thought to be in excess of US$3 billion in the 1980s. An agreement was reached in February 1990 with the USA to stop the planting of coca in some areas and instead to plant oil palms, but success has been limited and much still finds its way to Colombia for processing and re-export.

Peru once had the largest fish catch in the world and there are 70 canning factories. Anchoveta was the main target, but fishing was halted from 1976 until 1982 because of depleted stocks. In 1983 a warm current known as 'El Niño' ruined the fishing but recovery followed from 1986.

Several metals are exported, including silver, zinc

THE ANDES

Created 200 million years ago by the collision of the Nazca plate and the land mass of South America – and still moving at about 12.5 mm [0.5 in] each year – the Andes mountain system extends along the entire west side of the continent from the coast of the Caribbean to Tierra del Fuego for over 6,400 km [4,000 mls], making it the world's longest chain.

It is the highest range outside the Himalayas and Argentina's Cerro Aconcagua, at 6,960 m [22,834 ft], is the highest peak outside Asia. Argentina shares with Chile four of the ten highest summits. In the middle section there are two main chains and elsewhere three, with the breadth exceeding 800 km [500 mls] to the north of latitude 20°S.

Many of South America's great rivers, including the Orinoco, Negro, Amazon and Madeira, rise in the Andes.

THE INCA CIVILIZATION

The empire of the Incas, centring on Cuzco in the Peruvian Highlands, developed from millennia of earlier Andean civilizations that included the Chavin, the Nazca and the Tiahuanaco. The Incas began their conquests about AD 1350, and by the end of the 15th century their empire extended from central Chile to Ecuador. Perhaps some 10 million people owed allegiance to it when it fell to the plundering Spanish *conquistadores* in 1532.

The empire was military and theocratic, with the sun as the focus of worship. The people were farmers, using elaborate irrigation systems and terraced fields.

The Incas had no written script: buildings and terracing – notably those of 'the lost city' of Machu Picchu (*left*) northwest of Cuzco – and delicate gold and silver ornaments form their main memorials, though fragments of Inca culture and beliefs remain among the Quechua-speaking peoples of Peru and Bolivia.

and lead, with copper the most important earner. However, industrial unrest has reduced production dramatically. Exports of oil are growing, providing much-needed foreign capital for industrial development, now forthcoming after a lull following Peru's limiting of debt repayment in 1985. Peru's inflation rate – 3,400% in 1989 and a staggering 7,480% in 1990 – settled down to a modest 200% or so in 1991, the same year that many state industries were liberalized.

The economic problems facing Peru are coupled with the terrorist activity and involvement in the illegal drugs trade by the Maoist Sendero Luminoso ('Shining Path'), which began in 1980. Over 23,000 people have been killed since their activities began, and the government, among Latin America's most repressive, has taken strong action against the group, including the arrest of its leader, Abimael Guzmán, in September 1992 ■

ECUADOR

The Incas of Peru conquered Ecuador in the 15th century but in 1532 a colony was founded by the Spaniards in the territory, then called Quito. Independence from Spain was achieved in 1822, when it became part of Gran Colombia, and full independence followed in 1830.

Ecuador's name comes from the Equator, which divides the country unequally; Quito, the capital, lies just within the southern hemisphere. There are three distinct regions – the coastal plain (Costa), the Andes, and the eastern alluvial plains of the Oriente.

The coastal plain, averaging 100 km [60 mls] wide, is a hot, fertile area of variable rainfall. Recently cleared of forests and largely freed of malaria, it is now good farmland where banana farms, coffee and cocoa plantations and fishing are the main sources of income, with the country's commercial centre of Guayaquil a flourishing port.

The national flag flutters from the rooftop of a government building in Quito, the capital of Ecuador.

The Andes form three linked ranges across the country, with several of the central peaks rising above 5,000 m [16,400 ft]. Quito, an old city rich in art and architecture from a colonial past, has a backdrop of snow-capped mountains, among them Cotopaxi – at 5,896 m [19,340 ft] the world's highest active volcano – and Chimborazo (6,267 m [20,556 ft]). The Oriente, a heavily forested upland, is virtually unexploited except for recent developments of oil and natural gas.

Ecuador's economy was based on the export of bananas, for which the country was world leader, and is still the biggest exporter, but this changed from 1972 when oil was first exploited with the opening of the trans-Andean pipeline linking with the tanker-loading port of Esmeraldas.

Shortage of power limits much development in the manufacturing industry – even in the mid-1980s only 60% of the people had use of electricity ■

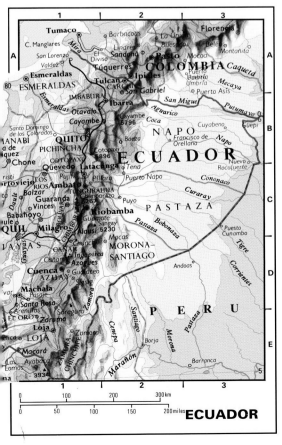

ECUADOR

GUYANA

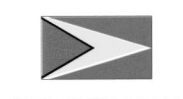

A traditional building appears incongruous in the industrial centre of Georgetown, the Guyanese capital and the country's chief port. The city has nearly a fifth of the total national population of 800,000.

The 'land of many waters' was settled by the Dutch between 1616 and 1621. The territory was ceded to Britain in 1814, and in 1831 British Guiana was formed. Independent since 1966, Guyana – the only English-speaking country in South America – became a republic in 1970. It is largely uninhabited and 95% of the population live within a few kilometres of the coast, leaving the interior virtually empty.

The vast interior, covering 85% of the land area, includes low forest-covered plateaus, the wooded Rupununi savannas, meandering river valleys, and the spectacular Roraima Massif on the Venezuela-Brazil border. The coastal plain is mainly artificial, reclaimed from the tidal marshes and mangrove swamps by dykes and canals.

Land reclamation for sugar and cotton planting began in the 18th century under Dutch West India Company rule, using slave labour, and continued through the 19th century after the British took over, with indentured Asian labour replacing slaves after emancipation. Today sugar remains the main plantation crop, with production largely mechanized, most of it in the lower Demerara River area.

The Asian community, however, who make up about half the total Guyanan population, are involved in rice growing. Bauxite mining and alumina production are well-established industries, combining with sugar production to provide 80% of the country's overseas earnings. But neither sugar nor rice provide year-round work and unemployment remains a stubborn problem. The economy, which is 80% state-controlled, entered a prolonged economic crisis in the 1970s, and in the early 1980s the situation was exacerbated by the decline in the production and the price of bauxite, sugar and rice. Following unrest, the government sought to replace Western aid by turning for help to socialist countries, but in the late 1980s Western aid and investment were again sought ∎

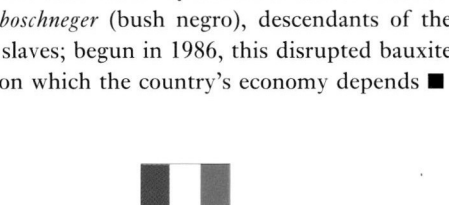

SURINAM

Although Spaniards visited as early as 1499, Surinam was first settled by British colonists in 1651. In 1667 it was ceded to Holland in exchange for Nieuw-Amsterdam, now New York, and was confirmed as a Dutch colony, called Dutch Guiana, in 1816.

Surinam has a coastline of 350 km [218 mls] of Amazonian mud and silt, fringed by extensive mangrove swamps. Behind lies an old coastal plain of sands and clays, bordering a stretch of sandy savanna. The heavily forested interior uplands further to the south are part of the Guiana Highlands, whose weathered soils form the basis of the bauxite industry.

Surinam's hot, steamy climate grows an abundance of bananas, citrus fruits and coconuts for export, with rice and many other tropical commodities for home consumption. Plantations were initially worked by African slaves, later by Chinese and East Indian indentured labour. Bauxite and its derivatives, shrimps and bananas are the main exports, but though 92% of the land is covered by forest – the world's highest figure – little is commercially exploited. There is also considerable potential for expansion of the tourist industry.

In 1980 there was a military coup and later, in 1982, after the execution of 15 opposition leaders and the banning of all political parties, the Netherlands broke off relations and suspended all aid; however, following elections, the Netherlands agreed to resume aid in 1988. This was badly needed because of a rebellion of *boschneger* (bush negro), descendants of the African slaves; begun in 1986, this disrupted bauxite mining on which the country's economy depends ∎

FRENCH GUIANA

The smallest country in South America, French Guiana has a narrow coastal plain comprising mangrove swamps and marshes, alternating with drier areas that can be cultivated; one such is the site of the capital, Cayenne. Inland, a belt of sandy savanna rises to a forested plateau.

A French settlement was established in 1604 by a group of merchant adventurers, and after brief periods of Dutch, English and Portuguese rule the territory finally became permanently French in 1817. In 1946 – a year after the closure of Devil's Island, the notorious convict settlement – its status changed to that of an overseas department of France, and in 1974 it also became an administrative region.

The economy is very dependent on France, both for budgetary aid and for food and manufactured goods. The French have also built a rocket-launching station near the coast at Kourou. Timber is the most important natural resource; bauxite and kaolin have been discovered but are largely unexploited. Only 104 sq km [40 sq mls] of the land is under cultivation where sugar, cassava and rice are grown. Fishing, particularly for shrimps, much of which are exported, is a leading occupation ∎

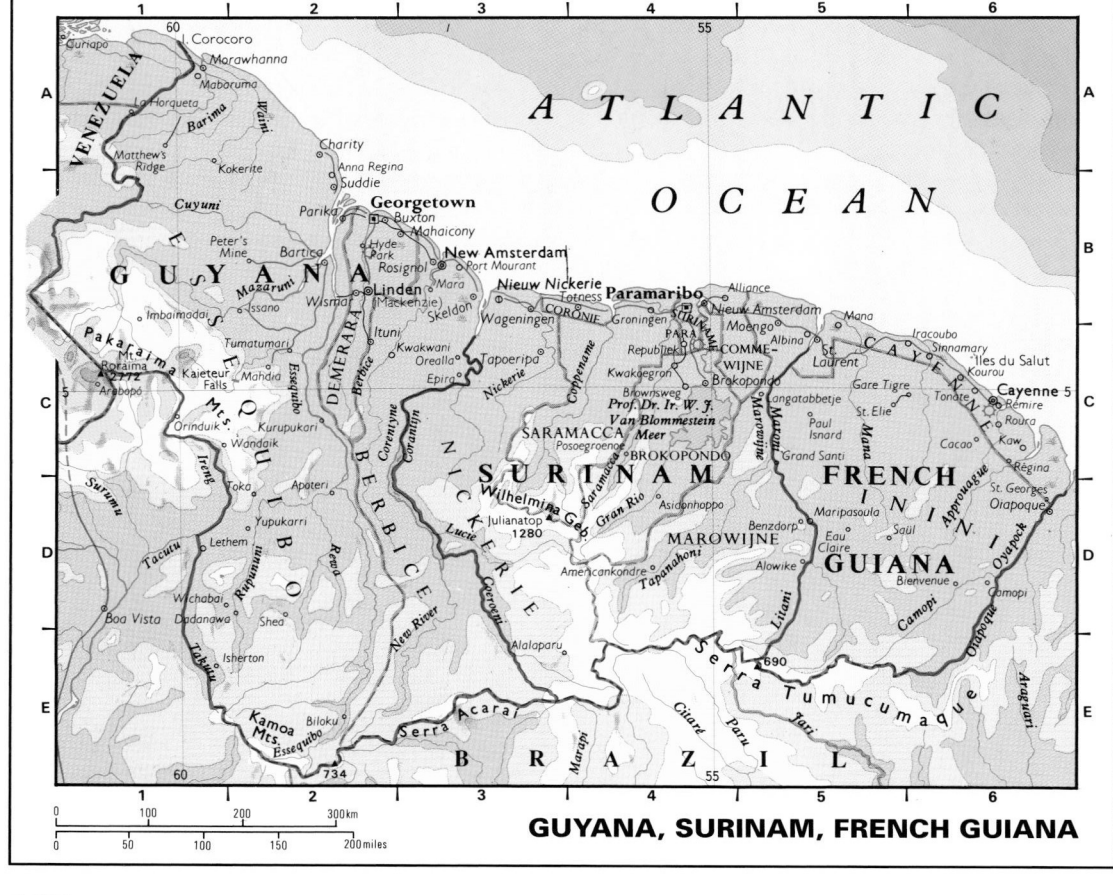

GUYANA, SURINAM, FRENCH GUIANA

BRAZIL

By any standards Brazil is a big country. The fifth largest in the world, it covers nearly 48% of South America. Structurally, it has two main regions. In the north lies the vast Amazon Basin, once an inland sea and now drained by a river system that carries one-fifth of the Earth's running water. In the centre and south lies the sprawling bulk of the Brazilian Highlands, a huge extent of hard crystalline rock deeply dissected into rolling uplands. This occupies the heartland (Mato Grosso), and the whole western flank of the country from the bulge to the border with Uruguay.

Landscape

The Amazon River rises in the Peruvian Andes, close to the Pacific Ocean, and many of its tributaries are of similar origin. Several are wide enough to take boats of substantial draught (6 m [20 ft]) from the Andean foothills all the way to the Atlantic.

The largest area of river plain lies in the upper part of the basin, along the frontier with Bolivia and Peru. Downstream the flood plain is relatively narrow, shrinking in width to a few kilometres where the basin drains between the Guiana Highlands in the north and the Brazilian Highlands in the south. Overall, only 1–2% of the Amazon Valley is alluvial flood plain; away from this the soils are heavily leached and infertile, and liable to be washed away by tropical rainstorms if the protective canopy of forest is felled: this, unfortunately, is happening at an increasingly alarming rate.

The undulating plateau of the northern highlands also carries poor soils; here rainfall is seasonal, and the typical natural vegetation is a thorny scrub forest, used as open grazing for cattle herds. Further south scrub turns to wooded savanna – the *campo cerrado* vegetation that covers 2 million sq km [770,000 sq mls] of the interior plateau. It extends into the basin of the Paraná River and its tributaries, most of which start in the coastal highlands and flow east, draining ultimately into the Plate estuary. The Mato Grosso, on the border with Bolivia, is part of this area and still largely unexplored. The north-eastern uplands are poor farming country; dry for at least half the year, they occasionally suffer long periods of drought.

Conditions are better in the south, with more reliable rainfall. The south-east includes a narrow coastal plain, swampy in places and with abundant rainfall throughout the year; behind rises the Great Escarpment (820 m [2,700 ft]), first in a series of steps to the high eastern edge of the plateau. Over 60% of Brazil's population live in four southern and south-eastern states that account for only 17% of the total area.

History and politics

Brazil was 'discovered' by Pedro Alvarez Cabral on 22 April 1500 and gradually penetrated by Portuguese missionaries, explorers and prospectors during the 17th and 18th centuries. Many of the semi-nomadic Indians indigenous to the country were enslaved for plantation work or driven into the interior, and some 4 million African slaves were introduced, notably in the sugar-growing areas of the north-east.

Little more than a group of rival provinces, Brazil began to unite in 1808 when the Portuguese royal

RIO DE JANEIRO AND SÃO PAULO

Much of Brazil's population is concentrated in a relatively small and highly developed 'corner' in the south-east of the country. Rio de Janeiro, discovered by the Portuguese in 1502, lies in a magnificent setting, stretching for 20 km [12 mls] along the coast between mountain and ocean, its harbour overlooked by Sugar Loaf Mountain (*above*, with Ipanema Beach) and, on Corcovado, the famous statue of Christ. Though no longer the capital, it remains the focus of Brazil's cultural life, attracting visitors with the great pre-Lent festival at carnival time.

São Paulo, its early growth fuelled by the coffee boom of the late 19th century, is the most populous city in the southern hemisphere and rivals Mexico City as the world's fastest growing and largest conurbation. Estimates state that the 1985 total of 15.5 million will increase to 23.6 million by the year 2000. In both cities the yawning gap between rich and poor is all too evident, the sprawling shanty towns (*favelas*) standing in sharp contrast to sophisticated city centres. Amazingly, despite endemic corruption, these cities have yet to witness revolution.

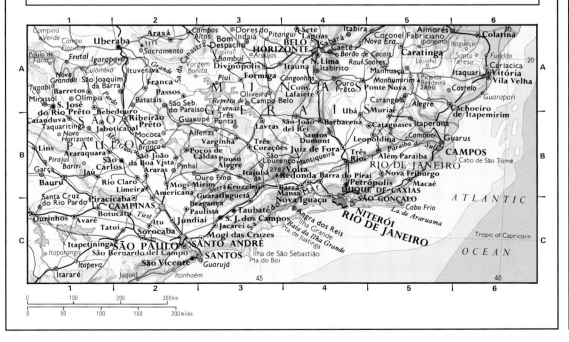

court, seeking refuge from Napoleon, transferred from Lisbon to Rio de Janeiro. The eldest surviving son of King Joàs VI of Portugal was chosen as 'Perpetual Defender' of Brazil by a national congress. In 1822 he proclaimed the independence of the country and was chosen as the constitutional emperor with the title Pedro I. He abdicated in 1831 and was succeeded by his son Pedro II, who ruled for nearly 50 years and whose liberal policies included the gradual abolition of slavery (1888).

A federal system was adopted for the United States of Brazil in the 1881 constitution and Brazil became a republic in 1889. Until 1930 the country experienced strong economic expansion and prosperity, but social unrest in 1930 resulted in a major revolt and from then until 1945 the country was under the control of President Vargas, who established a strong corporate state similar to that of fascist Italy, although Brazil entered World War II on the side of the Allies. Democracy, often corrupt, prevailed from 1956 to 1964 and from 1985; between were five military presidents of illiberal regimes.

A new constitution came into force in October 1988 – the eighth since independence from the Portuguese in 1822 – which transferred powers from the president to congress and paved the way for a return to democracy in 1990. Today the country comprises 23 states, each with its own directly elected governor and legislature, three territories and the Federal District of Brasilia, capital since 1960.

Economy and resources

For many decades following the early settlements Brazil was mainly a sugar-producing colony, with most plantations centred on the rich coastal plains of the north-east. Later the same areas produced cotton, cocoa, rice and other crops. In the south, colonists

THE AMAZON RAINFOREST

The world's largest and ecologically most important rainforest, covering some 6.5 million sq km [2.5 million sq mls, was still being destroyed at an alarming rate in the late 1980s, with somewhere between 1.5% and 4% disappearing each year in Brazil alone. Opening up the forest for many reasons (such as logging and mining) the Brazilian authorities did little in real terms when confronted with a catalogue of indictments: decimation of a crucial world habitat; pollution of rivers; destruction of thousands of species of fauna and flora; and the brutal ruination of the lives of the last remaining Amerindian tribes.

Once cut off from the world by impenetrable jungle, hundreds of thousands of Indians have been displaced in the provinces of Rondonia and Acre, principally by loggers and landless migrants, and in Para by mining, dams for HEP and ranching for beef cattle. It is estimated that five centuries ago the Amazon rainforest supported some 2 million Indians in more than 200 tribes; today the number has shrunk to a pitiful 50,000 or so, and many of the tribes have disappeared altogether.

penetrated the interior in search of slaves and minerals, especially gold and diamonds; the city of Ouro Prêto in Minas Gerais was built, and Rio de Janeiro grew as the port for the region.

During the 19th century São Paulo state became the centre of a huge coffee-growing industry; and while the fortunes made in mining helped to develop Rio de Janeiro, profits from coffee were invested in the city of São Paulo. Immigrants from Italy and Germany settled in the south, introducing farming into the fertile valleys in coexistence with the cattle-ranchers and gauchos whose herds dominated the plains.

The second half of the 19th century saw the development of the wild rubber industry in the Amazon Basin, where the city of Manaus, with its world-famous opera house, served as a centre and market; though Manaus lies 1,600 km [1,000 mls] from the mouth of the Amazon, rubber collected from trees in the hinterland could be shipped out directly to world markets in ocean-going steamers. Brazil enjoyed a virtual monopoly of the rubber trade until the early 20th century, when Malayan plantations began to compete, later with massive success.

Vast mineral resources exist, particularly in Minas Gerais and the Amazon area; they include bauxite, tin, iron ore, manganese, chrome, nickel, uranium, platinum and industrial diamonds. Brazil is the world's leading exporter of iron ore and there are reserves of at least 18,000 million metric tons including the world's biggest at Carajás. Discoveries of new reserves of minerals are frequently being made. The world's largest tin mine is situated in the Amazon region, 50% of the world's platinum is in Brazil, and 65% of the world's supply of precious stones are produced within the country.

The demand for energy has increased rapidly over the years and over a quarter of imports are for crude petroleum. An alternative energy was developed from 1976 made from sugar cane and cassava called ethanol (combustible alcohol) with the aim of reducing demand for petroleum, and in the eight years to 1987, some 3.5 million cars were manufactured to take this fuel; falling oil prices later made this uneconomic. Large investments have been made in hydroelectricity – 93% of the country's electricity is now from water – and the Itaipú HEP station on the Paraná, shared with Paraguay, is the world's largest.

Brazil is one of the world's largest farming countries, and agriculture employs 35% of the population and provides 40% of her exports. The main agricultural exports are coffee, sugar, soya beans, orange juice concentrates, beef, cocoa, poultry, sisal, tobacco, maize and cotton. While Brazil is no longer the leading exporter of coffee – a position now held by Colombia – the country is the world's biggest producer, as it is for sugar cane, bananas, oranges, sisal and castor oil.

The manufacturing industry includes the production of steel, chemicals, machinery, vehicles, pharmaceuticals, cement, timber, paper, shipping and consumer goods. There is also offshore oil production, and nearly 70% of the country's output comes from the continental shelf. The Amazon Basin is gradually being opened for the controversial exploitation of forests and mines, with Santarém a new focus of agriculture in a frontier land.

Road transport now accounts for 70% of the movement of freight and 97% of passenger traffic, replacing the 19th-century railways.

There are 35 deep-water ports in Brazil, and the two main oil terminals at São Sebastião and Madre de Jesus are being expanded. Though river transport now plays only a minor part in the movement of goods, for many years rivers gave the only access to the interior, and there are plans to link the Amazon and the Upper Paraná to give a navigable waterway across central Brazil.

The Iguazú Falls in the southern corner of Brazil, near the border with Paraguay.

Population

In 1872 Brazil had a population of about 10 million. By 1972 this had increased almost tenfold, and 1989 saw a figure of 147.4 million Brazilians – with a projected increase to 200 million by the end of the century. Of the economically active population (55 million in 1985), 15 million were engaged in agriculture, 9 million in the service industries, 8 million in manufacturing, 5 million in the wholesale and retail trade, and 3 million in construction.

On 21 April 1960 Rio de Janeiro ceased to be the capital and inland the new city of Brasília, built from 1956 onwards, in many ways encapsulated both the spirit and the problems of contemporary Brazil – a sparkling, dramatic, planned city, deliberately planted in the unpopulated uplands of Goías as a gesture of faith; modern, practical and beautiful, but still surrounded by the shanties of poverty and – beyond them – the challenge of an untamed wilderness. So much of the nation's wealth is still held by the élites of the cities, particularly those of the south-east, and despite grandiose development plans aimed at spreading prosperity throughout the country, the interior remains poor and underpopulated.

Although possessing great reserves, Brazil has not made the big jump from developing to developed country. The boom of 'the miracle years' from 1968 to 1973, when the economy grew at over 10% per annum, was not sustained. Falls in commodity prices and massive borrowing to finance large and often unproductive projects have combined to make Brazil the world's biggest debtor nation; despite paying back $69 billion between 1985 and 1991 – a huge drain on any economy – there was still over $120 billion owed. Inflation during early 1994 was over 3,000% and mismanagement and corruption still afflicted the administration. While Brazil does not have the huge population growths of many African and Asian countries, it does have poverty on a large scale ■

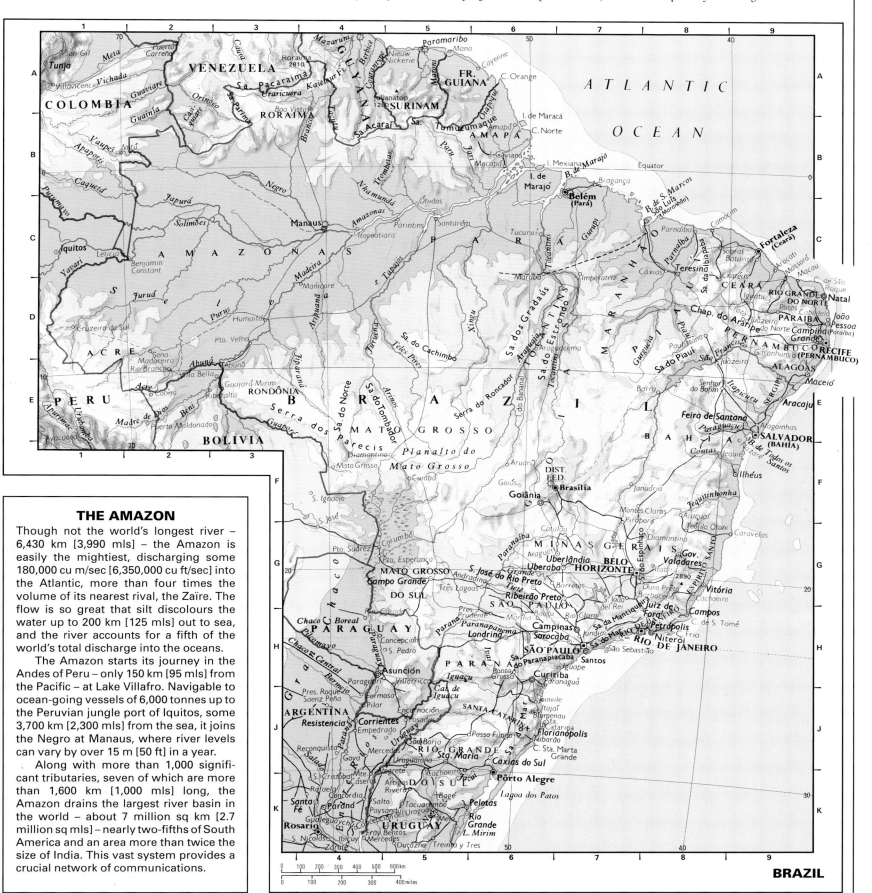

THE AMAZON

Though not the world's longest river – 6,430 km [3,990 mls] – the Amazon is easily the mightiest, discharging some 180,000 cu m/sec [6,350,000 cu ft/sec] into the Atlantic, more than four times the volume of its nearest rival, the Zaïre. The flow is so great that silt discolours the water up to 200 km [125 mls] out to sea, and the river accounts for a fifth of the world's total discharge into the oceans.

The Amazon starts its journey in the Andes of Peru – only 150 km [95 mls] from the Pacific – at Lake Villafro. Navigable to ocean-going vessels of 6,000 tonnes up to the Peruvian jungle port of Iquitos, some 3,700 km [2,300 mls] from the sea, it joins the Negro at Manaus, where river levels can vary by over 15 m [50 ft] in a year.

Along with more than 1,000 significant tributaries, seven of which are more than 1,600 km [1,000 mls] long, the Amazon drains the largest river basin in the world – about 7 million sq km [2.7 million sq mls] – nearly two-fifths of South America and an area more than twice the size of India. This vast system provides a crucial network of communications.

BOLIVIA

By far the larger of South America's two landlocked countries, Bolivia is made up of a wide stretch of the Andes and a long, broad Oriente – part of the south-western fringe of the Amazon Basin. The western boundary is the High Cordillera Occidental, crowned by Sajama at 6,520 m [21,400 ft] and many other volcanic peaks. To the east lies the Altiplano, a high plateau which in prehistoric times was a great lake. Eastwards again rises the majestic Cordillera Real, where Illimani, a glacier-covered peak of 6,462 m [21,200 ft], forms a backdrop to La Paz (The Peace), the world's highest capital. In the transmontane region to the north and east lies the huge expanse of the Oriente – foothills and plains extending from the semi-arid Chaco of the south-east through the savanna-like *llanos* of the centre to the high, wetter forests of the northern plains.

In pre-Conquest days Bolivia was the homeland of the Tiahuanaco culture (7th–11th centuries AD) and was later absorbed into the Inca empire; Quechua, the Inca language, is still spoken by large Amerindian minorities that constitute the highest proportion of any South American country. Famous for its silver mines, the high Andean area was exploited ruthlessly by the Spanish *conquistadores*; the mine at Potosí, discovered in 1545, proved the richest in the world, and Upper Peru (today's highland Bolivia) was for two centuries one of the most densely populated of Spain's American colonies. In 1824 the local population seized their independence, naming the country after Simón Bolívar, hero of other South American wars of independence. When the era of silver passed, the economy flagged (Bolivia now accounts for less than 2% of world production) and the country began to lose ground to its neighbours. The Pacific coast was lost to Chile and Peru in 1884 and large tracts of the Oriente were ceded to Brazil (1903) and Paraguay (1935).

Today Bolivia is the poorest of the South American republics, though it has abundant natural resources with large reserves of petroleum, natural gas and many mineral ores. Lack of investment both in these areas and in the agricultural sector do not help the comparatively poor development, but new irrigation schemes in the south-western Oriente may improve local production of staple foods. Over half the working population is engaged in agriculture, but mining still contributes significantly to the country's wealth. However, Bolivia, once the world's leading tin producer, now ranks fifth with just 7% of a rapidly dwindling total. Today's main export may well be coca and refined cocaine, which almost certainly employs 5% of the population; the government, with US help and co-operation with neighbours, is trying to stifle the growing industry. Initial results from the joint crackdown begun in 1990 and involving the USA and three Andean states – Bolivia, Peru and Colombia – were encouraging, with voluntary eradication quadrupling in Chapáte, where over 80% of the country's coca crop was grown. But although incentives helped shift farmers on to legal produce, policing the processing plants (using leaf from other countries) proved more difficult.

The collapse of the tin market was linked to the record inflation of 1985 – figures vary between 12,000% and over 20,000%, and the 1980–8 average was the world's worst at 483% – though the rates were more stable by the end of the decade. So, too, in a nation renowned for its political volatility (192 coups in 156 years from independence to 1981), was the government, desperately trying to lift Bolivia to the standards of its neighbours ∎

Aymara women with conventional hats and traditional bags in La Paz, at 3,625 m [11,893 ft] the world's highest national capital. Bolivia has a higher proportion of Indians in its population than any other South American country: Quechua (25%) is the largest group.

THE ALTIPLANO

A high, rolling plateau 3,600 m [12,000 ft] above sea level on the Peruvian border of Bolivia, the Altiplano stretches 400 km [250 mls] north to south between the eastern and western cordilleras of the Andes. Surrounded by high, snow-capped peaks, at its north end lies Lake Titicaca, the highest navigable body of water in the world and according to Indian legend the birthplace of the Inca civilization. To the south are smaller lakes, and extensive salt flats representing old lake beds. Though tropical in latitude the Altiplano is cold, windswept and bleak, by any standards a harsh environment, yet over half the population of Bolivia live there.

The natural vegetation is grassland merging at high levels to puna – small bushes and trees forming a harsh scrubland. Summer rains and winter snows bring enough moisture to support grass, and the Altiplano is grazed by guanaco and vicuña as well as many smaller herbivores – chinchillas, viscachas and guinea-pigs. Llama and alpaca, domesticated from guanaco-like ancestors, are herded to provide meat and wool for the peasant farmers. Small and tough, the local people are physiologically adapted for life at high altitude, with more blood, more oxygen-carrying haemoglobin and more efficient lungs than the Indians of the foothills.

BOLIVIA

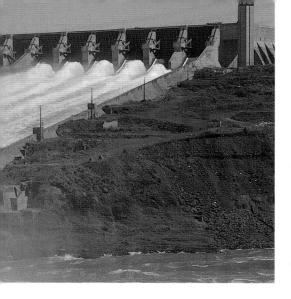

LEFT *The waters of the Paraná (South America's second longest river) roar through six of the 14 sluices of the Itaipú Dam. Straddling the Paraguay-Brazil border, this plant is the world's biggest power station, its turbines capable of generating 13,320 megawatts (million watts) of hydroelectricity for the two countries. In the mid-1990s, however, it will lose its ranking to Turukhansk, on the Yenisey in northern Siberia, which has a planned maximum of 20,000 megawatts.*

PARAGUAY

A landlocked nation, Paraguay is bounded mainly by rivers – the Paraná (South America's second longest) in the south and east, the Pilcomayo in the south-west, and the Paraguay and Apa rivers in the north-west. The middle reach of the Paraguay, navigable for vessels of 1,700 tonnes to Asunción, 1,610 km [1,000 mls] from the sea, divides the country unequally. The eastern third, an extension of the Brazilian plateau at a height of 300 to 600 m [1,000 to 2,000 ft], is densely forested with tropical hardwoods. The western two-thirds is the Northern Chaco, a flat, alluvial plain rising gently from the damp, marshy Paraguay river valley to semi-desert scrubland along the western border.

Paraguay was settled in 1537 by Spaniards attracted by the labour supply of the native Guarani Indians – and the chance of finding a short cut to the silver of Peru. Forming part of the Rio de la Plata Viceroyalty from 1766, Paraguay broke free in 1811 and achieved independence from Buenos Aires in 1813. For over a century the country struggled for nationhood, torn by destructive internal strife and conflict with neighbouring states: in 1865–70, war against Brazil, Argentina and Uruguay cost the country more than half its 600,000 people and much of its territory. At a time when most other South American countries were attracting European settlers and foreign capital for development, Paraguay remained isolated and forbidding. Some territory was regained after the Chaco Wars against Bolivia in 1929–35, and in 1947 a period of civil war was followed by political and economic stability.

In 1954 General Stroessner seized power and assumed the presidency. During his dictatorship there was considerable economic growth, particularly in the 1970s, and great emphasis was placed on developing hydroelectricity: by 1976 Paraguay was self-sufficient in electric energy as a result of the completion of the Acaray complex, and a second HEP project (the world's largest) started production in 1984 at Itaipú – a joint $20 billion venture with Brazil to harness the Paraná. Paraguay was now generating 99.8% of its electricity from water power, and another construction on the Paraná – in the south at Yacyreta (near Encarnación) and involving the world's longest dam – was commissioned.

However, demand slackened and income declined, making it difficult for Paraguay to repay foreign debts incurred on the projects, and high inflation and balance of payments problems followed. The economy is being adjusted and as there are no significant mineral sources a return to an agricultural base is planned for the 1990s.

Hopefully, this will be happening under the umbrella of democracy. Stroessner's regime was a particularly unpleasant variety of despotism, and he ruled with an ever-increasing disregard for human rights during nearly 35 years of fear and fraud before being deposed by his own supporters in 1989. The speeches about reform from his successor, General Andrés Rodríguez, sounded somewhat hollow, but at the end of 1991 Paraguayans did indeed go to the polls to elect a constituent assembly which would frame a new constitution incorporating a multiparty system. At the same time the country was given what amounted to a virtual clean bill of health by international human rights organizations.

In May 1993 the country's first free elections failed to dislodge the ruling Colorado Party from power, the right-wing establishment relying mainly on the rural, Gurani-speaking areas to secure its 40% of the vote ■

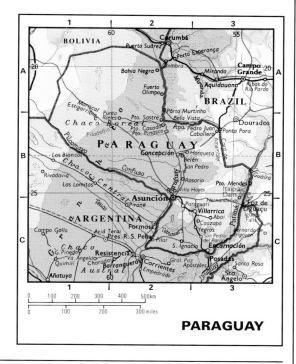

PARAGUAY

URUGUAY

A fter Surinam, Uruguay is the smallest South American state, a country of tall prairie grasses and riparian woodlands with the highest land less than 600 m [2,000 ft] above sea level. The Atlantic coast and River Plate estuary are fringed with lagoons and sand dunes; the centre of the country is a low plateau, rising in the north towards the Brazilian border. The Uruguay River forms the western boundary, and is navigable as far as the falls at Salto, 300 km [186 mls] from the Plate.

Originally little more than the hinterland to the Spanish base at Montevideo, Uruguay formed a buffer area between northern Portuguese and western Spanish territories. Though independent in 1828, internal struggles and civil war intervened before the country developed a basis for prosperity. European immigrants settled the coast and the valley of the Uruguay River, farming the lowlands and leaving the highlands for stock rearing.

Meat processing, pioneered at Fray Bentos in the 1860s, was the start of a meat-and-hide export industry that, boosted by railways to Montevideo and later by refrigerated cargo ships, established the nation's fortunes. Today a modern and moderately prosperous country, Uruguay still depends largely on exports of animal products – mostly meat, wool and dairy produce – for her livelihood.

Farming is thus the main industry, though four out of five Uruguayans are urban-living and almost half live in the capital. Moreover, although more than 90% of Uruguay's land could be used for agriculture, only 10% of it is currently under cultivation. The manufacturing industry today is largely centred on food processing and packing, though with a small domestic market the economy has diversified into cement, chemicals, leather, textiles and steel. Uruguay's trading patterns are changing, too, in an attempt to avoid reliance on Brazil and Argentina, and in 1988 trade agreements with China and the USSR were signed. With inadequate supplies of coal, gas and oil, the nation depends on HEP (90%) for its energy, and exports electricity to Argentina.

Since 1828 Uruguay has been dominated by two political parties – Colorados (Liberals) and Blancos (Conservatives) – and from 1904 has been unique in constitutional innovations aimed at avoiding a dictatorship. The early part of the 20th century saw the development of a pioneering welfare state which in turn encouraged extensive immigration. From 1973 until 1985, however, the country's military regime was accused of appalling human rights abuses ■

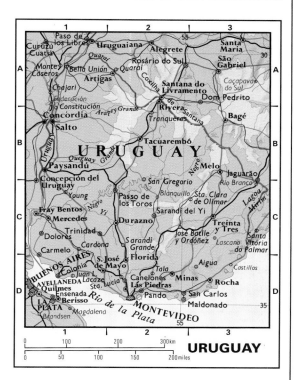

URUGUAY

CHILE

Extending in an extraordinary shape down the west coast of South America from latitude 17°30'S, well inside the tropics, to 55°50'S at Cape Horn, Chile falls into three parallel zones based on the longitudinal folding of the Andes, whose high peaks form the boundaries with Bolivia and Argentina. It is the world's 'thinnest' country, 25 times as long as it is wide.

From the Bolivian border in the north down as far as 27°S runs an extension of the high plateau of Bolivia. Several volcanic peaks of more than 6,000 m [19,680 ft] mark the edge of the western cordilleras. South of Ojos del Salado the ranges narrow and steepen, then gradually reduce in height as they approach Cape Horn.

The parallel coastal ranges create a rolling, hilly belt, rising to 3,000 m [10,000 ft] or more in the north but generally much lower. Between this belt and the Andes runs the sheltered and fertile central valley, most clearly marked southwards from Santiago; over 60% of the population live in an 800 km [500 ml] stretch of land here. Climatically the country divides readily into a desert north (the Atacama, where no recorded rain fell for almost 400 years), a warm-temperate centre and a cool-temperate south.

A Spanish colony from the 16th century, Chile developed as a mining enterprise in the north and a series of vast ranches, or haciendas, in the fertile central region. After Chile finally freed itself from Spanish rule in 1818, mining continued to flourish in the north, and in the south Valparaiso developed as a port with the farmlands of the southern valley exporting produce to the settlers of California and Australia.

The first Christian Democrat president was elected in 1964, but in 1970 he was replaced by President Allende, his administration, the world's first democratically elected Marxist government, was overthrown in a CIA-backed military coup in 1973 and General Pinochet took power as dictator, banning all political activity in a strongly repressive regime. A new constitution took effect from 1981, allowing for an eventual return to democracy, and free elections finally took place in 1989. President Aylwin took office in 1990, but Pinochet secured continued office as commander-in-chief of the armed forces.

Chile's economy continues to depend on agriculture, fishing and, particularly, mining: the country is the world's leading copper producer (17% of total) and copper accounts for nearly half of all export earnings. Magellanes, the southernmost region that includes Cape Horn and Tierra del Fuego (with Argentina), has oilfields that produce about half the country's needs. When the military took over in 1973 inflation was running at about 850%, despite government controls, and Pinochet reintroduced a market economy and abandoned agricultural reform. Economic decline began in 1981 – brought about, in part, by low world prices for minerals and primary products in general – but with great application the situation has steadily improved. ■

ABOVE Vicuñas search for food in the Andes foothills in the Lauca National Park of northern Chile. The wild guanaco and its domestic cousins – vicuña, alpaca and llama – are all members of the camel family.

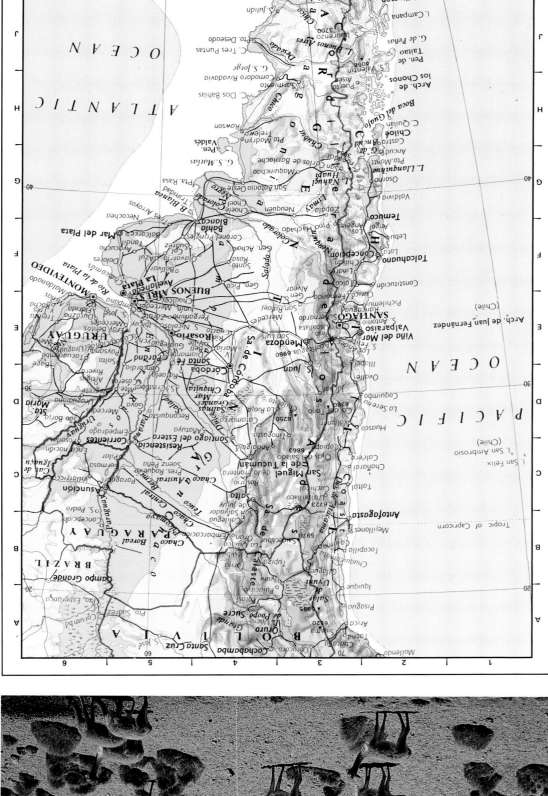

CHILE, ARGENTINA

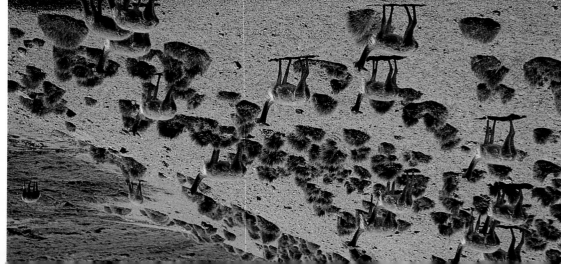

ARGENTINA

Largest of the Spanish-speaking countries of Latin America, but still less than a third of the size of Brazil, Argentina forms a wedge-shaped country from the Tropic of Capricorn to Tierra del Fuego. The western boundary lies high in the Andes, including basins, ridges and peaks of 6,000 m [19,685 ft] in the north. South of the latitude 27°S the ridges merge into a single high cordillera, the highest point being Aconcagua at 6,960 m [22,834 ft], the tallest mountain in the western hemisphere; south of 39°S the Patagonian Andes are lower, but include glaciers and volcanoes. Eastern Argentina is a series of alluvial plains, stretching from the Andean foothills to the sea. The Gran Chaco in the north slopes gradually towards the valley of the Paraná River, from the high desert in the foothills to lowland swamp forest.

Further south are the extensive pampas grasslands, damp and fertile near Buenos Aires, drier but still productive elsewhere. Southwards again, the pampas give way to the much rougher and less hospitable plateaus of Patagonia, areas of mixed volcanic, alluvial and glacial debris that form a harsh, windswept landscape. The climate varies dramatically from hot and humid in the north to bitterly cold, damp and stormy in the extreme south.

History and settlement
Formerly a dependency of Peru, Argentina ('land of silver') was settled first in the north-west around Salta and San Miguel de Tucumán with strong links to Lima. This area is unusual today in retaining a largely mestizo (mixed Indian and Spanish) population, a remnant of colonial times. In 1776 Argentina, Uruguay, Paraguay and southern Bolivia were disengaged from Peru to form a separate viceroyalty, with its administrative centre in Buenos Aires. After a long war of independence the United Provinces of the Rió de la Plata achieved self-government under Simón Bolívar, but Uruguay, Bolivia and Paraguay separated between 1814 and 1828; it took many years of warfare and turbulence before Argentina emerged as a national entity in 1816, united and centred on Buenos Aires.

Early prosperity, based on stock raising and farming, was boosted from 1870 by a massive influx of European immigrants, particularly Italians and Spaniards for whom the Argentine was a real alternative to the USA. They settled lands recently cleared of Indians and often organized by huge land companies. Britain provided much of the capital and some of the immigrants; families of English and Welsh sheep farmers, still speaking their own languages, are identifiable in Patagonia today. Development of a good railway network to the ports, plus steamship services to Europe and refrigerated vessels, helped to create the strong meat, wool and wheat economy that carried Argentina through its formative years and into the 20th century.

Politics and economy
A military coup in 1930 started a long period of military intervention in the politics of the country. The period from 1976 – the so-called 'dirty war' – saw the torture, wrongful imprisonment and murder ('disappearance') of up to 15,000 people by the military, and up to 2 million fled the country. In 1982 the government, blamed for the poor state of the economy, launched an ill-fated invasion of the Falkland Islands (Islas Malvinas), a territory they had claimed since 1820. Britain regained possession later that year by sending an expeditionary force, and President Galtieri resigned. Constitutional rule was restored in 1983 under President Raúl Alfonsin, though the military remained influential. The country's economic problems – with their classic Latin American causes of reliance on certain commodities, big borrowing ($62 billion foreign debt) and maladministration – were inherited by his Peronist successor, Carlos Menem, in 1989. His austerity programme took Argentina through inflation rates of 3,084% and 2,314% down to a modest 85% in 1991.

His policies of economic liberalization and reduction of state involvement were given a boost by his election victory in April 1994. Certainly Argentina is one of the richest of South America's countries in terms of natural resources, and its population – 85% of whom live in towns and cities – is not growing at anything like the rates seen in most of Africa and Asia ■

Smog hovers over the skyline of Buenos Aires – home to nearly a third of Argentina's 32.7 million people.

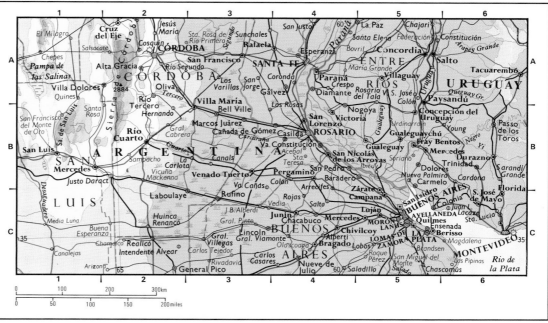

THE PAMPAS
'Pampa' is a South American Indian word describing a flat, featureless expanse: the pampas of South America are the broad, grassy plains – equivalent to the temperate grasslands of the North American prairies, the Central Asian steppes or the South African veld – that stretch between the eastern flank of the Andes and the Atlantic Ocean. Geologically they represent outwash fans of rubble, sand, silt and clay, washed down from the Andes by torrents and redistributed by wind and water. Fine soils cover huge expanses of pampas, providing good deep soils in the well-watered areas, but scrub and sandy desert where rainfall and ground-water are lacking.

Early Spanish settlers introduced horses and cattle, and later the best areas of pampas were enclosed for cattle ranching and cultivation. Now the pampas are almost entirely converted to rangelands growing turf-grasses or to huge fields producing alfalfa, maize, wheat and flax.

BERMUDA

Comprising about 150 small islands, the coral caps of ancient submarine volcanoes rising over 4,000 m [13,000 ft] from the ocean floor, Bermuda is situated 920 km [570 mls] east of Cape Hatteras in North Carolina. Some 20 are inhabited, with most of the population living on the biggest island of Great Bermuda, 21 km [13 mls] long and connected to the other main islands by bridges and causeways. The capital, Hamilton, stands beside a deep harbour.

Uninhabited when discovered by the Spaniard Juan Mermúdez in 1503, the islands were taken over by the British more than a century later (following a shipwreck) and slaves were brought in from Virginia to work the land. Today over 60% of the population is of African descent. The pleasant climate, coral sand beaches, historic buildings and pastel-coloured townships attract nearly 600,000 tourists each year, mainly from the USA; but if tourism is the mainstay of the economy, the islands are also a tax haven for overseas companies and individuals.

Food and energy needs dominate imports, while (legal) drugs and medicines account for over 50% of exports – though services are the main earners, offsetting a large deficit and giving the islanders an annual per capita income of US$25,000 ■

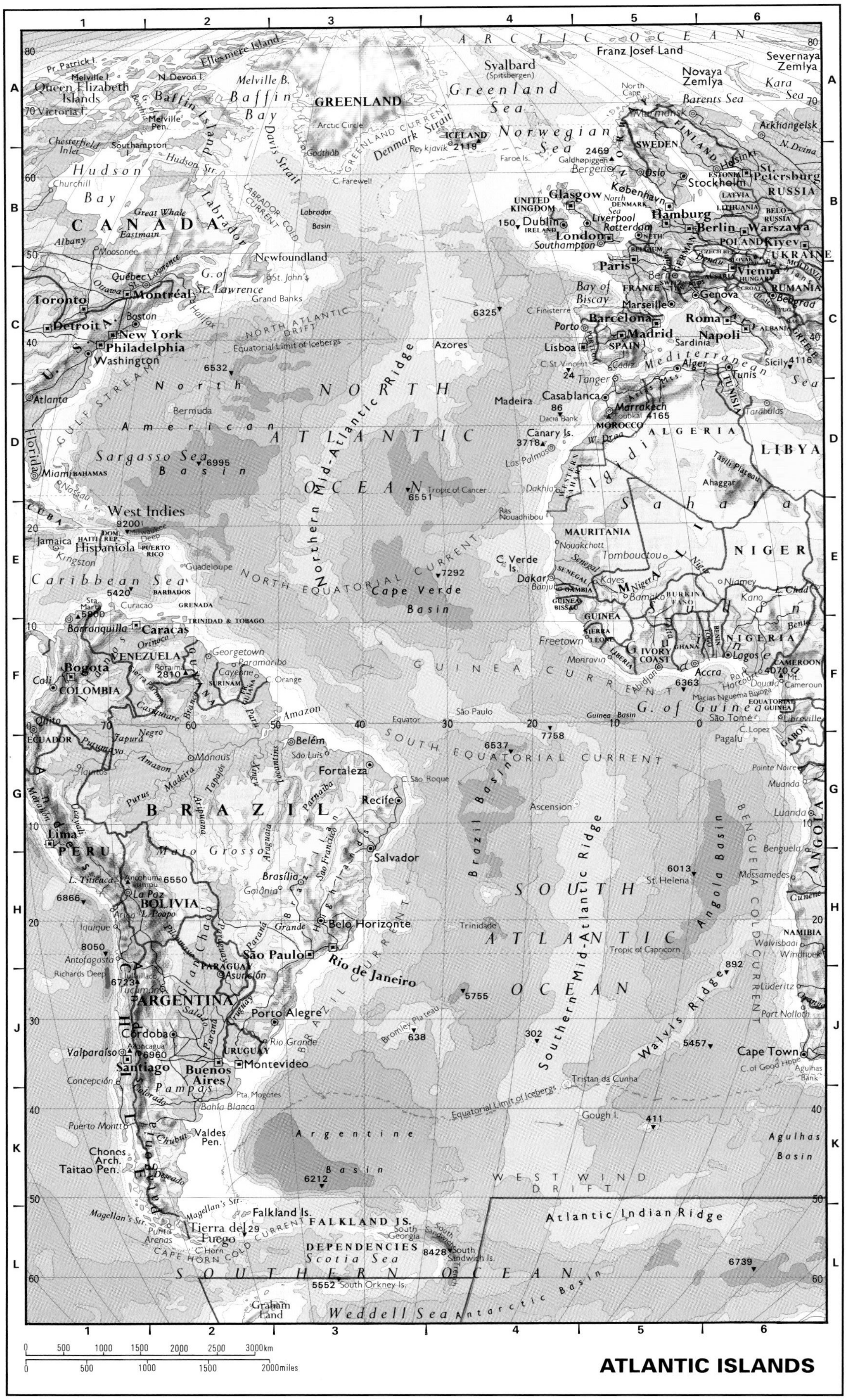

CAPE VERDE

An archipelago of ten large and five small islands, divided into the Barlavento (windward) and Sotavento (leeward) groups, Cape Verde lies 560 km [350 mls] off Dakar. They are volcanic and mainly mountainous, with steep cliffs and rocky headlands; the highest, Fogo, rises to 2,829 m [9,281 ft] and is active. The islands are tropical, hot for most of the year and mainly dry at sea level. Higher ground is cooler and more fertile, producing maize, groundnuts, coffee, sugar cane, beans and fruit when not subject to the endemic droughts that have killed 75,000 people since 1900. Poor soils and lack of surface water prohibit development.

Portuguese since the 15th century – and used chiefly as a provisioning station for ships and an assembly point for slaves in the trade from West Africa – the colony became an overseas territory in 1951 and independent in 1975. Linked with Guinea-Bissau in the fight against colonial rule, its Socialist single-party government flirted with union in 1980, but in 1991 the ruling PAICV was soundly trounced in the country's first multiparty elections by a newly legalized opposition, the Movement for Democracy.

Cape Verde's meagre exports comprise mainly bananas and tuna fish, but it has to import much of its food. The only significant minerals are salt and pozzolana, a volcanic rock used in making cement. Much of the population's income comes from foreign aid and remittances sent home by the 600,000 Cape Verdeans who work abroad – nearly twice the native population; in the last severe drought (1968–82), some 40,000 emigrated to Portugal alone. Tourism is still in its infancy – only 2,000 visitors a year – lagging well behind the Azores, Madeira and the Canaries. Economic problems are compounded by tens of thousands of Angolan refugees ■

ATLANTIC ISLANDS

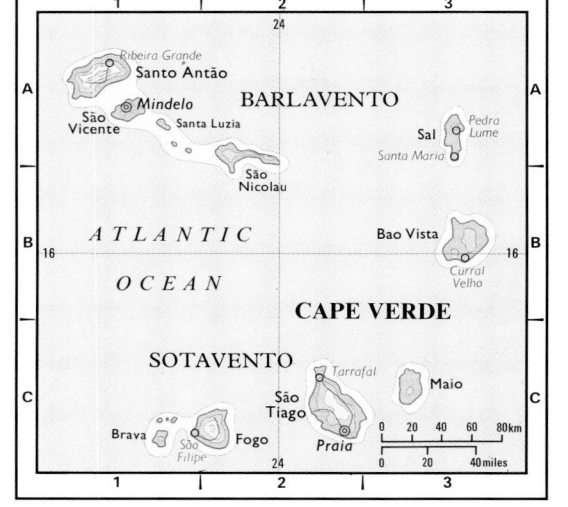

AZORES

Part of the Mid-Atlantic Ridge, the Azores are nine large and several small islands situated about 1,200 km [745 mls] west of Lisbon. They divide into three widely separated groups: São Miguel (759 sq km [293 sq mls] out of a total area of 2,247 sq km [868 sq mls]) and Santa Maria are the most easterly; 160 km [100 mls] to the north-west is the central cluster of Terceira, Graciosa, São Jorge, Pico and Faial; another 240 km [150 mls] to the north-west are Flores and the most isolated significant island of Corvo.

Of relatively recent volcanic origin, the islands are mostly mountainous, with high cliffs and narrow beaches of shell gravel or dark volcanic sand. The highest mountain (and Portugal's highest) is Pico Alto, a volcanic cone of 2,351 m [7,713 ft].

Well watered with an equable, temperate climate and fertile soils, the Azores produce food crops and vines, with all flat or slightly sloping land cultivated. Small-scale farming and fishing are the main occupations, with fruit, wine and canned fish exported (mostly to Portugal), but tourism is an increasingly important sector of the economy.

Like Madeira, the Azores have been Portuguese since the mid-15th century; there were no indigenous people, and its present population of 260,000 is mostly of Portuguese stock. Since 1976 they have been governed as three districts of Portugal, comprising an autonomous region. The capital is Ponta Delgada ∎

CANARY ISLANDS

The Canary Islands comprise seven large islands and numerous small volcanic islands situated off the coast of southern Morocco, the nearest within 100 km [60 mls] of the mainland. The 'inshore' islands of Lanzarote and Fuerteventura are low-lying, while the western group, including Gran Canaria and Tenerife, are more mountainous, the volcanic cone of Pico de Teide rising to 3,718 m [12,198 ft].

The islands, totalling 7,273 sq km [2,807 sq mls] in area, have a subtropical climate, pleasantly dry at sea level but damp on higher ground. Soils are fertile, supporting farming and fruit growing, mainly by large-scale irrigation. Bananas, sugar, coffee and citrus fruits are the main crops at lower levels, and temperate cereals, potatoes, tomatoes and vines grow in the cooler, damper air of the hills. Much of the produce is exported to Western Europe for the early spring market. Industries include food and fish processing, boat-building and crafts.

Known to ancient European civilizations as the Fortunate Islands, the picturesque Canaries are today a major destination for both winter and summer tourists. Claimed by Portugal in 1341, they were ceded to Spain in 1479 and since 1927 have been divided into two provinces under the name of their respective capitals, Las Palmas de Gran Canaria (at 372,000 population Spain's eighth biggest city) and Santa Cruz de Tenerife (population 191,000). The former (56% of the area) includes Gran Canaria, Lanzarote and Fuerteventura; the latter (44%) includes Tenerife, La Palma, Gomera and Hierro ∎

MADEIRA

Madeira is the largest of the group of picturesque volcanic islands of that name lying 550 km [350 mls] from the Moroccan coast and 900 km [560 mls] south-west of the national capital, Lisbon. Porto Santo and the uninhabited Ilhas Selvagens and Desertas complete the group, with a total area of 813 sq km [314 sq mls], of which Madeira itself contributes 745 sq km [288 sq mls].

With a warm temperate climate, adequate rainfall and good soils, Madeira was originally forested, but early settlers cleared the uplands for plantations. Farming is still the main occupation, producing sugar cane, wines, vegetables and both temperate and tropical fruits. The main exports are grapes (mainly for Madeira wine), bananas and sugar. Handicrafts and, increasingly, tourism are additional sources of revenue.

Known to the Genoese in the 14th century but colonized by the Portuguese from the 15th century, the islands have since 1976 formed an autonomous region of Portugal. The population is 280,000 ∎

A church peers down on the harbour at Funchal, capital of the Portuguese 'region' of Madeira.

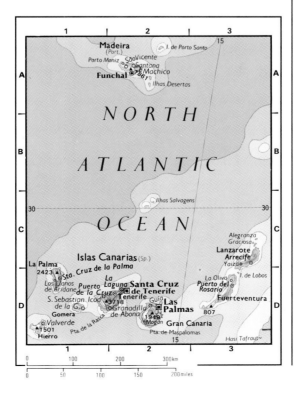

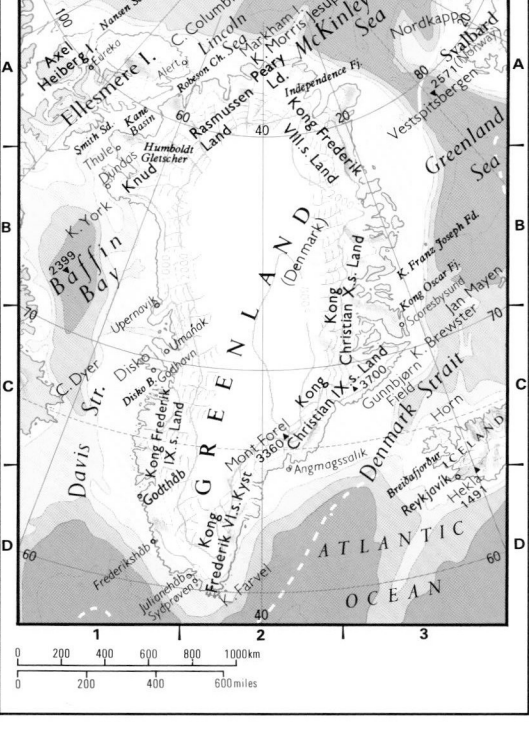

GREENLAND

Recognized by geographers as the world's largest island (the Australian mainland being considered a continental land mass), Greenland is almost three times the size of the second largest, New Guinea. However, more than 85% of the land is covered in continuous permafrost, an ice-cap with an average depth of about 1,500 m [5,000 ft], and though there are a few sandy and clay plains in the ice-free areas, settlement is confined to the narrow rocky coasts. The few towns, including the capital of Godthåb (Nuuk), are on the south-west coast, warmed by the southerly

currents of the Atlantic; on the east side, a northerly current from the Arctic chills the pack-ice and makes it inaccessible for most of the year.

The first recorded European to visit this barren desert was Eirike Raudi (Eric the Red), a Norseman from Iceland who settled at Brattahlid in 982. It was he who named the place Greenland – to make it sound attractive to settlers. Within four years, more than 30 ships had ferried pioneers there, founding a colony which would last five centuries.

Greenland became a Danish possession in 1380 and, eventually, an integral part of the Danish kingdom in 1953. After the island was taken into the EC in 1973 – despite a majority vote against by Greenlanders – a nationalist movement developed and in 1979, after another referendum, a home rule was

introduced, with full internal self-government following in 1981. Then, in 1985, Greenland withdrew from the EC – halving the Community's territory.

The economy still depends substantially on subsidies from Denmark, which remains its chief trading partner. The main rural occupations are sheep rearing and fishing – with shrimps, prawns and molluscs contributing over 60% of exports. The only major manufacturing is fish canning, which has drawn many Eskimos to the towns; few now follow the traditional life of nomadic hunters, and most Greenlanders (a mixture of Inuit Eskimo and Danish extraction) live between the primitive and the modern ∎

Polar hunters and their husky-powered sled avoid an ice-bank on Murchison Sound, in north-west Greenland.

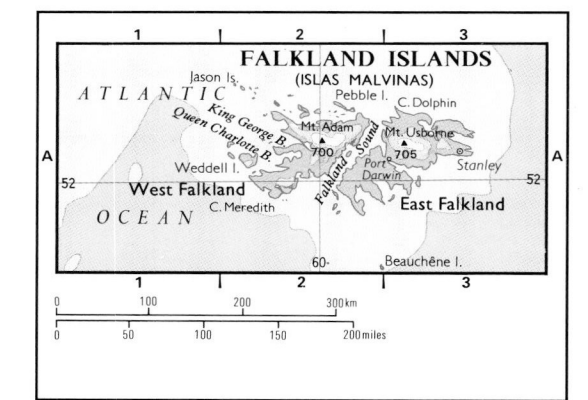

FALKLAND ISLANDS

Comprising two main islands and over 200 small islands, the Falkland Islands lie 480 km [300 mls] from South America. Windswept, virtually treeless, covered with peat moorland and tussock grass, the rolling landscape rises to two points of about 700 m [2,300 ft] – Mt Usborne in East Falkland and Mt Adam in West Falkland.

The prospect of rich offshore oil and gas deposits

from the 1970s aggravated the long-standing dispute between Britain and Argentina, and in 1982 Argentine forces invaded the Dependent Territory (Islas Malvinas in Spanish) and expelled the Governor. Two months later – after the loss of 725 Argentinians and 225 Britons – the UK regained possession. Anglo-Argentine diplomatic relations were restored in 1990, but the UK refuses to enter discussions on sovereignty.

Life has since been based on the presence of a large British garrison, but in normal times the economy is dominated by sheep-farming, almost the only industry, with over 40% of exports comprising high-grade wool, mostly to Britain ∎

ASCENSION

Ascension stands in isolation on the Mid-Atlantic Ridge, a triangular volcanic island of 88 sq km [34 sq mls], with a single high peak, Green Mountain (859 m [2,817 ft]), surrounded by hot low-lying ash and lava plains. The mountain climate is cool and damp enough to support a farm, which supplies vegetables for the local community of about 1,500. Ascension has no native population. Administered from St Helena since 1922, its inhabitants are British, St Helenian or American, many involved in telecommunications and servicing a mid-ocean airstrip ∎

ST HELENA

St Helena is an isolated rectangular, slab-sided island of old volcanic rocks, well off the main line of the Mid-Atlantic Ridge and measuring 122 sq km [47 sq mls]. A tableland deeply dissected by valleys, it has steep cliffs and ridges, and there is relatively little flat ground available. Standing in the trade winds, St Helena has a cool tropical maritime climate, dry at sea level but moist enough for limited farming on the heights. The population of about 7,000, mainly of East Indian descent, produce potatoes and other vegetables and raise cattle, sheep and goats on smallholdings ∎

TRISTAN DA CUNHA

Tristan da Cunha is the largest of four scattered islands towards the southern end of the Mid-Atlantic Ridge, a volcanic cone of 2,060 m [6,760 ft], ringed by a lava plain that drops steeply to the sea; a narrow strip of flat ground accommodates the settlement of about 300 inhabitants. The climate is mild and damp with frequent storms; the islanders grow potatoes and rear sheep and cattle for their own use. Like Ascension to the north, neighbours Nightingale, Inaccessible and Gough Islands are administered as dependencies of St Helena ∎

Index to Map Pages

The index contains the names of all the principal places and features shown on the country maps. Physical features composed of a proper name (Erie) and a description (Lake) are positioned alphabetically by the proper name. The description is positioned after the proper name and is usually abbreviated:

Erie, L. **148** E11

Where a description forms part of a settlement or administrative name however, it is always written in full and put in its true alphabetic position:

Lake Charles **159** J11

Names beginning St. are alphabetized under Saint, but Sankt, Sint, Sant', Santa and San are all spelt in full and are alphabetized accordingly.

The number in bold type which follows each name in the index refers to the number of the page where that feature or place will be found.

The letter and figure which are in bold type immediately after the page number give the imaginary grid square on the map page, within which the feature is situated. This is formed by joining the black ticks outside each map frame. It does not relate to the latitude nor longitude except in the case of the physical maps of the continents.

In some cases the feature itself may fall within the specified square, while the name is outside. Rivers carry the symbol → after their names. A solid square ■ follows the name of a country while an open square □ refers to a first order administrative area.

The abbreviations which follow the French département names are those used on the map of France on page 23.

Abbreviations used in the index

A.R. – Autonomous Region
B. – Baie, Bahía, Bay, Bucht
C. – Cabo, Cap, Cape, Coast
Cat. – Catarata
G. – Golfe, Golfo, Gulf, Guba, Gebel
I.(s) – Île, Ilha, Insel, Isla, Island, Isle
Kep. – Kepulauan
L. – Lac, Lacul, Lago, Lagoa, Lake, Limni, Loch, Lough
Mt.(e) – Mont, Monte, Monti, Montaña, Mountain
Oz. – Ozero
P. – Pass, Passo, Pasul, Pulau
Pen. – Peninsula, Péninsule
P-ov. – Poluostrov
Ra.(s) – Range(s)
Rep. – Republic
Res. – Reserve, Reservoir
Sd. – Sound
Str. – Strait, Stretto
Terr. – Territory
Vdkhr. – Vodokhranilishche
Wlkp. – Wielkopolski

A

Aachen 26 D1
Aalst 19 B3
Aarau 28 A3
Aare → 28 A3
Ābādān 71 D2
Abbeville 23 A5
Abbots Langley 13 B2
Abéché 110 D2
Abeokuta 119 E1
Aberdeen 14 C7
Aberystwyth 14 J5
Abidjan 116 D5
Abitibi L. 155 K11
Abu Dhabi = Abū Ẓāby 69 B3
Abū Ẓāby 69 B3
Abuja 119 D4
Acapulco 162 F5
Accra 117 D3
Achill I. 14 G1
Achinsk 59 H10
Acklins I. 169 B3
Aconcagua 188 E3
Acre □ 185 D1
Ad Dammām 67 C6
Ad Dawhah 68 D3
Adamaoua, Massif de l' 121 C2
Adam's Bridge 78 B1
Adana 62 C4
Adapazarı 62 A2
Addis Abeba 112 D3
Addlestone 13 D2
Adelaide, *Australia* 139 F2
Adelaide, *S. Africa* 131 H6
Aden = Al 'Adan 68 C1
Aden, G. of 53 G8
Adirondack Mts. 159 C16
Admiralty Is. 141 A2
Ado Ekiti 119 E2
Adoni 75 E3
Adour → 23 G3
Adrar 105 C3
Adriatic Sea 2 G9
Ægean Sea 2 H11
Aerhtai Shan 80 B5
Afghanistan ■ 72
'Afīf 67 D4
Agadez 109 C3
Agadir 104 D2
Agen 23 G4
Agra 74 B3
Agrigento 35 K5
Aguascalientes 162 D4
Agulhas, C. 131 H3
Ahaggar 105 E5
Ahmadabad 74 D1
Ahmadnagar 74 F2
Ahmadpur 73 D5
Ahvāz 71 C2
Ain (A.) □ 23 E8
Aïr 109 B4
Aisne (Ai.) □ 23 B6
Aisne → 23 B6
Aix-en-Provence 23 G8
Ajaccio 23 H9
Ajanta Ra. 74 F2
Ajmer 74 B2
Akashi 88 C5
Akita 89 D7
'Akko 64 B2
Akola 74 F3
Akranes 6 C2
Akron 159 D14
Aktyubinsk 58 H5
Akure 119 E2
Akureyri 6 B4
Akyab 91 E1
Al 'Adan 68 C1
Al Başrah 70 E6
Al Hasa 67 C6
Al Ḩudaydah 68 B1
Al Hufūf 67 C6
Al Jawf 67 B3
Al Jazirah 70 C3
Al Kūt 70 D5
Al Kuwayt 68 A1
Al Lādhiqīyah 65 B2
Al Madīnah 67 C3
Al Manāmah 68 C3
Al Mawşil 70 A3
Al Mubarraz 67 C6
Al Qaţīf 67 C6
Al Qunaytirah 65 D2
Al 'Ulā 67 C2
Alabama □ 159 H13
Alaska □ 161
Alaska, G. of 148 D5
Alaska Peninsula 161 B3
Alaska Range 161 B4
Alba Iulia 43 C3
Albacete 31 E6
Albania ■ 38
Albany, *Australia* 139 D3
Albany, *Ga., U.S.A.* 159 H14
Albany, *N.Y., U.S.A.* 157 A5
Albany → 155 J11
Albert, L. = Mobutu Sese Seko, L. 101 F7
Alberta □ 154 G5
Albi 23 G5
Ålborg 10 B2
Alborz, Reshteh-ye Kūhhā-ye 71 B3
Albuquerque 158 G7
Alcalá de Henares 31 D5
Aldabra Is. 101 G8
Aldan → 59 E14
Alderney 12 A2
Aldershot 13 D1
Aleksandrovsk-Sakhalinskiy 59 G17
Alençon 23 C4
Alès 23 G7
Alessándria 35 B2
Ålesund 8 E1
Aleutian Is. 161 B1
Alexander Arch. 161 B5
Alexandria = El Iskandarîya 107 A3
Alexandria 159 H11
Algarve 31 G1
Algeciras 31 H4
Alger 105 A4
Algeria ■ 105
Algiers = Alger 105 A4
Alicante 31 F7
Alice Springs 137 H11
Aligarh 74 B3
Alipur Duar 74 B8
Aliwal North 131 F6
Alkmaar 18 C3
Allahabad 74 C5
Allegheny → 157 C1
Allegheny, Mts. 148 F11
Allentown 157 C4
Alleppey 75 G2
Allier (Al.) □ 23 E6
Allier → 23 D6
Alma Ata 61 A8
Almelo 18 C6
Almería 31 G6
Alor 97 F12
Alpes-de-Haute-Provence (A.H.P.) □ 23 G8
Alpes-Maritimes (A.Mar.) □ 23 G9
Alphen 18 D3
Alps 2 F8
Alsace 23 C9
Altai = Aerhtai Shan 80 B5
Altay 80 B4
Alton 13 E1
Altoona 157 C2
Altun Shan 80 D3
Alwar 74 B3
Amadjuak L. 155 E11
Amagasaki 88 C5
Amarillo 158 G8
Amazon → 175 C4
Amazonas □ 185 C3
Ambala 75 B2
Ambikapur 74 D6
Ambon 97 D13
American Samoa ■ 145 G7
Amersfoort 18 D4
Amersham 13 B2
Amiens 23 B5
'Ammān 66 B2
Ampthill 13 A2
Amravati 74 E3
Amritsar 75 B2
Amroha 74 A4
Amsterdam, *Neths.* 18 C3
Amsterdam, *U.S.A.* 157 A5
Amudarya → 58 J4
Amundsen Gulf 154 C6
Amur → 59 G16
An Nafūd 67 B3
An Najaf 70 D4
An Nāşirīyah 70 E5
An Nhon 93 E5
An Nîl el Azraq □ 111 D5
An Uaimh 14 G3
Anadolu 62 B2
Anadyr 59 A17
Anadyrskiy Zaliv 59 A17
Anaheim 158 G3
Anambas, Kepulauan 96 B5
Anār 71 C4
Anatolia = Anadolu 62 B2
Anchorage 161 B4
Ancona 35 C5
Andalucía □ 31 G4
Andaman Is. 53 G13
Anderson 159 E13
Andes, Cord. de los 175 D2
Andhra Pradesh □ 75 E3
Andizhan 61 C5
Andorra ■ 31 B9
Andreanof Is. 161 B1
Ándria 35 F7
Andros I. 169 B1
Angara → 59 G10
Angarsk 59 J11
Ånge 8 E3
Angerman → 8 E4
Angers 23 D4
Anglesey 14 H5
Angmagssalik 192 D2
Angola ■ 128
Angoulême 23 E4
Angoumois 23 E4
Anguilla ■ 170 A1
Anhui □ 84 F4
Anjou 23 D4
Ankara 62 B3
Ann, C. 157 A6
Ann Arbor 159 D14
Annaba 105 A6
Annapolis 157 D3
Annecy 23 E8
Annobón 101 G4
Anshan 84 B6
Anshun 81 H7
Antalya 62 C2
Antananarivo 133 C2
Anticosti, I. d' 155 J14
Antofagasta 188 B3
Antrim 14 F3
Antrim, Mts. of 14 F4
Antsiranana 133 A3
Antwerpen 19 B3
Anvers = Antwerpen 19 B3
Anyang 84 E2
Anzhero-Sudzhensk 58 H9
Aomori 89 D7
Aparri 98 B3
Apeldoorn 18 D5
Apia 145 G6
Appalachian Mts. 159 F15
Appennini 35 D4
Appledore 13 E6
Appleton 159 C12
Ar Ramādī 70 C3
Ar Riyāḑ 67 C5
Ara 74 C6
Arabia 53 F8
Arabian Desert = Es Sahrâ' Esh Sharqîya 107 C5
Arabian Gulf = The Gulf 53 F9
Arabian Sea 53 G10
Aracaju 185 E9
Arad 43 B1
Arafura Sea 96 F16
Aragón □ 31 C7
Araguaia → 185 C7
Arāk 71 B2
Arakan Yoma 91 E2
Aral Sea = Aralskoye More 58 J4
Aralsk 58 J5
Aralskoye More 58 J4
Aran I. 14 E2
Ararat 139 G4
Arbīl 70 A4
Arbroath 14 C6
Arcachon 23 F3
Arctic Ocean 53
Arctic Red River 154 C5
Ardabīl 71 A2
Ardèche (Ar.) □ 23 F7
Ardenne 19 E4
Ardennes (Ard.) □ 23 B7
Ardingly 13 E3
Arendal 8 G1
Arequipa 180 F4
Argentina ■ 188
Århus 10 B2
Arica 188 A3
Ariège (Ari.) □ 23 H5
Arima 172 A3
Arizona □ 158 G4
Arkansas □ 159 G11
Arkansas → 159 G12
Arkhangelsk 58 D5
Arklow 14 H3
Arlberg 29 B1
Arles 23 G7
Arlon 19 F5
Armagh 14 F3
Armenia 178 C1
Armenia ■ 49 C5
Armidale 139 C8
Arnhem 18 D5
Arnhem Land 137 B3
Arnprior 152 B3
Arran 14 E4
Arras 23 A6
Artois 23 A6
Aru, Kepulauan 97 E16
Arun → 13 E2
Arunachal Pradesh □ 75 B6
Arusha 126 B2
As Salt 66 B2
Aş Şummān 67 C5
Asahigawa 89 B8
Asansol 74 D7
Asbestos 152 B6
Asbury Park 157 C5
Ascension I. 190 G4
Ascot 13 D1
Ash 13 D1
Ash Shāriqah 69 B3
Ashburton 143 G3
Ashburton → 137 C1
Ashdown Forest 13 E4
Ashford 13 E6
Ashkhabad 58 K3
Ashland 159 E14
Ashqelon 64 D1
Ashurstwood 13 E4
Asifabad 74 F4
'Asīr □ 67 E3
Asir, Ras 113 A3
Asmera 112 B3
Assam □ 75 C6
Assen 18 B5
Asti 35 B2
Aston Clinton 13 B1
Astrakhan 47 G8
Asturias □ 31 A3
Asunción 187 B2
Aswân 107 E5
Atacama, Desierto de 188 C3
Atbara 111 B5
'Atbara → 111 B5
Athabasca, L. 154 G6
Athenry 14 H1
Athens = Athínai 39 D3
Athínai 39 D3
Athlone 14 H2
Athy 14 H3
Atlanta 159 G14
Atlantic City 157 D5
Atlantic Ocean 190
Atlas Mts. = Haut Atlas 104 C5
Atyrau 58 H3
Aube (Aub.) □ 23 C7
Aube → 23 C6
Auburn 157 A3
Aubusson 23 E5
Auch 23 G4
Auckland 143 B5
Aude (Aud.) □ 23 H6
Aude → 23 H6
Augrabies Falls 131 E3
Augsburg 26 F4
Augusta, *Ga., U.S.A.* 159 G15
Augusta, *Maine, U.S.A.* 159 B18
Aunis 23 E3
Aurangabad, *Bihar, India* 74 C6
Aurangabad, *Maharashtra, India* 74 F2
Aurillac 23 F6
Aurora 159 D12
Austin 158 J9
Australia ■ 137
Australian Alps 139 G7
Australian Capital Territory □ 139 F7
Austria ■ 29
Autun 23 D7
Auvergne 23 F6
Auxerre 23 C6
Avallon 23 D7
Avellino 35 F6
Aveyron (Av.) □ 23 G6
Avignon 23 G7
Ávila 31 D4
Avranches 23 C3
Axminster 14 L6
Aylesbury 13 B1
Aylesford 13 D5
Ayr 14 E5
Az Zarqā 66 A2
Azamgarh 74 C6
Azerbaijan ■ 49 D8
Azores 190 C4
Azov, Sea of = Azovskoye More 47 G5
Azovskoye More 47 G5
Azuero, Pen. de 165 E5

B

Bābol 71 B3
Babuyan Chan. 98 B3
Bacău 43 B5
Bacolod 98 H4
Badajoz 31 E2
Badalona 31 C9
Baden-Württemberg □ 26 F3
Baffin B. 155 C10
Baffin I. 155 D10
Baghdād 70 C4
Bagshot 13 D1
Baguio 98 D2
Bahamas ■ 169
Baharampur 74 D8
Bahawalpur 73 D5
Bahía = Salvador 185 E9
Bahía □ 185 E8
Bahía Blanca 188 F4
Bahraich 74 B5
Bahrain ■ 68
Baia Mare 43 A3
Baikal, L. = Baykal, Oz. 59 J12
Baja California 162 A1
Bakersfield 158 F2
Bākhtarān 71 B2
Bakony Hegyseg 42 B3
Baku 49 C9
Balaghat 74 E4
Balaton 42 B2
Balboa 165 E5
Balbriggan 14 G3
Baldock 13 A3
Baleares, Is. 33 B4
Baleshwar 74 E7
Bali 96 F8
Balikeşir 62 B1
Balikpapan 96 C9
Balkan Mts. = Stara Planina 41 B2
Balkhash 58 K7
Balkhash, Ozero 58 K7
Ballarat 139 G4
Ballina 14 G1
Ballymena 14 F3
Balmoral 14 C6
Balrampur 74 B5
Balsas → 162 E4
Baltic Sea 2 D10
Baltimore 157 D3
Baluchistan □ 73 E2
Bam 71 D5
Bamako 108 F3
Bamberg 26 E4
Bamenda 121 D1
Bancroft 152 B3
Banda 74 C4
Banda, Kepulauan 97 E14
Banda Aceh 96 A1
Banda Sea 97 E14
Bandār 'Abbās 71 E4
Bandar-e Khomeyni 71 D2
Bandar Maharani 94 D2
Bandar Penggaram 94 D2
Bandar Seri Begawan 95 A3
Bandon 14 K1
Bandundu 123 D2
Bandung 96 F5
Banff 14 B6
Bangalore 75 F3
Banggai, Kepulauan 97 D12
Banghāzī 106 A4
Bangka 96 D5
Bangka, Selat 96 D5
Bangkok 91 H4
Bangladesh ■ 79
Bangor, *U.K.* 14 F4
Bangor, *U.S.A.* 159 B18
Bangui 110 C3
Bangweulu, L. 129 B4
Banja Luka 40 B5
Banjarmasin 96 D8
Banjul 114 C1
Banks I. 154 B7
Banks Pen. 143 G4
Bankura 74 D7
Bannu 73 B4
Banská Bystrica 44 C6
Bantry 14 K1
Banyak, Kepulauan 96 B1
Baoding 84 C3
Baoji 81 E7
Baotou 84 B1
Bar Harbor 159 B18
Bar-le-Duc 23 C7
Baran 74 C3
Barbados ■ 172
Barberton 131 C9

INDEX

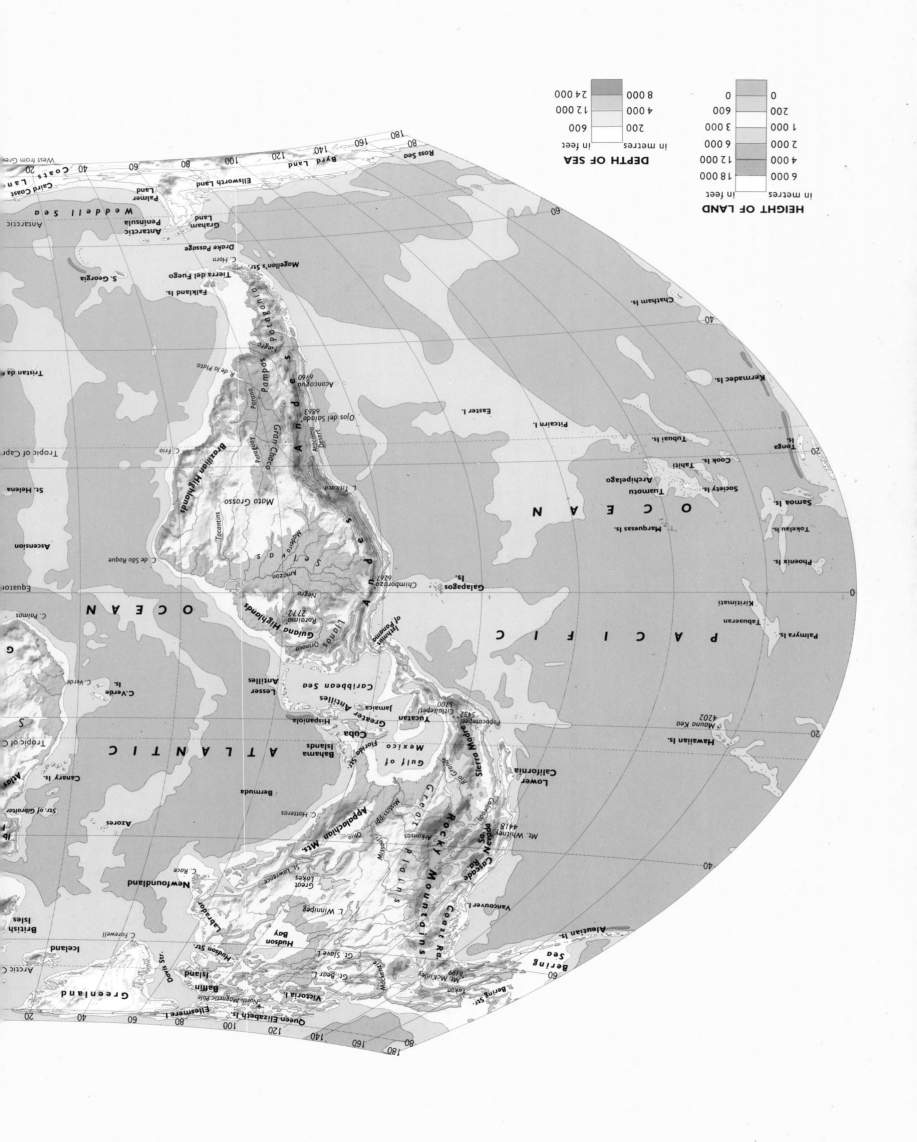

HEIGHT OF LAND

in metres		in feet	
6000		18 000	
4000		12 000	
2000		6000	
1000		3000	
200		600	
0		0	

DEPTH OF SEA

in feet		in metres	
200		600	
4000		12 000	
8000		24 000	

PACIFIC OCEAN

ATLANTIC OCEAN

Greenland

Rocky Mountains

Andes

Brazilian Highlands

Guiana Highlands

Antarctic Peninsula

Weddell Sea

Ross Sea